Lecture Notes in Computer Science 2374

Edited by G. Goos, J. Hartmanis, and J. van Leeuwen

Springer
Berlin
Heidelberg
New York
Barcelona
Hong Kong
London
Milan
Paris
Tokyo

Boris Magnusson (Ed.)

ECOOP 2002 – Object-Oriented Programming

16th European Conference
Málaga, Spain, June 10-14, 2002
Proceedings

 Springer

Series Editors

Gerhard Goos, Karlsruhe University, Germany
Juris Hartmanis, Cornell University, NY, USA
Jan van Leeuwen, Utrecht University, The Netherlands

Volume Editor

Boris Magnusson
University of Lund
Department of Computer Science
Box 118, 211 00 Lund, Sweden
E-mail: boris@cs.lth.se

Cataloging-in-Publication Data applied for

Die Deutsche Bibliothek - CIP-Einheitsaufnahme

Object oriented programming : 16th European conference ; proceedings / ECOOP
2002, Málaga, Spain, June 10 - 14, 2002. Boris Magnusson (ed.). - Berlin ;
Heidelberg ; New York ; Barcelona ; Hong Kong ; London ; Milan ; Paris ;
Tokyo : Springer, 2002
   (Lecture notes in computer science ; Vol. 2374)
   ISBN 3-540-43759-2

CR Subject Classification (1998): D.1-3, H.2, F.3, C.2, K.4, J.1

ISSN 0302-9743
ISBN 3-540-43759-2 Springer-Verlag Berlin Heidelberg New York

Springer-Verlag Berlin Heidelberg New York
a member of BertelsmannSpringer Science+Business Media GmbH

http://www.springer.de

© Springer-Verlag Berlin Heidelberg 2002
Printed in Germany

Typesetting: Camera-ready by author, data conversion by Olgun Computergrafik, Heidelberg
Printed on acid-free paper   SPIN 10870407   06/3142   5 4 3 2 1 0

Preface

Object-Orientation has for a number of years now been accepted as the industry standard in many areas. Coming from the area of simulation it showed its strengths in the design of graphical user interfaces and is now taken for granted in Internet applications. Object-oriented programming has positioned itself as the main programming paradigm in many universities and many students are introduced to programming through an Object-Oriented language. The importance of Object-Orientation and its fundamental ideas have now also been firmly recognized by the research community. This year both the IEEE John von Neumann Medal and the ACM Turing Award have been awarded to Ole-Johan Dahl and Kristen Nygaard for the pioneering work they did in the 1960s when designing the programming language Simula 67:

19 November 2001 – IEEE (Institute of Electrical and Electronic Engineers): Ole-Johan Dahl and Kristen Nygaard have been awarded the IEEE's 2002 John von Neumann Medal "For the introduction of the concepts underlying object-oriented programming through the design and implementation of SIMULA67."

New York, February 6, 2002 – The Association for Computing Machinery (ACM) has presented the 2001 A.M. Turing Award, considered the "Nobel Prize of Computing," to Ole-Johan Dahl and Kristen Nygaard of Norway for their role in the invention of object-oriented programming, the most widely used programming model today. Their work has led to a fundamental change in how software systems are designed and programmed, resulting in reusable, reliable, scalable applications that have streamlined the process of writing software code and facilitated software programming.

2002 will thus be remembered as an exceptional year in the history of Object-Orientation and it is an honor to have Kristen Nygaard as this year's banquet speaker.

This year we had 96 submitted papers of which 24 were accepted for publication after a thorough review process. In addition to the reviewed papers there are invited talks given by José Meseguer and Clemens Szyperski. The wide spread of topics in this year's conference will hopefully also illustrate the acceptance of Object-Orientation in all areas of Computer Science and Software Engineering and confirm ECOOP as a broad conference for all aspects of Object-Oriented Programming.

Organizing an international conference involves a lot of work carried out by a large group of people, most of which is not directly visible. I would like to extend my gratitude to the PC committee members, who spent endless hours reviewing the papers, Antonio Vallecillo and the local organization, who made everything work at the conference, and Richard van de Stadt, with his CyberChair system, which made my work so much easier when preparing these proceedings!

April 2002   Boris Magnusson

Organization

ECOOP 2002 was organized by the Department of Computer Science of the University of Málaga, and the Department of Computer Science of the University of Extremadura, under the auspices of AITO (Association Internationale pour les Technologies Objets).

Executive Committee

Conference Chair: José M. Troya (University of Málaga)
Program Chair: Boris Magnusson (Lund University)
Organizing Chair: Antonio Vallecillo (University of Málaga)

Organizing Committee

Tutorial Chairs: Ernesto Pimentel (University of Málaga)
Hanspeter Mössenböck (University of Linz, Austria)
Workshop Chairs: Juan Hernández (University of Extremadura)
Ana Moreira (Universidade Nova de Lisboa, Portugal)
Exhibit Chair: Manuel Díaz (University of Málaga)
Demonstration Chair: Lidia Fuentes (University of Málaga)
Poster Chair: Juan M. Murillo (University of Extremadura)
Panel Chair: Francisco Durán (University of Málaga)
Sponsorship Chair: Javier López (University of Málaga)
Advertizing, Web Site: Fernando Sánchez (University of Extremadura)
Registration Chair: Carlos Canal (University of Málaga)

Operational Support:

José M. Álvarez	Luis Llopis	Mónica Pinto
Mercedes Amor	Pablo López	Roberto Rodríguez
Manuel F. Bertoa	Antonio Maña	Bartolomé Rubio
Alfonso Gazo	Antonio Nebro	Blas C. Ruíz
Francisco Gutiérrez	Juan J. Ortega	

Program Committee

John Boyland	University of Wisconsin - Milwaukee, USA
Gilad Bracha	Sun Microsystems, USA
Krzysztof Czarnecki	DaimlerChrysler AG, Germany
Bjørn N. Freeman-Benson	University of Washington, USA
Svend Frølund	HP Labs, USA
Erich Gamma	OTI International, Switzerland
Görel Hedin	Lund University, Sweden
Urs Hölzle	University of California at Santa Barbara, USA
Eric Jul	University of Copenhagen, Denmark
Kai Koskimies	Tampere University of Technology, Finland
Kresten Krab Thorup	Trifork Technologies, Denmark
Doug Lea	State University of New York, USA
Jørgen Lindskov Knudsen	Mjølner Informatics, Inc., Denmark
Satoshi Matsuoka	Tokyo Institute of Technology, Japan
Mira Mezini	Technical University of Darmstadt, Germany
Ana Moreira	Universidade Nova de Lisboa, Portugal
Linda Northrop	Software Engineering Institute, USA
Arnd Poetzsch-Heffter	Fern Universität Hagen, Germany
Tore Risch	Uppsala University, Sweden
Houari A. Sahraoui	University of Montreal, Canada
Douglas Schmidt	University of California at Irvine, USA
Bran Selic	Rational Software Corporation, USA
Jan Vitek	Purdue University, USA
John Vlissides	IBM T.J. Watson Research Center, USA
Wolfgang Weck	Oberon microsystems, Switzerland

Sponsoring Organizations

Referees

João Araújo
Dirk Bäumer
Lars Bendix
Joshua Bloch
Salah Bouktif
Chandrasekhar Boyapati
Coral Calero Muñoz
Bogdan Carbunar
Gary Chastek
Shigeru Chiba
Robert Clark
Cliff Click
Sholom Cohen
Aino Corry
Erik Corry
Wim De Pauw
Misha Dmitriev
Karel Driesen
Torbjörn Ekman
Chapman Flack
Matthew Flatt
Alexander Garthwaite
Aaron Greenhouse
Dominik Gruntz
Pedro Guerreiro
Markku Hakala
Roger Henriksson
Scott Hissam
David Holmes
Wilson Hsieh
Yuuji Ichisugi
Anders Ive
Ralph Keller
Gregor Kiczales
Joseph Kiniry
Georgios Koutsoukos
Reed Little
Erkki Mäkinen
Kai-Uwe Mätzel
Eva Magnusson
Thomas Mailund
Jeremey Manson

Gergana Markova
Fuyuhiko Maruyama
Hidehiko Masuhara
Jörg Meyer
Hafedh Mili
Todd Millstein
Gabriel Moreno
Peter Mueller
Anders Nilsson
James Noble
Lennart Ohlsson
Kasper Østerbye
Krzysztof Palacz
Jens Palsberg
Tony Printezis
William Pugh
Awais Rachid
Nicole Rauch
William Retert
Sven Robertz
Jim Rumbaugh
Kenneth Russell
Markku Sakkinen
Alexandru Salcianu
Ichiro Sato
Ursula Scheben
Petri Selonen
Paulo Sérgio Almeida
Judith Stafford
Tarja Systä
Michiaki Tatsubori
Kenjiro Taura
Petko Valtchev
Tom VanDrunen
Andre Weinand
Adam Welc
Michel Wermelinger
Lei Wu
Francesco Zappa Nardelli
Tian Zhao
Yoav Zibin

Table of Contents

Invited Talk 2

Distributed Systems

Patterns and Architecture

Languages

Optimization

Theory and Formal Techniques

Semantic Models
for Distributed Object Reflection

José Meseguer[1] and Carolyn Talcott[2]

[1] Computer Science Department, University of Illinois at Urbana-Champaign,
Urbana IL 61801
[2] Computer Science Laboratory, SRI International, Menlo Park, CA 94025

Abstract. A generic formal model of distributed object reflection is proposed, that combines logical reflection with a structuring of distributed objects as nested configurations of metaobject that can control subobjects under them. The model provides mathematical models for a good number of existing models of distributed reflection and of reflective middleware. To illustrate the ideas, we show in some detail how two important models of distributed actor reflection can be naturally obtained as special cases of our generic model, and discuss how several recent models of reflective middleware can be likewise formalized as instances of our model.

1 Introduction

Distributed object reflection is a crucial technique for the development of a next generation of adaptive middleware systems, mobile languages, active networks, and ubiquitous embedded distributed systems. Semantic models for distributed object reflection can serve two important purposes. First of all, they can contribute to the *conceptual sharpening and unification* of reflective notions, so that existing reflective systems become easier to understand and, more importantly, so that the design of new systems can be done in a clear, simple, and principled way. A second important concern is *high assurance*, which is harder to achieve because of the complexity added by reflection to already complex distributed systems. This concern is real enough, because reflective systems, for all their nice properties, can become *Trojan horses* through which system security could be compromised in potentially devastating ways. Without semantic models any *mathematical* verification of highly critical system properties is of course impossible.

In this paper we propose a generic formal model of distributed object reflection that seems very flexible: it yields as special cases mathematical models for a good number of existing models of distributed reflection and of reflective middleware. The model is based on a simple *executable logic* for distributed system specification, namely rewriting logic [51,52]. Rewriting logic has high performance implementations [19,15], as well as an environment of formal tools including theorem provers [21], and model checkers such as the Maude LTL model checker. Therefore, the semantic model of a reflective distributed object

B. Magnusson (Ed.): ECOOP 2002, LNCS 2374, pp. 1–36, 2002.

system developed using the methods proposed here can be symbolically simulated, and can be formally analyzed using model checking and theorem proving tools.

One important feature of our generic model is the powerful combination of *distributed object reflection* and *logical reflection* that it provides. We discuss logical reflection in Section 3. In the rest of this introduction we first discuss earlier work on object-oriented reflection (Section 1.1) and on semantic models of distributed object reflection (Section 1.2). Then we explain in more detail the contributions of this paper (Section 1.3).

1.1   Object-Oriented Reflection

Research on computational reflection was initiated by work of Brian Smith [63] (3-Lisp) and Patty Maes [47] (3KRS). This work introduced ideas such as towers of reflection, and causal connection. An overview of research in computational reflection can be found in proceedings of several recent workshops and conferences [78,40,24,77,44].

Reflective Programming Languages. A number of reflective actor-based languages have been developed to support separation of concerns and high-level programming abstractions for distributed systems. The ABCL family of languages [76] explores different forms of reflection, including single-actor and group-based reflection. A layered reflection model (the *onion skin model*) [4,3] models different concerns such as application functionality, communication protocols and security requirements, and failure/dependability semantics separately and modularly as independent layers, providing services that may be composed, in various ways to achieve a desired overall behavior. This model has been used to support a number of high-level declarative programming abstractions such as synchronizers [32], actor spaces [2], real-time synchronizers [58], protocols that abstract over interaction patterns [66], and dynamic architectures [9]. Metaobject protocols [41] provide more restricted forms of reflective capability, providing interfaces to a language that give users the ability to incrementally modify the language's behavior and implementation. This approach has been generalized to the Aspect Oriented Programming paradigm [42] to facilitate separation of concerns, composition, and re-use in programming.

Operating Systems. A number of operating systems build on reflective distributed object models, thus allowing application objects to customize the system behavior. In the AL-D/1 reflective programming system [56] an object is represented by multiple models, allowing behavior to be described at different levels of abstraction and from different points of view. Additional examples are Apertos [38], Legion [34], and 2K [45].

Reflective Middleware. Adaptability and extensibility are prime requirements of middleware systems, and several groups are doing research on reflective middleware [44]. Reflective middleware typically builds on the idea of a metaobject protocol, with a metalevel describing the internal architecture of the middleware, and reflection used to inspect and modify internal components. Dynamic-Tao [43] is a reflective CORBA ORB [55] built as an extension of the Tao real-time CORBA ORB [61]. DynamicTao supports on-the-fly reconfiguration while maintaining consistency by reifying both internal structure and dependency relations using objects called configurators. In [74] the use of reflective middleware techniques to enhance adaptability in Quality of Service (QoS)-enabled component-based applications is discussed and illustrated using the Tao ORB. The distributed Multimedia Research Group at Lancaster University has proposed a reflective architecture for next-generation middleware based on multiple metamodels [13,12], and a prototype has been developed using the reflective capabilities of Python.

Middleware systems often contain components that are reflectively related to the application level and/or the underlying infrastructure. For example Quo [79,46] has *system condition objects* that provide interfaces to resources, mechanisms, orbs etc. that need to be observed, measured or controlled. Delegates reify method requests and evaluate them according to *contracts* that represent strategies for meeting service level agreements. Another example is the Grid Protocol architecture proposed in [31], in which the resource level contains protocols for query and control of individual resources.

1.2   Semantic Models of Distributed Object Reflection

Most of the work on computational reflection has focused on development of reflection mechanisms, and on design and use of reflective systems to achieve a variety of goals such as separation of concerns, extensibility, and dynamic adaptability. Much less work has been done on the underlying theory, although some initial efforts have been made toward developing semantic models, principles for reasoning and techniques for analysis.

A formal model of the ODP object reference model based on rewriting logic is given in [54], addressing key issues such as object binding. A translation of formal QoS specifications into monitors and controllers is discussed in [14]. In [48] a metaobject protocol for CORBA objects is formalized using the π-calculus. Such a formal model can be used to generate execution traces, and can be analyzed using existing tools for properties such as deadlock freedom. In [8] CSP is used to give a formal semantics to aspects and aspect weaving.

Two reflective architectures for actor computation have been used as a basis for defining and reasoning about composable services in dynamic adaptable distributed systems: the *onion skin* model and the *two-level actor machine (TLAM)* model. A formal executable semantics for the onion skin model of reflection is given in [26]. The TLAM [72,68,73,70] is a semantic framework for specifying, composing and reasoning about resource management services in open distributed systems. The two levels provide a clean separation of concerns and a natural basis for modeling and reasoning about customizable middleware and its integration with application activity. This model has been used to reason about distributed garbage collection [69], the safe composition of system-level activities such as remote creation, migration, and recording of global snapshots [71,72], and QoS-based multimedia services [68,70].

Maude has been used to formalize aspects of several existing distributed system standards. A method for integration with CORBA components is explained in [7] and Maude interaction with existing system components using SOAP is described in [6]. Using these ideas Maude executable specifications can plug and play with system components implemented on arbitrary platforms. Formal modeling of ODP enterprise and information viewpoints is illustrated in [28,29].

1.3   This Paper

Two important ingredients of our approach are the rewriting logic representation of distributed object systems (explained in Section 2) and the concept of logical reflection, including a logic-independent axiomatization of reflective logics in general, and rewriting logic reflection in particular (Section 3). Our generic model is then explained in Section 4. It combines two ideas:

1. a "Russian dolls" idea, in which distributed objects are structured in nested configurations of metaobjects that can control subobjects under them, with an arbitrary number of levels of nesting, so that a given metaobject may itself be a subobject of a metametaobject, and so on;
2. the use of logical reflection, so that subobjects may at times be metarepresented as *data*, again with an arbitrary number of levels of nesting; this, combined with the Russian dolls idea, greatly increases the reflective capabilities of a system, allowing, for example, a simple design of reflective systems that can be both mobile and adaptive.

The usefulness of any model has to be shown in its applications. We therefore show in detail how two important models of distributed actor reflection, the onion skin model, and the two-level actor machine model (TLAM) can be naturally obtained as special cases of our generic model (Section 5). Similarly, we discuss in Section 6 how several recent models of reflective middleware can be formalized in terms of our generic model. We finish the paper with some concluding remarks in Section 7.

2   Modeling Distributed Objects in Rewriting Logic

In this section we explain how distributed object systems are axiomatized in rewriting logic. In general, a rewrite theory is a triple $\mathcal{R} = (\Sigma, E, R)$, with (Σ, E) an equational specification with signature of operators Σ and a set of equational axioms E; and with R a collection of labelled rewrite rules. The equational specification describes the *static* structure of the distributed system's state space as an algebraic data type. The *dynamics* of the system are described by the rules in R that specify local concurrent *transitions* that can occur in the system axiomatized by $\mathcal{R}$, and that can be applied *modulo* the equations E.

Let us see in more detail how the state space of a distributed object system can be axiomatized as the initial algebra of an equational theory (Σ, E). That is, we need to explain the key state-building operators in Σ and the equations E that they satisfy. The concurrent state of an object-oriented system, often called a *configuration*, has typically the structure of a *multiset* made up of objects and messages. As we shall see in Section 4, there can be more general ways of structuring the distributed state than just as a *flat* multiset of objects and messages; however, the flat multiset structure is the simplest and will help us explain the basic ideas. Assuming such a structure, we can view configurations as built up by a binary multiset union operator which we can represent with empty syntax (i.e., juxtaposition) as

$$\_\ \_ : \texttt{Configuration} \times \texttt{Configuration} \longrightarrow \texttt{Configuration}.$$

(Following the conventions of mix-fix notation, underscore symbols (_) are used to indicate argument positions.) The operator $\_\ \_$ is declared to satisfy the structural laws of associativity and commutativity and to have identity $\emptyset$. Objects and messages are singleton multiset configurations, and belong to subsorts $\texttt{Object Msg} < \texttt{Configuration}$, so that more complex configurations are generated out of them by multiset union.

An *object* in a given state is represented as a term

$$\langle O : C \mid a_1 : v_1, \ldots, a_n : v_n \rangle$$

where O is the object's name or identifier, C is its class, the a_i's are the names of the object's *attribute identifiers*, and the v_i's are the corresponding *values*. The set of all the attribute-value pairs of an object state is formed by repeated application of the binary union operator $\_\ ,\ \_$ which also obeys structural laws of associativity, commutativity, and identity; i.e., the order of the attribute-value pairs of an object is immaterial. This finishes the description of some of the sorts, operators, and equations in the theory (Σ, E) axiomatizing the states of a concurrent object system. Particular systems will have additional operators and equations, specifying, for example, the data operators on attribute values, and perhaps other state-building operators besides multiset union.

The associativity and commutativity of a configuration's multiset structure make it very fluid. We can think of it as "soup" in which objects and messages float, so that any objects and messages can at any time come together and participate in a concurrent transition corresponding to a communication event of some kind. In general, the rewrite rules in R describing the dynamics of an object-oriented system can have the form

$$
\begin{aligned}
r: \quad & M_1 \ldots M_n \, \langle O_1 : F_1 \mid atts_1 \rangle \ldots \langle O_m : F_m \mid atts_m \rangle \\
& \longrightarrow \langle O_{i_1} : F'_{i_1} \mid atts'_{i_1} \rangle \ldots \langle O_{i_k} : F'_{i_k} \mid atts'_{i_k} \rangle \\
& \quad \langle Q_1 : D_1 \mid atts''_1 \rangle \ldots \langle Q_p : D_p \mid atts''_p \rangle \\
& \quad M'_1 \ldots M'_q \\
& \textit{if } C
\end{aligned}
$$

where r is the label, the Ms are message expressions, $i_1, \ldots, i_k$ are different numbers among the original $1, \ldots, m$, and C is the rule's condition. That is, a number of objects and messages can come together and participate in a transition in which some new objects may be created, others may be destroyed, and others can change their state, and where some new messages may be created. If two or more objects appear in the lefthand side, we call the rule *synchronous*, because it forces those objects to jointly participate in the transition. If there is only one object in the lefthand side, we call the rule *asynchronous*. The above rule format assumes again a *flat* multiset configuration of objects and messages. We shall see in Sections 4-5 more general rules specifying object interactions in nonflat state configurations.

For example, we can consider three classes of objects, Buffer, Sender, and Receiver. The buffer stores a list of numbers in its q attribute. Lists of numbers are built using an associative list concatenation operator, _._ with identity nil, and numbers are regarded as lists of length one. The name of the object reading from the buffer is stored in its reader attribute. The sender and receiver objects store a number in a cell attribute that can also be empty (mt) and have also a counter (cnt) attribute. The sender stores also the name of the receiver in an additional attribute. The counter attribute is used to ensure that messages are received by the receiver in the same order as they are sent by the sender even though communication between the two parties is asynchronous. Each time the sender gets a new message from the buffer, it increments its counter. It uses the current value of the counter to tag the message sent to the receiver. The receiver only accepts a message whose tag is its current counter. It then increments its counter indicating that it is ready for the next message. Using Maude syntax [19,20], the three classes above are defined by declaring the name of the class, followed by a "|", followed by a list of pairs giving the names of attributes and corresponding value sorts. Thus we have

```
class Buffer | q: List[Nat], reader: OId .
class Sender | cell: Default[Nat], cnt: Nat, receiver: OId .
class Receiver | cell: Default[Nat], cnt: Nat .
```

where OId is the sort of *object identifiers*, List[Nat] is the sort of lists of natural numbers, and Default[Nat] is a supersort of Nat adding the constant mt. Then, three typical rewrite rules for objects in these classes (where E and N range over natural numbers, L over lists of numbers, L.E is a list with last element E, and (to Z : E from (Y,N)) is a message) are

```
rl [read] : < X : Buffer | q: L . E, reader: Y >
                < Y : Sender | cell: mt, cnt: N >
            => < X : Buffer | q: L, reader: Y >
                < Y : Sender | cell: E, cnt: N + 1 > .

rl [send] : < Y : Sender | cell: E, cnt: N, receiver: Z >
          => < Y : Sender | cell: mt, cnt: N > (to Z : E from (Y,N)) .

rl [receive] : < Z : Receiver | cell: mt, cnt: N >
                  (to Z : E from (Y,N))
              => < Z : Receiver | cell: E, cnt: N + 1 > .
```

where the **read** rule is synchronous and the **send** and **receive** rules asynchronous. These rules are applied *modulo* the associativity and commutativity of the multiset union operator, and therefore allow both object synchronization and message sending and receiving events anywhere in the configuration, regardless of the position of the objects and messages. We can then consider the rewrite theory $\mathcal{R} = (\Sigma, E, R)$ axiomatizing the object system with these three object classes, and with R the three rules above (and perhaps other rules, such as one for the receiver to write its contents into another buffer object, that we omit).

Rewriting logic [51] then gives a simple inference system to deduce, for a system axiomatized by a rewrite theory $\mathcal{R}$, all the finitary concurrent computations possible in such a system. Such computations are identified with *proofs* of the general form $\alpha : t \longrightarrow t'$ in the logic. The intuitive idea is that such proofs/computations correspond to finitary concurrent behaviors of the distributed system so axiomatized. They are described as *concurrent rewritings*, where several rules may fire simultaneously in the distributed state, can be followed by other such simultaneous firing of other rules, and so on.

For example, a buffer object a, and sender and receiver objects b and c can be involved in a concurrent computation in which b reads a value from a and sends it to c, and then, simultaneously, c receives it and b reads a second value from a. Suppose that we begin with the following initial configuration C_0

```
< a : Buffer | q: 7 . 9, reader: b >
< c : Receiver | cell: mt, cnt: 1 >
< b : Sender | cell: mt, cnt: 0, receiver : c >
```

Then, the configuration C_0 is transformed by the above-mentioned concurrent rewriting into the following final configuration C_1:

```
< a : Buffer | q: nil, reader: b >
< b : Sender | cell: 7, cnt: 2, receiver : c >
< c : Receiver | cell: 9, cnt: 2 >
```

Under reasonable assumptions about the rewrite theory $\mathcal{R}$, such concurrent rewritings can be *executed*, either by *simulating* the concurrent rewriting as multiset rewriting in a sequential implementation of rewriting logic such as Maude [19,20], ELAN [15], or CafeOBJ [33]; or by *distributed execution* in a language such as Mobile Maude [27] in which the rewrite rules *are* the distributed code.

3   Logical Reflection

In logic, reflection has been studied by many researchers since the fundamental work of Gödel and Tarski (see the surveys [64,65]). One strand of computer science research on reflection is related, either implicitly or explicitly, to the logical understanding of reflection. The two areas where this strand has been mostly developed are: (1) declarative programming languages, where logical reflection is used in the form of *metacircular interpreters* [59]; and (2) theorem proving, where logical reflection can be used to increase in a disciplined and sound way the deductive power of theorem provers.

Different logics may be involved. For declarative languages one could mention, among others, reflective language designs based on the pure lambda calculus [53], equational logic [67], and Horn logic [36]. In theorem proving there has been a substantial body of research on logical reflection based on both first-order formalisms and higher-order logics, including, for example, [75,16,37,5,49,62,60].

An issue that only recently has received attention is axiomatizing the notion of a *reflective logic* in a *logic-independent* way, that is, within a metatheory of general logics [50], so that we can view and compare the different instances of logical reflection based on different formalisms as special cases of a general concept. This has been done by Clavel and Meseguer [22,17]. We present below the general notion of logic, called an *entailment system* [50], on which their actual definition of reflective logic is based.

3.1   Entailment Systems and Reflective Logics

We assume that logical syntax is given by a *signature* Σ that provides a grammar for building *sentences*. For first-order logic, a typical signature consists of a collection of function and predicate symbols which are used to build up sentences by means of the usual logical connectives. In general, it is enough to assume that for each logic there is a category **Sign** of possible signatures, and a functor *sen* assigning to each signature Σ the set $sen(\Sigma)$ of all its sentences.

For a given signature Σ in **Sign**, *entailment* (also called *provability*) of a sentence $\varphi \in sen(\Sigma)$ from a set of axioms $\Gamma \subseteq sen(\Sigma)$ is a relation $\Gamma \vdash \varphi$ that holds if and only if we can prove φ from the axioms Γ using the rules of the logic. We make this relation relative to a signature. In what follows, $|\mathcal{C}|$ denotes the collection of objects of a category $\mathcal{C}$.

Definition 1. [50] *An* entailment system *is a triple* $\mathcal{E} = (\mathbf{Sign}, sen, \vdash)$ *such that*

- **Sign** *is a category whose objects are called* signatures,
- *sen* : **Sign** $\longrightarrow$ **Set** *is a functor associating to each signature Σ a corresponding set of Σ-sentences, and*
- $\vdash$ *is a function associating to each $\Sigma \in |\mathbf{Sign}|$ a binary relation $\vdash_\Sigma \subseteq \mathcal{P}(sen(\Sigma)) \times sen(\Sigma)$ called Σ-entailment such that the following properties are satisfied:*
  1. *reflexivity: for any $\varphi \in sen(\Sigma)$, $\{\varphi\} \vdash_\Sigma \varphi$,*
  2. *monotonicity: if $\Gamma \vdash_\Sigma \varphi$ and $\Gamma' \supseteq \Gamma$ then $\Gamma' \vdash_\Sigma \varphi$,*
  3. *transitivity: if $\Gamma \vdash_\Sigma \varphi_i$, for all $i \in I$, and $\Gamma \cup \{\varphi_i \mid i \in I\} \vdash_\Sigma \psi$, then $\Gamma \vdash_\Sigma \psi$,*
  4. *$\vdash$-translation: if $\Gamma \vdash_\Sigma \varphi$, then for any signature morphism $H : \Sigma \longrightarrow \Sigma'$ in **Sign**, $sen(H)(\Gamma) \vdash_{\Sigma'} sen(H)(\varphi)$, where $sen(H)(\Gamma) = \{sen(H)(\varphi) \mid \varphi \in \Gamma\}$, as is standard.*

Given an entailment system $\mathcal{E}$, its category **Th** of *theories*[1] has as objects pairs $T = (\Sigma, \Gamma)$ with Σ a signature and $\Gamma \subseteq sen(\Sigma)$. A *theory morphism* (also called a *theory interpretation*) $H : (\Sigma, \Gamma) \longrightarrow (\Sigma', \Gamma')$ is a signature morphism $H : \Sigma \longrightarrow \Sigma'$ such that if $\varphi \in \Gamma$, then $\Gamma' \vdash_{\Sigma'} sen(H)(\varphi)$. By composing with the forgetful functor $sign : \textbf{Th} \longrightarrow \textbf{Sign}$, with $sign(\Sigma, \Gamma) = \Sigma$, we can extend the functor $sen : \textbf{Sign} \longrightarrow \textbf{Set}$ to a functor $sen : \textbf{Th} \longrightarrow \textbf{Set}$, i.e., we define $sen(T) = sen(sign(T))$.

Reflection can now be defined as a property of an entailment system. Although stronger requirements can be given (see [22,17,11]) the most basic property one wants is the capacity to metarepresent *theories and sentences* as expressions at the object level, and to then *simulate deduction* in those theories using the corresponding metarepresentations. This is captured by the notion of a *universal theory* defined below.

Definition 2. *([22,17]) Given an entailment system $\mathcal{E}$ and a nonempty set of theories $\mathcal{C}$ in it, a theory U is $\mathcal{C}$-universal if there is a function, called a representation function,*

$$\overline{(\_\vdash\_)} : \bigcup_{T \in \mathcal{C}} (\{T\} \times sen(T)) \longrightarrow sen(U),$$

such that for each $T \in \mathcal{C}, \varphi \in sen(T)$,

$$T \vdash \varphi \ \textit{iff}\ U \vdash \overline{T \vdash \varphi}.$$

If, in addition, $U \in \mathcal{C}$, then the entailment system $\mathcal{E}$ is called $\mathcal{C}$-reflective. Finally, a reflective logic *is a logic whose entailment system is $\mathcal{C}$-reflective for $\mathcal{C}$, the class of all finitely presentable theories in the logic.*

3.2   Reflection in Rewriting Logic and Maude

Rewriting logic is reflective in the precise axiomatic sense of Definition 2 above [17,23]. This is particularly useful for our purposes here, not only because of the advantages that this provides in a logically reflective language design such as Maude, but also because of the powerful ways in which, as explained in Section 4, logical reflection and distributed object-oriented reflection can be combined.

Indeed, as required by Definition 2, rewriting logic has a universal theory $\mathcal{U}$ and a representation function $\overline{(\_\vdash\_)}$ encoding pairs consisting of a rewrite theory $\mathcal{R}$ and a sentence in it as sentences in $\mathcal{U}$. Specifically, for any finitely presented rewrite theory $\mathcal{R}$ (including $\mathcal{U}$ itself) and any terms t, t' in $\mathcal{R}$, the representation function is defined by

$$\overline{\mathcal{R} \vdash t \longrightarrow t'} = \langle \overline{\mathcal{R}}, \overline{t} \rangle \longrightarrow \langle \overline{\mathcal{R}}, \overline{t}' \rangle,$$

where $\overline{\mathcal{R}}, \overline{t}$, and $\overline{t}'$ are ground terms in $\mathcal{U}$.

---

[1] What we call theories are sometimes called *theory presentations* in the literature.

Since $\mathcal{U}$ is representable in itself, we can achieve a "reflective tower" with an arbitrary number of levels of reflection, since we have

$$\mathcal{R} \vdash t \to t' \;\Leftrightarrow\; \mathcal{U} \vdash \langle \overline{\mathcal{R}}, \overline{t} \rangle \to \langle \overline{\mathcal{R}}, \overline{t'} \rangle \;\Leftrightarrow\; \mathcal{U} \vdash \left\langle \overline{\mathcal{U}}, \overline{\langle \overline{\mathcal{R}}, \overline{t} \rangle} \right\rangle \to \left\langle \overline{\mathcal{U}}, \overline{\langle \overline{\mathcal{R}}, \overline{t'} \rangle} \right\rangle \ldots$$

Reflection is systematically exploited in the Maude rewriting logic language implementation [19,18], that provides key features of the universal theory $\mathcal{U}$ in a built-in module called META-LEVEL. In particular, META-LEVEL has sorts Term and Module, so that the representations $\overline{t}$ and $\overline{\mathcal{R}}$ of a term t and a module $\mathcal{R}$ have sorts Term and Module, respectively. META-LEVEL has also functions meta-reduce($\overline{\mathcal{R}}, \overline{t}$), meta-rewrite($\overline{\mathcal{R}}, \overline{t}, n$), and meta-apply($\overline{\mathcal{R}}, \overline{t}, \overline{l}, \overline{\sigma}, n$) which return, respectively, the representation of the reduced form of a term t using the equations in the module $\mathcal{R}$, the representation of the result of rewriting a term t at most n steps with the default interpreter using the rules in the module $\mathcal{R}$, and the (representation of the) result of applying a rule labeled l in the module $\mathcal{R}$ to a term t at the top with the $(n + 1)$th match consistent with the partial substitution σ. As the universal theory $\mathcal{U}$ that it implements in a built-in fashion, META-LEVEL can also support a reflective tower with an arbitrary number of levels of reflection.

4   Semantic Models of Distributed Object Reflection

We first present, in Section 4.1, a "Russian dolls" model of distributed object reflection first sketched in [52]. We then motivate the need for logical reflection in Section 4.2 by explaining how mobility and code adaptation can be naturally supported. Our generic model of Russian dolls with logical reflection is then explained in Section 4.3 and is illustrated by means of the Mobile Maude [27] language design.

4.1   Distributed Object Reflection through Russian Dolls

In simple situations the distributed state of an object-based system can be conceptualized as a *flat configuration* involving objects and messages. As explained in Section 2, we can visualize this configuration as a "soup" in which the objects and messages float and interact with each other through asynchronous message passing and/or other synchronous interactions. In practice, however, there are often good reasons for *having boundaries* that circumscribe parts of a distributed object state. For example, the Internet is not really a flat network, but a *network of networks*, having different network *domains*, that may not be directly accessible except through specific gateways, firewalls, and so on. This means that in general we should not think of a distributed state as a *flat soup*, but as a *soup of soups*, each enclosed within specific boundaries. Of course, *soups can be nested within other soups* with any desirable depth of nesting. This suggests a *Russian dolls* metaphor: the charming Russian folk art dolls that contain inside other dolls, which in turn contain others, and so on.

Mathematically, this nested structuring of the state can be specified by *boundary operators* of the general form,

$$b : s_1 \ldots s_n \text{ Configuration} \longrightarrow \text{Configuration},$$

where $s_1 \ldots s_n$ are additional sorts, called the *parameters* of the boundary operator, that may be needed to endow the configuration wrapped by b with additional information. The simplest possible example is a boundary operator of the form,

$$\{\_\} : \text{Configuration} \longrightarrow \text{Configuration},$$

which just wraps a configuration adding no extra information. A more flexible, yet still simple, variant is provided by an operator

$$\{\_ \mid \_\} : \text{Location Configuration} \longrightarrow \text{Configuration},$$

where each wrapped configuration is now *located* in a specific location l of sort Location. The set of locations may then have additional structure such as, for example, being a free monoid. Another variant is an operator that adds an interface to a configuration of objects and messages

$$\{\_ \mid \_\} : \text{Interface Configuration} \longrightarrow \text{Configuration}.$$

An interface can be as simple as a pair of sets of object identifiers (ρ, χ) where ρ is a subset of identifiers of objects in the configuration called the *receptionists* and χ is the set of identifiers of objects external to the configuration but accessible from within the configuration. Only receptionists are visible from outside the wrapped configuration. An interface could be more complex, for example specifying the types of messages that can be received or sent.

Yet another quite general method for defining boundary operators is by means of *object classes with a configuration-valued attribute*. These are classes of the general form,

```
class C | conf : Configuration, ATTS .
```

with ATTS the remaining attribute declarations for the class. That is, a configuration is now *wrapped inside the state of a containing object*. We call such a containing object a *metaobject*, and the objects in its internal configuration its *subobjects*. Similarly, for other boundary operators b_1, b_2, objects O_1, O_2, remaining configurations C_1, C_2, and parameters $\vec{p}_1, \vec{p}_2$, whenever we have a nested configuration of the form,

$$b_1(\vec{p}_1, O_1 C_1 b_2(\vec{p}_2, O_2 C_2))$$

we call O_1 a *metaobject*, and O_2 is then one of its *subobjects*. Note that the metaobject-subobject relation can be both *many-to-many* and *nested*. For example in the nested configuration

$$b_1(\vec{p}_1, O_1 O_2 C_1 b_2(\vec{p}_2, O_3 O_4 C_2 b_3(\vec{p}_3, O_5 C_3)))$$

the objects O_1, O_2 are both metaobjects of O_3, O_4, which in turn are both metaobjects of O_5. We then say that O_1, O_2 are *meta-metaobjects* of O_5, and that O_5 is one of their *sub-subobjets*, and we can extend this terminology in the obvious way to any number of nesting levels.

Although the Russian dolls model of distributed object reflection is quite simple, it can provide a clear rewriting logic semantics allowing us to express quite sophisticated models of distributed object reflection already proposed in the literature as special instances of the general framework. In Sections 5 and 6 we discuss several such models that we have axiomatized this way. Their semantics is provided by specifying two things:

1. the specific *wrapping and nesting discipline* defining the allowable nested configurations (specified by an *equational theory*, with an associated *signature* of sorts, subsorts, and operators); and
2. the *interaction semantics* between objects and subobjects, which is typically specified by *boundary-crossing rewrite rules*.

By boundary-crossing rewrite rules we mean rewrite rules that allow objects and messages to interact across boundaries. For example, a metaobject O_1 may intercept and encrypt with a function k the contents of a message of the form $(M \triangleright O_3)$ sent to an outside object O_3 by its subobject O_2. This could be specified with a rewrite rule of the form,

$$b_1(\vec{p}_1, O_1 C_1 b_2(\vec{p}_2, O_2(M \triangleright O_3)C_2)) \rightarrow b_1(\vec{p}_1, O_1(k(M) \triangleright O_3)C_1 b_2(\vec{p}_2, O_2 C_2))$$

The reflective architecture thus defined is typically *very generic*, allowing the objects involved to belong to a wide range of object classes. Of course, some very general assumptions about object behavior in such classes (for example, communication by asynchronous message passing) may be required for correctness. Therefore, in each concrete instance of a reflective architecture of this kind, besides the generic interaction semantics provided by the boundary-crossing rewrite rules we have also an *application-specific semantics* provided by the rewrite rules for the concrete classes of objects involved in that specific instance. One of the great advantages of reflective architectures is of course the *modularity* and *separation of concerns* that they support, since the reflective interaction semantics is completely independent of the application-specific semantics of each instance.

Reflective architectures based on the Russian dolls paradigm are quite expressive, in the sense that metaobjects can perform a wide range of services and can control their subobjects in many different ways. For example, they can:

– provide security, fault-tolerance, and other communication service features (for example, different forms of quality-of-service properties) in a modular way;
– broadcast information to their subobjects, and gather and aggregate their responses;
– perform system monitoring in a distributed and hierarchical way, and take appropriate metalevel actions (for example, anomaly detection and response);

- control the execution of their underlying subobjects in different ways, including freezing[2], unfreezing, and scheduling of subobjects;
- create new subobjects or delete existing ones.

However, the Russian dolls model of reflection needs to be generalized in order to provide more powerful features for *code morphing*, *runtime dynamic adaptation*, and *mobility*. Models for such features require the use of *logical reflection*, as explained below.

4.2   Metaobjects with Logical Reflection

We can motivate the need for logical reflection by considering mobility. If objects don't move, their *code* can be static: it can typically be compiled once and for all to run on the execution engine available at the specific location where the object resides. By contrast, a *mobile object* has to carry with it its own code, which can then be executed in the different remote locations visited by the object. Code mobility is needed because the execution engines in those remote locations typically *have no a priori knowledge* of the mobile object's code.

How can this be formally specified in rewriting logic, and how can it be executed in a language like Maude? The key idea is to use logical reflection, and to regard mobile objects as *metaobjects whose code and state are metarepresented as values of some of their attributes*. We can for example define a class,

```
class Mobile | s : Term, mod : Module, ATTS .
```

where we assume that the module defining the class `Mobile` of mobile objects imports the `META-LEVEL` module. Then the value of the `mod` attribute is a term of sort `Module` in `META-LEVEL`, namely the meta-representation $\overline{\mathcal{R}}$ of the rewrite theory $\mathcal{R}$ containing the rules of the mobile object. Similarly the value of the `s` attribute is a term $\overline{C}$ of sort `Term` in `META-LEVEL`, namely the metarepresentation of a configuration C corresponding to the current state of the mobile object. In Mobile Maude [27] the configuration C contains an object *having the same name as that of its enclosing metaobject*, plus current incoming and outgoing messages; that its, the mobile metaobject contains the metarepresentation of an *homunculus subobject* with its same name.

How can mobile objects then be executed in different remote locations without prior knowledge of their code? The idea is that the execution engine of each remote location only needs to know about `META-LEVEL` and about the rewrite rules of the `Mobile` class; they need no knowledge whatever of the mobile object's code, that is, of the particular application-specific rewrite theory $\mathcal{R}$ specifying that code. We can illustrate this idea with the following key rule for the `Mobile` class [27]:

---

[2] Freezing of the state of subobjects can be specified by applying *frozen* operators, that forbid rewriting in any of their arguments, or by other type-theoretic means. Maude 2.0 supports the declaration of frozen operators with the `frozen` attribute.

```
rl [do-something] : < M : Mobile | s : T, mod : MOD > =>
    < M : Mobile | s : meta-rewrite(MOD,T,1), mod : MOD > .
```

where, as explained in Section 3.2, meta-rewrite(MOD,T,1) is a META-LEVEL expression that performs at the metalevel one rewrite step of the term metarepresented by T with the rewrite rules of the module metarepresented by MOD. One can easily imagine extra attributes ATTS for such mobile objects, as suggested above. For example, to prevent *runaway mobile objects* one may wish to have a gas attribute, indicating the overall amount of computational resources that the object will be allowed to use in a given location; then each application of the do-something rule could decrease the gas amount by one unit.

Another way of motivating the need for metaobjects that make an essential use of logical reflection is by considering *dynamic code adaptation*. Consider a class of adaptive objects which can change their code at runtime to deal with new situations. They may for example be mobile objects that—depending on the resources available at different physical locations and on other considerations such as security warnings or attacks—can change the protocols that they use to communicate with other objects. Furthermore, those changes need not be restricted to a fixed, finite repertoire of choices; they may be much more finely tunable by means of different *parameters*, allowing a possibly infinite range of code specializations. Again, the question is how to formally specify metaobjects that can adapt in this way. The answer is similar to the case of mobile objects, namely, such metaobjects should have their code and their state metarepresented. We can define a class, say,

```
class Adaptive | s : Term, mod : Module, ATTS .
```

where we assume that the module defining the class Adaptive of adaptive objects imports the META-LEVEL module. Therefore, as before, the value of the mod attribute will be a term of sort Module in META-LEVEL, namely the metarepresentation $\overline{\mathcal{R}}$ of the rewrite theory $\mathcal{R}$ containing the current rules of the adaptive object. Similarly the value of the s attribute will be a term $\overline{C}$ of sort Term in META-LEVEL, namely the metarepresentation of a configuration C corresponding to the current state of the adaptive object. Again, we may adopt the convention that the configuration C contains an object *having the same name as that of its enclosing metaobject*, plus current incoming and outgoing messages; that is, that the adaptive metaobject contains the metarepresentation of an *homunculus subobject* with its same name.

Adaptation may in fact occur along different dimensions and for different purposes. There may be a set of *adaptation policies* dictating which forms of adaptation are suitable at a given moment and with which parameters. Such policies may be implemented by invoking specific *adaptation functions*, which change the code and perhaps also the state representation. These adaptation functions have the general form,

$$a.mod : \text{Module } s_1 \ldots s_n \longrightarrow \text{Module},$$

$$a.s : \text{Term Module } s_1 \ldots s_n \longrightarrow \text{Term},$$

where $s_1 \ldots s_n$ are additional sorts used as *parameters* by the adaptation function. That is, *a.mod* takes (the metarepresentation of) a module and a list of parameters, and returns (the metarepresentation of) a transformed module as a result. Similarly, *a.s* takes (the metarepresentations of) a state and its corresponding module, plus a list of parameters, and returns (the metarepresentation of) a transformed state as a result. A particular policy may dictate that, under certain conditions, these functions are invoked on both the code and the state to adapt the object. For example, assuming that under the given policies a.mod-i and a.s-i are the ith pair of adaptation functions which should be invoked if a certain condition cond occurs, we can specify that particular adaptation by a rewrite rule of the general schematic form,

```
rl [a-i] : < O : Adaptive | s : T, mod : MOD, ATTS > =>
   < O : Adaptive | s : a.s-i(T,MOD,P), mod : a.mod-i(MOD,P), ATTS' >
                                                    if cond(X) .
```

where ATTS and ATTS' may be entire terms, and not just variables, and where P and X denote lists of variables.

The need for *several levels of logical reflection* may be illustrated by considering the case of objects that are *both mobile and adaptive*. The point is that mobility is a much more generic capability—applicable to object systems of many different classes with very few restrictions—than adaptation. Therefore, it seems reasonable to assume that a mobile language implementation will have the *generic code* supporting the execution and interaction of general mobile objects available in all execution engines at all locations. By contrast, adaptation is much more *application-specific*: it is not reasonable at all to assume a single class of rewrite rules for adaptation that would fit all objects and would be available everywhere. There may be many different classes of adaptive objects for different applications. This means that if an object is both mobile and adaptive, *the adaptation code must move with the object*.

How can this be done? By using *two levels of logical reflection*. There is a meta-metaobject that is a mobile object, say of class Mobile. The value of the mod attribute is now the metarepresentation $\overline{\mathcal{A}}$ of a rewrite theory $\mathcal{A}$ specifying a class, say, Adapt-app of adaptive objects for application app. Similarly, the value of the s attribute will now be the metarepresentation $\overline{C}$ of configuration C containing an *homunculus subobject* with the same name *which is itself an adaptive metaobject*. Therefore, such an homunculus subobject contains in its s attribute the metarepresentation $\overline{C'}$ of another configuration C' containing *another homunculus subobject*, namely the baselevel object that is both mobile and adaptive. We can visualize the two levels of logical reflection involved with the mobile meta-metaobject, the adaptive metaobject, and the baselevel object by considering that the mobile object state must have the form:

$$\langle O : \texttt{Mobile} \mid s : C_1 \langle O : \texttt{Adapt} - \texttt{app} \mid s : \overline{C_2 \langle O : Cl \mid ATTS \rangle}, ATT' \rangle, ATT'' \rangle ATT''' \rangle$$

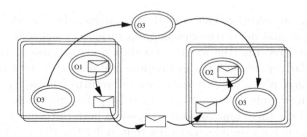

Fig. 1. Object and message mobility

4.3   The General Case: Russian Dolls with Logical Reflection

Having metaobjects with logical reflection allows us to do all that metaobjects without such reflection can do in the Russians dolls model presented in Section 4.1 and more. In particular, mobility and adaptation can be naturally modeled by logical reflection.

The two ideas of Russian dolls and logical reflection can be naturally combined and generalized into a model of *Russian dolls with logical reflection*. The idea is that the distributed state will still be a *nested and distributed soup of soups*—the Russian dolls—but now *the subobjects of a metaobject may or may not be metarepresented*, depending on the specific reflective needs of the application in question. As before, the metaobject-subobject relation can be both *many-to-many* and *nested*. Whether a subobject of a metaobject is metarepresented or not is a *purely local property* in the acyclic graph representing the metaobject-subobject relation. For example, a metaobject O_1 may contain a subobject O_2 that is metarepresented, but O_2 may itself be a metaobject containing a subobject O_3 which is *not* metarepresented. Of course, from O_1's perspective, both O_2 and O_3 are metarepresented; but they are metarepresented *at the same level*, that is, using only one level of reflection.

We can illustrate these ideas by explaining how the general model of Russian dolls with logical reflection becomes instantiated in the case of Mobile Maude [27]. In Mobile Maude the two key entities are *processes* and *mobile objects*. Processes are located computational environments where mobile objects can reside. Mobile objects can move between different processes in different locations, and can communicate asynchronously with each other by means of messages. As already explained, each mobile object contains its own code—that is, a rewrite theory $\mathcal{R}$—metarepresented as a term $\overline{\mathcal{R}}$, as well as its own internal state, also metarepresented as $\overline{C}$, for C a configuration containing the *homonimous homunculus subobject*.

Figure 1 shows several processes in two locations, with mobile object $o3$ moving from one process to another, and with object $o1$ sending a message to $o2$.

Note the double oval around each mobile object. This is a pictorial way of indicating that mobile objects consist of both the outer metaobject and its inner homonimous homunculus subobject.

From the perspective of our general model of reflection, note that:

- the top-level structure of a Mobile Maude distributed state is a *soup of processes*;
- each process is itself a metaobject, which contains an *inner soup of subobjects*, namely the mobile objects currently residing inside that process; furthermore, those subobjects are *not* metarepresented: since *processes do not move*, there is no need in this case to pay for an extra level of logical reflection;
- however, each mobile object is itself a metaobject whose homonimous homunculus subobject, as well as its rules, *are* metarepresented, since this is needed to support mobility.

The above description only mentions the first three levels of the metaobject-subobject relation. But nothing prevents the homunculus subobject of a mobile object from having other subobjects, and they in turn other subobjects, with no a priori bound on the number of nesting levels. Furthermore, at any level the corresponding subobject may or may not be metarepresented. We have already seen an example of this in Section 4.2, namely an adaptive mobile object whose homunculus subobject is itself an adaptive metaobject which contains another homunculus baseobject, also metarepresented.

5   Some Models of Distributed Reflection

The actor model of computation [35,10,1] is a natural model for open distributed systems. To support separation of concerns in developing and (dynamically) adapting open distributed systems, and to support high-level programming abstractions, a number of models of actor reflection have been proposed (see Section 1.1). In this section we show how two of these models, the onion skin [3,26] and the two-level actor machine (TLAM) [72,68], can be formalized using the ideas proposed in Section 4.

We will use the classic *ticker* example augmented with a meta-level monitor to illustrate how the two models work. A ticker has a counter which is incremented in response to a `tick` message. A ticker also replies to `time` requests.

```
Vars: c,t in Oid,  n in Nat
Messages:   tick, time@c, reply(n)
Rules:
    < t : Ticker | ctr: n > t <- tick
      ==>
    < t : Ticker | ctr: n+1 > t <- tick

    < t : Ticker | ctr: n > t <- time@c
      ==>
    < t : Ticker | ctr: n > c <- reply(n)
```

Here is a simple computation starting with a ticker and an object c that knows the ticker. Concurrently, the ticker processes a `tick` message, and c generates a `time` request. Then the ticker processes the request. We annotate the transition arrows with information describing the associated event.

```
< t : Ticker | ctr: 1 > t <- tick  < c : C | ... t ... >
   = deliver(t<-tick) | exe(c)=>
< t : Ticker | ctr: 2 > t <- tick t <- time@c < c : C | ... t ... >
   = deliver(time@c) =>
< t : Ticker | ctr: 2 > t <- tick c <- reply(2) < c : C | ... t ... >
```

Ticker Monitor Specification. A ticker monitor is a metaactor that observes delivery of `time` requests to a ticker and reports the current counter, the number of requests, and the reply address to its coordinator `mc`. The monitor can also be asked to reset the ticker.

```
Vars: c,mc,t,tm in Oids,  n,m in Nat
Messages: log(t,n,m,c), reset, reset-ack
Rules:
[log]
 < tm : Monitor | state: M(t,mc,m) >
   = [deliver(<t:Ticker|ctr:n>t<-time@c)/ ] =>
 < tm : Monitor | state: M(t,mc,m+1) > mc <- log(t,n,m+1,c)
[reset]
 < tm : Monitor | state: M(t,mc,m) > tm <- reset
   =[ /t:= ctr:0]=>
 < tm : Monitor | state: M(t,mc,0) > mc <- reset-ack
```

The metaactor rules are annotated with a pair [event/effect]. If event is nonempty it specifies the baselevel events that fire the rule. If effect is nonempty it specifies an update to the baselevel state. Thus the `log` rule fires when a baselevel transition delivers a `time` message to the monitored ticker. A metalevel message is sent, but there is no effect on the baselevel state. The effect part of the `reset` rule causes the ticker `ctr` attribute to be set to 0 when a `reset` message is delivered. If we add a monitor to the ticker configuration, and rerun the computation scenario we see that the first step is unchanged, but when the `time` request is delivered, the `log` rule of the monitor fires, and a `log` message is sent. We also add a `tm <- reset` message to the initial configuration to see the effect action.

```
< tm : Monitor | state: M(t,mc,0) > tm <- reset
< t : Ticker | ctr: 1 > t <- tick  < c : C | ... t ... >
   = deliver(t<-tick) | ..c.. =>
< tm : Monitor | state: M(t,mc,0) > tm <- reset
< t : Ticker | ctr: 2 > t <- tick t <- time@c < c : C | ... t ... >
   = deliver(t<-time@c) =>
< tm : Monitor | state: M(t,mc,1) > mc <- log(t,2,1,c)  tm <- reset
< t : Ticker | ctr: 2 > t <- tick c <- reply(2) < c : C | ... t ... >
   = deliver(tm<-reset) =>
< tm : Monitor | state: M(t,mc,1) > mc <- log(t,2,1,c)  mc <- reset-ack
< t : Ticker | ctr: 0 > t <- tick c <- reply(2) < c : C | ... t ... >
```

We will show how monitor semantics is modeled in two reflective models by desugaring the rule annotations and defining appropriate compositions of monitor with ticker.

5.1   The Onion Skin Model

In the onion skin model each actor has a metaactor that defines the semantics of its primitive actions. For example, a message send by the actor becomes a request to its metaactor to transmit the message. Dually, messages sent to the actor are first received by its metaactor, giving the metaactor the capability to control the receive semantics. If no explicit metaactor behavior is defined, the underlying system semantics provides a default metaactor behavior. An actor composed with its metaactor appears, from the outside, like a normal actor, and thus can be controlled by a further metalevel actor. This gives rise to layers of metalevels and hence the "onion skin" analogy. Distributed services for a group of actors can be expressed in terms of metaactor layers that coordinate to achieve some overall property.

The formalization of the onion skin model presented here is adapted from [26]. Onion skin layers are formalized using *tower objects* that implement individual layers of a tower of objects. Objects at the bottom of a tower represent application-level objects. Each metaobject has as a subobject the object tower immediately below. A top-level object implements the default metaactor and enables communication with the environment.

More precisely there are three object classes that structure towers: `Top`, `MetaTower`, and `Tower`. The class `Tower` has two attributes: in and out. The attribute in is a list of messages representing messages to be delivered to the object. The attribute out is a list of outgoing requests for message transmittal and object creation. Baseobjects have the form

```
< o : BTC | in: msgs, out: reqs, atts >
```

where BTC is a subclass of `Tower`, msgs is a list of messages, reqs is a list of requests (for creation of objects and transmission of messages) and atts stands for the additional internal state attributes. Baselevel rules have the form

```
< o : BTC | in: msgs, out: reqs, atts >
   =>
< o : BTC | in: msgs', out: reqs . reqs', atts >
```

where msgs' is a tail of msgs (the result of removing zero or more messages from the beginning), and reqs . reqs' is the concatenation of the original outgoing requests with newly generated requests, reqs'.

The class `MetaTower` is a subclass of the class `Tower`. It has an additional attribute, base, whose value is a tower object. The relation between a metaobject and its subobject is the same at each level of the tower—the base-meta relation, hence the name base for the attribute. `MetaTower` objects have the form

```
< o : MTC | in: msgs, out: reqs,  base: tobj, atts >
```

where MTC is a subclass of `MetaTower`, tobj is a tower object and atts holds additional internal state attributes. Metalevel rules have the form

```
< o : MTC | in: msgs, out: reqs,
      base: < o : TC | in: dmsgs, out: ureqs, tatts >,
      atts>
```

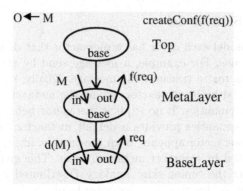

Fig. 2. A metaobject tower

```
  =>
< o : MTC | in: msgs', out: reqs . reqs',
      base: < o : TC | in: dmsgs . dmsgs', out: ureqs', tatts >,
      atts' >
```

where `msgs'` is a tail of `msgs`, `ureqs'` is a tail of `ureqs`, `dmsgs'` is a list of messages, and `reqs'` is a list of requests. The idea is that a metaobject can take a message from its `in` queue, or take a request from the `out` queue of its `base` subobject; and it can place requests in its own `out` queue or place messages in the `in` queue of its `base` subobject.

The class `Top` has one attribute, `base`, whose value is a tower object. `Top` objects only have rules for communication with the environment. These rules formalize the *default metaactor* behavior.

```
[in]
  o <- msg
  < o : Top | base: < o : TC | in: msgs, out: reqs,  tatts > >
    =>
  < o : Top | base: < o : TC | in: msgs . msg, out: reqs, tatts > >

[out]
  < o : Top | base: < o : TC | in: msgs, out: req . reqs, tatts > >
    =>
  < o : Top | base: < o : TC | in: msgs, out: reqs, tatts > >
  createConf(req)
```

where `createConf(req)` is the configuration whose creation is requested by `req`.

Figure 2 shows a two-level tower, with a message M coming in and being modified by the meta-level before delivering it to the base layer. There is also a request `req` going up from the base layer, being transformed by the meta layer and the processed by the top layer using the default semantics.

As a concrete illustration we model the ticker with monitor example as a tower. We apply a uniform transformation that maps actor objects to tower baseobjects. (This transformation is defined and proved to preserve semantics in [26].) The transformation maps the `Ticker` class to the `TTicker` class by adding the required in and out attributes. The ticker rules are then adapted to use these attributes as follows.

```
TowerTicker Rules:
    < t : TTicker | in: tick . msgs, out: reqs,  ctr: n >
      ==>
    < t : TTicker | in: msgs, out: reqs . (t <- tick),  ctr: n+1 >

    < t : TTicker | in: time@c . msgs, out: reqs,  ctr: n >
      ==>
    < t : TTicker | in: msgs, out: reqs . (c <- reply(n)),  ctr: n >
```

The ticker monitor is modeled using a subclass `TMonitor` of `MetaTower` obtained by adding in, out, and base attributes. The monitor rules are adapted as follows. The monitor forwards ticker messages to its ticker subobject and responds directly to `reset` messages. It also transmits all requests from the ticker, adding an appropriate `log` message in the case of a `reply` message.

```
< t : TMonitor | in: msg . mmsgs, out: mreqs,
                 base: < t : Ticker | in: msgs, out: reqs, ctr: n >
                 state: M(t,mc,m) >
=>
< t : TMonitor | in: mmsgs, out: mreqs,
                 base: < t : Ticker | in: msgs . msg, out: reqs, ctr: n >
                 state: M(t,mc,m) >
  if msg in (tick, time@c)

< t : TMonitor | in: reset . mmsgs, out: mreqs,
                 base: < t : Ticker | in: msgs, out: reqs, ctr: n >
                 state: M(t,mc,m) >
=>
< t : TMonitor | in: mmsgs, out: mreqs . (mc<-reset-ack),
                 base: < t : Ticker | in: msgs, out: reqs, ctr: 0 >
                 state: M(t,mc,0) >

< t : TMonitor | in: mmsgs, out: mreqs,
                 base: < t : Ticker | in: msgs, out: req . reqs, ctr: n>
                 state: M(t,mc,m) >
=>
< t : TMonitor | in: mmsgs, out: mreqs . req . qreq
                 base: < t : Ticker | in: msgs, out: reqs, ctr: n>
                 state: M(t,mc,m') >
  where
    if req := (c <- reply(n'))
    then qreq = (mc<-log(t,n',m+1,c)) and m' = m+1
    else qreq = mt and m' = m
```

A case study using the tower model to compose an encryption service and a client-server application in which the server may create helper objects and delegate requests to them can be found in [26].

5.2   The Two-Level Actor Machine Model

In the TLAM, a system is composed of two kinds of actors, baseactors and
metaactors, distributed over a network of processing nodes. *Baseactors* carry
out application level computation, while *metaactors* are part of the runtime
system which manages system resources and controls the runtime behavior of
the baselevel. Metaactors communicate with each other via message passing as
do baselevel actors. Metaactors may also examine and modify the state of the
baseactors located on the same node. Baselevel actors and messages have associated runtime annotations that can be set and read by metaactors, but are
invisible to baselevel computation. Actions which result in a change of baselevel state are called events. Metaactors may react to events occurring in their
node. A TLAM system configuration is a soup of nodes and messages with base
and metaactors forming subsoups inside the nodes. A node transition is either
a *communication transition* or an *execution transition*. A communication transition moves a message to actors on other nodes from the node's buffer to the
external soup or moves a message to an actor on the node from the external soup
into the node's mail buffer. An execution transition first applies either a base
or metalevel transition rule. If there is an associated baselevel event, then each
event-handling rule that matches the event must be applied (in an unspecified
order) and the associated annotation-update applied to the new local baselevel
configuration and messages.

Formally a TLAM is represented using a reflective object theory. Actors are
modeled as objects with identity and state, TLAM configurations as soups of
actors and messages, and actor behavior rules as rewrite rules. The trick is to
correctly model the metalevel observation of baselevel events and to ensure that
the event handling rules are applied when required. One way to do this is to use
metalevel strategies to describe the allowed computations. Another way is to
wrap the base and metaactor configurations of a node in operators that control
when rules can be applied. This works, but the resulting model is not so natural.
Here we show how the idea of Russian dolls with logical reflection allows a quite
natural modeling of the basic TLAM, an in fact provides a basis for natural
extensions to model scheduling, communication protocols and other concerns.

A baselevel actor system is represented quite directly as a special case of object module configurations. A baselevel actor is represented as an object in some
baseactor class BC. Messages have the form ba <- v, where ba is the identifier
of the intended recipient and v is the message contents. Baselevel actor rules are
constrained to have the form

```
< ba : BC | atts > [ ba <- v ] => < ba : BC' | atts' > bconf
   if  cond
```

where BC and BC' are baselevel classes, atts and atts' are attribute-value
sets appropriate for the corresponding classes, bconf is a configuration of newly
created baseactors and messages, and [ ] indicates that the message part is
optional.

A metaactor is an object in some metaactor class MC and metamessages have
the form ma <- mv where ma is the identifier of a metaactor. Metaactors are

grouped as subobject configurations of nodes, which in turn are metametaobjects. A *node* is an object of class TLAM-Node. A node has an attribute conf whose value is a configuration containing metaactors and messages. Each node has two special metaactors, one of class BMC that represents and controls the baselevel execution behavior, and the other of class CMC that represents and controls the baselevel communication semantics. These metaactors also implement the event handling semantics associated with baselevel events. Thus a node has the form

```
<nu : TLAM-Node | conf: <bma : BMC | ...> <cma : CMC | ...> mconf>
```

A metaobject of class BMC has attributes bMod, bConf, eReg, pendEv, and waitFor.

```
<bma : BMC | bMod: !BM, bConf: !bc, eReg: emap, pendEv: ev, waitFor: W>
```

The value of the attribute bMod is the metarepresentation of the baselevel module BM, and the value of the attribute bConf is the metarepresentation of the baselevel configuration bc. We use the convention that if foo denotes a baselevel entity then !foo denotes the metarepresentation of that entity. Thus !bc is the metarepresentation of bc. (This is the teletype analog of the overbar notation.)

The remaining attributes deal with execution event handling. An execution event is the modification of a node's baselevel actor configuration, resulting from applying either a base or a metalevel rule. An execution event is represented by a term of the form exe(!bconf, !update, cmap) where bconf is the initial baselevel configuration and update is a baselevel configuration that specifies new states for some existing baselevel actors, as well as newly created baselevel actors and messages. cmap maps newly created baselevel actors and messages to identifiers of existing baselevel actors on whose behalf the new elements are being created. This is used to maintain a model of the baselevel causality and acquaintance relations.

Event handling is modeled by sending notifications to metaactors registered for the event. A metaactor is registered for an event only if it has an event-handling rule matching this event that generates a reply to the notifying actor, in this case the behavior metaactor. The value emap of the attribute eReg maps an execution event to the set of names of metaactors that are registered to be notified about the event. The mapping is computed using the term apply(emap,event). The value ev of pendEv is either an execution event or the special constant none, indicating that no event handling is in progress. The value W of waitFor is the set of identifiers of metaactors for which a notification reply has not been received.

A communication metaactor (class CMC) has attributes sendQ, arriveQ, eReg, pendEv, and waitFor.

```
< cma : CMC | sendQ: smsgs, arriveQ: amsgs, eReg: emap,
              pendMsg: ev,  waitFor: W >
```

The value smsgs of sendQ is a list of pairs of the form (!msg,!sndr), representing requests from baselevel actor sndr to send msg. The value amsgs of arriveQ is a list of message arrivals, triples of the form (!msg,!sndr,amap) where amap is the message annotation map. The remaining attributes are event handling attributes analogous to those of the class BMC. A message arrival event has the form arrive(!(ba <- v), !sndr, amap) indicating the arrival at the node of a message for ba, sent by sndr and having annotations amap. A message send event has the form send(!(ba <- v), !sndr, amap) indicating that a message having annotations amap is to be sent to ba, by sndr[3].

In the TLAM *metalevel transition rules* have the form

$$mactor[mmsg] \xrightarrow[update]{baconf} mactor' \; mconf \; \textbf{if} \; \varphi$$

where *mactor* is a metaactor, $[mmsg]$ is an optional metalevel message addressed to the actor, *mactor'* is the same metaactor with its state possibly modified, *mconf* is a configuration of newly created baselevel actors and messages, and φ is a predicate constraining the actor-message pairs to which the rule applies. *update* is either empty or has the form $(bconf, cmap)$. When the rule is applied, *baconf* is bound to the baselevel actor configuration on the node where the metaactor is located.

Metaactor rules with empty *update* are represented directly as object rewrite rules.

```
< ma : MC | atts > [mmsg] => < ma : MC' | atts' >  mconf
if cond
```

Rules with non-empty update are represented using synchronization with the behavior actor.

```
< ma : MC | atts > [msg]
< bma : BMC | bMod: !BM, bConf: !bc, pendEv: none >
=>
< ma : MC | atts > [msg]
< bma : BMC | bMod: !BM, bConf: !bc, pendEv: evt,  started: false >
if evt := exe(!BM:!bc, !update, cmap)  and cond'
```

```
[startMEvent]
    < bma : BMC | eReg: emap, pendEv: evt,  started: false >
    =>
    < bma : BMC | eReg: emap, pendEv: evt, started: true, waitFor: W >
    notifyall(W,evt)
    if  evt =/= none and W = apply(emap, evt)
```

where notifyall(W,evt) is the set of messages ma <- notify(evt) for ma in W. The behavior metaactor also manages the scheduling of baselevel transitions. The general rule allows any enabled baselevel rule to be applied.

---

[3] We keep annotations at the metalevel. In the case of baseactor annotations we let the metaactors maintain them internally. Thus sharing of annotations must be by communication between metaactors. Shared annotations could be modeled as an additional attribute of the class BMC, but it seems cleaner to eliminate shared data. In the case of messages they are components of the metalevel messages that transport the baselevel message. This is consistent with the fact that annotations cannot be seen at the baselevel. By keeping them at the metalevel we avoid the need to extend baselevel modules with annotation data types.

```
[startExecution]
  < bma : BMC | bMod: !BM, bConf: !bc, pendEv: none >
  =>
  < bma : BMC | bMod: !BM, bConf: !bc, pendEv: evt, started: false >
  if (!ba, rname, subst) in enabled(!BM, !bc)
      and !update := Update(!BM, !bc, !ba, rname, subst)
      and cmap := makecmap(!update,!ba)
      and evt := exe(!BM:!bc, !update, cmap)
```

The condition
$$(!ba, rname, subst) \text{ in enabled}(!BM, !bc)$$
holds if
$$\text{meta} - \text{apply}(!BM, \text{restrict}(!bc, !ba), rname, subst, 0)$$
 succeeds, where `restrict(!bc,!ba)` is the term metarepresenting the sub-
configuration of `bc` containing the actor named `ba` and any pending messages
for that actor. `Update(!BM, !bc, !ba, rname, subst)` is the term metarepresenting the result of updating `bc` using the result of `meta-apply` as above. `cmap`
maps new actors and messages to the active actor `ba`. When an execution event
is being processed, the behavior metaactor waits for acknowledgments from the
registered metaactors.

```
[continueExecution]
  < bma : BMC | pendEv: evt,  started: true, waitFor: W ma >
   bma <- notified @ ma
  =>
  < bma : BMC | pendEv: evt,  started: true,  waitFor: W >
  if not(ma in W)
```

When all registered metaactors have acknowledged notification the behavior
metaactor completes the execution event by updating its model of the baselevel configuration, and transmitting newly sent messages to the communication
manager.

```
[completeExecution]
  < bma : BMC | bMod: !BM, bConf: !bc, started: true,
                pendEv: exe(!BM:!bc, !update, cmap), waitFor: mt >
  < cma : CMC | sendQ: smsgs >
  =>
  < bma : BMC | bMod: !BM, bConf: !bc', pendEv: none  >
  < cma : CMC | sendQ: smsgs . smsgs' >
```

where `bc'` is the result of applying `update` to `!bc`, and `smsgs'` contains elements
of the form `(!msg, cmap(!msg))` for each `msg` specified by `update`.

At the node level, baselevel messages are represented by requests to the
communications metaactor of the form `cma <- deliver(!msg, !sndr, amap)`.
These requests are queued for later processing.

```
[arriveQ]
  < cma : CMC |  arriveQ: amsgs > cma <- deliver(!msg, !sndr, amap)
  =>
  < cma : CMC |  arriveQ: amsgs . (!msg, !sndr, amap) >
```

For baselevel messages to be delivered, the communications metaactor first notifies registered metaactors.

```
[startArrival]
   < cma : CMC | arriveQ: (!msg, !sndr, amap) . amsgs,
                 eReg: emap, pendMsg: none >
   =>
   < cma : CMC | arriveQ: amsgs, pendMsg: !msg, waitFor: W >
   notifyall(W, evt)
   if evt := arrive(!msg, !sndr, amap) and  W := apply(emap, evt)
```

The communications metaactor waits for acknowledgments from all notified metaactors and then transmits the message to the behavior metaactor.

```
[continueArrival]
   < cma : CMC | pendMsg: !msg,  waitFor: W ma > cma <- notified(ma)
   =>
   < cma : CMC | pendMsg: !msg,  waitFor: W >  if not(ma in W)
```

```
[completeArrival]
   < cma : CMC | pendMsg: !msg,  waitFor: mt >
   < bma : BMC | bMod: !BM, bConf: !bc, pendEv: none >
   =>
   < cma : CMC | pendMsg: none >
   < bma : BMC | bMod: !BM, bConf: deliver(!BM,!bc,!msg) >
```

For each baselevel message to be sent, the communications metaactor notifies metaactors registered for send events, collects annotations, and then sends a `deliver` message to the communications metaactor co-located with the message target.

```
[startSend]
   < cma : CMC | sendQ: (!msg, !sndr) o smsgs, eReg: emap, pendMsg: none >
   =>
   < cma : CMC | sendQ: smsgs, pendMsg: (!msg, !sndr, mt),  waitFor: W >
   notifyall(W, evt)
   if evt := send(!msg, !sndr) and  W := apply(emap, evt)
```

```
[continueSend]
   < cma : CMC | pendMsg: (!msg, !sndr, amap), waitFor: W ma >
   cma <- notified(amap', ma)
   =>
   < cma : CMC | pendMsg: (!msg, !sndr, amap . amap'),  waitFor: W >
   if not(ma in W)
```

```
[completeSend]
   < cma : CMC | pendMsg: (!msg, !sndr, amap),  waitFor: mt >
   =>
   < cma : CMC | pendMsg: none,  waitFor: mt >
   mailQ(target(!msg)) <- deliver(!msg, !sndr, amap)
```

Notice that the communication metaactor can receive requests for message processing interleaved with the processing of a message event, but may not interleave processing of two or more message events. The two rules that involve synchronization with the behavior metaactor are the mechanism to ensure a consistent causal connection between base and metalevels.

Representing the ticker and monitor example in the TLAM model is now simple. The ticker itself is unchanged. The monitor rules are modified as follows.

```
TLAM Monitor Rules:
  < mt : Monitor | state: M(t,mc,m) >
  mt <- notify(send(!(c<-reply(n)), !t))@cma
  =>
  < mt : Monitor | state: M(t,mc,m+1) >
  cma <- notify-ack(mt) mc <- log(t,n,m+1,c)

  < mt : Monitor | state: M(t,mc,m) >  mt <- reset
  < bma : BMC | bMod: !BM, bConf: !bc, pendEv: none >
  =>
  < mt : Monitor | state: M(t,mc,m+1) >  mc <- reset-ack
  < bma : BMC | bMod: !BM, bConf: !bc, pendEv: evt,  started: false >
    if evt := ev(mt, !BM:!bc, ![t -> ctr -> 0])
```

Extensions of the TLAM model may modify the behavior of BMC to introduce scheduling algorithms and an interface to control scheduling. They may modify CMC to provide mechanisms for applying communications protocols and establishing policies for which protocols to apply.

6   Towards Semantically-Based Reflective Middleware

As indicated in Section 1.1 there are a number of ongoing efforts to develop reflective middleware systems. In the following we discuss three examples and indicate how they might be given semantics in our framework.

6.1   Anatomy of a Computational Grid

Grid computing addresses the problem of flexible, secure, coordinated resource sharing among dynamic collections of individuals, institutions, and resources, called *virtual organizations*. Grid programming applications include: multidisciplinary simulation, crisis management, and scientific data analysis. Middleware for Grid computing must provide a range of authentication, authorization, resource access, resource discovery, and collaboration services that cross platform and institution boundaries and allow participants to negotiate, manage, and exploit sharing relationships. In [31] a grid protocol architecture is proposed consisting of several layers as shown in Figure 3. The Grid Fabric layer provides the resources to which shared access is mediated by Grid protocols: for example, computational resources, storage systems, catalogs, network resources, and sensors. A "resource" may also be a logical entity, such as a distributed file system, computer cluster, or distributed computer pool. The Connectivity layer defines

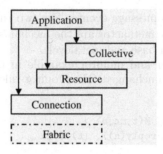

Fig. 3. Grid architecture

core communication and authentication protocols required for Grid-specific network transactions. Communication protocols enable the exchange of data between Fabric layer resources. Communication requirements include transport, routing, and naming. Authentication requirements include single sign on, delegation, integration with local security solutions, user-based trust relations. The Resource layer builds on Connectivity layer communication and authentication protocols to define protocols for the secure negotiation, initiation, monitoring, control, accounting, and payment of sharing operations on individual resources. Resource layer protocols are concerned entirely with individual resources. The Collective layer contains protocols and services that are global in nature and capture interactions across collections of resources. Examples include: directory services; co-allocation, scheduling, and brokering services; monitoring and diagnostics services; data replication services; and problem solving environments. The final layer is the Application layer.

This Grid architecture corresponds well to the TLAM model with the application layer corresponding to the baselevel, the collective, resource and communication layers, corresponding to the metalevel (middleware services), and the fabric layer corresponding to the TLAM infrastructure. The further layering of the middleware services is similar in spirit to the TLAM approach of identifying core services and building more complex global services on these foundations [68]. This correspondence to the TLAM suggests that techniques developed to compose and reason about TLAM specifications can be applied to formally specify and reason about grid-based systems.

6.2 Quality Objects

Quality Objects (QuO) [46,57] is a framework for including Quality of Service (QoS) in distributed object applications. QuO supports the specification of QoS contracts between clients and service providers, runtime monitoring of contracts, and adaptation to changing system conditions. QuO is based on the CORBA middleware standard. The operating regions and service requirements of an application are encoded in contracts, which describe the possible states the system might be in and actions to take when the state changes. QuO inserts delegates

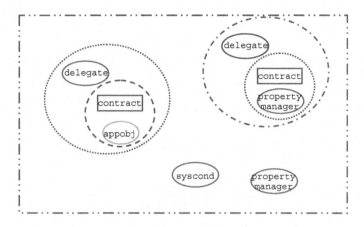

Fig. 4. Quo Architecture

in the CORBA functional path to support adaptive behavior upon method call and return. The delegate uses a set of contracts to check the state of the system and choose a behavior based upon it. System condition objects provide interfaces to system resources, mechanisms, and managers. They are used to capture the states of particular resources, mechanisms, or managers that are required by the contracts and to control them as directed by the contracts. QuO also provides a support for interfacing to below-the-ORB QoS mechanisms. Examples of property management below-the-orb are dependability management using replication, and bandwidth management using RSVP. These mechanisms also support intrusion detection systems via monitoring net traffic or resource access. QuO objects can themselves be subject to QoS contracts, thus leading to multiple levels of reflection.

Figure 4 indicates how parts of a QuO system configuration might be mapped to the Russian dolls model. The outer rectangle is a metaobject representing a node. It has a configuration of subobjects including system condition and property manager metaobjects (ovals with solid boundary). The circle on the left represents a delegate metaobject with its application subobject and the applications associated contract. The circle on the right shows the reflective aspect in which a critical property manager is a subobject protected by a contract.

6.3   OpenOrb

The OpenOrb reflective architecture [25,30] is based on the RM-ODP object model [39] and inspired by the AL-1/D reflective programming language for distributed applications [56]. An RM-ODP object may have multiple interfaces as well as being composed of nested interacting objects. In the OpenOrb architecture every object (interface) then has an associated metaspace supporting inspection and adaptation of the underlying infrastructure for the object. Following AL-1/D, this metaspace is organized as a number of closely related but

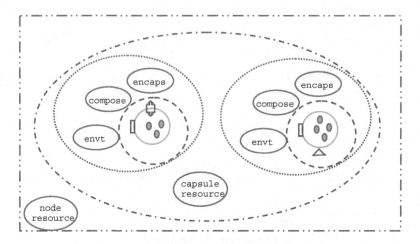

Fig. 5. The OpenOrb Reflective Architecture

distinct metaspace models. Currently there are four metamodels: compositional, environment, encapsulation, and resource. The compositional metamodel deals with the way a composite object is composed, i.e., how its components are interconnected, and how these connections are manipulated. There is one compositional metamodel per object. The environmental metamodel is in charge of the environmental computation of an object interface, i.e., how the computation is done. It deals with message arrivals, message selection, dispatching, marshaling, concurrency control, etc. The encapsulation metamodel relates to the set of methods and associated attributes of a particular object interface. Methods scripts can be inspected and changed by accessing this metamodel. Finally, the resource metamodel is concerned with both the resource awareness and resource management of objects in the platform.

The resource model includes abstract resources, resource factories and resource managers. Abstract resources explicitly represent system resources. In addition, there may be various levels of abstractions allowing higher level resources to be constructed on top of lower level resources. Resource managers are responsible for managing resources, that is, such managers either map or multiplex higher level resources onto lower level resources. Virtual task machines (VTMs) are top-level resource abstractions that may encompass several kinds of resources (e.g. CPU, memory and network resources) allocated to a particular task. Resource schedulers are a specialization of managers in charge of managing processing resources such as threads or virtual processors. Resource factories create abstract resources.

Note that objects/interfaces at the metalevel are also open to reflection and have an associated meta-metaspace. This process can be continued, providing a potentially infinite tower of reflection.

Figure 5 illustrates how an OpenOrb system configuration might be represented using the Russian dolls with logical reflection ideas. The outer rectangle is a node metaobject corresponding with its node resource manager. It has a configuration of capsule subobjects, of which the large oval is a representative. The capsule metaobject has a resource manager subobject and several application metaobjects, each containing the metaobjects for the three object specific metamodels, and an ODP object with its multiple interfaces and inner object graph. The shading of the inner objects indicates that these objects are metarepresented subobjects.

7 Concluding Remarks

We have proposed a generic model of distributed object reflection based on rewriting logic The model uses configuration-structuring mechanisms to organize distributed object configurations into hierarchies of metaobjects and subobjects, and logical reflection to treat subobjects as data for increased power, control, and adaptivity. We have also shown how this generic model specializes in natural ways to several well-known models of actor reflection and of reflective middleware.

We envision several directions for future work. One direction is to continue the analysis of reflective middleware to identify different nesting structures, required objects, if any, at each level, and interaction patterns, as expressed by allowed rule structure. One objective is to obtain a deeper understanding of base-meta interactions and principles leading to a useful balance of power and restraint.

A second direction is developing techniques for specification and analysis of reflective distributed systems. Challenges include modeling and reasoning about interactions of different metamodels and services; combining specifications of different aspects/concerns; and modular treatment of different reflective levels.

Acknowledgments

This work was supported in part by National Science Foundation Grants CCR-9900334 and CCR-9900326. The first author's work is supported in part by the ONR MURI Project "A Logical Framework for Adaptive System Interoperability."

The authors would like to thank our collaborators Gul Agha, Manuel Clavel, Grit Denker, Nalini Venkatasubramanian for their many contributions to the work leading to the results presented here. Thanks to Narciso Martí-Oliet both for fruitful collaboration and for help in proofreading. We also thank Doug Schmidt for insightful discussions regarding reflective middleware.

References

1. G. Agha. *Actors: A Model of Concurrent Computation in Distributed Systems.* MIT Press, Cambridge, Mass., 1986.
2. G. Agha and C. Callsen. Actorspace: An open distributed programming paradigm. In *Proc. ACM Symp. on Principles and Practice of Parallel Programming (PPOPP)*, volume (28:7), pages 23–32, July 1993.

3. G. Agha, S. Frølund, W. Kim, R. Panwar, A. Patterson, and D. Sturman. Abstraction and modularity mechanisms for concurrent computing. *IEEE Parallel and Distributed Technology: Systems and Applications*, 1(2):3–14, May 1993.

4. G. Agha, S. Frølund, R. Panwar, and D. Sturman. A linguistic framework for dynamic composition of dependability protocols. In *Proceedings of the 3rd IFIP Working Conference on Dependable Computing for Critical Applications*, Sept. 1992.

5. W. E. Aitken, R. L. Constable, and J. L. Underwood. Metalogical frameworks II: Using reflected decision procedures. Technical Report, Computer Sci. Dept., Cornell University, 1993; also, lecture at the Max Planck Institut für Informatik, Saarbrücken, Germany, July 1993.

6. A. Albarrán, F. Durán, and A. Vallecillo. From Maude specifications to SOAP distributed implementations: A smooth transition. In *VI Jornadas Ingenieria del Software y Bases de Datos (JISBD'01)*, pages 419–433, 2001.

7. A. Albarrán, F. Durán, and A. Vallecillo. Maude meets CORBA. In *Second Argentine Symposium on Software Engineering (ASSE'01)*, 2001.

8. J. Andrews. Process-algebraic foundations of separation-of-concerns programming. In *Third International Conference on Metalevel Architectures and Separation of Crosscutting Concerns, Reflection 2001*, Lecture Notes in Computer Science. Springer-Verlag, 2001.

9. M. Astley. *Customization and Composition of Distributed Objects: Policy Management in Distributed Software Architectures*. PhD thesis, University of Illinois, Urbana-Champaign, 1999.

10. H. G. Baker and C. Hewitt. Laws for communicating parallel processes. In *IFIP Congress*, pages 987–992. IFIP, Aug. 1977.

11. D. Basin, M. Clavel, and J. Meseguer. Rewriting logic as a metalogical framework. In S. Kapoor and S. Prasad, editors, *FST TCS 2000*, pages 55–80. Springer LNCS, 2000.

12. G. Blair, M. Clarke, F. Costa, G. Coulson, H. Duran, and N. Parlavantzas. The evolution of OpenORB. In Kon and Saikoski [44]. see http://www.comp.lancs.ac.uk/computing/users/johnstlr/rm2000/.

13. G. Blair, G. Coulson, P. Robin, and M. Papathomas. An architecture for next generation middleware. In *Middleware '98*, 1998.

14. L. Blair and G. Blair. Composition in multiparadigm specification techniques. In *3rd International Conference on Formal Methods for Open Object-Based Distributed Systems (FMOODS'99)*, pages 401–417. Kluwer, 1999.

15. P. Borovanský, C. Kirchner, H. Kirchner, P.-E. Moreau, and M. Vittek. ELAN: A logical framework based on computational systems. In J. Meseguer, editor, *Proc. First Intl. Workshop on Rewriting Logic and its Applications*, volume 4 of *Electronic Notes in Theoretical Computer Science*. Elsevier, 1996. http://www.elsevier.nl/cas/tree/store/tcs/free/noncas/pc/volume4.htm.

16. R. S. Boyer and J. S. Moore. Metafunctions: proving them correct and using them efficiently as new proof procedures. In R. Boyer and J. Moore, editors, *The Correctness Problem in Computer Science*, pages 103–185. Academic Press, 1981.

17. M. Clavel. *Reflection in Rewriting Logic: Metalogical Foundations and Metaprogramming Applications*. CSLI Publications, 2000.

18. M. Clavel, F. Durán, S. Eker, P. Lincoln, N. Marti-Oliet, and J. Meseguer. Metalevel Computation in Maude. In C. Kirchner and H. Kirchner, editors, *2nd International Workshop on Rewriting Logic and Its Applications, WRLA'98*, volume 15 of *Electronic Notes in Theoretical Computer Science*. Elsevier, 1998. http://www.elsevier.nl/locate/entcs/volume15.html.

19. M. Clavel, F. Durán, S. Eker, P. Lincoln, N. Martí-Oliet, J. Meseguer, and J. Quesada. Maude: specification and programming in rewriting logic. SRI International, January 1999, http://maude.csl.sri.com.

20. M. Clavel, F. Durán, S. Eker, P. Lincoln, N. Martí-Oliet, J. Meseguer, and J. Quesada. A tutorial on Maude. SRI International, March 2000, http://maude.csl.sri.com.

21. M. Clavel, F. Durán, S. Eker, and J. Meseguer. Building equational proving tools by reflection in rewriting logic. In *Proc. of the CafeOBJ Symposium '98, Numazu, Japan.* CafeOBJ Project, April 1998. http://maude.csl.sri.com.

22. M. Clavel and J. Meseguer. Axiomatizing reflective logics and languages. In G. Kiczales, editor, *Proceedings of Reflection'96, San Francisco, California, April 1996*, pages 263–288, 1996. http://jerry.cs.uiuc.edu/reflection/.

23. M. Clavel and J. Meseguer. Reflection in conditional rewriting logic. to appear in Theoretical Computer Science, Volume 304, Issues 1-2., 2002.

24. P. Cointe, editor. *Proceedings of Reflection'99*, volume 1616 of *Lecture Notes in Computer Science.* Springer, 1999.

25. F. M. Costa and G. S. Blair. Integrating meta-information management and reflection in middleware. In *Second International Symposium on Distributed Objects and Applications (DOA'00)*, pages 133–143, Sept. 2000.

26. G. Denker, J. Meseguer, and C. L. Talcott. Rewriting semantics of distributed meta objects and composable communication services. In *Third International Workshop on Rewriting Logic and Its Applications (WRLA'2000), Kanazawa, Japan, September 18 — 20, 2000*, volume 36 of *Electronic Notes in Theoretical Computer Science.* Elsevier, 2000. http://www.elsevier.nl/locate/entcs/volume36.html.

27. F. Durán, S. Eker, P. Lincoln, and J. Meseguer. Principles of Mobile Maude. In *Agent Systems, Mobile Agents, and Applications, ASA/MA 2000*, volume 1882 of *Lecture Notes in Computer Science*, pages 73–85. Springer-Verlag, 2000.

28. F. Durán and A. Vallecillo. Specifying the ODP information viewpoint using Maude. In H. Kilov and K. Baclawski, editors, *Proceedings of Tenth OOPSLA Workshop on Behavioral Semantics*, pages 44–57, October 2001.

29. F. Durán and A. Vallecillo. Writing ODP enterprise specifications in Maude. In J. Cordeiro and H. Kilov, editors, *Proceedings of Workshop On Open Distributed Processing: Enterprise, Computation, Knowledge, Engineering and Realisation (WOODPECKER'01)*, pages 55–68, July 2001.

30. H. A. Duran-Limon and G. S. Blair. The importance of resource management in engineering distributed objects. In *Second International Workshop on Engineering Distributed Objects (EDO2000)*, Nov. 2000.

31. I. Foster, C. Kesselman, and S. Tuecke. The anatomy of the grid: Enabling scalable virtual organizations. *International Journal of Supercomputer Applications*, 2001.

32. S. Frølund. *Coordinated Distributed Objects: An Actor Based Approach to Synchronization.* MIT Press, 1996.

33. K. Futatsugi and R. Diaconescu. *CafeOBJ Report.* World Scientific, AMAST Series, 1998.

34. A. Grimshaw and W. W. et al. The Legion Vision of a Worldwide Virtual Computer. *Communications of the ACM*, 40(1), Jan. 1997.

35. C. Hewitt, P. Bishop, and R. Steiger. A universal modular actor formalism for artificial intelligence. In *Proceedings of 1973 International Joint Conference on Artificial Intelligence*, pages 235–245, Aug. 1973.

36. P. Hill and J. Lloyd. The Gödel language. Technical Report CSTR-92-27, University of Bristol, Computer Science Department, 1992.

37. D. J. Howe. Reflecting the semantics of reflected proof. In P. Aczel, H. Simmons, and S. S. Wainer, editors, *Proof Theory*, pages 229–250. Cambridge University Press, 1990.

38. J.-I. Itoh, Y. Yokote, and R. Lea. Using meta-objects to support optimisation in the apertos operating system. In *USENIX Conference on Object-Oriented Technologies (COOTS)*, pages 147–158. USENIX Association, 1995.

39. ITU-T/ISO. Reference model for open distributed processing. Technical Report ITU-T X.901-X.904 — ISO/IEC IS 10746-(1,2,3), ITU-T/ISO, 1995.

40. G. Kiczales, editor. *Reflection'96*, 1996.

41. G. Kiczales, J. des Riviers, and D. G. Bobrow. *The Art of the Metaobject Protocol.* MIT Press, 1991.

42. G. Kiczales, J. Lamping, A. Mendhekar, C. Maeda, C. Lopes, J.-M. Loingtier, and J. Irwin. Aspect-oriented programming. In M. Aksit and S. Matsuoka, editors, *Proc. European Conference on Object-Oriented Programming (ECOOP'97), Finland*, volume 1241 of *Lecture Notes in Computer Science*, pages 220–242, 1997.

43. F. Kon, M. Román, P. Liu, J. Mao, T. Yamane, L. C. Magalhães, and R. H. Campbell. Monitoring, security, and dynamic configuration with the dynamicTAO reflective ORB. In *Proceedings of the IFIP/ACM International Conference on Distributed Systems Platforms and Open Distributed Processing (Middleware'2000)*, number 1795 in LNCS, pages 121–143, New York, April 2000. Springer-Verlag.

44. F. Kon and K. B. Saikoski, editors. *IFIP/ACM Middleware'2000 Workshop on Reflective Middleware*, New York, April 2000. Gordon Blair and Roy Campbell (co-chairs). see
http://www.comp.lancs.ac.uk/computing/users/johnstlr/rm2000/.

45. F. Kon, A. Singhai, R. H. Campbell, D. Carvalho, R. Moore, and F. J. Ballesteros. 2K: A Reflective, Component-Based Operating System for Rapidly Changing Environments. In *ECOOP'98 Workshop on Reflective Object-Oriented Programming and Systems*, Brussels, Belgium, July 1998.

46. J. Loyall, R. Schantz, J. Zinky, and D. Bakken. Specifying and measuring quality of service in distributed object systems. In *Proceedings of the First International Symposium on Object-Oriented Real-Time Distributed Computing (ISORC '98)*, Apr. 1998.

47. P. Maes. Concepts and experiments in computational reflection. In *OOPSLA*, pages 147–155, 1987. in ACM SIGPLAN Notices 22(12).

48. E. Marsden, J. C. R. García, and J.-C. Fabre. Towards validating reflective architectures: formalization of a metaobject protocol. In Kon and Saikoski [44]. see
http://www.comp.lancs.ac.uk/computing/users/johnstlr/rm2000/.

49. S. Matthews. Reflection in logical systems. In *IMSA'92*, pages 178–183. Information-Technology Promotion Agency, Japan, 1992.

50. J. Meseguer. General logics. In H.-D. E. et al., editor, *Logic Colloquium'87*, pages 275–329. North-Holland, 1989.

51. J. Meseguer. Conditional rewriting logic as a unified model of concurrency. *Theoretical Computer Science*, 96(1):73–155, 1992.

52. J. Meseguer. A logical theory of concurrent objects and its realization in the Maude language. In G. Agha, P. Wegner, and A. Yonezawa, editors, *Research Directions in Concurrent Object-Oriented Programming*, pages 314–390. MIT Press, 1993.

53. T. A. Mogensen. Efficient self-interpretation in lambda calculus. *Journal of Functional Programming*, 2(3):345–364, 1992.

54. E. Najm and J.-B. Stefani. Computational models for open distributed systems. In H. Bowman and J. Derrick, editors, *Formal Methods for Open Object-based Distributed Systems, Volume 2*, pages 157–176. Chapman & Hall, 1997.

55. Object Management Group. The Common Object Request Broker: Architecture and Specification, 2.3 ed., June 1999.
56. H. Okamura, Y. Ishikawa, and M. Tokoro. Al-1/d: A distributed programming system with multi-model reflection framework. In A. Yonezawa and B. C. Smith, editors, *Reflection and Meta-Level Architetures*, pages 36–47. ACM SIGPLAN, 1992.
57. P. P. Pal, J. Loyall, R. E. Schantz, J. Zinky, R. Shapiro, and J. Megquier. Using qdl to specify qos aware distributed (quo) application configuration. In *The 3rd IEEE International Symposium on Object-Oriented Real-time Distributed Computing, (ISORC 2000)*, Mar. 2000.
58. S. Ren. *An Actor-Based Framework for Real-Time Coordination*. PhD thesis, University of Illinois at Urbana-Champaign, 1997.
59. J. C. Reynolds. Definitional interpreters for higher-order programming languages. In *Proceedings, ACM national convention*, pages 717–740, 1972.
60. H. Rueß. *Formal Meta-Programming in the Calculus of Constructions*. PhD thesis, Universität Ulm, 1995.
61. D. C. Schmidt, D. Levine, and S. Mungee. The design of the Tao real-time object request broker. *Computer Communications*, 21, 1997. Special Issue on Building Quality of Service into Distributed Systems.
62. N. Shankar. *Metamathematics, Machines, and Gödel's Proof*. Cambridge University Press, 1994.
63. B. C. Smith. *Reflection and Semantics in a Procedural Language*. PhD thesis, MIT, 1982.
64. C. Smorynski. The incompleteness theorems. In J. Barwise, editor, *Handbook of Mathematical Logic*, pages 821–865. North-Holland, 1977.
65. R. M. Smullyan. *Diagonalization and Self-Reference*. Oxford University Press, 1994.
66. D. Sturman. *Modular Specification of Interaction Policies in Distributed Computing*. PhD thesis, University of Illinois at Champaign Urbana, 1996.
67. V. F. Turchin. *Refal-5: programming guide and reference manual*. New England Publishing Co., 1989.
68. N. Venkatasubramanian. *Resource Management in Open Distributed Systems with Applications to Multimedia*. PhD thesis, University of Illinois, Urbana-Champaign, 1998.
69. N. Venkatasubramanian, G. Agha, and C. L. Talcott. Scalable distributed garbage collection for systems of active objects. In *International Workshop on Memory Management, IWMM92, Saint-Malo*, LNCS, 1992.
70. N. Venkatasubramanian, G. Agha, and C. L. Talcott. A formal model for reasoning about adaptive QoS-enabled middleware. In *Formal Methods for Increasing Software Productivity (FME2001)*, 2001.
71. N. Venkatasubramanian and C. L. Talcott. A metaarchitecture for distributed resource management. In *Hawaii International Conference on System Sciences, HICSS-26*, Jan. 1993.
72. N. Venkatasubramanian and C. L. Talcott. Reasoning about meta level activities in open distributed systems. In *Principles of Distributed Computation (PODC '95)*, pages 144–153. ACM, 1995.
73. N. Venkatasubramanian and C. L. Talcott. A semantic framework for modeling and reasoning about reflective middleware, 2001. to appear in Distributed Systems Online.

74. N. Wang, M. Kircher, D. C. Schmidt, and K. Parameswaran. Applying reflective middleware techniques to optimize a QoS-enabled CORBA component model implementation. In *COMPSAC 2000 Conference, Taipei, Taiwan*, 2000.

75. R. W. Weyhrauch. Prolegomena to a theory of mechanized formal reasoning. *Artificial Intelligence*, 13:133–170, 1980.

76. A. Yonezawa. *ABCL: An Object-Oriented Concurrent System*. MIT Press, Cambridge Mass., 1990.

77. A. Yonezawa, editor. *Third International Conference on Metalevel Architectures and Separation of Crosscutting Concerns, Reflection 2001*. Lecture Notes in Computer Science. Springer-Verlag, 2001.

78. A. Yonezawa and B. C. Smith, editors. *Reflection and Meta-Level Architecture*. ACM SIGPLAN, 1992.

79. J. Zinky, D. Bakken, and R. Schantz. Architectural support for quality of service for CORBA objects. *Theory and Practice of Object Systems*, Apr. 1997.

AOP: Does It Make Sense?
The Case of Concurrency and Failures

Jörg Kienzle[1] and Rachid Guerraoui[2]

[1] Software Engineering Laboratory
[2] Distributed Programming Laboratory
Swiss Federal Institute of Technology in Lausanne (EPFL), Switzerland

Abstract. Concurrency and failures are fundamental problems in distributed computing. One likes to think that the mechanisms needed to address these problems can be separated from the rest of the distributed application: in modern words, these mechanisms could be *aspectized*. Does this however make sense?

This paper relates an experience that conveys our initial and indeed biased intuition that the answer is in general *no*. Except for simple academic examples, it is hard and even potentially dangerous to separate concurrency control and failure management from the actual application.

We point out the very facts that (1) an *aspect-oriented* language can, pretty much like a macro language, be beneficial for code factorization (but should be reserved to experienced programmers), and (2) concurrency and failures are particularly hard to aspectize because they are usually part of the phenomenon that objects should simulate. They are in this sense different than other concerns, like for instance tracing, which might be easier to aspectize.

Keywords. Aspect-oriented programming, abstraction, objects, concurrency, failures, exceptions, transactions.

1   Introduction

The job of any engineer is to manage complexity in designing and implementing systems. This is in particular true for software engineering: most research in the field has to do with how to manage the complexity of programs by providing better structuring mechanisms and methodologies.

Object-oriented programming comes with the intuitive idea that a program supposed to solve a real-world problem should be decomposed into a set of self-contained abstractions, each simulating a specific phenomena of the real-world problem. The abstraction is self-contained in the sense that it encapsulates state and behavior. One can follow the object-oriented programming discipline in any language, but object-oriented languages provide support to help such a programming discipline through mechanisms like encapsulation, sub-typing, inheritance, etc. [1].

Aspect-oriented programming (AOP) is the modern terminology given now to a branch of techniques that aim at deconstructing objects into several aspects (or concerns) and promoting each aspect to the level of a first-class citizen. Again, one could adopt this programming discipline in any language, but AOP languages help support

B. Magnusson (Ed.): ECOOP 2002, LNCS 2374, pp. 37–61, 2002.
© Springer-Verlag Berlin Heidelberg 2002

this kind of separation through mechanisms like join points, weaving, etc. [2]. Typically, one might talk about functional and non-functional aspects. The very notion of *functional part* has never been precisely defined, but is usually used to denote what average programmers are supposed to master. In essence, the notion of *functionality* is relative. These days, mechanisms that deal with concurrency and failures are, for instance, considered as *non-functional* aspects of the application. It is tempting to separate these aspects from the other functionalities of the application. This is very legitimate and it does not take long to convince any sensible programmer that such a separation would be great. The requirements of distributed applications vary tremendously, and it is appealing that concurrency control and failure management concerns can be configured separately by some distribution specialist to fit the application's needs.

Can the dream however come true? In other words, does it indeed make sense to use AOP techniques to separate concurrency control and failure management concerns from the other parts of a distributed application? The motivation of our work is precisely to address this question.

Our conclusion is that, except for simple (academic) examples, the answer is *no*. To get a reasonable behavior for any non-trivial distributed application, concurrency control, together with failure management, should in principle be dealt with as a full part of the application semantics, i.e., should be mixed up with the actual functionalities. One can indeed use an AOP language to achieve *some* level of syntactical separation, but the programmer should be aware of its very *syntactic-only* nature.

In our experiment, we use AspectJ [2] as a representative of aspect-oriented programming languages and *transactions* [3] as a fundamental paradigm to handle concurrency and failures. We proceed in an incremental manner, where we try to achieve three goals: from the most ambitious to the less ambitious one.

- First, we figure out the extent to which one can *aspectize transaction semantics*. That is, we figure out the extent to which one can completely hide transactional semantics from the programmer and have these semantics implicitly associated to the program a posteriori and in an automatic manner. This actually means that the programmer does not have to care about transactions. We give a set of illustrated examples why this is clearly impossible.
- Second, we figure out the extent to which one can *aspectize transaction interfaces*. That is, we figure out the extent to which one can completely separate transactional interfaces (*begin, commit, abort,* etc.) from the main (functional) object methods, and have these encapsulated within code invoked through specific aspects. We show by example that in certain cases this separation might be artificial, and that it leads to rather confusing code.
- Third and finally, we figure out the extent to which one can *aspectize transaction mechanisms*. That is, we figure out the extent to which one can completely separate the mechanisms needed to ensure the ACID [3] properties of transactions (i.e., concurrency control and failure management) from the main (functional) program (objects) and have these encapsulated within code invoked through specific aspects. We show that, syntactically speaking, an AOP language like AspectJ provides indeed a nice way of separating these mechanisms from the functional part of

the code. Just like with macros however [4], this separation should be handled with care, especially whenever the actual functionality does change. In short, the programmer must be aware that the physical separation does not imply a semantic decoupling.

It is important to notice that from our experience, especially in a non-rigorous area such as software engineering, we cannot draw any conclusion on the general applicability of AOP and AOP languages. The scope of our experience is indeed limited to (a) two concerns: concurrency and failures, (b) one paradigm to handle these concerns: transactions, and (c) a given subset of application scenarios that we have taken from our distributed computing background. The goal here is simply to provide some elements for a more general discussion of what dangers a misunderstanding of the capability of AOP might create, as well as what and when features of an AOP language might be useful *and* safe. The paper should be viewed as a warning to the new comers entering the AOP arena with very high expectations, rather than as an argumentation with AOP founders, who usually know the limitations.

The rest of the paper is organized as follows: Section 2 provides background information on AOP and transactions; Section 3 presents our experimental setting; Section 4 to Section 6 describe our attempts at achieving the three levels of aspectization mentioned above; Section 7 relates our experience to *Enterprise Java Beans* [5]; Section 8 discusses the limitation and possible generalization of our experiment, and Section 9 summarizes the results of this work.

2 Background

2.1 Aspect-Oriented Programming

Aspect-oriented programming (AOP) is the name given to a set of techniques based on the idea that software is better programmed by separately specifying the various *concerns (or aspects)*, properties, or areas of interest of a system, and describing their relationships [2]. Ultimately, the programmer relies on the underlying AOP environment to *weave* (or *compose*) the concerns together into a coherent program. Separating the expression of multiple concerns in programming systems promises increased readability, simpler structure, adaptability, customizability and better reuse.

One of the main elements of an AOP language is the *join point model*. It describes the "hooks" where enhancements may be added, and thus determines the structure of crosscutting concerns. AOP languages are supposed to provide means to identify join points, specify behavior at join points, define units that group together join point specifications and behavior enhancements, and provide means for attaching such units to a program.

2.2 Transactions

Transactions [3] have been used extensively to cope with concurrency and failures. A transaction groups an arbitrary number of simple actions together, making the whole appear indivisible with respect to other concurrent transactions. Using transactions, data updates that involve multiple objects can be executed without worrying about concurrency and failures. Transactions have the so-called ACID properties: *Atomicity, Consistency, Isolation* and *Durability* [3]. If something happens during the execution of a transaction that prevents the operation from continuing, the transaction is aborted, which will undo all state changes made on behalf of the transaction. A transaction can also be aborted voluntarily by the application programmer. The ability of transactions to hide the effects of concurrency, and at the same time act as firewalls for failures, makes them appropriate building blocks for structuring reliable distributed applications in general.

Multiple transactions may execute concurrently, but classic transaction models only allow one thread to execute inside a given transaction. Such models therefore support competitive concurrency only, since transactions, and hence the threads running within them, are isolated from each other. There is no way for threads to perform cooperative work inside the same transaction. More sophisticated transaction models, i.e., the *open multithreaded transaction model* [6, 7], allow multithreading inside a transaction. Threads participating in the same transaction can cooperate by accessing the same objects.

2.3 Transaction Interfaces

Typically, transactional systems offer a procedural interface to transactions including three operations:

- **void** beginTransaction(), which starts a new transaction or a nested transaction within an already ongoing one,
- **void** commitTransaction() **throws** TransactionAbortedException, which attempts to commit the current transaction,
- **void** abortTransaction(), which forces the transaction to rollback.

Multithreaded transaction models, e.g. open multithreaded transactions, provide additional operations to allow threads to join an ongoing transaction:

- **void** joinTransaction(Transaction t), which allows the calling thread to join the transaction t,
- **void** beginOrJoinTransaction(String name), which creates a new transaction with the name name, or, if a transaction with this name already exists, joins the calling thread by associating it with the same transaction context.

3 Experimental Setting

We briefly describe below the basic tools of our experimental setting: AspectJ and our OPTIMA transactional framework. We mainly overview here the elements that are used in our context.

3.1 AspectJ

We based our experiment on AspectJ [8], an aspect-oriented programming environment for the Java language.

In AspectJ, the join points are certain well-defined points in the execution flow of a Java program. These include method and constructor calls or executions, field accesses, object and class initialization, and others. *Pointcut designators* allow a programmer to pick out a certain set of join points, which can further be composed with boolean operations to build up other pointcuts. It is also possible to use wild cards when specifying, for instance, a method signature.

The following code defines a pointcut named `CallToAccount` that designates any call to a public method of the `Account` class:

```
pointcut CallToAccount () : call (public * Account.*(..));
```

To define the behavior at a join point, `AspectJ` uses the notion of *advice*. An advice contains code fragments that execute *before*, *after* or *around* a given pointcut. Finally, *aspects* are provided that, very much like a class, group together methods, fields, constructors, initializers, but also named pointcuts and advice. These units are intended to be used for implementing a crosscutting concern.

Since aspects potentially crosscut an entire application, the integration of aspects with the programming environment is of great importance. Programmers should get visual feedback of the effects of a given aspect on other parts of the program. The developers of `AspectJ` are aware of this, and hence provide extensions that integrate `AspectJ` with popular programming environments, such as Borland's JBuilder, Sun's Forte and GNU Emacs.

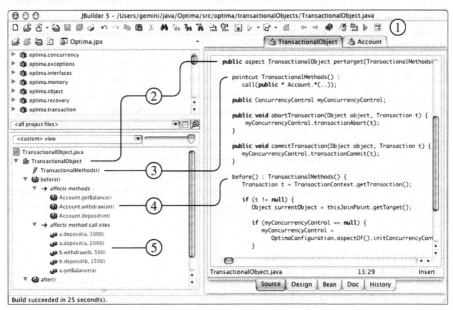

Fig. 1. AspectJ Integration with JBuilder 6 under Mac OS X

Figure 1 illustrates the integration of `AspectJ` with Borland JBuilder 6. The `AspectJ` plug-in adds buttons for compiling, running, and setting `AspectJ` preferences to JBuilder's toolbar ①. When the `AspectJ` environment is activated, the structure view of JBuilder is replaced with `AspectJ`'s structure view. It contains all elements of

JBuilder's structure view, but additionally allows a programmer to visualize aspect-specific constructs, e.g. pointcuts and advice.

In Figure 1, the structure of the `TransactionalObject` aspect is shown in the structure view ②: the definition of the `TransactionalMethods` pointcut ③, and a *before* advice. The next tab presents a list of all methods statically affected by the *before* advice, namely all public methods of the class `Account` ④. The following tab shows what actual calls are affected. In our test application, several calls are executed on `Account` objects a and b ⑤. Clicking on one of the method calls in the structure view makes the editor open the file that declares the call and jump to the corresponding line.

3.2 OPTIMA

Transactions require considerable run-time support. Our experiments make use of OPTIMA [6, 9], a highly configurable, object-oriented framework that provides support for open multithreaded transactions and guarantees the ACID properties for transactional objects.

Since transactions are nowadays used in different software domains, the requirements of applications using transactions vary tremendously. It is therefore important that the application programmer can configure a transaction support or middleware to fit the application's needs.

The OPTIMA framework has been designed along these lines. Hierarchies with classes implementing standard transactional behavior are provided, but a programmer is free to extent the hierarchies to tailor the framework to the application-specific needs. The framework supports, among other features, optimistic and pessimistic concurrency control, strict read / write or commutativity-based method invocation, different recovery strategies (Undo/Redo, NoUndo/Redo, Undo/NoRedo), different caching techniques, different logging techniques (physical logging and logical logging), different update strategies (in-place and deferred), and different storage devices.

For our experiment, a prototype of the OPTIMA framework has been implemented for Java. It offers a procedural interface that allows an application programmer to start, join, commit, and abort transactions (see Section 2.3). To guarantee the ACID properties, the framework must additionally be called before and after every method invocation on a transactional object.

4   Aspectizing Transactions

In this section, we relate our experience in trying to achieve the most ambitious of the three goals mentioned in the introduction, namely *aspectizing transaction semantics*. In other words, does it make sense to write a program without transactions, and then (somehow automatically) have the program run with transactions? Is it possible to take code written for and used in a non-transactional setting, and run it with transactions?

We discuss several reasons why this is clearly impossible. We point out the issue of local synchronization versus global synchronization, that is, transaction synchronization, then the issue of irreversible actions, and finally the impact of ensuring transactional semantics for all objects.

4.1 Cooperation vs. Competition

Concurrent systems can be classified into *cooperative* systems, where individual components collaborate, share results and work for a common goal, and *competitive* systems, where the individual components are not aware of each other and compete for shared resources [10, 11, 12].

Programming languages address collaboration and competition by providing means for communication and synchronization among threads. This can be done by using *shared objects*, also called *monitors* [13, 14]. Typically, two forms of synchronization are considered: *mutual exclusion* and *condition synchronization*.

- Mutual exclusion is a synchronization mechanism that ensures that while one thread is accessing the state of an object, no other thread can possibly gain access. In Java, this behavior is provided by classes that declare all their methods as being `synchronized`.
- Condition synchronization is necessary when a thread wishes to perform an operation that can only sensibly or safely be performed if another thread has itself taken some action or is in some defined state. For example, if a thread wants to pass some data to some other thread via a shared object, then the receiver thread must make sure that the sender has already stored the data in the shared object before trying to retrieve it. In this case, the receiver wants to synchronize with the sender, but the sender does not need to synchronize with the receiver. If the sender wants to know that the receiver has taken the data, then both threads must synchronize.

In Java, condition synchronization can be achieved by using the `wait()`, `notify()` and `notifyAll()` methods provided by all classes inheriting from `Object`. If a certain condition is not met, a thread executing one of the synchronized methods of a shared object can call `wait()` to suspend itself, thereby releasing the mutual exclusion lock. If some other thread modifies the condition, it should call `notify()`, which results in awakening the suspended thread.

In order to highlight the problems that arise when introducing transactions into previously non-transactional applications, let us consider the following example. Thread T1 wants to transfer money from bank account A to bank account B, whereas thread T2 wants to do the same from B to A. Without transactions, the program works just fine, provided that (1) no failure occurs during its execution, and (2) the `withdraw` and `deposit` methods are synchronized (ACID properties are of course not ensured without transactions).

Solvable Deadlock. To tolerate failures however, each thread must execute the two operations inside a transaction. If in this case the interleaving happens to be the one shown in Situation 1 of Figure 2, then a deadlock occurs. Fortunately, the deadlock can be broken by aborting one of the transactions and restarting it.

Unsolvable Deadlock. In situation 2, the withdraw operation is only performed if there is enough money on the account. In this case, an insufficient balance results in an unbreakable deadlock.

Situation 1 (solvable deadlock)		Situation 2 (unsolvable deadlock)	
T1:	T2:	T1:	T2:
`A.withdraw(Amount)`		`A.deposit(Amount)`	`B.deposit(Amount)`
	`B.withdraw(Amount)`	`while (B.getBalance()`	`while (A.getBalance()`
`B.deposit(Amount)`		`    <= Amount) { }`	`    <= Amount) { }`
	`A.deposit(Amount)`	`B.withdraw(Amount)`	`A.withdraw(Amount)`

Fig. 2. Possible Deadlock Situations caused by Transactions

Two different execution interleavings must be considered:

1. The first one is similar to the one presented before. T1 deposits the money on A, and T2 deposits the money on B. Both threads then try to execute `getBalance()`, but are blocked by the transaction support to prevent information smuggling (isolation property).
2. In the second scenario, T1 goes ahead, deposits the money on account A, queries the balance of account B, but then remains blocked in the while loop, because the balance of B is insufficient. The transaction support cannot allow T2 to call `deposit()` on B, otherwise the isolation property is violated. This deadlock is due to condition synchronization of T1 on T2.

Generally speaking, Java synchronized classes implement *linearizability* of *every single* operation [15], whereas transactions require *serializability* of *all* operations performed within a transaction [16].

The only way of circumventing this mismatch is to remove the isolation requirement between the two threads by executing them within the same transaction. Situation 2 in Figure 2 actually depicts a loose form of collaboration between the two threads. Either one can not perform its job without the help of the other.

To prevent unsolvable deadlocks, all threads that cooperate in some form must execute inside the same transaction. If transactions are to be introduced automatically and in a transparent manner, all such situations must be detected. For reasonably complex applications, this is clearly infeasible.

4.2 Irreversible Actions: I/O

Some method invocations are irreversible. Such a situation arises, for instance, in software controlled production cells. Invoking a method on an object that controls a forge might irreversibly shape some piece of metal. But even more conventional actions, such as displaying an alert message on the screen, cannot be undone. Admittedly, it is possible to remove the alert message on the screen, but perhaps some person has already read it and taken corresponding actions.

All I/O operations give rise to this kind of problems in transactional systems. Depending on the exact situation, different solutions are possible [17]. One solution is, for instance, to buffer irreversible method invocations, and only executing them on transaction commit[1]. Although it is possible to apply such techniques to objects with

---

[1] This, of course, assumes that the method itself cannot fail.

irreversible methods, it can obviously not be done completely transparently. Irreversible actions are therefore a clear argument against the complete aspectization of transactions.

4.3 Uniformity

A more practical-oriented reason why a complete aspectization is impossible is that, as a result of such aspectization, *all* application objects must be made *transactional*, i.e., provide concurrency control, undo-functionality, durability, etc.

In principle, this can be achieved in AspectJ by declaring an aspect as shown in Figure 3. The pointcut PublicMethodCall() captures all public method invocations of all objects in the system, except those declared in the OPTIMA framework. This restriction is necessary to prevent that the OPTIMA objects providing support for transactions are made transactional themselves, leading to a clear nonsense recursion.

```
aspect TransactionalObjects pertarget(PublicMethodCall()) {
    pointcut PublicMethodCall() : call(public * *.*(..)) &&
                                  !within(ch.epfl.lglwww.optima..*);
    // introduce fields here that link the object to the transaction support
    // i.e. concurrency control, recovery manager, storage, etc.
    before() : AllPublicMethodCalls() {...}
    after()  : AllPublicMethodCalls() {...}
}
```

Fig. 3. Capturing all Public Method Invocations on all Objects

At run-time, an instance of the TransactionalObjects aspect is associated with any object outside of OPTIMA that is the target of a public method invocation. The before() and after() advice make the necessary calls to the OPTIMA framework.

Although this approach looks reasonable, it might not be feasible in a particular setting. In our Java-based experiment, durability of the state of transactional objects is achieved using the Java serialization facility. Unfortunately, not all Java objects implement the Serializable interface, and hence making all objects transactional may not be possible.

An additional problem is memory usage. An instance of the aspect shown in Figure 3 is created for every accessed object in the system. Every object also needs, for instance, an associated concurrency control. This might end up adding a significant amount of memory use to applications composed of a large number of objects.

The issues raised in this subsection are fortunately not insurmountable. Some of them have been successfully addressed in [18].

5   Aspectizing Transaction Interfaces

In this section, we discuss the extent to which one can *aspectize transaction interfaces,* that is, completely separate transactional interfaces (*begin, commit, abort, etc.*) from the main (functional) object methods, and have these methods encapsulated within code invoked through specific aspects. We point out that this leads to very intricate programs because of the very nature of transaction terminations, their integration with exception handling mechanisms, and the difficulty in expressing thread collaboration.

The very need to consider worst-case situations for concurrency control and recovery typically also impacts performance.

5.1 Interactions with Transactions

Most of the time, an application programmer wants to commit his (her) transactions. In certain cases however, he (she) might want to abort a running transaction as illustrated by the example presented in Figure 4. The code shows a method `transfer()` that withdraws money from the bank account `source` and deposits it into the bank account `dest`. If there is not enough money on the source account, then the transaction is aborted.

```
void transfer(Account source, Account dest, int amount) {
    beginTransaction();
    try {
        source.withdraw(amount);
        dest.deposit(amount);
        commitTransaction();
    } catch (NotEnoughFundsException e) {
        abortTransaction();
    }
}
```

Fig. 4. Interacting with Transactions

If we separate the calls to the transaction support from the functional code, some other means must be found that allow the programmer to trigger a transaction abort.

One possibility is to use the exception mechanism provided in most modern programming languages. Transactions can be associated with exception handling contexts, typically methods [7, 19]. If the method ends normally, then the transaction is committed. If the method call terminates exceptionally, then the transaction is aborted.

The interaction problem might however also arise in the other direction. Even though a transaction is intended to commit, it may abort due to some failure in the system, i.e., the remote server that hosts the destination bank account is unreachable at commit time. In this case, the application programmer should be notified, for he (she) might want to take corresponding actions, i.e., execute an alternative transaction or retry the original one. Again, exceptions can be used to perform this notification, e.g., by means of a predefined exception `TransactionAbortedException`.

If this kind of integration is chosen, throwing exceptions has an additional meaning. The application programmer must be aware of the fact that an exception that crosses a transaction boundary results in a rollback. It seems clear to us that in this case it is preferable that the application programmer and the person that applies the transaction boundaries be the same person.

5.2 Making Methods Transactional Using AspectJ

When making the interface to transactions transparent, the calls to the transaction support must be completely hidden from the application programmer. They should execute automatically at certain points in the program.

Figure 5 shows an abstract aspect `TransactionalMethods` that wraps a transaction around a method invocation by making calls to the procedural interface of OPTIMA introduced in Section 2.3.

```
public abstract aspect TransactionalMethods {
    abstract public pointcut MethodToBeMadeTransactional();
    void around() : MethodToBeMadeTransactional() {
        ProceduralInterface.beginTransaction(); ①
        boolean aborted = false;
        try {
            proceed(); ②
        } catch (TransactionException e) {
            ProceduralInterface.abortTransaction(); ③
            aborted = true;
            throw e; ④
        } finally {
            if (!aborted) {
                ProceduralInterface.commitTransaction(); ⑤
            }
        }
    }
}
```

Fig. 5. Making Method Calls Transactional

The method call is encapsulated with the help of the around() advice. First, the beginTransaction() method is called to start a new (nested) transaction ①. The actual method call is placed inside a try-catch block and executed using the proceed() ② statement. If the original method call terminates with a Transaction-Exception, then the transaction is aborted ③, and the exception is thrown again ④. In any other case the transaction is committed ⑤. If the commit is not possible, the commitTransaction() method will throw the TransactionAbortedException exception.

In order to apply the TransactionalMethods aspect to a method, the programmer must extend the aspect and override the MethodToBeMadeTransactional pointcut. Figure 6 shows an aspect that makes all method invocations on the Account class transactional.

As a result, all method invocations on the Account class may now throw the TransactionAbortedException.

5.3 Java-Related Problems

Java has very strict rules for exception handling. Java exceptions are part of a method signature, i.e., a method or constructor must declare all exceptions it might throw during its execution. Forgetting to do so results in a compilation error. This rule applies to all exceptions apart from subclasses of Error or RuntimeException.[2]

In order to adhere to the Java exception rules, our aspect would have to modify the signature of the method it applies to. This is not possible in the current version of AspectJ (version 1.0.3), and we therefore had to declare the TransactionAborte-dException as a subclass of RuntimeException in order to avoid compilation errors. Unfortunately this work-around is not completely satisfying. A Java program-

---

[2] Exceptions of the class Error indicate serious problems, e.g. Virtual-MachineError. They should never occur and ordinary programs are not expected to recover from them. Subclasses of the class RuntimeException, e.g. ArithmeticException or NullPointerException, are thrown in case a language-defined check fails. These exceptions occur frequently, and hence the language designers decided that it would be cumbersome to force the programmer to declare them everywhere.

```
aspect MakeAccountMethodsTransactional extends TransactionalMethods {
    public pointcut MethodToBeMadeTransactional() :
        call (public * Account.*(..));
}
```

Fig. 6. Making Account Methods Transactional

mer, relying on the fact that important application exceptions are checked, might forget to handle the `TransactionAbortedException`, which results in an incorrect program behavior.

5.4 Collaboration among Threads

In the example presented in Section 5.2, every invocation of a method that has been specified as being transactional results in the creation of a new transaction. Unfortunately, this precludes any collaboration between threads as explained in Section 4.1.

In order to make collaboration possible, threads must be able to enter the same transaction. This can be achieved using a named transaction as shown in Figure 7.

```
public abstract aspect TransactionallyCollaboratingMethods {
    abstract public pointcut MethodToBeMadeTransactional();
    abstract public String initTransactionName();
    final String transactionName = initTransactionName();
    void around() : MethodToBeMadeTransactional() {
        ProceduralInterface.beginOrJoinTransaction(transactionName);
        // the rest of the code remains the same
    }
}
```

Fig. 7. Using Named Transactions

To apply this aspect to all `Account` objects, the programmer must define a concrete pointcut and provide a transaction name as follows:

```
aspect CollaboratingAccount extends TransactionallyCollaboratingMethods {
    public pointcut MethodToBeMadeTransactional() :
        call (public * Account.*(..));
    public String initTransactionName() {
        return "AccountTransaction";
    }
}
```

Fig. 8. Account Methods Collaborating Inside the Same Transaction

Now, a thread that executes `getBalance()` can proceed, even if some other thread has previously invoked `deposit()`, because they both participate in the same transaction named "`AccountTransaction`".

5.5 Transactional Objects

In Section 4.3 we argued that it makes no sense to turn *all* application objects into transactional objects. The situation here is different, since we aim only at aspectizing transaction interfaces. The programmer specifies which methods are to be executed transactionally, and therefore also knows which objects are accessed from within a transaction. Only these objects must be made transactional.

In OPTIMA, every transactional object must be associated with a recovery manager and a concurrency control. In order to guarantee the ACID properties, each time a method is invoked on a transactional object the following actions must be taken:

1. **Concurrency Control Prologue** — Call the preOperation() method of the concurrency control associated with the object. This allows, for instance, a lock-based concurrency control to suspend the calling thread in case the method to be called conflicts with other method calls made from other transactions.
2. **Recovery Prologue** — Call the recovery manager's preOperation() method. This allows the recovery manager to collect information for undoing the method call in case the transaction aborts later on.
3. **Method Execution** — Execute the actual method call.
4. **Recovery Epilogue** — Invoke the recovery manager's postOperation() method.
5. **Concurrency Control Epilogue** — Call the postOperation() method of the concurrency control associated with the object.

Using AspectJ, these actions can be encapsulated inside an aspect as shown in Figure 9. The TransactionalObject defines a pointcut TransactionalMethod, which in our example specifies that all calls to public methods of the Account class are to be intercepted ①, thus making all Account objects transactional.

```
aspect TransactionalObject pertarget(TransactionalMethod()) {
    pointcut TransactionalMethod() : call(public * Account.*(..));  ①
    private final RecoveryManager myRecoveryManager = ...;
    private final ConcurrencyControl myConcurrencyControl = new ...;  ②
    // other per-object info, e.g. recovery info
    public void abortTransaction(Object object, Transaction t) {
        myConcurrencyControl.transactionAbort(t);
    }
    public void commitTransaction(Object object, Transaction t) {
        myConcurrencyControl.transactionCommit(t);
    }
    before() : TransactionalObjectMethodCall() {  ③
        Transaction t = TransactionContext.getTransaction();  ④
        if (t != null) {
            Object currentObject = thisJoinPoint.getTarget();  ⑤
            myConcurrencyControl.preOperation(t);
            myRecoveryManager.preOperation(currentObject, t);  ⑥
        }
    }
    after() : TransactionalObjectMethodCall() {
        Transaction t = TransactionContext.getTransaction();
        if (t != null) {
            Object currentObject = thisJoinPoint.getTarget();
            myRecoveryManager.postOperation(currentObject, t);
            myConcurrencyControl.postOperation(t);
        }
    }
}
```

Fig. 9. Making Objects Transactional

The aspect itself is specified to be instantiated pertarget(Transactional-Method), meaning that an instance of the aspect is created for each account object that receives a public method call. Therefore, a separate copy of the private fields myRecoveryManager and myConcurrencyControl exist for each object. The fields are initialized when the aspect is instantiated, i.e. before a public method is invoked on the Account object for the first time ②.

The before() and after() advice encapsulate the actual method call. Any invocation of a public method on the Account class is intercepted, and the before advice is executed ③. First, the current transaction context is obtained from the transaction support ④. A reference to the transactional object itself is obtained by calling the getTarget() method of the thisJoinPoint object, which is an object offered by the AspectJ environment that provides information on the context of the advice's current join point ⑤. Next, the concurrency control prologue, and finally the recovery prologue are executed ⑥. The after() advice handles the epilogues in a similar way.

Although this aspect can be used to make any Java class transactional[3], it is nevertheless not a viable solution for an application that heavily relies on transactions. The transaction support does not get any knowledge on the frequency of use of the object, the size of its state and the semantics of its methods. As a result, worst-case assumptions must be made, which yields in poor performance. Exploiting such knowledge makes it possible to increase concurrency and decrease disk access, and therefore considerably improves performance.

6 Aspectizing Transaction Mechanisms

In this section, we discuss the extent to which one can *aspectize transaction mechanisms,* that is, separate the mechanisms needed to ensure the ACID properties of transactions (i.e., concurrency control and failure management) from the main (functional) program (objects) and have these encapsulated within specific aspects. We present how AspectJ aspects have been used to provide application-wide, per-class, and per-method customization of transaction mechanisms. We show that, although possible and elegant, this separation should be handled with care, especially whenever the actual functional part does change. In short, the programmer must be aware that the physical separation does not imply a semantic decoupling.

6.1 Configuring Application-Wide Transaction Preferences

Transactional systems guarantee atomicity and durability even in the presence of failures, i.e., crashes. Different techniques for recovering from a crash failure exist with different performance trade-offs.

To achieve durability, the state of transactional objects is stored on so-called stable storage [20]. To boost performance, the state of frequently used transactional objects is kept in a cache. On a system crash however, the content of the cache is lost, and there-

---

[3] Note that, in order to support durability, the class must implement the Serializable or Externalizable interface.

fore, in general, the state of the stable storage can be inconsistent for the following reasons:

- The storage does not contain updates of committed transactions.
- The storage contains updates of uncommitted transactions.

When recovering from a system crash, the former problem can be solved by *redoing* the changes made by the corresponding transactions, the latter by *undoing* the changes made by the corresponding transactions [21].

The Undo/Redo recovery strategy can handle both situations, and therefore gives the most freedom to the cache manager. However, the time needed for performing recovery is considerable. Other recovery strategies, e.g., NoUndo/Redo or Undo/NoRedo, perform better during recovery [22], but constrain the cache manager and hence may potentially slow down performance during normal processing.

In our OPTIMA framework, one can select the appropriate recovery manager by instantiating the corresponding class from the class hierarchy presented in Figure 10.

Fig. 10. The Recovery Manager Hierarchy

There must be a single recovery manager for the entire application, and it must be initialized during start-up. Using aspects, this initialization can be achieved by declaring an OptimaConfiguration aspect as shown in Figure 11.

```
public aspect OptimaConfiguration issingleton() {
    public RecoveryManager initRecoveryManager() {
        // instantiate your chosen recovery manager here
        // the parameters (omitted here) specify the desired log storage
        return new UndoNoRedoManager(...);
    }
    public final RecoveryManager recoveryManager = initRecoveryManager();
    // more code follows later
}
```

Fig. 11. Selecting a Recovery Manager

By using the modifier issingleton(), the aspect has exactly one instance that crosscuts the entire application. That instance is available at any time during execution of the program using the static method OptimaConfiguration.aspectOf().

6.2 Configuring Object Transactional Properties

Objects that are accessed from within a transaction must be capable of handling cooperative and competitive concurrency. In order to address cooperative concurrency, methods that update the state of an object must execute in mutual exclusion.

Competitive concurrency control, which guarantees the isolation property of transactions, can be *pessimistic (conservative)* or *optimistic (aggressive)* [23], both having

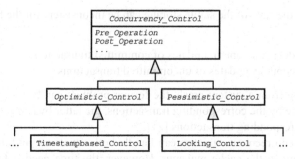

Fig. 12. The Concurrency Control Hierarchy

advantages and disadvantages. Figure 12 depicts an excerpt of the concurrency control class hierarchy of OPTIMA.

Every transactional object must have an associated concurrency control. In order to maximize concurrency, the kind of concurrency control must be configurable on a per-class (or even per-object) basis. However, in order to guarantee the serializability of transactions, the global serialization order must be the same for all concurrency controls used in a system [24].

To do this transparently, we have introduced an interface `CustomizedConcurrencyControl`, shown in Figure 13. An object that wants to specify its preferred concurrency control must implement this interface.

```
interface CustomizedConcurrencyControl {
    public ConcurrencyControl getConcurrencyControl();
}
```

Fig. 13. The `CustomizedConcurrencyControl` Interface

The following aspect does this transparently. It specifies a timestamp-based concurrency control for the `Account` class.

```
public aspect AccountConcurrencyControlAspect {
    declare parents: Account implements CustomizedConcurrencyControl;
    public ConcurrencyControl
      CustomizedConcurrencyControl.getConcurrencyControl() {
        return new TimestampbasedControl();
    }
}
```

Fig. 14. Selecting a Custom Concurrency Control for a Class

The default concurrency control can be set in the `OptimaConfiguration` aspect as shown in Figure 15.

The method `initConcurrencyControl` is called once for each object. In Figure 15, if the object does not implement the `CustomizedConcurrencyControl` interface, a `LockingControl` is instantiated.

6.3 Specifying Transactional Properties on a Per-method Basis

To optimize concurrency even further, the transaction support needs specific information about the semantics of each method of an object.

```
public aspect OptimaConfiguration issingleton() {
    // code shown in Figure 11
    public ConcurrencyControl initConcurrencyControl(Object o) {
        if (o instanceof CustomizedConcurrencyControl) {
            // get the customized ConcurrencyControl
            return ((CustomizedConcurrencyControl) o).getConcurrencyControl();
        } else {
            // instantiate your default concurrency control here
            return new LockingControl();
        }
    }
}
```

Fig. 15. Selecting a Default Concurrency Control for All Classes

A sophisticated concurrency control can, for instance, allow method invocations on the same object made from different transactions to execute concurrently, if it knows that no information smuggling will occur. For example, multiple getBalance() invocations on an Account object do not conflict. This is not surprising, since getBalance() does not modify the state of an account. However, two deposit() operations do not conflict either; they *commute*. Generally speaking, the decision of what methods may cause a conflict depends on the semantics of the method, the method input and output parameters, the structure of the object state, and the object usage [24].

Other parts of the transaction support can also benefit from the knowledge of method semantics. If, for instance, every method has an associated *inverse method*, which undoes the effects of the former one, then the recovery manager can perform logical logging instead of physical logging, if appropriate.

Obviously, such semantic knowledge about methods can not be guessed automatically. It must be provided by the application programmer. In OPTIMA, this information is encapsulated in the abstract Operation class. Subclasses of Operation must implement methods such as isCompatible(Operation op), which must determine if the current operation conflicts with the operation op passed as a parameter.

```
public class GetBalanceOperation extends Operation {
    boolean isCompatible(Operation op) {
        return (op instanceof GetBalanceOperation);
    }
}
```

Fig. 16. The GetBalanceOperation Class

Figure 16 depicts parts of the declaration code of the GetBalanceOperation class. It specifies that calls to the getBalance() method from one transaction are compatible with calls to getBalance() from other transactions, but incompatible with all other methods invocations on the Account class.

Following the same idea shown in Section 6.2 for customizing concurrency control, classes that want to customize their transactional behavior on a per-method basis must implement the CustomizedMethods interface shown in Figure 17.

```
public interface CustomizedMethods {
    public Operation getOperation(String name, JoinPoint jp)
        throws MethodCustomizationException;
}
```

Fig. 17. The CustomizedMethods Interface

The aspect shown in Figure 18 adds this functionality to the Account class. The implementation of the method getOperation may make use of the JoinPoint parameter jp. In AspectJ, JoinPoint objects provide access to run-time information, e.g., parameter values. In Figure 18, jp is used when the deposit method is invoked to extract the value of the parameter that holds the amount of money to be deposited.

```
public aspect AccountMethodAspect {
    declare parents: Account implements CustomizedMethods;
    public Operation CustomizedMethods.getOperation(String name, JoinPoint jp)
        throws MethodCustomizationException {
        if (name.equals("getBalance")) {
            return new GetBalanceOperation();
        } else if (name.equals("deposit")) {
            return new DepositOperation((Integer)jp.getArgs()[0]);
        } else {
            throw MethodCustomizationException;
        }
    }
}
```

Fig. 18. Customizing All Methods of the Account Class

If no operation subclass is defined for a given method, or if the class does not implement the CustomizedMethods interface, the default operation class is used as shown in Figure 19 ①. The default operation class assumes the worst: the operation is assumed to modify the state of the object, and is assumed to conflict with any other operation.

```
public aspect OptimaConfiguration issingleton() {
    // code shown in Figure 11 and Figure 15
    public Operation getOperation(Object o, JoinPoint jp) {
        if (o instanceof CustomizedMethods) {
            // get the customized Operation object
            Operation op;
            try {
                op = ((CustomizedMethods)o).getOperation
                    (jp.getSignature().getName(), jp);
            } catch (MethodCustomizationException e) {
                return new DefaultOperation();
            }
            return op;
        } else {
            return new DefaultOperation(); ①
        }
    }
}
```

Fig. 19. Default Operation Object for All Methods

6.4 Transactional Objects with Customization

The previous sections have shown how to add customization at the application, object and method level. To encapsulate transactional objects and at the same time provide customization, the aspect presented in Figure 9 has been extended. The result is shown in Figure 20.

The aspect CustomizedTransactionalObject is still specified to be instantiated pertarget(TransactionalMethods). At instantiation time, the recovery manager is initialized to the one given in the OptimaConfiguration aspect ①. The concurrency control for the transactional object is initialized when a public method is invoked from within a transaction for the first time by calling initConcurrency Control() ② (see Section 6.2).

Before the method is executed, the Operation object for the method is obtained by calling getOperation() ③. The returned Operation object is passed to the concurrency control preOperation() method ④.

```
aspect CustomizedTransactionalObject pertarget(TransactionalMethods()) {
    pointcut TransactionalMethods() : call(public * Account.*(..));
    private final RecoveryManager myRecoveryManager =
        OptimaConfiguration.aspectOf().recoveryManager; ①
    private ConcurrencyControl myConcurrencyControl;
    // other per-object info, e.g. recovery info
    public void abortTransaction(Object object, Transaction t) {
        myConcurrencyControl.transactionAbort(t);
    }
    public void commitTransaction(Object object, Transaction t) {
        myConcurrencyControl.transactionCommit(t);
    }
    before() : TransactionalObjectMethodCall() {
        Transaction t = TransactionContext.getTransaction();
        if (t != null) {
            Object currentObject = thisJoinPoint.getTarget();
            if (myConcurrencyControl == null) {
                myConcurrencyControl = OptimaConfiguration.aspectOf()
                    .initConcurrencyControl(currentObject); ②
            }
            Operation myOperation = OptimaConfiguration.aspectOf()
                .getOperation(currentObject, thisJoinPoint); ③
            myConcurrencyControl.preOperation(myOperation, t);
            myRecoveryManager.preOperation(currentObject, t); ④
        }
    }
    after() : TransactionalObjectMethodCall() {
        Transaction t = TransactionContext.getTransaction();
        if (t != null) {
            Object currentObject = thisJoinPoint.getTarget();
            myRecoveryManager.postOperation(currentObject, t);
            Operation myOperation = OptimaConfiguration.aspectOf()
                .getOperation(currentObject, thisJoinPoint);
            myConcurrencyControl.postOperation(myOperation, t);
        }
    }
}
```

Fig. 20. Making Objects Transactional with Customization

6.5 Extensibility

Care must be taken when modifying methods of transactional objects with customized transactional behavior, since modifications in the code might also modify the method semantics.

Consider a bank account that offers the usual deposit and withdraw operations, and an operation that returns the current interest rate getInterestRate. In general, bank accounts have fixed interest rates, and therefore invocations of getInterest-Rate do not conflict with deposit or withdraw. An implementation of such a bank account will exploit this property and implement customized methods to increase concurrency.

But what if a bank decides to offer better interest rates to "good" customers, meaning customers whose account balance exceeds a certain amount of money? In this case, calling `deposit` or `withdraw` might change the interest rate if the new balance passes the threshold. The point we want to make here is that such a modification inside a method of the `Account` class must be accompanied by a corresponding modification in the `AccountMethodAspect`; otherwise the ACID properties will be violated. Hence, although the transaction mechanisms are physically separated from the "functional" part of the account class, they remain semantically coupled. When performing maintenance, both parts must be updated in accordance.

7   Related Work

To the best of our knowledge, there has been no previously published work on providing support for transactions using AOP.

A widely used platform that promises what we called *transaction interface aspectization* is *Enterprise Java Beans* [5]. EJB is a higher-level component-based architecture for distributed business applications, which aims at simplifying the development of complex systems in Java by dividing the overall development process into seven different architecture roles that can be performed by different parties.

One of the architecture roles is the *Enterprise Bean Provider*. Typically performed by an application-domain expert, e.g. from the financial industry, the enterprise bean provider builds a component, called an *enterprise bean*, that implements the business methods without being concerned about the distribution, transaction, security, and other non-business-specific aspects of the application. The *EJB Container Provider* on the other hand is supposed to be an expert in distributed systems, transactions and security. The container provider must deliver tools for the deployment of enterprise beans, and a run-time system that provides the deployed beans with transaction and security management, distribution, management of resources, and other services. The other architecture roles are the *Persistence Manager Provider,* the *EJB Server Provider*, the *System Administrator*, the *Application Assembler*, and finally the *Deployer*.

Entity beans provide an object view of data in a database, and typically access this data from within a transaction. However, the methods of an enterprise bean do not handle transactions directly. Instead, transactional properties are specified in the *deployment descriptor* of a bean. Possible transaction policies are presented in figure 21.

The transaction policies can be set by the bean provider for the entire bean or for each method separately. But, surprisingly, these policies can later on be changed by the application assembler, or even by the deployer. It is also possible to change the isolation level for an entire bean, or even for each method separately. Isolation levels, however, are not standardized. In Visual Age for Java, for instance, possible isolation levels (from strongest to weakest) are TRANSACTION_SERIALIZABLE, TRANSACTION_REPEATABLE_READ, TRANSACTION_READ_COMMITTED, TRANSACTION_READ_UNCOMMITTED.

Based on our experience, changing the transaction policies and isolation levels defined by the bean provider is highly error-prone. Only the implementor of the bean knows the exact semantics of the methods, and is qualified to select the appropriate

Policy	Meaning
Tx_NOT_SUPPORTED	The method can not be called from inside a transaction.
Tx_SUPPORTED	The method can be called from inside a transaction.
Tx_MANDATORY	The method must be called from inside a transaction. If this is not the case, an exception is thrown to the caller.
Tx_REQUIRED	The method requires to be executed from inside a transaction. If this is not the case, a new transaction is created.
Tx_REQUIRES_NEW	The container creates a new transaction before executing the method.
Tx_BEAN_MANAGED	Session beans are allowed to manage transactions explicitly by calling javax.transaction.CurrentTransaction. This policy is not supported for entity beans.

Fig. 21. Enterprise Java Beans Transaction Policies

policies. Allowing a different person to fiddle with these properties at deployment time will inevitably lead to incorrect programs.

Another obvious drawback of the EJB approach is performance. When writing the entity bean methods, the bean provider does not have to worry about concurrent accesses by multiple transactions. The bean provider may assume that the container will ensure appropriate synchronization for entity objects that are accessed concurrently by multiple transactions.

Unfortunately, the container does not have any knowledge of the semantics of the methods of a bean, and therefore must make a "blind" choice when implementing concurrency control. The EJB specification mentions two different implementation strategies. The container can activate multiple instances of a bean, one for each transaction, and let the underlying database handle proper serialization. Depending on what kind of lock the ejbLoad method acquires, this may unnecessarily block read-only transactions, or lead to deadlocks. The other solution is to activate only a single instance of the entity bean, and serialize the accesses by multiple transactions to this instance, which also restricts concurrency among transactions dramatically.

8 Discussion

Our experience was limited to:

1. The use of AspectJ as a representative of AOP languages;
2. *Transactions* as a fundamental paradigm to handle concurrency and failures;
3. Our underlying OPTIMA transactional framework to implement concurrency control and failure management.

Hence, in principle, one can hardly draw any conclusion on using AOP to aspectize concurrency and failures in general. Furthermore, the very fact that we could not smoothly aspectize concurrency and failures does in no way mean that other techniques to aspectize those concerns are bound to fail.

We have, however, tried to explore different possibilities, and we considered mainly issues of general importance without focussing on technical issues related, for instance, to the current implementation of AspectJ. For example, the current AspectJ implementation only advises the parts of an application for which source code is available at compile time, excluding, for instance, code in precompiled libraries such as java.lang. This restriction is an additional reason why the *aspectizing transactions* approach presented in Section 4 is impossible. We also ignored technical problems like aliasing of transactional objects, serializing references to transactional objects, and static fields of classes.

Our underlying thesis is, however, that concurrency control and failure management are hard to aspectize in general, and we argue below that this is actually not surprising.

- On one hand, existing transactional languages, e.g. Argus [25], Arjuna [26], KAROS [27], Transactional Drago [28] or PJama [29, 30, 18], provide primitives for expressing transaction boundaries within methods, and not as separate concerns. Furthermore, even if the systems underlying those languages provide default mechanisms for handling concurrency and failures, most work on how to obtain effective mechanisms advocate the tight integration of the mechanisms within the actual methods or objects [21, 31, 32]. The difficulty of providing local concurrency control mechanisms and the strong integration with recovery management is pointed out in [25].
- On the other hand, object-oriented programming is about modeling real-world phenomenon with objects. Each object is supposed to encapsulate the state and the behavior of a real world phenomena, and concurrency and failures are usually parts of that phenomena. For instance, the very fact that a transaction should be aborted if there is not enough money in a bank account is a full part of the semantics of the bank account. Similarly, one would hate to get the actual balance of his bank account during a transfer.

9 Summary

We considered three levels of aspectization in our transactional context. The results of our experiment are summarized below:

Aspectizing transactions: Trying to automatically apply transactions to previously non-transaction code is doomed to failure, because of the incompatibility of the linearizability of method invocations provided by shared objects and transaction serializability, and because of the impossibility to automatically identify irreversible actions.

Aspectizing transaction interfaces: Separating transactional interfaces from the rest of the program can be achieved using aspect-oriented programming techniques. This separation, however, might seem artificial in situations where the "transactional aspect" actually is part of the semantics of the object it applies to. Each object is supposed to encapsulate the state and the behavior of a real world phenomena, and concurrency and failures are usually parts of that phenomena. In such situations, an indirect connection between functional and transactional concerns must be established, for instance by using exceptions. This, however, might lead to rather confusing code.

Another drawback of aspectizing transaction interfaces and not exposing transaction mechanisms is that default choices must be made by the underlying transaction support, which can considerably impact performance.

Aspectizing transaction mechanisms: AOP languages provide interesting features that can simplify the separation, at the syntactic level, of concurrency control and failure management mechanisms from the rest of the objects. Pretty much like an advanced macro language, however, these features should be reserved for smart programmers who have an advanced sense of the risk [4]. Physical separation does not necessarily imply semantic decoupling, and at least in the case of transactions, we believe that the application programmer and the programmer applying transactions using aspects must be the same person. Approaches such as the one taken by Enterprise Java Beans, where the application deployer can set or change transactional attributes for each Java bean, are error-prone, since they can easily lead to the violation of the ACID properties of transactions.

To prevent such problems, and to help aspect-oriented programmers, some guidelines and tool support would be useful, e.g., the ability to display "tightly coupled" aspects applying to an object whenever the implementation of the object changes. It might also be interesting to clearly emphasize that what can possibly be safely aspectized is probably what is not part of the object semantics, i.e., of the phenomena that the object is supposed to simulate, e.g., debugging and display. Drawing that borderline would be another interesting exercise.

In short, although the thesis underlying our experiment is not surprising, we believe nevertheless that the experiment itself provides some material for discussing what can be aspectized and what cannot. Given the growing interest in AOP, such a discussion can be of great value.

Acknowledgements

We are very grateful to Andrew Black and Pierre Cointe for many fruitful discussions on AOP. Besides the anonymous reviewers, we would also like to thank Bjorn Freeman-Benson, Gregor Kiczales and Mira Mezini for their comments on earlier drafts of this paper. Jörg Kienzle has been partially supported by the Swiss National Science Foundation project FN 2000-057187.99/1.

References

[1]   Madsen, O. L.; Møller-Pederson, B.: "What object-oriented programming may be - and what it does not have to be". In Gjessing, S.; Nygaard, K. (Eds.), *2nd European Conference on Object–Oriented Programming (ECOOP '88)*, pp. 1 – 20, Olso, Norway, August 1988, Lecture Notes in Computer Science **322**, Springer Verlag.

[2]   Elrad, T.; Aksit, M.; Kiczales, G.; Lieberherr, K.; Ossher, H.: "Discussing Aspects of AOP". *Communications of the ACM 44(10)*, pp. 33–38, October 2001.

[3]   Gray, J.; Reuter, A.: *Transaction Processing: Concepts and Techniques*. Morgan Kaufmann Publishers, San Mateo, California, 1993.

[4]   Guerraoui, R. "AOP = SMP (Structured Macro Programming)", Panel at the
      14th European Conference on Object–Oriented Programming (ECOOP '2000),
      Cannes, France, June 2000.
[5]   Shannon, B.; Hapner, M.; Matena, V.; Davidson, J.; Pelegri-Llopart, E.; Cable,
      L.: *Java 2 Platform Enterprise Edition: Platform and Component Specification.*
      The Java Series, Addison Wesley, Reading, MA, USA, 2000.
[6]   Kienzle, J.: *Open Multithreaded Transactions: A Transaction Model for Con-
      current Object-Oriented Programming.* Ph.D. Thesis #2393, Swiss Federal
      Institute of Technology, Lausanne, Switzerland, April 2001.
[7]   Kienzle, J.; Romanovsky, A.; Strohmeier, A.: "Open Multithreaded Transac-
      tions: Keeping Threads and Exceptions under Control". In *Proceedings of the
      6th International Worshop on Object-Oriented Real-Time Dependable Systems,
      Universita di Roma La Sapienza, Roma, Italy, January 8th - 10th, 2001*,
      pp. 209 – 217, IEEE Computer Society Press, 2001.
[8]   Kiczales, G.; Hilsdale, E.; Hugunin, J.; Kersen, M.; Palm, J.; Griswold, W. G.:
      "An Overview of AspectJ". In *15th European Conference on Object–Oriented
      Programming (ECOOP 2001)*, pp. 327 – 357, June 18–22, 2001, Budapest,
      Hungary, 2001.
[9]   Kienzle, J.; Jiménez-Peris, R.; Romanovsky, A.; Patiño-Martinez, M.: "Trans-
      action Support for Ada". In *Reliable Software Technologies - Ada-
      Europe'2001, Leuven, Belgium, May 14-18, 2001*, pp. 290 – 304, Lecture Notes
      in Computer Science **2043**, Springer Verlag, 2001.
[10] Lee, P. A.; Anderson, T.: "Fault Tolerance - Principles and Practice". In
      Dependable Computing and Fault-Tolerant Systems, Springer Verlag, 2 ed.,
      1990.
[11] Hoare, C. A. R.: "Parallel Programming: an Axiomatic Approach". In Bauer,
      F. L.; Samelson, K. (Eds.), *Proceedings of the International Summer School on
      Language Hierarchies and Interfaces*, pp. 11 – 42, Marktoberdorf, Germany,
      July 1975, Lecture Notes in Computer Science **46**, Springer Verlag.
[12] Horning, J. J.; Randell, B.: "Process Structuring". *ACM Computing Surveys
      5(1)*, pp. 5 – 30, March 1973.
[13] Brinch Hansen, P.: *Operating System Principles.* Prentice Hall, 1973.
[14] Hoare, C. A. R.: "Monitors: An Operating Systems Structuring Concept". *Com-
      munications of the ACM 17(10)*, pp. 549 – 557, October 1974.
[15] Herlihy, M.; Wing, J.: "Linearizability: a correctness condition for concurrent
      objects". *ACM Transactions on Programming Languages and Systems 12(3)*,
      pp. 463 – 492, July 1990.
[16] Papadimitriou, C.: "The serializability of concurrent database updates". *Journal
      of the ACM 26(4)*, pp. 631 – 653, October 1979.
[17] Romanovsky, A. B.; Shturtz, I. V.: "Unplanned recovery for non-program
      objects". *Computer Systems Science and Engineering 8(2)*, pp. 72–79, April
      1993.
[18] Daynès, L.: "Implementation of automated fine-granularity locking in a persis-
      tent programming language". *Software — Practice & Experience 30(4)*,
      pp. 325 – 361, April 2000.

[19] Romanovksy, A.; Kienzle, J.: "Action-Oriented Exception Handling in Cooperative and Competitive Object-Oriented Systems". In Romanovsky, A.; Dony, C.; Knudsen, J. L.; Tripathi, A. (Eds.), *Advances in Exception Handling Techniques*, pp. 147 – 164, Lecture Notes in Computer Science **2022**, Springer Verlag, 2001.

[20] Lampson, B. W.; Sturgis, H. E.: "Crash Recovery in a Distributed Data Storage System". *Technical report*, XEROX Research, Palo Alto, June 1979.

[21] Bernstein, P. A.; Goodman, N.: "Concurrency Control in Distributed Database Systems". *ACM Computing Surveys 13(2)*, pp. 185 – 221, June 1981.

[22] Bernstein, P. A.; Hadzilacos, V.; Goodman, N.: *Concurrency Control and Recovery in Database Systems*. Addison-Wesley, 1987.

[23] Kung, H. T.; Robinson, J. T.: "On Optimistic Methods for Concurrency Control". *ACM Transactions on Database Systems 6(2)*, pp. 213 – 226, June 1981.

[24] Ramamritham, K.; Chrysanthis, P. K.: "Advances in Concurrency Control and Transaction Processing". Los Alamitos, California, 1997.

[25] Liskov, B.: "Distributed Programming in Argus". *Communications of the ACM 31(3)*, pp. 300 – 312, March 1988.

[26] Shrivastava, S. K.: "Lessons Learned from Building and Using the Arjuna Distributed Programming System". In Birman, K.; Mattern, F.; Schiper, A. (Eds.), *Theory and Practice in Distributed Systems*, pp. 17 – 32, Lecture Notes in Computer Science **938**, 1995.

[27] Guerraoui, R.; Capobianchi, R.; Lanusse, A.; Roux, P.: "Nesting Actions through Asynchronous Message Passing: the ACS Protocol". In Madsen, O. L. (Ed.), *6th European Conference on Object–Oriented Programming (ECOOP '92)*, pp. 170 – 184, Utrecht, The Netherlands, June 1992, Lecture Notes in Computer Science **615**, Springer Verlag.

[28] Patiño-Martinez, M.; Jiménez-Peris, R.; Arévalo, S.: "Integrating Groups and Transactions: A Fault-Tolerant Extension of Ada". In *Reliable Software Technologies - Ada-Europe'98, Uppsala, Sweden, June 8-12, 1998*, pp. 78 – 89, Lecture Notes in Computer Science **1411**, 1998.

[29] Atkinson, M. P.; Daynès, L.; Jordan, M. J.; Printezis, T.; Spence, S.: "An orthogonally persistent Java". *ACM SIGMOD Record 25(4)*, pp. 68 – 75, December 1996.

[30] Daynès, L.: "Extensible Transaction Management in PJava". In *Proceedings of the First International Workshop on Persistence and Java, University of Glasgow, UK*, September 1996.

[31] Weihl, W. E.: "Local Atomicity Properties: Modular Concurrency Control for Abstract Data Types". *ACM Transactions on Programming Languages and Systems 11(2)*, pp. 249 – 283, April 1989.

[32] Guerraoui, R.: "Atomic Object Composition". In Tokoro, M.; Pareschi, R. (Eds.), *8th European Conference on Object–Oriented Programming (ECOOP '94)*, pp. 118 – 138, Bologna, Italy, June 1994, Lecture Notes in Computer Science **821**, Springer Verlag.

Difference-Based Modules:
A Class-Independent Module Mechanism

Yuuji Ichisugi[1] and Akira Tanaka[2]

[1] PRESTO, Japan Science and Technology Corporation(JST) /
National Institute of Advanced Industrial Science and Technology(AIST),
y-ichisugi@aist.go.jp
[2] National Institute of Advanced Industrial Science and Technology(AIST),
akr@m17n.org

Abstract. We describe a module mechanism, which we call *difference-based modules*, and an object-oriented language we call *MixJuice*. MixJuice is an enhancement to the Java language that adopts difference-based modules instead of Java's original module mechanism. Modules are units of information hiding, reuse and separate compilation. We have completely separated the class mechanism and the module mechanism, and then unified the module mechanism and the differential programming mechanism. Although this module mechanism is simpler than that of Java, it enhances ease with which programs can be extended, reused and maintained. Collaborations that crosscut several classes can be separated into different modules. Modules are composable in the same way as mixins. The composition of modules sometimes causes name collision and an interesting phenomenon, which we call *implementation defects*. We describe solutions to these problems.

1 Introduction

Modules are units of information hiding and reuse. Classes are templates of objects. These two notions are inherently different. However, in current object-oriented languages such as C++ and Java, the language construct "`class`" has the functions of a module. We call this type of module mechanism *class-based modules*. In large-scale programs, various problems occur when classes are used as modules.

One problem, pointed out by Szyperski[30], is that classes are inappropriate as units of information hiding. A class is appropriate as a unit of information hiding only if it is a simple abstract data type such as a stack. If one or more classes collaborate closely to realize a function, these classes are not appropriate as units of information hiding. In order to alleviate this problem, mechanisms such as packages and nested classes[10] have been introduced into Java. Even though these mechanisms have been introduced, class-based modules suffer a major problem. If the number of functions possessed by the software increases, the fields and methods needed for each class will also increase. This enlarges the size of the class, more specifically its scope, thus making system maintenance

B. Magnusson (Ed.): ECOOP 2002, LNCS 2374, pp. 62–88, 2002.
© Springer-Verlag Berlin Heidelberg 2002

more difficult. For example, the size of the source file of the class `TreeMap`, which is in the standard Java library, is about 1,000 lines, not including comment lines. Because all lines share a single name space, it is difficult to predict which parts of the source file will be influenced if a part of it is modified.

Another problem is that classes are inappropriate as units of reuse. Over the past few years, several studies have been made on this problem. The source-code related to a concern may crosscut more than one class[17]. In order to increase the reusability of the programs, such *crosscutting concerns* should be separated from the other parts of the program. Some systems such as AspectJ[16], Hyper/J[26], Demeter/Java[19] and DJ[25] have been proposed to support *separation of cross-cutting concerns*.

Other than these, some studies have focused on *collaborations* instead of classes as units of reuse[11,31,27,14,22,23]. A collaboration is a set of the fields and methods of two or more classes in relation to a certain function. In order to make collaborations into reusable units, the programming language should feature a *mixin*[3] or similar mechanism.

Mixins are fragments of classes. The programmers can define a new class by composing existing mixins. The use of mixins is a common programming technique used in programming languages that support multiple inheritance with class linearization, such as CLOS[28]. Mixins increase the reusability of programs because each mixin can be used as a part of more than one class.

VanHilst and Notkin have proposed a programming technique to implement mixins using C++ template mechanisms, in order to support collaboration-based design[31]. Mixin layers[27], however, are an improved programming technique that make the composition of the reusable parts much easier than in the Van-Hilst and Notkin method. Mixin layers are sets of mixins belonging to certain collaborations.

Independently, we have designed and implemented a mechanism named SystemMixins[14] on top of Java. SystemMixins are similar to mixin layers, which are sets of mixins belonging to certain collaborations. We have implemented an extensible Java pre-processor(EPP)[14,12] using this mechanism. The user can extend the language specification of Java by adding new collaborations to the pre-processor using the SystemMixin mechanism. A wide variety of language extensions have been implemented, including a data-parallel language[14], thread migration[2], parameterized types[12] and SystemMixin mechanism itself.

As a result of our experience with EPP implementation, we are convinced that collaborations are appropriate as units of reuse, especially for applications with extremely high extensibility, such as EPP.

As pointed out in [11,31], in collaborations, groups of objects cooperate to perform a task or to maintain an invariant. Therefore, collaborations must be suitable for not only units of reuse but also units of information hiding. However, both mixin layers and SystemMixins lack the function of information hiding.

In this paper, we propose a module mechanism which we call *difference-based modules*. We have designed and implemented an improved version of Java, which we call the *MixJuice* language[13], which adopts difference-based modules instead of Java's original module mechanism. We first completely separated the class mechanism and the module mechanism, and then unified the module mechanism and the differential programming mechanism. By applying difference-based modules, we have resolved the problems associated with the above-described conventional class-based modules. Using this module mechanism, collaborations can become units of information hiding and reuse instead of classes. This module mechanism is based on the three simple design principles: *difference definition, name-space inheritance* and *name-collision avoidance*.

The rest of this paper is organized as follows. In Section 2, we describe differential programming using this module mechanism. In Section 3, we describe the other feature of this module mechanism, information hiding. In Section 4, we explain an implementation defect phenomenon that may occur in highly extensible systems. In Section 5 we describe an application of MixJuice. Section 6 covers related work. We conclude with Section 7.

2 Differential Programming Using Difference-Based Modules

2.1 Principle and Merits

This module mechanism is based on the following design principle.

> **The principle of difference definition:** A module is the difference between the original program and the extended program. The difference is a set of definitions of new names and modifications of definitions of existing names[1].

Modules are units of reuse, information hiding and separate compilation. The executable application is constructed by linking of modules. In the case of difference-based modules, linking of modules means adding all differences defined by the modules to the empty program.

Difference-based modules can be applied to various programming languages. In many programming languages, a program consists of names and their definitions. For example, in the case of imperative languages, a program is a set of definitions of procedures and data structures. In the case of Java, a program is a set of definitions of classes, fields and methods. The MixJuice language is a modified Java language, which adopts difference-based modules instead of Java's original module mechanism. In other words, in MixJuice, a module is a set of additions and modifications of classes, fields and methods.

Modules may inherit other modules. In MixJuice, both the module-inheritance mechanism and the traditional class-inheritance mechanism can be independently available. Class inheritance and module inheritance are different, as described next. Class inheritance is a mechanism for describing the difference between classes. Module Inheritance is a mechanism for describing the difference

---

[1] Currently, the difference includes neither the renaming nor deletion of names.

between two programs consisting of one or more classes. Using class inheritance, the programmers can only define a new class which has a different name from that of the original class. By module inheritance, the programmers can modify the definitions of existing classes and methods without changing their names. Class inheritance is a mechanism for subtyping and safe late binding. Module inheritance is a mechanism for static reuse and information hiding as described in Section 3.

Classes no longer have the functions of modules. In other words, classes are no longer units of reuse, information hiding, or separate compilation.

Difference-based modules have the following merits compared with class-based modules.

- **High extensibility of applications**
  It is easy to write highly extensible applications. There are two reasons for this. One is that all class and method names act as "hooks" for programmers of extension modules. The other reason is that each extension module is composable as a mixin, using multiple inheritance of modules. (Details are described in Section 2.3.)
- **Class-independency of units of reuse**
  Programmers can define the units of reuse completely independently of boundaries of classes. The programmers can make codes that crosscut some classes, namely collaborations, units of reuse (Figure 1).

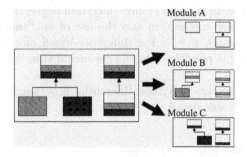

Fig. 1. Separation of crosscutting code.

- **Extensibility by third party programmers**
  Third party programmers can provide extension modules to extend existing applications. The programmers do not need to have the source-code of the original programs. (We give a more detailed account of this process in Section 2.5.)
- **Module-composability by end-users**
  End users can compose existing modules that provide selected functions to create their own customized applications. The composition of modules does not require any lines of "glue code". It only requires a set of module names. (Details are included in Section 5.)

```
module m1 {
  define class S {
    define S(){}
    define int foo(){ return 1; }
  }
  define class A extends S {
    define A(){}
    int foo(){ return original() + 10; }
  }
  class SS {
    void main(String[] args){
      A a = new A();
      System.out.println(a.foo());
    }
  }
}
module m2 extends m1 {
  class S { int foo(){ return original() + 2; } }
  class A { int foo(){ return original() + 20; } }
}
```

Fig. 2. Definitions of module m1 and module m2.

- **Flexibility of module grouping**
  The programmers can make groups of modules and give names to them to simplify their use. In the case of Java, a certain degree of grouping is possible due to the package mechanism and the use of an "import" declaration in the form of "import p.*;". For difference-based modules, however, more flexible grouping is possible. (Details are included in Section 2.3.)

The rest of this section describes differential programming using difference-based modules in greater detail.

2.2 Syntax of Module Definitions

Modules are defined as illustrated in Figure 2. The modules m1 and m2 are defined in Figure 2.

An "extends" declaration at the top of the module definition specifies the module to which the difference is intended to be added. The declared module is called a *super-module*. In Figure 2, the module m2 declares the module m1 to be a super-module of m2. At this time, we can say that "m2 is a sub-module of m1"; or "m2 inherits m1".

A module definition without an "extends" declaration, like module m1, denotes that the difference is assumed to be added to the empty program.

The module body, enclosed by braces, is the definition of the difference between the original program and the extended program. Specifically, a module can modify the program defined by its super-module as follows:

```
class $S1$ { int foo(){ return 1; } }
class S extends $S1$ { int foo(){ return super.foo() + 2; } }
class $A1$ extends S { int foo(){ return super.foo() + 10; } }
class A extends $A1$ { int foo(){ return super.foo() + 20; } }
class SS {
  void main(String[] args){
    A a = new A();
    System.out.println(a.foo());
  }
}
```

Fig. 3. A Java program almost equivalent to the program defined by module m2.

– Addition of new classes[2].
– Addition of fields to existing classes.
– Addition of methods to existing classes.
– Modification of existing methods by overriding.

In Figure 2, the module m2 extends the behavior of the method foo of class S and the method foo of class A by overriding those methods originally defined in the module m1.

The syntax of the inside of the module body is closely similar to Java; however, it differs from Java in the following ways.

The definitions of new names require the keywords "define". More accurately, the declarations of classes, fields, constructors and methods preceded by "define" denote they are the new definitions. The declarations of classes, constructors and methods without "define" denote them to be modifications of existing definitions. (Because the class SS and its method main are pre-defined names, they do not require "define".)

An expression "original()" is used when an overriding method invokes the overridden method. This is a similar mechanism to the method invocation of "super" in Java. In MixJuice, there are two kinds of method overriding. One is overriding by class inheritance, and the other is by module inheritance. In case of Figure 2, an "original()" in the module m1 is for the former, and two "original()" in the module m2 are for the latter.

In MixJuice, there is no use of package mechanisms or access modifiers (public, protected or private). How information hiding is achieved in MixJuice is described in Section 3.

The MixJuice program defined by module m2 is closely equivalent to the Java program as seen in Figure 3.

2.3 Multiple Inheritance of Modules

A module can inherit more than one super-module.

---

[2] In this paper, we do not mention "interfaces". Actually, the current implementation of MixJuice allows both extension of existing interfaces and addition of super interfaces to existing classes.

```
module m3 extends m1 {
  class S { int foo(){ return original() + 3; } }
  class A { int foo(){ return original() + 30; } }
}
module m4 extends m2, m3 {
  class S { int foo(){ return original() + 4; } }
  class A { int foo(){ return original() + 40; } }
}
```

Fig. 4. Multiple inheritance of modules.

Figure 4 is an example of multiple inheritance of modules. The module m3 defines, as well as m2, the difference between the extended program and the program defined by m1. The module m4 inherits both m2 and m3. In this case, the modules form a so-called "diamond inheritance" because both m2 and m3 inherit m1.

All modules are linearized by topological sort. This is similar to the class linearization done in some object-oriented languages with multiple-inheritance mechanisms such as CLOS[28].

For example, the program defined by the module m4 is constructed as follows. First of all, the set of the module m4 itself and the ancestor modules of m4 are found. The set is {m1, m2, m3, m4}. The set is then linearized by topological sort so that it preserves the order between super-modules and sub-modules. The result of this topological sort is called a *linearized list*. In this case, the linearized list may be (m1 m2 m3 m4). Finally, all differences defined by the modules are applied to the empty program ϕ, from the beginning of the linearized list to the end. That is, if the notation "$a \triangleleft b$" expresses the result of addition of a difference "b" to "a", the constructed program is expressed as:

$$((((\phi \triangleleft m1) \triangleleft m2) \triangleleft m3) \triangleleft m4)$$

A serious problem incurred by multiple inheritance is name collision. In MixJuice, this problem is completely resolved. The details are described in Section 3.7.

The multiple-inheritance mechanism of modules can be used as a grouping mechanism. To make the utilization of the group of modules more convenient, the programmer can define a group of modules and name it. For example, the following is the definition of a group named "m_x".

```
module m_x extends m_a, m_b, m_c, m_d {}
```

This mechanism is more flexible than Java's grouping mechanism using the declarations like "import p.*;", which is grouping based on packages. In addition, MixJuice allows definitions of groups of groups, which are not possible in Java.

```
class F {
  void branch(String s){
    if (s.equals("a")){ ... }
    else if (s.equals("b")){ ... }
    else { throw new Error(); }
  }
}
```

Fig. 5. Nested if-statements.

```
module framework {
  define class F {
    define void branch(String s){ throw new Error(); }
  }
}
module case_a extends framework {
  class F {
    void branch(String s){
      if (s.equals("a")){ ... } else { original(s); } }
  }
}
module case_b extends framework {
  class F {
    void branch(String s){
      if (s.equals("b")){ ... } else { original(s); } }
  }
}
```

Fig. 6. Modularized nested if-statements.

2.4 Programming Styles Specific to MixJuice

Using difference-based modules, programmers can write programs in modular style, even if the programs cannot be written in modular style using traditional class-based modules.

The programmer can add a new traversing code for the tree structure without modifying the original source-code, because modules can add new methods to existing classes. In traditional object-oriented languages, it is possible to add a new traversing code using Visitor pattern[8]; however, the use of Visitor pattern disables the addition of the new kind of nodes to the tree structure unless the source-code is modified.

The programmer can split a nested if-statement as in Figure 5 into the modules shown in Figure 6, if each condition is disjoint. This programming style enables the programmers to add new conditional clauses without modifying the source-code. With this style, for example, recursive-descent parsers become modular and highly extensible[14]. Another application of this style is in programs processing XML that normally have nested if-statements.

The programmer can split initialization codes, such as initialization of tables, into modules. Moreover, when initializing tables, the programmer can add new entries to a table without needing to modify the source-code, because the initialization method acts as a hook for the extension modules. These initialization codes tend to be concentrated in a single method in traditional object-oriented languages.

2.5   Execution Environment

This section describes the characteristics of MixJuice with respect to compiling, linking and execution.

Separate Compilation of Modules. Each module can be separately compiled. Although each module contains fragments of classes, such fragments are type-checked by the compiler. When compiling a module, the compiler requires the ancestor modules of the modules. More accurately, the source-codes or the compiled binaries[3] of the ancestor modules should be accessible by the compiler.

Because units of separate compilation are independent of class, MixJuice is ideal for realistic application development, which sometimes uses collaborations as development and testing units. In MixJuice, each collaboration can be written and tested by an independent development team.

Linking and Execution of Modules. In order to execute a program, all the modules that make up the program must be linked together. Current implementation of MixJuice features the `mj` command which links and executes the modules.

To execute a program defined by a module, the module name should be specified as an argument of the `mj` command. The `mj` command links the specified module and produces a executable Java program[4]. The `mj` command then loads the Java program to the JavaVM and executes it. The `mj` command invokes a `main` method of the class `SS` by default.

The `mj` command automatically links all the ancestor modules of the specified module[5]. For example, if the module m2 is specified as an argument, the module m1 is automatically linked. Below is an example of execution of the modules m1, m2, m3 and m4.

```
% mj m1
11
% mj m2
33
% mj m3
44
% mj m4
110
```

---

[3] In the current implementation, the result of compilation of a module is represented by a set of class files of the Java language.

[4] The current implementation performs byte-code translation to compose fragments of classes.

[5] In the current implementation, the linker finds the required modules from the `CLASSPATH`.

Actually, the mj command automatically links modules of a type other than ancestor modules, *complementary modules*, which are described in Section 4.

Composition of Selected Modules. The end-users of an application can select specific modules and construct their own configured applications without having to write any lines of code.

For example, end-users can compose the module m2 and m3, which might be independently developed modules. To compose selected modules, the "-s" option of the mj command is used as follows.

```
% mj -s m2 m3
66
```

The mj command makes a virtual module named "_bottom" which extends all the selected modules specified as arguments. In the above case, the definition of the module "_bottom" would look like the following.

```
module _bottom extends m2, m3 {}
```

The mj command then executes the program defined by the module "_bottom". That is, the program expressed as

$$(((\phi \lhd \mathtt{m1}) \lhd \mathtt{m2}) \lhd \mathtt{m3})$$

is executed.

End users can select more than two modules by specifying the "-s" option more than once. (The current version of MixJuice does not permit the addition of a difference defined by a module more than once.)

In this way, end-users can compose existing modules that provide chosen functions in order to build their own customized applications. Traditionally, this type of customization is achieved by the mechanism of conditional compilation, such as "#ifdef", or patching onto the source-code. These mechanisms are processed at string level; difference-based modules, conversely, are more reliable because they are processed at the language level. In addition, difference-based modules have the advantage of not requiring the source-codes of extension modules to be available to the public.

3   Information Hiding Using Difference-Based Modules

In this section, we describe how the module mechanism of MixJuice is more powerful than that of Java with respect to information hiding.

3.1   Principle and Advantages

The module mechanism of MixJuice is based on the following design principle concerning information hiding.

> **The principle of name space inheritance:** All names that are de-
> fined at a module are visible from the module itself and its descendant
> modules, and are invisible from the other modules.

More specifically, "names" means the class, field and method names. The
module mechanism of MixJuice enables more flexible name space management
than that of Java by means of this simple rule concerning visibility.

Classes are no longer the units of information hiding in the source-code. All
fields in a class are accessible from the defining module and the descendant
modules of the module, even if the accessor class is different from the owner
of the fields. In MixJuice, there are no access modifiers (`public`, `protected` or
`private`), package mechanisms or nested class mechanisms[6].

Difference-based modules have the following advantages with respect to information hiding compared with Java.

- **Class-independency of units of information hiding**
  Programmers can make the boundaries of information hiding independent of
  class boundaries. For example, programmers can make collaboration units
  of information hiding. (Details are described in Section 3.6.) In addition, to
  improve the maintainability of the source-code, a programmer can minimize
  the size of the name space on which their source-code depends. This is especially effective if the number of functions of classes increases and the size
  of the classes thus becomes bigger and bigger.
- **Flexibility of name space structures**
  The name spaces can form nested structures and, giving a more general structure than nesting, overlapping structures. This characteristic makes Java's
  nested class mechanism unnecessary, with the result that the language specification is radically simplified. (Details are described in Section 3.4 and
  Section 3.5.)
- **Ease of code-moving**
  Programmers can easily move code between modules. This is due to a characteristic of difference-based modules: moving code between a super-module
  and a sub-module does not affect the semantics of the linked modules. As
  a result, the programmer can perform a kind of refactoring[7] with a high
  degree of flexibility and without changing the structure of the classes. For
  example, inter-dependent classes can be split into non-inter-dependent modules without changing the structure of the classes. (Details are described in
  Section 3.6.) Ease of code-moving enables smooth shifting from a monolithic
  prototyping source-code to a modular and extensible source-code.
- **Simplicity**
  Names are inherited only by one mechanism: module inheritance. On the
  other hand, the specification of Java concerning names is extremely complex. For example, four kinds of classes can be referred to by simple names:
  (1) Classes belonging to the same package. (2) Classes declared by `import`

---

[6] To be precise, MixJuice supports a kind of nested class, anonymous classes which
are often used for GUI programming in Java.

```
module point {
  define class Point {
    // abstract constructor:
    define abstract Point(int x, int y);
    // abstract methods:
    define abstract void move(int dx, int dy);
    define abstract int getX();
    define abstract int getY();
  }
}
module point.implementation extends point {
  class Point {
    define int x;
    define int y;
    Point(int x, int y){ this.x = x; this.y = y; }
    void move(int dx, int dy){ x += dx; y += dy; }
    int getX(){ return x; }
    int getY(){ return y; }
  }
}
```

Fig. 7. The specification module and the implementation module.

declarations. (3) Member classes of the outer classes. (4) Member classes of the ancestor classes. The relation between these four mechanisms is far from intuitive.

The rest of this section describes the details of information hiding using difference-based modules.

3.2 Black-Box Reuse

In MixJuice, the programmer can utilize existing classes in a manner called *black-box reuse*. We define black-box reuse as a style of utilization of existing classes only depending on the external interface of the classes.

A class can be defined as two separate modules. One module is called the *specification module*, which only defines the external interface of the class using *abstract constructors* and *abstract methods*; and the other is called the *implementation module*, which defines the internal implementation of the class. Abstract constructors, which do not appear in Java, are introduced to separate the interface and the implementation of constructors.

The program in Figure 7 is a definition of a class Point which consists of two modules: a specification module, point and an implementation module, point.implementation[7]. The module point defines the interfaces of the con-

---

[7] The character "." contained in the module name point.implementation is merely a punctuator. In MixJuice, the hierarchical structure of module names does not affect the semantics of the program.

```
module point.test extends point {
  define class Test {
    define void test(){
      Point p = new Point(1, 2);
      p.move(10, 10);
      ...
    }
  }
}
```

Fig. 8. An example of black-box reuse.

structor and the methods of the class `Point`. The module `point.implementation` implements the constructor and methods.

Other modules can utilize the class `Point` in the style of black-box reuse, by means of inheriting the specification module of the class `Point`. In Figure 8, the module `point.test` is an example of black-box reuse. The module `point.test` inherits the module `point`, and does not inherit `point.implementation`.

3.3   White-Box Reuse

In MixJuice, programmers can utilize existing classes in the manner of *white-box reuse*, in addition to black-box. We define white-box reuse as a style of utilization of existing classes depending not only on the external interface of the classes, but also on the internal implementation of the classes.

In Java, a class can serve for both black-box reuse and white-box reuse due to the `protected` access modifier. By defining the internal implementation of a class with the `protected` modifiers, a programmer can make internal implementation accessible by the subclasses of the class, but inaccessible by classes other than the subclasses.

In MixJuice, the programmer utilizes a class in the style of white-box reuse by inheriting the implementation module of the class. `protected` modifiers are no longer used in MixJuice. Figure 9 is an example of white-box reuse. The `ColorPoint` class is a subclass of the class `Point` defined in the program illustrated in Figure 7. The module `colorPoint.implementation` inherits not only the module `colorPoint`, but also the module `point.implementation`. The inheritance graph of these modules is illustrated in Figure 10. This inheritance structure enables the programmer to utilize the internal implementation of the class `Point` when implementing the class `ColorPoint`.

In MixJuice, the programmer can choose either black-box reuse or white-box reuse when implementing a class, independently of the inheritance relation of classes. For example, if the module `point.test` in Figure 8 inherits the module `point.implementation`, the style is white-box reuse; if the module `colorPoint.implementation` in Figure 9 does *not* inherit the module `point.implementation`, the style is black-box reuse.

With white-box reuse, the programmer can utilize the internal implementation of other classes; however, white-box reuse has the following disadvantages.

```
module colorPoint extends point {
  define class ColorPoint extends Point {
    define abstract ColorPoint(Color c, int x, int y);
  }
  define class Color {...}
}
module colorPoint.implementation extends colorPoint,
point.implementation{
  class ColorPoint {
    define Color c;
    ColorPoint(Color c, int x, int y){ super(x, y); this.c = c; }
    ...
  }
}
```

Fig. 9. The definition of the class `ColorPoint`.

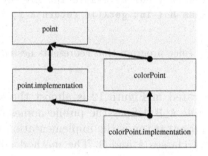

Fig. 10. The module diagram of the class `Point` and `ColorPoint`.

If the internal implementation on which a module written by a programmer depends is modified, the programmer must rewrite the module. In addition, if the programmer accesses the internal implementation of other classes, the programming needs to be done more carefully in order to preserve the class invariants of the classes.

Currently, MixJuice does not have a mechanism for preventing careless inheritance of implementation modules: such mistakes are prevented by the naming convention, in which the implementation modules are given long names such as `point.implementation`.

3.4 Nested Name Spaces

Nested name spaces, which are expressed by nested classes in Java, are expressed by module inheritance in MixJuice.

The Java program illustrated in Figure 11 is an example of nested name space expressed as nested classes. The field `x` of class `A` is not accessible from outside of class `A` because it is not a public field; it is, however, accessible from class B which is a member of class A.

```
public class A {
  protected static int x = 0;
  public static class B {
    public int getX(){ return x; }
  }
}
```

Fig. 11. A Java program with nested classes.

```
module A_B {
  define class A { }
  define class B {
    define abstract int getX();
  }
}
module A_B.implementation extends A_B {
  class A { define static int x = 0; }
  class B { int getX(){ return A.x; } }
}
```

Fig. 12. A MixJuice program that represents nested name spaces.

The program illustrated in Figure 12 is almost the same program written in MixJuice. The module A_B defines the public names of class A and class B. The module A_B.implementation is the implementation module, which defines the protected names of classes A and B. The method getX in class B directly accesses the static field of class A, using the expression "A.x". In this way, all names defined in a module can be accessed from the inside of the module (and the descendant modules of the module) even if the accessor class is a different class.

Similarly, n-levels of nesting of name spaces can be expressed using n-levels of module inheritance (Figure 13).

3.5   Overlapping Name Spaces

With multiple inheritance of modules, overlapping name spaces can be expressed, which have a more general structure than nested name spaces.

For example, the programs in Figure 2 and Figure 4 form overlapping name spaces as seen in Figure 14. That is to say, the lowest module, m4, is inside the name spaces defined by the modules m1, m2 and m3.

In the case of class-based modules, programmers are often forced to make names public to a greater extent than actually necessary because of the low degree of flexibility of name spaces. For example, some method names are often defined as public methods even though they are accessed by only members of a collaboration. A programmer can sometimes encapsulate such names using nested classes; however, the use of nested class mechanisms damages the maintainability of the classes because the scope of the field names defined by the classes expands.

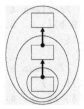

Fig. 13. The nested name spaces formed by inheritance of modules.

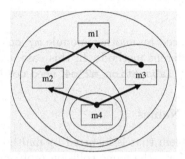

Fig. 14. The overlapping name spaces formed by multiple inheritance of modules.

In the case of difference-based modules, the programmers can minimize the size of scope of names. In addition, programmers can easily uncover the dependency relation between the modules because it is explicitly declared by the "extends" declaration.

3.6   Collaboration-Based Modularization

The programmers can define a collaboration that crosscuts more than one class as a separate module, since classes and modules are completely orthogonal in MixJuice.

Consider the program in Figure 15 written in Java. Two classes, classes A and B, depend on each other; however, these classes actually contain two independent collaborations.

The program can be modularized as in Figure 16. The program contains two unrelated modules, collaboration_m1_m3 and collaboration_m2_m4.

Modularization based on collaborations has the following advantages:

- The volume of the source-code on which each module depends decreases. In general, this leads to increased maintainability.
- Because collaboration_m1_m3 and collaboration_m2_m4 do not depend on each other, one of the two modules can be compiled and executed even if the other module does not exist. Therefore, these two modules can be developed and tested by different development teams.
- Other variations of application can be provided by means of implementing different versions of collaborations. For example, the module collaboration

```
class A {  // class A uses class B
  void m1(B b){ ... b.m3(); ...}
  void m2(){...}
}
class B {  // class B uses class A
  void m3(){...}
  void m4(A a){ ... a.m2(); ...}
}
```

Fig. 15. Inter-dependent classes containing two collaborations.

_m1_m3 can be replaced by another module `my_collaboration` which contains completely different methods. In this case, existing modules, such as modules `A_B` and `collaboration_m2_m4`, need not be re-compiled.

3.7   Fully-Qualified-Names

The name-collision problem that is incurred by multiple inheritance is fully resolved in MixJuice. In Java, the name-collision problem caused by `import` declarations is resolved by the idea of *fully-qualified-names* (FQNs) of classes. In MixJuice, this idea is applied to all names including field and method names in order to resolve the problem.

In difference-based modules, all names are processed based on the following design principle.

> **The principle of name-collision avoidance:** Each name has a unique FQN. Each FQN consists of "the module name which first defined the name" and "a simple name". If a simple name is used at one point in the source-code and more than one candidate which has the same simple name is accessible at that point, the compiler will report an error because the reference is ambiguous. Two names defined at different places are never regarded as identical by the compiler. A name definition never shadows another name. If an error is reported because of an ambiguous reference to a name, the programmer can always avoid this error by using the FQN of the name instead of the simple name.

We assume that the uniqueness of the module names is guaranteed by other mechanisms or rules, such as the naming convention adding as a prefix the domain name of the vendor, as in Java.

In MixJuice, an FQN which consists "the defining module name m" and "the simple name n" is expressed as "`FQN[m::n]`"[8].

---

[8] The syntax of FQN shown in this paper is ugly. The reason is the parsing problem caused by the character "`.`" used as both the punctuator of module names and the access operator for fields and methods in Java. In actual programming in MixJuice, FQNs are seldom used because the scope of names becomes smaller than that in traditional object-oriented languages.

```
module A_B {
  define class A {}
  define class B {}
}
module collaboration_m1_m3 extends A_B {
  class A { define void m1(B b){ ... b.m3(); ...} }
  class B { define void m3(){...} }
}
module collaboration_m2_m4 extends A_B {
  class A { define void m2(){...} }
  class B { define void m4(A a){ ... a.m2(); ...} }
}
```

Fig. 16. Modularized inter-dependent classes.

```
module m1 {
  define class A { define A(){} }
}
module m2 extends m1 {
  class A { define int m(){ return 1; } }
}
module m3 extends m1 {
  class A { define int m(){ return 2; } }
}
module m4 extends m2, m3 {
  class A {
    int FQN[m2::m](){ return original() + 3; }
    int FQN[m3::m](){ return original() + 4; }
  }
  class SS {
    void main(String[] args){
      A a = new A();
      //System.out.println(a.m()); // ambiguous
      System.out.println( a.FQN[m2::m]() ); // 4
      System.out.println( a.FQN[m3::m]() ); // 6
    }
  }
}
```

Fig. 17. An example of FQNs.

The FQNs of methods are used not only for method invocations, but also for method overriding. The program in Figure 17 is an example of overriding and invocations of the two methods m independently defined at the module m2 and m3.

Although a similar notation, "c::n" is used in C++[29] to resolve name-collision, its semantics is quite different from that of MixJuice. In C++, the expression "a.c::n()" is not a virtual function call. In MixJuice, the expression "a.FQN[m2::m]()" is a normal method invocation with late binding. In addition,

```
module m1 {
  // S and a subclass A.
  define abstract class S { }
  define class A extends S { }
}
module m2 extends m1 {
  // Add a new subclass of S.
  define class B extends S { }
}
module m3 extends m1 {
  // Add a new method of S.
  class S { define abstract int m(); }
  class A { int m(){ return 1; } }
}
```

Fig. 18. An example of an implementation defect between two modules.

in C++, it is impossible to override two virtual functions with the same name as in Figure 17 because separately defined virtual functions with the same name are regarded as identical by the C++ compiler.

4   Implementation Defects and Complementary Modules

4.1   Implementation Defects

When the end user composes two modules, an interesting phenomenon, which we call an *implementation defect*, may occur. Consider the program in Figure 18. The module m1 defines an abstract class S and its subclass A. The module m2 adds a new subclass B. On the other hand, the module m3 adds a new abstract method m to the class S and an implementation of the method m to the class A. Both m2 and m3 are the complete program which will not result in a link-time error; however, if the end user selects both modules simultaneously, the linker reports a link-time error because the method m in the class B is not implemented. As in this example, the phenomenon where the composition of two correct modules produces un-implemented abstract methods is called an implementation defect.

4.2   Complementary Modules

In general, it is impossible to complement an implementation defect automatically. Someone who understands the specification needs to implement abstract methods to make the program executable. Modules that complement an implementation defect between other modules are called *complementary modules*.

The program in Figure 19 is an example of a complementary module m23 which complements the implementation defect between m2 and m3. The complementary module is defined as a module that has a "**complements**" declaration that declares the modules that cause the implementation defect. The compiler

```
module m23 complements m2, m3 {
  class B { int m(){ return 2; } }
}
```

Fig. 19. The complementary module.

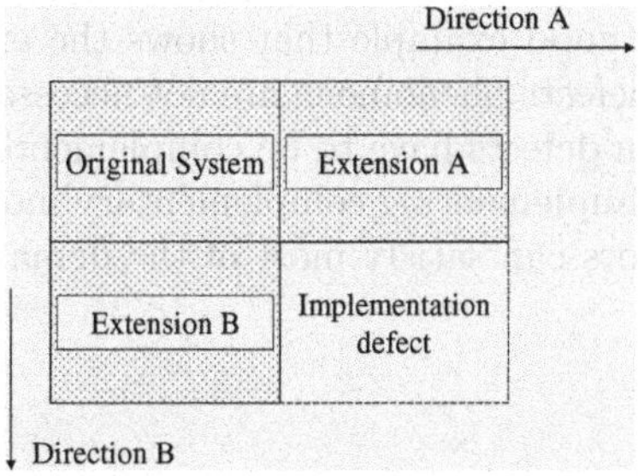

Fig. 20. Two directions of extension and their implementation defect.

processes the "`complements`" declaration in the same way as an "`extends`" declaration, except that the compiler adds information of module names to be complemented to the compiled binary.

The linker of MixJuice supports automatic linking of complementary modules in order to enhance the usability of end users who compose existing modules. Suppose that the complementary module as in Figure 19 is implemented by someone and the compiled binary is placed where the linker is able to access it. If an end user tries to compose m2 and m3 as follows, the linker automatically finds the complementary module m23 and links the complementary module together with m2 and m3.

```
% mj -s m2 m3
```

As shown above, if the complementary modules are properly installed, the end users do not have to be aware of the implementation defect problem when composing modules. By this mechanism, the end users can customize applications easily without requiring detailed knowledge of implementation of the modules.

4.3   Implementation Defect and Complementary Modules in Other Systems

The implementation defect problem occurs not only in MixJuice, but also in other highly extensible systems. To be precise, it occurs in extensible systems that have two or more directions of extension (Figure 20).

One example can be seen in the extensible interpreter using monad transformers [18], which are composable extension modules. Monads are abstract data types which become extensible by a technique called monad transformers in order to extend their data-structure and applicable operations. When composing two monad transformers, "lifting of operators" are sometimes required to make the monad complete. This is what we call a complementary module.

Another more familiar example can be seen in personal computers (PCs). The users of a PC can choose their OS and peripherals; however, the device drivers corresponding to the selected OS and the peripherals need to be obtained and installed in order to make them work. These device drivers are what we call complementary modules.

The latter case is a good example that shows the extensible systems which cause implementation defects phenomena are not necessarily impractical. Not all possible implementation defects have to be complemented by the vendors of the extension modules. By implementing complementary modules between relatively popular modules, vendors can satisfy most of the demand for customization by the end users.

5   Application

As an example of a typical object-oriented application, we now describe a drawing tool[9]. The source-code of the tool contains a class hierarchy: an abstract class `Figure` and subclasses of the `Figure` corresponding to each kind of figure such as circles and rectangles.

This program is extensible by adding extension modules. Extension modules can add new kinds of figures or new kinds of operations to the figures.

The module that adds a new kind of figure contains the following code: (1) A definition of a new subclass of the class `Figure`. (2) An extension of the method that displays the buttons to select the figure to draw. The programmer can add a new button without modifying the source-code because the method that displays buttons is a "hook" for extension.

The module that adds a new kind of operation to the figures contains the following code: (1) The definition of an abstract method of the class `Figure` and the implementation of the method of all the subclasses of the class `Figure`. (2) An extension of the method that displays the buttons to select the operation to perform.

Currently, the following 11 modules have been implemented.

`base` : Framework of the drawing tool
`select` : Selection of a figure
`delete` : Deletion of a selected figure
`move` : Moving of a selected figure
`dump` : Dumping of information of the displayed figures
`area` : Display of the total area of the displayed figures
`line` : Lines
`rect` : Rectangles
`elli` : Ellipses
`tri` : Triangles
`oct` : Octagons

---

[9] The source-code of this drawing tool and demonstration as Java applets are accessible from the following URL. http://staff.aist.go.jp/y-ichisugi/mj/demo.html

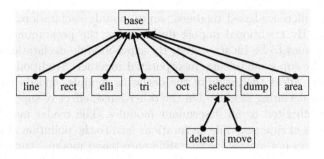

Fig. 21. The module diagram of the drawing tool.

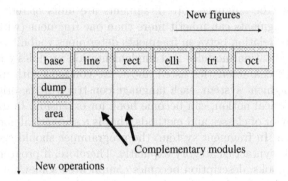

Fig. 22. Complementary modules for the drawing tool.

The module **base** contains the definitions of a class **Figure** and a class that displays a canvas, menus and buttons. The module **base** can itself be executed as an application; however, it displays no buttons for selecting the figure to draw or buttons to select the type of operation. All other modules are defined as sub-modules of this module (Figure 21).

The combination of modules which add a figure and an operation causes implementation defects that need to be complemented. We have implemented 10 complementary modules which complement defects between the modules which add figures (**line**, **rect**, **elli**, **tri** and **oct**) and the modules which add operations (**dump** and **area**), as illustrated in Figure 22.

Although the modules **select**, **delete** and **move** are modules that add operations to the figures, they do not require complementary modules, since these operations are implemented as non-abstract methods of the class **Figure**.

More than 2^9 varieties of applications can be realized because all modules except **base** and **select** can be arbitrarily selected.

6   Related Work

Some traditional languages including Modula-3[1] and Java have *import declarations*, which incorporate names defined at other modules into the current module. In difference-based modules, super-module declarations provide similar function. By traditional import declarations, the programmer can specify individual names to be incorporated. By super-module declarations, all names defined by the super-module are incorporated together. Traditional import declarations only affect the inside of the declaring module, and do not affect the clients of the declaring module. On the other hand, effect of super-module declarations is inherited to all descendant modules. The reader may think these characteristics of super-module declarations lead to the pollution of name space. Actually it does not matter because difference-based modules can minimize the scope of names, and the name collision can be avoided by fully-qualified-names.

Fragment system of BETA language[20] is a module mechanism that is independent from the language core. Fragments are units of reuse and separate compilation. Fragments can inherit more than one fragment (with restrictions). The inheritance relation between fragments determines visibility of names. Separation of specification modules and implementation modules enables information hiding. All characteristics listed above are common with difference-based modules. In fragment system, each language construct in the original program, that is a syntactical notion, can become hook for extension. In difference-based modules, behavior of classes and methods, that is a semantical notion, is the target of extension. In fragment system, the programmer should specify names of hooks and their syntactic category explicitly. Therefore, if programmer wants to provide many hooks, description becomes complicated somewhat. In difference-based modules, the increase of hooks does not make the program complicated because existing class and method names act as hooks.

Virtual classes[21] are mechanism of BETA, which enables extension of inner classes of nested classes by means of overriding by the subclass of the outer class. In order to make applications as extensible as MixJuice does, modules in MixJuice may be expressed as outer classes in BETA and classes in MixJuice may be expressed as inner classes in BETA. Virtual classes are covariant types, which require runtime-check because it is not type safe. On the other hand, MixJuice is type safe because the original class hierarchy and the extended class hierarchy do not exist simultaneously in an application. Virtual classes in gbeta language enable family polymorphism[6], which is polymorphism over a group of objects, which is not supported by MixJuice.

A programming technique of mixin layers[27] supports collaboration-based design. A mixin layer is a set of mixins that is related to a collaboration. The programming technique does not require a special language, because it only uses the standard C++ template mechanism. The programming style using mixin layers is quite similar to that in MixJuice; however, mixin layers support neither information hiding nor separate compilation. In addition, the ingenious programming using the template mechanism makes debugging difficult. In MixJuice programming, there are no essential difficulties with debugging.

AspectJ [16], Hyper/J [26], Demeter/Java [19], DJ [25], Adaptive Plug-and-Play Components(AP&PC)[22] and Pluggable Composite Adapters(PCA)[23] are Java based systems which supports separation of crosscutting concerns. All these systems inherit Java's original information hiding mechanism and extend it. In contrast, MixJuice removes it and successfully makes the language specification simpler.

AspectJ[16] treats two kind of crosscutting concerns. One is about dynamic concerns related to the call graph and the other is static concern supported by a mechanism called *introduction*. The former is orthogonal to the MixJuice features and the latter is basically the same as the differential programming mechanism of MixJuice.

Hyper/J[26] is a tool that extracts more than one concern from compiled Java programs and applies them to the other compiled programs. MixJuice solves the problem of "the tyranny of the dominant decomposition", that is pointed out by [26], in a different way. If there are n-dimension of orthogonal concerns, the programmer can divide the source-code into n orthogonal directions. For example, the drawing tool in Section 5 has two dimensions of concerns: data concern and operation concern. The source code of the drawing tool is divided into two orthogonal directions as illustrated in Figure 22.

Hyper/J supports non-invasive extraction of concerns from existing applications; however, MixJuice does not. We think enhancing refactoring[7] tools is more promising approach for extracting concerns from existing applications. MixJuice is a suitable language for this approach because it makes refactoring easier than languages with class-based modules.

Demeter/Java[19] and DJ[25] enables definition of traversing concerns which is independent from concrete tree structures. As described in Section 2.4, it is possible to separate traversing code in MixJuice too.

AP&PC[22] enables definition of collaborations that are independent from concrete class structures. PCA[23] is an enhancement of AP&PC, which supports dynamic application of collaborations. In contrast, current MixJuice does not support dynamic loading of modules.

In mixin layers, Hyper/J and AP&PC, it is possible to apply a collaboration to more than one class hierarchies. On the other hand, it is not possible in the current MixJuice because module definitions include concrete class names to be applied to. This restriction of reusability simplifies definition and composition of modules compared with above systems.

BCA[15] is a system using byte-code translation to enhance the reusability of existing class libraries. The programmers can modify the existing classes without source-code by describing the difference, called *delta files*. This implementation technique is similar to that of MixJuice. Separate type-checking of the delta files has not yet been implemented.

In some object-oriented languages such as CLOS[28] and Smalltalk[9], it is a common programming practice to add methods to existing classes; however, differential extension of existing methods, as in MixJuice, is not common practice. In addition, these languages do not support static type-checking.

Cecil[4], Dubious[24] and MultiJava[5] are object-oriented languages that support multi-methods. They have class-independent module mechanisms that support separate compilation. These languages support a feature called *open*

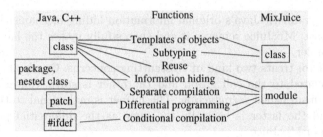

Fig. 23. The functions of classes and modules.

class that enables modules to add methods to existing classes[24]; however, they
do not support differential extension of existing methods.

7   Conclusion

We have described a module mechanism, which we call difference-based modules, and an object-oriented language MixJuice. MixJuice is an enhancement of
the Java language which adopts difference-based modules in preference to Java's
original module mechanism. We have completely separated the class mechanism and the module mechanism, and then unified the module mechanism and
the differential programming mechanism. This module mechanism enhances the
extensibility, reusability and maintainability of programs. In particular, collaborations, which crosscut several classes, can be separated into different modules
that can be developed and tested by independent development teams.

Figure 23 shows how the functions in object-oriented languages are supported
by class-based modules and difference-based modules. As shown in Figure 23,
the responsibility of classes and modules is clearly separated in difference-based
modules. In addition, difference-based modules support differential programming
and conditional-compilation features, which are not supported by the language-
core of the traditional languages.

We have already written more than 20,000 lines of code in MixJuice. We
have not found any major problems with difference-based modules. Their only
disadvantage might be readability problems when the code of a class is split
into several modules. This problem is the same as the readability problem in the
current object-oriented languages that is incurred by code splitting into superclasses and subclasses. Sometimes there is a tradeoff between readability and
reusability. These readability problems should be alleviated by documents using
UML or similar, as in current object-oriented languages. Actually, we found
that if the roles of classes and methods are made clear, the code becomes more
readable, because related codes are located in the same module.

Because the design principles of difference-based modules are very simple,
they can be applied to languages other than Java. In addition, because the
MixJuice language is still simple, there are numerous possibilities for language
extensions, such as introducing parameterized modules.

References

1. Modula–3 home page. http://research.compaq.com/SRC/modula-3/html/.
2. Hirotake Abe, Yuuji Ichisugi, and Kazuhiko Kato. An implementation scheme of mobile threads with a source code translation technique in Java. In *IPSJ:PRO*, volume 41, pages 29–40. IPSJ, March 2000. in Japanese.
3. Gilad Bracha and William Cook. Mixin-based inheritance. In *Proc. of the OOPSLA/ECOOP '90*, pages 303–311, October 1990. Published as ACM SIG-PLAN Notices, volume 25, number 10.
4. Craig Chambers and Gary T. Leavens. Typechecking and modules for multimethods. *ACM Transactions on Programming Languages and Systems*, 17(6):805–843, November 1995.
5. Curtis Clifton, Gary T. Leavens, Craig Chambers, and Todd Millstein. Multi-Java: modular open classes and symmetric multiple dispatch for Java. In *Proc. of the OOPSLA2000*, pages 130–145, October 2000. Published as ACM SIGPLAN Notices, volume 35, number 10.
6. Erik Ernst. Family polymorphism. In *Proc. of the ECOOP'2001*, LNCS 2072, 2001.
7. Martin Fowler, Kent Beck, John Brant, William Opdyke, and Don Roberts. *Refactoring: Improving the Design of Existing Code*. Addison-Wesley, 1999.
8. E. Gamma, R. Helm, R. Johnson, and J. Vlissides. *Design Patterns*. Addison-Welsley, 1995.
9. A. Goldberg and D. Robson. *Smalltalk–80: The language and its implementation*. Addison-Wesley, 1983.
10. James Gosling, Bill Joy, Guy L. Steele, and Gilad Bracha. *The Java language specification*. Java series. Addison-Wesley, second edition, 2000.
11. R. Helm, I. Holland, and D. Gangopadhyay. Contracts: Specifying behavioral compositions in object oriented systems. In *Proc. of the ECOOP/OOPSLA'90, Ottawa*, pages 169–180, October 1990. Published as ACM SIGPLAN Notices, volume 25, number 10.
12. Yuuji Ichisugi. EPP home page. http://staff.aist.go.jp/y-ichisugi/epp/.
13. Yuuji Ichisugi. MixJuice home page. http://staff.aist.go.jp/y-ichisugi/mj/.
14. Yuuji Ichisugi and Yves Roudier. The extensible Java preprocessor kit and a tiny data-parallel Java. In *ISCOPE'97, California*, LNCS 1343, pages 153–160, December 1997.
15. R. Keller and U. Höelzle. Binary component adaptation. In *Proc. of the ECOOP'98*, LNCS 1445, pages 307–329, 1998.
16. G. Kiczales, E. Hilsdale, J. Hugunin, M. Kersten, J. Palm, and W. Griswold. An overview of AspectJ. In *Proc. of the ECOOP2001*, 2001.
17. G. Kiczales, J. Lamping, A. Mendhekar, C. Maeda, C. V. Lopes, J.M. Loingtier, and J. Irwin. Aspect-oriented programming. In *Proc. of the ECOOP'97*, LNCS 1241, pages 220–242, 1997. Invited Talk.
18. Sheng Liang, Paul Hudak, and Mark Jones. Monad transformers and modular interpreters. In *Proc. of the POPL'95*, pages 333–343, January 1995.
19. Karl J. Lieberherr and Doug Orleans. Preventive program maintenance in Demeter/Java (research demonstration). In *International Conference on Software Engineering*, pages 604–605, 1997.
20. M. Löfgren, J. Lindskov Knudsen, B. Magnusson, and O. Lehrmann Madsen. *Object-Oriented Environments - The Mjølner Approach*. Prentice Hall, 1994.

21. Ole Lehrmann Madsen and Birger Møller-Pedersen. Virtual classes - a powerful mechanism in object-oriented programming. In *Proc. of the OOPSLA'89*, October 1989. Published as ACM SIGPLAN Notices, volume 24, number 10.

22. M. Mezini and K. Lieberherr. Adaptive plug-and-play components for evolutionary software development. In *Proc. of the OOPSLA'98*, pages 97–116, October 1998.

23. Mira Mezini, Linda Seiter, and Karl Lieberherr. Component integration with pluggable composite adapters. In Mehmet Aksit, editor, *Software Architectures and Component Technology: The State of the Art in Research and Practice*. Kluwer Academic Publishers, 2000. University of Twente, The Netherlands.

24. Todd Millstein and Craig Chambers. Modular statically typed multimethods. In *Proc. of the ECOOP'99*, LNCS 1628, pages 279–303, 1999.

25. Doug Orleans and Karl Lieberherr. DJ: Dynamic adaptive programming in Java. In *Reflection 2001: Meta-level Architectures and Separation of Crosscutting Concerns*, LNCS 2192, pages 73–80, Kyoto, Japan, September 2001.

26. H. Ossher and P. Tarr. Multi-dimensional separation of concerns and the hyperspace approach. In *Proc. of the Symposium on Software Architectures and Component Technology: The State of the Art in Software Development, Kluwer*, 2000.

27. Yannis Smaragdakis and Don Batory. Implementing layered designs with mixin layers. In *Proc. of the ECOOP'98*, LNCS 1445, pages 550–570, 1998.

28. G.L. Steele. *Common Lisp the Language, 2nd edition*. Digital Press, 1990.

29. Bjarne Stroustrup. *The C++ programming language*. Addison-Wesley, third edition, 1997.

30. C.A. Szyperski. Import is not inheritance – why we need both: Modules and classes. In *Proc. of the ECOOP'92*, LNCS 615, 1992.

31. Michael VanHilst and David Notkin. Using role components to implement collaboration-based designs. In *Proc. of the OOPSLA'96*, October 1996. Published as ACM SIGPLAN Notices, volume 31, number 10.

Dynamically Composable Collaborations
with Delegation Layers

Klaus Ostermann

Siemens AG, CT SE 2, D-81730 Munich, Germany
`Klaus.Ostermann@mchp.siemens.de`

Abstract. It has been recognized in several works that a slice of behavior affecting a set of collaborating classes is a better unit of reuse than a single class. Different techniques and language extensions have been suggested to express such slices in programming languages. We propose delegation layers, an approach that scales the OO mechanisms for single objects, such as delegation, late binding, and subtype polymorphism, to sets of collaborating objects. Technically, delegation layers combine and generalize delegation and virtual class concepts. Due to their runtime semantics, delegation layers are more flexible than previous compile time approaches like mixin layers.

1 Introduction

In the early days of object-oriented programming there has been a general agreement that the class should be the primary unit of organization and reuse. However, over the years it has been recognized that a slice of behavior affecting a set of collaborating classes is a better unit of organization than a single class. In the face of these insights, mainstream programming languages have been equipped with lightweight linguistic means to group sets of related classes, for example name spaces in C++ [11] or packages and nested classes in Java [1]. On the other hand, the research community has developed a great deal of models related to *collaboration-* or *role-model based design*, for example [4,15,29,34].

Our point of view is that we should not try to invent a completely new kind of module for grouping classes just to realize (sooner or later) that we need means to express variants, hide details, have polymorphism etc. Instead, we propose a model within which all the concepts that proved so useful for *single* classes/objects, for example inheritance, delegation, late binding, and subtype polymorphism, automatically apply to *sets* of collaborating classes and objects.

In particular, we deal with the question of how sets of collaborating classes can be defined and composed in terms of different variants (*layers*) of a base collaboration. The running example in this paper is a graph collaboration with classes like `Node` and `Edge` and variations of this collaboration for colored graphs and weighted graphs.

One of the most advanced approaches with respect to our goals is the *mixin layer* approach by Smaragdakis and Batory [31]. Mixin layers allow (a) sets of classes (which represent a particular collaboration and are implemented as nested classes of an outer class) to inherit from other sets of classes, and (b) the composition of different variants of a base collaboration. With regard to our running

B. Magnusson (Ed.): ECOOP 2002, LNCS 2374, pp. 89–110, 2002.
© Springer-Verlag Berlin Heidelberg 2002

example, this means we can (a) implement a `Graph` collaboration with `Node` and `Edge` classes and refine the `Graph` collaboration to `ColoredGraph` or `Weighted-Graph` via inheritance, and (b) combine `ColoredGraph` and `WeightedGraph` to a `ColoredWeightedGraph`.

Technically, the most important difference between our *delegation layer* approach and mixin layers is that the mixin layer notion of multi-class mixin-inheritance is replaced by multi-object delegation[1]. For those readers who have never heard of mixin-inheritance [5] or delegation [20] (we will elaborate on that in the paper), this can be tentatively summarized as: With mixin layers, everything happens on classes at compile time, whereas with delegation layers, everything happens on objects at runtime.

This has a deep impact on the semantics and expressiveness of the model. In particular, delegation layers have the following two properties:

- **Polymorphic runtime composition**: In our approach, a collaboration is composed at runtime by combining different delegation layers. Since delegation layers are subject to subtype polymorphism, the code which combines the layers is decoupled from the specific layers to be composed. For example, we may combine a `ColoredGraph` with a `Graph` g, but at runtime, g may actually refer to an instance of `WeightedGraph`.
- **Local on-the-fly extensibility**: We can extend a group of collaborating objects' behavior on-the-fly, whereby these behavior extensions are local, meaning that after the extension both the original and modified behavior of the object group are simultaneously accessible. For example, we may have an existing graph instance g with a set of node and edge objects and extend g with all its nodes and edges to be a colored graph cg. After the extension, the nodes and edges of the graph behave as a colored graph if they are accessed via cg and as a usual graph if they are accessed via g. We may even have multiple independent color extensions of a specific graph denoting different colorings of the same graph.

These properties are consequences of the runtime semantics of delegation layers. In addition, our approach eliminates two subtle flaws of the mixin layer approach related to polymorphism and consistency:

- **Polymorphism**: We define a notion of subtyping among collaborations which guarantees substitutability and allows us to use a compound collaboration where an instance of a particular layer is expected if and only if this layer is a part of the compound collaboration. For example, a graph that is both colored and weighted can be used where a colored graph is expected. Thus the advantages of standard OO subtyping (reusability, decoupling etc.) are transferred to collaboration inheritance. In general, this property does not apply for mixin layers.

---

[1] Please note that in contrast to the frequent use of the term delegation as a synonym for forwarding semantics, in this paper it stands for dynamic, object-based inheritance as defined in [20].

- **Composition consistency**: Our approach guarantees that all operations inside a compound collaboration are applied to the composite collaboration rather than to a specific layer alone. In particular, this proposition holds for constructor calls, thereby eliminating a composition anomaly of mixin layers.

Composing and extending collaborations at runtime yields type safety and consistency questions not emerging with compile time composition. In order to give answers to these questions, our model combines delegation techniques with virtual classes [21], family polymorphism [12], and a wrapper technique that is based on the idea of lifting and lowering as described in [25]. Although - to the best knowledge of the author - delegation has never been combined with virtual classes before, the interplay between these two mechanisms is elegant and natural.

The rest of this paper is structured as follows: Sect. 2 elucidates the concept of composable collaborations and gives a short overview of mixin layers. In addition, it emphasizes the weaknesses of mixin layers with respect to the aforementioned benefits we aim at. Sect. 3 and 4 introduce simple variants of delegation and virtual classes with family polymorphism as extensions of Java [1]. Sect. 5 shows how delegation and virtual classes interact and introduces the notion of delegation layers. Sect. 6 elaborates on on-the-fly extensions and the impact of delegation layers on sharing and aliasing. Sect. 7 discusses related work. Sect. 8 summarizes and indicates areas of future work.

2   Collaboration Composition and Mixin Layers

The rationale behind collaboration composition is that sets of collaborating classes can be defined and composed in terms of different variants (*layers*) of a base collaboration. Consider the situation in Fig. 1. It shows two collaborations `ColoredGraph` and `WeightedGraph` that inherit from a base collaboration `Graph`. The `Graph` collaboration defines classes `Node`, `Edge` and `UEdge`. The graphs in this example are assumed to be directed in general, and the class `UEdge` represents undirected edges which enter themselves in the adjacency list of *both* nodes. The subcollaborations `ColoredGraph` and `WeightedGraph` extend the base collaborations by defining classes that extend (i.e., are subclasses of) the base collaborations' classes. For example, the class `ColoredGraph.Edge` extends `Graph.Edge` by an additional association to `Color`. The class `WeightedGraph.Edge` adds a field `float weight` and `WeightedGraph.Node` overrides the inherited short-estPath() method in order to consider the edge weights.

The key issue is the ability to compose different variants of a base collaboration. For example, we may want to create a graph that is both colored and weighted by means of the collaborations in Fig. 1. Fig. 2 demonstrates the desired semantics of a combination `WeightedGraph(ColoredGraph(Graph))`: The collaborations are organized in layers according to the order in the composition expression; i.e. the outermost `WeightedGraph` collaboration is at the bottom, in the middle the `ColoredGraph`, and the `Graph` collaboration on top.

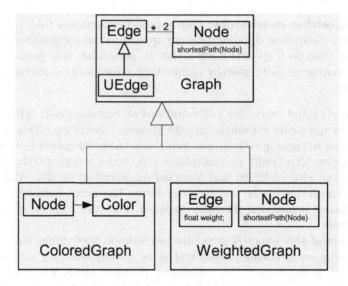

Fig. 1. Collaboration inheritance

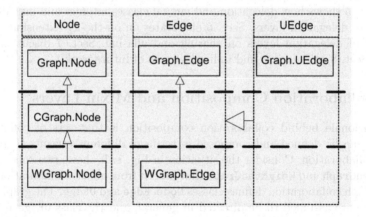

Fig. 2. Layer combination: `WeightedGraph(ColoredGraph(Graph))`:

All inner classes are organized according to the definition of the outer abstractions. For example, in the context of the compound collaboration in Fig. 2, `WeightedGraph.Edge` is a subclass of `ColoredGraph.Edge`, and the compound `UEdge` is a subclass of the *compound* `Edge` class rather than of `Graph.Edge`.

In other words, superclasses of the collaboration classes are replaced by subclasses of the annotated superclass. This kind of class combination is commonly known as *mixin-inheritance* [5]. Mixin-inheritance relaxes the strong coupling between a class and its superclass by enabling the instantiation of a class with different superclasses. This property renders mixin-inheritance suitable for defining and combining uniform incremental extensions of a class.

```
class Graph {
  public:
  class Node {
    public:
    NodeList shortestPath(Node *t) {...}
  };
  class Edge { ... };
  class UEdge: public Edge { ... };
};
template <class SuperGraph>
class ColoredGraph : public SuperGraph {
public:
  class Node: public SuperGraph::Node {
    Color color;
    ...
  }
};
template <class SuperGraph>
class WeightedGraph : public SuperGraph {
  class Edge: public SuperGraph::Edge {
    float weight;
    ...
  }
  class Node: public SuperGraph::Node {
    public:
    NodeList shortestPath(Node *t) {...}
  }
};
typedef ColoredGraph<WeightedGraph<Graph> > CWG;
typedef ColoredGraph<Graph> CG;
```

Fig. 3. Graph Example with C++ mixin layers

Mixin layers [31] scale this concept to multi-class granularity. In [31], the authors propose the usage of C++ [11] to implement mixin layers. Fig. 3 shows C++ mixin layers corresponding to Fig. 1 and 2. The basic technique is that the collaborating classes are implemented as nested classes of an outer class representing the collaboration. Subcollaborations are implemented as template classes with a parameterizable superclass. This superclass also determines the superclasses of the nested classes. Since C++ does not support F-bounded polymorphism [8], the template parameters are not explicitly bounded, but they should be thought of as being restricted to subclasses of Graph. The typedef statements at the bottom of Fig. 3 compose different collaboration variants. The type CG designates a colored graph, and CWG designates a colored weighted graph.

In the following, we want to elaborate on the two flaws of mixin layers mentioned in the introduction.

```
class Client {
  void createTransitiveHull(Graph *g, Graph::Node *n) {
  ... Graph::Node *m = currentNode->neighbor(i); ...
  if ( ! n->isNeighbor(m)) {
    Graph::Edge *e = new Graph::Edge(n,m); ...
  }
  }
};
```

Fig. 4. Restricted polymorphism in the mixin layer approach

- **Polymorphism**: Mixin layers have two flaws concerning polymorphism. First, subtyping among collaborations is too restrictive. Consider for example the two types CWG and CG in Fig. 3. Although a colored weighted graph of type CWG has all features of a colored graph type (CG), the former one is no subtype of the latter one[2]. Secondly, in the cases where subtyping is possible, the effect of substitution is not as expected. Consider the example in Fig. 4. If the method createTransitiveHull is called with an instance of a colored graph CG, the new statements will still create instances of Graph.Node and Graph.Edge rather than of their corresponding implementations for colored graphs. The problem is that the constructors in a new statement are statically bound to a specific implementation and we have no means to express that the new statements should instantiate the classes that are appropriate in the specific collaboration represented by g. Please note that the factory pattern [13] is in general no satisfactory solution because this pattern needs to anticipated and cannot be applied to superclasses (i.e., we cannot retrieve the superclass of a nested class via a factory object).
- **Composition consistency**: Inside a compound collaboration, all operations should be applied to the composite collaboration rather than to a specific layer. This is in general not true for constructor calls in mixin layers. Consider for example the compound UEdge class in Fig. 2. In a weighted graph, the weight property should of course also apply to UEdge. This means that in the context of a weighted graph, UEdge should inherit from the *compound* Edge rather than from Graph.Edge (see also Fig. 2). The same argument also applies to new statements inside a collaboration. If the class to be created is a participant of the collaboration, we expect a corresponding new statement to create an instance of the respective *compound* participant class. However, in the mixin layer approach the constructor calls refer to a fixed implementation in both cases. For example, the UEdge class in Fig. 3 is always a subclass of Graph.Edge and not of WeightedGraph.Edge, even in the context of the weighted graph collaboration.

The second problem has also been acknowledged in [31]. We think that it can be seen as a variant of the *self problem* [20], a.k.a. *broken delegation* [14]: In a

---

[2] However, this flaw can be attributed to the C++ template implementation and is no conceptual weakness of mixin layers

```
class Graph {
  private String info = "SomeInfo";
  public String setInfo(String s) { info = s; }
  String toString() { return "Graph, info="+info; }
  void printInfo() { print(this.toString()); }
}
class ColoredGraph extends Graph {
  String toString() { return "Colored"+super.toString();}
}
class WeightedGraph extends Graph {
  String toString() { return "Weighted"+super.toString();}
}
// demo code
Graph g = new WeightedGraph();
g.printInfo(); // prints "WeightedGraph, info=SomeInfo"
Graph cg = new ColoredGraph();
cg.printInfo(); // prints "ColoredGraph, info=SomeInfo"
Graph wg = new WeightedGraph<cg>();
wg.printInfo(); // prints "WeightedColoredGraph, info=SomeInfo"
cg.setInfo("OtherInfo");
wg.printInfo(); // prints "WeightedColoredGraph, info=OtherInfo"
ColoredGraph cg2 =
  (ColoredGraph) wg; // succeeding cast due to transparency
```

Fig. 5. Code example for delegation

composite component, all actions should be applied to the composite component, rather than to an individual part of it. The original formulation of the self problem refers to method calls; in our case, it refers to constructor calls.

3   Delegation

This section introduces the first building block of delegation layers, namely a simple variant of delegation as an extension of Java. Delegation means that objects inherit from other objects, with roughly the same semantics as classes which inherit from other classes. An object o that inherits from (*delegates to*) another object p is called *child* of p, and p is a *parent* of o.

To make the discussion simple, we restrict ourselves to *static delegation*, meaning that the parent of an object can be set at runtime, but once the parent reference is initialized, it cannot be changed, similar to a final variable in Java. This restriction avoids many problems which are not in the scope of this paper; see [19,27].

Consider the situation in Fig. 5. It shows classes Graph, ColoredGraph and WeightedGraph as well as some demonstration code that uses delegation. In our approach, we unify standard inheritance and delegation as follows: In a new WeightedGraph() expression for a class WeightedGraph as in Fig. 5, we may *optionally* specify a parent object (delimited by <>) that has to be a subtype of the

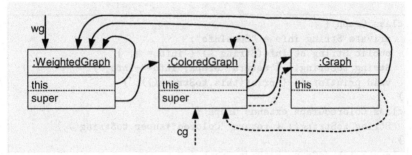

Fig. 6. Meaning of `this` and `super` in a delegation relationship as in Fig. 5. The non-dashed lines represent the behavior if the objects are accessed via `wg` and the dashed lines represent the behavior if the objects are accessed via `cg`.

original superclass `Graph`. For example, let `ColoredGraph` be another subclass of `Graph`. Then `new WeightedGraph()` creates an instance of `WeightedGraph` with superclass `Graph` (usual semantics), and `new WeightedGraph<cg>()` creates an instance of `WeightedGraph` with parent `cg` (see Fig. 5). In the latter case, the parent object replaces the superclass.

The unification of delegation and inheritance has two advantages. First, the usage of a class with a different superclass as initially intended does not have to be anticipated. Second, we have a *default* superclass/parent, so that it becomes easier to create instances of such a class. In the following, we will treat the direct instantiation of an object (without specifying a parent object) as an abbreviation for assigning an instance of the superclass as parent object. For example, `new ColoredGraph()` is an abbreviation for `new ColoredGraph<new Graph()>()`[3]. The parent object of an object `o` is always available via the implicit `super` field `o.super`.

The key issue in combining classes and objects via delegation is the treatment of the `this` and `super` pseudo variables. This is illustrated in the demonstration code in Fig. 5 and in Fig. 6: The `this` pseudo variable refers to the *receiver* of a method call, and `super` refers to the (possibly dynamically assigned) parent/superclass. The implications are illustrated by the `printInfo()` calls in Fig. 5. It is important to understand that the "value" of `this` is not fixed but depends on the receiver of a message. For example, in the context of a method call to `cg`, all `this` pointers refer to the instance of `ColoredGraph` rather than to the `WeightedGraph` instance.

Delegation is more than just composing classes at runtime. An important property of delegation is that parent objects may be *shared*. In Fig. 5, both the `cg` instance variable and the parent reference of `wg` refer to the same object. This is demonstrated by the `cg.setInfo()` call which affects `wg` due to the shared `ColoredGraph` object.

---

[3] For the sake of simplicity we assume that every class has only a single no-argument constructor.

```
class Graph {
  virtual class Node {
    void foo() { Edge e = new Edge(); }
    NodeList shortestPath(Node n) { ... }
  }
  virtual class Edge { ... }
  virtual class UEdge extends Edge { ...}
}

class ColoredGraph extends Graph {
  override class Node { Color color; ... }
}

class WeightedGraph extends Graph {
  override class Node {
    NodeList shortestPath(Node n) {...}
  }
  override class Edge { float weight; ... }
}
```

Fig. 7. Virtual classes

A property of delegation that has been postulated by Büchi and Weck [3] is *transparency*, meaning that an object is a subtype of the *dynamic* type of its parent. This property is relatively straightforward in the context of static delegation[4]. In our example (Fig. 5), transparency means that the dynamic cast in the last line succeeds. We will see that incorporation of transparency supports the elimination of polymorphism problem indicated in Sect. 2 ("better support for polymorphism").

For further details about the integration of delegation into a statically typed language, we refer to the existing approaches, e.g., [18,3,27].

4   Virtual Classes

Virtual classes are the second important building block for delegation layers. Virtual classes are a concept from the Beta programming language [21,22] (in Beta known as *virtual pattern*). The basic idea is that the notions of overriding and late binding should also apply to nested classes, similarly to overriding and late binding of methods.

Consider the class Graph in Fig. 7. The nested classes Node, Edge and UEdge are declared as *virtual classes* with a virtual modifier (corresponds to :< in Beta), meaning that these classes can be overridden by subclasses of the enclosing class. In contrast to methods in Java, nested classes are not virtual by default, because a virtual class has important typing implications.

---

[4] In models that support full dynamic delegation, transparency implies serious typing problems.

```
class Graph {
  virtual class Node {
    void foo() { Graph.this.Edge e = new Graph.this.Edge(); }
    NodeList shortestPath(Graph.this.Node n) { ... }
  }
  virtual class Edge { ... }
  virtual class UEdge extends this.Edge { ...}
}

class ColoredGraph extends Graph {
  override class Node extends super.Node { Color color; ... }
}

class WeightedGraph extends Graph {
  override class Node extends super.Node {
    NodeList shortestPath(WeightedGraph.this.Node n) {...}
  }
  override class Edge extends super.Node { float weight; ... }
}
```

Fig. 8. Virtual classes are properties of *objects* of the enclosing class.

The classes `ColoredGraph` and `WeightedGraph` in Fig. 7 override virtual classes of their superclass. The meaning of an `override` declaration (corresponds to `::<` in Beta) such as the `override class Node` declaration in `ColoredGraph` is that - in the context of `ColoredGraph` - the class `Graph.Node` is replaced by the class `ColoredGraph.Node`. The latter one is automatically a subclass of the former one, and hence has all methods and fields of `Graph.Node` plus an additional color field. Since an overriding virtual class is automatically a subclass of the overridden class, the single inheritance link is already allocated, such that an overriding class cannot extend another class.

As mentioned before, the rationale behind virtual classes is that overriding and late binding should uniformly apply to methods as well as virtual classes. Late binding of *methods* means that the receiver *object* determines the method implementation to be executed. If this principle is applied to virtual classes, it becomes clear that virtual classes should also be properties of *objects* of the enclosing class, rather than properties of the enclosing class itself. This is in the vein of the family polymorphism approach [12].

Virtual classes being properties of an object means that all references to a virtual class are resolved via an instance of the enclosing class. In our approach, we apply the Java scoping rules for method calls to virtual classes as well, meaning that all references to a virtual class are implicitly resolved via the corresponding `this`. Fig. 8 makes the implicit scoping of Fig. 7 explicit. For example, the type declaration `Edge e` in `foo()` is a shorthand for `Graph.this.Edge` (the notation `Graph.this` refers to the instance of the enclosing class). Similarly, `UEdge` in `Graph` is a subclass of `this.Edge` (rather than of `Graph.Edge`) and `Colored-Graph.Node` extends `super.Node` (rather than `Graph.Node`).

```
class Client {
  void createTransitiveHull(final Graph graph, graph.Node n) {
    ... graph.Node m = currentNode.neighbor(i); ...
    if ( ! n.isNeighbor(m)) {
      graph.Edge e = new graph.Edge(n,m); ...
    }
  }
}
```

Fig. 9. Family polymorphism version of Fig. 4

Consequently, `Graph.Node` is no longer a valid type annotation: The treatment of virtual classes as properties of objects stretches out to the client code of a class as well. For example, the family polymorphism version of Fig. 4 is shown in Fig. 9: Type annotations and constructor calls for virtual classes are all redirected via an instance of the enclosing class.

For type checking reasons, variables that are used inside type declarations have to be `final`. Otherwise, the type `g.Node` of a variable could change due to an update of g.

In contrast to Fig. 4, `createTransitiveHull` in Fig. 9 works with arbitrary subclasses of graph and without compromising type safety. Similarly, a statement like `node1.shortestPath(node2)` can be statically proved type-safe, if `node1` and `node2` are both of type `g.Node`, although at runtime g may refer to an instance of an arbitrary *subclass* of `Graph`. This demonstrates that the treatment of virtual classes as properties of objects is an alternative to other approaches for retaining type safety in the presence of virtual classes, such as final bindings [33] or type-exact variables [7].

For more details about virtual classes with family polymorphism, we refer to [12].

5   Delegation Layers

Delegation layers are the result of combining delegation with virtual classes. In the following, we want to elaborate on the interplay between these two mechanisms.

Reconsider the semantics of our virtual class mechanism as demonstrated in Fig. 7 and 8. All references to virtual classes are actually resolved via the implicit this and super pseudo variables of the enclosing object.

Our delegation mechanism implies that the "meaning" of this and super can be altered at runtime. Consider the second new expression in Fig. 10. It creates an instance of `WeightedGraph` and assigns an instance of `ColoredGraph` as parent of the weighted graph object. The meaning of this and super in the context of g has already been illustrated in Fig. 6.

The crucial point is that virtual classes and delegation, if combined, interact due to their influence/dependency on the semantics of this and super. The

```
main() {
  Graph cg = new ColoredGraph();
  Graph g = new WeightedGraph<cg>();
  g.Node n = ...;
  new Client().createTransitiveHull(g,n);
  ColoredGraph cg2 = (ColoredGraph) g; // succeeding dynamic cast
}
```

Fig. 10. Delegation layers

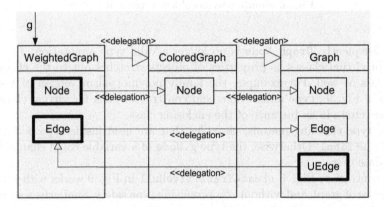

Fig. 11. Recursive delegation

semantics of this interaction, which is illustrated in Fig. 11, can be derived from Fig. 6 and 8. Consider, for example, the superclass declaration "extends super.Node" in WeightedGraph.Node (Fig. 8). In the context of g, super refers to an instance of ColoredGraph, therefore the parent of WeightedGraph.Node is an instance of ColoredGraph.Node. Similarly, the superclass declaration "extends this.Edge" in Graph.UEdge binds the parent of UEdge to an instance of WeightedGraph.Edge. The boxes with bold frame in Fig. 11 represent the composite classes g.Node, g.Edge, and g.UEdge.

Generally speaking, the combination of virtual classes and delegation effects the delegation relationship to spread to the nested virtual classes of the enclosing object. This is exactly the semantics that is required to obtain the composition behavior indicated in Fig. 2; cf. Fig. 2 and Fig. 11.

Let us revisit the delegation layer approach with respect to the goals stated in the introduction (except on-the-fly extensibility, which is the subject of the next section).

– **Polymorphic runtime composition**: Due to the use of delegation, the composition happens at runtime, and the composition code does not need to know the exact classes of the layers. Note, for example, that the static type of the parent reference cg in Fig. 10 is Graph, although it actually refers to an instance of ColoredGraph, which might have been passed as a method argument as well.

```
class Graph {
  Node n;
  Node getNode() { return n; }
  void setNode(Node n) { this.n = n; }
  ... // as in Fig. 7
}
// demo code
final Graph g = new Graph();
g.setNode(new g.Node());
g.Node node       = g.getNode(); // OK
final ColoredGraph cg = new ColoredGraph<g>();
cg.Node cnode     = cg.getNode();  // Type Error ?
cnode.color       = Color.RED;     // ??
```

Fig. 12. Potential problems due to hot state

- **Polymorphism**: In Sect. 2 we stated two different shortcomings related to polymorphism with mixin layers. The first one is the restricted subtyping. For example, a colored weighted graph CWG is no subtype of a colored graph CG in Fig. 3. Compare this with the last line in Fig. 10. Due to the introduction of transparency (see Sect. 3), an instance of a compound collaboration can be dynamically casted to the type of all participants. In general, if $C = C_1(C_2(...(C_n)...))$ is a composed collaboration, C is a subtype of C_i for $i = 1, ..., n$ in the delegation layer approach. With mixin layers, on the other hand, C is only a subtype of $C_i(C_{i+1}(...(C_n)...))$ for $i = 1, ..., n$.
  The second flaw is that the effect of subsumption is not as expected, exemplified by Fig. 4. This problem ceases to exist in our approach, because the class which is instantiated in response to a constructor call is determined at runtime, depending on the instance of the enclosing class (see Fig. 9).
- **Composition consistency**: We postulated that inside a compound collaboration, all operations should be applied to the composite collaboration rather than to a specific layer. With mixin layers, this property is violated, cf. the discussion in Sect. 2. With delegation layers, the class UEdge is a subclass of the *compound* Edge class (see Fig. 11), and the new Edge() statement in foo() creates an instance of the *compound* Edge (cf. Fig. 7 and 8).

6   Hot State and On-the-fly Extensions

So far, we have avoided to introduce state into the classes in our examples. At first sight, it seems as if this implies both a semantic and a typing problem. Consider the code in Fig. 12. The Node n instance variable is initialized to an instance of Graph.Node (and not ColoredGraph.Node). However, if this graph instance was extended by an instance of ColoredGraph, the same (identical) node would suddenly have to be a colored node.

The cause of this problem is that the type of the instance variable Node n is non-constant. Recall that Node n is an abbreviation for this.Node n (see

```
class Graph {
  // begin internal structure pseudocode
  Graph.Node liftNode(Graph.Node n) { return n; }
  Graph.Node lowerNode(Graph.Node n) { return n; }
  Graph.Edge liftEdge(Graph.Edge e) { return e; }
  Graph.Edge lowerEdge(Graph.Edge e) { return e; }
  // end internal structure pseudocode
}
class ColoredGraph extends Graph {
  // begin internal structure pseudocode
  private Map nodeMap = new HashMap();

  ColoredGraph.Node liftNode(Graph.Node n) {
    ColoredGraph.Node result = (ColoredGraph.Node) nodeMap.get(n);
    if (result == null) {
      result = new ColoredGraph.Node<super.liftNode(n)>();
      nodeMap.put(n,result);
    }
    return result;
  }
  Graph.Node lowerNode(ColoredGraph.Node n) {
    Graph.Node result = super.lowerNode(n.super);
    nodeMap.put(result, n);
    return result;
  }
  // end internal structure pseudocode
}
```

Fig. 13. Lifting details

Sect. 4). Hence this refers to an instance of Graph if n is accessed via g, and refers to an instance of ColoredGraph if n is accessed via cg. We call such state whose type depends on the enclosing this *hot state*.

We found a mechanism that turns this problem into a feature. It is based on the idea of *lifting* and *lowering* as described in [25] but adapted to the specific needs of our model. The basic idea is that, in the context of a colored graph, a node n can be automatically lifted to a colored node by creating an instance of ColoredGraph.Node that delegates to n. In order to make this approach sound, it is essential that two subsequent liftings for the same node yield the same colored node.

Fig. 13 shows pseudo code indiciating the operational semantics of the lifting and lowering operation. Please note that the programmer does not write this code: The code is just an illustration of the language semantics in terms of OO constructs.

Every class C maintains a map (hashtable) for every virtual class which is overridden in that class. For example, ColoredGraph has a map nodeMap, and WeightedGraph has the maps nodeMap and edgeMap. In addition, a class C has a lifting and a lowering operation liftV(V v) resp. lowerV(V v) for each virtual class V that is (a) defined or (b) overridden in C. In case (a), the lifting and lowering operations simply return their argument. In case (b), the lifting operation lifts an instance of the base virtual class (e.g., Graph.Node) to an instance of the overriding virtual class (ColoredGraph.Node), and the lowering operation lowers an instance of the overriding virtual class (e.g., ColoredGraph.Node) to an instance of the base virtual class (Graph.Node).

The semantics of the lifting and lowering operations is indicated in Fig. 13: The lifting and lowering operations in Graph simply return their argument. The more interesting case are the lifting and lowering operations in ColoredGraph, which override their corresponding implementations in Graph.

In liftNode(), a lookup in the map determines whether the same node has ever been lifted before. In this case, the corresponding instance of Colored-Graph.Node is directly returned. Otherwise, an instance of ColoredGraph that delegates to the node instance is created, stored in the map, and returned. The lookup in the map ensures that subsequent liftings for the same node yield the same ColoredNode wrapper.

The lowerNode() operation is the counterpart of liftNode(). It stores the ColoredGraph part of the node in the map and recursively asks its parent super to lower the parent of the node (n.super).

In the liftNode() operation, the parent object of the wrapper object is super.liftNode(n) rather than n, and in lowerNode(), the method returns super.lowerNode(n.super) rather than n.super. This ensures the mechanism will work when a class C overrides a virtual class that has already been overridden in the superclass of C. The anchor of the recursions are the liftNode() and lowerNode operations in the class that introduces the virtual class (in this case Graph, which simply return their argument, see Fig. 13).

What are the appropriate places to apply lifting and lowering operations? We think that the only reasonable solution is to apply it whenever hot state is evaluated; that is, the r-value of a hot instance variable in an expression node is actually liftNode(node), and the l-value of a hot variable in an assignment node = anExpression is actually node = lowerNode(anExpression). In our example, this means that the implementation of getNode() returns this.liftNode(n) rather than n, and the implementation of setNode() assigns the result of lowerNode(n) to this.n.

The calls to liftNode() and lowerNode are subject to late binding, because the respective implementations of ColoredGraph overrides the implementations in Graph. For example, the call g.getNode() in Fig. 12 yields a call to Graph.liftNode(), while the call cg.getNode() yields a call to Colored-Graph.liftNode().

An important invariant of lifting and lowering is that the function combination lowerV(liftV(v)) is the identity function, such that a statement like node = node, which translates to node = lowerNode(liftNode(node)), has the expected meaning.

This approach preserves static type safety because the lifting operation ensures that the evaluation of a hot instance variable yields an instance of the

```
class Graph {
  Node[] nodes;
  void setNode(Node n, int i) {
    nodes[i] = n; // efectively assigns this.lowerNode(n)
  }
  Node getNode(int i) {
    return nodes[i]; // effectively returns this.liftNode(nodes[i])
  }

  virtual class Node {
    Edge[] edges;
    Edge getEdge(int i) {
      return edges[i]; // effectively returns this.liftEdge(edges[i])
    }
  }
  virtual class Edge {
    Node n1, n2;
    Node getTargetNode() {
      return n2; // effectively returns this.liftNode(n2)
    }
  }
}
class ColoredGraph extends Graph ... // as in Fig. 7
```

Fig. 14. A graph with hot state

type which is appropriate for the respective context by dynamically creating and maintaining wrappers that delegate to the base objects. The hash table guarantees that we do not loose the state and identity of the individual parts of a delegation chain. Finally, the lowering operation guarantees consistency in the sense that all objects will only interact with other objects from the same family. For example, if we would execute the statement g.setNode(new cg.Node()) with g and cg as in Fig. 12, and we would *not* apply lowering, we would suddenly have a colored node in a context g that does not assume color properties. A subsequent call like g.getNode().setNeighbor(new g.Node()) would expose the inconsistency because the original colored node would assume that its neighbor nodes would also be colored nodes.

However, this approach is much more than a fix to preserve type safety. Let us look at a more interesting example. Consider the code in Fig. 14. It shows a graph class which stores a graph as a list of nodes. A node has a list of incident edges and an edge stores its source and target node. The comments in the code indicate the places where the lifting and lowering actually takes place.

Let us suppose we want to determine the chromatic number[5] and/or a corresponding coloring for a specific graph. Let us further suppose we have an appropriate algorithm in a class GraphColoring as indicated in Fig. 15. Of course,

---

[5] The minimum number of colors needed to color the vertices of a graph such that no two adjacent vertices have the same color.

```
class GraphColoring {
  int chromaticNumber(final ColoredGraph g) {
    ...
    g.Node node = g.getNode(i);
    node.color = Color.RED;  // statically safe
    ...
  }
  void randomColoring(final ColoredGraph g) {
    ...
  }
}
// demo code
Graph g = ...;
GraphColoring coloring = new GraphColoring();
ColoredGraph cg1 = new ColoredGraph<g>();
int i = coloring.chromaticNumber(cg1);
...
ColoredGraph cg2 = new ColoredGraph<g>();
coloring.randomColoring(cg2);
```

Fig. 15. Independent on-the-fly extensions of a graph

the algorithm is directly applicable to any graph which has been instantiated as `ColoredGraph`. However, let us suppose that this is not the case for our sample graph because, say, we just want to know the chromatic number and are not interested in the coloring itself and do not want to waste the corresponding memory. Another reason might be that we want a graph that has different independent colorings with different meanings.

The demo code in Fig. 15 shows how an arbitrary graph can be extended on-the-fly with the mechanisms of our approach. The color extension is only visible via `cg1` and `cg2`, respectively. The state and behavior of the graph remains unchanged if it is accessed via `g`. Please note how easy it is to create two completely independent colorings (chromatic and random coloring) for a specific graph instance. Due to subtype polymorphism, these extensions are also decoupled from the specific graph instance in the sense that `g` may also refer to an instance of `WeightedGraph` or even `ColoredGraph`. In the latter case, the extension would yield a coloring which is independent from the original coloring of `g`.

The last example in this section does not introduce new features but emphasizes two important properties of our approach: The ability to extend a collaboration which has already been extended (orthogonality), and transparent simultaneous behavior extensions for all objects of a collaboration instance.

Suppose we want to observe the progress of the coloring algorithm on the screen in case the respective graph is currently displayed. In other words, we want to be notified whenever the `setColor()` method is invoked for a node of that graph.

Consider the code in Fig. 16. It introduces an appropriate interface `ColorObserver` that is implemented by `GraphDisplay`. The class `NotifyingGraph`

```
interface ColorObserver {
  void colorChanged(final ColoredGraph cg, cg.Node node, Color color);
}
class GraphDisplay implements ColorObserver { ... }
class NotifyingGraph extends ColoredGraph {
  ColorObserver o;
  public NotifyingGraph(ColorObserver o) { this.o = o; }

  override class Node {
    void setColor(Color color) {
      super.setColor(color);
      o.colorChanged(NotifyingGraph.this, this, color);
    }
  }
}
// demo code
Graph g = ...; GraphDisplay display = ...;
GraphColoring coloring = new GraphColoring();
ColoredGraph cg1 = new ColoredGraph<g>();
if (screenDisplay) cg1 = new NotifyingGraph<cg1>(display);
int i = coloring.chromaticNumber(cg1);
```

Fig. 16. Adding notifier functionality

extends the behavior of all color nodes such that the `ColorObserver` is notified whenever the color of that node is changed. The demonstration code creates a `Graph g` and extends `g` to be a colored graph in the context of `cg1`. The colored graph `cg1` is again extended with the notifier behavior if the variable `screenDisplay` evaluates to `true`.

Please note that the graph `cg1` that is potentially extended with the `NotifyingGraph` functionality is already an extended version of the original graph instance `g`.

The type of `cg1` is `ColoredGraph` and not `NotifyingGraph`. Nevertheless, the extensions defined by `NotifyingGraph` spread through all further actions via `cg1`. In particular, all `setColor()` invocations in the coloring algorithm are dispatched to the `setColor()` redefinition in `NotifyingGraph`, although the author of the coloring algorithm does not know anything about the existence of `NotiyingGraph`.

The powerful expressiveness of on-the-fly extensions is due to the fact that delegation layers allow simultaneous behavior extensions for *sets* of objects. To the best knowledge of the author, delegation layers are the first approach that enables such kind of operations.

7 Related Work

The relation to mixin layers [31], virtual classes [21], family polymorphism [12], and delegation [20,18,3,27] has already been discussed in Sect. 1-4.

Java Layers [6,9] are a Java-based implementation of mixin layers. Java Layers extend Java by supporting constrained parametric polymorphism and mixins. The authors acknowledge the composition consistency problem and propose different solutions (called *sibling pattern*), including a limited variant of virtual types and a naming convention approach, to cope with this problem. An interesting approach in Java Layers, which might also be useful for delegation layers, is their notion of *deep conformance*, which extends Java's concept of interfaces to include nested interfaces.

Jiazzi [23] is a system that does also allow classes to be composed in a mixin layer style at compile time. Jiazzi is especially related to our work because it addresses both the composition consistency and the polymorphism problem (see Sect. 2). Their proposal for the composition consistency problem is based on the *open class pattern*, a kind of design pattern that mimicks the constructor semantics of virtual types. An application that uses a particular layer (*package* in the terminology of [23]) can be parameterized with different variants of this layer, thereby eliminating the polymorphism flaw of the original mixin layer idea. This is similar to the idea of parameterizing a method with a family object, as shown in Fig. 9. However, in contrast to delegation layers, composition and polymorphism in Jiazzi are pure compile-time / link-time concepts, there is no notion of subtyping polymorphism and subsumption among different variants of a layer.

In comparison with delegation layers, a practical advantage of all aforementioned compile-time approaches [31,6,9,23] is that it is very much easier to create an efficient implementation with little or no runtime overhead.

In general, *virtual classes* are an interesting alternative or complement to parametric polymorphism. Please note that this is not the main focus of our approach, in contrast to the approaches in [32] and [7]. Therefore we do not introduce additional language means to express virtual classes defined outside the enclosing class, e.g., virtual classes like `StackItem` that are later overridden with `String` or `Point` in order to create a stack of strings or a stack of points.

Pluggable composite adapters (PCA) [25] are a language construct for on-the-fly adaptation of frameworks. A set of base objects can be dynamically extended with the functionality provided by a particular framework. The relations between base objects and framework objects are maintained by a lifting technique that is similar to the one proposed in this paper. However, in PCA, objects are lifted to types that are in general unrelated to their original type, whereas with delegation layers, objects are lifted to subtypes that delegate to the original object. In contrast to delegation layers, it is not possible to *change* the behavior of the lifted objects.

Delegation layers can also be seen as a form of *aspect-oriented programming* [17]. A delegation layer defines functionality that affects the behavior of a set of different classes and can thus be seen as a module for crosscutting concerns. In comparison with AOP languages like AspectJ [2], delegation layers have a very limited joinpoint model. On the other hand, delegation layers are much more dynamic than other AOP languages. For example, in AspectJ it would also be possible to extend the `Graph` class with color functionality. However, in this case *all* graphs would automatically be colored graphs; it would not be possible offhand to access a graph simultaneously both as a graph and a colored graph, or create independent colorings as in Fig. 15. The same argument applies to the notification extension in Fig. 16. In AspectJ, the notification would automatically apply to *all* graphs and it would require additional measures (e.g., conditional statements in the form of `if (notifyEnabled)` ...) to be able to choose at runtime which graphs feature the notification behavior.

A number of approaches focus on the evolution of single objects or single classes. The basic idea of the *context relationship* [30] is that if a class C is context-related to a base class B, then B-objects can get their functionality dynamically altered by C-objects. A C-object may be explicitly attached to a B-object, or it may be implicitly attached to a group of `B-objects` for the duration of a method invocation. In *Rondo* [26], the behavior of single objects can be altered at runtime by means of so-called *adjustments*. With *predicate classes* [10], an object is automatically an instance of a predicate class whenever it satisfies a predicate expression associated with the predicate class. If an object is modified, the classification of an object can change, yielding in a different behavior of the object.

There have been a number of proposals related to *collaboration-* or *role-based design* [28,4,15,29,16,24]. In contrast to these approaches, delegation layers focus on the definition and on-the-fly runtime combination of collaboration *variants*.

8   Summary and Future Work

In this paper, we proposed delegation layers, a new mechanism to define and combine sets of collaborating classes and objects. Since the modules to group such sets are classes and objects themselves, the concepts that proved so useful for single classes and objects - inheritance, delegation, late binding, instantiation, subtype polymorphism etc. - apply to sets of collaborating classes and objects as well.

Due to their strong runtime semantics, delegation layers are extremely flexible. In particular, the ability for local on-the-fly extensions, with which we can change the behavior of a *set* of objects (instead of a single object with classical delegation) seems to be very promising. We think that this is especially interesting with respect to the idea of aspect-oriented programming [17]. Current AOP approaches are frequently working on the basis of sophisticated source- or byte-code transformations and have little or no runtime semantics. We hope that delegation layers are a first step towards aspects with rich runtime semantics. We are currently working towards this goal.

Acknowledgements

We thank the anonymous reviewers for numerous helpful comments and Erik Ernst for insightful discussions which revealed serious shortcomings of previous drafts.

References

1. K. Arnold and J. Gosling. *The Java Programming Language*. Addison-Wesley, 1996.
2. AspectJ homepage, 2001. http://aspectj.org.
3. M. BCchi and W. Weck. Generic wrappers. In *Proceedings of ECOOP 2000, LNCS 1850*, pages 201–225. Springer, 2000.
4. K. Beck and W. Cunningham. A laboratory for teaching object-oriented thinking. In *Proc. OOPSLA '89*, 1989.
5. G. Bracha and W. Cook. Mixin-based inheritance. In *Proceedings OOP-SLA/ECOOP'90, ACM SIGPLAN Notices 25(10)*, pages 303–311, 1990.
6. A. Brown, R. Cardone, S. McDirmid, and C. Lin. Using mixins to build flexible widgets. In *1st International Conference on Aspect-Oriented Software Development AOSD '02*, 2002.
7. K. B. Bruce, M. Odersky, and P. Wadler. A statically safe alternative to virtual types. In *Proceedings ECOOP '98*, 1998.
8. P. S. Canning, W. Cook, W. L. Hill, J. C. Mitchell, and W. G. Olthoff. F-bounded polymorphism for object-oriented programming. In *Proceedings of the ACM Conference on Functional Programming and Computer Architecture*, pages 273–280, 1989.
9. R. Cardone and C. Lin. Comparing frameworks and layered refinement. In *Proceedings of the 23rd International Conference on Software Engineering ICSE '01*, 2001.
10. C. Chambers. Predicate classes. In W.Olthoff, editor, *Proceedings ECCOP '93*, LNCS 707, pages 268–297. Springer, 1993.
11. M. Ellis and B. Stroustrup. *The Annotated C++ Reference Manual*. Addison-Wesley, 1995.
12. E. Ernst. Family polymorphism. In *Proceedings of ECOOP '01*, LNCS 2072, pages 303–326. Springer, 2001.
13. E. Gamma, R. Helm, R. Johnson, and J. Vlissides. *Design Patterns*. Addison Wesley, 1995.
14. W. Harrison, H. Ossher, and P. Tarr. Using delegation for software and subject composition. Technical Report RC 20946(92722), IBM Research Division T.J. Watson Research Center, Aug 1997.
15. R. Helm, I. M. Holland, and D. Gangopadhyay. Contracts: Specifying behavioural compositions in object-oriented systems. In *Proceedings OOPSLA/ECOOP'90, ACM SIGPLAN Notices*, pages 169–180, 1990.
16. I. M. Holland. Specifying reusable components using contracts. In *Proceedings ECOOP '93, LNCS 615*, pages 287–308, 1992.
17. G. Kiczales, J. Lamping, A. Mendhekar, C. Maeda, C. Lopes, J.-M. Loingtier, and J. Irwin. Aspect-oriented programming. In M. Aksit and S. Matsuoka, editors, *Proceedings ECOOP'97*, LNCS 1241, pages 220–242, Jyvaskyla, Finland, 1997. Springer-Verlag.
18. G. Kniesel. Type-safe delegation for run-time component adaptation. In R. Guerraoui, editor, *Proceedings of ECOOP '99*, LNCS 1628. Springer, 1999.
19. G. Kniesel. *Dynamic Object-Based Inheritance with Subtyping*. PhD thesis, University of Bonn, Institute for Computer Science III, 2000.
20. H. Liebermann. Using prototypical objects to implement shared behavior in object-oriented systems. In *Proceedings OOPSLA '86, ACM SIGPLAN Notices*, 1986.

21. O. L. Madsen and B. Müller-Pedersen. Virtual classes: A powerful mechanism in object-oriented programming. In *Proceedings of OOPSLA '89*. ACM SIGPLAN, 1989.
22. O. L. Madsen, B. Møller-Pedersen, and K. Nygaard. *Object Oriented Programming in the Beta Programming Language*. Addison-Wesley Publishing Company, 1993.
23. S. McDirmid, M. Flatt, and W. Hsieh. Jiazzi: New age components for old fashioned java. In *Proceedings of OOPSLA '01*, 2001.
24. M. Mezini and K. Lieberherr. Adaptive plug-and-play components for evolutionary software development. In *Proceedings OOPSLA '98, ACM SIGPLAN Notices*, 1998.
25. M. Mezini, L. Seiter, and K. Lieberherr. Component integration with pluggable composite adapters. In M. Aksit, editor, *Software Architectures and Component Technology: The State of the Art in Research and Practice*. Kluwer, 2001. University of Twente, The Netherlands.
26. M. Mezini. Dynamic object evolution without name collisions. In *Proceedings ECOOP '97, LNCS 1241*, pages 190–219. Springer, 1997.
27. K. Ostermann and M. Mezini. Object-oriented composition untangled. In *Proceedings OOPSLA '01*, 2001.
28. T. Reenskaug. *Working with Objects: The OOram software Engineering Method*. Manning, 1995.
29. D. Riehle and T. Gross. Role model based framework design and integration. In *Proceedings OOPSLA '98*, 1998.
30. L. M. Seiter, J. Palsberg, and K. Lieberherr. Evolution of object behavior using context relations. *IEEE Transactions on Software Engineering*, 24:79–92, 1998.
31. Y. Smaragdakis and D. Batory. Implementing layered designs with mixin-layers. In *Proceedings of ECOOP '98*, pages 550–570, 1998.
32. K. K. Thorup. Genericity in Java with virtual types. In *Proceedings ECOOP '97*, 1997.
33. M. Torgersen. Virtual types are statically safe. In *5th Workshop on Foundations of Object-Oriented Languages*, 1998.
34. M. VanHilst and D. Notkin. Using role components to implement collaboration-based design. In *Proceedings OOPSLA 96*, 1996.

Space- and Time-Efficient Implementation of the Java Object Model

David F. Bacon, Stephen J. Fink, and David Grove

IBM T.J. Watson Research Center
P.O. Box 704, Yorktown Heights, NY 10598, USA
dfb@watson.ibm.com, {sjfink,groved}@us.ibm.com

Abstract. While many object-oriented languages impose space overhead of only one word per object to support features like virtual method dispatch, Java's richer functionality has led to implementations that require two or three header words per object. This space overhead increases memory usage and attendant garbage collection costs, reduces cache locality, and constrains programmers who might naturally solve a problem by using large numbers of small objects.

In this paper, we show that with careful engineering, a high-performance virtual machine can instantiate most Java objects with only a single-word object header. The single header word provides fast access to the virtual method table, allowing for quick method invocation. The implementation represents other per-object data (lock state, hash code, and garbage collection flags) using heuristic compression techniques. The heuristic retains two-word headers, containing thin lock state, only for objects that have synchronized methods.

We describe the implementation of various object models in the IBM Jikes Research Virtual Machine, by introducing a pluggable object model abstraction into the virtual machine implementation. We compare an object model with a two-word header with three different object models with single-word headers. Experimental results show that the object header compression techniques give a mean space savings of 7%, with savings of up to 21%. Compared to the two-word headers, the compressed space-encodings result in application speedups ranging from -1.5% to $+2.2\%$. Performance on synthetic micro-benchmarks ranges from $+23\%$ due to benefits from reduced object size, to -12% on a stress test of virtual method invocation.

1 Introduction

The choice of *object model* plays a central role in the design of any object-oriented language implementation. The object model dictates how to represent objects in storage. The best object model will maximize efficiency of frequent language operations while minimizing storage overhead.

A fundamental property of object-oriented languages is that the operations performed on an object depend upon the object's *run-time* type, rather than its compile-time type. Therefore, in any object model, each object must at a

B. Magnusson (Ed.): ECOOP 2002, LNCS 2374, pp. 111–132, 2002.
© Springer-Verlag Berlin Heidelberg 2002

minimum contain some sort of run-time type identifier, typically a pointer to a virtual method table.

Some modern object-oriented languages, like Java[1], require additional per-object state to support richer functionality including garbage collection, hashing, and synchronization. Conventional wisdom holds that since an object's virtual method table is accessed so frequently, any attempt to encode extra information into that header word would seriously degrade performance. Therefore, existing Java systems all require at least two words (and in some cases three words) of header space for each object.

This paper makes the following contributions regarding object models for Java and similar object-oriented languages:

- we describe a variety of composable header compression techniques;
- we show how these techniques can be composed into a variety of object models requiring only one word of space overhead per object;
- we show how the object models can all be implemented in one plug-compatible framework; and
- we show that the compressed object headers can improve mean run-time performance up to 2.3%, and even the most aggressive space compression leads to a mean run-time slowdown of only 1.6% while reducing space consumption by a mean of 7% (14% ignoring two programs that mainly manipulate very large arrays).

In summary, our work shows that in the presence of a high-quality JIT compiler, conventional wisdom is wrong: encoding the method table pointer, when engineered carefully, has a negligible run-time performance impact while saving significant space. This result is significant in that once adopted, it will encourage programmers to use large numbers of small objects more freely. This in turn will improve the quality and maintainability of code.

Our results should apply to other object-oriented languages, such as Small-talk, Modula-3, SELF, Sather, and Oberon, with the obvious caveat that the more similar the language is to Java, the more directly translatable the results should be.

We have implemented the pluggable object model framework and four different object models in the Jikes[2] Research Virtual Machine [15] (formerly known as Jalapeño [6]), and present detailed measurements from this implementation. The Jikes RVM is an open-source Java virtual machine that includes a high-quality optimizing JIT compiler. The object model framework and implementations described in this paper are available in the open-source release of Jikes RVM version 2.0.4 and later.

The rest of the paper is organized as follows: Section 2 describes the abstract, plug-compatible object model. Section 3 describes the various header compression techniques that we use. Section 4 describes the four object models that

---

[1] Java[TM] and all Java-based trademarks and logos are trademarks or registered trademarks of Sun Microsystems, Inc. in the United States, other countries, or both.

[2] Jikes[TM] is a trademark or registered trademark of International Business Machines Corporation in the United States, other countries, or both.

we implemented: a standard object model with a two-word header, and three different object models with single-word headers. Section 5 presents our measurements in detail. Section 6 compares related work, and is followed by our conclusions.

2 Object Model Abstraction

Any object model implementation must provide a basic set of functionality for other parts of the virtual machine. In this study, we will assume that any object model implementation must instantiate a common abstract object model. The object model provides access to the following abstract fields for each heap-allocated object:

TIB Pointer. The TIB (Type Information Block) holds information that applies to all objects of a type. Each object points to a TIB, which could be a class object or some other related object. In the Jikes RVM, the TIB includes the virtual method table, a pointer to an object representing the type, and pointers to a few data structures to facilitate efficient interface invocation [4] and dynamic type checking [5].

Default Hash Code. Each Java object has a default hash code.

Lock. Each Java object has an associated lock state. This could be a pointer to a lock object or a direct representation of the lock.

Garbage Collection Information. Each Java object has associated information used by the memory management system. Usually this consists of one or two mark bits, but this could also include some combination of a reference count, forwarding pointer, etc.

Additionally, each array object provides a *length* field, and in certain experimental configurations each object header may contain one or more fields for profiling.

This paper explores various implementations of this abstract object model.

For example, one could implement an object model where each object has a four-word header, with one word devoted to each abstract field. This implementation would support 2^{32} distinct values for each field. This is usually overkill, as other considerations restrict the range of distinct values for each field.

2.1 Pluggable Implementation

In order to facilitate an apples-to-apples comparison of different object models in a high performance virtual machine, we have modified the Jikes RVM to delegate all access to the object model through a (logically) abstract class, called VM_ObjectModel. The fact that the Jikes RVM is implemented in Java made introducing this new abstraction fairly straightforward. We select and plug in a VM_ObjectModel implementation at system build time, allowing the system-building compiler to specialize all components of the virtual machine for the chosen object model implementation.

The VM_ObjectModel class provides the following services to the rest of the the virtual machine:

Getters and setters for each field in the abstract object model.
The Jikes RVM runtime services (class loaders, garbage collectors, compilers, etc.) perform all accesses to the fields through these methods.

Compiler inline code generation stubs. For high performance dynamic type checks and virtual method dispatch, the compilers must generate inline code to access an object's TIB. VM_ObjectModel provides small callbacks for the compilers to generate the appropriate inline code sequence.

Locking entry points. Since the synchronization implementation depends on the object model, all locking calls delegate to VM_ObjectModel.

Allocator support. VM_ObjectModel provides services to the memory management system to compute the size of an object and to initialize a chunk of raw memory as an object of a given type.

Note that the system-building compiler inlines the getter, setter, and other forwarding methods, so that abstracting the object model in this fashion has no runtime costs.

3   Header Compression Techniques

In this section we describe various compression techniques for each of the object header components.

3.1   TIB Pointer

The virtual machine uses the TIB pointer for virtual method calls, dynamic type checks, and other operations based on the object's run-time type. We examine three basic compression techniques that can be applied to the TIB pointer: *bit-stealing*, *indirection*, and *implicit type*.

Bit-stealing exploits the property that some bits of the TIB pointer always have the same value (usually 0) and allocates those bits for other uses. When bit-stealing, the virtual machine must perform a short sequence of ALU operations (on PowerPC[3], a single rotate-and-mask instruction) to extract the TIB pointer from the object header. Most commonly, the implementation can steal the low-order two or three bits, since TIBs are generally aligned on four- or eight-byte boundaries. The implementation may steal high order bits of the word as well, if the TIB always resides in a particular memory segment.

The bit-stealing technique has the advantages of low runtime overhead and not requiring any additional loads. The technique's main disadvantage is that it generally frees only a few bits for other uses.

---

[3] **PowerPC**[TM] is a trademark or registered trademark of International Business Machines Corporation in the United States, other countries, or both.

A more general technique, indirection, represents the TIB pointer as an index into a table of TIB pointers. Usually, indirection can free more bits than bit-stealing, since the table can pack TIB pointers more densely than TIB objects can be packed in memory. Furthermore, the total number of types should be several orders of magnitude smaller than the number of objects.

The disadvantages of indirection are that it requires an extra load to access the TIB pointer, and the table both consumes space and imposes a fixed limit on the number of TIBs.

A third technique, the implicit type method [11], reserves a range of memory for objects that all share the same type. If the memory range is a page, then the TIB pointer can be computed by shifting the object address to obtain a page number that is used as an index into a table that maps pages to TIB pointers.

The main advantage of this approach is that it frees all 32 bits typically associated with the TIB pointer, potentially allowing objects with no header space overhead. Like indirection, it requires only a single ALU operation followed by a single load to obtain the TIB pointer. The disadvantage is that it can lead to significant fragmentation of the heap, since all the objects on a page must be of the same type.

3.2   Synchronization State

In previous work, Bacon et al. [7] showed that using an in-object "thin lock" for the common case when locking does not involve contention can yield application speedups of up to a factor of two for Java programs due to the thread-safe design of many core libraries. The thin lock consists of a partial word used by inlined code that attempts to lock the object using a compare-and-swap style atomic operation. Out-of-line code handles the uncommon case when the compare-and-swap fails.

While fast, a thin lock for every object introduces a space cost in each object's header. Furthermore, in most programs, the majority of objects are never locked. We observe that in most cases, a simple static heuristic can predict whether an object of a particular class is likely to be locked. The heuristic predicts that an object of a class C is likely to be locked if and only if C has at least one synchronized method, or if any of its methods contain synchronized(this) statements.

Put another way, we consider locks as instance variables that are implicitly defined in the first class in the hierarchy that has a synchronized method or statement. Objects without the implicit lock variable (in particular, arrays), will not have a synchronization instance variable and must always resort to a more heavyweight locking scheme, mediated through a hash table.

Note that all synchronized methods and synchronized statements whose argument types have lock instance variables can always have the offset of the lock variable generated as a compile-time constant, leading to highly efficient inline locking code. Also note that since the space overhead of lock words is eliminated from most objects, there is no need for locking schemes that attempt to use only a small number of bits until the object is locked, such as meta-locks [1].

This heuristic will not catch a common idiom where program uses an object of type java.lang.Object as a lock. For such cases, we provide a type Synchronizer with a dummy synchronized method that forces allocation of a thin lock in the object header. Naturally, legacy code using this idiom will still suffer performance degradation. One could provide tool support with static or dynamic analysis to help identify troublesome cases. Alternatively, as a subject for future work, an adaptive optimization system could detect excessive locking overhead dynamically and introduce a thin lock word for particular object instances as needed.

The Lock Nursery. To implement the lock space optimization, we introduce the *lock nursery*, a data structure holding lock state for objects that do not have thin locks allocated in the object header. The implementation finds an object's entry in the lock nursery via its hash code.

Hash-table based locking schemes are notoriously slow. The original Sun Java Virtual Machine used a hash table scheme in which locking an object required acquiring two locks: first on the hash table and then on the object itself. Performance suffered both due to long path length and to contention on the hash table lock.

So, for good performance, either lock nursery access must be infrequent, or we must address inherent inefficiencies in hash-based locking. First, is the lock prediction heuristic sufficiently accurate that we rarely result to the lock nursery? If so, a simple lock nursery implementation suffices, since performance will not be critical. Our measurements in Section 5 show that is indeed the case for the benchmarks considered.

However, even if applications arise for which synchronized blocks turn out to be a performance bottleneck, we present two techniques that can address the problem.

In a copying collector, we can *evacuate* an object from the lock nursery when it moves, reformatting the object header to allocate an inline lock word in the object. Especially in a generational collector, this technique will convert long-lived locks to thin locks in a relatively short time period. The only vulnerability of this approach is to programs that invoke a large number of synchronized blocks on a large number of short-lived objects. This seems unlikely.

In a non-copying collector, if the simple lock nursery does not perform well enough, we can employ a more sophisticated implementation. Essentially, we define each slot in the hash table as holding either a surrogate thin lock for a single object hashed to that slot, or in the case of collisions, as a pointer to a list of lock objects, one for each object that maps to that hash slot.

When no object in the lock nursery maps to a particular slot, then that entry holds 0. When a single object is in the thin-locked state, the hash table slot contains a triple

$$(threadId, objectId, lockCount).$$

When $lockCount \neq 0$, the system can recover the object pointer from this information by computing

$$(objectId \times tableSize) + slotNumber.$$

When *lockCount* = 0, the rest of the word contains a pointer to (or index of) a list of fat locks for that hash code.

Note that since the majority of objects should be synchronized via the in-object thin locks allocated by the static lock prediction heuristic, the hash table will be far less dense than previous hash table based approaches to synchronization for Java.

3.3 Default Hash Code

For non-moving collectors such as mark-and-sweep, the system can define the default hash code of an object to be its address, or more generally, a function thereof.

For moving collectors, we can use the tri-state encoding technique from Bacon et al. [7] (also developed independently by Agesen and used in the Sun EVM), where the states of an object are *unhashed*, *hashed*, and *hashed-and-moved*. For the first two states, the hash code of the object is the address. When the collector moves an object whose state is *hashed*, it changes its state to *hashed-and-moved* and copies the old address to the end of the new version of the object.

If space is available, the system can encode hash code state in two bits in the object header.

If space is not available in the header, we can encode the state by using different TIB pointers which point to blocks that have different hashCode() method implementations. The additional TIB blocks are generated on demand, since most classes are never hashed. Therefore, the space cost for the extra TIB blocks should be minimal.

Note that if fast class equality tests are implemented by comparing TIB pointers, the class equality test must be modified so that if the TIBs do not match then the class pointers are compared before a false result is returned.

3.4 Garbage Collector State

Usually, garbage collectors require the ability to mark objects in one or more ways. For instance, one bit may indicate that the object has been reached from the roots by the garbage collector, and another bit may indicate that the object has been placed in a write buffer by a generational collector (as a way of avoiding duplicate entries).

Because the amount and type of garbage collector state depends heavily on the collector implementation, for this paper, we assume that the collector requires two bits of state information for each object, and provide those bits in all but one of the object models that we implement. We consider the one exception of a garbage collector that uses an alternative method to represent the marks. There are many well-known alternatives, particularly bit maps, that often benefit locality in addition to removing state from the object header [16].

3.5   Forwarding Pointers in Copying Collectors

In a copying collector, it is generally necessary for the object in from-space to temporarily contain a forwarding pointer to its replica in to-space. In object models with multi-word headers, the forwarding pointer is usually placed in the word that normally contains the lock state and hash code. However, when a single-word object model is used, there is generally only one choice: to use the space normally occupied by the TIB pointer.

As a result, the type of the object is not directly available during collection and must be obtained by following the forwarding pointer. This is generally not a problem if the run-time system is written in another language, like C or C++. However, if the run-time system is itself written in Java, as is the case for Jikes RVM, then the presence of forwarding pointers complicates matters considerably.

In particular, an object that is being used by one processor to perform the task of collection may be forwarded by another processor which copies it into to-space. As a result, the TIB of the first processor's object will become a forwarding pointer and virtual method dispatch and other run-time operations will fail.

There are a number of ways to address this problem. The simplest is to always check whether the word contains a forwarding pointer, but this is prohibitively expensive. We chose instead to mark those classes used by the garbage collector, and generate the checks only for methods in those classes and only in object models that require it (namely copying collectors with one-word headers). The result is a slight slow-down in operations on some virtual machine classes, but unimpeded performance for user classes.

3.6   Atomicity

The previous techniques all describe methods to pack sub-word fields into a single word. However, in a multi-processor system, the techniques must also consider atomicity of access to these fields. Mainstream CPUs provide atomic memory access at the word or sometimes byte granularity; they do not provide atomic access at the granularity of a single bit. Thus, if we pack two logically distinct fields into the same byte or word, we must be sure to guard updates to the individual fields to ensure that concurrent writes are not lost.

Note that if the TIB field remains constant after object initialization, stealing bits from the TIB field does not cause a race condition. The other fields may be subject to concurrent writes, and so require care in their layout and access.

4   The Object Models

In this section we describe the various object models implemented for this paper. Figure 1 illustrates the various models[4]. For all object models, arrays include an extra header word which contains the length of the array.

---

[4] The diagrams show the data as always following the header, but in fact in the Jikes RVM the data precedes the header for non-arrays and follows the header for arrays. This allows trap-based null checking and optimized array access [6].

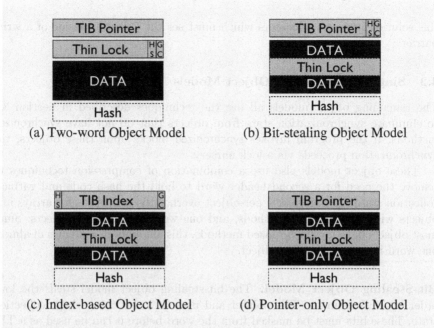

Fig. 1. Object models compared in this paper. Fields in dashed lines are optional and usually absent, including the thin lock in models (b), (c), and (d), in which it is treated as an instance variable. GC and HS are two-bit fields encoding garbage collection and hash code state.

All object models we implemented define the hash code to be an object's address, shifted right by two. For the copying semispace collector, we use the tri-state hashcode encoding described in Section 3.3.

4.1 Two-Word Header Object Model

Each scalar object in this object model has a two-word header. The first word contains the TIB pointer, and the second word contains all the other per-object state: lock state (24 bits) and garbage collection state (2 bits). Additionally, for the semispace collector, the second word holds two bits for the tri-state hash code information. The remaining bits are unused.

The advantages of the two-word header object model are that it is relatively simple, allows direct access to the TIB with a single *load* instruction, and only requires two words of overhead for non-arrays and three words of overhead for arrays.

If a copying collector changes GC bits during mutation, this model faces an atomicity issue since the GC state bits and the hash code bits reside in the same byte. The Jikes RVM generational collectors face this problem, since the write barriers may mutate the GC bit for objects in mature space. One option would be to always update the hash bits and GC state bits with atomic operations; but this solution hampers allocators which must set the GC state inside of a write barrier.

4.2 Single-Word Header Object Models

The remaining object models all use the techniques described in Section 3.2 to eliminate synchronization state from objects that do not have synchronized methods. If the program invokes synchronized blocks upon these objects, the synchronization proceeds via a lock nursery.

These object models also use a combination of compression techniques to remove the need for a second header word to hold the hash code and garbage collection state. Therefore, the per-object overhead is two words for arrays and objects with synchronized methods, and one word for all other objects. Since most objects have no synchronized methods, this amounts to a savings of almost one word for every allocated object.

Bit-Stealing Object Model. The bit-stealing object model steals the low-order two bits from the TIB pointer and uses them for the garbage collection state. These bits must be masked from the word before it can be used as a TIB pointer.

In addition, for the copying collectors, we need to encode the hash code state. In our implementations, we did this by aligning all TIBs on 16-byte boundaries, making the 4 low-order bits of TIB pointers available to the object model. Since TIBs are of moderate size and occur infrequently relative to instance objects, the space cost is negligible.

Note that for a generational copying collector, if the hash code and GC bits reside in the same byte, this model faces the same atomicity issue between GC bits and hash code state bits as described in Section 4.1. However, if the high-order bit of the TIB address is guaranteed to be fixed (e.g. 0), and the TIB address is fixed, then the system can update this high-order bit with non-atomic byte operations, without introducing a race condition with the hash bits. The current Jikes RVM admits this solution by allocating all TIBs in a non-moving space in a low memory segment.

Indexed Object Model. The indexed object model uses a TIB index instead of a TIB pointer, requiring an extra *load* instruction to obtain the TIB pointer indirectly.

The advantages of this object model are that more state can be packed into the header word. Furthermore, in our implementation for the generational copying collector, we use the *high-order* bits for hash code state and the *low-order* bits for GC state. Since the two logical fields do not inhabit the same byte of memory, there are no issues with atomic updates during mutation.

Since the TIB index does not change, the JIT compiler could fold the TIB index as a compile-time constant, further improving the speed of dynamic type tests.

TIB Pointer Only. The TIB-only object model provides a minimalist object model that applies when both the GC and hash code state can be eliminated from the object. An example is a mark-and-sweep collector that uses side-arrays of bits to mark objects, rather than marking the objects themselves.

Since a mark-and-sweep collector does not move objects, it can use a function of the object address as the hash code, eliminating the need for the hash code state.

The Jikes RVM includes just such a collector; in fact it uses a side array of bytes rather than bits; this allows parallelization of the marking phase without the need for atomic operations to update the mark bits (since the target architecture is byte-atomic). In this case, the increased parallel garbage collector performance justified the cost of an extra byte per object.

5 Measurements

To evaluate the different object models, we implemented them in a common modular framework in the Jikes RVM version 2.0.4 [15]. All measurements are for the Jikes JIT compiler at optimization level 2, and are run in a non-adaptive configuration to remove non-deterministic effects due to the adaptive sampling which drives re-compilation. Other than the object model, all other facets of the implementation and the machine environment were held constant.

All performance results reported below were obtained on an IBM RS/6000 Enterprise Server model F80 running AIX[5] 4.3.3. The machine has 4GB of main memory and six 500MHz PowerPC RS64 III processors, each of which has a 4MB L2 cache.

Table 1 lists the benchmarks used to evaluate the various object models. They include the full SPECjvm98 [25] benchmark suite, the SPECjbb2000 [26] benchmark which is commonly used to measure multi-processor transactional workloads, and two commonly cited synthetic benchmarks. The results reported do *not* conform to the official SPEC run rules, so our results do not directly or indirectly represent a SPEC metric. Note that the average object size ranges between 22 and 36 bytes, except for two codes that mostly create large arrays (compress and CaffeineMark).

With the exception of SPECjbb2000, the lock, space usage, and hash code statistics reported below were gathered using a measurement harness that ran the benchmark multiple times, clearing the counters after each run. This enables us to remove distortions caused by Jikes RVM during the first run (in particular optimizing compilation) and accurately report statistics for only the benchmark itself. Since SPECjbb2000 ran for over 30 minutes, the startup effects of compilation should not significantly impact the overall statistics. Since the Jikes RVM itself is implemented in Java, the statistics do include locks, allocations, and hash code operations performed by the JVM itself on behalf of application code.

---

[5] **AIX**[TM] is a trademark or registered trademark of International Business Machines Corporation in the United States, other countries, or both.

Table 1. The benchmarks used to evaluate the object models. The benchmarks include the complete SPECjvm98 suite and represent a wide range of application characteristics. The average object size reported assumes a two-word header for scalars and a three-word header for arrays.

Program	Description	Applic. Size	Allocation (MB)	Avg. Obj. Size	Lock Operations
jBYTEmark	Synthetic benchmark	71 KB	35.5	36.2	336,933
CaffeineMark	Synthetic benchmark	33 KB	966.1	307.0	1,606,773
201.compress	Compression	18 KB	105.7	2,973.3	23,856
202.jess	Expert system shell	11 KB	231.7	34.5	4,811,737
209.db	Database	10 KB	62.5	24.2	45,236,755
213.javac	Bytecode compiler	688 KB	198.6	31.7	15,109,145
222.mpegaudio	MPEG coder/decoder	120 KB	1.1	34.6	17936
227.mtrt	Multithreaded raytracer	57 KB	80.4	22.4	1,357,819
228.jack	Parser generator	131 KB	279.8	39.4	9,672,868
SPECjbb2000	TPC-C style workload	821 KB	18,514.3	26.4	1,376,606,250

5.1   Use of Lock Nursery

Figure 2 shows the distribution of lock operations, using a lock nursery for synchronized blocks that operate on objects that have no synchronized methods. The figure reports the percentage of dynamic lock operations by type: nursery lock, fat (contended) lock, slow thin lock (recursive, no contention), and fast thin lock (non-recursive, no contention).

Nursery locks account for about 0.5% of all lock operations on SPECjbb2000. For all other benchmarks, the number of nursery locks is so small as to be invisible on the graph. This indicates that the use of a lock nursery should have a negligible impact on performance.

Based on these results, we relied on an exceedingly simple lock nursery implementation: a hash table guarded by a single global lock.

The other statistics for locking operations are consistent with those reported in our and other related work on fast locking: more than 95% of all lock operations are handled by the inlined fast path; virtually all of the remaining cases are handled by the slow path for thin locks that handles nested locking. Contention (and the correspondent use of fat locks) is negligible.

5.2   Space Savings

Figure 3 shows how well two single-word object models reduce space consumption. The first bar shows the percentage of allocated objects whose size we have reduced by a word: arrays and objects without synchronized methods. Clearly, the simple heuristic effectively saves header space. Although we almost never resort to the lock nursery, we have eliminated the space for the thin lock from 97.5% of all objects in the system.

The second bar reports the space savings, as a percentage of the total number of bytes allocated. The one-word object models reduce mean allocated space by

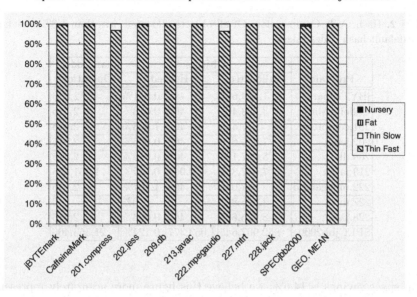

Fig. 2. Lock Usage. The lock nursery accounts for 0.5% of lock operations in SPECjbb2000 and is insignificant for all other programs, indicating that performance impact will be minimal.

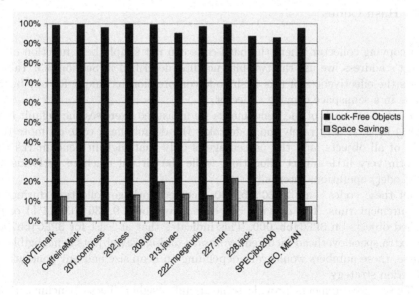

Fig. 3. Object compaction and its effects. Overall 97.5% of objects can be allocated without a lock word; the result is a mean space savings of about 7%. Excluding the two codes that mainly create large arrays, the mean space savings is 14.6%.

about 7%, although on some benchmarks the savings was as high as 21%. Excluding the two array-based codes, compress and CaffeineMark, the (geometric)

Table 2. Hash Code Compression. Of all objects allocated, less than 1.3% ever have their default hash codes taken.

	Objects			hashCode()
Program	Allocated	Hashed		Operations
jBYTEmark	1,184,687	488	0.041%	2,636
CaffeineMark	3,483,406	469	0.013%	2,515
201.compress	37,419	469	1.253%	2,515
202.jess	7,959,679	469	0.006%	2,515
209.db	3,247,129	469	0.014%	2,515
213.javac	7,517,852	9,961	0.132%	1,961,835
222.mpegaudio	37,018	469	1.267%	2,515
227.mtrt	4,565,881	0	0%	0
228.jack	8,225,623	469	0.006%	2,515
SPECjbb2000	852,907,645	1,053,377	0.124%	21,363,400

mean space savings is 14.6%; we believe this figure more accurately represents the expected savings from codes written in an object-oriented style.

5.3   Hash Codes

In a copying collector where the hash code can not simply be a function of the object's address, we use the two-bit encoding described in Section 3.3. Table 2 shows the effectiveness of this hash code compression technique for our benchmarks in a semispace copying collector.

First of all, each of the benchmarks we measured exercises the default hash-Code() method very rarely: no code takes the default hash code on more than 1.3% of all objects, and the percentage is only that high in benchmarks that perform very little object allocation, while the virtual machine performs 469 hashCode() operations internally.

Of these codes, only SPECjbb2000 incurred garbage collection during the measurement runs. The copying collector moved only 9,736 (0.0011%) of the hashed objects on SPECjbb2000. This indicates that at least for SPECjbb2000, the extra space overhead incurred by *hashed-and-moved* objects is negligible. Of course, these numbers would vary depending on heap size and any generational collection strategy.

These measurements provide some useful insights. These benchmarks use default hash codes rarely, indicating that the virtual machine should place a premium on a compact hashcode representation and a simple implementation. While the two-bit encoding scheme we measured works well, in some cases the extra two bits may not be available in the object header; in this case, it may be better to represent the hash code state with multiple TIBs as described in Section 3.3. Unfortunately this strategy would somewhat complicate other portions of the virtual machine.

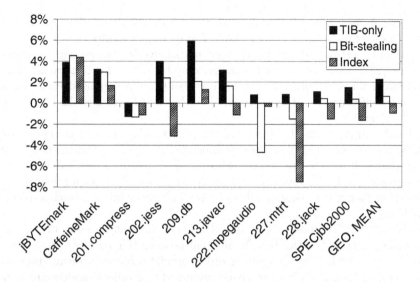

Fig. 4. Speedup obtained by the one-word object models with a non-copying mark-and-sweep collector, relative to the standard two-word Jikes RVM object model. Measurements are for optimized code.

For future language designs, it might be better to omit hashing as a feature of all objects in the system, and instead require an explicit declaration. Then hash codes could be treated like instance fields, as we do for lock words.

5.4   Run-Time Performance: Non-moving Collector

Figure 4 shows the performance of the various object models, relative to the two-word header object model. These measurements are all taken in a non-moving mark-and-sweep collector.

Figure 4 shows that none of the single-word header object models introduces more than a 8% slowdown on any benchmark, as compared to the two-word header object model. However, we did observe slowdowns of 4% and 12% for the Bit-stealing and Index object models, respectively, on the `Method` component of the `CaffeineMark` micro-benchmark. This component represents a worst-case measurement of object-model induced virtual dispatch overhead. However, the overall performance results indicate that between compiler optimizations that eliminate redundant TIB loads and instruction-level parallelism in the hardware that can perform the extra ALU operations, packing the TIB pointer in with other information only has a minor performance impact on normal workloads. This goes against the common folklore of object-oriented run-time systems design.

Secondly, across these benchmarks, one-word headers improve performance more often than they degrade performance. This indicates that better cache locality and less frequent garbage collection can have a significant positive performance impact. The jBYTEmark, 202.jess, and 209.db benchmarks show significant speedups (over 4%) with the TIB-only object model.

In some sections of the micro-benchmarks, we saw large performance increases (23% on Float in CaffeineMark and 14% on LU Decomposition in jBYTEmark for TIB-only). This probably results from increased cache locality and more effective use of memory bandwidth for codes that make heavy use of small objects.

Krall and Tomsich [18] have argued that the header size of Java objects should not impose a significant performance penalty on Java floating point codes, since they will mostly use arrays. However, our measurements indicate that in some cases exactly the opposite holds: header size matters most for floating point codes that manipulate large numbers of small arrays or objects (such as complex numbers).

Overall, the TIB-only object model leads to a mean speedup of 2.3% (not surprising since it has the benefit of small headers but pays no extra cost for TIB lookup), while the bit-stealing object model achieves a mean speedup of 0.6%. Taken together with the space savings, these object models are a clear improvement over the baseline two-word object header.

The indexed object model suffers a 0.9% mean run-time slowdown, and the space saving may justify this implementation choice in some scenarios. However, on codes where the TIB field is frequently accessed, the indexed object model pays a much higher price than the bit-stealing object model.

For mtrt, where the indexed model suffers almost 8% slowdown, the TIB accesses are primarily due to guarded inlining performed with the method test [9]; on IA32 Jikes RVM inlines these methods with a code patching guard [14] and thus does not access the TIB. Alternatively, the inlining could be performed with a type test which simply compared the TIB indexes instead of a method test, which would also eliminate the additional cost.

The 1.2% slowdown on 201.compress for all one-word object models and the 4.7% slowdown on 222.mpegaudio for the bit-stealing object model are due to cache effects.

Even though it makes non-trivial use of the lock nursery (0.5% of all locking operations), the performance of SPECjbb2000 still improves with the TIB-only and bit-stealing object models. The space saved by the one word object models enables a 13% decrease in the number of garbage collections.

5.5   Run-Time Performance: Copying Collector

Figure 5 shows the performance of the Bit-stealing and Index object models, relative to the object model with a two-word header. These measurements are all taken in a non-generational semispace copying collector.

We did not implement the TIB-only object model in the copying collector because the copying collector does not naturally have mark arrays external to the objects, although this could certainly be done.

Overall, the performance trends are similar to those obtained with the mark-and-sweep collector. The bit-stealing object model improved mean performance

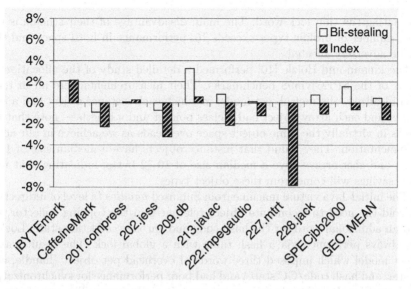

Fig. 5. Speedup obtained by the one-word object models, with a semi-space copying collector, relative to the standard two-word Jikes RVM object model. Measurements are for optimized code.

by 0.4%, while the indexed object model degraded performance by 1.6%. The difference in relative performance, when compared to the same object models under the non-moving collector, may be due to the cost of checking for forwarding pointers on TIB access within the virtual machine run-time system classes, or may simply be the result of variations in locality and similar effects.

The performance inversions on 201.compress and 222.mpegaudio observed with the mark-and-sweep collector did not occur with the semispace collector, but 227.mtrt once again payed a high cost for TIB lookup with guarded inlining.

6   Related Work

To our knowledge this work is the first comprehensive study to explore alternative implementations of the Java object model. Previous work has been implicit in work on other parts of the system, primarily locking and garbage collection.

Most closely related to this paper is the work of Shuf et al. [22], in which they studied the opportunities for space savings made possible by the classification of certain types as *prolific*. Prolific types are assigned a short (4-bit) type index, which is stored in a compressed header word along with lock, hash, and garbage collection state. If the type index is 0, an extra header word is the full 32-bit TIB pointer. They presented measurements of potential space savings that agree with ours, but did not implement the scheme.

One way of understanding the difference between our work and that of Shuf et al. is that they are usually compressing the TIB pointer, while we are usually eliminating the thin lock word. The main disadvantage of their scheme is that if the number of prolific types exceeds 16, performance in both space and time will be adversely affected.

Dieckmann and Hölzle [10] performed a detailed study of the allocation behavior of the SPECjvm98 benchmarks. Their measurements were all in terms of an idealized, abstract object model in which each instance object had a class pointer and each array object had a class pointer and a length — note that this results in virtually the same object space overheads as we achieve in our actual implementation. They found that instance objects have a median size of 12-24 bytes, and char arrays have a median size of 10-72 bytes, indicating that most space savings will come from these object types.

The initial Java virtual machine from Sun used *handles* (a level of indirection) to avoid the need to recompute object references in the copying collector, and used an additional word for the hash code and garbage collection state. Locking was always performed via a hash table with a global lock. The result was an object model which imposed three words of overhead per object (handle, class pointer, and hash code/GC state) and had poor performance for synchronization, which turned out to be ubiquitous in many Java programs. The use of handles led each object to reside in two cache lines, significantly reducing effective cache size.

6.1   Run-Time Monitor Optimizations

Krall and Probst [17] were the first to attack the synchronization overhead in a systematic manner in the CACAO JIT compiler. Since their locks were represented as three-word structures, it was unacceptable to place them inline in the object header. Instead, the system accessed the locks via an external hash table, severely limiting the potential speedup.

With *thin locks*, Bacon et al. [7] attacked the synchronization overhead by allocating 24 bits within each object for lock state, and using atomic compare-and-swap operations to handle the most common cases: locking unlocked objects and locking objects already owned by the current thread. In these cases, the lock was in its thin state, and the 24 bits represented the thread identifier of the lock owner and the lock nesting level. In rare cases (deeply nested locking, contention between threads, or use of wait and notify operations), the high bit of the lock state is set to 1, indicating that the lock is a fat lock, and the other 23 bits are an index into a table of fat locks.

To make room for the thin lock, the system employed the two-bit hash code state encoding described in Section 3.3, and the remaining 6 bits of the word were reserved for garbage collection state. The implementation was done in a Sun-derived JVM modified by the IBM Tokyo Research Lab to eliminate handles. The resultant system had an object model with two words of space overhead per object and good lock performance.

Thin locks have the potential drawbacks of excessive space consumption due to lack of deflation and excessive spinning due to busy-waiting on inflation. Subsequent work by Onodera and Kawachiya [20] attempted to ameliorate these problems, at the expense of complicating the locking protocol and requiring an extra bit in the object header in a separate word from the lock. Subsequently, Gagnon and Hendren [13] showed how the extra bit could be stored on a per-thread rather than a per-object basis.

The alternative approach to lightweight Java locking that is most similar to thin locks is that of Yang et al. [28] in the LaTTe virtual machine, which used a 32-bit lock word in each object. Unlike thin locks, the format of the lock word never changes, and includes a count of waiting threads. If the count is non-zero, the queue is found via a hash table.

In the *meta-lock* approach of Agesen et al. [1] in the Sun Exact VM, one 32-bit word in the header normally contains a 25 bit hash code, a five bit age (for generational collection), and a two bit lock (which is 0 in the normal state). When the lock is non-zero, the other 30 bits point to an auxiliary structure, either a lock structure or a thread structure of the thread that is changing the lock state. In the latter case the object is considered meta-locked, and the per-object lock, hash code, and garbage collection state are temporarily unavailable. Meta-locked objects are always in the process of making short transitions between other states. When the object is locked, the auxiliary structure contains the relocated hash code and garbage collection state.

Fitzgerald et al. [12] describe the Marmot static compiler for Java, which uses a two word object header that includes a class pointer and a word containing synchronization state and hash code.

All of these various techniques are compatible with the object compression techniques described in this paper, which could be used to generate single-word object models that use different synchronization techniques.

6.2 Compile-Time Monitor Optimizations

There has also been significant work on elimination of synchronization via compile-time analysis [2,3,8,21]. This work can in some cases be highly effective at reducing or (in the case of single-threaded programs) eliminating synchronization operations. Therefore these optimizations are complementary to the run-time techniques described above.

While none of the cited work investigated the potential for reducing object size, this could certainly be done, complementing the work presented in this paper.

6.3 Other Languages

Previous work [23,19] describes object models for C++, primarily addressing complications due to multiple inheritance. C++ does not support synchronization, hashing, and garbage collection at the language level.

Tip and Sweeney [27] describe how C++ class hierarchy specialization can improve the efficiency of object layout. In a subsequent study [24], they show that a significant number of data members are never actually used at run-time, and can be identified and removed at compile-time.

7 Conclusions

We have shown that a fundamental piece of folklore about the design of object-oriented run-time systems is wrong: when engineered carefully in conjunction with a high-quality optimizing JIT compiler, encoding the method table pointer does not lead to any significant performance penalty. Our techniques do not depend on any particular implementation of lightweight synchronization or garbage collection, and so long as a high-quality compiler is used, should apply to other object-oriented languages.

Experimental results show that header compression can yield significant space savings while simultaneously either improving run-time performance by a mean of 2.3% or at worst degrading it by 1.6% (depending on the details of the implemented object model). Programs that use large numbers of small objects show significant performance improvement. The availability of space-efficient Java run-time systems should encourage programmers to more freely apply object-oriented abstraction to small objects.

We have also shown that treating the lock as an instance field, implicitly defined by synchronized methods, is a highly effective way of eliminating the space overhead of in-object locks, while retaining their performance benefits in 99% of the cases.

As an added benefit, we have shown how to engineer a high performance virtual machine with a pluggable, parameterized object model, without any loss in run-time efficiency. This feature allows an implementer to substitute various object models according to their fit with the rest of the system design, especially the garbage collector. The object model plug-ins are available via the IBM Jikes RVM open-source release to encourage future experimental studies of object model variants.

References

1. AGESEN, O., DETLEFS, D., GARTHWAITE, A., KNIPPEL, R., RAMAKRISHNA, Y. S., AND WHITE, D. An efficient meta-lock for implementing ubiquitous synchronization. In *OOPSLA'99 Conference Proceedings: Object-Oriented Programming Systems, Languages, and Applications* (Denver, Colorado, Oct. 1999). *SIGPLAN Notices, 34*, 10, 207–222.
2. ALDRICH, J., CHAMBERS, C., SIRER, E. G., AND EGGERS, S. J. Static analyses for eliminating unnecessary synchronization from Java programs. In *Static Analysis: Sixth International Symposium* (Venice, Italy, Sept. 1999), A. Cortesi and G. Filé, Eds., vol. 1694 of *Lecture Notes in Computer Science*, Springer Verlag, pp. 19–38.
3. ALDRICH, J., SIRER, E. G., CHAMBERS, C., AND EGGERS, S. Comprehensive synchronization elimination for Java. Tech. Rep. UW-CSE-00-10-01, Department of Computer Science, University of Washington, 2000.
4. ALPERN, B., COCCHI, A., FINK, S., GROVE, D., AND LIEBER, D. Efficient implementation of Java interfaces: invokeinterface considered harmless. In *Proceedings of the ACM SIGPLAN Conference on Object-Oriented Programming Systems, Languages, and Applications* (Tampa, Florida, Oct. 2001). *SIGPLAN Notices, 36*, 10, 108–124.

5. ALPERN, B., COCCHI, A., AND GROVE, D. Dynamic type checking in Jalapeño. In *Proceedings of the Java Virtual Machine Research and Technology Symposium* (Monterey, California, Apr. 2001), pp. 41–52.

6. ALPERN, B., ET AL. The Jalapeño virtual machine. *IBM Syst. J. 39*, 1 (2000), 211–238.

7. BACON, D. F., KONURU, R., MURTHY, C., AND SERRANO, M. Thin locks: Featherweight synchronization for Java. In *Proceedings of the SIGPLAN Conference on Programming Language Design and Implementation* (Montreal, Canada, June 1998). *SIGPLAN Notices, 33*, 6, 258–268.

8. BOGDA, J., AND HÖLZLE, U. Removing unnecessary synchronization in Java. In *Conference Proceedings: Object-Oriented Programming Systems, Languages, and Applications* (Denver, Colorado, Oct. 1999). *SIGPLAN Notices, 34*, 10, 35–46.

9. DETLEFS, D., AND AGESEN, O. Inlining of virtual methods. In *Thirteenth European Conference on Object-Oriented Programming* (1999), vol. 1628 of *Lecture Notes in Computer Science*, Springer Verlag, pp. 258–278.

10. DIECKMANN, S., AND HÖLZLE, U. A study of the allocation behavior of the SPECjvm98 Java benchmarks. In *Proceedings of the Thirteenth European Conference on Object-Oriented Programming* (Lisbon, Portugal, 1999), R. Guerraoui, Ed., vol. 1628 of *Lecture Notes in Computer Science*, Springer-Verlag, pp. 92–115.

11. DYBVIG, R. K., EBY, D., AND BRUGGEMAN, C. Don't stop the BIBOP: Flexible and efficient storage management for dynamically-typed languages. Tech. Rep. 400, Indiana University Computer Science Department, 1994.

12. FITZGERALD, R. P., KNOBLOCK, T. B., RUF, E., STEENSGAARD, B., AND TARDITI, D. Marmot: an optimizing compiler for Java. *Software – Practice and Experience 30*, 3 (2000), 199–232.

13. GAGNON, E., AND HENDREN, L. SableVM: A research framework for the efficient execution of Java bytecode. In *Proceedings of the Java Virtual Machine Research and Technology Symposium* (Monterey, California, Apr. 2001), pp. 27–40.

14. ISHIZAKI, K., KAWAHITO, M., YASUE, T., KOMATSU, H., AND NAKATANI, T. A study of devirtualization techniques for a Java Just-In-Time compiler. In *OOPSLA'2000 Conference Proceedings: Object-Oriented Programming Systems, Languages, and Applications* (Tampa, Florida, Oct. 2000). *SIGPLAN Notices, 35*, 10, 294–310.

15. Jikes RVM 2.0.4. http://www.ibm.com/developerworks/oss/jikesrvm.

16. JONES, R. E., AND LINS, R. D. *Garbage Collection*. John Wiley and Sons, 1996.

17. KRALL, A., AND PROBST, M. Monitors and exceptions: how to implement Java efficiently. *Concurrency: Practice and Experience 10*, 11–13 (1998), 837–850.

18. KRALL, A., AND TOMSICH, P. Java for large-scale scientific computations? In *Proceedings of the Third International Conference on Large-Scale Scientific Computing* (Sozopol, Bulgaria, June 2001), S. Margenov, J. Wasniewski, and P. Y. Yalamov, Eds., vol. 2179 of *Lecture Notes in Computer Science*, Springer Verlag, pp. 228–235.

19. MYERS, A. C. Bidirectional object layout for separate compilation. In *OOPSLA'95 Conference Proceedings: Object-Oriented Programming Systems, Languages, and Applications* (Oct. 1995). *SIGPLAN Notices, 30*, 10, 124–139.

20. ONODERA, T., AND KAWACHIYA, K. A study of locking objects with bimodal fields. In *OOPSLA'99 Conference Proceedings: Object-Oriented Programming Systems, Languages, and Applications* (Denver, Colorado, Oct. 1999). *SIGPLAN Notices, 34*, 10, 223–237.

21. RUF, E. Effective synchronization removal for Java. In *Proceedings of the SIG-PLAN Conference on Programming Language Design and Implementation* (Vancouver, British Columbia, June 2000). *SIGPLAN Notices*, *35*, 5, 208–218.

22. SHUF, Y., GUPTA, M., BORDAWEKAR, R., AND SINGH, J. P. Exploiting prolific types for memory management and optimizations. In *Conference Record of the ACM Conference on Principles of Programming Languages* (Portland, Oregon, Jan. 2002), pp. 295–306.

23. STROUSTROUP, B. *The Annotated C++ Reference Manual.* Addison-Wesley, 1990. Chapter 10, section 10.

24. SWEENEY, P. F., AND TIP, F. A study of dead data members in C++ applications. In *Proceedings of the SIGPLAN Conference on Programming Language Design and Implementation* (Montreal, Canada, June 1998). *SIGPLAN Notices*, *33*, 6, 324–332.

25. THE STANDARD PERFORMANCE EVALUATION CORPORATION. SPEC JVM98 Benchmarks. http://www.spec.org/osg/jvm98, 1998.

26. THE STANDARD PERFORMANCE EVALUATION CORPORATION. SPEC JBB 2000 Benchmark. http://www.spec.org/osg/jbb2000, 2000.

27. TIP, F., AND SWEENEY, P. F. Class hierarchy specialization. In *OOPSLA'97 Conference Proceedings: Object-Oriented Programming Systems, Languages, and Applications* (Denver, Colorado, Oct. 1997). *SIGPLAN Notices*, *32*, 10, 271–285.

28. YANG, B.-S., LEE, J., PARK, J., MOON, S.-M., AND EBCIOĞLU, K. Lightweight monitor in Java virtual machine. In *Proceedings of the Third Workshop on Interaction between Compilers and Computer Architectures* (San Jose, California, Oct. 1998). *SIGARCH Computer Architecture News*, *21*, 1, 35–38.

Atomic Instructions in Java

David Hovemeyer, William Pugh, and Jaime Spacco

Dept. of Computer Science, University of Maryland, College Park, MD 20742 USA
{daveho,pugh,jspacco}@cs.umd.edu

Abstract. Atomic instructions atomically access and update one or
more memory locations. Because they do not incur the overhead of lock
acquisition or suspend the executing thread during contention, they may
allow higher levels of concurrency on multiprocessors than lock-based
synchronization. Wait-free data structures are an important application
of atomic instructions, and extend these performance benefits to higher
level abstractions such as queues. In type-unsafe languages such as C,
atomic instructions can be expressed in terms of operations on memory addresses. However, type-safe languages such as Java do not allow
manipulation of arbitrary memory locations. Adding support for atomic
instructions to Java is an interesting but important challenge.

In this paper we consider several ways to support atomic instructions
in Java. Each technique has advantages and disadvantages. We propose
idiom recognition as the technique we feel has the best combination of
expressiveness and simplicity. We describe techniques for recognizing instances of atomic operation idioms in the compiler of a Java Virtual
Machine, and converting such instances into code utilizing atomic machine instructions. In addition, we describe a runtime technique which
ensures that the semantics of multithreaded Java [11] are preserved when
atomic instructions and blocking synchronization are used in the same
program. Finally, we present benchmark results showing that for concurrent queues, a wait-free algorithm implemented using atomic compare-
and-swap instructions yields better scalability on a large multiprocessor
than a queue implemented with lock-based synchronization.

1   Introduction

Wait-free data structures and algorithms have been an active area of research in
recent years [3,6,12,18], and have spawned a variety of applications [4,8,9]. They
have the desirable property that when multiple threads access a wait-free data
structure, stalled threads cannot prevent other threads from making progress.
This avoids a variety of problems encountered with lock-based (blocking) synchronization, such as priority inversion and formation of convoys. Wait-free synchronization is especially useful when a data structure must be accessed in a
context from which blocking is impossible or undesirable.

Wait-free data structures generally work by making small changes atomically, such that before and after the atomic operation the data structure is
in a consistent state. These atomic operations are usually implemented using

B. Magnusson (Ed.): ECOOP 2002, LNCS 2374, pp. 133–154, 2002.

atomic machine instructions, in which one or more memory locations are accessed and updated atomically. For example, many architectures support an atomic *compare-and-swap*, or 'CAS', instruction. CAS atomically compares the contents of a single memory location against an input value, and if they are equal stores a second value in the memory location.

Atomic memory operations are easy to express in languages such as C and C++, in which it is possible to determine the address of any variable, array element, or field. (It is necessary to resort to assembly language to implement these operations, but most compilers support some form of inline assembly.) However, type-safe languages such as Java do not permit manipulation of arbitrary memory locations, nor do they permit the direct execution of arbitrary machine instructions. The problem of how to express atomic memory operations in such languages in a way that respects the language's safety guarantees is thus more challenging.

In this paper we consider several techniques for supporting atomic memory operations in the Java programming language [7]. We propose *idiom recognition* as a lightweight technique for expressing atomic instructions in a way that is simple to implement and is fully compatible with the semantics of the language.

While much of our discussion is specific to Java, the same basic techniques could also be used in other type-safe virtual machines, such as Microsoft's CLR (Common Language Runtime).

The structure of the paper is as follows. In Sect. 2, we give a general overview of atomic instructions and how they are used in wait-free algorithms. In Sect. 3, we describe several techniques for supporting atomic instructions in the Java virtual machine. In Sect. 4 we discuss several questions of strategy that arise in supporting atomic instructions. In Sect. 5, we describe an algorithm for recognizing instances of idioms which can be translated into atomic machine instructions within the Java virtual machine. In Sect. 6 we show performance results that show that support for atomic instructions allow the implementation of a concurrent queue that is more scalable than a comparable queue implemented with blocking synchronization. In Sect. 7 we describe related work. Finally, in Sect. 8 we summarize our findings and describe possibilities for future work.

2   Atomic Instructions

Atomic machine instructions atomically access and modify one or more memory locations. They have two primary advantages over using a lock to guarantee atomicity:

1. an atomic instruction is generally faster than equivalent lock-based code, and
2. atomic instructions execute in a finite amount of time, whereas acquiring a lock may block the executing thread for an unbounded period of time

For these reasons, atomic instructions are valuable in situations where a small update is made to a shared data structure, especially when the use of a lock

Table 1. Examples of atomic instructions.

Instruction	Semantics	Supported by
Compare-and-swap	Compare two values, update if equal	Sparc, IA32
LL/SC	Two instruction version of CAS	Alpha, PPC, MIPS
Double CAS	CAS on two memory locations	none
Atomic increment	Atomically increment an integer value	IA32
Atomic exchange	Exchange register and memory location	Sparc, IA32

might significantly reduce potential concurrency. Table 1 lists examples of atomic instructions and common commercial architectures in which they are supported in hardware[1].

One promising application of atomic instructions is in the implementation of wait-free data structures and algorithms. A wait-free algorithm is one in which any thread attempting an operation on a shared data structure is guaranteed to succeed in a finite number of steps, regardless of the actions of other threads. Examples of algorithms and data structures for which efficient wait-free implementations exist include queues [12,18], double ended queues [6], and union find [3].

A variety of applications have been implemented using wait-free algorithms and data structures. For example, because wait-free data structures do not block, they are ideal for communication between execution contexts that run at different priorities. This makes them useful for operating systems [8,9], where high priority system threads (such as interrupt handlers) may need to access data structures that are also accessed by low priority threads. A wait-free double ended queue has also been used successfully in a work-stealing parallel fork/join framework [4].

Ad-hoc implementations of atomic instructions have also found their way into commercial implementations of the Java programming language. Several companies have determined that use of compare-and-swap in the implementation of `java.util.Random` could substantially improve performance on some benchmarks, and perhaps some real applications as well.

Considering the growing interest in wait-free algorithms and the potential of atomic instructions to increase the performance of Java libraries, we believe that there is a demonstrated need for a general-purpose mechanism to support atomic instructions in Java.

A note on terminology: in this paper, we will use the term 'atomic operation' to refer to an operation on one or more memory locations that takes place atomically. We will use the term 'atomic instruction' to refer to the implementa-

---

[1] 'LL/SC' stands for load linked/store conditional. Note that although double compare-and-swap, or DCAS, is not currently implemented as a hardware instruction on any mainstream architecture, it is a significantly more powerful primitive than single word CAS. Recent research [6,8] suggests that DCAS would enable more effective wait-free algorithms, and therefore it is possible that in the future it will be implemented on commercial architectures in hardware.

tion of an atomic operation by a machine instruction or instructions. (Note that even when a particular atomic operation is not available as a single hardware instruction, it may be possible to synthesize from simpler instructions.)

3   Supporting Atomic Instructions in Java

In this section we discuss several ways of supporting atomic instructions in Java. After weighing the alternatives (see Sect. 3.2), we chose *idiom recognition* as the preferred approach. Idiom recognition is a semantically transparent compiler-based approach, in which instances of atomic idioms are translated into atomic instructions.

Before describing the alternatives we considered, it is worth discussing the criteria we used to evaluate them. We did not want to change the syntax or semantics of the language. More generally, we realized that support for atomic instructions was likely to be relevant only to specialized applications and libraries. Thus, we wanted a technique that was simple to implement, did not require expensive program analysis, and had no impact on programs that do not use atomic instructions. Finally, we wanted a technique that was not limited in the kinds of atomic operations which it could express.

3.1   Idiom Recognition

Our approach is to look for synchronized blocks that can be recognized as an idiom that can be implemented via an atomic operation. An example is shown in Fig. 1. The code shown is part of the implementation of a wait-free queue implementation based on an algorithm developed by Valois in [18].

To allow the programmer to indicate which blocks should be implemented using to atomic instructions, we define a new class, `javax.atomic.AtomicLock`. If the compile-time type of an object being synchronized on is a subtype of `AtomicLock`, we consider this a signal to the JVM to try to implement the synchronized block using atomic operations. If the JVM is unable to implement the block using an atomic instruction, it can issue a warning to the user. We refer to synchronized blocks implemented as atomic instructions as 'atomic synchronized blocks', and all others as 'ordinary synchronized blocks'.

Note that it is illegal to allow both atomic and ordinary synchronized blocks to use the same `AtomicLock`. If we did allow such sharing, atomic synchronized blocks might execute concurrently with ordinary synchronized blocks, a violation of Java's guarantee of mutual exclusion for blocks synchronized on the same lock. In Sect. 4.1 we discuss a runtime technique to ensure that atomic instructions are only executed if they respect Java semantics.

While this approach is semantically transparent, it isn't transparent from a performance point of view; it will not provide equal performance across all platforms. If a user writes code implemented using a DCAS (double compare-and-swap) idiom, that code can only use DCAS instructions on platforms that support them.

```
import javax.atomic.*;
public class WFQ {
    // This lock marks blocks we want to implement using CAS.
    AtomicLock casLock = new AtomicLock();

    private static class Node {
        Node next;
        Object value; }

    // Head field of the queue.  The head node's next field
    // points to the node that contains the next value to
    // be dequeued.
    private volatile Node m_head = new Node();

    // Tail field of the queue.
    private volatile Node m_tail = m_head;

    public Object dequeue() {
        Node next, head;

        // try to advance the head pointer, until
        // either we observe an empty list or we succeed
        while ( true ) {
            head = this.m_head;
            next = head.next;

            if (next == null)
                return null; // We observed an empty queue

            // Attempt to use CAS to update head pointer to point
            // to the next node in the list.
            synchronized (casLock) {
                if (this.m_head == head) {
                    this.m_head = next;
                    break; // CAS succeeded!
                }
            }
        }

        // Head successfully updated; get value from new head node
        return next.value;
    }

    public void enqueue( Object value ) { ... }
}
```

Fig. 1. Part of wait-free-queue implementation.

```
package javax.atomic; // provided by the runtime
public final class AtomicMutableInteger {
  private int value;
  // method implementations omitted
  public AtomicMutableInteger(int initialValue);
  public int getValue();
  public void setValue(int newValue);
  public void increment(void);
  public void decrement(void);
  public int exchange(int newValue);
  public boolean CAS(int expect, int update);
  public boolean DCAS(int expect1, int update1,
        AtomicMutableInteger other,
        int expect2, int update2);
}
```

Fig. 2. A special class to support atomic instructions on integer values.

3.2 Alternative Approaches

Before we delve further into the use of idiom recognition, we briefly describe alternative approaches to support for atomic operations.

Special Classes. A simple way to support atomic instructions in Java would be as methods of special object types. For example, the Java runtime could provide a class called `AtomicMutableInteger`, shown in Fig. 2. This class supports get and set, atomic increment and decrement, atomic exchange, compare-and-swap, and double compare-and-swap. The default implementation of this class in the class library would use a private lock object to ensure the atomicity of its methods[2], in order to allow programs using the `AtomicMutableInteger` class to work as expected on any JVM. At runtime, an optimized JVM would convert the method calls into atomic machine instructions.

The main advantage of this approach is simplicity of implementation. It is easy for a JVM to recognize special method calls and convert them to atomic instructions in the generated machine code. It is also easy for programmers to understand.

The main disadvantage of this approach is its inflexibility; only those atomic operations explicitly named in the API would be supported. We would like to support as many operations as possible, but we do not want to clutter the API with operations that are only supported on a few platforms. Another problem is the duplication that would result from extending this approach to the full range of basic types supported by Java. For example, we would need a `AtomicMutableReference` class for operations on references, etc. This problem becomes worse when operations that operate on multiple independent memory

---

[2] Care must be taken to avoid potential deadlocks in the `DCAS()` method, since two locks would be involved.

```
package java.lang.reflect;
public class Field {
  // ...

  // exception specification omitted for brevity
  public boolean CAS(Object obj, Object expect, Object update);

  // ...
}
```

Fig. 3. Adding support for compare-and-swap to `java.lang.reflect.Field`.

locations are considered. For example, supporting double compare-and-swap for all combinations of operand types would require methods for the entire Cartesian product of basic types.

Furthermore, using special classes would introduce an additional level of indirection and memory consumption. If an application needed to perform CAS operations on an array of integers, the array would instead need to contain references to AtomicMutableIntegers. In addition to the performance penalty of this indirection, the additional allocation becomes more difficult in situations such as real-time Java where memory allocation is much more complicated (e.g., having to decide which `ScopedMemory` to allocate the `AtomicMutableIntegers` in).

Reflection. Another possible technique to support atomic instructions is via Java's *reflection* mechanism. To support atomic operations, we could add additional methods to the `Field` class in `java.lang.reflect`. An example of how the `Field` class could support compare-and-swap is shown in Fig. 3. Note that the types of the operations' parameters are checked dynamically. Similar methods could be added to the `Array` reflection class to support atomic operations on array objects.

The main advantage of this approach is that it avoids the explosion of method variations needed in a statically typed approach, such as special classes. However, it does so at the price of requiring primitive types to be wrapped when used as arguments to atomic operations, and requiring dynamic type checks of operands.

There are many disadvantages to this approach. The primary problem is that under Java's synchronization semantics, it doesn't make sense to talk about an atomic memory operation in isolation. In particular, say you have an algorithm that needs, in different places, to read, to write or to CAS a field. How do you link those operations so that the write will be visible to the CAS? If you use synchronized blocks and idiom recognition, you just synchronize on the same lock object. But with the reflection based approach, you have normal reads/writes that need to interact with the CAS implemented through reflection.

Another disadvantage is that reflection can make it very hard for either programmers or static analysis to understand a program (most forms of static analysis are unsound in the presence of reflection).

A third disadvantage is that it is difficult to implement reflection in a way that doesn't incur a substantial performance penalty over standard field access.

Finally, reflection also suffers from the problem that the API can support only a fixed set of atomic operations.

Magic. As shown in the preceding two sections, both static and dynamic typing of method-based interfaces for atomic operations lead to difficulties. We could avoid these difficulties by bypassing the type system altogether, and allowing direct unsafe access to heap memory. For example, IBM's Jikes Research Virtual Machine [2,10] (formerly known as Jalapeño) has a VM_Magic class which allows direct access to an object's memory, and Sun's HotSpot VM has similar sun.misc.Unsafe class (as of the 1.4 implementation). This class could be extended to support atomic operations. While it is reasonable for a JVM or runtime library to allow such unsafe operations to be called from core libraries that implement VM functionality, it is not reasonable to allow access to unsafe operations from application code.

4   Implementation Strategies

This section describes our high-level strategies for supporting atomic instructions in Java.

4.1   Runtime Issues

Recall from Sect. 3.1 that atomic synchronized blocks are atomic with respect to each other, but not with respect to ordinary (lock-based) synchronized blocks. Therefore, the JVM must prevent an AtomicLock from being used by both atomic and ordinary synchronized blocks.

We considered trying to use escape analysis [19] to prove that all synchronizations on a particular AtomicLock could be implemented using atomic operations. But we believe it would be impossible to devise an effective static analysis for this purpose that would be sound in the presence of dynamic class loading, native methods, reflection, and data races.

Instead, we depend upon run-time techniques to detect and handle standard monitor operations on subclasses of AtomicLock. Instances of AtomicLock are created by the JVM as though they are already locked; thus, any thread attempting to acquire a newly created atomic lock will be immediately suspended. Periodically (perhaps at each garbage collection), the system will check to see if any threads are blocked trying to acquire an atomic lock. If so, a bit is set in the lock to indicate that it is *spoiled*. Once the spoiled bit is set (and all threads are guaranteed not to be executing blocks synchronized on the lock, atomic or otherwise), the atomic lock reverts to ordinary blocking synchronization wherever it is used.

In JVMs using *thin locks* [5], spoiling a lock may be implemented by simply inflating it, avoiding the need for a dedicated spoiled bit in the lock data.

Because the JVM relies on a runtime technique to ensure the correctness of generated atomic instructions, it must preserve the original lock-based code for

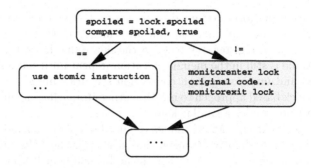

Fig. 4. Code generation pattern to check lock spoiled bit.

each atomic synchronized block, as shown in Fig. 4. It is important that when the system checks spoils an `AtomicLock`, all other threads are suspended and no thread is suspended at a point between checking the spoiled bit and performing the atomic operation.

A consequence of this approach is that if an `AtomicLock` object is used in a way that cannot be supported using atomic operations, there will be a delay the first time the object is used in this way.

We could attempt to translate all synchronized blocks into atomic instructions; however, this strategy suffers from a number of complications. First, all potential atomic blocks must have the object they lock created as though it were locked until spoiled. Thus, all synchronized blocks suffer a performance hit the first time they are executed while the lock is spoiled, in addition to a small overhead for each execution in the form of an extra check and corresponding branch on the spoiled bit. Since many if not all synchronized blocks in a typical program will not be eligible for atomic substitution, we feel this approach is too heavy handed for our lightweight approach.

A necessary but useful feature of our design is graceful degradation. Assume you have a class that needs CAS operations for many of its functions, but also needs DCAS for one function. If the platform is unable to efficiently support DCAS using atomic instructions, it must implement it through lock-based mechanisms. However, while a lock-based DCAS operations is being performed, the system must not perform a CAS operation on one of the fields involved in the DCAS. With our implementation, rather than saying that the presence of a synchronization block that requires DCAS prevents us from translating any of the synchronized blocks into atomic operations, we can translate those that we support. If the code requiring the DCAS is involved, the system will revert to using lock-based synchronization for all blocks protected by the now spoiled `AtomicLock`.

4.2   Translation Issues

In some cases, it is possible to synthesize an atomic operation out of lower-level instructions. For example, if a block is recognized as an atomic increment, and the execution platform doesn't directly support atomic increment but does support CAS, we can implement atomic increment via CAS (load the value, perform increment in register, try to CAS the new value in on the assumption that the old value is still in the memory location, repeat until success). Now, this code can loop and under very high contention scenarios might be undesirable. However, the lock based approach to implementing atomic increment would likely perform even worse under a similar load.

It is also possible to use AtomicLocks to guard simple reads and writes. This would give semantics slightly stronger that declaring the field volatile, which might be useful in some cases [17]. It has the additional benefit that you can also guard reads/writes of array elements (which can't be declared as volatile), and interacts correctly with other operations on the field guarded by the same lock. This is a side benefit of using idiom recognition to support atomic instructions, and is possible because atomic locks simply mark places where it is possible for a synchronized block to be implemented without blocking.

4.3   Memory Model Issues

The Java Memory Model [11] defines the semantics of synchronization to include not only mutual exclusion, but also visibility of reads and writes. We provide exactly the same semantics for synchronized blocks implemented through atomic instructions. This is handled straightforwardly in our technique; generated atomic operations are treated as both compiler and processor memory barrier instructions; neither the compiler nor the processor must allow heap reads/writes to be reordered across an atomic operation. In some cases it may be necessary for the code generator to emit explicit memory barrier instructions to guarantee correct behavior.

5   Implementing Idiom Recognition

This section describes techniques for recognizing instances of atomic idioms and transforming them to use atomic instructions.

5.1   Recognizing Instances of Atomic Idioms

In order to transform instances of atomic operations into atomic instructions, the JVM must recognize them. Because it is not possible to express atomic instructions directly in Java bytecode, a technique for recognizing instances of atomic idioms in the JVM compiler's intermediate representation (IR) is needed.

Basics. Figure 5 shows a template for how a compare-and-swap operation would look in a JVM's IR. We assume that the JVM's intermediate representation is a graph of basic blocks using three-address style instructions. We also assume that the IR is in single assignment form, since this greatly simplifies the task of determining the lifetime of a value in the IR. The template begins with a

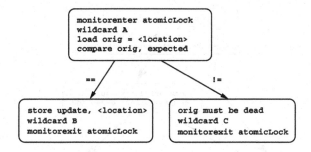

Fig. 5. A template for compare-and-swap in a JVM's IR.

`monitorenter` on an atomic lock, which is simply an object whose static type is `javax.atomic.AtomicLock` or a subtype. The essential features of the CAS idiom are a load of a value from memory, a comparison against an expected value, a store of an updated value to the same location if the original and expected values were equal, and finally a `monitorexit` to release the atomic lock on both branches of the comparison. Additional instructions, indicated by `wildcard`, may be present provided they do not access or modify the heap or have effects observable by other threads; we refer to such instructions as 'incidental'. Note that the variable `atomicLock` appears three times in the template. We require that any template variable occurring multiple times matches the same code variable or constant value in each occurrence. In the context of the template, this ensures that the same lock is used for both the `monitorenter` and `monitorexit` instructions. Any part of an IR graph that matches this template may be transformed to use a hardware compare-and-swap or load linked/store conditional[3].

Our recognition algorithm works by treating each path through a potential idiom instance as a string to be matched by a corresponding path through the template pattern. We place some restrictions on the structure of potential idioms: we do not allow loops, and the only branching constructs we allow are `if` (comparing for equality or inequality only) and `goto`. This language is powerful enough to express all common atomic operations.

A complication arises for atomic operations which access multiple memory locations. For example, in a double compare-and-swap operation there are two ways the operation could fail, one for each comparison. However, the implementation of DCAS (either as a hardware instruction or an emulation in software) is likely to provide only a true or false result for the operation as a whole. This means that a valid instance of the DCAS idiom must use a single code sequence for handling the failure of the operation. In other words, a valid instance of DCAS must be structured as a DAG, rather than a tree. An example of a DCAS template is shown in Fig. 6. There are two paths through the template which reach the block containing the failure code. When matching a potential instance

---

[3] Note that if LL/SC is used, it is not possible to know the contents of the memory location if the SC fails. For this reason, the variable matched by `orig` in the template must be dead when the failure code for the operation is executed.

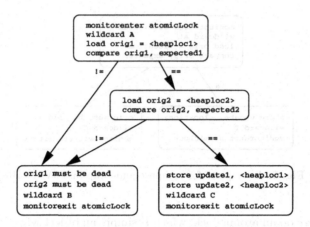

Fig. 6. An IR template for double compare-and-swap.

of the DCAS idiom, the recognition algorithm must ensure that the IR code being matched is also structured with a single code sequence handling failure. Later on we will explain how we handle DAG-shaped templates.

Language and Algorithm. In order to test our pattern matching technique on code generated by a real JVM, we implemented a prototype within the Jikes Research Virtual Machine which analyzes methods for possible instances of atomic idioms and transforms them into atomic machine instructions[4]. The template patterns used in the prototype's idiom recognizer resemble instructions in Jikes RVM's optimizing compiler intermediate representation. The goal of the recognizer is to match the template against a method's IR. If a successful match is found, the matched part of the IR is transformed to use an atomic instruction or instructions[5].

Figure 7 shows the code generated by Jikes RVM for the dequeue() method from Fig. 1; comments indicate the start and end of the CAS idiom. Figure 8 shows how the template pattern for CAS is expressed using an augmented version of the same IR language. (This pattern is represented by a graph data structure within the prototype's idiom recognizer.) The WILDCARD template instructions match 0 or more 'incidental' instructions in the code. Incidental instructions do not directly affect the instructions comprising the atomic operation, but may help convey the result of the operation. Wildcards are labeled so that the matched instructions can be regenerated when the code is transformed. The

---

[4] The examples of IR code shown in this paper were produced by Jikes RVM; we have modified the format of its output to make it more concise and to eliminate redundant goto instructions, but have not otherwise removed or modified any generated instructions.

[5] We have not yet implemented the runtime check described in Sect. 4.1 to ensure the legality of the transformation.

```
label0:
  ir_prologue      local0 =
  yldpt_prologue
  bbend            bb0 (ENTRY)
label1:
  yldpt_backedge
  getfield         temp17 = local0, <WFQ.m_head>
  null_check       temp4(GUARD) = temp17
  getfield         temp18 = temp17, <WFQ$Node.next>, temp4(GUARD)
  ref_ifcmp        temp7(GUARD) = temp18, <null>, !=, label11
  goto             label9
  bbend            bb1
label11:
  ref_move         temp21 = temp18
  goto             label3
  bbend            bb11
label3:
  getfield         temp8 = local0, <WFQ.casLock>
  null_check       temp10(GUARD) = temp8
  monitorenter     temp8, temp10(GUARD)  ; *** start of CAS idiom ***
  bbend            bb3
label4:
  getfield         temp22 = local0, <WFQ.m_head>
  ref_ifcmp        temp13(GUARD) = temp22, temp17, !=, label6
  goto             label5
  bbend            bb4
label5:
  putfield         temp21, local0, <WFQ.m_head>
  null_check       temp25(GUARD) = temp8
  bbend            bb5
label15:
  monitorexit      temp8, temp25(GUARD)  ; *** end of CAS idiom ***
  goto             label8
  bbend            bb15
label6:
  null_check       temp29(GUARD) = temp8
  bbend            bb6
label16:
  monitorexit      temp8, temp29(GUARD)  ; *** end of CAS idiom ***
  goto             label1
  bbend            bb16
label7:
  get_exception    temp11 =
  null_check       temp30(GUARD) = temp8
  monitorexit      temp8, temp30(GUARD)
  null_check       temp15(GUARD) = temp11
  athrow           temp11
  bbend            bb7 (catches for bb15 bb5 bb16 bb6)
label8:
  getfield         temp16 = temp21, <WFQ$Node.value>, temp7(GUARD)
  bbend            bb8
label9:
  phi              temp31 = <null>, bb2, temp16, bb8
  return           temp31
  bbend            bb9
```

Fig. 7. IR produced by Jikes RVM for the `dequeue()` method from Fig. 1.

```
;;; Template for the compare-and-swap idiom.
;;; Variable 'lock' must be an AtomicLock.
label0:
  monitorenter lock, gv1(GUARD)
  WILDCARD A
  LOAD orig = <heaploc>
  IFCMP gv2(GUARD) = orig, expected, !=, label2
  goto label1
  bbend bb0 (ENTRY)
label1:
  STORE update, <heaploc>
  WILDCARD B
  monitorexit lock, gv3(GUARD)
  FINISH
  bbend bb1
label2:
  ASSERTDEAD orig
  WILDCARD C
  monitorexit lock, gv4(GUARD)
  FINISH
  bbend bb2
```

Fig. 8. Template pattern for the CAS idiom, expressed in the IR of Jikes RVM.

LOAD and STORE template instructions access heap locations, and are an abstractions of `getfield/putfield` and `aload/astore` instructions, allowing atomic operations to be expressed on both fields and array locations. The IFCMP template instruction matches any if comparison (of which there are multiple variants in the Jikes RVM IR). The ASSERTDEAD template instruction ensures that the original value read from the heap location is not accessed in the failure branch, since when LL/SC is used to implement compare-and-swap, this value will not be available. (Note that ASSERTDEAD does not correspond to any actual code instruction.) Finally, the FINISH instruction indicates the termination of a path in the template graph.

The recognition algorithm is essentially a regular-expression match of each path through the template with a corresponding path in the IR code. Each template instruction is matched with a corresponding code instruction, except for WILDCARD, which may match a variable number of code instructions, and ASSERTDEAD, which does not match any code instructions. Each time a template instruction is matched, it is mapped to its corresponding code instruction(s), and any variables used in the template instruction are mapped to the corresponding variables in the code instruction. These maps are used by the algorithm to enforce two important properties.

First, the algorithm must ensure that the structure of the code graph is compatible with the structure of the template graph. Recall that recognizer templates may be DAGs, meaning that the same template instruction(s) will be applied multiple times. When this is the case, we need to ensure that each template instruction maps to a single point[6] in the code graph, even if it is reached on multiple paths through the template graph. For example, in a template for the DCAS idiom (Fig. 6), we need to ensure that there is only a single code sequence to handle failure.

Second, it must ensure that a match results in a consistent mapping of template variables to code variables. For this purpose, our algorithm builds maps of variables in the template graph to variables, values, and heap locations in the code graph. These maps are used to detect inconsistent mapping of template variables to code values; for example, to ensure that the same lock is used for `monitorenter` and `monitorexit`, or to ensure that the same heap location is accessed by a `getfield` and a `putfield`.

Handling Heap References. The template language uses 'heap variables' to name heap locations (such as fields and array elements). IR instructions may access the heap in three ways: through instance fields, static fields, and array elements. Because we require the IR to be in single-assignment form, heap references in the analyzed code can be modeled simply as tuples which store the type of reference, object reference variable, index value, and field name; each heap variable in the template is mapped to one such tuple.

Integration with the JVM. Our prototype is integrated into Jikes RVM as follows. The idiom recognizer looks for places where a `monitorenter` instruction accesses a value whose type is `AtomicLock` or a subtype. All known template patterns for atomic operations are applied at these locations[7]. If a template matches, the code is transformed to use an atomic instruction instead of ordinary blocking synchronization (as explained in Sect. 5.2).

Note that in general, a given template pattern will not match every code idiom that could possibly be implemented as an atomic instruction. Therefore, the JVM should document the exact form required to trigger the generation of an atomic instruction at runtime. Ideally, it should provide a stand alone program to check programs offline. Each attempted idiom (marked by synchronization on an atomic lock) would be matched against known templates; any failures would be reported.

5.2   Code Generation

Currently, our prototype implements the code transformation of a matched instance of an atomic idiom using ad-hoc code, based on information collected by the idiom recognizer. A more general approach to code generation would be to use a third graph called the generation template, the structure of which is

---

[6] For this purpose, chains of `goto` instructions and their eventual target instruction are considered equivalent, since the `goto` instructions' only observable effect is to change the program counter of the executing thread.

[7] Currently, only compare-and-swap is implemented.

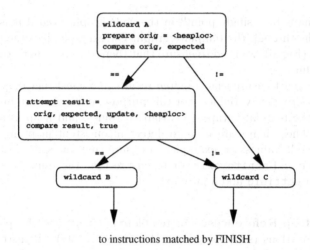

Fig. 9. Code generation template for compare-and-swap.

similar to the recognition template graph. An example of a generation template is shown in Fig. 9. Note that Jikes RVM uses `prepare` and `attempt` instructions to support atomic compare-and-swap. These instructions contain redundant information that allow code to be generated both for systems supporting a real compare-and-swap instruction as well as those supporting only LL/SC. To create IR code from the generation template, the JVM would substitute uses of template variables with their matching code variables, and expands code matched by `WILDCARD` instructions. The original `monitorenter` instruction would be replaced by the first generated instruction in the generation template's entry block, and each generated exit block would be connected to the instruction matched by the code instruction matched by the corresponding `FINISH` instruction in the recognition template.

6   Performance Results

To collect empirical evidence of the potential benefits of supporting atomic instructions in Java, we performed two experiments.

6.1   A Random Number Generator

In the first experiment, we measured the performance of a simple pseudo-random number generator class with an integer field for the seed[8]. We implemented two methods to generate the next random number in the sequence. The `nextInt-CAS()` method uses the CAS idiom to update the seed, and the `nextIntSynch()`

---

[8] We based the algorithm on the `rand()` function from FreeBSD's C library. Originally, we intended to use the `java.util.Random` class from a commercial Java implementation; however, it uses a 64 bit seed, requiring a 64-bit CAS operation, which was not possible to support using Jikes RVM.

```
public class Random32 {
    private volatile int seed;
    private final AtomicLock atomicLock = new AtomicLock();
    private static int nextSeed( int origSeed ) { ... }

    public int nextIntCAS() {
        while ( true ) {
            int origSeed = this.seed;
            int newSeed = nextSeed( origSeed );
            synchronized ( atomicLock ) {
                if ( this.seed == origSeed ) {
                    this.seed = newSeed;
                    return newSeed;
                } } } }

    public synchronized int nextIntSynch() {
        int origSeed = this.seed;
        int newSeed = nextSeed( origSeed );
        this.seed = newSeed;
        return newSeed;
    }
}
```

Fig. 10. CAS and lock based implementations of a random number generator.

method is marked using the Java **synchronized** keyword. The code for these methods is shown in Fig. 10. We found that using Jikes RVM on a uniprocessor Power Macintosh G3, we could generate 1,000,000 random numbers in 312 milliseconds using the nextIntCAS() method, whereas it took 345 milliseconds to generate 1,000,000 random numbers using the nextIntSynch() method. This shows that the overhead of a CAS instruction is less than the overhead of acquiring and releasing a lock in the uncontended case. This result suggests that atomic instructions may be useful for expressing fine-grained optimistic concurrency in real code.

6.2   A Concurrent Queue

In the second experiment, we tested the performance of a wait free queue algorithm implemented with CAS instructions (developed by Valois [18]) against a lock-based queue (developed by Michael and Scott [12]). Because the lock-based queue uses two locks, it permits enqueue and dequeue operations to proceed in parallel, and was found by Michael and Scott to be the most scalable lock-based queue in their experiments.

To add support for CAS, we modified OpenJIT [13,14] to replace calls to special CAS methods with the Sparc **casa** instruction; essentially, this is the 'special classes' approach. However, the bodies of the CAS methods were in precisely the same form as the CAS idiom shown in Fig. 1, so our code would also work using idiom recognition to guide the transformation.

The benchmark consists of a number of threads performing pairs of enqueue and dequeue operations on a single queue. To simulate work associated with the queue items, after each enqueue and dequeue there is a call to a `think()` method, which spins in a loop adding to the value of one of the thread's fields. A 'think time' of n corresponds to $10n$ iterations of this loop. The enqueued objects were preallocated and the tests run with a large heap to ensure that object allocation and garbage collection did not affect the results. We also performed a dry run with one thread before collecting timing results, to remove dynamic compilation overhead.

We performed this experiment on a Sun Microsystems SunFire 6800 with 24 750 MHz UltraSparc-III processors and 24 GB of main memory. We tested three JVM versions:

- Sun JDK 1.2.2, Classic VM, using our modified version of OpenJIT
- Sun JDK 1.4, Hotspot Client VM
- Sun JDK 1.4, Hotspot Server VM

Figure 11 shows throughput for the wait-free and two-lock queues for the Classic and Hotspot VMs. 'Throughput' is a measure of the average rate at which the threads in the experiment perform enqueue/dequeue pairs.

The first graph shows throughput results for 0 think time, using increasing numbers of threads (up to the number of physical processors). Because there was no simulated work between queue operations, this scenario shows the behavior of the queue implementation under maximum contention. The wait-free queue using CAS shows demonstrates much better scalability than the lock-based implementation.

The second graph of Fig. 11 illustrates how the different queue and JVM implementations scale under more realistic conditions, where work is performed between queue operations. The HotSpot server VM, which contains an aggressively optimizing JIT compiler, significantly outperforms the other JVMs until we use 13 processors, at which point the HotSpot server performance tails off to closely match the performance of HostSpot client JIT. This occurs when contention for locks, rather than code quality, becomes the bottleneck. The throughput of the wait-free queue implementation shows nearly linear scalability.

This experiment demonstrates the potential of wait-free data structures implemented using atomic instructions to achieve significantly better scalability than lock-based synchronization when there is high contention. The results also suggest that the combination of a high performance compiler and support for atomic instructions would yield superior performance for any amount of contention.

7   Related Work

There has been a large amount of work on wait-free algorithms and data structures in recent years [3,6,12,18], which have found a variety of applications [4,8,9]. This work has generally been based on type-unsafe languages such as

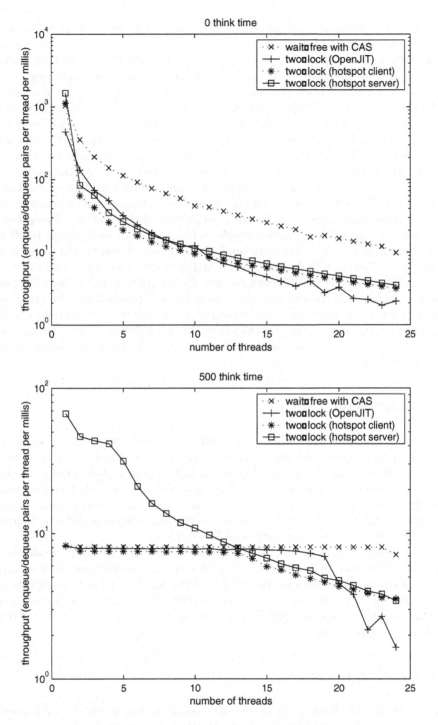

Fig. 11. Throughput results for 0 and 500 think time.

C and C++. Because type-safe languages such as Java use garbage collection, they avoid a variety of implementation difficulties associated with wait-free algorithms, such as requiring type-stable memory. Our work has focused on trying to combine the strengths of type-safety and non-blocking synchronization.

In [1], Agesen *et. al.* describe a protocol for implementing low-level synchronization in Java. Their approach uses atomic instructions to implement a 'metalock' to protect the synchronization data for a lock object. While useful for building locks whose acquire and release operations are fast in the absence of contention, their work does not enable truly nonblocking synchronization.

In [16], Rinard describes a technique for automatically converting instances of lock-based synchronization into optimistic synchronization based on the CAS operation. His approach is based on *commutivity analysis*, which attempts to detect latent fine-grained parallelism in single-threaded object-based programs. In contrast, our approach uses a simple technique (idiom recognition) to allow the programmer to explicitly mark small blocks of code as constituting an atomic operation, allowing wait-free algorithms and data structures to be expressed.

In [15], Pottenger and Eigenmann describe an application of idiom recognition to enable code transformations in an automatic parallelizing Fortran compiler. Their work serves as a good example of the benefit of recognizing idioms in order to perform targeted optimization. Our work differs in that the kinds of idioms we recognize are simpler, and are marked explicitly by the programmer (by atomic locks).

8   Conclusion

Atomic instructions have important applications, and can yield higher levels of concurrency than lock-based synchronization. This paper has presented a lightweight technique for supporting atomic instructions in Java without changing the syntax or semantics of the language. We also presented performance results from a microbenchmark which demonstrate that a wait-free queue implementation written in Java using atomic instructions is more scalable on a large multiprocessor than a comparable lock-based queue.

For future work, we would like to implement our run time check (spoiled bit) in Jikes RVM, and replace the current ad-hoc code generation code with a more general template-based approach. We would also like to explore to possibility of using atomic instructions in the implementation of standard Java classes (such as the collection classes), to determine if we can improve the performance of real concurrent applications.

Acknowledgments

We would like to thank Doug Lea for discussions on atomic instruction support in Java. We also would like to thank Matthew Katsouros for loaning us the Power Macintosh G3 we used to run Jikes RVM.

References

1. Ole Agesen, David Detlefs, Alex Garthwaite, Ross Knippel, Y. S. Ramakrishna, and Derek White. An Efficient Meta-Lock for Implementing Ubiquitous Synchronization. In *ACM Conference on Object-Oriented Systems, Languages, and Applications*, Denver, CO, 1999.
2. B. Alpern, C. R. Attanasio, J. J. Barton, M. G. Burke, P.Cheng, J.-D. Choi, A. Cocchi, S. J. Fink, D. Grove, M. Hind, S. F. Hummel, D. Lieber, V. Litvinov, M. F. Mergen, T. Ngo, J. R. Russell, V. Sarkar, M. J. Serrano, J. C. Shepherd, S. E. Smith, V. C. Sreedhar, H. Srinivasan, , and J. Whaley. The Jalapeño Virtual Machine. *IBM System Journal*, 39(1), February 2000.
3. Richard J. Anderson and Heather Woll. Wait-free Parallel Algorithms for the Union-Find Problem. In *ACM Symposium on Theory of Computing*, 1991.
4. Nimar S. Arora, Robert D. Blumofe, and C. Greg Plaxton. Thread Scheduling for Multiprogrammed Multiprocessors. In *ACM Symposium on Parallel Algorithms and Architectures*, pages 119–129, 1998.
5. David F. Bacon, Ravi B. Konuru, Chet Murthy, and Mauricio J. Serrano. Thin Locks: Featherweight Synchronization for Java. In *SIGPLAN Conference on Programming Language Design and Implementation*, pages 258–268, 1998.
6. David Detlefs, Christine H. Flood, Alex Garthwaite, Paul Martin, Nir Shavit, and Guy L. Steele, Jr. Even Better DCAS-Based Concurrent Deques. In *International Symposium on Distributed Computing*, pages 59–73, 2000.
7. James Gosling, Bill Joy, Guy L. Steele, and Gilad Bracha. *The Java Language Specification*. Java series. Addison-Wesley, Reading, MA, USA, second edition, 2000.
8. Michael Greenwald and David R. Cheriton. The Synergy Between Non-Blocking Synchronization and Operating System Structure. In *Operating Systems Design and Implementation*, pages 123–136, 1996.
9. Michael Hohmuth and Hermann Härtig. Pragmatic Nonblocking Synchronization for Real-Time Systems. In *Proceedings of the USENIX Annual Technical Conference*, pages 217–230, 2001.
10. Jikes RVM, http://oss.software.ibm.com/developerworks/projects/jikesrvm, 2001.
11. Jeremy Manson and William Pugh. Semantics of Multithreaded Java. Technical Report CS-TR-4215, Dept. of Computer Science, University of Maryland, College Park, March 2001.
12. Maged M. Michael and Michael L. Scott. Simple, Fast, and Practical Non-Blocking and Blocking Concurrent Queue Algorithms. In *Symposium on Principles of Distributed Computing*, pages 267–275, 1996.
13. Hirotaka Ogawa, Kouya Shimura, Satoshi Matsuoka, Fuyuhiko Maruyama, Yukihiko Sohda, and Yasunori Kimura. OpenJIT: An Open-Ended, Reflective JIT Compiler Framework for Java. In *European Conference on Object-Oriented Programming*, Cannes, France, 2000.
14. OpenJIT: A Reflective JIT Compiler for Java, http://www.openjit.org, 2000.
15. W. Pottenger and R. Eigenmann. Parallelization in the Presence of Generalized Induction and Reduction Variables. Technical Report 1396, Univ. of Illinois at Urbana-Champaign Center for Supercomputing Research & Development, January 1995.
16. Martin C. Rinard. Effective Fine-grain Synchronization for Automatically Parallelized Programs Using Optimistic Synchronization Primitives. *ACM Transactions on Computer Systems*, 17(4):337–371, 1999.

17. Robert Strom and Joshua Auerbach. The Optimistic Readers Transformation. In *European Conference on Object Oriented Programming*, June 2001.
18. J. D. Valois. Implementing Lock-Free Queues. In *Proceedings of the Seventh International Conference on Parallel and Distributed Computing Systems*, pages 64–69, Las Vegas, NV, 1994.
19. John Whaley and Martin Rinard. Compositional Pointer and Escape Analysis for Java Programs. In *ACM Conference on Object-Oriented Systems, Languages, and Applications*, Denver, CO, 1999.

Code Sharing among Virtual Machines

Grzegorz Czajkowski[1], Laurent Daynès[1], and Nathaniel Nystrom[2]

[1] Sun Microsystem Laboratories,
2600 Casey Avenue, Mountain View CA 94043, USA
{Grzegorz.Czajkowski,Laurent.Daynes}@sun.com
[2] Computer Science Department,
Cornell University, Ithaca NY 14853, USA
nystrom@cs.cornell.edu

Abstract. Sharing of code among applications executing in separate virtual machines can lead to memory footprint reductions and to performance improvements. The design of a general and acceptable sharing mechanism is challenging because of several constraints: performance considerations, the possibility of dynamic class loading, dependencies between shared code and the runtime system, and the potential of adverse impact on the runtime's reliability and on ease of maintenance. This paper analyzes these tradeoffs in the context of two modifications to the Java^{TM} virtual machine (JVM^{TM}). The first allows for sharing of bytecodes and class information across multiple virtual machines, each of which executes in a separate operating system process, using shared memory. The second additionally enables the sharing of dynamically compiled code. Their design and performance are evaluated against two other approaches: running each application in a separate instance of an unmodified virtual machine, and running all applications in a single instance of a multitasking virtual machine.

1   Introduction

The idea of sharing executable code gained widespread acceptance in the mid-1980s, with the introduction of shared libraries [1,9]. Shared libraries lower the system-wide memory footprint and enable faster application start-up. Providing support for shared libraries at the operating system (OS) level frees programmers from having to implement the sharing themselves. Today, shared libraries are an entrenched concept, available in optimized forms in most OSes. Due to the popularity of the Java^{TM} platform, it is common to come across a computer running many applications written in the Java^{TM} programming language [10] at any given time. One might ask whether in these settings the sharing of executable code across multiple virtual machines is as beneficial for the scalability of the JVM as shared libraries are for OSes.

In the context of the JVM, executable code includes the runtime representation of classes, methods and their bytecodes, and compiled code for methods generated by a just-in-time or dynamic compiler. Several characteristics of the

B. Magnusson (Ed.): ECOOP 2002, LNCS 2374, pp. 155–177, 2002.

Java programming language and of the JVM make sharing executable code challenging. First, dynamic class loading makes the granularity of sharing small, at most a class. Second, the size and format of executable code evolve during program execution as the JVM identifies targets for optimizations and compiles them. Third, executable code is often intertwined with the runtime state of a program (e.g., pointers to objects subject to garbage collection can be embedded in executable code). Despite these difficulties, code sharing remains attractive because of its potential to decrease the memory footprint of virtual machines and to amortize costs related to on-demand class loading (e.g., parsing, verification, dynamic link resolution) and the architecture neutrality of class files (e.g., runtime quickening of interpreted code and runtime compilations), leading to both improved application execution time and to faster start-up time. This potential can be realized in differing degrees by sharing various forms of code (bytecode, quickened bytecode, compiled code, etc.)

This paper explores some of these issues by analyzing ShMVM. In ShMVM, each application is executed by a virtual machine running in a separate OS process. Executable code is shared among cooperating virtual machines using shared memory. Two versions of ShMVM have been designed and implemented: ShMVM-B allows for class information and method bytecode sharing while ShMVM-C additionally allows for compiled code sharing. This paper describes the design of ShMVM, highlighting the rationale for certain decisions. ShMVM was implemented by retrofitting an existing high-performance virtual machine with cross-process sharing capabilities; the discussion differentiates between issues inherent in the problem of sharing code and those due to the choice of the base virtual machine. The complexity of the internals of the chosen virtual machine swayed some design decisions towards minimizing the number of changes, and in several cases the outcome may be sub-optimal.

Two other architectures are used to evaluate the performance and robustness of ShMVM: (i) the currently standard way of executing multiple virtual machines, each in a separate process, without any sharing among them, and (ii) MVM [7], which transparently co-locates multiple applications in the same process. ShMVM and MVM are modifications of the same virtual machine. This enables meaningful quantitative discussion. We also analyze qualitatively the robustness of ShMVM. The use of shared memory may lead to degradation of robustness when compared to separate isolated JVMs.

This paper should be of interest to implementers of resource sharing virtual machines. In particular we conclude that while sharing code among processes has its advantages, the approach of MVM is better than ShMVM as a long-term solution to the effective use of resources by virtual machines. The rest of this paper is organized as follows. Sections 2 through 4 describe the design of ShMVM-B and ShMVM-C. Section 5 describes relevant code sharing details of MVM. Performance is the topic of Sect. 6. Robustness issues are the focus of Sect. 7. A general discussion is presented in Sect. 8. An overview of related work is given in Sect. 9.

2   Design Overview

Two versions of ShMVM have been implemented: ShMVM-B, which allows for sharing of class meta-data, including bytecodes, among virtual machines, and ShMVM-C, which additionally allows for sharing of compiled code. No distinction is made with respect to sharing between core (system) classes and application classes. The virtual machines participating in the sharing must be identical and must use the same version of the JDK classes. Both systems were implemented as modifications to the HotSpot Java^{TM} virtual machine [18] (referred to as HSVM from now on) version 1.3.1, client compiler, for the Solaris^{TM} Operating Environment executing on the SPARC^{TM} processor. Details specific to the two versions of ShMVM are described in the next two sections. Common design principles are discussed here.

In ShMVM each application is executed by a JVM in a separate OS process. The virtual machines cooperatively maintain a shared area that holds shared data. Whenever a virtual machine needs an item not found in the shared area, it computes the item and stores it there. The shared area is implemented as a memory mapped file. The first ShMVM process to map the file declares itself the primary and initializes the meta-data. After initialization, all processes are equally privileged to use the shared area. The shared area is mapped at the same virtual address by each participating JVM. This ensures that pointers to shared objects are valid across all JVMs. Often, shared data structures need to refer to data which are created as needed by each JVM and stored in their private area. Such shared-to-private references must encode a one-to-many mapping between one shared data structure and many private data structures, one per JVM. Direct pointers to the private area cannot be used for such references for two reasons. First, it would require each private data structure referenced from a shared object to be mapped at the same virtual address in all processes, which is impractical. Second, it prevents garbage collection to relocate private object referenced from a shared object. Our approach is to allocate an indirection table at a fixed location in the private space of each process.

Figure 1 shows how the address space of each process executing ShMVM is divided up into a private area, a shared area, and an indirection area. The last two must be at the same virtual address in all processes. The shared area holds objects that are shared across all processes. The private area contains all data private to a process, including the garbage-collected heap and thread stacks. Objects in any area can reference objects in the shared area directly, using their virtual memory addresses (e.g., pointers p_2 and p_4 holds the address of shared object o_2 in Fig. 1). Objects in the private area of a process can also directly reference objects in the private area of the same process (e.g., p_1). However, pointers to objects of the private area of any process (e.g., pointer p_{3a} in process A, or p_{3b} in process B) cannot be stored in the shared area, since they hold a virtual memory address that may not correspond to the same object in different processes. To solve this problem, each process maintains a private indirection table mapped at the same virtual address (i_1 in Fig. 1): objects in the shared area reference objects in the private area via an entry in the indirection table

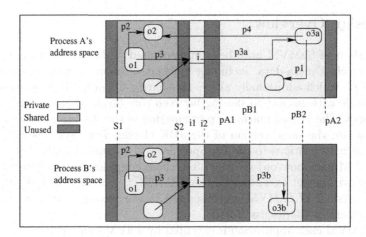

Fig. 1. The layout of memory areas in ShMVM.

(an indirection). Addresses to indirections (e.g., p_3 in Fig. 1) are valid across all processes, and therefore, can be stored in shared objects (e.g., o_1). Each indirections holds the virtual address of the object associated with it, which can be different for each process. For instance, shared object o_1 refers to indirection i, which has the same address p_3 in all processes; i holds the address of o_{3a} in process A and of o_{3b} in B.

Indirections are allocated as needed, when shared data that need to reference private ones are stored in the shared area. A field of a shared object that references a private object either holds a null value or the address to an indirection. JVMs initialize the entries of their indirection table to null. When a JVM uses a shared object for the first time, it initializes the indirections referenced from that object. Indirections may also be initialized lazily, in which case the null value is used to detect whether an indirection has been initialized. The garbage collector running in one process can relocate a private object referenced from the shared area independently of other processes by updating the indirections of its copy of the indirection table. This solution leverages virtual memory to efficiently support the one-to-many mapping between shared and private data.

Appropriate locks guard initialization, updates and look-ups in the shared area. A crash of one process holding a lock on a shared resource must not block forever other processes that are waiting for the lock to be freed. ShMVM's locking mechanisms relies on the atomic compare-and-swap instruction to implement non-blocking synchronization. To acquire a lock, the identifier of the locking process is atomically stored in the lock variable if the lock is not held by another process. The process will spin, yielding the processor, until the lock is available. Processes that terminated while holding a lock are detected by periodically asking for the process groups of all lock holders.

We assume that objects allocated in the shared area never become garbage, and thus are never collected. This assumption is roughly equivalent to preventing the unloading of shared classes and their compiled methods.

Finally, issues common to the design of both versions of ShMVM and of MVM are class initialization barriers and constant pool resolution barriers. A class initialization barrier tests whether a class has been initialized and triggers its initialization if it has not; in particular, the static initializer of this class is executed at this point. A constant pool resolution barrier tests whether a symbol in a class's constant pool has been resolved, and if not, proceeds to resolve it. Since both types of barriers always succeed except for the first time the barrier is encountered, JVM implementations commonly use dynamic code rewriting techniques, such as bytecode quickening [13] and native code patching to dynamically remove these barriers upon their first execution. Problems created by these barriers and respective solutions are described in the next three sections.

3   ShMVM-B Details

In ShMVM-B class information and method bytecodes are shared among virtual machines. The design revolves around the use in HSVM of a very infrequently collected area of the heap, called *permanent generation*, to store the runtime representation of classes, which includes descriptors for fields and methods, symbolic links, class constants and static variables, and method bytecodes. In ShMVM-B the permanent generation is split into a shared generation, shared by all JVM processes, and a private generation. Each process maps the shared generation at the same address. To minimize changes to garbage collection data structures, the shared generation is allocated contiguously to the private generation. Two kinds of objects are stored in the shared generation: (i) summaries of certain information about classes, and (ii) methods (including bytecodes).

3.1   Sharing Classes

In HSVM, the majority of the objects that collectively make up the runtime representation of a class are allocated in the garbage-collected heap. Each heap object starts with a header that includes a pointer to a klass object. The klass object understands the layout of a specific object type and knows how to reclaim it. To amortize the costs of class loading, we initially attempted to put as many objects of the runtime representation of a class (most notably klass, constant pool, and method objects) as possible in the shared generation. This approach presented several challenges: (i) klasses include a pointer to a C++ virtual function table located in private space, (ii) the resolved entries of the constant pool of a klass contain pointers to other klasses, to instances of `java.lang.String`, and to symbols (special objects used by HSVM to represent class symbols), and (iii) if klasses are shared, then the system dictionary, used to locate loaded classes, should be shared as well. For the reasons described below, in each case we decided against sharing.

The first problem is that each klass object contains a pointer to a C++ virtual method table (or *vtable*). Since the vtable is allocated in the process's data segment, it is in the private part of the address space. Indirectly accessing vtables via the indirection table would require changing the virtual method dispatch of

C++, which is not realistic. One solution is to copy the vtable into the same area as the indirection table and to adjust the vtable pointer of klass objects upon their allocation. Unfortunately, the exact size of the vtable is difficult to compute without compiler support. Another, arguably clumsy solution would be to ensure that the vtables are loaded at the same addresses in all the virtual machines.

Sharing only the unresolved part of a constant pool requires changing its resolved entries so that they reference entries of the indirection table. However, the unresolved part amounts to only a fraction of the space occupied by the constant pool. So in effect, allocating one indirection per resolved constant pool entry is equivalent, in terms of space consumption, to replicate the constant pool for each process. The alternative is to share the whole constant pool and to directly reference resolved strings and symbols. This in turn requires pulling those strings and symbols in the shared area, as well as the table used to internalize them. The table of interned strings also records strings explicitly interned by applications via the `intern()` method of the `java.lang.String` class. This complicates sharing substantially, not the least by adding much more cross-process synchronization.

HSVM keeps track of all the klass objects in a system dictionary. If klass objects are stored in the shared area, the system dictionary needs to move there as well. The system dictionary contains private heap-allocated objects. If the system dictionary is shared, we must ensure that classes loaded by custom class loaders (i.e., not by the bootstrap or system class loaders) are isolated; allocating these classes in private space can accomplish this. Also, we would have to ensure that the protection domain of a class is not shared.

In addition to the difficulties it brings, sharing klass and constant pool objects would result in numerous cascading modifications to the existing run-time system, which goes against our goal of minimizing the changes to HSVM. The solution we finally opted for was to store klass summary objects in the shared area. Klass summary objects contain all information found in the class file as well as size information that is computed when a klass object is constructed. Klass information specific to an instance of the virtual machine, such as the class initialization state, and information that can be easily recomputed, are not stored in the summary object. The system dictionary is modified to look up summary objects in the shared generation. If a summary object is found, it is used to construct a klass object; otherwise, the runtime attempts to load the class file. To avoid class versioning problems, summary objects are only added to the shared heap for classes loaded with the bootstrap or system class loader.

The klass summary object contains a pointer to a copy of the class's constant pool. Unlike a klass object's constant pool, this copy does not have pointers to resolved classes or to instances of `String`, since link resolution should be performed at runtime by the individual virtual machines. The copy contains pointers to symbols in the shared heap. Tables of interned strings and symbols are privately maintained by each process, and do not contain any of the symbol objects of the shared area. Because of this, in ShMVM, shared and private symbols are compared using their values instead of their addresses.

The klass summary also contains pointers to shared symbols for the names of the class's super class, interfaces, and source file. These symbols are handled in the same way as shared symbols pointed to by the constant pool. Other objects pointed to by klass objects, namely field description array, the inner class description array, and method descriptions, are shared with the klass summary object. The first two of these object types are immutable arrays of integers, so sharing them pose no problem. Sharing method descriptors is more complicated and will be discussed in Sect. 3.2.

Let us consider an object in a garbage-collected heap. This object has a klass pointer. Since all klasses reside in the private area of the JVM process, if the object is shared, its klass pointer must be indirected through the indirection table. If the object is private we do not need the extra indirection to access the klass object. However, we do not necessarily know statically if an object is shared or private. One alternative is to check if an object is shared when dereferencing the klass pointer. We could also do bounds checks on the shared space. The bounds of the shared space are compile-time constants, so the checks can be implemented without any additional loads. However, at least one branch would be required. Another solution would be to allocate an additional field in the object header that points to the private klass pointer. If the object is shared, the additional field points to the indirection table entry. If the object is private, the field points to the klass pointer field in the same object. This would increase the memory footprint of all heap-allocated objects, diluting one of the purposes of this work. Instead, we allocate an extra `self` field in each klass. This field contains a pointer back to the klass object itself. In each private object we store a pointer to its klass object. In each shared object, we instead store a pointer to the indirection table entry for the klass object adjusted by the offset of the `self` field in a klass object. Figure 2 shows the layout of these data structures. The instruction sequence for loading a klass object, identical for both shared and private objects, adds one load:

```
ld [this+4], klass_indirect
ld [klass_indirect + offset], klass
```

For private objects, the second indirection is redundant; thus, if it is known statically that an object is private, the second indirection can be eliminated. This is the case for all dynamically compiled code (not shared in ShMVM-B). Objects instantiated by the application (such as program data heap objects) are also never shared, and no additional cost is paid to obtain their klass pointers.

3.2   Sharing Methods

HSVM appends bytecodes at the end of objects representing methods. One option for sharing bytecode is to split the bytecodes out of the method object. This required changing a considerable amount of code. Instead, we allocate the entire method object in the shared region. Other issues of interest include bytecode quickening, sharing invocation counters, and dealing with virtual method tables (*vtables*).

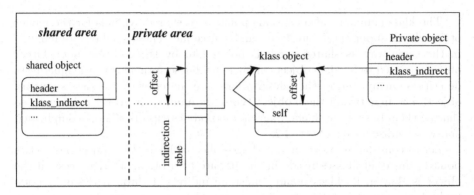

Fig. 2. Accessing klass objects in ShMVM.

Bytecode Quickening. Bytecode rewriting, or quickening, is used to remove class initialization and constant pool resolution barriers. On its first execution, a given bytecode instruction executes the barrier operation, which sets up state for the corresponding quickened operation, and then overwrites the opcode of the instruction with that of another bytecode instruction; on subsequent executions of the fast instruction, the barrier operation is not performed. For constant pool resolution barriers, the state for the fast instruction is stored in a constant pool cache. Since bytecodes are shared, one virtual machine may quicken a bytecode and then another may execute the quickened bytecode without performing the barrier operation. This will cause the second virtual machine to crash since certain initialization actions are not performed. Disabling quickening completely ensures the barriers are always executed correctly. However, quickening is integrated tightly into the structure of the HSVM interpreter; the un-quickened versions of the bytecodes only perform the barrier operation while implementation of the actual bytecode operation is left to the quickened version of the bytecode. Our solution is to dynamically un-quicken bytecodes if the barrier operation has not been executed.

To simplify the implementation, quickening of the `new` bytecode and of the bytecode sequence `aload_0; getfield` was completely disabled. Unlike most of the other bytecodes, quickening of these bytecodes is not required for correct execution of HSVM. Quickening of the `ldc` bytecode for non-string constants need not be disabled at all. The slow version of these bytecodes is used solely to determine the type of the constant so that the correct load instruction is executed by the quickened bytecode. In HSVM, the slow version of `ldc` for string constants may construct a `String` instance and install a pointer to it in the constant pool. In ShMVM-B the fast version of this bytecode also performs this operation.

The other bytecodes that may be quickened perform class constant pool resolution barriers or class initialization barriers. When executed, these bytecodes update the constant pool cache and then rewrite the bytecode. When a quickened bytecode is executed, we test if the constant pool cache for that bytecode is valid. If the cache is valid, the execution of the quickened bytecode can continue. Otherwise, the execution is dispatched to the un-quickened version of the bytecode. The bytecode is not re-written with the un-quickened version since this may result in a race condition. The code for the un-quickened bytecode will rewrite the bytecode with the fast bytecode, but this is safe since the same quickened opcode will be written. Testing the constant pool cache entry validity requires only a null pointer check.

Sharing of Invocation Counters. HSVM uses method invocation counters to determine which methods are frequently invoked. A method is compiled when its counter reaches a certain threshold value. In ShMVM-B the invocation counter of a method may be shared (default) or private, depending on a runtime flag.

If counters are shared, methods "hot" in one application may cause compilation of the method by another virtual machine. Hopefully, such methods will be hot in other applications as well. Virtual machines that start later will compile hot methods earlier than they would have with private invocation counters. Less time will be spent executing interpreted code while the invocation counter rises toward the compilation threshold. However, compilation may occur in several virtual machines that execute a given method even if in an individual application the method would not have reached the compilation threshold. This compilation may decrease the aggregate throughput. If the shared region exists for a long enough time, a new virtual machine attaching to it may behave as if all of the methods it executes required compilation on first invocation.

Private invocation counters are implemented by creating a one-element array in private space and a pointer to it through the indirection table in the method description object. This requires two extra indirections to access the counter compared to the path length of accessing shared counters. Since only the interpreter uses the counters, the overhead of these extra loads is negligible.

Method Vtable Index. Klass object embeds a vtable that contains pointers to method descriptors. Each descriptor includes the index to the vtable entry where its pointer is stored. Because method descriptors are shared, vtable indexes must be valid for all virtual machines.

In HSVM, the vtable is ordered by comparing addresses of the symbols holding each method name. Symbols are allocated in the permanent generation and their relative order remains fixed. However, two processes may allocate symbols at different addresses. The vtable sorting implementation was consequently changed in ShMVM to do string comparisons on method names.

4   Details on ShMVM-C

ShMVM-C extends ShMVM-B with the ability to share dynamically compiled code. In particular, a virtual machine can execute the native code of a method already compiled by another virtual machine, without having to interpret the method at all. In HSVM compiled methods (called nmethods) are stored in a contiguous area of memory called the code cache. In ShMVM-C this area is mapped at the same address in all virtual machines. Since only method description objects (already located in the shared area – Sect. 3.2) contain references to their corresponding nmethods, no new infrastructure for finding nmethods had to be implemented. In particular, whereas ShMVM-B needs an indirection from a method object to its nmethod, ShMVM-C can use a direct pointer, like HSVM.

Sharing the code cache raises several issues. First, the code cache refers to many data structures dynamically allocated outside of the code cache or the garbage collected heap. Examples of such data structures include small fragments of code, maps of object references, and caches of exception handler locations. These data structures must be accessible to all processes using the code cache and were therefore moved into the code cache for simplicity. References in these data structures to objects stored in the garbage collected were indirected.

Second, the dynamic compiler embeds pointers to objects allocated in the garbage-collected heap in the code that it emits. This includes pointers to klasses, methods, instances of `java.lang.String` and `java.lang.Class`, and objects implementing inline caches. In ShMVM-C, all such embedded pointers must refer to locations shared between processes in order for the compiled code to be sharable.

Method objects are already in the shared generation, and thus can be left embedded in compiled code. Inline cache objects serve an optimization that significantly speeds up the dispatch of virtual methods. For both simplicity and efficiency, they were moved into the shared generation so that they can be referenced directly. Klass objects, for reasons already explained in Sect. 3.1, are not shared, and therefore the indirection mechanism (Sect. 2) is used to access them. That is, pointers to the indirection table entries for instances of private klass objects are embedded in the compiled code. The generated code was modified to properly handle the double dereferencing to get to klass objects. Whenever a virtual machine executes a method for the first time and that method has already been compiled by another virtual machine, the first dereference (following a pointer embedded in the compiled code) will return a null value. In this case, the code is dispatched to a routine that finds the corresponding method and properly initializes the entry in the indirection table.

The only instances of `java.lang.String` for which a reference is embedded in compiled code are resolved strings from the constant pool of the class of the compiled method. For each such string, the corresponding `ldc` bytecode instruction contains the constant pool index for this string. As for classes, pointers to these strings are replaced with pointers to entries in the indirection table. After each dereference of such a pointer, the compiler inserts a null pointer test that branches to an upcall to the runtime. The upcall specifies the index of the constant pool where the string may be found. Thus, when a process dereferences this embedded pointer for the first time the upcall to the runtime will find the corresponding local string and update the indirection table entry accordingly before resuming execution of the compiled code. With these changes, compiled code does not contain any direct pointers to virtual memory areas that are private to one process, making it sharable across virtual machines.

Another issue is related to class initialization barriers. Each klass whose pointer can be embedded in compiled code is associated with two consecutive entries in the indirection table. Each of these entries can contain either a null value or the pointer to the klass object private to the current process. The first entry corresponds to the loaded status (the null value indicates that the class has not been loaded yet) and the second one to the initialized status (the null value indicates that the class has not been initialized yet). Upon loading of a class the "loaded" entry is updated with the klass pointer, but its "initialized" entry is left set to the null value. Compiled code must test the value of the second entry at places that may trigger the initialization of a class, i.e., in code generated for `new`, `getstatic`, `putstatic`, and `invokestatic` bytecode instructions. Using this organization, access to a class at points requiring test for class initialization adds only two instructions to the original sequence generated by HSVM:

```
sethi hi(ind_tbl_entry_addr), entry
ld [entry + lo(ind_tbl_entry_addr)], k
brz,k,a class_initialization_stub
ld [entry+4], k
```

The original pair of `sethi`/`add` instructions is replaced with a pair `sethi`/`ld` to embed a pointer to an entry in the indirection table, instead of a pointer to a klass object. A branch on a register value tests the result of the introduced load added to obtain the klass pointer from the indirection. When the class is not already initialized, the load in the annulled delay slot of the branch instruction stores the contents of the second entry in the register, and control is transferred to a stub that invokes the runtime class initialization routine.

5   Code Sharing in MVM

MVM [7] is an implementation of the JVM capable of executing many programs simultaneously within a single OS process. MVM supports all the features and APIs of the Java platform. Multiple invocations of the standard invocation API within a single process actually result in the creation of multiple instances of the JVM within that process, each capable of executing a program. Each JVM instance, referred as a task hereafter, is a set of data structures that captures the part of the execution context of a program that cannot be shared (e.g., static variables, class initialization status, etc.). The aggressive sharing of the JVM data structures and of the runtime representation of classes, including dynamically compiled code, contributes to making the size of a program execution context small. Privileged programs can create and control tasks using a preliminary version of the application isolation API [12].

For the purpose of comparison with the other approaches to code sharing explored in this paper, only the changes to the runtime representation of classes, to the interpreter, and to the dynamic compiler are described in what follows.

5.1   Shared Class Runtime Representation

Sharing heap-allocated runtime representations of classes is problematic in ShMVM because each program executes in different address space. MVM does not suffer from this since all tasks execute in the same address space and have access to the heap. Therefore, sharing data accross tasks does not require using a different pointer format or removing objects from under the contol of the garbage collector. As a result, MVM barely changes the runtime representation of classes used in HSVM.

Most of the runtime representation of a class is already independent of any particular execution context and can therefore be shared as is. This sharable portion includes the constant pool, debugging information, the descriptions of methods and fields, including information resolved at runtime such as the offset of an instance variable from the beginning of an object or the index of a method in a virtual table, and, given appropriate changes to the interpreter, the bytecode of methods. The runtime constant pool cache (a subset of the runtime constant pool optimized for use by both the interpreter and code produced by the runtime compiler) can also be shared after a few minor modifications.

Data that cannot be shared across program execution contexts, that is, the task-dependent data, are relatively small, and include the storage for static variables, the objects that constitute the program-visible representation of classes, such as instances of `java.lang.Class` and other relevant objects (e.g., class loader, signers, etc.), and data describing the initialization state of the class. In HSVM, all of the above is either embedded in, or referenced from, a single heap-allocated klass object (Sect. 3.1).

MVM replaces the task-dependent data of each klass object with a single reference to an array of references to taskKlassMirror objects (TKMs). Each TKM encapsulates the task-dependent part of a class for a given task. Both TKM tables and TKMs are heap-allocated. TKM tables are sized to correspond to the maximum number of tasks supported. Tasks are uniquely identified within the virtual machine using an index to a task table that keeps track of ongoing tasks. Each program thread is tagged with the unique identifier of its task and always runs in the context of the same task. Obtaining the TKM corresponding to a given task is a matter of indexing the TKM table of the corresponding klass with the current task's identifier stored in the current thread.

5.2   Task-Reentrant Initialization Barriers

Class initialization barriers cannot be entirely eliminated in MVM because both bytecodes and the code generated by the dynamic compiler are shared by multiple tasks, which may each be at different stages of initialization for a given class. Testing whether a task has initialized a class amounts to checking whether the entry in the class's task table for that task is non-null. The testing part of the class initialization barrier takes three instructions: loading a unique internal task identifier from the current thread data structure, loading the address of the corresponding TKM from the class's task table (indexed by the task identifier), and then branching to the appropriate class initialization code if the returned address is null.

Both the initialization status of a class and the thread initializing it are kept in the TKM. The main issue is to locate the TKM corresponding to the initializing task when one of its threads is dispatched to the runtime to initialize the class. The entry in the TKM table cannot be used to store the TKM created by the task during class load but before the class is initialized for this task, because this would invalidate the null pointer test performed upon a class initialization barrier. A scheme similar to the one described in Sect. 4 addresses this issue: the TKM table holds two references to the same TKM for each task. Each reference is set up at a different time: the first one is set up during class loading, and the second one once the class is fully initialized. Class initialization barriers test the second entry only: when the test performed by the barrier fails, the TKM for the current task can be simply obtained from the first entry. The first entry is also useful for accessing the static variables of a class for a given task when the task is not fully initialized (e.g., an access to the static variable may be required by the thread initializing the class while executing a static initializer of the class).

5.3   Bytecode Interpretation

MVM leaves the interpretation of all standard bytecodes unchanged. Modifications are required only for the interpretation of some of the quick versions of bytecodes, and for the handling of synchronized static methods, which requires finding the instance of `java.lang.Class` that represents the class for the current task in order to enter its monitor.

As explained in Sect. 5.2, all class initialization barriers that are eliminated by bytecode quickening need to be re-introduced. This affects four bytecodes only: the quick versions of `new`, `invokestatic`, `getstatic`, and `putstatic`. The first two require an additional load instruction before the barrier code described in Sect. 5.2 in order to fetch the TKM table of the class. The net increase in the path-length of these bytecodes is thus 4 instructions. The quickened versions of `getstatic` and `putstatic` need, in addition to the class initialization barrier, the TKM of the current task to access the static variables of the class. A cost-free side effect of the barrier is to set a register to the TKM of a class. Thus, once the barrier is passed, the static variable can be obtained with a single memory load. This only adds 3 instructions to the path-length of `getstatic` and `putstatic` because the constant pool cache entries for these instructions have been modified to store a reference to a class's TKM table instead of a reference to a klass.

5.4   Sharing Compiled Code

Because MVM executes all programs in the same address space, it did not introduce many of the compiler-related problems that were encountered during the design of ShMVM-C. In particular, no changes were necessary to deal with embedded pointers (see Sect. 4). The code originally emitted by HSVM's compiler can almost be shared as is between tasks. The only aspect that needed care is class initialization barriers.

MVM addresses this problem by augmenting the compiler with a set of simple optimizations that determine, independently of any runtime state, when a class initialization barrier is necessary, and generate a task re-entrant class initialization barrier if so. In particular, class initialization barriers are omitted if their target is one of (i) the class defining the method being compiled, (ii) a super-class of the above, (iii) a class initialized at virtual machine startup whose initialization was not triggered by the method being compiled, or (iv) a class for which a barrier has been already emitted upward the instruction stream of the method being compiled. Because the dynamic compiler now generates code that does not make any assumptions about the initialization state of classes, new tasks entering the system can immediately start executing the native code of a method already compiled by other tasks, without having to interpret the method at all.

Two additional modifications to the compiler make the compiled code task re-entrant. First, code generated to access static variables is modified to obtain the reference to the TKM corresponding to the current task, where the static variables are stored. The reference to the TKM is either obtained via a class initialization barrier (if present), or more directly, by indexing the class's TKM table with the current task's identifier. Second, code generated to enter and to exit a class's monitor is modified to locate the appropriate instance of java.lang.Class.

6   Performance

To gain insight into the performance of ShMVM, we measured its start-up time, the performance of the SPEC JVM98 benchmarks [17], and the footprint savings. The experimental setup consists of a Sun Enterprise^{TM} server with four UltraSPARC^{TM} II processors, with 4GB of main memory, running the Solaris Operating Environment, version 8. The code base of HSVM (Sect. 2) is used as the implementation basis for ShMVM and for MVM.

6.1   Start-Up Latency

We define start-up latency as the time elapsed between issuing the java command and the moment when the main method of the class specified in command line argument begins execution. For HSVM this was measured by recording the total execution time required to execute *JustReturn*, an application that has only the return statement in its main method. This captures the process startup time and the bootstrapping of the virtual machine present in each execution. The same approach was used to measure the start-up latency of ShMVM. The typical use of ShMVM is as a number of virtual machines collectively maintaining a shared area; since only the first of them will initialize bootstrap-related information in the shared area, the start-up latency reported here is for a subsequent execution

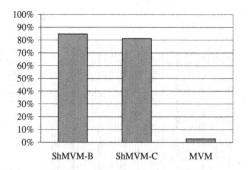

Fig. 3. Startup latency of ShMVM-B, ShMVM-C, and MVM relative to HSVM.

of ShMVM. For MVM the following strategy was used: a simple application manager, which executes as a task, listens on a socket. Whenever a request arrives, the manager immediately starts a new task to execute *JustReturn* and replies with an "ok" message upon termination of that task. The time elapsing between sending the request and receiving the reply is reported as MVM's start-up time. This reflects the intended use of MVM as a multi-tasking virtual machine, in contrast to the HSVM and ShMVM models, in which JVM OS processes are started for each new application.

The results relative to the start-up time of HSVM are presented in Fig. 3. The modest decrease gained in ShMVM is a result of a faster bootstrap sequence, which does not require loading system classes shared in this architecture. However, the bulk of the startup latency is related to starting an OS process and initializing the runtime. In MVM these issues are not present in the start-up of a task. As a consequence, the start-up latency result is only 2.7% of the time necessary to start up HSVM.

6.2 Application Performance

Total application execution time is another measure of performance impact. The same experimental strategy as with start-up latency measurements was used to execute SPEC JVM98 benchmarks. The execution time may differ depending on how many times a given benchmark has been executed before.

For ShMVM-B, the first execution will typically be longer, as it needs to compute the data stored in the shared area. Since no new classes are loaded after the first execution of the benchmark, the execution time of the second and subsequent executions (instances) of the benchmark are the same. For ShMVM-C, the execution time of any instance of the benchmark can be faster than the previous one as more compiled methods may become available. Similar effects can be observed for MVM for the same reasons.

We ran both versions of ShMVM with shared and with private invocation counters (Sect. 3.2). We have not noticed any significant differences in the execution time between these two schemes, which implies that for these programs the effect of shared invocation counters is negligible. Results are reported on Fig. 4.

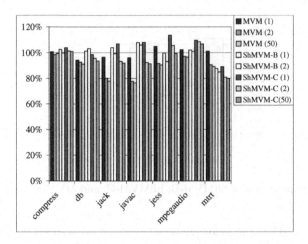

Fig. 4. Performance of ShMVM-B, ShMVM-C, and MVM relative to HSVM.

For ShMVM and for MVM the numbers in parentheses indicate which instance of the benchmark was measured. Several observations can be made. First, for both MVM and ShMVM-C the difference in execution time between the second and the fiftieth instance of any of the benchmarks is much smaller than the difference between the first and the second instance. This indicates that all the "hot" methods are compiled during the first execution and the subsequent compilations of "colder" methods do not impact performance for these programs. The situation may be different for other programs, with more dynamic and less predictable class loading and method execution behavior. Second, MVM is faster than any of the versions of ShMVM for all but one benchmark. The reason for mtrt behaving this way is not clear. In the case of ShMVM-B the slowdown relative to MVM is understandable, since it does not enjoy the benefits of shared compiled code. Shared-to-private references planted in the generated code make ShMVM-C slower than MVM. In particular, two such references are followed on a non-static method invocation.

These measurements indicate that the costs of handling shared-to-private references outweigh the benefits of sharing compiled code. Finally, when compared to HSVM, the first execution of a benchmark under MVM executes on the average in the same time as with HSVM, while ShMVM-B and ShMVM-C are typically slower than HSVM. This is due to the cost of storing data in the shared area.

6.3   Memory Footprint

The sizes of shared areas are shown in Table 1. The first column contains the size of the shared generation in ShMVM-B after the execution of the first instance of a benchmark. This does not change after later executions for the same benchmark, since for the SPEC JVM98 programs the set of loaded classes is always the same. The next three columns contain, respectively: the size of the code cache after

Table 1. Size (in KB) of the shared generation and code cache in ShMVM.

	ShMVM-B	ShMVM-C (1)	ShMVM-C (2)	ShMVM-C (50)
compress	297	96	96	96
db	304	126	137	686
jack	363	858	859	921
javac	492	1487	1500	1629
jess	392	409	415	582
mpegaudio	364	510	511	577
mtrt	340	396	434	467
JustReturn	266	42	42	42

the execution of the first, second, and fiftieth execution of the benchmark in ShMVM-C (to get the total size of shared code in ShMVM-C, these values must be added to the first column, as ShMVM-C is an extension of ShMVM-B).

The memory savings due to sharing bytecodes are uniform across the benchmark programs, in the range of 300-500KB. For ShMVM-C, the size of the code cache varies much more across the benchmark programs. This indicates that the size of loaded bytecodes and the size of compiled "hot" methods are not strictly correlated. Moreover, in some scenarios the size of data in the shared generation is larger than the total size of compiled code but in some others is smaller, which precludes giving a clear verdict on what is more important to share from a footprint standpoint: bytecode or compiled code.

The savings reported in Table 1 are effective when at least two instance of the same program execute simultaneously. However, bootstrap classes are necessary for executing any application. The last row reports their size (the data was obtained by running *JustReturn*). Bootstrapping stores about 266KB-worth of methods and klass summaries in the shared generation, and a further 42KB of compiled methods in the code cache. These savings are applicable to any application executed in ShMVM. For applications using large sets of classes, such as the Swing package, the savings would be much bigger.

It is interesting to compare these numbers and the memory footprint of a virtual machine process. For instance, the pmap utility reports that for HSVM running *JustReturn*, the size of resident memory pages due to C/C++ libraries (both system libraries, such as libc and libCrun, and JVM-specific ones) is 5.06MB, out of which 4.14MB are attributed to shared pages. This means that starting a new instance of ShMVM (either ShMVM-B or ShMVM-C) incurs almost 1MB of memory footprint due to non-shareable (private) segments of libraries necessary for virtual machine's startup. Thus, unless an application generates a large amount of code, the savings realized by sharing in ShMVM are smaller than the footprint of a new process. This should be contrasted with MVM, where, in addition to sharing class information (including bytecode) and compiled code, private segments of libraries are shared as well.

7   Robustness

ShMVM sacrifices robustness for scalability when compared to executing each application in its own JVM OS process with no sharing among the JVMs. First, errant native code in any of the virtual machines may write over the shared area, corrupting it and potentially causing other virtual machine processes to crash. This problem can be somewhat mitigated by write-protecting the shared area between writes to it. However, this solution only decreases the window of opportunity for the problem occurring at the expense of potentially high performance overhead. Weakened robustness is mostly a result of having a writeable shared area, but on the other hand the largest win in memory footprint reduction comes from sharing things that are writeable, e.g., the resolved constant pool, compiled code, the system dictionary, etc. The largest gain in terms of runtime cost results from eliminating compilation and interpretation by sharing compiled code. However, in HSVM as well as in ShMVM, compiled code evolves at runtime (inline caches, safe-point traps and fix-up of embedded pointers at garbage collection time are the main examples of this; recompilations and de-optimizations are other, more elaborate possible cases). Frequent code rewriting is very likely to make the use of virtual memory protection in order to improve robustness too expensive.

Several approaches may be used to address this problem. First, read-only meta-data images can be generated and then memory-mapped by virtual machines. For instance, desktop applications using a large number of GUI components can benefit from such a solution as all the Swing classes can be put into the shared area. Another approach would be to store meta-data in a server process and access it via copying inter-process communication. This will not decrease the footprint, but performance may improve. A more difficult problem is surviving virtual machine crashes when at the point of crash a shared resource was accessed. While we can detect and deal with locks on shared resources being held during crashes, a limitation of our locking scheme is that a process holding a lock can die, leaving a shared data structure in an inconsistent state. Using recoverable memory, such as RVM [15] or Rio Vista [14], can address this problem. Recoverable memory provides atomic updates and persistence for a region of virtual memory, and allows programs to manipulate permanent data structures safely in their native, in-memory form. A simple, lightweight layer that handles atomicity and persistence is also provided. These transactional guarantees simplify programming by restricting the number of states in which a crash can leave the system. The feasibility of implementing shared meta-data areas for ShMVM with a low-overhead recoverable memory system, depends on what is actually shared.

Yet another alternative would be to encode shared meta-data in shared libraries. Immutable parts of shared libraries can be used to store pre-quickened bytecodes, while the mutable parts, lazily turned from shared to private by the copy-on-write mechanism, would store resolved data forming the constant pool cache. Some of the properties of the shared library mechanism and the optimized support provided by modern OSes makes this approach promising, especially for class meta-data. Sharing compiled code may be more problematic, especially in the presence of code rewriting.

8 Discussion

Even though improvements are certainly possible to our design and implementation, we have enough data for a general summary of the opportunities and broadly defined costs associated with designs similar to ShMVM. In the following discussion, properties of ShMVM are contrasted with those of MVM, since both systems aim at improving the resource utilization of the JVM.

Let us first look at the effort associated with modifying a high-performance, industrial-strength virtual machine. Less design and implementation effort was required for MVM than for ShMVM. Splitting klass data structures in MVM was greatly simplified by not having to deal with different address space issues, and by leaving the resulting data structures in the garbage-collected heap. This led to virtually no modifications to the garbage collector. Also, because of the single address space assumption, practically the entire runtime representation of a class was shared and sharing of compiled code was simpler. For instance, no changes were necessary to the inline cache optimization, and embedding of pointers into compiled code was left unchanged except for places requiring access to static variables and to class initialization barriers. In these cases, embedded pointers to klass objects were simply replaced with embedded pointers to TKMs. Dealing with class initialization barriers in MVM was relatively simple: the only difficulty was augmenting the compiler with an analysis to eliminate unnecessary barriers. Implementing the other parts of MVM, such as fast paths for class loading, linking, and initializing, and accessing mutable parts of classes was much simpler than the corresponding changes for ShMVM.

The use of multiple address spaces has been the main source of problem in ShMVM. Code sharing was particularly challenging. In ShMVM splitting klasses proved much more difficult because of data structures located in the garbage-collected heap in HSVM that had to be moved to the shared area in ShMVM. This resulted in substantial changes to both the garbage collector and the dynamic compiler. Although bytecodes are shared, most of the runtime representation of a class had to be replicated, as well symbol tables, system dictionary etc. As a consequence, other issues, such as the computation of virtual method tables, emerged and had to be addressed.

Choosing MVM or ShMVM shifts the optimization effort to different parts of the virtual machine. For instance, in ShMVM the main issue is handling shared-to-private pointers. Optimizing for this and minimizing the number of indirect references can significantly impact the design of klass objects, of inline caches, of the code executed to interpret quickened bytecodes, and of the mechanism to detect whether a class initialization barrier can be removed. Only the last of these issues is present in the design of MVM. However, MVM virtualizes non-constant parts of classes, and optimizing their access path is important. The differences in design and optimization focuses are likely to become even more pronounced when rolling both systems forward to target a more sophisticated compiler. For instance, a larger number of direct references, such as references to Java objects on the heap, can be embedded in the compiled code. Optimizing ShMVM is challenging in this case. Certain optimizations, beneficial in the case of a single non-shared address space, are difficult to deal with in the presence of both the shared and private areas, and the approach of ShMVM may preclude some of these optimizations. Both MVM and ShMVM would be impacted by more aggressive virtual method inlining and by de-optimizing when an optimistic assumption, such as assuming a class has only one subclass, fails.

MVM is better than either version of ShMVM on all performance-related metrics (more data on MVM can be found in [7]). It is also worth pointing out that ShMVM currently does not have any scheme to change protection of the shared area's pages to increase robustness, which would have a negative impact on its performance, especially for ShMVM-C. However, the following three points must also be weighed in. First, MVM is just another OS process, with a single set of permissions for accessing the file system, etc. This is not an issue for the construction of MVM-based Web servers, application servers, and for single-user desktop scenarios, but the construction of multi-user environments is more challenging. In ShMVM, each virtual machine can have its own set of permissions, which facilitates the handling of multi-user requirements. Second, in MVM user-supplied native code transparently executes in a separate process, which may adversely impact performance. In ShMVM this may also be an issue since errant native code can clobber the shared area. Protecting and un-protecting these areas may be expensive if the shared data is frequently updated. Third, robustness is an issue in the presence of virtual machine bugs: a bug in the runtime system can corrupt or crash all the tasks co-located in MVM. This is also the issue for ShMVM although it has a lower likelihood that the effects of such a bug are not isolated to one application only.

Achieving as much sharing as accomplished with MVM but with cross-address space sharing à la ShMVM requires a great deal of changes to the underlying virtual machine; so much in fact that a from-scratch re-design looks like an attractive option. MVM was easier to engineer, and required fewer changes for better results than ShMVM. Following the ShMVM model may quickly turn into a slippery slope: when one item is shared, it is tempting to share objects pointed to by that item. No matter how the graph of references among runtime data structures is cut by the boundaries of shared and private address spaces, the issue of dealing with references and dependencies spanning these spaces is difficult, especially given the complexity of modern high-performance virtual machines. Minimizing the number of such inter-space references is important for performance, for implementation complexity, and for robustness (if the shared area is writeable). Our experience suggests that removing inter-space references and co-locating all of them in a single address space in a MVM-like style is the most attractive long-term solution.

9   Related Work

Quite a number of projects have aimed at conserving resource consumption of the JVM. The majority of these efforts focus on co-locating applications in the same virtual machine. Detailed overview of these efforts can be found, for instance, in [2,3,5,6,11].

The only account of work similar to ours we have found is [8], which describes IBM's implementation of the JVM for OS/390. This system, aimed at server applications, is interesting in several respects. Multiple JVMs can share system data (e.g., classes, method tables, constant pools, etc) stored in a shared memory region, called the shared heap. The shared heap is designed to store system data but can also store application data that can be reused across multiple instances of the JVM. The shared heap is never garbage collected, and cannot be expanded. The JVMs use the shared heap to load, link, and verify classes. A JVM need not perform any of these actions for any class that has been loaded by another JVM; this includes the bootstrap and system classes. A common class loader is used to share name spaces across a set of JVMs. Compiled code is not shared. The account presented in [8] briefly discusses these issues at a high level, without expounding on challenges and alternatives; it also does not discuss the performance of the system. It would be very interesting to compare the design and problems faced in that work with the issues we had in building ShMVM. This system presents another interesting approach to conserving resources: each JVM is executed in a large outer loop, which accepts requests to execute programs. After a program has been executed and it is determined that it has not left any residual resources behind (e.g., threads, open files, etc), the JVM can be immediately used to execute another request. Thus, multiple virtual machines can concurrently share resources through the shared heap, but additionally, each of them reduces start-up latency via sequential execution of applications.

A similar system is described in [4]. Performance data presented there are promising from the perspective of reduced start-up time, but monitoring and managing the transition to "clean slate" virtual machine can be a challenging task. Compiled code is shared in [4], but no account is given of the complexity and benefits of this feature in their system.

The Quicksilver quasi-static compiler [16] aims at removing most of the costs of compiling bytecodes. Pre-compiled code images of methods are generated off-line. During loading they need to be "stitched", that is, incorporated into the virtual machine using relocation information generated during the compilation. Stitching removes the need for an extra level of indirection since relevant offsets in stitched code are replaced with the actual addresses of data structures in the virtual machine. These design decisions form an interesting comparison with ShMVM, where code compiled on-line is shared in order to lower memory footprint and where the sharing of compiled code introduces an extra level of indirection in certain cases. The approach of Quicksilver may also be complementary to ShMVM and to MVM: certain meta-data can be computed off-line and used to pre-populate shared areas.

10   Summary

This paper discusses the design, selected implementation details, and performance of ShMVM, an architecture that allows Java virtual machines to share executable code. The implementation is based on an existing high-performance virtual machine. Partitioning the runtime data structures across shared (located in shared memory) and private heaps creates numerous problems when introduced into a complex, well-tuned runtime designed with an implicit, inherent, and pervasive assumption of a single, uniform, non-shared address space. After addressing these issues and after the evaluation of our results we conclude that JVM architectures promoting multitasking in a single process are much more attractive as a long-term approach to improving the scalability of the virtual machine. This is, in a way, a negative result of significant value, as various groups have recently contemplated improving the efficiency of their virtual machines by designs similar to ShMVM. Hopefully our findings will lead to faster, leaner, and more robust future virtual machine architectures.

Acknowledgements

The authors are grateful to Dave Dice, Misha Dmitriev, Mick Jordan, Fred Oliver, Glenn Skinner, Pete Soper and Mario Wolczko for their comments and suggestions.

Trademarks. Sun, Sun Microsystems, Inc., Java, JVM, HotSpot, and Solaris are trademarks or registered trademarks of Sun Microsystems, Inc., in the United States and other countries. SPARC and UltraSPARC are a trademarks or registered trademarks of SPARC International, Inc. in the United States and other countries. UNIX is a registered trademark in the United States and other countries, exclusively licensed through X/Open Company, Ltd.

References

1. Arnold, J.: Shared Libraries on UNIX System V. Summer USENIX Conference (1986), Atlanta, GA.
2. Back, G., Hsieh, W., Lepreau, J.: Processes in KaffeOS: Isolation, Resource Management, and Sharing in Java. 4th Symposium on Operating Systems Design and Implementation (2000), San Diego, CA.
3. Balfanz, D., Gong, L.: Experience with Secure Multi-Processing in Java. Technical Report 560-97, Department of Computer Science, Princeton University (1997).
4. Borman, S., Paice, S., Webster, M., Trotter, M., McGuire, R., Stevens, A., Hutchinson, B., Berry, R.: A Serially Reusable Java Virtual Machine Implementation for High Volume, Highly Reliable, Transaction Processing. Technical Report TR29.4306, IBM Corporation.
5. Bryce, C., Vitek, J.: The JavaSeal Mobile Agent Kernel. 3rd International Symposium on Mobile Agents (1999), Palm Springs, CA.
6. Czajkowski, G.: Application Isolation in the Java Virtual Machine. ACM OOPSLA (2000), Minneapolis, MN.
7. Czajkowski, G., Daynès, L.: Multitasking without Compromise: A Virtual Machine Evolution. ACM OOPSLA (2001), Tampa, FL.

8. Dillenberger, W., Bordawekar, R., Clark, C., Durand, D., Emmes, D., Gohda, O., Howard, S., Oliver, M., Samuel, F., St. John, R.: Building a Java Virtual Machine for Server Applications: The JVM on OS/390. IBM Systems Journal, Vol. 39, No 1, 2000.
9. Gingell, R., Lee, M., Dang, X., Weeks, M.: Shared Libraries in SunOS. Summer USENIX Conference (1987), Phoenix, AZ.
10. Gosling, J., Joy, B., Steele, G., Bracha, G.: The Java Language Specification. 2nd edn. Addison-Wesley (2000).
11. Hawblitzel, C., Chang, C-C., Czajkowski, G., Hu, D., von Eicken, T.: Implementing Multiple Protection Domains in Java. USENIX Annual Conference (1998), New Orleans, LA.
12. Java Community Process.: JSR 121: Application Isolation API Specification. http://jcp.org/jsr/detail/121.jsp.
13. Linholm, T., Yellin, F.: The Java Virtual Machine Specification. 1st edn. Addison-Wesley (1996).
14. Lowell, D., Chen, P.: Free Transactions with Rio Vista. 16th ACM Symposium on Operating Systems Principles (1997), Saint-Malo, France.
15. Satyanarayanan, M., Mashburn, H., Kumar, P, Steere, D., Kistler, J.: Lightweight Recoverable Virtual Memory. 14th ACM Symposium on Operating Systems Principles (1993), Asheville, NC.
16. Serrano, M., Bordawekar, R., Midkiff, S., Gupta, M.: Quicksilver: A Quasi-Static Compiler for Java. ACM OOPSLA (2000), Minneapolis, MN.
17. Standard Performance Evaluation Corporation.: SPEC Java Virtual Machine Benchmark Suite (1998). http://www.spec.org/osg/jvm98.
18. Sun Microsystems, Inc.: Java HotSpot^{TM} Technology. http://java.sun.com/products/hotspot.

J-Orchestra: Automatic Java Application Partitioning

Eli Tilevich and Yannis Smaragdakis

Center for Experimental Research in Comp. Science (CERCS), College of Computing
Georgia Institute of Technology, Atlanta, GA 30332
{tilevich, yannis}@cc.gatech.edu
http://j-orchestra.org

Abstract. J-Orchestra is an automatic partitioning system for Java programs. J-Orchestra takes as input Java applications in bytecode format and transforms them into distributed applications, running on distinct Java Virtual Machines. To accomplish such automatic partitioning, J-Orchestra uses bytecode rewriting to substitute method calls with remote method calls, direct object references with proxy references, etc. Using J-Orchestra does not require great sophistication in distributed system methodology—the user only has to specify the network location of various hardware and software resources and their corresponding application classes. J-Orchestra has significant generality, flexibility, and degree of automation advantages compared to previous work on automatic partitioning. For instance, J-Orchestra can correctly partition almost any pure Java program, allowing any application object to be placed on any machine, regardless of how application objects access each other and Java system objects. This power is due to the novel way that J-Orchestra deals with unmodifiable code (e.g., native code in the Java system classes). Additionally, J-Orchestra offers support for object migration and run-time optimizations, like the lazy creation of distributed objects.

We have used J-Orchestra to successfully partition several realistic applications including a command line shell, a ray tracer, and several applications with native dependencies (sound, graphics).

1 Introduction

Application partitioning is the task of breaking up the functionality of an application into distinct entities that can operate independently, usually in a distributed setting. Application partitioning has been advocated strongly in the computing press [11] as a way to use resources efficiently. Traditional partitioning entails re-coding the application functionality to use a middleware mechanism for communication between the different entities. In this paper, we present an *automatic partitioning system* for Java applications. Our system, called J-Orchestra, utilizes compiler technology to partition existing applications without manual editing of the application source code.

Automatic partitioning aims to satisfy functional constraints (e.g., resource availability). For instance, an application may be getting input from sensors, storing it in a database, processing it, and presenting the results on a graphical screen. All four hardware resources (sensors, database, fast processor, graphical screen) may be on different machines. Indeed, the configuration may change several times in the lifetime of the application. Automatic partitioning can accommodate such requirements without needing to hand-modify the application source code. Thus, automatic partitioning is a

B. Magnusson (Ed.): ECOOP 2002, LNCS 2374, pp. 178–204, 2002.
© Springer-Verlag Berlin Heidelberg 2002

sophisticated alternative to input-output re-direction protocols (Java servlets, telnet, X-Windows [15]). Automatic partitioning can do whatever these technologies do, with the additional advantage that the partitioning of the application is completely flexible—different parts of the application can run on different machines in order to minimize network traffic or reduce server load. For instance, instead of using X-Windows to send graphics over the network, one can keep the code generating the graphics on the same site as the graphics hardware.

J-Orchestra operates at the Java bytecode level and rewrites the application code to replace local data exchange (function calls, data sharing through pointers) with remote communication (remote function calls through Java RMI [18], indirect pointers to mobile objects). The resulting application is guaranteed to have the same behavior as the original one (with a few, well-identified exceptions). J-Orchestra receives input from the user specifying the network locations of various hardware and software resources and the code using them directly. A separate profiling phase and static analysis are used to automatically compute a partitioning that minimizes network traffic.

Although the significance of J-Orchestra may appear Java-specific, there is a general conceptual problem that J-Orchestra is the first system to solve. This is the problem of supporting transparent reference indirection in the presence of unmodifiable code. More specifically, J-Orchestra is one of many systems that work by changing all direct references to objects into indirect references (i.e., references to proxy objects). This approach is hard to implement transparently when the program consists partly of unmodifiable code. We show that J-Orchestra can "work around" unmodifiable code, ensuring that it is clearly isolated from modifiable code by dynamically "wrapping" direct references to make them indirect (and vice versa), when the references are passed from unmodifiable to modifiable code (and vice versa).

The result of solving the problems with unmodifiable code is that J-Orchestra is the first automatic partitioning system that imposes no partitioning constraints on application code. (We make a clear distinction between "automatic partitioning" systems and general "Distributed Shared Memory" mechanisms in our related work discussion.) Unlike previous systems (e.g., Addistant [19]—the most mature and closest alternative to J-Orchestra in the design space) J-Orchestra can partition any Java application, allowing any *application object* to be placed on any machine, regardless of how application objects interact among them and with system objects. Any *system object* can be remotely accessed from anywhere in the network, although it has to be co-located with system objects that may potentially reference it. (The terms "application" and "system" objects roughly correspond to instances of regular classes of a Java application, and of Java system classes with native dependencies, respectively.)

In this paper, we present the main elements of the J-Orchestra rewrite engine. We describe the J-Orchestra rewrite algorithm, discuss its power and detail how J-Orchestra deals with various features of the Java language. Finally, we examine some J-Orchestra optimizations and present performance measurements that demonstrate the advantage of J-Orchestra over input/output redirection with X-Windows.

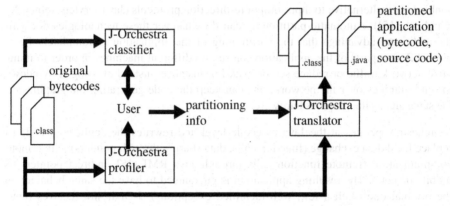

Fig. 1. An overview of the J-Orchestra partitioning process

2 System Overview

We will give here a high-level overview of the operation of J-Orchestra from the perspective of a user (see Fig. 1). Many important details are elided—they will be added in the next few sections. Some low-level details will be left unspecified as they may soon change. For instance, currently the interaction of the user and the J-Orchestra system is done using scripts and XML-based configuration files, but a complete GUI that will hide many of these details will be available by the time of publication.

The user interaction with the J-Orchestra system consists of specifying the mobility properties and location of application objects. J-Orchestra converts all objects of an application into *remote-capable* objects—i.e., objects that can be accessed from a remote site. Remote-capable objects can be either *anchored* (i.e., they cannot move from their location) or *mobile* (i.e., they can migrate at will). For every class in the original application, or Java system class potentially used by application code, the user can specify whether the class instances will be mobile or anchored. For mobile classes, the user needs to also describe a migration policy—a specification of when the objects should migrate and how. For anchored classes, the user needs to specify their location. Using this input, the *J-Orchestra translator* modifies the original application and system bytecode, creates new binary packages, produces source code for helper classes (proxies, etc.), compiles that source code, and creates the final distributed application.

Specifying the properties (anchored or mobile, migration policy, etc.) of an application or system class is not a trivial task. A wrong choice may yield an inefficient or incorrect distributed application. For instance, many system classes have interdependencies so that they all need to be anchored on the same site for the application to work correctly. To ensure a correct and efficient partitioning, J-Orchestra offers two tools: a *profiler* and a *classifier* (Fig. 1).

The profiler is the simpler of the two: it reports to the user statistics on the interdependencies of various classes based on (off-line) profiled runs of the application. With this information, the user can decide which classes should be anchored together and where. J-Orchestra includes heuristics that compute a good partitioning based on profiling data—the user can run these heuristics and override the result at will.

The J-Orchestra classification algorithm is responsible for ensuring the correctness of the user-chosen partitioning. The classifier analyzes classes to find any dependencies that can prevent them from being fully mobile. One of the novelties of J-Orchestra is that regular application classes can almost always be mobile. Nevertheless, Java system classes, as well as some kinds of application classes, may have dependencies that force them to be anchored. As discussed in Section 4, example dependencies include an implementation in native (i.e., platform-specific) code, possible access to instances of the class from native code, inheriting from a class that is implemented in native code, etc. The interaction of the user with the classifier is simple: the classifier takes one or more classes and their desired locations as input and computes whether they can be mobile and, if not, whether the suggested locations are legal and what other classes should be co-anchored on the same sites. The user interacts with the classifier until all system classes have been anchored correctly.

In the next sections, we describe the J-Orchestra classification and translation algorithms in detail.

3 Rewrite Strategy Overview

3.1 Main Insights

J-Orchestra creates an abstraction of shared memory by allowing references to objects on remote JVMs. That is, the J-Orchestra rewrite converts all references in the original application into *indirect references*—i.e., references to *proxy objects*. The proxy object hides the details of whether the actual object is local or remote. If remote methods need to be invoked, the proxy object will be responsible for propagating the method call over the network. Turning every reference into an indirect reference implies several changes to application code: for instance, all new statements have to be rewritten to first create a proxy object and return it, an object has to be prevented from passing direct references to itself (this) to other objects, etc. If other objects need to refer to data fields of a rewritten object directly, the code needs to be rewritten to invoke accessor and mutator methods, instead. Such methods are generated automatically for every piece of data in application classes. For instance, if the original application code tried to increment a field of a potentially remote object directly, as in o1.a_field++, the code will have to change into o1.set_a_field(o1.get_a_field()+1). (This rewrite will actually occur at the bytecode level.)

The above indirect reference techniques are not novel (e.g., see JavaParty [8], as well as the implementation of middleware like Java RMI [18]). The problem with indirect reference techniques, however, is that they do not work well when the remote object and the client objects are implemented in *unmodifiable code*. Typically, code is unmodifiable because it is native code—i.e., code in platform specific binary form. For instance, the implementation of many Java system classes falls in this category. Unmodifiable code may be pre-compiled to refer directly to another object's fields, thus rendering the proxy indirection invalid. One of the major novel elements of J-Orchestra is the use of indirect reference techniques even in the presence of unmodifiable code.

3.2 Handling Unmodifiable Code

To see the issues involved, let us examine some possible approaches to dealing with unmodifiable code. We will restrict our attention to Java but the problem (and our solution) is general: pre-compiled native code that accesses the object layout directly will cause problems to indirect reference approaches in any setting.

- If the client code (i.e., holder of a reference) of a remote object is not modifiable, but the code of the remote object is modifiable, then we can use "name indirection": the proxy class can assume the name of the original remote class, and the remote class can be renamed. This is the "replace" approach of the Addistant system [19]. The problem is that the client may expect to access fields of the remote object directly. In this case, the approach breaks.
- If the client code (i.e., holder of a reference) of a remote object is modifiable but the code of the remote object is not, then we can change all clients to refer to the proxy. This is the "rename" approach of the Addistant system. This case does not present any problems, but note that the Addistant approach is "all-or-none". *All* clients of the unmodifiable class must be modifiable, or references cannot be freely passed around (since one client will refer to a proxy object and another to the object directly).
- If the client code (i.e., holder of a reference) of a remote object is not modifiable and the code of the remote object is also not modifiable, no solution exists. There is no way to replace direct references with indirect references. Nevertheless, the key observation is that unmodifiable clients can refer to the remote object directly, while modifiable clients refer to it indirectly. In this way, although unmodifiable objects cannot be placed on different network sites when they reference each other, modifiable objects can be on a different site than the unmodifiable objects that they reference. *This is the approach that J-Orchestra follows.* A direct consequence is that (unlike the Addistant rewrite) the semantics of the application does not affect its ability to be partitioned. An application object (instance of a modifiable class) can be placed anywhere on the network, regardless of which Java system objects it accesses and how.

  For this approach to work, it must be possible to create an indirect reference from a direct one and vice versa, at application run time. The reason is that references can be passed from modifiable to unmodifiable code and vice versa by using them as arguments or results of a method call. Fortunately, this conversion is easy to handle since all method calls are done through proxies. Proxies for unmodifiable classes are the only way to refer to unmodifiable objects from modifiable code. When a method of such a proxy is called, the reference arguments need to be *unwrapped* before the call is propagated to the target object. Unwrapping refers to creating a direct reference from an indirect one. Similarly, when a method of such a proxy returns a reference, that reference needs to be *wrapped*: a new indirect reference (i.e., reference to a proxy object) is created and returned instead.

A consequence of the J-Orchestra rewrite algorithm is that is supports object mobility. If an object can only be referenced through proxies, then its location can change transparently at run-time. Thus, for instance, regular application objects in a "pure Java" application can migrate freely to other sites during application execution. (An exception is the case of application classes that extend system classes other than the default subtyping root, java.lang.Object—see Section 4.2.2.) In contrast, many instances of Java system classes are remotely accessible but typically cannot migrate, as they may be accessed directly by native code.

4 Rewrite Mechanism

In this section, we discuss in concrete detail the J-Orchestra rewrite model. As described in Section 2, J-Orchestra distinguishes between anchored and mobile classes. Unmodifiable classes have to be anchored, but modifiable classes can be either anchored or mobile. The J-Orchestra mechanisms of *classification* and *translation* are entirely separate. The purpose of the J-Orchestra classifier is to determine whether an object should be anchored (and where) or mobile. This algorithm could change in the future, while the translation mechanism for mobile classes, anchored unmodifiable classes, and anchored modifiable classes stays the same. Similarly, the translation mechanism for the three categories of classes can change, even if the way we determine the category of a class remains the same.

In the following sections, we will blur the distinction between classes and their instances when the meaning is clear from context. For instance, we write "class A refers to class B" to mean that an instance of A may hold a reference to an instance of B.

4.1 Classification

Classes may have to be anchored if they have native methods or if they may potentially be manipulated by native code. For example, J-Orchestra's rewrite engine deems java.lang.ThreadGroup anchored because a reference to a ThreadGroup can be passed to the constructor of class java.lang.Thread, which has native methods.

Fig. 2 shows the different categories in which classes are classified by J-Orchestra. The classification criteria for the vast majority of classes can be summarized as follows. (Some exceptions will be discussed individually.)

- *Anchored Unmodifiable Classes*: A class C is anchored unmodifiable if it has native methods, or references to C objects can be passed between modifiable code and an anchored unmodifiable class U. In the latter case, classes C and U need to be anchored on the same network site.

  For simplicity, we assume in this paper that the application to be partitioned is written in pure Java (i.e., the only access to native code is inside Java system

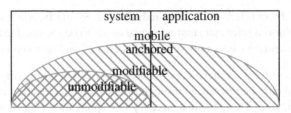

Fig. 2. The possible categories of classes. Unmodifiable classes need to be anchored, but both system and application classes can be modifiable and even modifiable classes may be anchored (by need or by choice). For simplicity, we ignore the possibility of unmodifiable application classes.

classes). Thus, application classes are modifiable—only system classes can be unmodifiable. This is the standard usage scenario for J-Orchestra. It is straightforward to generalize our observations to applications that include native code.[1]

- *Anchored Modifiable Classes*: A class is anchored modifiable if it is a modifiable application class that extends an anchored unmodifiable class (other than java.lang.Object). These classes need to be anchored on the same site as their superclasses.

  Additionally, a modifiable class may be anchored by choice (see Section 5.1).

- *Mobile Classes*: Mobile classes are all classes that do not fall in either of the above two categories. All classes in a pure Java application that do not extend system classes are mobile. Note, however, that Java system classes can also be mobile, as long as they do not call native code and they cannot be passed to/from anchored system classes. In this case, instances of the system class are used entirely in "application space" and are never passed to unmodifiable code. The implementation of such classes can be replicated in a different (non-system) package and application code can be rewritten to refer to the new class. The system class can be treated exactly like a regular application class using this approach.

Note that static inspection can conservatively guarantee that references to a system class C never cross the system/application boundary. As long as no references to C or its superclasses (other than java.lang.Object) or to arrays of these types appear in the signatures of methods in anchored system classes, it is safe to create a mobile "application-only" version. (Interface access or access through or java.lang.Object references is safe—a proxy object is indistinguishable from the original object in these cases.) As a consequence, the categorization of system classes into mobile and anchored is robust with respect to future changes in the implementation of Java library classes—the partitioning remains valid as long as the interfaces are guaranteed to stay the same.

---

1. If the application includes native code, our guarantees will need to be adjusted. For an extreme example, if native code in a single method accesses fields of all application classes directly, then no partitioning can be done, since all application classes will need to be anchored on the same site.

compute_co-anchored (A) {
  AS := set of all mutable system classes and all array types
  A := A ∪ Superclasses(A) ∪ Subclasses(A)
  do {
    AS := AS - A
    AArg := MethodArguments(A)
    AArg := AArg ∪ Superclasses(AArg) ∪ Subclasses(AArg) ∪ Constituents(AArg)
    ArgS := AS ∩ AArg
    A := A ∪ ArgS
  } while (ArgS ≠ ∅)
  return A
}

Fig. 3. J-Orchestra algorithm to compute anchored unmodi able classes

More concretely, the J-Orchestra algorithm to compute anchored unmodifiable classes can be seen in set pseudo-code notation in Fig. 3. This algorithm finds the classes that need to be anchored on the same site as any one of the classes of an initial set A. By changing the input set A, we adapt this algorithm for several different purposes throughout J-Orchestra. The auxiliary set routines used in this algorithm are defined as follows: *Super(Sub)classes(X)* returns the set of all super(sub)classes of classes in set X; *MethodArguments(X)* returns the set of all argument and return types of all methods of all classes in X; *Constituents(X)* returns the set of all constituent types of all array types in X. For instance, an array type T[][] has constituent types T[] and T.

We should mention that, anchoring system classes together with other related system classes typically does not inhibit the meaningful partitioning of system resources. For instance, we have used J-Orchestra to partition several applications so that the graphics display on one machine, while disk processing, sound output, keyboard input, etc. are provided on remote computers. This is possible because classes within the same Java system package reference mostly each other and very rarely system classes from other packages. This property means that anchoring group boundaries commonly coincide with package boundaries. For example, all the classes from the java.awt package can be anchored on the same machine that handles the user interface part of an application. This arrangement allows anchored system classes to access each other directly while being remotely accessible by application classes through proxies.

As an advanced technical note, we should mention that less conservative classification rules can also be applied to guarantee that more system classes can be made mobile. For instance, if a system class never accesses native code, never has its fields directly referenced by other system classes (i.e., all access is through methods), and its instances are passed from application classes to system classes but not the other way, then the class can be mobile by using a "subtype" approach: a subtype of the system class can be created in an application package. The subtype is used as a proxy—none of its original data fields are used. Nevertheless, the subtype object can be safely passed to system code when the supertype is expected. The subtype object itself propagates all method calls to an actual mobile object. This technique is applicable as long as the original system class is not `final`. We already use this technique in J-Orchestra but not automatically—manual intervention is required to enable this transformation on a case-by-case basis when it seems warranted. A good example is the `java.lang.Vector` class. Vectors are used very often to pass data around and it would be bad for performance to restrict their mobility: vectors should migrate where they are needed. Nevertheless, many graphical applications pass vectors to Swing library anchored system classes—e.g., the `javax.swing.table.DefaultTableModel` class has methods that expect vectors. All the aforementioned conditions are true for vectors: the `Vector` class has no native methods, classes in the Swing library do not access fields of vector objects directly (only through methods), and vectors are only passed from application to system code, but not the other way. Therefore, `Vector` can be safely turned into a mobile class in this case.

For a more accurate determination of whether system classes can be made mobile, data flow analysis should be employed. In this way, it can be determined more accurately whether instances of a class flow from application code to system code. So far, we have not needed to exploit such techniques in J-Orchestra—the type system has been a powerful enough ally in our effort to determine which objects can be made mobile.

4.2 Translation

4.2.1 Anchored Unmodifiable (System) Classes

J-Orchestra does not modify anchored system classes but produces two supporting classes per anchored system class. These are a proxy class and a *remote application-system translator* (or just *application-system translator*). A proxy exposes the services of its anchored class to regular application classes. A remote application-system translator enables remote execution and handles the translation of object parameters between the application and system layers.[2] Both proxy classes and remote application-system translator classes are produced in source code form and translated using a regular Java compiler. We will now examine each of these supporting classes in detail.

A proxy is a front-end class that exposes the method interface of the original system class. It would be impossible to put a proxy into the same package as the original system class: system classes reside in system packages that J-Orchestra does not modify. Instead, proxies are placed in a different package and have no relationship to their system classes. Proxy naming/package hierarchies are isomorphic to their corresponding system classes. For example, aproxy for `java.lang.Thread` is called

---

2. The existence of a separate application-system translator is an RMI-specific implementation detail—under different middleware, the translator functionality could be folded inside the proxy. Under RMI, classes need to explicitly declare that they are remotely accessible (e.g., by inheriting from class `UnicastRemoteObject`). Therefore, unmodifiable system classes cannot be made remotely accessible, but their translator can. Separate application-system translators simplify our implementation because system classes wrapped with an application-system translator can be treated the same as application classes.

anchored.java.lang.Thread. To make remote execution possible, all modifiable classes that reference the original system class have to now reference the proxy class instead. This is accomplished by consistently changing the constant pools of all the modifiable binary class files. The following example demonstrates the effect of those changes as if they were done on the source code level for clarity reasons.

```
//Original code: client of java.lang.Thread
java.lang.Thread t = new java.lang.Thread (...);
void f (java.lang.Thread t){ t.start (); }

//Modified code
anchored.java.lang.Thread t =
  new anchored.java.lang.Thread (...);
void f (anchored.java.lang.Thread t) { t.start (); }
```

All the object parameters to the methods of a proxy are either immutable classes such as java.lang.String or other proxies. The rewrite strategy ensures that proxies for anchored system classes do not reference any other anchored system classes directly but rather through proxies.

The only data member of an anchored system proxy is an interface reference to the remote application-system translator class. A typical proxy method delegates execution by calling an appropriate method in the remote instance member and then handles possible remote exceptions. For instance, the setPriority method for the proxy of java.lang.Thread is:

```
public final void setPriority(int arg0){
  try { _remoteRef.setPriority (arg0); }
  catch (RemoteException e) { e.printStackTrace (); }
}
```

The _remoteRef member variable can point to either the remote application-system translator class itself or its RMI stub. In the first case, all method invocations will be local. Invocations made through RMI stubs go over the network, eventually getting handled by the system object on a remote site.

Application-system translators enable remote invocation by extending java.rmi.server.UnicastRemoteObject.[3] Additionally, they handle the translation of proxy parameters between the application and user layers. Before a proxy reference is passed to a method in a system class, it needs to be unwrapped. Unwrapping is the operation of extracting the original system object pointed to by a proxy. If a system class returns an instance of another system class as the result of a method call, then that instance needs to be wrapped before it is passed to the application layer. Using wrap-

---

3. While this is not the only way to achieve remote semantics (a class can simply implement java.rmi.Remote and then use javax.rmi.PortableRemoteObject.export() to export objects later on), UnicastRemoteObject provides several important services (e.g., identity), and so far we have chosen to avoid re-implementing them.

ping, J-Orchestra manages to be oblivious to the way objects are created. Even if system objects are created by unmodifiable code, they can be used by regular application classes: they just need to be wrapped as soon as they are about to be referenced by application code.

The following example demonstrates how "wrapping-unwrapping" works in methods `setForeground` and `getForeground` of the application-system translator for `java.awt.Component`.

```
public void setForeground (anchored.java.awt.Color arg0) {
  _localClassRef.setForeground
    ((java.awt.Color)Anchored.unwrapSysObj (arg0));
}

public anchored.java.awt.Color getForeground () {
  return
    (anchored.java.awt.Color)
      Anchored.wrapSysObj(_localClassRef.getForeground());
}
```

`_localClassRef` points to an instance of the original system class (`java.awt.Component`) that handles all method calls made through the application-system translator.

4.2.2 Anchored Modifiable Classes

Anchored modifiable classes are the application classes that inherit from anchored system classes or any otherwise modifiable class that is anchored by choice. Anchored modifiable classes are handled with a translation that is identical to the one for anchored unmodifiable classes, except for one aspect. The defining distinction between unmodifiable and modifiable anchored classes is that the latter can be changed so that, if they access other classes' fields directly, such accesses can be replaced with calls to accessor and mutator methods. In this way, other classes referenced by anchored modifiable classes do not need to be anchored.

4.2.3 Mobile Classes

Mobile classes are able to migrate to various network sites during the run of a program. The migration currently supported by J-Orchestra is *synchronous*: objects migrate in response to run-time events, such as passing a mobile object as a parameter to a remote method. Migration allows us to exploit data locality in an application. For instance, when a remote method call occurs, it can be advantageous to have a mobile object parameter move temporarily or permanently to the callee's network site. All standard object mobility semantics (e.g., call-by-visit, call-by-move [10]) can be supported in an application rewritten by J-Orchestra.

J-Orchestra translates mobile classes in the original application (and the replicated mobile system classes) into a *proxy class* and a *remote class*. Proxy classes are created in source code form, while remote classes are produced by bytecode rewriting of the original mobile class. Proxies for mobile classes are very similar to the ones for anchored classes. The only difference is that *a mobile proxy assumes the exact name and method interface of the original class.* J-Orchestra adds an "__remote" suffix to the original class name. The clients of a mobile class access its proxy in exactly the same way as they used to access the original class.

Mobile class proxies mimic the inheritance structure of their original classes. The remote semantics is achieved by changing the superclass of the base (topmost) proxy from java.lang.Object to java.rmi.server.UnicastRemoteObject.

The example below summarizes the rewrite in source code form (although in reality the original class and the remote class only exist in bytecode form).

```
//Original class declaration
class A extends B implements I {...}

//Proxy class declaration.
//B or one of its ancestors inherit from UnicastRemoteObject
class A extends B implements I, Proxy { ... }

//Remote class declaration
//body of A__remote is same as body of original A
class A__remote extends B__remote implements I, Remote {...}
```

Some care needs to be taken during binary modification of a class, to ensure that the types expected match the ones actually used. For instance, the name of a class A needs to change to A__remote, but most references to type A (e.g., as the type of a method parameter) need to continue referring to A—the proxy type is the right type for references to A objects in the rewritten application.

4.3 Handling of Java Language Features

In this section, we describe how J-Orchestra handles various Java language features. Some of the techniques described here are similar to the ones used by JavaParty (but JavaParty operates at the source code level while J-Orchestra is a bytecode translator). Due to lack of space, we omit some of the more involved topics, like dealing with arrays and object identity. The interested reader can find more information in [20].

Maintaining exactly the local execution semantics is not always possible or efficient. We will identify the few features for which J-Orchestra will not guarantee, by need or by choice, that the partitioned application will behave exactly like the original one.

4.3.1 Static Methods and Fields

J-Orchestra has to handle remote execution of static methods. This also takes care of remote access to static fields: just like with member fields, J-Orchestra replaces all direct accesses to static fields of other classes with calls to accessor and mutator methods. In order to be able to handle remote execution of static methods, J-Orchestra creates static delegator classes for every original class that has any static methods. Static delegators extend java.rmi.server.UnicastRemoteObject and define all the static methods declared in the original class.

```
//Original class
class A {
  static void foo (String s) {...}
  static int bar () {...}
}

//Static Delegator for A--runs on a remote site
class A__StaticDelegator
 extends java.rmi.server.UnicastRemoteObject {
  void foo (String s) { A__remote.foo (s); }
  int bar () { return A__remote.bar (); }
}
```

For optimization purposes, a static delegator for a class gets created only in response to calling any of the static methods in the proxy class. If no static method of a class is ever called during a particular execution scenario, the static delegator for that class is never created. Once created, the static delegator or its RMI stub is stored in a member field of the class's proxy and is reused for all subsequent static method invocations.

A static delegator for a class shares the mobility properties of the class itself. While a static delegator for an anchored class must be co-anchored on the same site, the static delegator of a mobile class can potentially migrate at will, irrespective of the locations of the existing objects of its class type.

4.3.2 Inheritance

Proxies, remote application-system translator classes, and remote classes all mimic the inheritance/subtyping hierarchy of their corresponding original classes. Replacing direct references with references to proxies preserves the original execution semantics: a proxy can be used when a supertype instance is expected. Since it is not known which particular proxy is going to be used to invoke a method, only the base class contains the interface reference that is used for method delegation. This field is accessible to all the subclasses' proxies by having the `protected` access modifier.

4.3.3 Object Creation

Creating objects remotely is a necessary functionality for every distributed object system. J-Orchestra proxies' constructors work differently from other methods in order to implement distribution policies (i.e., create various objects on given network sites). First, a proxy constructor calls a special-purpose do-nothing constructor in its super class to avoid the regular object creation sequence. A proxy constructor creates objects using the services of the *object factory*. J-Orchestra's object factory is an RMI service running on every network node where the partitioned application operates. Every object factory is parameterized with configuration files specifying a symbolic location of every class in the application and the URLs of other object factories. Every *object factory client* keeps remote references to all the object factories in the system. Object factory clients determine object locations, handle remote object creations, and maintain various mappings between the created objects and their proxies. The following example shows a portion of the constructor code in a proxy class A.

```
public  A () {
  //call super do-nothing constructor
  super ((BogusConstructorArg)null);

  //check if we are already initialized or are
  //called from a subclass
  if ((null != _remoteRef) || (!getClass ().equals (A.class)))
    return;
  ...
  //Call ObjectFactory
  try { _remoteRef = (A) ObjectFactory.createObject("A"); }
  catch (RemoteException e) { ... }
}
```

4.3.4 "this"

Under the J-Orchestra rewrite, an object can refer to its own methods and variables directly. That is, no proxy indirection overhead is imposed for access to methods through the this reference. Nevertheless, this means that J-Orchestra has to treat explicit uses of this specially. Recall that remote objects are generated by changing the name of the original class at the bytecode level. When the name of a class changes so does the type of all of its explicit this references. Consider the following example showing the problem if no special care is taken:

```
//original code
class A { void foo (B b) { b.baz (this); } }
class B { void baz (A a) {...} }

//generated remote object for A
class A__remote {
  void foo (B b) { b.baz (this); } //"this" is of type A__remote!
}
```

Method baz in class B expects an argument of type A, hence the call b.baz(this) will fail, as this is of type A__remote. J-Orchestra detects all such explicit uses of this and fixes the problem by looking up the corresponding proxy object and replacing this with it. Furthermore, we can store the result of the proxy lookup in a local variable and use that variable instead of this in future expressions. For example, the rewritten bytecode for foo in this case would be:

```
aload_0        //pass "this" to locateProxy method
invokestatic Runtime.locateProxy
checkcast "A"  //locateProxy returns Object, need a cast to "A"
astore_2       //store the located proxy object for future use
aload_1        //load b
aload_2        //load proxy (of type A)
invokevirtual B.baz
```

At the bytecode level, it is somewhat involved to detect when the transformation should be applied. Recognizing explicit uses of `this` (as opposed to instances of the `aload_0` instruction used to reference the object's own methods) requires a full stack machine emulator for the bytecode instructions. The emulator needs to reconstruct operations and operands from the bytecode stack-machine instruction architecture. This is the only instance where we have found our transformations to be harder to apply at the bytecode level than at the source code level (e.g., like JavaParty does).

4.3.5 Multithreading and Synchronization

The handling of synchronization is an important issue in guaranteeing regular Java semantics for a partitioned multithreaded application. Java has no support for remote synchronization: RMI does not support transparency of synchronization references—all `wait`/`notify` calls on remote objects are not propagated to the remote site (see [18], section 8.1). Nevertheless, it is possible to build a distributed synchronization mechanism that will guarantee semantics identical to regular Java for all partitioned applications. On the other hand, such a mechanism will likely be complex and inefficient, especially if the distribution relies on an unmodified version of Java RMI. One of the noteworthy issues with synchronization is the possibility of self-deadlocks if thread identity is not maintained when the flow of control moves over the network. We will not describe here the complications of distributed synchronization—a good description of both the problems and the possible solutions (also applicable to J-Orchestra) can be found in the documentation of version 1.05 of JavaParty [8].

In the near future, we plan to evolve the J-Orchestra synchronization mechanism, making this description of transient interest. The current mechanism is rudimentary and incomplete. First, thread identity is not maintained when the flow of control crosses the network, creating the possibility of deadlocks. Second, the identity of locks is guaranteed when `synchronized` *methods* are used (which is the most common Java synchronization technique) but not necessarily when `synchronized` *code blocks* are used. When code blocks are used, lock identity is maintained per-site: if all `synchronized` blocks are executed on the same machine, synchronization will work correctly (barring the problems caused by not maintaining thread identity across machines).

The translation to maintain these properties is as follows: for synchronized methods, we only have to ensure that the proxy "forwarder" method is not synchronized—the original method on the remote object will perform the synchronization. For handling `wait`/`notify`/`notifyAll` calls on proxies, we globally detect all such calls and replace them with calls to specially generated methods in the proxy objects (the original `wait`/`notify`/`notifyAll` in `java.lang.Object` are `final` and cannot be overridden). Proxies propagate all `wait`/`notify`/`notifyAll` calls to the remote objects they represent. All remote objects (`__remote` objects for mobile classes or system/application translators for anchored classes) export methods that implement `wait`/`notify`/`notifyAll` semantics on the object.

4.3.6 Reflection and Dynamic Loading

Reflection can be used explicitly to render the J-Orchestra translation incorrect. For instance, an application class may get an `Object` reference, query it to determine its actual type, and fail if the type is a proxy. Nevertheless, the common case of reflection that is used only to invoke methods of an object is compatible with the J-Orchestra rewrite—the corresponding method will be invoked on the proxy object. In fact, one of the first example applications distributed with J-Orchestra—the JShell command line shell—uses reflection heavily.

We should note that offering full support for correctness under reflection is possible and we have not done so for pure engineering reasons. For example, it is possible to create a J-Orchestra-specific reflection library that will mimic the interface of the regular Java reflection routines but will take care to always hide proxies. All reflection questions on a proxy object will instead be handled by the remote object. With bytecode manipulation, we can replace all method calls to Java reflection functionality with method calls to the J-Orchestra-specific reflection library. We have considered this task to be too complex for the expected benefit.

Similar observations hold regarding dynamic class loading. J-Orchestra is meant for use in cases where the entire application is available and gets analyzed, so that the J-Orchestra classification and translation are guaranteed correct. Currently, dynamically loading code that was not rewritten by J-Orchestra may fail because the code may try to access remote data directly. Additionally, dynamically loading code that calls J-Orchestra rewritten code may violate the security guarantees of the original application (we discuss the problem in more detail in [20]). Nevertheless, one can imagine a loader installed by J-Orchestra that takes care of rewriting any dynamically loaded classes before they are used. Essentially, this would implement the entire J-Orchestra translation at load time. Unfortunately, classification cannot be performed incrementally: unmodifiable classes may be loaded and anchored on some nodes before loading another class makes apparent that the previous anchorings are inconsistent. The only safe approach would be to make all dynamically loaded classes anchored on the same network site.

4.3.7 Garbage Collection

Distributed garbage collection is a tough problem. J-Orchestra relies on the RMI distributed reference counting mechanism for garbage collection. This means that cyclic garbage, where the cycle traverses the network, will never be collected. Nevertheless, this aspect is orthogonal to the goal of J-Orchestra—the system just inherits the garbage collection facility of the underlying middleware.

4.3.8 Inner Classes

On the Java language level, inner classes have direct access to all member fields (including private and protected) of their enclosing classes. In order to enable this access, the Java compiler introduces *synthetic* methods that access and modify member fields of enclosing classes. Synthetic methods are not visible during compilation. This clearly presents a problem for J-Orchestra since synthetic methods also need to be accessed through a proxy. The code inside a synthetic proxy method accesses the synthetic method of its remote class. Since proxies are created in source code form, no Java compiler would be able to successfully compile them. Removing the synthetic attributes from methods in remote classes eliminates the problem. The removal does not violate the Java security semantics because there are no access restrictions for synthetic methods to begin with.

4.3.9 System.out, System.in, System.err, System.exit, System.properties

The java.lang.System class provides access to standard input, standard output, and error output streams (exported as pre-defined objects), access to externally defined "properties", and a way to terminate the execution of the JVM. In a distributed environment, it is important to modify these facilities so that their behavior makes sense. Different policies may be appropriate for different applications. For example, when any of the partitions writes something to the standard output stream, should the results be visible only on the network site of the partition, all the network sites, or one specially designated network site that handles I/O? If one of the partitions makes a call to System.exit, should only the JVM that runs that partition exit or the request should be applied to all the remaining network sites? J-Orchestra allows defining these policies on a per-application basis. For this purpose, J-Orchestra provides classes called RemoteIn, RemoteOut, RemoteErr, RemoteExit, and RemoteProperties whose implementation determines the application-specific policy. For example, all references to System.out are replaced with RemoteOut.out() in all the rewritten code. An implementation of RemoteOut.out() can return a stream that redirects all the messages to a particular network site, for example.

5 Performance

5.1 Overhead and Limited Rewrite

As mentioned earlier, modifiable classes may be anchored by choice. In fact, it is a common usage scenario for J-Orchestra to try to make mobile only very few classes. We call this the J-Orchestra *limited rewrite* model. The reason to limit which classes are mobile has to do with performance. The J-Orchestra rewrite adds some execution overhead even when mobile objects are used entirely locally. The most significant overheads of the J-Orchestra rewrite are one level of indirection for each method call to a different application object, two levels of indirection for each method call to an anchored system object, and one extra method call for every direct access to another object's fields. The J-Orchestra rewrite keeps overheads as low as possible. For instance, for an application object created and used only locally, the overhead is only one interface call for every virtual call, because proxy objects refer directly to the target object and not through RMI. Interface calls are not expensive in modern JVMs (only about as much as virtual calls [1]) but the overall slowdown can be significant.

The overall impact of the indirection overhead on an application depends on how much work the application's methods perform per method call. A simple experiment puts the costs in perspective. Table 1 shows the overhead of adding an extra interface indirection per virtual method call for a simple benchmark program. The overall overhead rises from 17% (when a method performs 10 multiplications, 10 increment, and 10 test operations) to 35% (when the method only performs 2 of these operations).

Table 1. J-Orchestra indirection overhead as a function of average work per method call (a billion calls total)

Work (multiply, increment, test)	Original Time	Rewritten Time	Overhead
2	35.17s	47.52s	35%
4	42.06s	51.30s	22%
10	62.5s	73.32s	17%

Penalizing programs that have small methods is against good object-oriented design, however. Furthermore, the above numbers do not include the extra cost of accessing anchored objects and fields of other objects indirectly (although these costs are secondary). To get an idea of the total overhead for an actual application, we measured the slowdown of the J-Orchestra rewrite using J-Orchestra itself as input. That is, we used J-Orchestra to translate the main loop of the J-Orchestra rewriter, consisting of 41 class files totalling 192KB. Thus, the rewritten version of the J-Orchestra rewriter (as well as all system classes it accesses) became remote-capable but still consisted of a single partition. In local execution, the rewritten version was about 37% slower (see Table 2). Although a 37% slowdown of local processing can be acceptable for some applications, for many others it is too high.

By anchoring classes by choice, we ensure that their objects can refer to all other objects on the same site with no overhead. These anchored classes will still be remotely accessible, but their proxies are only used for true remote access. The limited rewrite is particularly successful when most of the processing in an application occurs on one network site and only some resources (e.g., graphics, sound, keyboard input) are accessed remotely. We have used the limited rewrite to partition several applications that follow this pattern (e.g., a GUI-driven demo of the Java speech API, a graphical display of real time statistics from another machine, etc.). In all cases, the execution overhead from J-Orchestra indirection was practically zero.

5.2 Optimization: Lazy Remote Object Creation

Recall that remote objects extend `java.rmi.server.UnicastRemoteObject` to enable remote execution. The constructor of `java.rmi.server.UnicastRemoteObject` exports the remote object to the RMI run-time. This is an intensive process that significantly slows down the overall object creation. J-Orchestra tries to avoid this slowdown by employing lazy remote object creation for all the objects that might never be invoked remotely. If a proxy constructor determines that the object it wraps is to be created on the local machine, then the creation process does not go through the object factory. Instead, a *lazy* version of the remote object is created directly. A lazy object is identical to a remote one with the exception of having a different name and not inheriting from java.rmi.server.UnicastRemoteObject. A proxy continues to point to such a lazy object until the application attempts to use the proxy in a remote method call. In that case, the proxy converts its lazy object to a remote one using a special conversion constructor. This constructor reassigns every member field from the lazy object to the remote one. All static fields are kept in the remote version of the object to avoid data inconsistencies.

Although this optimization may at first seem RMI-specific, in fact it is not. Every middleware mechanism suffers significant overhead for registering remotely accessible objects. Lazy remote object creation ensures that the overhead is not suffered until it is absolutely necessary. In the case of RMI, our experiments show that the creation of a remotely accessible object is over 200 times more expensive than a single constructor invocation. In contrast, the extra cost of converting a lazy object into a remotely accessible one is about the same as a few variable assignments in Java. Therefore, it makes sense to optimistically assume that objects are created only for local use, until they are actually passed to a remote site. Considering that a well-partitioned application will only move few objects over the network, the optimization is likely to be valuable.

The impact of speeding up object creation is significant in terms of total application execution time. We measured the effects using the J-Orchestra code itself as a benchmark. The result is shown below (Table 2). The measurements are on the full J-Orchestra rewrite: all objects are made remote-capable, although they are executed on a single machine. 767 objects were constructed during this execution. The overhead for the version of J-Orchestra that eagerly constructs all objects to be remote-capable is 58%, while the same overhead when the objects are created for local use is less than 38% (an overall speedup of 1.15, or 15%).

Table 2. Effect of lazy remote object creation and J-Orchestra indirection

Original time	Indirect lazy	Overhead	Indirect non-lazy	Overhead
6.63s	9.11s	37.4%	10.48s	58.1%

5.3 Performance Comparison to X-Windows

J-Orchestra is an attractive alternative to input/output redirection technologies like X-Windows and telnet. A good partitioning using J-Orchestra can avoid transferring redundant data (e.g., graphics that do not change, or inefficient representations) over the network. In this section, we compare the performance of J-Orchestra to X-Windows, used to display graphics on a remote host.

All the experiments described are partitioned using the J-Orchestra limited rewrite: only a handful of classes are made mobile, most classes are made remotely accessible and get anchored on different sites. In all experiments, we measured the run time of the original Java application, as well as the run time of the rewritten (i.e., remote-capable) version of the application but executing in a single partition. These two baseline results were identical—the limited rewrite only adds indirection to a tiny proportion of the total objects created in our example programs.

We used JDK 1.3 on two Sun Ultra 10 machines (Sparc II 440MHz processor) connected with a 100Mbit Ethernet network for these experiments.

5.3.1 Window Drawing

We created three different tests of window operations. The first opens an empty remote window. The second opens a remote window and displays 100 text buttons on it. The third opens a remote window and displays 100 graphical buttons on it. In all three cases, the window is repainted 10 times. Each of the three experiments has two versions: one where all drawing operations are initiated from the window object itself and one where the (re-)painting is initiated from a different object. The reason for this last distinction is that we want to produce a more "realistic" comparison by initiating the operations remotely. That is, in the J-Orchestra case, there will be operations over the network for each re-painting, although the graphics for the buttons themselves will never need to be transferred over the network.

The results (run times) are shown below (all numbers are averages of 3 runs that varied by at most 0.5s). The baseline is the run time of a local version.

Table 3. Version 1 of window experiments

Experiment/System	Empty window	Window + 100 text buttons	Window + 100 graphics buttons
Baseline	2.9s	7.2s	6.6s
X-Windows	4.7s	8.2s	15.8s
J-Orchestra	3.1s	7.7s	6.6s

Table 4. Version 2 of window experiments

Experiment/System	Empty window	Window + 100 text buttons	Window + 100 graphics buttons
Baseline	2.7s	7.6s	6.8s
X-Windows	4.5s	8.5s	16.3s
J-Orchestra	4.9s	8.4s	7.7s

Version 1 of the above experiment shows the benefit of J-Orchestra, but the partitioning can be considered "unfairly optimal". All the graphics are produced in response to a single network operation. Therefore, J-Orchestra performs very close to the baseline in the Version 1 experiment. Version 2, however, is more realistic: all re-drawing is initiated over the network. In this case, J-Orchestra performs about the same as X-Windows, except for the case of graphics buttons. In this case, X-Windows has to transfer the graphical icon over the network, while J-Orchestra avoids this overhead altogether. As a result, J-Orchestra is more than twice as fast as X-Windows. Of course, a slower network (e.g., 10Mbit ethernet, ISDN, or modem connection) would accentuate these results dramatically. We should mention that the window with text buttons displays incorrectly (empty window) in the case of X-Windows.

5.3.2 Simple Animation

In this benchmark, we test a small but fully usable third-party application. This experiment is representative of the way X-Windows and J-Orchestra will be used in practice to graphically display real time data on a different machine from the one producing them. It consists of a Java analog clock program (one of the many written as Java graphics demos). The program draws a simple face of a digital/analog clock (4 hour numbers, three moving clock hands, and a digital representation of the current time). With X-Windows, we just run the clock application on one machine and display the results on another. With J-Orchestra, however, we can transfer only the interesting data (a Date object) over the network and do all the drawing locally. To turn this into a useful benchmark, we changed it very slightly, so that the clock updates the time on the screen as quickly as possible—i.e., the program keeps polling the system for time as often as it can and displays the results. The measured quantity is then the frames-per-second attained on the remote display. In other words, we are treating the clock display as a real-time animation and measure the animation quality.

The measurements (frames per second) for this benchmark appear in Table 5. Apart from the original clock, we also created two stripped-down versions that only display the "analog" part of the clock. The first only draws the clock hands. The second draws the clock hands as well as the numbers "3", "6", "9", and "12" on the face of the clock.

Table 5. Clock Experiment

Experiment/System	Original clock	Clock with just hands	Clock with hands and hours
Baseline	86 fps	294 fps	87 fps
X-Windows	22 fps	289 fps	32 fps
J-Orchestra	64 fps	175 fps	70 fps

For the original clock application, J-Orchestra is almost three times faster than X-Windows. The reason is that X-Windows needs to transfer over the network a lot of graphical information that does not change (e.g., the kind of font used for the displayed text, text that does not change on the screen, etc.). When just the clock hands are drawn, J-Orchestra is a little slower than X-Windows. When, however, as little as the four hour numbers (3, 6, 9, and 12) need to be drawn on the face of the clock, J-Orchestra again is more than twice as fast as X-Windows.

5.3.3 Analysis

We analyzed the network traffic in order to show the trade-off in the above experiments. Due to lack of space, we cannot present the full results (bytes per request, effect of clustering, etc.) but the main observations are clear: X-Windows has a lower overhead per network transfer, but J-Orchestra has the flexibility to place the drawing code on the machine where the graphics will be displayed. More specifically, the X protocol [15] is fairly inefficient in terms of the amount of data transferred in order to send graphics over the network. Nevertheless, compared to a heavyweight implementation of general purpose middleware like Java RMI, the X protocol is much better suited for transferring graphics. A major difference is that RMI is a synchronous protocol: most X protocol requests do not generate replies, but RMI remote method calls will always need to generate network traffic when an operation completes. Additionally, the X protocol allows multiple remote drawing requests to be clustered together and sent in a single TCP segment. J-Orchestra outperforms X-Windows only because it transfers much less data over the network (e.g., only the current time instead of full graphical information for the clock display, no font information, etc.).

6 Related Work

Distributed computing has been the main focus of systems research in the past two decades. Therefore, there is a wealth of work that exhibits similar goals or methodologies to ours. We will separate closely related work (approaches that use similar techniques to ours) from indirectly related work (work with similar goals but significantly different approaches).

6.1 Directly Related Work

Several recent systems other than J-Orchestra can also be classified as automatic partitioning tools. In the Java world, the closest approaches are the Addistant [19] and Pangaea [16] systems. The Coign system [9] has promoted the idea of automatic partitioning for applications based on COM components.

Addistant [19] is the closest alternative to J-Orchestra in the design space. J-Orchestra has three advantages over Addistant. First, J-Orchestra has a far more general rewrite engine allowing arbitrary partitioning of the application: we discussed earlier how J-Orchestra allows any partitioning along application boundaries. In contrast, Addistant imposes limitations based on dependencies on unmodifiable code. For instance, Addistant cannot make a class remotely accessible when the class is unmodifiable and has unmodifiable clients. Second, J-Orchestra allows object mobility, allowing to take advantage of locality. With Addistant, objects are created and used on the same network site—they cannot move to be co-located with other objects that access them. Third, J-Orchestra includes automatic analyses that ensure the correctness of a partitioning and relieve the user from having to specify policies for each class. The Addistant user has to explicitly specify whether instances of an unmodifiable class are created only by modifiable code, whether an unmodifiable class is accessed by modifiable code, whether instances of a class can be safely passed by-copy, etc. This information is application-specific and getting it wrong results in a partitioning that violates the original application semantics.

Coign [9] is an automatic partitioning system for software based on Microsoft's COM model. Although Coign is a pioneering system, it suffers from two drawbacks. First, Coign is not applicable to many real-world situations: although Windows software often exports coarse-grained COM components, very few real-world applications are written as collections of many fine-grained COM components. The applications that constitute success cases for Coign (mainly the Octarine word processor) were experimental and written specifically to showcase that COM is a viable platform for developing applications from many small components. The second drawback is technical. Coign does not try to solve the hard problems of automatic partitioning: it does not distribute components when they share data through memory pointers. Such components are deemed non-distributable and are located on the same machine. Practical experience with Coign [9] showed that this is a severe limitation for the only real-world application included in Coign's example set (the Microsoft PhotoDraw program). The Coign approach would be impossible in the case of Java: almost all program data are accessed through references in Java. No support for synchronous data mobility exists in Coign, but the application can be periodically repartitioned based on its recent behavior.

Pangaea [16][17] is an automatic partitioning system that has very similar goals to J-Orchestra. Pangaea is based on the JavaParty [13] infrastructure for application partitioning. Since JavaParty is designed for manual partitioning and operates at the source code level, Pangaea is also limited in this respect. Thus, Pangaea cannot be used to make Java system classes (which are supplied in bytecode format) remotely accessible. Therefore, Pangaea has little applicability to real world situations, especially with limited manual intervention. For instance, much data exchange in Java programs happens through system classes (e.g., collection classes, like java.util.Vector). If such classes are not remotely accessible, all their clients need to be located on the same site, making partitioning almost impossible for realistic applications.

Finally, we should mention that the JavaParty infrastructure [13][8] is closely related to J-Orchestra. The similarity is not so much in the objectives—JavaParty only aims to support manual partitioning and does not deal with system classes. The techniques used, however, are very similar to J-Orchestra, especially for the newest versions of JavaParty [8].

6.2 Indirectly Related Work

Automatic partitioning is essentially a *Distributed Shared Memory (DSM)* technique. Just like traditional DSM approaches, we try to create the illusion of a shared address space, when the data are really distributed across different machines. Nevertheless, automatic partitioning differs from traditional DSM work in one major aspect: *only the application is allowed to change, not the run-time environment.* Traditional DSM systems like Munin [5], Orca [3], and, in the Java world, CJVM [2], and Java/DSM [23] use a specialized run-time environment in order to detect access to remote data and ensure data consistency. The deployment cost of DSMs has restricted DSM applicability to high-performance parallel applications. In contrast, automatically partitioned Java applications work on original, unmodified Java Virtual Machines (JVMs), possibly shipped with Web browsers. All modifications necessary are made directly to the application, using compilation techniques. In this way, automatic partitioning has no deployment cost, allowing it to be applied to regular applications and compete with lightweight technologies like X-Windows.

Among distributed shared memory systems, the ones most closely resembling the J-Orchestra approach are object-based DSMs, like Orca [3]. The Orca system has a dedicated language and run-time system, but also has similarities to J-Orchestra in its treatment of data at the object level, and its use of static analysis.

Mobile object systems, like Emerald [4][10] have similarities with J-Orchestra. Many of the J-Orchestra ideas on implementing mobile objects and choosing appropriate semantics for method invocations (synchronous object migration) have originated with Emerald.

The Doorastha system [6] represents another piece of work closely related to automatic partitioning. Doorastha allows the user to annotate a centralized program to turn it into a distributed application. Unfortunately, all the burden is shifted to the user to specify what semantics are valid for a specific class (e.g., whether objects are mobile, whether they can be passed by-copy, etc.). The Doorastha annotations are quite expressive in terms of how method arguments, different fields of a class, etc., are manipulated. Nevertheless, programming in this way is tedious and error-prone: a slight error in an annotation may cause insidious inconsistency errors.

The need for infrastructure to support application partitioning has been recognized in the systems community. Proposals for such infrastructure (most recently, Protium [22]) usually try to address different concerns from those covered by J-Orchestra. High performance is an essential element, with the infrastructure trying to hide the latency of remote accesses. J-Orchestra aims at a much higher degree of automation, but for applications with more modest network performance requirements.

Finally, we should mention that the overall approach of programming distributed systems as if they were centralized ("papering over the network") has been occasionally criticized (e.g., see the best known "manifesto" on the topic [21]). The main point of criticism has been that distributed systems fundamentally differ from centralized systems because of the possibility of partial failure, which needs to be handled differently for each application. Nevertheless, J-Orchestra can address this problem, at least partially: although the input of the system is a binary application, the proxies for remote-capable classes are produced in source code. Application-specific partial-failure handling can be effected by manually editing the source code of the proxy classes and handling the corresponding Java language exceptions. Thus, although J-Orchestra hides much of the complexity of distribution, it allows the user to handle distribution-specific failure exactly like it would be handled through manual partitioning. Alternatively viewed, the user can concentrate on the part of the application that really matters for distributed computing: partial failure handling. This part is the only code that needs to be written by hand in order to partition an application.

7 Status and Conclusions

J-Orchestra is work-in-progress, but most of the back-end functionality is in place, as described in this paper. We have already used J-Orchestra to partition several realistic, third-party applications. Among them are "J-Shell" (a command line shell implementation for Java), a graphical demo of the Java speech API (the user selects parameters and a sound synthesizer composes phrases), an application for monitoring server load and displaying real-time graphical statistics, and some small graphical demos and benchmarks. All of the above were partitioned in a client-server model, where the I/O part of the functionality (graphics, text, etc.) is displayed on a client machine, while processing or execution of commands takes place on a server. Our client machine is typically a hand-held iPAQ PDA, running Linux. This environment is good for showcasing the capabilities of J-Orchestra—even relatively uninteresting centralized applications become exciting demos when they are automatically turned into distributed applications, partly running on a hand-held device that communicates over a wireless network with a central server.

In the future, we intend to continue work on the J-Orchestra back-end, but at the same time develop more front-end functionality. Currently, J-Orchestra uses Java RMI as its distribution middleware. RMI has been criticized for its inefficiency, but offers useful features for transparent distribution (e.g., distributed reference counting). In the future, we may select a more efficient middleware implementation (e.g., KaRMI [12]) when such alternatives become more mature. Any middleware, however, will perform badly if the application is not partitioned well and object mobility is not coordinated optimally. Therefore, the greatest future challenge for J-Orchestra will be to develop mechanisms that automatically infer detailed object migration strategies in response to synchronous events. (For example, a strategy could be as detailed as "when a method foo is called, all its arguments and all data reachable from its arguments in up to three indirections should migrate to the method's execution site.")

A common question we are asked concerns our choice of the name "J-Orchestra". The reason for the name is that there is a strong analogy between application partitioning and the way orchestral music is often composed. Many orchestral pieces are not originally written for orchestral performance. Instead, only a piano score is originally composed. Later, an "orchestration" process takes place that determines which instruments should play which notes of the completed piano score. There are many examples of orchestrating piano music that was never intended by its composer for orchestral performance. There are several examples of piano pieces that have several brilliant but totally different orchestrations. With J-Orchestra, we provide a state-of-the-art "orchestration" facility for Java programs. Taking into account the unique capabilities of network nodes (instruments) we partition Java applications for harmonious distributed execution. We believe that automatic application partitioning represents a huge promise and that J-Orchestra is a general and powerful automatic partitioning tool.

Acknowledgments

Austin (Chun Fai) Chau, Dean Pu Mao, Kane See, Hailemelekot Seifu, and Marcus Handte have all contributed to the J-Orchestra front-end (GUI and profiler) as well as the partitioning and set up of current J-Orchestra demo applications. Their enthusiasm helped us stay on track. We would also like to thank Kresten Krab Thorup and the anonymous referees for their valuable comments that helped strengthen the paper.

This work has been supported by the Yamacraw Foundation, by DARPA/ITO under the PCES program, and by a Raytheon E-Systems faculty fellowship.

References

[1]   Bowen Alpern, Anthony Cocchi, Stephen Fink, David Grove, and Derek Lieber, "Efficient Implementation of Java Interfaces: Invokeinterface Considered Harmless", in Proc. *Object-Oriented Programming, Systems, Languages, and Applications (OOPSLA)*, 2001.

[2]   Yariv Aridor, Michael Factor, and Avi Teperman, "CJVM: a Single System Image of a JVM on a Cluster", in Proc. *ICPP'99*.

[3]   Henri E. Bal, Raoul Bhoedjang, Rutger Hofman, Ceriel Jacobs, Koen Langendoen, Tim Ruhl, and M. Frans Kaashoek, "Performance Evaluation of the Orca Shared-Object System", *ACM Trans. on Computer Systems*, 16(1):1-40, February 1998.

[4]   Andrew Black, Norman Hutchinson, Eric Jul, Henry Levy, and Larry Carter, "Distribution and Abstract Types in Emerald", in *IEEE Trans. Softw. Eng.*, 13(1):65-76, 1987.

[5]   John B. Carter, John K. Bennett, and Willy Zwaenepoel, "Implementation and performance of Munin", *Proc. 13th ACM Symposium on Operating Systems Principles*, pp. 152-164, October 1991.

[6]   Markus Dahm, "Doorastha—a step towards distribution transparency", *JIT*, 2000. See http://www.inf.fu-berlin.de/~dahm/doorastha/ .

[7]   James Gosling, Bill Joy, Guy Steele, and Gilad Bracha, *The Java Language Specification, 2nd Ed.*, The Java Series, Addison-Wesley, 2000.

[8]   Bernhard Haumacher, Jürgen Reuter, Michael Philippsen, "JavaParty: A distributed companion to Java", http://wwwipd.ira.uka.de/JavaParty/

[9]   Galen C. Hunt, and Michael L. Scott, "The Coign Automatic Distributed Partitioning System", *3rd Symposium on Operating System Design and Implementation (OSDI'99)*, pp. 187-200, New Orleans, 1999.

[10]   Eric Jul, Henry Levy, Norman Hutchinson, and Andrew Black, "Fine-Grained Mobility in the Emerald System", ACM Trans. on Computer Systems, 6(1):109-133, February 1988.

[11] Nelson King, "Partitioning Applications", *DBMS and Internet Systems* magazine, May 1997. See http://www.dbmsmag.com/9705d13.html.

[12] Christian Nester, Michael Phillipsen, and Bernhard Haumacher, "A More Efficient RMI for Java", in Proc. *ACM Java Grande Conference*, 1999.

[13] Michael Philippsen and Matthias Zenger, "JavaParty - Transparent Remote Objects in Java", *Concurrency: Practice and Experience*, 9(11):1125-1242, 1997.

[14] Robert W. Scheifler, and Jim Gettys, "The X Window System", *ACM Transactions on Graphics*, 5(2): 79-109, April 1986.

[15] Robert W. Scheifler, "X Window System Protocol, Version 11", *Network Working Group RFC 1013*, April 1987.

[16] Andre Spiegel, "Pangaea: An Automatic Distribution Front-End for Java", 4th *IEEE Workshop on High-Level Parallel Programming Models and Supportive Environments (HIPS '99)*, San Juan, Puerto Rico, April 1999.

[17] Andre Spiegel, "Automatic Distribution in Pangaea", *CBS 2000*, Berlin, April 2000. See also http://www.inf.fu-berlin.de/~spiegel/pangaea/

[18] Sun Microsystems, Remote Method Invocation Specification, http://java.sun.com/products/jdk/rmi/, 1997.

[19] Michiaki Tatsubori, Toshiyuki Sasaki, Shigeru Chiba, and Kozo Itano, "A Bytecode Translator for Distributed Execution of 'Legacy' Java Software", *European Conference on Object-Oriented Programming (ECOOP)*, Budapest, June 2001.

[20] Eli Tilevich and Yannis Smaragdakis, "J-Orchestra: Automatic Java Application Partitioning", Georgia Tech, CoC Tech. Report, GIT-CC-02-17, 2002.

[21] Jim Waldo, Geoff Wyant, Ann Wollrath, and Sam Kendall, "A note on distributed computing", Technical Report, Sun Microsystems Laboratories, SMLI TR-94-29, November 1994.

[22] Cliff Young, Y. N. Lakshman, Tom Szymanski, John Reppy, David Presotto, Rob Pike, Girija Narlikar, Sape Mullender, and Eric Grosse, "Protium, and Infrastructure for Partitioned Applications", *Eighth IEEE Workshop on Hot Topics in Operating Systems (HotOS-VIII)*. May 20—23, 2001, Schoss Elmau Germany, pp. 41-46, IEEE Computer Society Press, 2001.

[23] Weimin Yu, and Alan Cox, "Java/DSM: A Platform for Heterogeneous Computing", *Concurrency: Practice and Experience*, 9(11):1213-1224, 1997.

Supporting Unanticipated Dynamic Adaptation
of Application Behaviour

Barry Redmond and Vinny Cahill

Distributed Systems Group,
Department of Computer Science,
Trinity College Dublin
{barry.redmond,vinny.cahill}@cs.tcd.ie

Abstract. The need to dynamically modify running applications arises in systems that must adapt to changes in their environment, in updating long-running systems that cannot be halted and restarted, and in monitoring and debugging systems without the need to recompile and restart them. Relatively few architectures have explored the meaning and possibilities of applying behavioural modifications to already running applications without static preparation of the application. The desirable characteristics of an architecture for dynamic modification include support for non-invasive association of new behaviour with the application, support for modular reusable components encapsulating the new behaviour and support for dynamic association (and de-association) of new behaviour with any class or object of the application. The Iguana/J architecture explores unanticipated dynamic modification, and demonstrates how these characteristics may be supported in an interpreted language without extending the language, without a preprocessor, and without requiring the source code of the application. This paper describes the Iguana/J programmer's model and how it addresses some acknowledged issues in dynamic adaptation and separation of concerns, describes how Iguana/J is implemented, and gives examples of applying Iguana/J.

1   Introduction

Dynamic adaptation of a running application allows the application's behaviour to be changed without stopping and restarting it. Systems that benefit from being able to do this include systems that must adapt to short-term changes in their environment, such as mobile systems, and systems that cannot tolerate being halted but must be updated on the fly, such as financial systems or real-time monitoring and control systems. Dynamic adaptation can also be a very useful debugging tool, allowing experimental modifications or monitoring code to be inserted into the software under test without the normal edit-compile-restart process.

It is possible to design an application to be adaptable in ways that can be fully specified at design time, by using approaches such as the strategy pattern [9][7], but it is difficult, if not impossible, to anticipate all the ways in which it may be required to adapt some applications. Some of the requirements for a dynamic adaptation architecture are explored in [25], as part of an examination of dynamic aspects and advanced separation of concerns. A dynamic adaptation technique should not require

B. Magnusson (Ed.): ECOOP 2002, LNCS 2374, pp. 205–230, 2002.

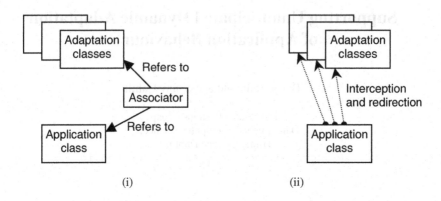

Fig. 1. A separate associator refers to adaptation classes and an application class at load time or runtime, and links them to each other

any special preparation of the application code, as this would imply anticipation of the modifications. It must be non-invasive in the sense that it must not require the addition or modification of any application code before the application starts to run. This implies that the technique must support the insertion of the modification mechanisms at runtime.

Just as for other software components, modularity and reusability of components that implement new behaviour are desirable characteristics. To maximize reusability it should be possible to design such components to encapsulate the new behaviour without specific knowledge of the application to which they will be applied, and without knowledge of the other dynamic adaptation components with which they will be used. As we are considering a dynamic environment, the reusability of these components should extend to runtime. In other words, the dynamic adaptation components will be most useful if they remain reusable even in their compiled state. This separation of concerns between the application and the dynamic adaptation components supports a high level of separation between the roles of the application programmer, the adaptation component programmer, and the adaptation component user who applies them to the application.

To be independently reusable the components must not contain static references to of each other or to any part of the application. This implies that the associations between dynamic adaptation components and the points in the application to which they are to be applied must be created at runtime, and therefore that the dynamic adaptation approach must have a runtime platform that can carry out the dynamic manipulation of the associations. The runtime platform must be able to intercept identified operations at arbitrary points in the application, and redirect them to the dynamic adaptation components for handling.

The Iguana/J architecture [21] attempts to provide a dynamic adaptation platform for the Java language that has the characteristics described above. Iguana/J is based on the Iguana reflective language [12] and on a later revision, Iguana/C++ [22], implemented for the C++ language. Iguana/J supports changes to the internal behaviour of classes and objects; it does not support modifications to their external interfaces. It allows new behaviour to be implemented as standard Java classes,

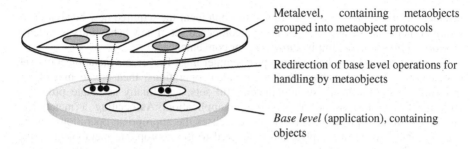

Metalevel, containing metaobjects grouped into metaobject protocols

Redirection of base level operations for handling by metaobjects

Base level (application), containing objects

Fig. 2. The two levels of the Iguana/J model

without language extensions, and without dependencies on the application software with which it will be used. The adaptation classes may be compiled without knowledge of the application, and are reusable in their compiled form. Separate association mechanisms make the connection between specified operations in the running application and the adaptation classes at runtime, and may supply specialization parameters to the adaptation classes. Fig. 1(i) illustrates an association mechanism referring to reusable adaptation classes and an unprepared application class. Fig. 1(ii) shows the result of the association. The selected operations in the application class are linked to the appropriate adaptation classes so that the operations will be intercepted and redirected to them. By keeping the association mechanism separate from both the application classes and the adaptation classes Iguana/J improves the support for reusable adaptation components. A similar technique is used by Aspectual Components [15] to maintain the reusability of the components.

In this paper we describe the Iguana/J programmer's model, we give examples of using Iguana/J to address acknowledged challenge problems, and we discuss the implementation and performance of the architecture. Due to space limitations some details of the model and implementation are not included in this paper.

2   Programmers' Model

In Iguana/J new behaviours are expressed as Java classes that are associated (and de-associated) with existing application classes and objects at runtime. The architecture can be most usefully viewed as two programs in two separate layers (Fig. 2). The lower layer is the application whose behaviour is to be modified, while the upper layer represents the new behaviour. Appropriate objects in the upper layer are associated with specified operations such as method invocation or object creation in specified classes and objects in the application (the lower layer). When an application operation that has an associated upper layer object is attempted the operation is intercepted and transferred to the associated upper layer object to be handled. This transfer completely replaces the original application operation, and therefore the operation may be modified in any required way by suitable design of the handler objects in the upper layer.

We refer to the application (lower) layer as the *base level*, and to the upper layer as the *metalevel*. The operation handler objects in the metalevel are called *metaobjects*, instances of *metaobject classes* designed to implement the required new behaviour. A group of metaobject classes representing a composed set of new behaviours is called a *metaobject protocol*, or simply a *protocol* for convenience.

To create and use new behaviour a programmer must first create metaobject classes implementing the new behaviour for individual operations, then create metaobject protocols that compose these into meaningful sets, and finally associate protocols with identified classes and objects in the application. Associating a metaobject protocol with an application class or object causes the appropriate operations on the class or object to be intercepted and redirected to the appropriate metaobject of the protocol. The concepts and procedures involved in using Iguana/J are described in more detail in the sections below.

2.1   Separation of Concerns

To support dynamic adaptation of applications in unanticipated ways the Iguana/J architecture provides a strong runtime separation between the application classes and the metaobject classes, thus maintaining a high level of modularity and reusability of all the elements of the architecture. The application classes do not require any preprocessing or preparation of any kind, and no modifications are required in the application source code. Iguana/J may be used to apply new behaviour to application classes for which no source code is available.

Metaobject classes and metaobject protocols may be designed to implement behaviour such as synchronisation, argument checking, logging, persistence, and distribution as general concepts, without explicit reference to the application classes with which they will be associated. The association of a protocol and its metaobjects with a specific application class occurs solely and completely at runtime, ensuring that they are reusable in their compiled form.

Iguana/J's support for separation of concerns and modularity also establishes a sharp distinction between the responsibilities of the application programmer, the metalevel programmer and the system integrator. The application may be created without any regard for any metalevel program that may be used with it. The metalevel programmer may create metaobject classes and metaobject protocols to implement particular behaviour without any knowledge of the specific application classes with which they will be used. Finally, the system integrator causes the dynamic association of application classes with metaobject protocols to apply new behaviour to the application.

2.2   Interception and Handling

The present version of Iguana/J supports modification of seven categories of application operations. The seven categories are object creation and deletion, method call (send), dispatch and invocation (receive), and field read and write. When a metaobject protocol is associated with an application object then all operation categories declared in that protocol are intercepted in the application object and redirected to the appropriate metaobject of the associated protocol. In the prototype version of Iguana/J operations can be intercepted on class members whether they are public, protected or private. The metaobject handles the operation, and returns control to the application object. The handling by the metaobject occurs in the same thread as the intercepted operation, and any return value expected from the operation can be returned from the metaobject. The application object is effectively unaware of the fact that the operation has been intercepted and handled by a metaobject.

2.3 Metaobject Classes

Metaobjects handle operations intercepted in an application class or object. Metaobjects encapsulate new behaviour, and must be instances of the Iguana/J metaobject classes, or instances of subclasses of them. There are seven metaobject classes in the current version of Iguana/J (table 1). Each class is used to handle a different category of intercepted operation, and each class has a handler method appropriate to the class's purpose. The handler methods in each of these seven classes implement the operation in the 'normal' manner, so the appropriate metaobject class must be subclassed and its handler method overridden to implement new behaviour.

For example, the handler method `execute()` of the class `MExecute` carries out a normal execution of the method whose execution was intercepted, giving the same effect as if it had not been intercepted. To change the behaviour the metalevel programmer must subclass `MExecute`, overriding its `execute()` method to implement the new behaviour. Then instances of the derived metaobject class may be used to handle method execution in selected classes and objects in the application. An intercepted application operation is completely replaced by the redirection to the metaobject, so that the metaobject has full control over how the operation is carried out. The metaobject may decide to proceed with the operation, replace it with some other operation, or skip it. The metaobject may also carry out extra steps before or after the intercepted operation. Where the intercepted operation is expected to return a value the handler method of the metaobject returns a value to take its place.

The handler methods of metaobject classes receive arguments representing the intercepted operation. There may be up to three arguments passed to the handler method, representing the target object, the target method or field, and the marshalled arguments of the intercepted operation. Iguana/J uses the Java reflection classes to represent methods and fields, and uses the same array-of-objects technique as the Java reflection API to marshal operation arguments. This allows the metaobject to examine and manipulate the intercepted operation using the Java reflection API.

Every metaobject class inherits a `proceed()` method. `proceed()` takes the same arguments as passed into the handler method (the target object, the target method or field, and the array of marshalled arguments) but the handler method may

Table 1. Intercepted operations and corresponding metaobject classes (handlers)

Intercepted operation	Metaobject class (handler)	Handler method
object creation	`ie.tcd.iguana.MCreate`	`create()`
object deletion	`ie.tcd.iguana.MDelete`	`delete()`
method call (send)	`ie.tcd.iguana.MSend`	`send()`
method dispatch	`ie.tcd.iguana.MDispatch`	`dispatch()`
method execution	`ie.tcd.iguana.MExecute`	`execute()`
field read	`ie.tcd.iguana.StateRead`	`read()`
field write	`ie.tcd.iguana.StateWrite`	`write()`

```
public class VerboseDebug extends MExecute {
   public Object execute(Object o, Object[] args,
                         Method m)
                         throws InvocationTargetException {
      System.out.println("Entering method: " &
                         m.getName());
      System.out.println("Number of args: " &
                         args.length);
      Object result = proceed(o,args,m);
      System.out.println("Return type: " &
                         result.getClass().getName());
      return(result);
   }
}
```

Fig. 3. A simple verbose metaobject

be designed to replace or modify any of these before calling proceed(). The value returned by proceed() is the return value from the operation, and it may be examined and modified by the metaobject before it is returned. The handler methods in each of the seven metaobject classes in the Iguana/J library implement the default behaviour for the corresponding operation by containing only a call to the class's proceed() method, passing on the interception arguments unchanged and passing back the return value unchanged. For example, the execute() method of MExecute is:

```
public Object execute(Object o, Object[] args, Method m)
                      throws InvocationTargetException {
   return(proceed(o,args,m));
}
```

The example in fig. 3 illustrates how a metaobject class may be used to add behaviour to the execution of a method, and how the Java reflection API may be used to examine the arguments and return value of the intercepted method execution. This example also illustrates the separation of concerns supported by Iguana/J. The metaobject does not include any static reference to the application class, and therefore it may be reused with any application class without recompilation.

A metaobject may examine the execution context of the intercepted operation by using the Iguana/J CallStack and StackFrame classes. These classes support examination of the chain of method calls leading to the intercepted operation, and allow a metaobject to make decisions based on the context in which the operation has occurred. Context examination addresses issues such as the *jumping aspects* [4] problem, described in section 4.2. The example in fig. 4 is a metaobject that illustrates the use of this to detect method invocations from outside the application object's class. The getCallStack() method is inherited into every metaobject class, and returns an instance of CallStack representing the method call stack of the current thread. Instances of StackFrame are used to represent individual frames on the call stack.

```
public class Detector extends MExecute {
   public Object execute(Object o, Object[] args, Method m)
                     throws InvocationTargetException {
   //Construct fully qualified name, with wildcard method part:
      String fqname = o.getClass().getName() & ".*";
      if(!getCallStack().containsCallTo(fqname)) {
         System.out.println(fqname & " called from inside
               object's class");
      }
      return(proceed(o,args,m));
   }
}
```

Fig. 4. Example of context examination by a metaobject

2.4   Metaobject Protocols

Metaobject protocols bring together a group of metaobject classes into a single unit representing some coherent new behaviour. Each metaobject class in the protocol implements new behaviour to be applied to one category of intercepted operation, so a protocol allows the metalevel programmer to create new behaviour that cuts across different types of operations on a class or object.

Metaobject protocols are created declaratively. Each protocol declaration specifies which operation categories are to be intercepted by the protocol, and the metaobject classes to be used to handle the intercepted operations. Fig. 5 is a simple example protocol that declares that an instance of MyMCreate should be used to handle intercepted creation operations, and that an instance of MyMExecute should be used to handle intercepted execution (method receive) operations. The metaobject class specified for an operation category must be a subclass of the Iguana/J metaobject class for that category.

Keywords local and shared may be used in protocol declarations to affect the scope of individual metaobjects of the protocol. A *local* metaobject is instantiated once for each instance of an application class with which the protocol is associated. The metaobject is associated with just one application object, and therefore the metaobject has object scope. A *shared* metaobject is instantiated only once for all instances of an application class. The single metaobject is associated with all the instances of the class and therefore has class scope. Local metaobjects may be used to hold state information for individual application objects. Shared metaobjects may be used to support coordination of the behaviour of instances of an application class, or to minimize the number of metaobjects created.

```
protocol MyProtocol {
  reify Creation: MyMCreate;
  reify Invocation: MyMExecute;
}
```

Fig. 5. A simple protocol declaration.

```
protocol P1 {
  reify Creation: MyCreate1;
  reify Invocation: MyExecute1;
}

protocol P2 {
  reify Invocation: MyExecute2;
}

protocol P3 : P1, P2 {
  reify Creation: MyCreate3;
  reify StateRead: MyRead3;
}
```

Fig. 6. Derivation of protocol P3 from P1 and P2

Protocol declarations are not expressed in Java and are not placed in Java source files. They are placed in separate protocol files that must be compiled by the Iguana/J protocol compiler before they can be used. The protocol compiler converts each declaration to a subclass of ie.tcd.iguana.Meta and compiles it to bytecode, and therefore a compiled protocol may be referred to in the same way as a Java class.

2.5   Protocol Derivation and Metaobject Composition

Only one protocol may be associated with an application class or object at any one time, but a number of protocols may be explicitly composed to give a new protocol that represents all of them. This is supported by the protocol derivation mechanism. As illustrated in the examples in fig. 6 a protocol declaration may include one or more protocols whose declarations are to be inherited into this declaration. Protocol P3 is derived from P1 and P2, and also declares additional metaobjects. Unlike class inheritance in C++ or Java, inherited metaobject declarations cannot be overridden. Instead, the inherited metaobject declarations for each operation category are composed with any explicit metaobject declarations for the category to give a set of metaobject classes to handle an operation. This structure is part of Iguana/J's metatyping model (section 2.7) and ensures that derived protocols cannot remove behaviour introduced by a protocol higher in the derivation tree. In the example, protocol P3 will contain metaobjects to handle three categories of operations. It will handle creation using a composition of MyCreate1 and MyCreate3, it will handle invocation using a composition of MyExecute1 and MyExecute2, and it will handle field reads using just MyRead3.

Composition of metaobjects uses a simple chain structure. An intercepted operation is passed along the chain, so that each metaobject has an opportunity to process it. The passing mechanism is implemented by the proceed() method of each metaobject. If there is a next metaobject on the chain then this method will pass the operation to that metaobject and will return the value returned by that metaobject. If there is no next metaobject on the chain then proceed() will carry out the operation using the arguments passed to it.

```
public class MyExecute extends MExecute {
  private String methodname;
  public MyExecute(String name) {
    methodname = name;
  }
  public Object execute(Object o, Object[] args,
                        Method m) throws . . . {
    . . .    // Uses methodname.
  }
}
```

Fig. 7. Metaobject class with constructor to accept specialization parameters

If we consider handler methods in metaobjects to consist of some *before* code, a call to proceed() and some *after* code, then the composition chain passes the intercepted operation down the chain through all the *before* code sections, carries out the operation, and then passes the result back up the chain through all the *after* code sections. The *before* code of each metaobject may examine or change the target application object, the target method or field, and the operation's arguments. The *after* code of each metaobject may examine or change the result of the operation. The order of metaobjects on the composition chain is determined by the structure of the protocol declarations. In this simple composition model any metaobject may terminate the chain by not calling proceed().

2.6   Protocol Parameters

Many useful metaobject classes need specific information about the associated application class in order to operate, but if we make this information explicit then the metaobject class is not reusable with other application classes. For example, a metaobject class to apply persistence to a short-term storage management class needs to be able to detect invocations of the put and get methods of the storage manager. However, if we include in the metaobject class explicit mention of the names of the put and get methods then the metaobject class is usable only with application classes that use those method names.

To overcome this Iguana/J provides protocol parameters. A metaobject protocol may be declared to expect a number of parameters to be supplied when it is associated with a specific application class or object. These parameters are passed (at association time) to constructors of the metaobjects that make up the protocol. The following example protocol declares that it expects two parameters, and that they are to be passed separately to the constructors of the two metaobjects:

```
protocol MyProtocol(String s, int i) {
    reify Creation: MyCreate(i);
    reify Invocation: MyExecute(s);
}
```

The metaobject classes must have constructors that take arguments that match the number and type of the parameters passed to them in the protocol declaration. Typically, the constructors will store the parameter value for use by the handler method of the metaobject when an application operation is intercepted, as illustrated by the fragment of a metaobject class in fig. 7. A metaobject class may have a number of constructors, to allow it to be constructed with different types or numbers of parameters from a protocol declaration.

2.7   The Metatyping Model

Iguana/J applies two strict typing rules governing the relationships between metaobject protocols associated with related classes and their instances. The rules may be summarized as follows:

1. The protocol associated with a class must be derived from or equal to the protocol associated with its superclass.
2. The protocol associated with an object must be derived from or equal to the protocol associated with its class.

These rules impose a typing structure at the metalevel that parallels the typing structure at the application level. They ensure that new behaviour applied to an application class will also apply to all its instances and to all its subclasses, no matter what protocols may be associated later with any of its instances or subclasses. We use the term *metatype* to refer to the type of the protocol associated with an application class or object. Two objects have the same metatype if they are associated with the same protocol. Just as the type of a class or object represents its public interface, the metatype of the class or object represents its behaviour. Unlike its type, its metatype may be changed dynamically. Changing a component's metatype does not alter its public interface, but it may alter its internal behaviour. Iguana/J's metatyping system ensures that behavioural changes, identified by metatype, are dynamically inherited in a manner similar to the static inheritance of external interfaces that is part of the conventional class structure.

To provide consistency for this metatype structure Iguana/J includes the concept of a *null metaobject protocol*. Every application class and object that is not associated with a real metaobject protocol is automatically associated with the null metaobject protocol. The null protocol does not intercept any application operations and does not have any metaobjects, so it represents the normal or default behaviour of the class or object. Every metaobject protocol that is not explicitly derived from another protocol is conceptually derived from the null protocol, and therefore every protocol is ultimately derived from the null protocol.

2.8   Associating Protocols with Classes

Association of an Iguana/J protocol with an application class has two separate general effects. The first is that instances of the metaobjects are created and associated with appropriate static operations on the class. In this context, object creation is considered to be a static operation and therefore any creation metaobject in the protocol associated with the class will be used to handle creation of instances of the class. The second general effect of associating a protocol with a class is that all instances of the class will be associated with the same protocol as they are created. In other words,

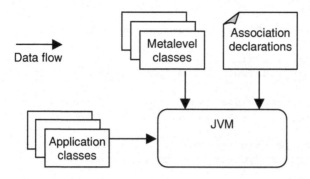

Fig. 8. The JVM looks up the association declarations as application classes are loaded

when a new instance of the class is created a set of metaobjects will be automatically created and associated with it. It may be argued that being able to associate two protocols with a class, one to intercept static operations and one as the initial protocol for instances of the class, would be useful, but this version of Iguana/J associates a single protocol for both purposes.

Two techniques are provided to associate a protocol with a class: a semi-static technique and a dynamic technique. The semi-static technique is the simplest to use. The required associations are declared in a special text file that is read by the Iguana/J runtime engine at JVM startup, and are used to associate protocols with application classes as the classes are loaded by the JVM (Fig. 8). The declaration file does not need to be processed in any way. It is read directly, as text. As each application class is loaded the JVM checks whether a protocol association is declared for it, and if so the protocol and metaobject classes are also loaded and the association with the class is created. This technique allows associations between arbitrary application classes and arbitrary protocols without writing special software to establish them.

Each association declaration names one application class and one protocol to be associated with each other. The declarations apply globally, so the names must be fully qualified. The application class name may be replaced by a wildcard, indicating that all classes of the package are to be associated with the named protocol, and the declaration may optionally include protocol parameters. Fig. 9 contains some association declarations that illustrate these possibilities.

Declarations of association are inherited by application classes, so any subclass of an application class mentioned in an association declaration will also be associated with the named protocol. If there is a declaration specifically for the class then that will be used in place of an inherited association. Inheritance of protocol association means that new behaviour associated with any class will be automatically associated with its subclasses too. A metalevel programmer does not have to be aware of all subclasses when applying new behaviour, and the protocol associations do not have to be updated if a new subclass is introduced. The inherited association of the protocol will apply the new behaviour even to overridden members in the subclasses. This addresses the *inheritance anomaly* identified by [16], by ensuring that behaviour such as synchronization applied to an application class cannot be removed from subclasses by overriding methods.

```
// Simple:
com.foo.bar.SomeClass ==> com.foo.mops.SomeProtocol;

// With parameters:
com.foo.bar.ClassTwo ==> com.foo.mops.PTwo("hello", 4);

// With wildcard class name to select whole package:
com.foo.project.* ==> com.foo.mops.ProtThree;

// Override package select for one class:
com.foo.project.MyClass ==> com.foo.mops.MyProtocol;
```

Fig. 9. Four association declarations

The second technique for associating a class with a protocol is dynamic association. It may be used to associate (or de-associate) an application class with a protocol during runtime. The technique uses a static method of the Iguana/J API, as illustrated in fig. 10. As for the association declaration technique described above, wildcard class names may be used to mean all classes in a package, and protocol parameters are supported. The two examples in fig. 10 are equivalent to the first two declarations in fig. 9.

While association using the dynamic technique is essentially the same as using the semi-static declarative technique there are some extra issues that must be dealt with. The differences arise because when a declarative association is applied the class is just being loaded and it has no previous protocol association and has no instances, while when a dynamic association is applied the class may have a protocol already and it may have instances. The semantics of associating a protocol with a class are that it affects static operations on the class and non-static operations on existing and future instances of the class. Therefore dynamic association changes any existing protocol associated with the class to the new protocol, and also changes any protocol associated with each existing instance of the class to the new protocol.

In associating metaobject protocols with application classes, whether using the declarative technique or the dynamic technique, we must adhere to the Iguana/J metatyping structure. In particular we must ensure that at all times the metaobject protocol associated with an application class is derived from or equal to the protocol associated with its superclass. The metatyping rules can complicate making dynamic changes to protocol associations when existing protocols are associated with two or more application classes related to each other by inheritance. To avoid the need for the metalevel programmer to create convoluted sequences of changes to protocol associations the dynamic association operation is enhanced. It changes not just the protocol associated with the named application class but also the protocols associated with each subclass (direct and indirect) of the named application class. In other words, the semantics of dynamic association includes inheritance of the new association into subclasses of the application class, just as declarative association does. The metalevel programmer must still ensure that a new metaobject protocol is derived from or equal to the protocol associated with the application superclass. If it is not then a runtime exception will be thrown.

```
// Basic dynamic association:
Meta.associate("com.foo.bar.SomeClass",
                    "com.foo.mops.SomeProtocol");

// Dynamic association including protocol parameters:
Object[] args = new Object[2];
args[0] = "hello";
args[1] = new Integer(4);
Meta.associate("com.foo.bar.ClassTwo",
                    "com.foo.mops.PTwo", args);
```

Fig. 10. Two examples of dynamically associating a class with a protocol

2.9   Associating Protocols with Objects

Associating metaobject protocols with application objects affects the behaviour of individual objects according to the metaobjects and operation categories declared by the protocol. The association causes a set of metaobjects to be instantiated for that object (although some metaobjects may be *shared*) and linked to the appropriate operations in the object.

There are three ways that an application object can become associated with a metaobject protocol. The first two are a consequence of associating a protocol with an application class, declaratively or dynamically. Associating a protocol using either technique causes all future instances of the class to be associated automatically with the same protocol as they are created. Dynamically associating a protocol with an application class also causes all existing instances of the class to become associated with the protocol, replacing any previous protocol associated with those instances. Associating a protocol with an application class can be considered as meaning association of the protocol with all existing and future instances of the class.

The third way that an application object can become associated with a metaobject protocol is by using the explicit object association mechanism. A static method of class Meta allows the metalevel programmer to dynamically associate any single object with a named protocol. The following example causes the object referred to by x to be associated with the metaobject protocol com.foo.mops.MyProtocol:

```
Object x = new Object();
...
Meta.associate(x, "com.foo.mops.MyProtocol");
```

This association will affect only one application object. It will not affect other objects of the same class. However, the Iguana/J metatyping rules must be observed in making the association. In particular, the new metaobject protocol must be equal to or derived from the protocol associated with the object's class. If it is not then a runtime exception will be thrown. This restriction ensures that dynamic association with an object can only be used to widen the object's initial metatype, not to narrow it. The protocol association of an object may be changed as often as required, as long as the metatyping rules are observed at all times.

3   Implementation

3.1   Approach

Runtime reflective architectures, such as Iguana/J, can be regarded as supporting dynamic aspect oriented programming (AOP) [6]. AOP allows cross-cutting behaviour to be modularised and *woven* with the basic application in some suitable way. Dynamic AOP performs weaving at runtime, and is a kind of dynamic adaptation of the application. Dynamic AOP architectures (e.g. [20]) use interception and redirection techniques similar to those used by runtime reflection, while many runtime reflective architectures can be used to implement dynamic aspects. Because of the overlap in objectives and implementation techniques we consider both types of architecture here.

There are two basic approaches to implementing dynamic aspect systems or runtime reflective systems for interpreted languages [3]. The first is to transform the application code (in source or binary form) to introduce the interception mechanisms required at runtime. This approach has been used by AspectJ [14], Hyper/J [26], Aspectual Components [15], JAC [19], Kava [29], OpenJava [27] and Reflex [24]. It has the major advantage of leaving the system's portability unaffected, as it will run on a standard interpreter for the language. However, it has the disadvantage of being a static transformation of the application, and therefore it limits the scope for dynamic adaptation. The second implementation approach is to leave the application code unchanged, but to modify or extend the interpreter to create the interception mechanisms. This is used by Guaraná [18], MetaXa [11], MetaclassTalk [2] and PROSE [20]. The advantage of this approach is that it provides access to low level operations and data in the interpreter and therefore greater flexibility in the level of support that can be provided for dynamic adaptation. On the other hand, portability is reduced because it usually requires a modified interpreter to run.

Iguana/J uses the extended interpreter approach, although the technique used (described below) means that the JVM can be extended without modifying its source code. This approach was chosen because it provides the best opportunities for dynamic adaptation of arbitrary classes and objects in unanticipated ways. The resulting portability restrictions were not regarded as critical because this prototype implementation of Iguana/J is intended only to be a research platform.

Although Iguana/J requires a runtime engine very closely integrated into the virtual machine, it was decided not to modify existing JVM source code, or create a new JVM from scratch, in order to avoid diverting research efforts into issues not central to the objectives. The implementation technique selected was to make use of the JIT Compiler Interface [30] available on the JVM in the Sun J2SE development kit. This interface was originally intended to support just-in-time compilation of Java bytecode, and provides very low level access to the interpreter. A native code library can be connected to the interface by specifying the library on the command line when the JVM is started, and the JVM will give the library low level access to all classes as they are loaded. Although the interface is intended for use by a JIT compiler, it may be used for anything that requires interception of class loading and low level access to JVM data structures. The JIT compiler interface is not part of the Java standard, and is not supported on all JVMs. While it is supported on Sun JVMs up to version 1.3 the shift by Sun from add-on JIT compilers to the integrated HotSpot technology means that the JIT interface is likely to disappear. This is not a serious problem for Iguana/J because the JIT interface is only an implementation technique, not an integral part of the model. The JIT interface is only available in the *classic* mode of the Sun JVM, so this implementation of Iguana/J cannot take advantage of the runtime improvements provided by the HotSpot mode of the JVM.

Iguana/J consists of two main elements. The first is a set of Java classes to be used as the basis for metaobject classes and protocols, and the second is the runtime engine. Iguana/J does not extend the Java language, so there is no preprocessor. New behaviours are implemented as metaobject classes, and compiled as standard Java. The only development time support provided as part of Iguana/J is the protocol compiler which is used to convert protocol declarations into compiled Java classes. The Iguana/J runtime engine is a native dynamic library that is integrated very closely with the interpreter, via the JIT compiler interface, and that effectively extends the JVM.

3.2   Association and Interception

As each class is being loaded by the JVM it is passed to the Iguana/J runtime engine for any required processing. The runtime engine consults the association declaration file to find any explicit or inherited association for the class being loaded, and it examines its superclass to check any protocol associated with it. If a metaobject protocol is to be associated then the runtime engine creates the required metaobjects, inserts interception mechanisms in the class being loaded, and creates the links from the class to the metaobjects. There are two useful and interesting results of this technique. Firstly, no execution time overhead whatever is incurred by a class that has no associated protocol. Neither the class nor its interpretation are modified, so it executes as normal. Secondly, even Java system classes may be associated with metaobject protocols. This is in sharp contrast with approaches that use class loaders to modify classes as they load (e.g. [15], [19], [24] and [29]). The Iguana/J runtime engine becomes integrated with the JVM as it initializes and therefore it is given the opportunity to process all classes, including system classes.

Iguana/J uses a number of mechanisms to intercept operations in an application. These mechanisms are inserted and removed dynamically, in response to association at class load time via the association declarations and in response to association after class load time via Meta.associate(). Invocation of methods and constructors is intercepted by altering the pointer to the JVM *invoker function* for the method or constructor. The data structure for every method or constructor includes a pointer to the function in the JVM that is to be used to invoke it. The JVM uses this technique because it has a number of possible method invokers, each optimized for methods with different combinations of characteristics such as synchronized, compiled, or native. To intercept invocation of a method Iguana/J simply changes its invoker pointer to point to a special function in the Iguana/J runtime engine. This allows Iguana/J to marshal arguments and redirect the invocation to the appropriate metaobject. Iguana/J saves the old invoker pointer, and restores it if the interception is no longer required by a protocol dynamically associated with the class at a later time.

Interception and redirection of object creation is more complex. It is intercepted by changing the invoker pointer for constructors of the class, but there is a difficulty in allowing the handler metaobject to completely replace the object creation in any way

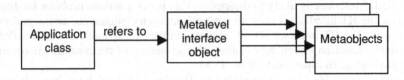

Fig. 11. Runtime structures

it wishes. The problem is caused by the fact that when the constructor is called the new object has already been created (but not fully initialized), and the normal constructor behaviour does not support replacement of the new object. To support complete replacement of the new object by the handler metaobject Iguana/J accepts a new object back from the handler and performs an object swap. The original partially initialized object is discarded, and the one returned by the handler is inserted instead.

Interception of operations such as method call (send), and field read and write uses bytecode modification to insert hooks at the originating point in the application code. Unlike bytecode modifications carried out by a preprocessor or a class loader, Iguana/J performs the modifications dynamically if required by a dynamically associated protocol and replaces the original bytecode dynamically if the interception is no longer needed.

The semantics of dynamically associating a metaobject protocol with a class include causing the same protocol to be dynamically associated with every existing instance of the class. As the JVM does not keep track of all instances of a given class the Iguana/J implementation must explicitly address the problem of finding all instances of the class. A number of possible techniques were considered, but the one selected was to search the object pool for instances when the dynamic association is being carried out. While this may result in a significant time overhead in a large system, the delays occur only when dynamic association with a class is carried out.

3.3   Metalevel Structure at Runtime

At runtime each application class and object with an associated metaobject protocol contains a hidden pointer to an object called the *metalevel interface object* (Fig. 11). The pointer is inserted by modifying the JVM data structure representing the class or object. The metalevel interface object is an instance of a subclass of ie.tcd. iguana.Meta. The subclass is created by the Iguana/J protocol compiler, and is the runtime representation of the protocol. Each metalevel interface object contains references to the metaobjects that make up the protocol, arranged into one chain of metaobjects per operation category intercepted by the protocol.

3.4   Performance

Some initial performance measurements have been made on prototype implementations of Iguana/J. The prototype implementation techniques are not compatible with the Sun HotSpot JVM, or with the use of a JIT compiler with the JVM, so no runtime optimizations were carried out. Compiler optimizations of native code were turned off, to facilitate testing and debug.

The measurements showed that Iguana/J has no impact whatever on classes and objects that have no metaobject protocol associated with them. Even where a protocol is associated with an application class or object there is no delay for operations that are not intercepted by the protocol. One exception to this is object creation which encounters a significant delay, a factor of about 25, when a protocol is associated with the class. The reason for this is that a new set of metaobjects must be created when a new application object is created, even if object creation is not handled by the protocol.

Measurements of interception and handling of method execution by Iguana/J show that it suffers a slowdown of about 24 times. It is important to note that this factor applies only to the call to and return from the method. The execution of the body of the method is not affected. The source of the delay is mainly in the marshalling of method arguments, the invocation of metaobject methods, and the use of the Java reflection API to carry out the intercepted invocation.

Published performance figures for other runtime reflective architectures indicate delays of the same order. Guaraná gives a delay factor of over 40 for method invocation on a comparable platform when a JIT compiler is not used (more when a JIT compiler is used) [18]. PROSE gives a delay factor of 70 or more for method invocation [20]. MetaXa performance figures give a slowdown of 28 times for method invocation [10].

These figures indicate that, as expected, support for dynamic adaptation has a significant runtime cost. However the Iguana/J figures show that the cost can be limited to parts of the application that use dynamic adaptation, and that it does not have to increase with increasing dynamic functionality. We are confident that the initial performance figures for Iguana/J can be significantly improved by more careful coding of the Iguana/J runtime engine, by moving most of the Iguana/J classes from Java to native code, and by enabling compiler optimization of native code. In the longer term, integration into the source code of the JVM will provide the best performance.

4   Examples

4.1   Challenge Problems

The characteristics of Iguana/J allow it to address a number of challenge problems that have been identified [25] in the areas of dynamic aspects and advanced separation of concerns. In particular, Iguana/J's strong separation between new behaviours and the application, its support for dynamic manipulation of the links between them, and its metatyping model address identified issues such as binary reusability, "jumping aspects", non-invasive weaving, semantic join points, dynamic weaving, and the "inheritance anomaly".

The three examples given here illustrate how Iguana/J may be used to address some of these issues. It should be noted that although the examples are laid out as single blocks here, each example contains a number of separate elements, including two alternative ways to cause association between the application classes and the protocol. In practice the classes would be compiled separately, the protocol declaration would be compiled by the Iguana/J protocol compiler, dynamic associat-

```
[1]        // Application class:
[2]        public class List {
[3]          public void addOne(ListItem l) { ... }
[4]          public void addAll(ListItem[] la) {
[5]            ... // addAll() uses addOne().
[6]          }
[7]        }
[8]      }

[9]        // Metaobject class:
[10]       public class GenEvent extends MExecute {
[11]         private String name;
[12]         private Announcer announcer;
[13]         public GenEvent(String c, String m) {
[14]           name = m;
[15]           announcer = EventControl.getAnnouncer(c);
[16]         }
[17]         public Object execute(Object o,Object[] args,Method m)
[18]               throws InvocationTargetException {
[19]           Object result = proceed(o,args,m);
[20]           if(!getCallStack().containsCallTo(name)) {
[21]             Event e = new Event(o);
[22]             announcer.notify(e);   // Generate the event.
[23]           }
[24]           return(result);
[25]         }
[26]       }

[27]       // Metaobject Protocol:
[28]       protocol EventProtocol(String cls, String meth) {
[29]         reify Invocation: GenEvent(cls, meth);
[30]       }

[31]       // Declarative association:
[32]       List ==> EventProtocol("List", "List.addAll");

[33]       // Dynamic association (alternative to declarative):
[34]       Object[] args = new Object[] {"List", "List.addAll"};
[35]       Meta.associate("List", "EventProtocol", args);
```

Fig. 12. A metaobject that examines execution context

ion code would be included in some other class, and the association declarations would be read by the JVM at startup.

4.2   Context Examination

The examination of execution context when an application operation is intercepted is an important facility, as has been highlighted by the *jumping aspects* problem [4]. The difficulty occurs when new behaviour must be applied to two public methods, one of which uses the other. In the example in fig. 12, adapted from [4] and [25], these two methods are in class `List`, and are used to add items to a list. If we want to notify some other component when something has been added to the list then we can do this by using a metaobject to handle invocation of methods on `List` instances. However, for efficiency we would like to generate only one event whether `addOne()` or `addAll()` was called by the client. To do this we need to apply the event generation behaviour to both methods, but make the event generation in `addOne()` conditional on the call not coming from `addAll()`.

Iguana/J addresses this problem by allowing the metaobject to examine the execution context to determine whether or not a call to `addAll()` is on the call stack of the current thread. This example also uses protocol parameters and a metaobject constructor to maintain the reusability of the metaobject class, specializing it for the application class at association time. The protocol may be associated with the application class declaratively or dynamically.

The example uses classes `EventControl`, a central repository of event generator objects, and `Announcer`, an event generator, to generate and listen for events from classes, such as `List`, that are not themselves designed as event sources.

4.3   Reusability

The separation that Iguana/J provides between metaobject classes and the declarative or dynamic association mechanisms, and the support that it provides for runtime specialization of metaobjects via protocol parameters, allow metaobject classes to be reusable in their compiled form.   The example in fig. 13, based on a reusability challenge problem in [25], illustrates this with a metaobject class that applies synchronization to any specified methods of any application class. The protocol takes an array of the names of the methods to which synchronization should be applied. The array is passed to the constructor of the metaobject class, which checks the method name against this array each time it intercepts an invocation.

The example includes two different application classes (`Stack` and `Fifo`), with no naming consistency between their methods, to which the synchronization behaviour is applied by associating the metaobject protocol with them. The association can be made declaratively or dynamically as convenient. The Iguana/J runtime engine dynamically creates the array when it detects a load of the application class specified in the declaration. If the association is made dynamically the metalevel programmer must explicitly create and fill the array

The example in fig. 13 also demonstrates Iguana/J's solution to the inheritance anomaly problem [16]. Associating the synchronization behaviour with any class will automatically associate it with subclasses. Synchronization will be applied to the specified methods in all subclass even if a subclass overrides the methods.

4.4   Dynamic Adaptation

Fig. 14 is an example that dynamically adapts an application to use a new communications API. The original communications API is a class called `Channel`, with

```
[1]  // Two separate application classes (not thread safe):
[2]  public class Stack {
[3]      void push(Object o) { ... }
[4]      Object pop() { ... }
[5]  }
[6]  public class Fifo {
[7]      void enqueue(Object o) { ... }
[8]      Object dequeue() { ... }
[9]  }

[10] // Metaobject class:
[11] public class Sync extends MExecute {
[12]     private String[] names; // Method names.
[13]     public Sync(String[] s) {
[14]         names = s;
[15]     }
[16]     public Object execute(Object o,Object[] args,Method m)
[17]                 throws InvocationTargetException {
[18]         if(inNames(m.getName())) {
[19]             synchronized(o) { return(proceed(o,args,m)); }
[20]         }
[21]         else return(proceed(o,args,m));
[22]     }
[23]     private boolean inNames(String mname) {
[24]         for(int i=0; i < names.length; i++) {
[25]             if(mname.equals(names[i]) return(true);
[26]         }
[27]         return(false);
[28]     }
[29] }

[30] // Protocol declaration:
[31] protocol SyncProtocol(String[] s) {
[32]     reify Invocation: Sync(s);
[33] }

[34] // Declarative associations:
[35] Stack ==> SyncProtocol({"pop","push"});
[36] Fifo ==> SyncProtocol({"dequeue","enqueue"});

[37] // Dynamic associations (alternative to declarative):
[38] Object[] params = new Object[1];
[39] params[0] = new String[] {"pop", "push"};
[40] Meta.associate("Stack", "SyncProtocol", params);
[41] params[0] = new String[] {"dequeue", "enqueue"};
[42] Meta.associate("Fifo", "SyncProtocol", params);
```

Fig. 13. A reusable metaobject class to apply synchronization `send()` and `receive()` methods that use an instance of `Message` to hold the information. The example dynamically replaces this with a class called `NewChannel`, with `write()` and `read()` methods that use an instance of `Block` to hold the information. The metaobject class `RedirectExecute` redirects all invocations of `send()` and `receive()` on an instance of `Channel` to methods `write()` and `read()` on an instance of `NewChannel`, converting arguments and return values as required. The instance of `NewChannel` is created by the metaobject the first time that a method execution on the original instance of `Channel` is intercepted.

The protocol declaration `RedirectChannel` declares that method execution on instances of `Channel` is to be handled by a metaobject of class `Redirect Execute`. It also declares that the metaobject is to be local rather than shared, so there will be one instance of `RedirectExecute` for each instance of `Channel`. This is required because `RedirectExecute` holds a reference to the instance of `NewChannel` that replaces one instance of `Channel`.

The adaptation may be applied at startup time, via an association declaration, or it may be applied dynamically at any time after startup. In both cases it affects all future clients of `Channel`, and if it is applied dynamically it is also effective for all existing clients. There are no typing implications for clients as they still hold only a reference to an instance of the original class. This allows any application class to be associated with any protocol, without anticipation of the specific association.

5   Related Work

A range of possible approaches to aspect oriented programming (AOP) are possible, from completely static to completely dynamic [25], and giving varying trade-offs between functionality and cost. This range may be understood in terms of the concepts of binding time and binding mode defined by [6]. Binding time describes when the weaving or association occurs, and may be compile time, load time or runtime. Binding mode describes the permanency of the binding, and may be static or dynamic. Static mode means that the binding cannot be undone, whereas dynamic mode means that it may be undone and redone. The completely static end of the range of AOP approaches supports static binding at compile time, while the completely dynamic end supports dynamic binding at runtime. It is acknowledged [5] that there is a lack of support at the dynamic end of the range at present.

At the static end of the range architectures such as AspectJ [14], Hyper/J [26] and Knit [8] provide support for encapsulation of cross-cutting concerns during system implementation, but they provide very limited support, if any, for dynamic adaptation. These approaches focus on helping the application programmer to modularize design concerns or system features that would otherwise cut across the conventional class structure of the application. The cross-cutting concerns or features are statically woven or associated with the appropriate parts of the application at compile time or load time. The aspects are essentially static components. While they may be reusable before runtime, there is very little support for manipulation of them while the system is running.

```
[1]  // Old API:
[2]  public class Channel {
[3]      public boolean send(Message m) { ... }
[4]      public Message receive() { ... }
[5]  }
[6]  public class Message { ... }  // Data structure.

[7]  // New API:
[8]  public class NewChannel {
[9]      public boolean write(Block b) { ... }
[10]     public Block read() { ... }
[11] }
[12] public class Block { ... }  // Data structure.

[13] // Invocation metaobject:
[14] public class RedirectExecute extends MExecute {
[15]     private NewChannel nc;
[16]     public Object execute(Object o,Object[] args,Method m)
[17]                  throws InvocationTargetException {
[18]         if(nc == null) nc = new NewChannel( ... );
[19]         String mname = m.getName();
[20]         if(mname.equals("send")) {
[21]             Message msg = (Message)args[0];
[22]             ...   // Convert msg to new Block.
[23]             return(nc.write(blk));
[24]         }
[25]         else if(mname.equals("receive") {
[26]             Block blk = nc.read();
[27]             ...   // Convert blk to new Message.
[28]             return(msg);
[29]         }
[30]         else return(proceed(o,args,m));
[31]     }
[32] }
[33] // Protocol:
[34] package com.foo.adapters;
[35] protocol RedirectChannel {
[36]     local: reify Invocation: RedirectExecute;
[37] }

[38] // Dynamic association:
[39] Meta.associate("com.acme.comms.Channel",
[40]                "com.foo.adapters.RedirectChannel");
```

Fig. 14. Dynamic update of a communications API

LEAD++ [1] is a reflective language that implements a dynamic adaptation model by extending the Java language. It supports dynamic adaptation of the structure of an application in response to specified changes in the state of the runtime environment, but the adaptations must be anticipated in the design of the application.

In the middle of the range, a number of reflective or dynamic AOP architectures use load time translation of binary code to introduce the hooks needed for runtime. These architectures make use of tools such as Binary Component Adaptation (BCA) [13] or Javassist [28] to perform the translation, but in general they are limited in the range of dynamic modifications supported because they establish the association mechanisms before runtime. Architectures that use this approach include Aspectual Components [15], Java Aspect Components (JAC) [19], Kava [29] and Reflex [24]. The first two are AOP architectures, while the second two are reflective architectures.

Aspectual Components supports reusable aspects for Java by separating the weaving declarations from the aspects itself. It uses BCA to perform the weaving at load time. It does not support runtime weaving or un-weaving, and therefore is a static aspect architecture. JAC also uses load time modification of selected application classes to insert the weaving mechanism. Once the mechanism has been inserted into a class the architecture supports a range of dynamic operations to weave and un-weave aspects at runtime, and thus it supports dynamic aspects. If a class has not been modified at load time then it is not possible to associate aspects with it.

Kava supports some dynamic manipulation of metaobjects, but only for application classes and operations that have been anticipated at load time. Reflex is a reflective architecture for Java that modifies bytecode to create reflective classes (with interception hooks) to replace the original classes. This can be done statically, or it can be done dynamically, but the application programmer must explicitly use the reflective class instead of the original one. Reflex supports dynamic manipulation of the metalevel, but it requires invasive changes to the base level program. AL-1/D [17] provides a strong separation between base and meta levels, but supports only limited dynamic manipulation of associations between the levels.

Architectures at the dynamic end of the range provide a more sophisticated dynamic adaptation model, usually by tightly integrating a runtime support engine into a virtual machine. Three such architectures are Guaraná [19], MetaclassTalk [2] and PROSE [20]. Guaraná uses a specialized JVM to provides runtime reflective facilities. The Guaraná JVM is based on a modified version of the Kaffe open source JVM (http://www.kaffe.org), and supports a wide range of dynamic operations to add and remove new behaviour. Guaraná focuses on metaobject composition and security. The metaobjects, representing new behaviour, that are associated with new application objects are influenced by the creating object rather than by the new object's class, and there is no explicit support for changing the behaviour of all instances of a class.

MetaclassTalk is a dynamic reflective architecture based on Smalltalk. It maintains runtime separation by implementing the metalevel as metaclasses, and the metalevel behaviour is applied to application objects by using the metaclasses as the classes of the application objects. Metaclasses may be written to be independent of specific application object types, and configuration properties are used to parameterize them for particular base level classes.

PROSE is a dynamic aspect architecture for Java. It retains portability by using the JVM Debug Interface (JVMDI) [23] to manipulate the JVM at runtime. PROSE supports dynamic association of Java classes, representing aspects, with arbitrary application classes. It also supports reusable aspects by allowing association details to be separately specified in *specializer* classes. It has some limitations, particularly in manipulation by an aspect of the value returned from an operation.

Iguana/J is also at the dynamic end of the range, but it addresses some of the weaknesses of the architectures described above by having a combination of a very strong separation of concerns, support for dynamic manipulation of associations with both classes and individual objects, and a structured metatyping model.

6   Conclusion

Iguana/J supports dynamic adaptation of the behaviour of arbitrary classes and objects in unanticipated ways, exploring the meaning of behavioural change in the context of a running application. It performs the association of the new behaviour with the target class or object on demand at runtime, with no preparation before runtime, so the source code of the application is not required. The architecture supports reusable new behaviour by providing a mechanism to specialize generic behaviours at association time, using protocol parameters, and by separating the specification of the association from the definition of the new behaviour. It does this without extending the Java language, allowing the programmer to implement new behaviour using familiar syntax. Iguana/J directly addresses acknowledged issues in dynamic adaptation and separation of concerns such as non-invasive association, reusability, context sensitivity, and the inheritance anomaly.

In common with other dynamic AOP and runtime reflection architectures Iguana/J has a significant execution time cost, but the implementation technique used ensures that a cost is only incurred for individual classes and objects that use dynamic adaptation. Comparisons of figures for other architectures also show that Iguana/J is of equal or better performance.

While Iguana/J can be used to apply new behaviour representing aspects of the application design, it does not inherently support the capture of cross-cutting concerns in the same way that static aspect architectures such as AspectJ and Hyper/J do. Iguana/J does not attempt to support direct structural changes to the application classes, on the basis that altering the public interface of a class dynamically is of limited use because of the difficulty making the changes usable by other classes. Iguana/J focuses on behavioural rather than structural changes.

References

1. Amano, N., Watanabe, T.: Reflection for Dynamic Adaptability: A Linguistic Approach Using LEAD++. In: Pierre Cointe, editor, Meta-Level Architectures and Reflection, Vol. 1616 of Lecture Notes in Computer Science, pages 138-140. Springer-Verlag (1999)
2. Bouraqadi, N.: Concern Oriented Programming using Reflection. Workshop on Advanced Separation of Concerns at OOPSLA 2000 (position paper)
3. Bouraqadi-Saâdani, N., Ledoux, T.: How to Weave? Workshop on advanced separation of concerns at ECOOP 2001 (position paper)
4. Brichau, J., de Meuter, W, de Volder, K.: Jumping Aspects. Workshop on aspects and dimensions of concern at ECOOP 2000 (position paper)
5. Brichau, J., Glandrup, M., Clarke, S., Bergmans, L.: Advanced Separation of Concerns. Report of workshop on advanced separation of concerns at ECOOP'2001. http://trese.cs.utwente.nl/Workshops/ecoop01asoc/ws.pdf

6. Czarnecki, K., Eisenecker, U.W.: Generative Programming. Addison Wesley (2000)
7. Dowling, J., Schäfer, T., Cahill, V., Haraszti, P, Redmond, B.: Using Reflection to Support Dynamic Adaptation of System Software. In: Cazzola, W., Stroud, R.J., Tisato, F. (eds): Reflection and Software Engineering, Vol. 1826 of Lecture Notes in Computer Science, pages 171-190. Springer-Verlag (2000)
8. Eide, E., Reid, A., Flatt, M., Lepreau, J.: Aspect Weaving as Component Knitting: Separating Concerns with Knit. Workshop on Advanced Separation of Concerns in Software Engineering at ICSE 2001 (position paper).
9. Gamma, E., Helm, R., Johnson, R., Vlissides, J.: Design Patterns: Elements of Reusable Object-Oriented Software. Addison-Wesley (1995)
10. Golm, M.: Design and Implementation of a Meta-Architecture for Java. Master's Thesis, Dept. of Computer Science, Friedrich-Alexander-University, Erlangen-Nuremberg (1997)
11. Golm, M., Kleinöder, J.: Jumping to the Meta Level: Behavioural Reflection can be Fast and Flexible. In: Cointe, P. (ed): Meta-Level Architectures and Reflection, Vol. 1616 of Lecture Notes in Computer Science, pages 22-39. Springer-Verlag (1999)
12. Gowing, B., Cahill, V.: Meta-object protocols for C++: The Iguana approach. In: Proceedings of Reflection '96, pages 137-152. XEROX Palo Alto Research Center (1996)
13. Keller, R., Hölzle, U.: Binary Component Adaptation. In: Jul, E. (ed): ECOOP'98 - Object-Oriented Programming, Vol. 1445 of Lecture Notes in Computer Science, pages 307-329. Springer-Verlag (1998)
14. Kiczales, G., Hilsdale, E., Hugunin, J., Kersten, M., Palm, J., Griswold, W.G.: An Overview of AspectJ. In: Knudsen, L.J. (ed): ECOOP 2001 - Object-Oriented Programming, Vol. 2072 of Lecture Notes in Computer Science, pages 327-353. Springer-Verlag (2001)
15. 15.Lieberherr, K., Lorenz, D., Mezini, M.: Programming with Aspectual Components. Technical report NU-CCS-99-01, College of Computer Science, Northeastern University, Boston MA (1999)
16. Matsuoka, S., Yonezawa, A.: Analysis of Inheritance Anomaly in Object-Oriented Concurrent Programming Languages. In: Agha, G., Wegner, P., Yonezawa, A. (eds): Research Directions in Concurrent Object-Oriented Programming, pages 107-150. MIT Press (1993)
17. 17.Okamura, H., Ishikawa, Y., Tokoro, M.: AL-1/D: A Distributed Programming System with Multi-Model Reflection Framework. In: Yonezawa, A., Smith, B.C. (eds): Proceedings of the IMSA'92 Workshop on Reflection and Metalevel Architecture. Tokyo (1992)
18. Oliva, A., Buzato, L.: The Implementation of Guaraná on Java. Technical report IC-98-32 of Instituto de Computação, Universidade Estadual de Campinas, Brazil (1998)
19. Pawlak, R., Seinturier, L., Duchien, L., Florin, G.: JAC: A Flexible Solution for Aspect-Oriented Programming in Java. In: Yonezawa, A., Matsuoka, S. (eds): MetaLevel Architectures and Separation of Crosscutting Concerns, Vol. 2192 of Lecture Notes in Computer Science, pages 1-24. Springer-Verlag (1999)
20. Popovici, A., Gross, T., Alonso, G.: Dynamic Homogenous AOP with PROSE. Technical report, Department of Computer Science, Federal Institute of Technology, Zurich (2001)
21. 21.Redmond, B., Cahill, V.: Iguana/J: Towards a Dynamic and Efficient Reflective Architecture for Java. Presented at ECOOP'00 workshop on Reflection and Meta-Level Architectures. Cannes, 2000. (position paper) http://www.dsg.cs.tcd.ie/~redmondb/iguanaj
22. Schäfer, T.: Supporting Meta-types in a Compiled Reflective Programming Language. PhD Thesis, Department of Computer Science, University of Dublin, Trinity College (2001)
23. Java Virtual Machine Debug Interface Refererence. Sun Microsystems (2000) http://java.sun.com/products/jdk/1.2/docs/guide/jvmdi/jvmdi.html .
24. Tanter, E., Bouraqadi-Saâdani, N., Noyé, J.: Reflex - Towards an Open Reflective Extension of Java. In: Yonezawa, A., Matsuoka, S. (eds): MetaLevel Architectures and Separation of Crosscutting Concerns, Vol. 2192 of Lecture Notes in Computer Science, pages 25-43. Springer-Verlag (2001)

25. Tarr, P., D'Hondt, M., Bergmans, L., Videira Lopes, C.: Workshop on Aspects and Dimensions of Concern. In: Malenfant, J., Moisant, S., Moreira, A. (eds): Object-Oriented Technology, Vol. 1964 of Lecture Notes in Computer Science, pages 203-240. Springer-Verlag (2000)
26. Tarr, P., Osher, H.: Hyper/J User and Installation Manual. IBM Research (2000)
27. Tatsubori, M., Chiba, S., Killijian, M., Itano, K.: OpenJava: A Class-based Macro System for Java. In: Cazzola, W., Stroud, R.J., Tisato, F. (eds): Reflection and Software Engineering, Vol. 1826 of Lecture Notes in Computer Science, pages 117-133. Springer-Verlag (2000)
28. Tatsubori, M., Sasaki, T., Chiba, S., Itano, K.: A Bytecode Translator for Distributed Execution of "Legacy" Java Software. In: Knudsen, L.J. (ed): ECOOP 2001 - Object-Oriented Programming, Vol. 2072 of Lecture Notes in Computer Science, pages 236-255. Springer-Verlag (2001)
29. Welch, I., Stroud, R.J.: Kava - Using Byte code Rewriting to add Behavioural Reflection to Java. In: proceedings of 6th USENIX Conference on Object Oriented Technologies and Systems. San Antonio, USA, January (2001)
30. Yellin, F.: The Java Native Code API. Sun Microsystems (1996)
    http://java.sun.com/docs/jit_interface.html

A Simple and Practical Approach
to Unit Testing: The JML and JUnit Way

Yoonsik Cheon and Gary T. Leavens

Department of Computer Science, Iowa State University
226 Atanasoff Hall, Ames, IA 50011-1040, USA
{cheon,leavens}@cs.iastate.edu

Abstract. Writing unit test code is labor-intensive, hence it is often
not done as an integral part of programming. However, unit testing is a
practical approach to increasing the correctness and quality of software;
for example, the Extreme Programming approach relies on frequent unit
testing.

In this paper we present a new approach that makes writing unit tests
easier. It uses a formal specification language's runtime assertion checker
to decide whether methods are working correctly, thus automating the
writing of unit test oracles. These oracles can be easily combined with
hand-written test data. Instead of writing testing code, the programmer
writes formal specifications (e.g., pre- and postconditions). This makes
the programmer's task easier, because specifications are more concise
and abstract than the equivalent test code, and hence more readable
and maintainable. Furthermore, by using specifications in testing, specification errors are quickly discovered, so the specifications are more likely
to provide useful documentation and inputs to other tools. We have implemented this idea using the Java Modeling Language (JML) and the
JUnit testing framework, but the approach could be easily implemented
with other combinations of formal specification languages and unit test
tools.

1 Introduction

Program testing is an effective and practical way of improving correctness of
software, and thereby improving software quality. It has many benefits when
compared to more rigorous methods like formal reasoning and proof, such as
simplicity, practicality, cost effectiveness, immediate feedback, understandabil-
ity, and so on. There is a growing interest in applying program testing to the
development process, as reflected by the Extreme Programming (XP) approach
[4]. In XP, unit tests are viewed as an integral part of programming. Tests are
created before, during, and after the code is written — often emphasized as
"code a little, test a little, code a little, and test a little ..." [3]. The philosophy
behind this is to use regression tests [22] as a practical means of supporting
refactoring.

B. Magnusson (Ed.): ECOOP 2002, LNCS 2374, pp. 231–255, 2002.
© Springer-Verlag Berlin Heidelberg 2002

1.1   The Problem

However, writing unit tests is a laborious, tedious, cumbersome, and often difficult task. If the testing code is written at a low level of abstraction, it may be tedious and time-consuming to change it to match changes in the code. One problem is that there may simply be a lot of testing code that has to be examined and revised. Another problem occurs if the testing program refers to details of the representation of an abstract data type; in this case, changing the representation may require changing the testing program.

To avoid these problems, one should automate more of the writing of unit test code. The goal is to make writing testing code easier and more maintainable.

One way to do this is to use a framework that automates some of the details of running tests. An example of such a framework is JUnit [3]. It is a simple yet practical testing framework for Java classes; it encourages the close integration of testing with development by allowing a test suite be built incrementally.

However, even with tools like JUnit, writing unit tests often requires a great deal of effort. Separate testing code must be written and maintained in synchrony with the code under development, because the test class must inherit from the JUnit framework. This test class must be reviewed when the code under test changes, and, if necessary, also revised to reflect the changes. In addition, the test class suffers from the problems described above. The difficulty and expense of writing the test class are exacerbated during development, when the code being tested changes frequently. As a consequence, during development there is pressure to not write testing code and to not test as frequently as might be optimal.

We encountered these problems ourselves in writing Java code. The code we have been writing is part of a tool suite for the Java Modeling Language (JML). JML is a behavioral interface specification language for Java [25,24]. In our implementation of these tools, we have been formally documenting the behavior of some of our implementation classes in JML. This enabled us to use JML's runtime assertion checker to help debug our code [6,9]. In addition, we have been using JUnit as our testing framework. We soon realized that we spent a lot of time writing test classes and maintaining them. In particular we had to write many query methods to determine test success or failure. We often also had to write code to build expected results for test cases. We also found that refactoring made testing painful; we had to change the test classes to reflect changes in the refactored code. Changing the representation data structures for classes also required us to rewrite code that calculated expected results for test cases.

While writing unit test methods, we soon realized that most often we were translating method pre- and postconditions into the code in corresponding testing methods. The preconditions became the criteria for selecting test inputs, and the postconditions provided the properties to check for test results. That is, we turned the postconditions of methods into code for test oracles. A *test oracle* determines whether or not the results of a test execution are correct [31,34,37]. Developing test oracles from postconditions approach helped avoid dependence of the testing code on the representation data structures, but still required us to write lots of query methods. In addition, there was no direct connection between the specifications and the test oracles, hence they could easily become inconsistent.

These problems led us to think about ways of testing code that would save us time and effort. We also wanted to have less duplication of effort between the specifications we were writing and the testing code. Finally, we wanted the process to help keep specifications, code, and tests consistent with each other.

1.2 Our Approach

In this paper, we propose a solution to these problems. We describe a simple and effective technique that automates the generation of oracles for unit testing classes. The conventional way of implementing a test oracle is to compare the test output to some pre-calculated, presumably correct, output [16,30]. We take a different perspective. Instead of building expected outputs and comparing them to the test outputs, we monitor the specified behavior of the method being tested to decide whether the test passed or failed. This monitoring is done using the formal specification language's runtime assertion checker. We also show how the user can combine hand-written test inputs with these test oracles. Our approach thus combines formal specifications (such as JML) and a unit testing framework (such as JUnit).

Formal interface specifications include class invariants and pre- and postconditions. We assume that these specifications are fairly complete descriptions of the desired behavior. Although the testing process will encourage the user to write better preconditions, the quality of the generated test oracles will depend on the quality of the specification's postconditions. The quality of these postconditions is the user's responsibility, just as the quality of hand-written test oracles would be.

We wrote a tool to automatically generate JUnit test classes from JML specifications. The generated test classes send messages to objects of the Java classes under test; they catch assertion violation exceptions from test cases that pass an initial precondition check. Such assertion violation exceptions are used to decide if the code failed to meet its specification, and hence that the test failed. If the class under test satisfies its interface specification for some particular input values, no such exceptions will be thrown, and that particular test execution succeeds. So the automatically generated test code serves as a test oracle whose behavior is derived from the specified behavior of the target class. (There is one complication which is explained in Section 4.) The user is still responsible for generating test data; however the generated test classes make it easy for the user to add test data.

1.3 Outline

The remainder of this paper is organized as follows. In Section 2 we describe the capabilities our approach assumes from a formal interface specification language and its runtime assertion checker, using JML as an example. In Section 3 we describe the capabilities our approach assumes from a testing framework, using JUnit as an example. In Section 4 we explain our approach in detail; we discuss design issues such as how to decide whether tests fail or not, test fixture setup, and explain the automatic generation of test methods and test classes. In Section 5 we discuss how the user can add test data by hand to the automatically generated test classes. In Section 6 we discuss other issues. In Section 7 we describe related work and we conclude, in Section 8, with a description of our experience, future plans, and the contributions of our work.

2   Assumptions about the Formal Specification Language

Our approach assumes that the formal specification language specifies the interface (i.e., names and types) and behavior (i.e., functionality) of classes and methods. We assume that the language has a way to express class invariants and method specifications consisting of pre- and postconditions.

Our approach can also handle specification of some more advanced features. One such feature is an *intra-condition*, usually written as an **assert** statement. Another is a distinction between normal and exceptional postconditions. A *normal postcondition* describes the behavior of a method when it returns without throwing an exception; an *exceptional postcondition* describes the behavior of a method when it throws an exception.

The Java Modeling Language (JML) [24,25] is an example of such a formal specification language. JML specifications are tailored to Java, and its assertions are written in a superset of Java's expression language.

Fig. 1 shows an example JML specification. As shown, a JML specification is commonly written as annotation comments in a Java source file. Annotation comments start with //@ or are enclosed in /*@ and @*/. Within the latter kind of comment, at-signs (@) on the beginning of lines are ignored. The spec_public annotation lets non-public declarations such as private fields **name** and **weight** be considered to be public for specification purposes[1]. The fourth line of the figure gives an example of an invariant, which should be true in each publicly-visible state.

In JML, method specifications precede the corresponding method declarations. Method preconditions start with the keyword **requires**, frame axioms start with the keyword **assignable**, normal postconditions start with the keyword **ensures**, and exceptional postconditions start with the keyword **signals** [18,24,25]. The semantics of such a JML specification states that a method's precondition must hold before the method is called. When the precondition holds, the method must terminate and when it does, the appropriate postconditions must hold. If it returns normally, then its normal postcondition must hold in

---

[1] As in Java, a field specification can have an access modifier determining the visibility. If not specified, it defaults to that of the Java declaration; i.e., without the spec_public annotations, both **name** and **weight** could be used only in private specifications.

```
public class Person {
   private /*@ spec_public @*/ String name;
   private /*@ spec_public @*/ int weight;
   //@ public invariant name != null && name.length() > 0 && weight >= 0;

   /*@ public behavior
     @   requires n != null &&  name.length() > 0;
     @   assignable name, weight;
     @   ensures n.equals(name) && weight == 0;
     @   signals (Exception e) false;
     @*/
   public Person(String n) { name = n; weight = 0; }

   /*@ public behavior
     @   assignable weight;
     @   ensures kgs >= 0 && weight == \old(weight + kgs);
     @   signals (IllegalArgumentException e) kgs < 0;
     @*/
   public void addKgs(int kgs) { weight += kgs; }

   /*@ public behavior
     @   ensures \result == weight;
     @   signals (Exception e) false;
     @*/
   public /*@ pure @*/ int getWeight() { return weight; }

   /* ... */
}
```

Fig. 1. An example JML specification. The implementation of the method addKgs contains an error to be revealed in Section 5.2. This error was overlooked in our initial version of this paper, and so is an example of a "real" error.

the post-state (i.e., the state just after the body's execution), but if it throws an exception, then the appropriate exceptional postcondition must hold in the post-state. For example, the constructor must return normally when called with a non-null, non-empty string n. It cannot throw an exception because the corresponding exceptional postcondition is false.

JML has lots of syntactic sugar that can be used to highlight various properties for the reader and to make specifications more concise. For example, one can omit the requires clause if the precondition is true, as in the specification of addKgs. However, we will not discuss these sugars in detail here.

JML follows Eiffel [27,28] in having special syntax, written \old(e) to refer to the pre-state value of e, i.e., the value of e just before execution of the body of the method. This is often used in situations like that shown in the normal postcondition of addKgs.

For a non-void method, such as getWeight, \result can be used in the normal postcondition to refer to the return value. The method getWeight is specified to be *pure*, which means that its execution cannot have any side effects. In JML, only pure methods can be used in assertions.

In addition to pre- and postconditions, one can also specify intra-conditions with `assert` statements.

2.1   The Runtime Assertion Checker

The basic task of the runtime assertion checker is to execute code in a way that is transparent, unless an assertion violation is detected. That is, if a method is called and no assertion violations occur, then, except for performance measures (time and space) the behavior of the method is unchanged. In particular, this implies that, as in JML, assertions can be executed without side effects.

We do not assume that the runtime assertion checker can execute all assertions in the specification language. However, only the assertions it can execute are of interest in this paper.

We assume that the runtime assertion checker has a way of signaling assertion violations to a method's callers. In practice this is most conveniently done using exceptions. While any systematic mechanism for indicating assertion violations would do, to avoid circumlocutions, we will assume that exceptions are used in the remainder of this paper.

The runtime assertion checker must have some exceptions that it can use without interference from user programs. These exceptions are thus reserved for use by the runtime assertion checker. We call such exceptions assertion violation exceptions. It is convenient to assume that all such assertion violation exceptions are subtypes of a single assertion violation exception type.

JML's runtime assertion checker can execute a constructive subset of JML assertions, including some forms of quantifiers [6,9]. In functionality, it is similar to other design by contract tools [23,27,28,35]; such tools could also be used with our approach.

To explain how JML's runtime checker monitors Java code for assertion violations, it is necessary to explain the structure of the instrumented code compiled by the checker. Each Java class and method with associated JML specifications is instrumented as shown by example in Fig. 2. The original method becomes a private method, e.g., `addKgs` becomes `internal$addKgs`. The checker generates a new method, e.g., `addKgs`, to replace it, which calls `internal$addKgs` inside a `try` statement.

The generated method first checks the method's precondition and class invariant, if any[2]. This check throws either `JMLEntryPreconditionException` or `JMLInvariantException` if these assertions are not satisfied. After the original method is executed in the `try` block, the normal postcondition is checked, or, if exceptions were thrown, the exceptional postconditions are checked in the

---

[2] To handle old expressions (as used in the postcondition of `addKgs`), the instrumented code evaluates each old expression occurring in the postconditions from within the `checkPre$addKgs` method, and binds the resulting value to a private field of the class. The corresponding private field is used when checking postconditions.

```
public void addKgs(int kgs) {
  checkPre$addKgs(kgs); // check precondition
  checkInv(); // check invariant
  boolean rac$ok = true;
  try {
    internal$addKgs(kgs);
    checkPost$addKgs(kgs); // check normal postcondition
  } catch (JMLEntryPreconditionException e) {
    rac$ok = false;
    throw new JMLInternalPreconditionException(e);
  } catch (JMLAssertionException e) {
    rac$ok = false;
    throw e;
  } catch (Throwable e) {
    try { // check exceptional postcondition
      checkExceptionalPost$addKgs(kgs, e);
    } catch (JMLAssertionException e1) {
      rac$ok = false; // an exceptional postcondition violation
      throw e1;
    }
  } finally {
    if (rac$ok) {
      checkInv(); // check invariant
    }
  }
}
```

Fig. 2. The top-level of the run-time assertion checker's translation of the addKgs method in class **Person**. (Some details have been suppressed.)

third `catch` block. To make assertion checking transparent, the code that checks the exceptional postcondition re-throws the original exception if the exceptional postcondition is satisfied; otherwise, it throws a `JMLPostconditionException`. In the `finally` block, the class invariant is checked again. The purpose of the first `catch` block is explained below (see Section 4.1).

Our approach assumes that the runtime assertion checker can distinguish two kinds of precondition assertion violations: *entry precondition violations* and *internal precondition violations*. The former refers to violations of preconditions of the method being tested. The latter refers to precondition violations that arise during the execution of the tested method's body. Other distinctions among assertion violations are useful in reporting errors to the user, but are not important for our approach.

In JML the assertion violation exceptions are organized into an exception hierarchy as shown in Fig. 3. The ultimate superclass of all assertion violation exceptions is the abstract class `JMLAssertionException`. This class has several subclasses that correspond to different kinds of assertion violations, such as precondition violations, postcondition violations, invariant violations, and so on. The entry precondition violation and the internal precondition violation of

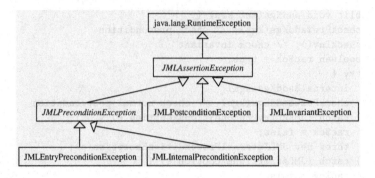

Fig. 3. A part of the exception hierarchy for JML runtime assertion violations.

our assumptions correspond to the types `JMLEntryPreconditionException` and `JMLInternalPreconditionException`. Both are concrete subclasses of the abstract class `JMLPreconditionException`.

3   Assumptions about the Testing Framework

Our approach assumes that unit tests are to be run for each method of each class being tested. We assume that the framework provides *test methods*, which are methods used to test the methods of the class under test. For convenience, we will assume that test methods can be grouped into test classes.

In our approach, each test method executes several test cases for the method it is testing. Thus we assume that a test method can indicate to the framework whether each test case fails, succeeds, or was meaningless. The outcome will be meaningless if an entry precondition violation exception occurs for the test case; details are given in Section 5.2.

We also assume that there is a way to provide test data to test methods. Following JUnit's terminology, we call this a test fixture. A *test fixture* is a context for executing a test; it typically contains several declarations for test inputs and expected outputs.

For the convenience of the users of our approach, we assume that it is possible to define a global test fixture, i.e., one that is shared by all test methods in a test class. With a global test fixture, one needs ways to initialize the test inputs, and to undo any side effects of a test after running the test.

JUnit is a simple, useful testing framework for Java [3,20]. In JUnit, a test class consists of a set of test methods. The simplest way to tell the framework about the test methods is to name them all with names beginning with "`test`". The framework uses introspection to find all these methods, and can run them when requested.

Fig. 4 is a sample JUnit test class, which is designed to test the class `Person`. Every JUnit test class must be a subclass, directly or indirectly, of the framework class `TestCase`. The class `TestCase` provides a basic facility to write test classes,

```
import junit.framework.*;
public class PersonTest extends TestCase {
  private Person p;
  public PersonTest(String name) {
    super(name);
  }
  public void testAddKgs() {
    p.addKgs(10);
    assertEquals(10, p.getWeight());
  }
  protected void setUp() {
    p = new Person("Baby");
  }
  protected void tearDown() {
  }
  public static Test suite() {
    return new TestSuite(PersonTest.class);
  }
  public static void main(String args[]) {
    String[] testCaseName = {PersonTest.class.getName()};
    junit.textui.TestRunner.main(testCaseName);
  }
}
```

Fig. 4. A sample JUnit test class.

e.g., defining test data, asserting test success or failure, and composing test methods into a test suite.

One uses methods like `assertEquals`, defined in the framework, to write test methods, as in the test method `testAddKgs`. Such methods indicate test success or failure to the framework. For example, when the arguments to `assertEquals` are not equal, the test fails. Another such framework method is `fail`, which directly indicates test failure. JUnit assumes that a test succeeds unless the test method throws an exception or indicates test failure. Thus the only way a test method can indicate success is to return normally.

JUnit thus does not provide a way to indicate that a test execution was meaningless. This is because it is geared toward counting executions of test methods instead of test cases, and because hand-written tests are assumed to be meaningful. However, in our approach we need to extend JUnit to allow the counting of test case executions and to track which test cases were meaningful. We extended the JUnit framework to do this by writing a class `JMLTestRunner`, which tracks the meaningful test cases executed.

JUnit provides two methods to manipulate the test fixture: `setUp` creates objects and does any other tasks needed to run a test, and `tearDown` undoes otherwise permanent side-effects of tests. For example, the `setUp` method in Fig. 4 creates a new `Person` object, and assigns it to the test fixture variable p. The `tearDown` method can be omitted if it does nothing. JUnit automatically invokes the `setUp` and `tearDown` methods before and after each test method is executed (respectively).

The static method `suite` creates a *test suite*, i.e., a collection of test methods. To run tests, JUnit first obtains a test suite by invoking the method `suite`, and then runs each test method in the suite. A test suite can contain several test methods, and it can contain other test suites, recursively. Fig. 4 uses Java's reflection facility to create a test suite consisting of all the test methods of class `PersonTest`.

4 Test Oracle Generation

This section presents the details of our approach to automatically generating a JUnit test class from a JML-annotated Java class. We first describe how test outcomes are determined. Then we describe the convention and protocol for the user to supply test data to the automatically generated test oracles in the test classes. After that we discuss in detail the automatic generation of test methods and test classes.

4.1 Deciding Test Outcomes

A test class has one test method, $testM$, for each method, M, to be tested in the original class. The method $testM$ runs M on several test cases. Conceptually, a *test case* consists of a pair of a receiver object (an instance of the class being tested) and a sequence of argument values; for testing static methods, a test case does not include the receiver object.

The outcome of a call to M for a given test case is determined by whether the runtime assertion checker throws an exception during M's execution, and what kind of exception is thrown. If no exception is thrown, then the test case succeeds (assuming the call returns), because there was no assertion violation, and hence the call must have satisfied its specification.

Similarly, if the call to M for a given test case throws an exception that is not an assertion violation exception, then this also indicates that the call to M succeeded for this test case. Such exceptions are passed along by the runtime assertion checker because it is assumed to be transparent. Hence if the call to M throws such an exception instead of an assertion violation exception, then the call must have satisfied M's specification, specifically, the exceptional postcondition. With JUnit, such exceptions must, however, be caught by the test method $testM$, since any such exceptions are interpreted by the framework as signaling test failure. Hence, the $testM$ method must catch and ignore all exceptions that are not assertion violation exceptions.

If the call to M for a test case throws an assertion violation exception, however, things become interesting. If the assertion violation exception is not a precondition exception, then the method M is considered to fail that test case.

However, we have to be careful with the treatment of precondition violations. A precondition is an obligation that the client must satisfy; nothing else in the specification is guaranteed if the precondition is violated. Therefore, when a test method $testM$ calls method M and M's precondition does not hold, we do not consider that to be a test failure; rather, when M signals a precondition exception, it indicates that the given test input is outside M's domain, and thus is inappropriate for test execution. We call the outcome of such a test execution "meaningless" instead of calling it either a success or failure. On the other hand, precondition violations that arise inside the execution of M should still be considered to be test failures. To do this, we distinguish two kinds of precondition violations that may occur when test M runs M on a test case, $(o, \vec{x})$:

- The precondition of M fails for $(o, \vec{x})$, which indicates, as above, that the test case $(o, \vec{x})$ is outside M's domain. As noted earlier, this is called an *entry* precondition violation.
- A method f called from within M's body signals a precondition violation, which indicates that M's body did not meet f's precondition, and thus that M failed to correctly implement its specification on the test case $(o, \vec{x})$. (Note that if M calls itself recursively, then f may be the same as M.) Such an assertion violation is an *internal* precondition violation.

The JML runtime assertion checker converts the second kind of precondition violation into an internal precondition violation exception. Thus, test M decides that M fails on a test case $(o, \vec{x})$ if M throws an internal precondition violation exception, but rejects the test case $(o, \vec{x})$ as meaningless if it throws an entry precondition violation exception. This treatment of precondition exceptions was the main change that we had to make to JML's existing runtime assertion checker to implement our approach. The treatment of meaningless test case executions is also the only place where we had to extend the JUnit testing framework.

To summarize, the outcome of a test execution is "failure" if an assertion violation exception other than an entry precondition violation is thrown, is "meaningless" if an entry precondition violation is thrown, and "success" otherwise.

4.2   Setting up Test Cases

In our approach, a test fixture is responsible for constructing test data, i.e., constructing receiver objects and argument objects. For example, testing the method addKgs of class Person (see Fig. 1) requires one object of type Person in the test fixture, and one value of type int. The first object will be the receiver of the message addKgs, and the second will be the argument. In our approach, a test fixture does not need to construct expected outputs, because success or failure is determined by observing the runtime assertion checker, not by comparing results to expected outputs.

How does the user define these objects and values in the test fixture, for use by the automatically generated test methods? There are three general approaches to answering this question: (i) one can define a separate fixture for each test method, (ii) a global test fixture shared by all methods, or (iii) a combination of both. In the first approach, each test method defines a separate set of test fixture variables, resulting in more flexible and customizable configuration. However this makes more work for the user. Thus, we take the second approach. Other than execution time, there is no harm to run a test execution with a test fixture of another method if both are type-compatible; it may turn out to be more effective. The more test cases, the better! One might worry that some of these inputs may violate preconditions for some methods; recall, however, that entry precondition violations are not treated as test failures, and so such inputs cause no problems.

Our implementation defines test fixture variables as one-dimensional arrays. The test fixture variables are defined to be `protected` fields of the test class so that users can initialize them in subclasses of the automatically generated test classes. To let test fixtures be shared by all test methods, we adopt a simple naming convention. Let C be a class to be tested and $T_1, T_2, \ldots, T_n$ be the formal parameter types of all the methods to be tested in the class C. Then, the test fixture for the class C is defined as[3]:

C[] `receivers`; T_1[] vT_1; $\ldots$; T_n[] vT_n;

The first array named `receivers` is for the set of receiver objects (i.e., objects to be tested) and the rest for argument objects.

If a particular method has formal parameter types $A_1, A_2, \ldots, A_m$, where each A_i is drawn from the set $\{T_1, \ldots, T_n\}$, then its test cases are:

$$\{\langle \mathtt{receivers}[i], vA_1[j_1], \ldots, vA_m[j_m] \rangle \mid 0 \le i < \mathtt{receivers.length},$$
$$0 \le j_1 < vA_1.\mathtt{length}, \ldots, 0 \le j_m < vA_m.\mathtt{length}\}$$

For example, the methods to be tested from the class `Person` (that are shown in Fig. 1) have only one type of formal parameter, which is the type `int` (in the method `addKgs`). Therefore, the class `Person`'s fixture is defined as follows:

```
protected Person[] receivers; // objects to be tested
protected int[] vint;         // arguments
```

So the test cases for the method `addKgs` are

$$\{\langle \mathtt{receivers}[i], \mathtt{vint}[j] \rangle \mid 0 \le i < \mathtt{receivers.length}, 0 \le j < \mathtt{vint.length}\}$$

whereas those of the method `getWeight`, are

$$\{\langle \mathtt{receivers}[i] \rangle \mid 0 \le i < \mathtt{receivers.length}\}.$$

The test fixture variables such as `receivers` and `vint` will be initialized and reset by the methods `setUp` and `tearDown` respectively (see Section 4.4 for more details).

4.3 Test Methods

Recall that there will be a separate test method, `test`M for each target method, M, to be tested. The purpose of `test`M is to determine the outcome of calling M

---

[3] For array types we use the character $ to denote their dimensions, e.g., `vint_$_$` for `int[][]`.

```
public void testM() {
  final A₁[] a₁ = vA₁;
    ...
  final Aₙ[] aₙ = vAₙ;
  for (int i₀ = 0; i₀ < receivers.length; i₀++)
    for (int i₁ = 0; i₁ < a₁.length; i₁++)
      ...
      for (int iₙ = 0; iₙ < aₙ.length; iₙ++) {
        if (receivers[i₀] != null) {
          try {
            receivers[i₀].M(a₁[i₁], ..., aₙ[iₙ]);
          }
          catch (JMLEntryPreconditionException e) {
            /* ... tell framework test case was meaningless ... */
            continue;
          }
          catch (JMLAssertionException e) {
            String msg = /* a String showing the test case */;
            fail(msg + NEW_LINE + e.getMessage());
          }
          catch (java.lang.Throwable e) {
            continue; // success for this test case
          }
          finally {
            setUp(); // restore test cases
          }
        } else {
          /* ... tell framework test case was meaningless ... */
        }
        ...
      }
}
```

Fig. 5. A skeleton of generated test methods.

with each test case and to give an informative message if the test execution fails for that test case. The method **test**M accomplishes this by invoking M with each test case and indicating test failure when the runtime assertion checker throws an assertion violation exception that is not an entry precondition violation. Test methods also note when test cases were rejected as meaningless.

To describe our implementation, let C be a Java class annotated with a JML specification and C_JML_Test the JUnit test class generated from the class C. For each instance (i.e., non-**static**) method of the form:

$$T \; M(A_1 \; a_1,\ldots, \; A_n \; a_n) \; \textbf{throws} \; E_1,\ldots, \; E_m \; \{ \; /* \; \ldots \; */ \; \}$$

of the class C, a corresponding test method **test**M is generated in the test class C_JML_Test.

The generated test method **test**M has the code skeleton shown in Fig. 5. The test method first initializes a sequence of local variables to the test fixture variables corresponding to the formal parameters of the method under test. The local variables are named the same as the formal parameters of the method under test. The local variables are not necessary, but they make the resulting code more comprehensible if one should ever try to read the generated test class. For each test case, given by the test fixture, the test method then invokes the method under test in a `try` statement and sees if the JML runtime assertion checker throws an exception. As described above, an assertion violation exception (`JMLAssertionException`) other than an entry precondition violation exception means a failure of the test execution; thus an appropriate error message is composed and printed. The message contains the failed method name, the failed test case (i.e., the values of receiver and argument objects), and the exception thrown by the JML runtime assertion checker. The `finally` block restores test cases to their original values (see Section 5). It prevents side-effects of one test execution, e.g., mutation of the receiver or argument objects, from being carried over to another.

A similar form of test methods are generated for static methods. For static methods, however, test messages are sent to the class itself, therefore, the outermost `for` loop is omitted and the body of the `try` block is replaced with $C.M(a_1[i_1], \ldots, a_n[i_n])$.

Test methods are generated only for public and package visible methods. That is, no test methods are generated for private and protected methods, although these may be indirectly tested through testing of the other methods. Also, test methods are not generated for a `static public void` method named `main`; testing the main method seems inappropriate for unit testing. Furthermore, no test methods are generated for constructor methods. However, we should note that constructor methods are implicitly tested when the test fixture variable `receivers` is initialized; if the pre- or postconditions of a constructor are violated during initialization, the test setup will fail, and the user will be led to the error by the message in the assertion violation exception.

Fig. 6 is an example test method generated for the method `addKgs` of the class `Person`. We use a very simple convention to name the generated test methods. We prefix the original method name with the string "`test`" and capitalize the initial letter of the method name[4].

4.4   Test Classes

In addition to test fixture definition and test methods described in the previous sections, a JUnit test class must have several other methods. Let C be a Java class annotated with a JML specification and C_JML_Test the JUnit test class generated from the class C.

A JUnit test class should inherit from the JUnit framework's class `TestCase`. The `package` and `import` definitions for C_JML_Test are copied verbatim from the class C. As a result, the generated test class will reside in the same package.

---

[4]   If necessary, the tool appends a unique suffix to prevent a name clash due to method overloading.

```
public void testAddKgs() {
  final int[] kgs = vint;
  for (int i = 0; i < receivers.length; i++)
    for (int j = 0; j < kgs.length; j++) {
      if (receivers[i] != null) {
        try {
          receivers[i].addKgs(kgs[j]);
        }
        catch (JMLEntryPreconditionException e) {
          /* ... tell framework test case was meaningless ... */
          continue;
        }
        catch (JMLAssertionException e) {
          String msg = /* a String showing the test case */;
          fail(msg + NEW_LINE + e.getMessage());
        }
        catch (java.lang.Throwable e) {
          continue;
        }
        finally {
          setUp();
        }
      } else {
        /* ... tell framework test case was meaningless ... */
      }
    }
}
```

Fig. 6. Code generated for testing the method **addKgs** of the class **Person**. Details of generating the error messages and telling the framework about meaningless test cases are suppressed.

This allows the test class to have access to package-private members of the class under test. In addition to the copied import definitions, several **import** statements are generated that import JUnit-specific packages.

The test class includes several boilerplate methods that are the same in all the generated test classes. A constructor, a main method, and a method for test suites are automatically generated, as shown in Fig. 7.

As explained in the previous section, test fixture variables are defined as protected member fields. A test fixture definition is accompanied by a default **setUp** method. The **setUp** method must be redefined by a subclass to populate the test fixture with actual test data. Let $T_1, T_2, \ldots, T_n$ be the formal parameter types of all the methods to be tested in the class C. Then, the test fixture for the class C and the **setUp** method are defined as in Fig. 8 (see also Section 4.2).

For example, the generated code for the test fixture definition and test fixture setup methods of the test class, **Person_JML_Test**, generated for our example class **Person**, will be as shown in Fig. 9.

```
public C_JML_Test(String name) {
  super(name);
}
public static void main(String[] args) {
    org.jmlspecs.jmlunit.JMLTestRunner.run(suite());
}
public static Test suite() {
    return new TestSuite(C_JML_Test.class);
}
```

Fig. 7. Boilerplate methods for JUnit test class for testing class C.

```
protected C[] receivers;
protected T1[] vT1;
  ...
protected Tn[] vTn;

protected void setUp() {
  receivers = new C[0];
  vT1 = new T1[0];
    ...
  vTn = new Tn[0];
}
```

Fig. 8. Skeleton of the automatically generated test fixture.

```
protected Person[] receivers;
protected int[] vint;

protected void setUp() {
  receivers = new Person[0];
  vint = new int[0];
}
```

Fig. 9. Example of an automatically generated test fixture, for Person.

Test fixture variables are initialized to empty arrays so that the test class can be run "out of the box," although it is not very useful to do so. At least the setUp method, and sometimes the tearDown method (inherited from the class TestCase), should be overridden in subclasses to populate the fixture with actual test data (see Section 5).

5   Supplying and Running Test Cases

To perform actual test executions, the user must supply reasonable test inputs by initializing the test fixture variables. This can be done either by directly editing the setUp method of the generated test class or by subclassing and redefining the setUp method. We recommend the subclassing approach. The subclassing

```
import junit.framework.*;
import junit.extensions.*;

public class PersonTestCase extends Person_JML_Test
{
  public PersonTestCase(String name) {
    super(name);
  }

  protected void setUp() {
    receivers = new Person[4];
    receivers[0] = new Person("Baby");
    receivers[1] = new Person("Cortez");
    receivers[2] = new Person("Isabella");
    receivers[3] = null;
    vint = new int[] { 10, -22, 0, 1, 55, 3000 };
  }

  public static Test suite() {
    return new TestSuite(PersonTestCase.class);
  }

  public static void main(String[] args) {
    org.jmlspecs.jmlunit.JMLTestRunner.run(suite());
  }
}
```

Fig. 10. The user-defined class that defines the test fixture for the class `Person`.

approach prevents the user from losing test cases if the test class is regenerated. In addition, the user can tune the testing by adding hand-written test methods to subclasses. The JUnit framework collects and exercises the added test methods together with the automatically generated methods.

5.1 Populating the Test Fixture with Test Data

A test input can be any type-correct value. For example, we can set the test fixture variables for the class `Person` as written in Fig. 10. Remember that the test class for the class `Person` has two test fixture variables `receivers` and `vint`, of types `Person[]` and `int[]` respectively.

As shown, test inputs can even be `null`. Also there can be aliasing among the test fixture variables, although this is not shown in our example. With the above test fixture, the `addKgs` method is tested 24 times, one for each pair of `receivers[i]` and `vint[j]`, where $0 \leq i < 4$ and $0 \leq j < 6$.

5.2 Running Test Cases

It is very simple to perform test execution with user-defined test cases such as the class `PersonTestCase` shown in Fig. 10. It is done in three steps as follows.

```
.F..
Time: 0.041
There was 1 failure:
1) testAddKgs(PersonTestCase)junit.framework.AssertionFailedError:
        Method 'addKgs' applied to
        Receiver receivers[0]: Person("Baby",-22)
        Argument 'kgs' (vint[1]): -22
        Caused org.jmlspecs.jmlrac.runtime.JMLPostconditionException
        Assertion of method 'addKgs' of class 'Person' specified at
        Person.java:16:25
        at Person_JML_Test.testAddKgs(Person_JML_Test.java:57)
        at Person_JML_Test.run(Person_JML_Test.java:24)
        at org.jmlspecs.jmlunit.JMLTestRunner.run(JMLTestRunner.java:114)
        at PersonTestCase.main(PersonTestCase.java:22)


FAILURES!!!
Tests run: 3,  Failures: 1,  Errors: 0
Test cases run: 8/10 (meaningful/total)
```

Fig. 11. Output from running the tests in `PersonTestClass`.

```
public void addKgs(int kgs) {
    if (kgs >= 0)
        weight += kgs;
    else
        throw new IllegalArgumentException("Negative Kgs");
}
```

Fig. 12. Corrected implementation of method `addKgs` in class `Person`.

1. Generate an instrumented Java class for the class to be tested, e.g., class `Person`, using the `jmlc` script.
2. Generate and compile a JUnit test class for the target class, e.g., class, `Person_JML_Test`, using the `jmlunit` script and `javac`.
3. Compile and run the user-defined test case class, e.g., class `PersonTestCase`, using `javac` and `java`.

The first two steps can also be done using the command `jtest`; for example, the command "`jtest Person.java`" does them assuming that the class `Person` is stored in the file `Person.java`. Of course, the last step can be done with any Java compiler and interpreter.

Fig. 11 shows the result of running the test cases of Fig. 10, i.e., the class `PersonTestCase`. It reveals the error that we mentioned in the caption of Fig. 1.

As the above output shows, one test failure occurred for the method `addKgs`. The test data that caused the failure is also printed, i.e., the receiver, an object of class `Person` with name `Baby`, and the argument of value -22.

A corrected implementation of the method `addKgs` is shown in Fig. 12. (Compare this with the specification and the faulty implementation shown in Fig. 1.)

To report the numbers of test successes or failures, the framework counts the number of test methods. This is not the right measure in our approach, because each test method runs the method under test with all possible combinations of test data. To get more accurate report, one can use our specialized test runner class, `JMLTestRunner`, instead of a JUnit's test runner class such as `junit.framework.textui.TestRunner` (see Fig. 10). The class `JMLTestRunner` reports the number of meaningful test runs and the total number of test runs in terms of test data, as shown in the last line of Fig. 11. Such a report prevents the user having a wrong impression that the class under test satisfied all tests when in fact no test has actually be executed due to all test cases being inapplicable[5].

6 Discussion

What should the outcome of a test case be if a method detects an invariant is violated in at the beginning of a method's execution? Such a situation can arise if clients can directly write an object's fields, or if aliasing allows clients to manipulate the object's representation without calling its methods. The question is whether such invariant violations should be treated as a test failure or as a rejection of the test data (i.e., as a "meaningless" test). One reason for rejecting the test data is that one can consider the invariant to be part of the precondition. One may also consider an object malformed if it does not satisfy the invariant. However, treating such violations as if the test case were meaningless seems to mask the underlying violation of information hiding, and so our current implementation treats these as test failures.

7 Related Work

There are now quite a few runtime assertion checking facilities developed and advocated by many different groups of researchers. One of the earliest and most popular approaches is Meyer's view of Design By Contract (DBC) implemented in the programming language Eiffel [29,27,28]. Eiffel's success in checking pre- and postconditions and encouraging the DBC discipline in programming partly contributed to the availability of similar facilities in other programming languages, including C [35], C++ [12,15,33,38], Java [2,13,14,21,23], .NET [1], Python [32], and Smalltalk [7]. These approaches vary widely from a simple assertion mechanism similar to the C `assert` macros, to full-fledged contract enforcement capabilities. Among all that we are aware of, however, none uses its assertion checking capability as a basis for automated program testing. Thus, our work is unique in the DBC community in using a runtime assertion checking to automate program testing.

Another difference between our work and that of other DBC work is that we use a formal specification language, JML, whose runtime assertion checker supports manipulation of abstract values. As far as we know, all other DBC

---

[5] We thank an anonymous referee for pointing out this problem.

tools work only with concrete program values. However, in JML, one can specify behavior in terms of abstract (specification) values, rather than concrete program values [6,24,25]. So-called *model variables* — specification variables for holding not concrete program data but their abstractions — can be accompanied by **represents** clauses [24]. A **represents** clause specifies an abstraction function (or relation) that maps concrete values into abstract values. This abstraction function is used by the runtime assertion checker in JML to manipulate assertions written in terms of abstract values.

The traditional way to implement test oracles is to compare the result of a test execution with a user supplied, expected result [16,30]. A test case, therefore, consists of a pairs of input and output values. In our approach, however, a test case consists of only input values. And instead of directly comparing the actual and expected results, we observe if, for the given input values, the program under test satisfies the specified behavior. As a consequence, programmers are freed from not only the burden of writing test programs, often called *test drivers*, but also from the burden of pre-calculating presumably correct outputs and comparing them. The traditional schemes are constructive and direct whereas ours is behavior observing and indirect.

Several researchers have already noticed that if a program is formally specified, it should be possible to use the specification as an oracle [31,34,37]. Thus, the idea of automatically generating test oracles from formal specifications is not new, but the novelty lies in employing a runtime assertion checker as the test oracle engine. This aspect seems to be original and first explored in our approach. Peters and Parnas discussed their work on a tool that generates a test oracle from formal program documentation [31]. The behavior of program is specified in a relational program specification using tabular expressions, and the test oracle procedure, generated in C++, checks if an input and output pair satisfies the relation described by the specification. Their approach is limited to checking only pre and postconditions, thus allowing only a form of black-box tests. In our approach, however we also support *intra-conditions*, assertions that can be specified and checked within a method, i.e., on internal states [24]; thus our approach supports a form of white-box tests. As mentioned above, our approach also support abstract value manipulation. In contrast to other work on test oracles, our approach also supports object-oriented concepts such as specification inheritance.

There are many research papers published on the subject of testing using formal specifications [5,8,10,19,22,34,36]. Most of these papers are concerned with methods and techniques for automatically generating test cases from formal specifications, though there are some addressing the problem of automatic generation of test oracles as noted before [31,34,37]. A general approach is to derive the so-called *test conditions*, a description of test cases, from the formal specification of each program module [8]. The derived test conditions can be used to guide test selection and to measure comprehensiveness of an existing test suite, and sometimes they even can be turned into executable forms [8,10]. The degree of support for automation varies widely from the derivation of test cases, to the actual test execution and even to the analysis of test results [10,34]. Some approaches use existing specification languages [17,19], and others have their own (specialized) languages for the description of test cases and test execution [8,10,34,36]. All of these works are complimentary to the approach described in this paper, since, except as noted above, they solve the problem of defining test cases which we do not attempt to solve, and they do not solve the problem of easing the task of writing test oracles, which we partially solve.

8   Conclusion and Future Work

We presented a simple but effective approach to implementing test oracles from formal behavioral interface specifications. The idea is to use the runtime assertion checker as the decision procedure for test oracles. We have implemented this approach using JML, but other runtime assertion checkers can easily be adapted to work with our approach. There are two complications. The first is that the runtime assertion checker has to distinguish two kinds of precondition violations: those that arise from the call to a method and those that arise within the implementation of the method; the first kind of precondition violations is used to reject meaningless test cases, while the second indicates a test failure. The second is that the unit testing framework needs to distinguish three possible outcomes for test cases: a test execution can either be a success, a failure, or it can be meaningless.

Our approach trades the effort one might spend in writing code to construct expected test outputs for effort spent in writing formal specifications. Formal specifications are more concise and abstract than code, and hence we expect them to be more readable and maintainable. Formal specifications also serve as more readable documentation than testing code, and can be used as input to other tools such as extended static checkers [11].

Most testing methods do not check behavioral results, but focus only on defining what to test. Because most testing requires a large number of test cases, manually checking test results severely hampers its effectiveness, and makes repeated and frequent testing impractical. To remedy this, our approach automatically generates test oracles from formal specifications, and integrates these test oracles with a testing framework to automate test executions. This helps make our implementation practical. It also makes our approach a blend of formal verification and testing.

In sum, the main goal of our work —to ease the writing of testing code— has been achieved.

A main advantage of our approach is the improved automation of testing process, i.e., generation of test oracles from formal behavioral interface specifications and test executions. We expect that, due to the automation, writing test code will be easier. Indeed, this has been our experience. However, measuring this effect is future work.

Another advantage of our approach is that it helps make formal methods more practical and concretely usable in programming. One aspect of this is that

test specifications and target programs can reside in the same file. We expect
that this will have a positive effect in maintaining consistency between test
specifications and the programs to be tested, although again this remains to be
empirically verified.

A third advantage is that our approach can achieve the effect of both black-
box testing and white-box testing. White-box testing can be achieved by specifying intra-conditions, predicates on internal states in addition to pre- and postconditions. Assertion facilities such as the `assert` statement are an example
of intra conditions; they are widely used in programming and debugging. JML
has several specification constructs for specifying intra-conditions which support
white-box testing.

Finally, in our approach a programmer may extend and add his own testing
methods to the automatically generated test oracles. This can be done easily by
adding hand-written test methods to a subclass of the automatically generated
test class.

Our approach frees the programmer from writing unit test code, but the
programmer still has to supply actual test data by hand. In the future, we
hope to partially alleviate this problem by automatically generating some of
test inputs from the specifications. There are several approaches proposed by
researchers to automatically deriving test cases from formal specifications. It
would be very exciting to apply some of the published techniques to JML. JML
has some features that may make this future work easier, in particular various
forms of specification redundancy. In JML, a *redundant* part of a specification
does not itself form part of the specification's contract, but instead is a formalized
commentary on it [26]. One such feature are formalized examples, which can be
thought of as specifying both test inputs and a description of the resulting post-
state. However, for such formalized examples to be useful in generating test data,
they would: (a) have to be specified constructively, and (b) it would have to be
possible to invert the abstraction function, so as to build concrete representation
values from them.

Another area of future work is to gain more experience with our approach.
The application of our approach so far has been limited to the development of the
JML support tools themselves, but our initial experience seems very promising.
We were able to perform testing as an integral part of programming with minimal
effort and to detect many kinds of errors. Almost half of the test failures that we
encountered were caused by specification errors; this shows that our approach
is useful for debugging specifications as well as code. However, we have yet to
perform significant, empirical evaluation of the effectiveness of our approach.

JML and a version of the tool that implements our approach can be obtained
through the JML web page at http://www.jmlspecs.org.

Acknowledgments

The work of both authors was supported in part by a grant from Electron-
ics and Telecommunications Research Institute (ETRI) of South Korea, and by

grants CCR-0097907 and CCR-0113181 from the US National Science Foundation. Thanks to Curtis Clifton and Markus Lumpe for comments on an earlier draft of this paper.

References

1. Karine Arnout and Raphael Simon. The .NET contract wizard: Adding design by contract to languages other than Eiffel. In *Proceedings of TOOLS 39, 29 July -3 August 2001, Santa Barbara, California*, pages 14–23. IEEE Computer Society, 2001.

2. D. Bartetzko, C. Fischer, M. Moller, and H. Wehrheim. Jass - Java with assertions. In *Workshop on Runtime Verification held in conjunction with the 13th Conference on Computer Aided Verification, CAV'01*, 2001.

3. Kent Beck and Erich Gamma. Test infected: Programmers love writing tests. *Java Report*, 3(7), July 1998.

4. Kent Beck. *Extreme Programming Explained*. Addison-Wesley, 2000.

5. Gilles Bernot, Marie Claude Claudel, and Bruno Marre. Software testing based on formal specifications: a theory and a tool. *Software Engineering Journal*, 6(6):387–405, November 1991.

6. Abhay Bhorkar. A run-time assertion checker for Java using JML. Technical Report TR #00-08, Department of Computer Science, Iowa State University, Ames, IA, May 2000.

7. Manuela Carrillo-Castellon, Jesus Garcia-Molina, Ernesto Pimentel, and Israel Repiso. Design by contract in Smalltalk. *Journal of Object-Oriented Programming*, 9(7):23–28, November/December 1996.

8. Juei Chang, Debra J. Richardson, and Sriram Sankar. Structural specification-based testing with ADL. In *Proceedings of ISSTA 96, San Diego, CA*, pages 62–70. IEEE Computer Society, 1996.

9. Yoonsik Cheon and Gary T. Leavens. A runtime assertion checker for the Java Modeling Language (JML). Technical Report 02-05, Department of Computer Science, Iowa State University, March 2002.

10. J. L. Crowley, J. F. Leathrum, and K. A. Liburdy. Isues in the full scale use of formal methods for automated testing. *ACM SIGSOFT Software Engineering Notes*, 21(3):71–78, May 1996.

11. David L. Detlefs, K. Rustan M. Leino, Greg Nelson, and James B. Saxe. Extended static checking. SRC Research Report 159, Compaq Systems Research Center, 130 Lytton Ave., Palo Alto, Dec 1998.

12. Carolyn K. Duby, Scott Meyers, and Steven P. Reiss. CCEL: A metalanguage for C++. In *USENIX C++ Technical Conference Proceedings*, pages 99–115, Portland, OR, August 1992. USENIX Assoc. Berkeley, CA, USA.

13. Andrew Duncan and Urs Holzle. Adding contracts to Java with Handshake. Technical Report TRCS98-32, Department of Computer Science, University of California, Santa Barbara, CA, December 1998.

14. Robert Bruce Findler and Matthias Felleisen. Behavioral interface contracts for Java. Technical Report CS TR00-366, Department of Computer Science, Rice University, Houston, TX, August 2000.

15. Pedro Guerreiro. Simple support for design by contract in C++. In *Proceedings of TOOLS 39, 29 July -3 August 2001, Santa Barbara, California*, pages 24–34. IEEE Computer Society, 2001.

254   Yoonsik Cheon and Gary T. Leavens

16. R. G. Hamlet. Testing programs with the aid of a compiler. *IEEE Transactions on Software Engineering*, 3(4):279–290, July 1977.
17. Teruo Higashino and Gregor v. Bochmann. Automatic analysis and test case derivation for a restricted class of LOTOS expressions with data parameters. *IEEE Transactions on Software Engineering*, 20(1):29–42, January 1994.
18. Bart Jacobs and Eric Poll. A logic for the Java modeling language JML. In *Fundamental Approaches to Software Engineering (FASE'2001), Genova, Italy, 2001*, volume 2029 of *Lecture Notes in Computer Science*, pages 284–299. Springer-Verlag, 2001.
19. Pankaj Jalote. Specification and testing of abstract data types. *Computing Languages*, 17(1):75–82, 1992.
20. JUnit. Http://www.junit.org.
21. Murat Karaorman, Urs Holzle, and John Bruno. jContractor: A reflective Java library to support design by contract. In Pierre Cointe, editor, *Meta-Level Architectures and Reflection, Second International Conference on Reflection '99, Saint-Malo, France, July 19–21, 1999, Proceedings*, volume 1616 of *Lecture Notes in Computer Science*, pages 175–196. Springer-Verlag, July 1999.
22. Bogdan Korel and Ali M. Al-Yami. Automated regression test generation. In *Proceedings of ISSTA 98, Clearwater Beach, FL*, pages 143–152. IEEE Computer Society, 1998.
23. Reto Kramer. iContract – the Java design by contract tool. *TOOLS 26: Technology of Object-Oriented Kanguages and Systems, Los Alamitos, California*, pages 295–307, 1998.
24. Gary T. Leavens, Albert L. Baker, and Clyde Ruby. Preliminary design of JML: A behavioral interface specification language for Java. Technical Report 98-06p, Iowa State University, Department of Computer Science, August 2001. See www.jmlspecs.org.
25. Gary T. Leavens, Albert L. Baker, and Clye Ruby. JML: A notation for detailed design. In Haim Kilov, Bernhard Rumpe, and Ian Simmonds, editors, *Behavioral Specifications of Businesses and Systems*, chapter 12, pages 175–188. Kluwer, 1999.
26. Gary T. Leavens and Albert L. Baker. Enhancing the pre- and postcondition technique for more expressive specifications. In J. Davies J.M. Wing, J. Woodcock, editor, *FM'99 - Formal Methods, World Congress on Formal Methods in the Development of Computing Systems, Toulouse, France, September 1999. Proceedings, Volume II*, volume 1708 of *Lecture Notes in Computer Science*, pages 1087–1106. Springer-Verlag, September 1999.
27. Bertrand Meyer. *Eiffel: The Language*. Object-Oriented Series. Prentice Hall, New York, N.Y., 1992.
28. Bertrand Meyer. *Object-oriented Software Construction*. Prentice Hall, New York, N.Y., second edition, 1997.
29. B. Meyer. Applying design by contract. *IEEE Computer*, 25(10):40–51, October 1992.
30. D.J. Panzl. Automatic software test driver. *IEEE Computer*, pages 44–50, April 1978.
31. Dennis Peters and David L. Parnas. Generating a test oracle from program documentation. In *Proceedings of ISSTA 94, Seattle, Washington, August, 1994*, pages 58–65. IEEE Computer Society, August 1994.
32. Reinhold Plosch and Josef Pichler. Contracts: From analysis to C++ implementation. In *Proceedings of TOOLS 30*, pages 248–257. IEEE Computer Society, 1999.

33. Sara Porat and Paul Fertig. Class assertions in C++. *Journal of Object-Oriented Programming*, 8(2):30–37, May 1995.
34. Debra J. Richardson. TAOS: Testing with analysis and oracle support. In *Proceedings of ISSTA 94, Seattle, Washington, August, 1994*, pages 138–152. IEEE Computer Society, August 1994.
35. David R. Rosenblum. A practical approach to programming with assertions. *IEEE Transactions on Software Engineering*, 21(1):19–31, January 1995.
36. Sriram Sankar and Roger Hayes. ADL: An interface definition language for specifying and testing software. *ACM SIGPLAN Notices*, 29(8):13–21, August 1994. Proceedings of the Workshop on Interface Definition Language, Jeannette M. Wing (editor), Portland, Oregon.
37. P. Stocks and D. Carrington. Test template framework: A specification-based test case study. In *Proceedings of the 1993 International Symposium on Software Testing and Analysis (ISSTA)*, pages 11–18. IEEE Computer Society, June 1993.
38. David Welch and Scott Strong. An exception-based assertion mechanism for C++. *Journal of Object-Oriented Programming*, 11(4):50–60, July/August 1998.

Objectively: Components versus Web Services

Clemens Szyperski

Microsoft

Abstract. We are observing a dramatic confluence of several different aspects: software components, software as a service, and an ever growing space of Internet and Web standards. Over the past year all major players in the software industry have announced their support of XML Web Services in one form or another. So, are services here to displace components? And what about our good old objects?

Drawing boundaries that help to understand the key concepts without obstructing the path towards future development is important but challenging. Concepts such as contracts, specifications, and perhaps even the very notion of correctness need to be rethought. Or are they? A strange feeling of deja vue spreads as we see computer science and software engineering rediscovered - this time at your service.

After years of both academic and entrepreneurial experience, Clemens Szyperski has joined Microsoft Research in Redmond, Washington in early 1999, where he works on furthering the principles, technologies, and methods supporting component software. He is the author of the award-winning book

"Component Software: Beyond Object-Oriented Programming" (Addison Wesley), now in its second edition, and of numerous other publications. He has served on program committees for major international conferences, including ECOOP, ICSE, and OOPSLA and he is a frequent speaker at events of both academic and industrial nature.

Clemens received his Masters in Electrical Engineering in 1987 from the Aachen Institute of Technology, in Germany. He received his PhD in Computer Science in 1992 from ETH Zurich under the guidance of Niklaus Wirth. After a postdoctoral fellowship at the International Computer Science Institute at UC Berkeley, he was tenured as associate professor at the Queensland University of Technology, Australia, where he continues to hold an adjunct professorship. He is a cofounder of Oberon Microsystems, Inc., Zurich, with its recent spinoff, esmertec inc, also Zurich.

Clemens' homepage is at: www.research.microsoft.com/~cszypers/programming.

B. Magnusson (Ed.): ECOOP 2002, LNCS 2374, p. 256, 2002.
© Springer-Verlag Berlin Heidelberg 2002

Modular Internet Programming with Cells

Ran Rinat and Scott Smith

Department of Computer Science
The Johns Hopkins University
Baltimore, Maryland, USA
{rinat,scott}@cs.jhu.edu
http://www.cs.jhu.edu/~scott/cells

Abstract. The success of Java in recent years is largely due to its targeting as a language for the Internet. Many of the network-related features of Java however are not part of the core language design. In this paper we focus on the design of a more parsimonious Internet programming language, which supports network integration smoothly and coherently as part of its core specification.

The key idea is to center these extensions around the unified notion of a *cell*. Cells are deployable containers of objects and code, which may import (*plugin*) and export (*plugout*) classes and operations. They may be dynamically linked and unlinked, locally or across the network. Cells may be dynamically loaded, unloaded, copied, and moved, and serve as units of security. At first approximation, cells can be thought of as a hybrid between modules and components. Here we concentrate on the design of *JCells*, a language which builds cells on top of the fundamental Java notions of class, object, and virtual machine.

1   Introduction

In the history of programming languages, fundamentally new concepts have never been implemented correctly the first time or even the first several times. FORTRAN was very difficult to parse because parsing theory was not developed. Lisp first implemented higher-order functions, but with dynamic scoping; Scheme was created partly to correct this flaw in the Lisp design. In a similar spirit, our goal is to take a second look at important new features that have arisen in the Java JDK, and to create a more parsimonious language expressing these features smoothly and coherently as part of the core specification. Features of Java which are relatively new include explicit dynamic class loading, object serialization and RMI, an explicit security architecture, Java Bean components, and mobile Applet code.

At the core of our quest for an improved language platform is the concept of a *cell*. Here is a brief definition.

> **Cells** are deployable containers of objects and code. They expose typed linking interfaces (*connectors*) that may import (*plugin*) and export (*plugout*) classes and operations. Via these interfaces, cells may be dynamically linked and unlinked, locally or across the network. Standard client-server

B. Magnusson (Ed.): ECOOP 2002, LNCS 2374, pp. 257–280, 2002.

style interfaces (*services*) are also provided for local or remote invocations. Cells may be dynamically loaded, unloaded, copied, and moved. Cells serve as principals to which security policies may be applied.

In terms of existing concepts, cells can be thought of as an internet-aware, security-geared hybrid between the concepts of *component* and *module*.

In this paper we define *JCells*, a language which builds cells on top of the fundamental Java notions of class, object, and virtual machine. We build on top of Java here for two purposes: we need not detail many aspects of JCells since it is identical to Java; and, by implementing on top of Java we can more easily get a prototype. We aim to get to examples as quickly as possible to define what is meant by the above description. First we help set the stage by relating cells to known concepts.

1.1   Relating Cells to Existing Concepts

Cells combine ideas from disparate domains of research, so they need to be viewed from several angles to see their merit. As already mentioned, cells aim to capture aspects of existing module and component systems, but also aspects of distributed object systems, mobile code systems, persistent object systems, and distributed security architectures.

Cells are similar to some module interface designs [MFH01,FF98,CDG+88]. Like modules, cells have fixed interfaces ("connectors") to the outside which import and export ("plug-in" and "plug-out") items, and cells are persistently linked to one another. However, unlike modules, cells separate the notions of loading and linking. Cells are loaded in unlinked form, and then are explicitly linked by the JCells link ...at ... command. They may also later be unlinked and unloaded. Cells may link across the network; module linking is confined to a single process. Cells may contain objects and so have state and thus a run-time presence; modules are purely code with little if any run-time presence. The module aspects of cells were partly inspired by Units [FF98], which recently have been implemented for Java as Jiazzi [MFH01].

Cells are related to component systems [Szy98] such as Corba [Gro01] and COM/DCOM: they are larger-grained than objects and have run-time interfaces (*connectors and services*) for interaction. Like Corba and COM/DCOM objects, cells support local and distributed service invocations, a client-server mode of interaction. Unlike components, they are designed to make long-term interactions explicit by forming persistent peer-to-peer links with one another, via connectors. Cells also "own" a collection of objects and thus have state; components don't. Several considerations led us to make cells stateful. Cells can dynamically link and unlink, and as such must have the state of the connections kept at run-time. The modularity of components and module systems is "shallow" in the sense that it exists at compile-time only; cells are "deeply" modular in that run-time objects are also grouped. We believe that when engineering software, this extra dimension of modularity will help factor functionality and clarify meaning. Lastly, migrating cells can directly "walk to" their new locations without the need for an additional protocol to move their state; this is similar to the design of other mobile code systems, discussed next.

Cells support a notion of mobile code which is a generalization of Java Applets: mobile code packages are *serialized cells*, which may include objects as well as code, and cells may actively migrate from one host to another. Here we have been inspired by the numerous mobile object systems also aimed to support such generalized functionality [JLH90,Car95,Whi94,VT97,LO98]. Third-party references to a cell are maintained after a cell moves.

Cells support a clean messaging protocol between virtual machines; in this sense they are related to Java's RMI [Sun] and other research in distributed object-passing systems [JLH90,BNOW93,Gro01]. In contrast to RMI, we believe that remote objects should not generally be used to support services invoked by non-local users: objects are too light-weight to support the sizable burden of remote invocation. Instead we advocate the use of cells in the place of remote objects: one cell may easily invoke a service on a remote cell to which it holds a reference. In this sense cells act like a distributed Corba or DCOM component. We still support the notion of object method invocation across the network (via what we call a *modulated reference*) for cases of lightweight servers implemented as objects.

Security is a main focus in the cell architecture. First, the act of bringing cells together—linking—is subject to a runtime authentication protocol. Secondly, cells aim to isolate objects that should not directly interact with one another. Our approach to object isolation is related to J-Kernel [HCC+98]; other related work includes [BR00,WCC+74]. Cells also support a capability-based layer of security across the network, as in [vDABW96]. The goal of object isolation inside a cell wall also has parallels in several abstract theories of distributed system security [Car99,VC99].

Cells are designed to cleanly support persistence: cells *own* their objects, and so a cell can be archived by serializing it and all of "its" objects. Persistent object database systems [ZM90] generally allow any object to be persistent; we instead have a per-cell notion of persistence. Like object databases, cells are a good level of granularity on which to place transaction processing protocols.

Cells also are related to prototype-based object languages such as Self [US87] in the sense that they can in some ways be viewed as heavyweight prototype-style objects: cells have no notion of inheritance, and copies can be generated from a prototype cell. Self's transporter mechanism for serializing objects is also related to how cells serialize their "own" objects, but ownership is more *ad hoc* in Self since without something like cells it is hard to define what objects should own what other objects. A more elegant self transporter mechanism is stated as future work [Ung95]; we believe cells make a step toward such an improvement.

In terms of the general goals, cells are also intended to provide open internet services on a wide-area network. Such services have clear, published modes for interaction, and directories for looking up services. In this sense cells can be viewed as a toolkit with a similar purpose to the XML/SOAP/UDDI/WSDL standards now being developed. Cells are more expressive than the above technologies, but the above are at the bottom text-based messaging protocols and so are more widely

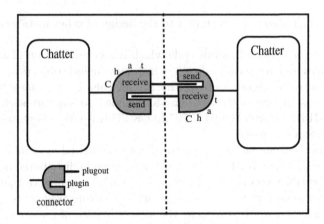

Fig. 1. Two chatters communicating over the network

adaptable across platforms. So the two address a different target set of problems. For loosely-coupled systems a simple protocol is often preferable, but for more tightly-coupled systems, the additional expressivity of cells may be necessary.

There are many projects in addition to those named above that share at least a fraction of our goals. JavaSeal [BV01] is built around the concept of a *seal*, which encapsulates objects and code much like cells do. Seals own their objects, just like cells. Our focus is more on module/component technology, and individual cells can be large immobile components consisting of many classes, whereas seals are more intended for mobile units. Our module focus means we support cross-network linking and our component focus means we support remote service invocation. Serialized cells are similar to passive seals. Seals may be nested; we may add nesting to cells in the future.

ArchJava [ACN02] is another module/component system extension to Java which supports code-embedded architectural design and guarantees the compatibility of implementations. ArchJava components have *ports*, which are similar to our plugins and plugouts. Their focus however is more on static architectural aspects and less on runtime and networking.

2   Cells by Example

In this section we introduce JCells through a running **Chatter** example modeled on an internet chat system such as ICQ, Odigo, or Yahoo Messenger. The base scenario is two **Chatter** cells running in different virtual machines which link to one another across the network to carry out a chat conversation; see Fig. 1.

Each **Chatter** has a *connector* named **Chat** with send and receive operations. The **receive** operation is a *plugout*, i.e. provided to anyone who connects to it, and **send** is a *plugin*, i.e. expected from connecting cells. When the individual **Chatter** cells are first loaded, their connectors are not linked. Later, an explicit **link** command will connect them across the network (the dashed line in the figure is the network boundary), linking the **send** of one to the **receive** of the other. From this time on, one cell calling its plugin **send** will invoke the plugout **receive** of the other **Chatter**, passing the message as parameter. When the two cells are done chatting, they can be **unlinked**.

The **Chatter** is expressed by the following JCells syntax.

```
// File Chatter.csc

cell Chatter {
{ // begin cell header

//-----------------Cell Connector Declaration -----------------

connector Chat {  // connector which another chatter links on to chat
    plugins {
        void send (String aMessage);
    }
    plugouts {
        void receive (String aMessage);
    }
}

} // end cell header

//===================== Cell Chatter Body =====================

{ // begin cell body

// ----------------------- Cell Operations--------------------
// (Operations defined for the cell; some, e.g. receive, may be plugged out)

void linkToAnotherChatter(String userID) {
    cell Chatter otherChatter = ... get chatter for userID;  detailed later ...
    link otherChatter at Chat [receive->send, send<-receive] ;

void UnLinkFromOtherChatter() {
    unlink at Chat;
}

// sendMessage is activated by the GUI's send button event handler
void sendMessage() {
    String msg = ... // get message from GUI window
    send (msg) ;     // call send plugin. receive of linked chatter is thus invoked.

}

void receive (String aMessage) {
    ... implementation for plugout operation receive: display aMessage ...
}

...

} // end cell body

}   // end cell Chatter
```

The code above is in a cell source file **Chatter.csc**. A .csc file contains the definition of a single cell, in analogy to a .java file holding one class. A cell's definition consists of a *header* and a *body*. The header contains declarations, and the body contains implementations. Every plugout must be implemented in the body (or, itself plugged in on some other connector). The only declaration in the header here is of the **Chat** connector with the **send** operation as plugin and **receive** as plugout. The cell body contains the operation implementations. **receive** implements the plugout, `linkToAnotherChatter` is a local cell operation responsible for linking this chatter to another chatter, and `sendMessage` sends a message by invoking the `send` plugin. Note that a call to a plugin is the same syntax as a call to a local operation.

The body of operations mostly follows standard Java syntax, with only a few modifications. In `linkToAnotherChatter`, the variable `otherCell` has *cell type* cell `Chatter`. The keyword `cell` is used to distinguish cell types from class and interface names. As with classes, the definition of cell `Chatter` also defines a type by the same name. The statement

```
link otherChatter at Chat [receive->send, send<-receive]
```

is a JCells extension to Java syntax which dynamically links the current cell with `otherChatter` via connector `Chat`, and hooks `receive` into `send` in both sides. For the chat application, this link will be across the network, but local and nonlocal linking share the same syntax and largely the same semantics. Even though linking is dynamic, we do not want to lose the advantages of static types and typchecking: since `send` and `receive` are linked, we require their types to be the same. In general, a link at a connector requires the types in all connected plugin/plugout pairs to correspond.

Cells execute in a *Cell Virtual Machine* (CVM), which is similar to a Java JVM. One important property of cells is cross-network linking: the two chatter cells are are running in different CVMs at different network locations, but still can be linked. The `Chatter.csc` file above is compiled into a `Chatter.cell` file which can then be loaded into two different CVMs; one chatter then can `link` to the other to form the configuration of Fig. 1. A `.cell` file is at first approximation analogous to a Java `.class` file, but it contains a cell *including* its classes and objects.

CVMs only execute cells, so every object and operation must be part of some cell. There can be many cells loaded into a given CVM.

Library Linking. Cells serve both as components and as modules, thus code libraries are also cells. `Chatter` will need to plug in libraries, in this example an audio-visual support library extending the chatter's basic text capability. The audio-visual cell is likely to arrive to the local machine as a downloaded `AV_Extension.cell` file, perhaps some time after the basic `Chatter.cell` system has been installed. The `AV_Extension.cell` is a mobile cell, which generalizes Java's Applets: it may include state (in the form of objects) along with code.

We now expand the above example to link to an audio-visual library, pictured in Fig. 2 (cell `ChatCentral` at the bottom of the figure is introduced later). The syntax is as follows.

```
cell Chatter {

{ // Begin Cell Header

//---------------Class Signature Declarations------------
// (Class signatures declared here for typechecking purposes)

class MediaPlayer {
    void play();      // (No code is given in a class signature)
```

```
        void pause();
        ...
}

interface Cert {
    ... Java interface for certificates ...
}

//---------- Cell Signature Declarations ------------
// (Like class signatures, need to declare types of other cells for typechecking)

cell AV_Extension {
    connector AudioVideo {
        plugouts { MediaPlayer, ... }
    }
    service Cert getCertificate();

}


//---------- Connectors for Cell Chatter ------------

connector AudioVideo {  // For plugging in audio-video library code
    plugins {
        MediaPlayer, ...  // MediaPlayer is a class plugin
    }
    // special verify predicate: verify the extension comes from a reliable source
    boolean verify(cell AV_Extension other) {
        Cert cert = other <- getCertificate();
        ... return true only if cert is satisfactory ...
    }
}

connector Chat { ... as before ... }

} // End Cell Header

//================ Cell Chatter Body ================

{ // Begin Cell Body

//-----------------Cell Fields----------------------
// (Cell fields allow cells to have their own state)

cell AV_Extension theAV_Extension ;

//-----------------Cell Operations------------------

void onLoad() {  // this hook is invoked when the cell is loaded
    theAV_Extension = (cell AV_Extension) lookup("AV_Extension");

    link theAV_Extension at AudioVideo;  // links plugins with like-named plugouts

}

void linkToAnotherChatter(String userID) { ... as before... }
void UnLinkFromOtherChatter() { ... as before ... }
void receive(String aMessage) { ... as before ... }

//--------------Cell Internal Class Definitions-------------
// (Cells can define their own classes either for internal use
// or for plugging out and use by others)

class ChatMediaPlayer extends MediaPlayer { // internal class extending a plugin class
    ....
}

} // End Cell Body

} // End Cell Chatter
```

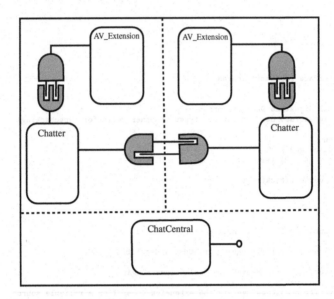

Fig. 2. The complete chatter example

Looking first at `Chatter`'s connectors declared above, a new connector for the `AV_Extension` library cell is defined. This connector declares plugins through which various classes such as `MediaPlayer` are plugged-in, showing how classes as well as operations may appear on connectors. In the providing cell `AV_Extension` (whose code we don't give), these classes should have been declared as plugouts and defined in its body. In `Chatter`'s body, there is now a class `ChatMediaPlayer` which extends the plugin class `MediaPlayer`—cross-cell inheritance is an important feature of JCells.

One important security aspect of cell connections is that link time is a point at which authentication should occur. This is one of the points in allowing persistent connections via `link`: security checks happen only at `link` time, not at every invocation. The connector `AudioVideo` includes a special `verify` predicate for this purpose. `verify` is called by the CVM whenever a link at this connector is initiated. This is one example of the per-cell approach we take to security. Note that the `Chat` connector should certainly also be verified in a real implementation since it is a cross-network link. In this example, verification of a library is sensible because the A/V library is a downloaded plug-in which cannot always be trusted.

In the code of `verify`, `other <- getCertificate()` invokes a *service* on the other cell. Services are direct cell operations which one can use without linking; they are used for more transient interactions. Services are described in more detail below. The signature for `AV_Extension` declares the service `getCertificate()`.

Upon loading a cell, the CVM calls the hook operation `onLoad()` if it is defined. Here `onLoad()` looks up and then links the `AV_Extension` library cell via `link theAV_extension at AudioVideo`. Since here plugouts are plugged into plugins by the same name, there is no need for a plugging map (`[...<-...]`). `lookup` is a *built-in* operation, found on all cells in analogy to the methods of `Object` which all objects respond to. `lookup` is a nameserver which maps strings to cells.

Cell source files are compilation units, and so they must know the types of all cells and classes they interact with. For simplicity, we now require each cell to directly declare the signatures of all these cells and classes. Class and cell signature information is given above in the header of the cell definition. A class signature is a class without method bodies, and similarly a cell signature is a cell without a body. Note that these declarations are solely for compile time typechecking; in order for actual code linking to occur, cells must explicitly link their connectors at runtime. Realistic cells will have very long signature declaration blocks, and a mechanism for abbreviating and sharing signatures is a topic for future work.

A Full Chatter System. We now flesh out the example above by showing how a central server (`ChatCentral`) is used to complete the picture of a chat framework, by allowing individual `Chatter` cells to learn about one another. In this full example, we also show how song archives may be traded amongst chatters, without having to send entire archives across the network, and without compromising security. Lastly, the example also illustrates cell persistence: a `Chatter` can be unloaded along with its state, and then reloaded at a later time.

The full architecture is shown in Fig. 2. It includes the `ChatCentral` cell, on which we only invoke services. Here is the code for the full example.

```
cell Chatter {

{ // Begin Cell Header

//--------------Class/interface Signature Declarations------------

  ... as before plus:

interface User {          // interface for chat user data
    String getID();
    String getName();
    String getIntention();  // romance, friendship, chat etc.
    String getHobbies();
    int getAge();
    ...
}

interface SongArchive {    // for song archives shared amongst chatters
    setGenre(String musicGenre);
    setArtist(String anArtist);
    setLanguage(String aLanguage);
    Collection getSongs(); // returns songs matching criteria
    ...
}

//----------- Cell Signature Declarations --------------

cell AV_Extension { ... as before ... }

cell ChatCentral {    // Clearinghouse for chatters to find other users to connect to
    // declaration of ChatCentral's services
    service String registerNewChatter(copy User aUser, cell Chatter aCell);
    service void logon (cell Chatter aChatter);
    service void logoff(cell Chatter aChatter);
    service copy User getUser (String userID);
    service void updateUserDetails(User aUser);
```

```
    service cell Chatter getChatter(String userID);
    service Collection getUsersByCriteria(String Criteria); // returns set of users

}

//----------- Connectors for Cell Chatter --------------------

... connectors Windowing, AudioVideo as before ...

// Chat connector expanded to include song archive capability

connector Chat {
    plugins {
        void send (String aMessage);
        modulate songArchive requestSongs(); // modulated (proxy) reference returned
    }
    plugouts {
        void receive (String aMessage);
        modulate songArchive provideSongs();
    }
}


} // End Cell Header

//================= Cell Chatter Body ==================

{ // Begin Cell Body

//-----------------Cell Fields-----------------------

cell ChatCentral theChatCentral;
cell GUI theGUI;
cell AV_Extension theAV_Extension ;

String myUserID;
User me;                        // an object holding this user's details
SongArchive mySongArchive;      // this user's SongArchive

boolean firstLoad = true;

//------------------Cell Operations ------------------

void onLoad() {

    // get cell references via lookup

    theChatCentral  = (cell ChatCentral) lookup("ChatCentral");
    theAV_Extension = (cell AV_Extension) lookup("AV_Extension");

    // link to library

    link theAV_Extension at AudioVideo;

    // if first time, get user details and register with ChatCentral

    if (firstTime) {
        me = getUserDetails();      // obtain user details by input from user
        // register new user via ChatCentral service ; fresh user ID is returned:
        myUserID = theChatCentral <- registerNewUser(me, thisCell);
        firstTime = false;
    }

    // logon to chatCentral
    theChatCentral <- logon(thisCell);   // let ChatCentral know we're ready to chat

void onUnload() {      // a hook run just before cell is unloaded
```

```
    // logoff upon unload since user will not be available for chat
    theChatCentral <- logoff(thisCell);
}

void linkToAnotherChatter(String userID) {

    cell Chatter otherChatter = theChatCentral <- getChatter(userID);
    // link chatters as before but more plugins and plugouts to map:
    link otherChatter at Chat [receive->send, send<-receive,
                               provideSongArchive->requestSongArchive,
                               requestSongArchive<-provideSongArchive] ;

void UnLinkFromOtherChatter() { ... as before ... }

// operations which implement plugouts

void receive(String aMessage) { ... }

modulate songArchive provideSongs { .... };

//--------------Cell Internal Class Definitions-------------

// As before, plus:

class SongArchiveObj implements SongArchive {
    ...
}

class UserObj implements User {
    ...
}

}    // End Cell Body

}    // End Cell Chatter
```

ChatCentral is a server cell that exclusively provides *services*. Services are the other means of communication with cells: they are operations that users can invoke without linking, in a client-server fashion. The group of services of a given cell act like a COM/Corba interface on the cell. Like connectors, services must be listed in the cell's header, and like plugouts, they must be implemented in the body or listed as plugins.

Each loaded cell has a *cell identifier* (cid) which identifies it globally across all CVMs. Cell variables at run-time hold cid's. Users wishing to join the chatting network proceed as follows: first they obtain the Chatter.cell file with no cid, an *anonymous* cell. When it is then loaded, the CVM automatically generates a fresh cid for the cell and executes its onLoad() hook. Using a boolean flag firstTime, onLoad() recognizes that it is the first time this cell is being loaded, and so asks the user for his/her details, including name, age, hobbies, etc. It then invokes the service registerNewUser() on ChatCentral to register this new user. This service returns a fresh userID generated by ChatCentral, which identifies the user in the chatting network. Next, onLoad() calls the service logon() on ChatCentral, letting it know that it is active and willing to chat.

At some later point the Chatter cell may be unloaded into a .cell file by invoking unload(aStream); the resulting .cell file will now contain the cell's cid, as well as its state, including the userID, the fields me and mySongArchive, etc. The full unload process is as follows: the CVM first unlinks all connectors, the code in the onUnload() hook is run (which in this case logs the user off from ChatCentral), and the whole cell including its state is then serialized into a .cell file. When the same cell is later loaded into the CVM, its state is fully restored and cid preserved.

While logged on, ChatCentral allows individual chatters to learn about each other and to update their own details via ChatCentral services. If one chatter wants to chat with another, it obtains a reference to it (i.e., a cid) from ChatCentral using getChatter(String userID), where userID has been obtained previously, for example by using ChatCentral's getUsersByCriteria(aCriteria) service. The chatting itself is done by the two cells linking directly at connector Chat. (Note that Chatter cells could have alternatively used a persistent connector to interact with ChatCentral; we chose a service interface here to illustrate cell services.)

The result type of getUser() is declared to be copy User; the keyword copy indicates a copy of the result is returned. Since this service is invoked from another network node, the link would fail without this declaration; unlike RMI, there is no implicit serialization of objects upon remote invocation.

This example also demonstrates a use of *modulated* object references, another means by which parameters can be passed and results returned across the network. A modulated reference is an RMI-like proxy through which one cell may refer to an object inside another cell. Each cell implicitly maintains a *modulation table* holding the objects it is letting outside cells access; these references can be revoked when the Chat connector is unlinked. Revocability of modulated references is an important security feature—when one cell is done interacting with another, backdoor channels via modulated references may be closed. Modulation is, unlike RMI, designed for either local or remote access; locally, the stronger security properties make it useful for *e.g.* agent interaction.

Here, a plugin requestSongArchive and a plugout provideSongArchive have been added to the Chat connector. The return value of these operations is a modulated SongArchive object which one chatter passes into the other while chatting: the keyword modulate in the connector declaration indicates a modulated proxy is to be returned and not the actual object. While linked, the receiving chatter may browse the other chatter's song archive by invoking methods on the modulated SongArchive object it holds. If the song archive were instead returned by copy, the whole archive would have to be copied across the network.

3   JCells Programs

This section describes JCells programs, already introduced informally in the example of the previous section. In the subsequent section we describe the run-time behavior of cells.

3.1   Cell Source Files and Static Scoping

Each cell is defined in its own distinct .csc (cell source code) file. Cells are the unit of source definition in JCells; each class is defined as part of some cell, and so .csc files replace .java files. A .csc file is compiled to a .cell file with no cid and with an empty state (see Sect. 4.3).

Cell definitions are statically closed name spaces on two levels. At the first level, every identifier mentioned in the header must be declared in the header. So, if a service, a plugin, or a plugout has a parameter of type A, A must be declared in the header. At the second level, identifiers mentioned in the cell's body must either be declared in the header or defined in the body.

All top level identifiers declared inside a cell are unique and thus referable anywhere within the cell without qualification. The top level identifiers of a cell are its name, the names of cell signatures declared inside, connector names, plugin/plugout names, services, and the names of all elements defined in the body. The uniqueness requirement entails that there may not be two plugins with the same name (even on different connectors), and the names of all internal classes, operations, and interfaces must be different from all plugin names. Plugouts and services must be defined in the body, and a given plugout name may be listed in more than one connector (but implemented by one element in the body).

3.2 JCells Syntax

The syntax is very similar to Java, with the `cell` definition, `link`/`unlink` statements, and service invocations `aCell <- aService()` being the primary new syntax. We informally described this new syntax when presenting the example.

A cell definition consists of a *header* and a *body*. The header mainly contains declarations of connectors and services, but also cell, class, and interface signatures for compile-time typechecking. Connectors list plugins and plugouts which may be classes or operations. Services are always operations. All plugouts and services must either be defined within the body or declared as plugins.

The body defines fields, classes, operations, and interfaces, some of which implement the plugouts and services, and some of which are purely internal. In the body, plugins are referable as if they are defined internally. In particular, an internal class may inherit from a plugin class.

The built-in operations are listed in Appendix A. The electronic version of this paper contains a link to the full JCells grammar.

3.3 Typing

Cells are strongly typed, meaning that "message not understood" errors do not arise at run-time. Additionally, cell linking never fails due to plugin-plugout type mismatch. Cell type casting *may* fail dynamically, just like object downcasting may fail at run-time in the JVM.

Cell Types and Subtyping. The only new types introduced in JCells are *cell types*. A definition of a cell implicitly derives a cell type by the same name with connectors and services as specified in the cell's header, much in analogue with how class definitions in Java implicitly define a type. Cell types may in addition be declared directly via *signatures*, see below.

Cell types are referred to in the program as `cell ACellName`, with the prefix `cell` added to distinguish them from class types.

A *subtyping* relation is supported between cell types. Unlike class/interface subtyping in Java, cell type subtyping is structural, not by name: one cell is a subtype of another if every service and every connector appearing in the supertype cell also appears in the subtype cell, and with the same or more plugouts and the same or fewer plugins on each connector. Structural subtyping is important because of the open-ended nature of cells: it is possible to interact with an external cell for which only one connector type is known; the types of all connectors are not needed. The empty cell type `cell Cell` is a supertype of all cell types.

   Casting on cell types is also supported, but in contrast with Java typecasting, it is of a purely *structural* nature: a cell may be cast to a type consistent with its header. That is, the cell at run-time must have all the connectors and services specified by the cell type it is being cast to. By subtyping (subsumption), it may have more. As with Java type casts, upcasts entail no runtime overhead but downcasts require a run-time verification that the cell indeed has the indicated and so-typed connectors and services. Type `cell Cell` is useful in analogy to `Object` in that polymorphism on cells can be crudely modeled by using type `cell Cell` and then casting as appropriate. For instance, the built-in operation `load` to load a `.cell` file returns a cell of type `cell Cell` which then must be cast to be used.

Type Signatures in Cells. Because cells are statically-typed closed namespaces, a cell definition must declare the types of all cells and all classes/interfaces it refers to. This is done by declaring cell and class/interface type *signatures*. Cell type signatures are simply cells without a body. Class signatures are analogously classes without method bodies. Signatures may appear only within a cell's header. Because cell signatures are defined within an enclosing cell, they may refer to other signatures declared in that cell. This makes it possible to declare cell types that recursively reference each other. One property of this requirement is that there will be many class signatures written out in cell definitions and cell types. We plan on adding type abbreviation mechanisms to the language in the future.

Type Checking Cell-Related Statements. A simple link statement

`link   aCell at   aConnector`

is statically typechecked: both the cell containing the link command and *aCell* need to have a connector named *aConnector*, with compatible types. That is, the connector *aConnector* on each cell must have a plugout A for every plugin A on the other cell's *aConnector*, and with identical type. There may be unused plugouts on either connector. In addition, the type `cell A` of the argument to `verify(cell A aCell)` in each cell must be a supertype of the other cell's type. `unlink` statements are typechecked similarly to `link`.

   A service invocation

aCell `<- s` (*args*)

is typechecked w.r.t *aCell*'s type in analogy to how object method invocation is typechecked. The concepts underlying cell types are generally well-understood: import/export interfaces subtyping, and typecast. So, we do plan on evantually proving the system sound, but is it not a priority.

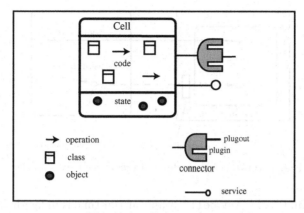

Fig. 3. A cell at run-time

4   JCells Semantics

In this section we outline the semantics of cells, elaborating on what was presented in the example. Since all of the concepts are interlinked, this section by necessity contains many cross-references.

4.1   Cells and the Cell Virtual Machine

Each cell executes within a *Cell Virtual Machine* (CVM). CVMs are responsible for loading, linking, and executing cells—much like JVMs w.r.t. classes. The major difference is that cell linking is triggered by explicit `link` commands in the program and is not done automatically upon loading: directly after being loaded, a cell is not connected to any other cells. In addition, linking is performed through cell connectors, which act as explicit interfaces to cells. In our implementation of JCells, each CVM is implemented by a JVM. CVMs contain cells exclusively—there is no possibility of a class or an object to be in a CVM but not part of some cell.

A cell in a CVM interacts with other cells via its connectors and services, and internally contains classes, operations, and objects, see Fig. 3. Connectors list plugins and plugouts, and may be used to link to cells with compatible connectors (Secs. 4.8,3.3). Linking will typically be used for more long term, security sensitive interactions. After linking, references to plugins in one cell are resolved to the connected plugout on the other. Services are operations which may be invoked directly, in a client-server fashion. The set of operations of a given cell act like a COM/CORBA interface to the cell. Services will typically be used for more light-weight, short term, and less security sensitive interactions.

Internally, a cell has code in the form of classes and operations, and state consisting of the state of its cell fields, the objects it owns (4.5), and the modulation table for its modulated references (4.4).

4.2   Cell Identifiers (cid's)

When a cell is loaded into a CVM, it is assigned a *cell identifier* (cid). The cid identifies a CVM and a cell within that CVM, so it identifies a cell uniquely and

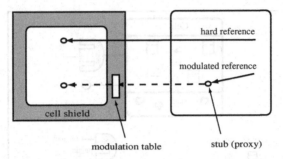

Fig. 4. Hard versus modulated references between cells

globally across all CVMs. Any `cell` variable at run-time is in fact holding a cid. We elaborate more on the need for and use of cid's in Sect. 5, where distributed cells are discussed.

4.3   .cell Files

A cell is loaded into a CVM from a stream called a *.cell file* (In analogy with .class files, we use this terminology even though the stream may not actually come from a file). A `.cell` file contains all the information needed to create a cell in memory. This includes the static part of the cell (functions, classes, Java interfaces) as well as the dynamic part (cell fields, owned objects, table of modulated objects). A `.cell` file may also contain a cid identifying the cell; if there is no cid the cell is *anonymous*.

Compiling and serializing a cell both result in a `.cell` file. In this sense, `.cell` files unify two distinct ideas in Java, the `.class` file and a file of serialized objects. Compiling a `.csc` file results in an anonymous `.cell` file with `null` state. Serializing a cell (see Sect. 4.6) results in a `.cell` file that contains a cid and the cell state.

4.4   Object References

CVMs support two kinds of references to objects: *hard* and *modulated* references. A hard reference is a normal Java object reference: a pointer to an object in memory. Hard references can span cell boundaries, but cannot span CVM boundaries. They allow direct and full access to the referenced object.

A modulated reference is a proxy to an object which may be in a different cell, see Fig. 4. Internally, a modulated reference has the form (cid, oid) where cid is the cid of the modulating cell and oid is the identity of the object within the modulating cell. From a programmer's point of view, modulated references are transparent: they are accessed as if they were local, like RMI objects. Behind the scenes, the proxy forwards method calls to the modulating cell which in turn forwards it to the real object.

The modulation of references is an important security construct: a cell may invalidate a reference it is modulating at any time. This is typically programmed to happen when a connector through which the reference was passed is unlinked; Unlinking a connector signifies the end of a tightly-coupled relationship, and object-object connections made between the two cells via the connector should be broken.

The idea of revokable proxy object access is a common theme of object security models [HCC+98]. The co-existence of hard and modulated references allows the programmer to control the degree of isolation of a given cell.

In the implementation of modulated references, each cell holds a *modulation table* mapping the oids of objects it is modulating to their actual locations in memory.

4.5 Cells as Containers: Object Ownership

Cells are both containers of static elements—functions, classes, interfaces—and dynamic elements—objects. The static elements contained by a given cell are those textually contained by it. The objects contained in a cell are given by an *ownership* relation between cells and objects: every object is owned by a unique cell, its *owner*. The owner of an object is set at object creation time to be the cell containing the **new** command that instantiated the object. Ownership is important for cell serialization purposes (see Sect. 4.6): when a cell is serialized, all the objects it owns come along.

4.6 Serialization

One of the fundamental features of cells is the ability to control them *as a whole*. Cells can be unloaded to be re-loaded later, they can be copied, and they can be moved. Underlying all these operations is the *serialization* process, i.e., turning a cell with everything it contains into a .cell file. All cells are in principle serializable.

When a cell is serialized, both its static elements—functions, classes, interfaces—and its dynamic elements—fields, owned objects, modulation table—are streamed into a .cell file. Streaming the object state consists of deeply serializing all cell fields and objects owned by the cell until either a *basic value* (including integer, boolean, cell reference, modulated reference) is reached, or an object not owned by the cell is reached. There are three built-in operations for serialization, which differ in the way they handle the latter case. serialize(aStream) serializes a cell and into aStream and raises an exception if a non-owned object is encountered. serializeWithNull(aStream) serializes a cell putting null in fields of non-owned objects. serializeByModulate(aStream) serializes a cell and requests that all non-owned objects be modulated by their owner (by calling o.getOwner() ←modulate(o)). All of these operations fail if the cell has any active connections at the time of serialization.

4.7 Cell Loading and Unloading

A cell is loaded into a CVM from a .cell file. Loading is accomplished by the built-in service operations load(aStream) and loadWithoutCid(aStream), differing on whether a fresh cid is assigned to the cell upon loading or not. load(aStream) loads the cell into memory. If the stream contains a cid, it is assigned to the loaded cell; an exception is raised if there is already a loaded cell with that cid. If the stream is anonymous, i.e., does not contain a cid, load() generates a fresh one for it. loadWithoutCid(aStream) loads a cell into memory, generating a fresh cid for the cell even if aStream contains a cid. Loading a cell entails loading the cell's classes, the objects owned by the cell, and the modulation table of the cell from the

.cell file into memory. Once the cell is loaded, the cell's hook onLoad() is invoked if present. If a .cell file with cid is loaded via load(aStream), other cells who knew this cell's cid may immediately begin interacting with it now that it is (again) loaded.

Cells may also be unloaded, which means removing them from the CVM, while possibly serializing into a stream. Built-in operation unload(aStream) unloads thisCell. If aStream is not null, the cell is also serialized onto aStream by invoking built-in operation serialize(aStream). A Cell may be unloaded only if it has no active connections. So, unload first unlinks any linked connections. Before a cell is unloaded, the hook onUnload() is run.

Unloading a cell entails also unloading all objects owned by the cell. If an object that is loaded holds a reference to an object that has been unloaded, the object appears in a *zombie* state: all object access results in an "object unloaded" exception being thrown. Zombie objects cannot be restored; if the cell is re-loaded its objects are restored, but at new locations. A cell may however hold *modulated* references to objects in unloaded cells, and these references will function upon re-loading of the cell, even if at a different location.

4.8   Cell Linking and Unlinking

Linking of cells is an operation which is not implicitly implied by loading. In order for two cells to be linked, each must already be running in some CVM. Linking can be either an intra- or inter-CVM operation, *i.e.*, the two cells being linked may be in different CVMs. intra- and inter-CVM linking is similar; here we define intra-CVM linking, and Sect. 5 describes how inter-CVM linking differs.

The cell linking protocol is as follows.

1. Cell connection is initiated by the atomic syntax link *linkee* at *aConnector* being invoked from within the *linker* cell. We use the terms *linker/linkee* to distinguish the two parties involved.
2. Multiple connections can be established at a given connector. However, the connection attempt aborts if as a result of the linking there would exist a plugin with more than one connected plugout (i.e. a plugout can be linked to multiple plugins, but a plugin must be linked to a unique plugout.).
3. To verify the connection passes security checks, the verify predicate of the linkee is first run, and if it succeeds, the verify predicate of the linker is run. Both the linker and the linkee have a chance to refuse the linking via the verify predicate.
4. If both verify operations succeed, the plugin/plugout connections are made, the onConnect() operation of the linkee connector is run, followed by the onConnect() operation of the linker connector.
5. Lastly, references to plugin classes, operations, and interfaces on either side of the connection are resolved to refer to the connected plugout on the other cell and the link command is complete.

The cell link protocol is asymmetric; for a perfectly symmetric model where both cells ask for the connection (as in e.g. process algebra synchronization) each cell must have its own thread in which each can simultaneously request a connection. Since each additional thread complicates the architecture, we do not assume a thread-per-cell model. So, one cell—the linker—initiates the process and the other—the linkee—responds.

A connector may have more than one cell linked to it, *provided* item 2. above is not violated. This supports reuse of a library-style cell with only plugouts by multiple cells. Cells are unlinked by the JCells command `unlink` *linkee* at `aConnector`. This first runs the `onDisconnect()` hooks of the linkee and linker in turn and then un-resolves the references to plugged-in operations. So, after disconnection is complete, any reference to plugin operations on the disconnected connector will raise an exception. Classes that are unplugged will also get an exception upon `new`.

Class loading and Linking. In Java, the loading of classes is performed by the class loader. Because a run-time type in Java is determined by the combination of class loader and class name, class loaders introduce multiple name spaces into Java ([LB98]). This way of managing class names and their actual code is low-level and is not related to the structure of the system at hand.

In JCells, on the other hand, there is only a cell loader, and not a class loader: classes are loaded as part of some cell, which acts as its complete namespace. Different cells may have different internal definitions of the same-named class, which causes no conflict. Classes also can be shared between cells by explicit links which plug in/out the classes. Cells thus hold classes both statically, by their definition within a cell, and dynamically, by how class names are resolved at run-time.

Type Consistency Across Cells. As explained above, different cells may have different interpretations for a given class identifier. This is a problem when an instance of class A is copied from one cell to another one, which has a different notion of A. This problem is analogous to an RMI A-instance being sent to another location in the network, where there may be a different A. This inconsistency will be detected at runtime similarly to how RMI handles type compatibilty: the receiving cell matches its type against a type hash value carried by the copied object.

4.9 Parameter Passing and modulation

Each object parameter or returned value on a method or operation can be passed in one of three ways:

1. by hard reference: the usual and the default case of Java.
2. by `copy`: the object and all objects it refers to, transitively, are copied.
3. by `modulate`: the cell holding the reference modulates it and passes this modulated reference; modulated references are defined in Sect. 4.4.

A `copy` parameter is deeply copied at method/operation invocation time. Copying is similar to serialization, but does not stop at non-owned objects.

5   Distribution

JCells is explicitly designed to support distribution of cells; in particular, CVM processes may be running on different nodes on a network, and cells in one CVM may directly hold references to cells in other CVMs. Additionally, cells may be copied or moved across the network, cells in different locations may be `linked` across the network, and cells in one location can hold (modulated) references to objects in other locations. In what follows, we use the terms *CVM* and *location* interchangeably.

Each cell is universally addressable, and has a *home CVM*—the CVM that initially loaded it and generated its cid. We can elaborate on cids in this context: a cid is a bit sequence which is a pair (`CVM_locator,id`), where `CVM_locator` globally identifies a CVM, and `id` identifies a cell with that CVM as its home. The `id` portion of a cid is random and "long enough" to make it, and thus cell identifiers, practically unguessable. For example, a cid of a cell in cvm1 in machine.cs.jhu.edu could have cid

(`cvm1.machine.cs.jhu.edu,20348320483559172034054855532639`)

Within one cell, a `Cell` variable holds a cid which may either be local, *i.e.*, refers to a cell at home on the executing CVM, or remote, i.e., refers to a cell which has its home on another CVM, which in turn may be on another machine. Built-in service `home()` may be used to dynamically determine any cell's home CVM. Every CVM has a running thread for handling remote cell operations. The protocol for linking to and invoking services on remote cells is the same as the local in-CVM protocol except for the issues which we now outline.

Inter-CVM Connections. One of the main points of the cell `link` protocol is that it can be used to persistently link two cells in different locations on the internet. As such it is a high-level analogue to `ftp` and other persistent socket-based internet protocols. An *interlocation* connector is one which is suitable for interlocation, that is inter-CVM, linking. Not all connectors are so suitable: hard object references are not sensible as parameters between CVMs, and so the connector must not contain such references. Additionally, we disallow classes being plugged in across CVMs: code for an object must be local, so a remote class reference is not sensible.

An *interlocation* connector is thus a connector with the following properties:

1. It has no class plugins or plugouts.
2. All non-basic parameters on operation plugins or plugouts are either `copy` or `modulate` parameters; similarly for return values.

An *interlocation* service is one in which all non-basic parameters are passed by `copy` or `modulate`. `copy` object parameters may be serialized to the remote CVM, and modulated parameters may be sent as (`cid,oid`) bit sequences.

The semantics of interlocation linking is the same as intra-location linking, except the connectors must first be verified to be interlocation connectors. This check is dynamic because `cell MyCell aCell` may either be local or not; this information is not declared in the type and the cell could have in fact initially been local and later moved to another CVM.

Loading and Cell Movement. Cells can be moved between locations by `unloading` and then re-`loading` them in a different location. In order for references to the moved cell to be transparent, the home CVM must be notified upon re-load at a new location. It then forwards any reference to that cid to the CVM where the cell is currently loaded. The home CVM is again notified if the cell is later unloaded. The home CVM is thus responsible for tracking the cell, wherever it might be loaded, throughout its lifetime.

Security. In a distributed setting, security is of particular concern. Cells were designed from the beginning as units on which security policies can be defined; this was in fact one of the inspirations of the design. Classes and objects are arguably too fine-grained for every class and object to hold an advanced security policy; components and modules are just code and directly support code-level security only.

Recall that cells mutually authenticate each other at link time via `verify` clauses, and the linking succeeds only if both sides verify the connection is legitimate. Verification is particularly important for inter-CVM linking. Cells are also secured by cid: cid's are unguessable and so cells know only other cells they have been explicitly told about. Finally, remote object references in JCells take the form of modulated references, which are dynamically revocable. These principles are however only the infrastructure on which a detailed security policy is to be placed. We are currently developing a complete policy built on the SDSI/SPKI open standard [EFL+97], where each cell is a SDSI/SPKI principal. Under any policy it is still unavoidable that some trust must be placed in the CVM by cells running on it. If the CVM has not itself been tampered with, integrity of individual cells running on the CVM is guaranteed.

6 Conclusions

Contributions. This work makes a number of contributions, which we now summarize. We unify the compile-time and run-time notions of module/component: modules are well-structured at compile time but largely disappear at run-time, whereas components have relatively less structure at compile-time but have clear interfaces at run-time; cells importantly have both a strong compile-time and run-time presence. Module principles of code reuse are also preserved by cells: a class in one cell may inherit from a class it has plugged in.

Java allows some programmer control over loading via class loaders; we complete what Java started by separating loading from linking and by putting both fully under high-level programmatic control. Cells support unlinking, a function absent from module systems. We extend the notion of module linking to a network context by allowing two cells running on different network nodes to link with one another.

Cells give an excellent foundation for a new security architecture because each cell itself is sensibly a principal to be secured; in particular, cell reference and cell linking are both privileged operations which may be restricted in JCells. The concept of a modulated reference allows for security-controlled access to objects in other, possibly remote cells.

We introduce the concept of multiple object spaces within a single virtual machine at run-time by requiring each object to be "owned" by a particular cell; this helps focus policies of security and persistence. We work persistence more directly into the design by having a standard definition of how cells and their objects may be serialized.

We believe the above elements in the cell architecture result in a more parsimonious language, in which modular Internet programming is supported as part of the core design. In particular, Java's RMI, `ClassLoader`, security manager, packages, Java Beans, and applets are not needed in JCells because cell functionality subsumes their responsibilities: cell references and modulated references replace RMI (and cell nameserver `lookup` replaces the RMI registry), cell loading replaces class loading, the cell security policy (currently under development) will replace the Java security manager, cells replace Java Beans and applets, and cells are also used in place of Java packages. The cell parallel of java package importing is future work.

Implementation. The design outlined in this paper clearly needs to be implemented to verify its soundness and workability in practice. So far we have implemented a limited prototype [Lu02] on top of an unmodified JVM. We have implemented cells with connections, a `.cell` file format with an XML manifest, loading of cells from `.cell` files, and dynamic linking and unlinking of cells. We have yet to implement ownership of objects by cells, serialization, modulated references, and distributed cells. Reflection is needed to implement plugin operations. A more complete implementation of JCells is currently in progress.

Future Work. This is a large project and we were forced to leave out topics that were not critical to the core architecture. A full cell security policy is currently under development. An explicit protocol for sharing cell signatures is needed, possibly via cell signature nameservers. This will provide the Java-like package import functionality for cells. Currently we lack any notion of cell version control, a critical issue for component systems.

Acknowledgements

The authors would like to thank the ECOOP reviewers for helpful comments on this work.

References

ACN02.   Jonathan Aldrich, Craig Chambers, and David Notkin. Archjava: Connecting software architecture to implementation. In *ICSE 2002*, 2002.

BNOW93.   A. Birell, G. Nelson, S. Owicki, and E. Wobber. Network objects. In *14th ACM Symposium on Operating System Principles*, pages 217–230, 1993.

BR00.   Ciaran Bryce and Chrislain Razafimahefa. An approach to safe object sharing. In *OOPSLA*, pages 367–381, 2000.

BV01.   Ciaran Bryce and Jan Vitek. The javaseal mobile agent kernel. *Autonomous Agents and Multi-Agent Systems*, 4:359–384, 2001.

Car95.   L. Cardelli. A language with distributed scope. *Computing Systems*, 8(1):27–59, January 1995.

Car99.   Luca Cardelli. Abstractions for mobile computation. In Jan Vitek and
                Christian Jensen, editors, *Secure Internet Programming: Security Issues for
                Mobile and Distributed Objects*, volume 1603 of *Lecture Notes in Computer
                Science*, pages 51–94. Springer, 1999.
CDG⁺ 88.   Luca Cardelli, James Donahue, Lucille Glassman, Mick Jordan, Bill Kalsow,
                and Greg Nelson. Modula-3 report. Technical Report 31, Digital Equipment
                Corporation, Systems Research Center, August 1988.
EFL⁺ 97.   Carl M. Ellison, Bill Frantz, Butler Lampson, Ron Rivest, Brian M. Thomas,
                and Tatu Ylonen. Simple public key certificate. Internet Engineering Task
                Force Draft IETF, July 1997.
FF98.   Matthew Flatt and Matthias Felleisen. Units: Cool modules for HOT lan-
                guages. In *Proceedings of the ACM SIGPLAN '98 Conference on Program-
                ming Language Design and Implementation*, pages 236–248, 1998.
Gro01.   Object Management Group. *The Common Object Request Broker: Architec-
                ture and Specification*, revision 2.5 edition, September 2001.
HCC⁺ 98.   C. Hawblitzel, C.-C. Chang, G. Czajkowski, D. Hu, and T. von Eicken.
                Implementing multiple protection domains in Java. In *1998 USENIX Annual
                Technical Conference*, pages 259–270, New Orleans, LA, 1998.
JLH90.   Eric Jul, Henry Levy, and Norman Hutchinson. Fine-grained mobility in the
                emerald system. In *Readings in Object Oriented Databases*, pages 317–328.
                ACM, 1990.
LB98.   Sheng Liang and Gilad Bracha. Dynamic class loading in the java virtual
                machine. In *OOPSLA '98*, pages 36–44, 1998.
LO98.   D. Lange and M. Oshima. *Programming and Deploying Java Mobile Agents
                with Aglets*. Addison-Wesley, 1998.
Lu02.   Xiaoqi Lu. Report on the cell prototype project. (Internal Report), March
                2002.
MFH01.   Sean McDirmid, Matthew Flatt, and Wilson Hsieh. Jiazzi: New age compo-
                nents for old fashioned java. In *OOPSLA 2001*, 2001.
Sun.   Sun Microsystems. Java RMI. http://java.sun.com/products/jdk/rmi/.
Szy98.   Clemens Szyperski. *Component Software: Beyond Object-Oriented Program-
                ming*. ACM Press and Addison-Wesley, New York, NY, 1998.
Ung95.   D. Ungar. How to program self 4.0 a guide to the programming environment,
                June 1995.
                http://research.sun.com/self/release/documentation.html.
US87.   D. Ungar and R. Smith. Self: the power of simplicity. In *OOPSLA 1987*,
                pages 227–241, 1987.
VC99.   Jan Vitek and Giuseppe Castagna. Seal: A framework for secure mobile
                computations. In *Internet Programming Languages*, 1999.
vDABW96.   L. van Doorn, M. Abadi, M. Burrows, and E. Wobber. Secure network
                objects. In *IEEE Symposium on Security and Privacy*, May 1996.
VT97.   J. Vitek and C. Tschudin. *Mobile Objects Systems: Towards the Pro-
                grammable Internet*, volume 1222. Springer-Verlag, Berlin, Germany, 1997.
WCC⁺ 74.   W. Wulf, E. Cohen, W. Corwin, A. Jones, R. Levin, C. Pierson, and F. Pol-
                lack. Hydra: The kernel of a multiprocessor. *Communications of the ACM*,
                17(6):337–345, 1974.
Whi94.   J. E. White. Telescript technology: The foundation for the electronic mar-
                ketplace. White paper, General Magic, Inc., 2465 Latham Street, Mountain
                View, CA 94040, 1994.
ZM90.   S. Zdonik and D. Maier. *Readings in Object-Oriented Database Systems*.
                Morgan Kaufmann, San Mateo, CA, 1990.

A Built-in Protocols

Cells have built-in services and operations for important functions, and the Object protocol is also enriched in JCells. In this Appendix we summarize the protocols.

Built-in Services. Cells have several built-in services to support system functions. This is in analogy to class Object public methods. Several of them have been already described above. Here we list the full metaprotocol available.

- cell Cell clone()—returns of a copy of the cell.
- cell Cell modulate(Object o)—returns a modulated reference to o.
- copy CVM home()—returns the home CVM of the cell.
- copy CVM location()—returns the current CVM where the cell is located.

Built-in Operations. Some in-cell built-in operations are also supported. These may not be invoked by outsiders, i.e. they are not services.

- Cell cell [] cellsAt(String aConnector)—returns the set of cells connected at thisCell's aConnector.
- cell Cell invoker()—the cell which invoked the currently executing cell operation.
- cell Cell revokeModulationOn(Object mo)—removes modulated reference mo from thisCell's modulation table.
- cell Cell load(aStream)—cell load preserving the cid
- cell Cell loadWithoutCid(Stream s)—a cell is loaded off of stream s, ignoring cid.
- void unload(Stream s)—thisCell is serialized to s and then unloaded from the CVM. If s is null, the cell is just unloaded.
- void serialize(Stream s)—serialize thisCell unto the stream s; variants serializeWithNull(Stream s) and void serializeByModulate(Stream s).
- cell Cell lookup(String s)—lookup a cell via name server.
- cell Cell register(String s)—register this cell with the name server as s.

Supported Hooks. The following hooks are supported by the CVM:

- onUnload()—This operation, if it is defined, is invoked just before a cell is unloaded.
- onLoad()—This operation, if it is defined, is invoked immediately after a cell is loaded off a stream, and can for instance be used to re-link the cell to libraries or other services.

Object Protocol. There are also a few additional object protocols, messages which all objects in a CVM respond to.

1. cell Cell o.getOwner() returns the cell owning object o.
2. Boolean o.isModulated() returns true iff o is a modulated reference.
3. Boolean o.isZombie() returns true iff o is a zombie.

Lana: An Approach
to Programming Autonomous Systems

Ciarán Bryce, Chrislain Razafimahefa, and Michel Pawlak

Centre Universitaire d'Informatique, University of Geneva,
Switzerland.
{bryce,razafima,pawlak}@cui.unige.ch

Abstract. Networks today are dynamic (e.g. devices join and leave P2P communities or Bluetooth piconets) so programs need to be autonomous. This means that they must be able to continue working despite changes in the network. To provide autonomy, developers require a programming model where the communication primitives are non-blocking, where there is support for information lookup in a program's current network and where network outages are considered natural rather than as errors. This paper presents Lana, a programming model based on Java, that includes concepts for communication, mobility, security and connection recovery in order to support autonomy.

1 Introduction

A major design goal of the Java language [4] is to support robust and secure distributed computing [20]. Robustness is desirable since outages by the network or its machines should not cause the whole system to fail. Security is desirable since we do not want our machines to collapse under a virus. However, robust and secure distributed programming is challenging. With regard to robustness, if a machine must tolerate the failure of others, then programmers have to think about what should happen when a machine goes down, and code recovery logic into their application. With regard to security, programmers have to code security logic into the application that minimizes the risk of application data being stolen or corrupted by malicious programs.

Today's distributed systems are becoming even harder to program because several networks exist where machines can join and leave spontaneously. For example, a user may be using the Internet via his mobile phone. If he is passing through an area where the telephone signal is weak, then he may temporarily lose contact with the network. Another example is a Bluetooth piconet [37] where a user's PDA may lose contact with other PDAs as the user wanders around the piconet area. Yet another example is an Internet peer-to-peer system where a user can connect and disconnect his PC from the community at any time. In these examples, a machine losing contact with the network is not necessarily an "error", and the disconnection may only be temporary.

B. Magnusson (Ed.): ECOOP 2002, LNCS 2374, pp. 281–308, 2002.

An *autonomous system* is a distributed system composed of machines that may join and leave the network at any time. Disconnection can be frequent, unforeseen and unannounced. The key to the programming model for these systems is to minimize a program's dependence on other programs. This entails being able to cut a program's links to its environment, as well as the environment's links to the program, without crashing either the environment or the program. Further, network outage must not be considered as an error; rather, the programming model must enable programs to resume communication should the network reappear. Finally, the model must contain mechanisms to maximize the potential for programs to locate information in a dynamic network where the set of machines available at any moment is arbitrary.

The goal of this paper is to propose a programming model called Lana for autonomous systems. Lana programs communicate using *asynchronous method calls* – thus a program need not block awaiting a method return message that might never come. An *associative information search* tool – based on a collection of message boards – is used by programs to find information in their current network irrespective of the current composition of the network and independently of any naming scheme. Programs are *mobile*, which increases disconnection toleration by permitting a machine to have programs left elsewhere on the network before it disconnects. Regarding security, *protection domains* prevent a program from gaining access to another program's data, and each inter-program communication is mediated by a *security policy*. A network outage does not crash a Lana program: the requesting program is notified via an event of the outage and can securely recover a lost connection in case the network becomes available again, or delegate that task to another program. We will argue in this paper that the combination of these features gives very useful properties for autonomous systems.

We contend that Java has shortcomings when used to program autonomous systems. For instance, loss of the network in a Java application leads to an exception interrupting the communicating programs. The exception does not help the programs to find each other later or to recover lost data. The onus is rather on the application programmer to code the logic that is needed to recover. Another shortcoming is that there is no clearly defined boundary between the objects that belong to individual programs (or threads). This makes security harder since aliasing can allow malicious programs to gain access to a program's internal data. A program can hardly be considered autonomous if it can be attacked in this manner. Support for network searching in Java is not provided in the language, but rather in frameworks such as Jini [5] and JXTA [19]. However, partly due to Java shortcomings, the implementations of these tools do not meet all of the requirements that we have set out above for programming autonomous systems.

This paper is organized as follows. Section 2 motivates the need for a new programming model for autonomous systems. The Lana model is then presented in Section 3 and we explain how it satisfies our requirements for autonomy. We implemented Lana as a Java framework and this is described in Section 4. We consider related work in Section 5 and conclude in Section 6.

2   Autonomous Systems

This section looks at the characteristics of current system environments. It then analyzes these characteristics in the aim of identifying features required for a programming model for autonomous systems.

2.1   Trends

Programming languages evolve because the environments we program evolve also. There are three major trends in distributed environments that we have considered when designing Lana: personal devices, wireless networks and peer-to-peer computing.

Personal devices such as mobile telephones are becoming fully-fledged computers. The *Nokia Communicator* for instance contains a complete keyboard, at least 32MB of memory and runs the Symbian operating system with an eclectic suite of applications. Several telephone devices now have both GSM and GPRS for communication, and even Bluetooth [37] for short-range data exchange. The GSM/GPRS connections enable Internet access though this can be perturbed for a mobile users since the strength of GSM/GPRS signals can vary greatly. The fact that each telephone carries a smartcard means that sensitive processing – such as data signing for electronic commerce – can potentially be carried out using the phone. This means that telephones can become more secure personal computers than traditional laptops. The SAGEM MC 840 (Triple Slot Phone) for instance can run data signing functions on its SIM card. By 2004, 17% of the world's population (70% in Europe and America) will be carrying mobile telephones [30], so these devices are obviously now a major class of personal computer.

In addition to these new people area networks, more run-of-the-mill machines are carrying embedded processors. Up to 98% of today's processors are embedded [12]. The wide variety of computers that results endorses the Java requirement for "write once, run anywhere" code [20], since we can expect them to be heterogeneous in size, architecture and computing power.

Another observable trend is that *Wireless networks* are omnipresent today. Wireless LANs are replacing cabled Ethernets, GSM and GPRS are spreading, and Bluetooth enables device communication over short distances. Though wireless networks have existed for a long time, they are now used to connect and to program a critical mass of devices. For instance, it is estimated that 40% of Internet accesses will be made via GSM/GPRS connections in the next few years [30]. Wireless communication will also make embedded devices easier to control.

Another important implication of wireless is that it tends to support device mobility, so devices that have never met each other before can form networks. This is typically the case for a Bluetooth piconet of PDAs where people and devices can directly exchange personal information. Another use of Bluetooth is for PDAs to contact a fixed network: this is done through Bluetooth cards (e.g., such as 3Com Bluetooth USB adaptors) that connect to standard PCs. A PDA can communicate with any PC in its neighborhood that has such a card.

In *Peer-to-Peer computing* (P2P) users share resources on their PC with others in the community. The P2P idea was popularized by Napster [23] – designed for the sharing of music files – and Gnutella [1]. Other kinds of resources that can be shared in P2P systems include: video files, disk space (more and more people in the operating systems community see P2P as a good solution to the disk backup problem, e.g., [11]), CPU time (e.g., the SETI project [2] asks community members to loan them CPU time to run programs that analyze radio signals from outer space). The most interesting aspect of P2P is that it implements a philosophy in which a user accepts that other users browse his PC for shared resources.

2.2   Programming Model Requirements

There are important lessons in these trends for the design of a programming model. These lead to a set of requirements for distribution, robustness and security, and raise concerns over the suitability of Java for autonomous systems.

Distribution. Machines in the examples presented can join and leave the network at any moment. A consequence of this is that a program must minimize its dependence on other programs and machines. A program must not be blocked awaiting a communication that may never come because its partner has left the network. Similarly, a program should not have to rely on any server even for information lookup since that directory server or the information it references may disappear from the program's network neighborhood. Finally, from a *resource discovery* perspective, a machine that joins a network must have some way of locating references to information or servers in that network.

Robustness. The spontaneous nature of network composition poses the question about how we consider "failure". In Java, the loss of a communication link generates an exception in the application that interrupts the communicating program. The exception implies a failure: something is wrong with the network and needs to be fixed. How it is fixed is something that the programmer must decide upon and code into his application. In contrast, the loss of ability to communicate in an autonomous system just means that communication cannot happen at that time. The application has not necessarily failed so rather than generating an error, the program should be allowed to continue its execution and to try again later. Thus, an autonomous program must remain robust to changes in its environment.

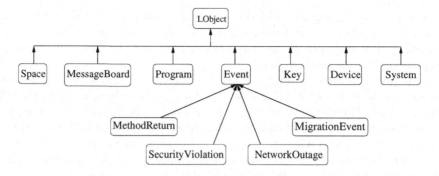

Fig. 1. The hierarchy of principal Lana classes.

Security. It might be impossible to prevent machines entering into an autonomous system network, e.g., a PC connecting to a P2P community or a Bluetooth PDA entering into a piconet. This means that a user will not be able to trust all other programs in the network. It is crucial therefore that measures be provided to prevent a malicious program from gaining access to a program's data. In addition, the confidentiality and integrity of messages exchanged between programs must be enforced. This means that only the designated receiver may gain access to the contents of a message, and a program may not alter the contents of a message generated by another program.

3   The Lana Model

Lana is designed to meet the requirements set out in Section 2.2. We chose to model Lana on Java because of its object-orientation, strong typing, security features, its exception handling mechanism that allows exceptions to be treated as first-class values, as well as its bytecode interpretation (and runtime compilation) approach that allows programs to run on heterogeneous platforms. This section describes the Lana programming model. We begin with an overview before describing the individual features in more detail. An implementation of Lana is described in Section 4.

3.1   Lana in a Nutshell

Like in Java, a Lana platform is structured from a basic hierarchy of classes. The core Lana classes are illustrated in Figure 1, where the arrows denote subclass relations.

LObject is the superclass of all classes in Lana. This class only contains a few basic methods, such as for printing its value to a standard output and for calculating a hashcode.

A Lana environment runs a set of concurrent *programs*. Programs may be mutually mistrusting so the Lana kernel prevents a program from gaining direct access to another program's objects. They can communicate using method calls though a security policy controls each of these calls. Finally, programs are mobile, meaning that they can be moved between machines. In Lana, machines are represented by the Device class.

Method calls between programs are *asynchronous*. When a method is called, the kernel generates a fresh Key object that is immediately returned to the calling program. The method call request is then dispatched to the called program. Assuming that all goes well, the invoked method will terminate. When this happens, the Lana kernel will generate an *event* to signal the method's completion.

Events are used to asynchronously signal information. Basic events include the return of a method call, the raising of a security violation when a call is made on a program for which the calling program does not possess an access right, the migration of a program to another device, or the disappearance of the network. Unlike exceptions, events need not be caught meaning that a program can choose to handle events only if they are important to its execution.

Each event generated in Lana is *locked* with a key. Only a program that possesses a matching key can observe the event. A key object is immutable and cannot be fabricated by a malicious program. In the case of method termination, the event generated – *MethodReturn* – holds the return value of the method call. Locking of events is needed to prevent malicious programs intercepting events destined to other programs.

A second communication mechanism is the MessageBoard. Each Lana device contains one message board. This is an associative object container in which programs can place and retrieve object copies (in byte array form) and object references. For security reasons, each object placed in the board is locked with a key; only a program possessing the key used to lock an object in the board may read that object. A second function of the message board is *resource discovery*: when a device joins a network, its programs typically search the message boards of other devices in the network to see what resources are available.

A program can contact a device's message board as soon as it detects the device. The Device class contains code for searching its environment for other devices.

Finally, a Space is composed of a set of objects shared between programs. Spaces are needed to enforce access control on objects and to curtail the effects of undetected aliasing. Every Lana object belongs to a space or to a program. The objects in a space have the same sharing constraints imposed by the system's security policy. A program or object can only invoke a method of an object in a space if it has been explicitly granted the right for that space. An example Lana environment illustrating programs, spaces and message boards is given in Figure 2.

3.2   Programs and Spaces

Programs are executable units in Lana. They each contain a thread and can be accessed via a call on one of their methods. A space is a collection of objects that are grouped together for protection and mobility reasons. Spaces contain

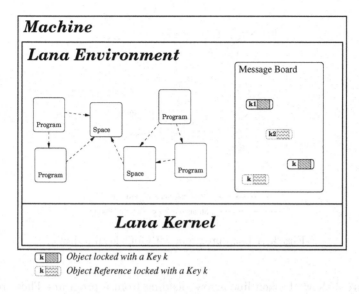

Fig. 2. An environment with programs, spaces and a message board.

objects that can be shared between programs without having to use a copy-by-value. Both programs and spaces implement *protection domains* in Lana. Access to a domain is controlled by a security policy, and both the `Program` and `Space` classes implement the interface `Domain`.

Programs. A program is an instance of `lana.lang.Program` or any of its subclasses. It is a unit of security, mobility and accountability in Lana. This means that each access to a program is controlled by a security policy. Regarding mobility, a program can be stopped, *wrapped* and sent to another device. Regarding accountability, each object and the thread in a program belongs to only that program; a program that consumes too much space can thus be stopped and removed from the system, without undermining other programs.

Security, mobility and accountability are essential – though not quite sufficient – for program autonomy. Concerning security, a program is hardly autonomous if another program can steal or corrupt its data. Concerning mobility, a program is not autonomous if it is bound to a device and has to put up with outages of that device. Concerning accountability, a program lacks autonomy if it must share responsibility for another program's resource usage.

The structure of a program is illustrated in Figure 3. It possesses an execution thread and a set of local objects. Objects inside of a program name each other using normal or *strong* references. If object $\mathcal{O}_1$ holds a strong reference for object $\mathcal{O}_2$, then $\mathcal{O}_1$ may invoke methods on $\mathcal{O}_2$. Method calls on objects named with strong references are synchronous: as in Java, the calling object is blocked until the invoked method returns. Strong object references are denoted in Figure 3 by complete-line arrows.

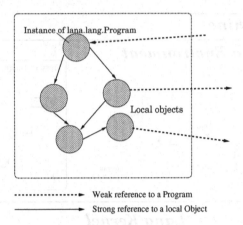

Weak reference to a Program
Strong reference to a local Object

Fig. 3. A Lana program, with four local objects.

Figure 3 shows broken line arrows leading from a program. These represent *weak references*. A program uses a weak reference to denote another program object. There are two important differences between weak and strong references:

1. Possession of a weak reference does not necessarily imply that the holder may invoke the referenced program. A method call on the program may fail because the caller does not have permission to call the program. It may also fail because the called object has moved and the system is unaware of its current location.
2. Method calls on weak references are asynchronous. Thus the caller does not wait for the return message. Rather, each method call generates a fresh *key* that is returned to the caller. This key becomes associated with the method call and can be used by the program to detect the presence of the method return message later in the environment.

```
class Me extends Program{

  You p;     /* You is a subclass of Program */
  Key k;
  Event e;

  public void run(){
    p = new You();
    k = p.yourName();

    System.println(''Method has been sent'');

    e = observe(k);    /* The program awaits an event locked with k */

    System.println(''Got return message of type: '' + e.toString());
    if(e instanceof MethodReturn)
```

```
       System.println(''Return value is '' + e.extract());

  if(e instanceof MigrationEvent)
      System.println(''The program has gone away :-('');
 }
}
```

In this program, Me queries another program – of class You – for its name. Every program contains a run method. On program creation, a new thread is created to execute this method. Once the run method terminates, the thread is free to service method calls from the outside. The program has three local variables: p denotes the program being called; e will denote the event of the call returning, and k is the key generated by the method invocation.

The run method first creates a You program. Then, in the second line, it invokes the method yourName on the program. Since programs are referenced using weak references, this call is asynchronous. A key is generated by the system and bound to k, which immediately continues to the println command. At this point, the method call is being concurrently serviced.

The program executes the observe command to block until the arrival of an event locked with k. If everything went well in the method's execution, this event is of type MethodReturn. However, it could be that the method call led to a security violation, or that the invoked program has disappeared due to mobility. In these cases, the system generates an event of class SecurityViolation (respectively MigrationEvent).

The reason for the k in observe(k) command is that each event generated by the system is *locked* with a key. Only a program that possesses a matching key can observe – and gain access to – that event. The motivation for keys is security, and we return to this issue in Section 3.3.

Spaces. Even though programs are prevented from gaining direct access to objects in other programs for security reasons, programs do typically need to share information to accomplish their tasks. Sharing in object-oriented systems can either be *by-reference* or *by-value*. The former is an integral part of the object model [22] where objects name each other via references that can be exchanged via method calls. Copy-by-reference allows an object to be reached for invocation via different paths. However, aliasing can arise in subtle ways and it can be difficult to know how many copies of a reference exist in the system. This makes security difficult to implement [33].

Copy-by-value is used in object-oriented systems to contain the effects of aliasing. In this scheme, the runtime makes copies of all objects exchanged between programs, so no inter-program object references exist. In Java, copy-by-value is known as serialization and is used to exchange data between applets [18]. However, copy-by-value is an awkward programming style since shared mutable data must be constantly copied between the sharing programs. This is inefficient and can lead to timing errors.

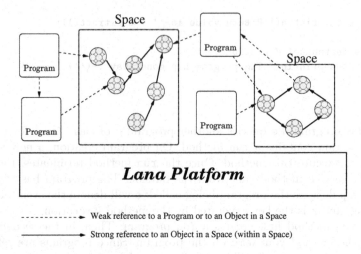

Fig. 4. Programs and spaces. All references to objects from outside their space are weak.

The compromise solution adopted for Lana is to permit copy-by-reference but to control the method invocations made on references. This entails adding access control to the system and in Lana this is done using *spaces*. A space is an instance of class `Space` and is a container for a set of objects. All objects in the container have the same access rights for objects in other spaces. Each object in Lana belongs to a space or is a local object to a program.

In order to maintain a boundary around the space, objects in a space are referenced from the outside using weak references. Objects in the same space name each other using strong references. Whenever a strong reference that an object holds on another object of its space is passed outside of the enclosing space, the kernel transforms this reference to a weak version. As was the case with programs, method calls on weakly referenced objects are asynchronous, with a fresh key being immediately returned to the caller. Figure 4 illustrates a system with programs and spaces.

Access Control. The set of programs and spaces running over a Lana kernel is organized into a hierarchy. Thus, when the kernel is booted, it creates a root program that itself can create other programs or object spaces. There is a single unique hierarchy per device: like others [29,10], we feel that the hierarchy offers a convenient way of structuring a multi-program environment. In Lana, the objects in a child space are not directly visible to the parent. Rather, the hierarchy implies that an object in the parent space may alter the security policy that governs access to objects in child spaces.

An example of the hierarchy is shown in Figure 5. The kernel runs a program that has created two children spaces, S1 and S2, and a child program `Prog1`. In this scenario, an object in space S2 creates a child program `Prog2`, and `Prog1`

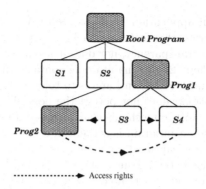

Fig. 5. A hierarchy of `Programs` and object `Spaces`.

creates two child spaces S3 and S4. The lines denote the parent relation. The dotted lines with arrows denote access permissions: `Prog1` has granted `Prog2` and objects of Space S3 the right to invoke methods on objects in Space S4. Similarly, an object in Space S2 has granted objects in Space S3 the right to invoke methods on `Prog2`.

As method calls are asynchronous, the access right of the caller is verified at the moment that the call is scheduled rather than at the time that the call is made. In this way, a method will not be scheduled after the access right of the caller has been revoked. Method calls on a program that originate from a remote device are prohibited by default, though may be enabled using the `permit` method (see Figure 6).

Mobility. Program and space domains are also the units of mobility between devices. Only a parent domain has the right to move a child domain. Mobility is useful for several reasons. First, since PDAs are generally not powerful devices, it allows devices to delegate programs to more powerful servers. Second, a client program can be migrated to the device of a server it is using; this enables the application to continue despite network interruptions. Third, dynamic program deployment is useful for supporting application evolution.

To move a domain, the thread in the program or object is stopped and its code and objects are *wrapped*. The packaged domain can then be sent to a remote site for re-instantiation. When a domain is wrapped, then all sibling domains are recursively wrapped along with it. In Figure 5 for instance, if `Prog1` is wrapped, then spaces S3 and S4 are wrapped along with it.

A program that moves can cause (weak reference) links to "break". The kernel makes a minimal effort to keep track of migrated domains. If `Prog2` of Figure 5 moves to a new device, the kernel associates the name of the new device with the weak reference held by objects of Space S3. Subsequent method calls on this reference are forwarded to this device and the result is shipped back to the calling device. If the program moves again, then this reference becomes out of date: a method call on the reference will lead to a `MigrationEvent` object being generated. If an application needs to keep track of where programs are, then it needs to program this feature as a Lana service. The kernel thus does not provide relocation transparency, nor does it use proxy objects or techniques such as DCOM Monikers [21] for maintaining contact with service objects.

The goal of program mobility in Lana is to tolerate the loss of sites over the network. Java, in contrast, does not permit the possibility of moving programs or threads. The only capture mechanism in Java is data capture – *serialization* in Java parlance. When a program is serialized, a copy is made of the objects. The thread's state is not captured, and even the classes of the objects are not included in the serialized state. Thus a site is expected to have its own copy of the classes when the object is activated at the receiving site. This requirement contradicts the autonomy requirement because devices can be disconnected from their code source.

Corresponding API. Figure 6 shows the API of core Lana classes (of our implementation). **Program** contains a **run** method that executes on program start-up at creation and following a migration. For reasons we explain in Section 4, programs are referenced using **Capability** objects in our Java implementation. **Capability** and **Space** implement the **Domain** methods. The **grant** and **revoke** methods give (respectively remove) the right to another domain for the current domain. The **permit** and **restrict** methods open (respectively close) the domain to calls from remote devices.

3.3   MessageBoards and Keys

As we mentioned in Section 2.2, autonomous systems require a communication mechanism that allows devices that meet for the first time to exchange data, i.e., *resource discovery*. In Lana, this mechanism is provided using message boards. After introducing this concept, we review events, as these are a third class of inter-program communication.

Resource Discovery. Since a device's neighborhood can change dynamically, a device cannot rely on any other device for searching the network for information, but must take a proactive approach. Further, the heterogeneous nature of the system means that it is impossible to agree upon a common naming scheme for identifying resources.

To this end, each Lana platform contains a single **MessageBoard** object (see Figure 2). This resembles a Linda shared data space or *board* [16] where programs can place object copies (in byte array form) or weak references for other programs to retrieve. The message board is searched in an associative manner. This is how devices that meet get to know each other: programs on each device can obtain references for objects on the other device and then start method calling, thus enabling mutually unknown programs to communicate. Message boards implement resource discovery without the need for a centralized lookup service. Lookups in Lana are distributed and therefore scalable. Scalability is important since the number of devices present on the network can be potentially large and can grow dynamically.

Resource discovery in autonomous systems first requires that devices be able to detect other devices in their neighborhood. In Lana, each device is represented by a `Device` object. This class' static method `getNetworkNeighbours` which scans the device's network for other Lana devices and returns an array of `Device` objects. In a Bluetooth network, this is implemented using the Bluetooth protocol search [37]. In an IP network, this searching is simulated using multicast addresses, as we explain in Section 4.

Message boards in Lana serve several purposes. First, they allow devices that meet to exchange initial data. Second, they give programs the possibility of exchanging data by-value, in addition to the sharing by reference implemented by method calls. Third, the message board is used to store lost messages. For instance, if a program makes a method call on an object on another device, and the network is lost during method execution, then the return message is stored in the message board of the called device. The key used to lock this message in the board is the key that is generated at the calling side when the call is made. Thus, the caller can search for its response whenever it comes back into the network. The final use of the message board is program and space migration: either is migrated by placing a wrapped copy in the destination device's message board.

Keys. In Lana, keys appear at several places. They identify individual method calls, and, as seen from Figure 2, objects in a message board are locked with keys. This means that a program can only read an entry in the board if it possesses a matching key. The goal here is to balance a requirement for security on the one hand with the flexibility of associative information lookup on the other.

Lana has two kinds of keys. *Fixed* keys are generated with a specific value using the `Key(long value)` or `Key(String value)` constructor (See Figure 6). *Floating* keys are generated with the `Key()` constructor. The value of a fixed key is that specified in the constructor. Two fixed keys are equal if they contain the same value. In contrast, a floating key has a value that is unique: two floating keys can never match and a fixed key can never match with a floating key. In fact, a floating key can only match with a duplicate of itself (generated using the `duplicate` method). The keys generated by method calls are floating keys; thus a malicious program cannot generate a false key to intercept a method return message.

Fixed keys are mainly used for exchanging basic information in the message board. For instance, when PDAs meet, a particular application – like a business card application – might have its reference stored in a message board locked with a key with a well known value, e.g., `Key(''Business Cards'')`. In this way, an initial set of object references can be locked with "well known" key values. Once these references have been exchanged, a normal method calling conversation can be established.

Keys in Lana are first class values, which means that they can be exchanged between programs. This allows a program to delegate the handling of a method call return to another program, by transferring a copy of the key to that program.

This feature is useful for autonomy since a device can leave a network though still have work carried out for it by other devices on the network.

API for `MessageBoard` and `Key` are given in Figure 6. The message board can store either object copies or weak references. If a program or space is `put` into a device's message board, the system suspends the executing thread and wraps up the associated objects – this is how program and space migration is achieved. Note also that a weak reference can be exported to a remote message board. Lana supports calls on weak references even when the referenced space or program is on a remote device. Finally, the `firewall` method can be used for self-protection: when invoked, it means that the message board will only accept to store objects locked with the specified set of keys. The goal here is to reduce the potential for denial of service attacks that saturate the memory space of the board.

3.4 Events

An *event* in Lana is a signal that is asynchronously sent and which may carry a value. An event is asynchronous in the sense that the program that generates it does not wait for the event to be *observed* by another program.

Events are used often in Lana. The return message from a method call is an event, as is the failure to make a call due to a `SecurityViolation` or a `MigrationEvent`. These are all subclasses of `Event` defined in the package `lana.lang`. Events are secure in the sense that they are locked with keys, and can only be accessed by a program that knows the key. An event can carry an object payload. In the case of `MethodReturn`, the payload carries the return value of the method. The `extract` method returns the event's payload.

An event is not the same thing as an *exception*. An exception is something that must be caught, e.g., division by zero, or `NullPointerException`, since the program cannot logically continue in its presence. On the other hand, an event like `MethodReturn` or `lana.net.NetworkOutage` need not be caught - it is explicitly caught by the program only if it chooses to know about it.

Though the Lana core packages contain event classes, user programs may also define their own event kinds. An event is generated with the `signal` command, and caught with `observe`. Note that a timeout value can be specified for the `observe` to avoid blocking indefinitely.

```
signal(Key k, Event e),
Event e = observe(Key k) /* or */ Event e = observe(Key k, long timeout)
```

Events are also used for program synchronization, even for programs on different devices. The command `observe(k)` causes a program to block until an event locked with `k` is signaled. Once this event is generated, only a single program that is blocked awaiting such an event will observe it. To synchronize on a number of events, *key rings* – a Boolean combination of keys – can be used.

```
public class Program implements Domain{
      public void run();
      /* From LObject */
      protected Event observe(Key);
      protected Event observe(KeyRing);
      protected Event observe(Key, className);
      protected void signal(Key, Event);
}

public final class Key {
      public Key();
      public Key(long value);
      public Key(String value);
      public Key duplicate();
      public void makeEncryptionKey();
}

public class Event{
      public Event(Object); // Create an event and its content
      public Object extract();
}

public final class Device{
      public Device(Address, portNumber); // Create a reference to remote device
      public static Device[] getNetworkNeighbours();
      public static Device getLocalDevice();
}

public final class Space implements Domain{
      public Space();
      public void permit();
      public void restrict();
      public void grant(Domain);
      public void revoke(Domain);
      public Capability newInstance(String); // Creates an object in another space
}

public final class MessageBoard {
      private MessageBoard(); // No user-visible constructor: one MessageBoard per device
      public static void put(Key, Object);
      public static void put(Device, Key, Object) throws NetworkException;
      public static void putReference(Key, Object);
      public static void putReference(Device, Key, Object);
      public static Object read(Device, Key, Object) throws NetworkException;;
      public static Object readReference(Device, Key, Object) throws NetworkException;;
      public static Object readReference(Key, Object);
      public static void firewall(Key[]);
      ...
}

public class Capability implements Domain{
      public void grant(Domain);
      public void revoke(Domain);
      public void permit();
      public void restrict();
      public Capability duplicate();
}
```

Fig. 6. The core Lana class API.

```
Key k1, k2, k3;
KeyRing kr1 = new KeyRing();
KeyRing kr2 = new KeyRing();
...
kr1.and(k1, k2);
kr2.or(kr1, k3);    /* Build expression of keys (k1 and k2) or k3 */
Event e = observe(kr2)
```

In this extract, two key rings kr1 and kr2 are defined from keys k1, k2 and k3. The observe command blocks awaiting any event locked with the key ring kr2. In other words, the program blocks until an event is observed that is either locked with key k1 *and* k2, or else with key k3.

3.5   Short Example

The following scenario illustrates some of the Lana concepts. A program "server" running on a machine creates a program of class HelloWorld. The code of this class is not shown; suffice to say that it contains a method printHello which returns a string. Note that Server does not directly create an instance of class HelloWorld, but rather a capability for the program of class HelloWorldCap. The reason for this comes from our current implementation that is described in the next section. (The code extracts shown are from programs that were run on a local area network of Sun machines). In its run method, the Server creates a HelloWorld program (via a capability) and places a reference for this in its device's message board. Note that the reference is locked with a fixed key whose value is "Hello World Agent".

```
public class Server extends Program {

  public void run() {

    // Create an agent capability and place reference
    // in the local message board
    HelloWorldCap agent = new HelloWorldCap();

    agent.permit(); // Allow Hello World program to be remotely called

    MessageBoard.putReference(new Key(''Hello World Agent''), agent);
  }// end run
}
```

A client program is started on some other machine of the network. The goal of Client is to contact HelloWorld programs on the network. The program begins by querying its network for devices using the getNetworkNeighbours method (with a timeout value of 5000 milliseconds). In each of the located devices, a reference locked with the key whose value is "Hello World Agent" is looked for. This lookup uses an associative search. It is assumed here that all devices wishing to advertise use of their HelloWorld programs will lock the references using a

key with this value. The string "Hello World Agent" is the only information
that a program needs to know to locate the programs. We omit the code that
treats the case where `readReference` returns no value since no object is locked
with this key, or where a value of a different type is returned. After importing
the reference, the client invokes the `HelloWorld` program on the remote device,
awaits a reply (of class `MethodReturn`), and finally prints the string returned.

```
public class Client extends Program {

  Key k; Event e;
  HelloWorldCap agent;

  public void run() {

   Device[] devices = Device.getNetworkNeighbours(5000);

   lana.lang.System.println(''Found '' + devices.length
                                       + '' neighbour(s)'');

   for (int i = 0; i < devices.length; i++) {
      System.println("Device's " + i + " address and port: "
          + devices[i].getHostAddress()
                      + devices[i].getCommunicationPort());

      agent = (AgentCap)MessageBoard.
              readReference(new Key(''Hello World Agent''), devices[i]);

      k = agent.printHello();
      e = observe(k, ''lana.lang.MethodReturn'');
      System.println((String)e.extract());
   }

  }// end run
}
```

4   Implementation

We have implemented Lana as a set of Java packages. The advantage of an
implementation over Java is rapid prototyping and portability of the platform.
The Lana kernel thus runs as a program over the Java virtual machine, which in
turn loads and runs Lana programs. The implementation contains around 8 000
lines of Java source code and 90KB of class files. Despite being implemented in
Java, Lana is a subset of Java in that several basic JDK classes are prohibited
from user programs for security and mobility reasons. The Lana class loader
verifies the absence of forbidden classes.

Lana runs over Java 1 and Java 2. Since PDAs are an important element of
autonomous systems, our goal is to have Lana running on small devices. Thus,

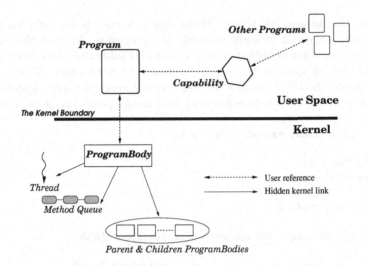

Fig. 7. The user/kernel boundary.

though we prototyped over Java 2, we adapted the platform to run over Java 1 because embedded Java systems are mostly based on this. Porting Lana to Java 1 meant axing several `java.util` classes from the platform, such as `LinkedList`, `HashSet`, etc. and replacing them with our own versions. This however proves advantageous since we effectively remove over-weight `java.util` classes. With regards to our support for embedded platforms, we feel that 90KB is a reasonable size for the Lana kernel. Lana has also been ported to the Compaq iPAQ PDA.

In this section we overview the main elements of the implementation. In particular, we explain how programs are implemented, as well as how security and disconnected operation are supported.

4.1   Programs and Communication

Programs are instances of `lana.lang.Program` subclasses. The class `Program` contains critical information such as references to the program's parent and children, a pointer to the access list (containing the names of the domains that possess an access right for the program), a reference to the program's thread, and a list of the pending method calls that the thread must service. Since `Program` is not final, we must prevent user programs from gaining access to this information. Further, we must also prevent users from introducing Trojan Horse programs by loading `Program` subclasses that alter a program's basic functionality. For this reason, each program has a corresponding `ProgramBody` object in the kernel (packages) which is protected from user code tampering. The protection boundary is illustrated in Figure 7.

Programs issue asynchronous method calls on other programs. On a call, the system creates a method request object containing the parameters and the

```
class Me extends Program{

    Event e; Key k;
    YouCap you;

    public void run(){

        you = new YouCap();

        k = you.setPartner(self);

        Device.println("The call is made !!"));

        e = observe(k, "MethodReturn");

        Device.println("Got Reply : " + e.extract());
    }
}
```

```
class You extends Program{

    Capability partner;
    public String setPartner(MeCap p){

        partner = p;
        return "Partner set!";
    }
}
```

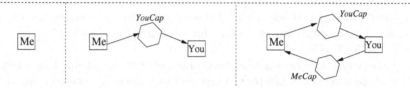

Fig. 8. The example of the previous section revisited.

method name, and places it in the method queue of the invoked program. The called program's thread reads this request, verifies that the caller possesses the access right and if so, dispatches the method. When the method completes, the kernel places a `MethodReturn` event in its environment's message board that carries the method's result as a parameter.

It is noteworthy that the calling program immediately returns with a `Key` object, even though the interface of the called method can specify a different return type. What in fact happens is that a *capability* object is interposed between programs, a technique also used in the J-Kernel [35] for controlling access to program domains. A program never references another program directly – that is, the former never holds a Java reference for the latter. Instead, a program holds a reference to a capability object, which in turns holds a reference to the designated program. The capability for a program contains all of the methods defined in its program's class, except that return types for methods are always of class `Key`. Once a call is made on a capability, it is the capability's implementation that places the method request in `ProgramBody`'s method queue, and which creates and returns a fresh key to the caller.

An example of capabilities is given in Figure 8, which revisits an example of the previous section. The class `Me` is shown, with two differences compared to the former version. First, it uses a `YouCap` class which is a capability class for the `You` class. Further, the method `setPartner` allows the caller to transmit a capability for itself to `You`, which it does using the `self` keyword. In Lana, the `this` keyword has the same meaning as in Java: it evaluates to return a pointer to the enclosing object. On the other hand, the value of `self` is a `Capability` on the current object. This expression is needed to enable a program to pass pointers to itself outside of the program. The evolution of the program is also illustrated in Figure 8. The program Me creates an instance of You indirectly via the capability. The method call involves the interposition of a capability object in You on Me.

All capability classes subclass lana.lang.Capability whose interface is given in Figure 6. From a programming viewpoint, a program that uses a program of class You, simply declares a capability variable of class YouCap. A program's capability class is automatically generated from the program's source file by lanac. This is our pre-compiler that extracts the interface and the class and super-class names from the program's source file and generates the capability source file. The capability classes have a hierarchy that mirrors the hierarchy of program classes. For example, if a program class B subclasses A, then the capability class for B, say B_C, subclasses A_C. After generating the capability classes, lanac simply invokes javac for all source files. We implemented lanac using SableCC [15].

Concerning events, both signal and observe are defined as final and protected methods in LObject. These methods are implemented using the message board: they write to (respectively read from) the message board using the key given as a parameter. Similarly, events generated by the system – such as method returns – are placed in the MessageBoard locked with the key created for the associated method call. The message board also possesses daemon threads for servicing requests from remote devices.

We do not detail the implementation of spaces here. Suffice to say that weak references are implemented using capabilities. The reader is referred to [8] for a discussion of implementation issues.

4.2 Security and Mobility

As seen in Section 4.1, programs and objects in spaces can only be accessed via capabilities. The interposition of the capability means that no field accesses to the program can occur, so we do not need to explicitly detect these accesses in the security infrastructure. On each call, the capability verifies that the parameters passed are either of type capability or are basic types. This check complements the work of the loader verifier for ensuring isolation.

The capability mechanism imposes a control of object aliasing, required because this is the cause of many security leaks in object systems. However, as pointed out elsewhere [35,9,33], even stronger controls need to be enforced to ensure isolation. For instance, static variables must be prohibited in user programs since they permit direct sharing between objects of the class – even if these objects belong to different programs. Similarly, the java.lang.Thread class cannot be directly referenced by user code since it allows indirect access to critical data like the class loader, the thread group and the program ID used by the Lana kernel to identify the program.

The capability mechanism requires that programs not be able to gain direct access to program objects, since this would allow a program to bypass the access controls. This constraint is enforced by the Lana loader which verifies all classes loaded that do not belong to the `lana.*`, Lana kernel or `java.lang` packages. The loader checks that a class does not import or export `lana.lang.Program` objects (or its subclasses), that there are no variables of this type and that there are no class casts to `Program`. Capability subclasses are the only user classes that may have a reference to `Program` objects so that communication between programs can occur, but they may not export this reference. Finally the loader checks for the presence of forbidden native or static methods and variables.

Regarding the JDK classes, we allow only a few classes in Lana programs. We even forbid `System` (`lana.lang.System` does input/output). Other forbidden classes include `Process`, `ThreadGroup`, `SecurityManager`, `ClassLoader` as well as the `java.io` (except for the Serializable interface) and `java.net` classes. The `java.io` and `java.net` packages are removed since all Lana communication uses either the message board or method calling. These restrictions are required to prevent direct sharing between programs through static variables and thus to prevent access to classes that could compromise Lana semantics. Nevertheless, some *service* programs can run in a liberal mode – having access to these forbidden classes - in order to interface between Lana and the outside world, as such services typically require access to socket and GUI code.

Another fundamental security concept in Lana is the `Key` class. We have two conflicting requirements for keys. On the one hand, key value comparison must be implemented efficiently since key comparison occurs often during a search of a message board. On the other hand, we must prohibit the falsification of keys.

When operating within the type-safe confines of a Lana platform, these constraints are relatively simply met. Each key has a private long field that represents the key's value. Key comparison comes down to comparing longs, and falsification is prohibited using scoping since the (long) value field is private to key objects. Apart from this ID field, a key contains a flag that indicates whether it is a fixed key or a floating key.

In the case of autonomous distributed environments we cannot prevent keys from being lost or even stolen from devices whose kernel has been tampered with. The only guarantee that we provide at the kernel level is that an encryption key can be linked with a Lana key (using the `makeEncryptionKey` method and a specified encryption library[1]). The idea for stronger security is to use real encryption to implement locking semantics. Thus, instead of exporting $\prec k, O \succ$ which represents a key and object pair, the encryption key associated with k encrypts the object that it locks. We are modifying the kernel so that it can be configured to generate $\{O\}_k$ (which represents the object O in byte array form encrypted with the encryption key bound to k) [7] whenever the object O is locked with k.

As mentioned, a program (or space) is moved by having it `put` into a remote message board. This is implemented using Java serialization and by copying the resulting byte array and the class archive in the message board entry. Wrapping capabilities is safe in that the system ensures that referenced programs are only

---

[1] For instance, we currently use the Bouncy Castle encryption library [28].

wrapped if they are children of the current domain. This prevents a program from accidentally serializing another program.

4.3 Disconnected Operation

As said, one Lana goal is that a device be able to minimize its dependence on others. This is the reason for message boards, asynchronous method calls, etc. However, this goal has also to be respected at the implementation level, where choices made cannot lead to implicit connections. One example of this is that the code of user classes is transmitted with the wrapped data; thus, even if the receiving device disconnects, it can still continue to execute programs since all required code is local.

Another example of this design principle applied is that no socket connection is ever left open for longer than the length of a communication. Though programs only communicate through the message board or method calls, the kernel uses sockets to implement remote method calls and message board accesses. A socket is opened for a message send, and if no response is immediately awaited, the socket is closed.

If failure occurs during a method execution then a `NetworkOutage` event locked with the key of the method call is generated at the calling side. The calling program can observe this, and may choose to query the called device's message board for the method result if the network returns. In the case of method calls on remote message boards, exceptions are generated if the network fails during data transfer. On the calling side, the caller's code can retry on receiving this exception. On the called side, the `read` result is thrown away if the error occurs when returning the result. Network outage is an issue even for fixed Internet machines since we tolerate users switching off their machines or disconnecting their Ethernet cable.

Another feature that we use in Lana is device detection. While this is an integral part of Bluetooth, it has to be simulated on a fixed network. This is done using multicast addressing. In effect, when the platform is launched a multicast address is assigned to it (via the platform's `properties` file). The `Device.getNetworkNeighbours()` method sends "Who is out there?" messages to this address. Lana platforms listen on this address for such messages from other devices. The "Who is out there?" messages contain the machine IP address of the sender and the number of the port used by the sending Lana platform to service remote `read` and `put` requests as well as method calls.

4.4 Future Implementation Work

We are currently developing a virtual machine for Lana. This virtual machine is being done in Java through a reengineering of the Joeq VM [36]. The goal behind this is to improve speed and space efficiency. For instance, capabilities could be implemented in the object layout, thus avoiding the need for separate objects, as is the case in the current version of Lana. A VM implementation would allow us to implement object field accesses to objects in other spaces with verification by the security policy. The VM implementation will also allow us to optimize the verification process. Verifying a Lana program or capability requires that all parent classes be loaded and verified. Classes are linked when Lana verification is completed. Java verification then occurs which also constructs a class hierarchy for its verification. A modified Java verifier that combines both the Java and Lana verification steps would certainly be more efficient. Other reasons for the virtual machine implementation are that the implementation becomes independent of Java and its virtual machine, and we desire a reference implementation to facilitate our work on formalizing Lana semantics and on developing applications for autonomous systems.

Concerning applications, Lana is being deployed in the Dilemma system [26]. The goal of Dilemma is to federate the databases of collaborating Innovation Relay Center (IRC) companies[2]. Thus, if a client is unable to find the requested information in one IRC database, his request may be serviced by another IRC. The IRC companies collaborate though do not necessarily grant the same access rights to each other for browsing their database. Lana programs are used to carry database requests and schemas between centers. The program carries sufficient client information to authenticate itself at the server. Lana was chosen for Dilemma because a client program agent and the server can interact without the need for the client's site to be on-line, and also because of the security guarantees that Lana provides.

There is also on-going work on the development of autonomous applications. One example is a peer-to-peer application for the Internet, where our goal is to use Lana mobile programs to improve the efficiency of resource location in the network. A search program can be programmed to note the hot resources it sees on each of the sites it visits, and to replicate them if permitted. In the current version, a search program that arrives on a local network uses getNetworkNeighbours to search the network. Thus, any machine in the local area network can be designated in a particular search to query the network. This yields a very decentralized search approach. We are also developing Lana applications for the iPAQ including a search application that allows a user to specify classes of information that he wants his PDA to actively search for in his environment. The kind of information includes business cards, company profiles, headline news, etc.

5   Related Work

This section compares Lana to other distributed programming models. Lana is obviously related to Java [4] and its frameworks, which we examine in Section 5.1. Other systems are looked at in Section 5.2.

---

[2] An Innovation Relay Center is a company that acts as a mediator between companies that produce new technologies, and companies that seek technologies and competencies.

5.1   Java and Its Frameworks

Jini is an infrastructure that runs over Java to support a distributed working group of machines and services. It provides a set of protocols for discovery of a lookup service on the network, the publication of a service endpoint in the lookup service, querying the lookup server for a service, and finally connection to a service. Jini tools include transactions, JavaSpaces (a Java implementation of the Linda message board model) [14], and a server to client event model.

JXTA is a Java environment for peer-to-peer computing [19]. It provides a set of protocols that allow programs to publish information (in XML) about sharable resources on their machines, and to program discovery services.

Both Jini and JXTA are frameworks built with specific goals. Our belief is that resource lookup and peer-to-peer are fundamentally important in today's programming environment, and so should be considered at the programming model level. Lana provides support for resource discovery at this level, and combines this with other required features such as security and mobility.

We mentioned the key differences with the Java language at several points in this paper. Basically, Java programs cannot be isolated from each other [35,8], which makes security hard to enforce due to the possibility of aliasing [22]. Aliasing also prohibits program mobility because there is no way to guarantee that the transitive closure of the set of objects referenced by a thread is disjoint from other threads' closures. These issues are handled in Lana since programs and spaces are protection domains where no direct references can exist from outside of the domain to objects on the inside.

One way to counteract aliasing in Java is to assign programs to different *loader domains*. Java uses a `ClassLoader` object to load program classes, and each program can have its own loader. A feature of Java's typing is that classes loaded by one loader are considered as possessing a distinct type to classes loaded by another. In this way, an attempt by a program object to reference an object in another program is signaled as a type violation (i.e., `java.lang.ClassCastException`). Class domains cannot share objects by reference - rather, all objects must be exchanged by value (i.e., by deep copy)[3]. This is awkward for the programmer, especially when the objects being shared in this fashion are highly mutable. Our goal in Lana is to introduce direct but controlled object sharing. This means that invocations on objects in different programs be controlled by a security policy. In Lana, safe copy-by-reference and copy-by-value are handled by the `Space` and `MessageBoard` concepts.

The shortcomings of Java manifest themselves in the Java frameworks. For instance, one of the problems with Jini is that it is too "connection-oriented": it does not provide suitable support for disconnected operation. Jini uses Remote Method Invocation (RMI) [31] for communication; this is basically a remote implementation of a synchronous method call. If ever the client or server become disconnected from each other, then irrespective of whether the disconnection is

---

[3] In fact, classes loaded by the basic *system* loader can be shared, though this can lead to security leaks [8].

voluntary or not, only an exception is locally generated on each site. There is no information implicitly retained concerning the connection that can allow communication to be re-established.

5.2 Programming Models

Emerald was the first object-oriented language to treat object mobility [25]. Emerald is designed to program applications for a local area distributed system. Objects can be migrated between platforms, the goal being to cluster closely cooperating objects so that method dispatch can be optimized. To this end, Emerald contains an object group notion, which works by having objects *attached* to each other. When an object is moved to a site, then its attached objects are moved along with it.

Distribution in Emerald is transparent, in that an object that invokes a method need not be aware that the invoked object is on another site. In a local area network, transparency is understandable. Since failures are quite rare, and the cost of remote access is still "acceptable", then why complicate the programmer's life with information that he does not really need to know. In an autonomous environment, distribution must not be transparent because programmers need to prepare for the effects of the call failing for security or mobility reasons.

The Salsa system [32], derived from the Actor model family [3], has similarities with Lana. Salsa is a programming model for the Internet where nodes may join and leave the network. Salsa actors are mobile and are globally named with universal resource names. Basic communication between actors uses token passing continuation, which is a form of message passing. Salsa actors can synchronize using join patterns [13]: this allows an actor to await a result from a number of other actors before continuing. Like Lana, Salsa has been implemented over Java. In contrast to Lana, security and resource discovery issues are not treated in Salsa.

Polyphonic C-Sharp is a variant of C-Sharp that contains new concurrency abstractions for distributed programming [6]. Recognizing the importance of asynchronous communication in recent systems, the language extension contains asynchronous methods. Join patterns, or *chords*, are a second proposal of the language that allows a thread to synchronize on the actions of several program threads. A chord specifies a set of asynchronous methods and a single synchronous method that must all be called before the declared method body can be executed. For example, in a class `Stack`, the following chord defines a method body that returns the contents of the top element of the stack. A call on `pop` blocks until a call to `push` is made. In Lana, join-like patterns are implemented using the key ring and the `observe` command.

```
string pop() & async push(String s){
    return s;
}
```

J-Kernel [35] is a system providing direct object sharing between protection domains through capabilities. Lana provides the same functionality through the notions of space and weak reference. In J-Kernel, the focus is on controlling access between domains that share a single address space. In contrast to Lana, J-Kernel was not explicitly designed to deal with distribution. Therefore it does not provide Lana features such as asynchronous calls and mobility, concepts that are useful for autonomy.

The Lana platform can be seen as a *mobile agent system* [34]. In principle, an *agent* is a software component that executes on behalf of a user somewhere on the network, without the need for direct user intervention – in much the same way that a human agent does in the real world, e.g., travel agent or police agent. Though the AI community adopts this view of agents, the distributed computing community tends to see an agent as an object or program that can be shipped between and executed on different Internet sites. Agent mobility is different to the Emerald approach since the object can be shipped to heterogeneous environments; an agent must therefore be programmed to adapt to each environment that it visits. The key advantages of agent technology is that moving closely communicating agents close together can reduce the overhead of network communication. Well-known examples of agent platforms include Voyager [17], Aglets [27], and Tacoma [24]. The Lana project is itself influenced by the JavaSeal agent platform that we developed in our group [9].

The majority of agent platforms around today are Java-based; the platform runs over Java and an agent is a Java object. Consequently, they tend to suffer from the security and mobility weaknesses of Java that we discussed in Section 5.1.

6   Conclusions

Emerging environments always challenge existing programming models. At some point, models no longer reflect the programming environment and must evolve. Autonomous systems present an environment that Java was not designed for. An important challenge for today's language designer is to find efficient programming concepts for these.

This paper has presented Lana, a programming model for autonomous systems, and its implementation. Autonomy is an important feature of today's systems, including personal area networks, embedded networks and peer-to-peer communities. The key characteristics of these systems are that devices are independent, and that network composition is dynamic and *ad hoc*. In Lana, autonomy is supported through asynchronous method calling, protection domains, an associative message board for communication by value and an event model that allows programs to securely delegate the handling of events to others.

Acknowledgements

Lana is supported by the Swiss National Science Foundation under grant number 2100-061405 and by the European Union 5th Framework through the Dilemma project (number IST-1999-10092).

References

1. Gnutella protocol. http://gnutella.wego.com/.
2. Seti project. http://setiathome.ssl.berkeley.edu/.
3. Gul A. Agha. *Actors: A Model of Concurrent Computation in Distributed Systems.* PhD thesis, University of Michigan, Computer and Communication Science, 1985. also MIT AI Laboratory Technical Report 844.
4. Ken Arnold and James Gosling. *The Java Programming Language.* The Java Series. Addison-Wesley, Reading, MA, second edition, 1998.
5. Ken Arnold, Ann Wollrath, Bryan O'Sullivan, Robert Scheifler, and Jim Waldo. *The Jini Specification.* Addison-Wesley, Reading, MA, USA, 1999.
6. Nick Benton, Luca Cardelli, and Cedric Fournet. Modern Concurrency Abstractions for C#, January 2002.
7. Ciaran Bryce, Manuel Oriol, and Jan Vitek. A Coordination Model for Agents Based on Secure Spaces. In P. Ciancarini and A. Wolf, editors, *Proc. 3rd Int. Conf. on Coordination Models and Languages,* volume 1594 of *Lecture Notes in Computer Science,* pages 4–20, Amsterdam, Netherland, April 1999. Springer-Verlag, Berlin.
8. Ciarán Bryce and Chrislain Razafimahefa. An Approach To Safe Object Sharing. In *Proceedings of the 15th Conference on Object-Oriented Programming, Systems, Languages, and Applications (OOPSLA-2000),* volume 35, pages 367–381, October 2000.
9. Ciarán Bryce and Jan Vitek. The JavaSeal Mobile Agent Kernel. *Autonomous Agents and Multi-Agent Systems,* 4(1):359–384, January 2001.
10. Luca Cardelli and Andrew D. Gordon. Mobile Ambients. In Maurice Nivat, editor, *Foundations of Software Science and Computational Structures,* number 1378 in LNCE, pages 140—155. Springer-Verlag, 1998.
11. Frank Dabek, Frans Kaashoek, David Karger, Robert Morris, and Ion Stoica. Wide Area Cooperative Storage with CFS. In *18th Symposium on Operating Systems Principles,* pages 116–128, October 2001.
12. Deborah Estrin, Ramesh Govindan, and John Heidemann. Embedding the Internet. *Communications of the ACM,* 43(5):39–41, May 2000.
13. Cédric Fournet. *The Join-Calculus: a Calculus for Distributed Mobile Programming.* Ph.D. thesis, Ecole Polytechnique, 1998.
14. Eric Freeman, Susanne Hupfer, and Ken Arnold. *JavaSpaces Pinciples, Ptterns, and Pactice.* Addison-Wesley, Reading, MA, USA, 1999.
15. Etienne M. Gagnon and Laurie J. Hendren. SableCC:An Object-Oriented Compiler Framework. In *Proceedings of the IEEE Tools Conference,* pages 140–154, Berkley, USA, April 1998. USENIX Association.
16. David Gelernter. Generative Communication in Linda. *ACM Transactions on Programming Languages and Systems,* 7(1), January 1985.
17. G. Glass. VOYAGER: The New Face of Distributed Computing. *OBJECT magazine,* June 1997.
18. Li Gong. Java security: Present and Near Future: Coping with the rapidly evolving security issues of cross-platform computing. *IEEE Micro,* 17(3):14–19, May/June 1997.
19. Li Gong. JXTA : A Network Programming Environment. *IEEE Internet Computing,* 5(3):88–95, May 2001.
20. James Gosling and Henry McGilton. The Java language environment – A White Paper. Technical report, Sun Microsystems, October 1995.

21. Henry Eddon Guy Eddon. *Inside Distributed Com.* Microsoft Programming Series. Microsoft Press, 1998.
22. John Hogg, Doug Lea, Alan Wills, Dennis deChampeaux, and Richard Holt. The Geneva Convention on the Treatment of Object Aliasing. *OOPS Messenger*, 3(2):11–16, April 1992.
23. Napster Inc. http://www.napster.com/.
24. D. Johansen, R. van Renesse, and F. B. Schneider. An Introduction to the TACOMA Distributed System. Technical Report 95-23, University of Tromso, June 1995.
25. Eric Jul, Henry Levy, and Norman Hutchinson. Fine-Grained Mobility in the Emerald System. In *Readings in Object Oriented Databases*, pages 317–328. ACM, 1990.
26. Dimitri Konstantas, Ciaran Bryce, Jean-Henry Morin, Christian Kobel, Apostolos Vontas, Panos Hatzaras, and Adamantios Koumpis. A framework for Building Agent-Based Industrial Applications. In Szpytko & Banaszak Zaremba, editor, *Intelligent Manufacturing Systems 2001, Proceedings of the 6th Workshop, April 24-26 2001, Poznan, Poland.* Elsevier Science Publishers B.V. (North-Holland), November 2001.
27. Danny B. Lange and Mitsuru Oshima. *Programming and Deploying Java Mobile Agents with Aglets.* Addison-Wesley, 1998.
28. The Legion. The Bouncy Castle Project. http://www.bouncycastle.org.
29. Rob Pike, Dave Presotto, Ken Thompson, Howard Trickey, and Phil Winterbottom. The Use of Name Spaces in Plan 9. *Operating System Review*, 27(2):72–76, April 1993.
30. Merlin Stone. Pervasive or Invasive - Managing the Customer on the Move. Technical report, IBM Corporation, 2001.
31. Sun. Java Remote Method Invocation Specification, 1997. http://www.javasoft.com.
32. Carlos Varela and Gul Agha. Programming Dynamically Reconfigurable Open Systems with SALSA. In Cindy Norris and Jr. James B. Fenwick, editors, *Proceedings of the 2001 ACM Conference on Object Oriented Programming Systems, Languages and Applications (OOPSLA-01)*, volume 36, 12 of *ACM SIGPLAN notices*, pages 20–34, New York, October 14–18 2001. ACM Press.
33. Jan Vitek and Boris Bokowski. Confined Types. *ACM SIGPLAN Notices*, 34(10):82–96, October 1999.
34. Jan Vitek and Christian Tschudin. *Mobile Objects Systems.* Springer Verlag, Berlin, 1997.
35. T. Von Eicken, C.-C. Chang, G. Czajkowski, and C. Hawblitzel. J-Kernel: A Capability-Based Operating System for Java. *Lecture Notes in Computer Science*, 1603:369–394, 1999.
36. John Whaley. Joeq Virtual Machine. *http://joeq.sourceforge.net*, 2001.
37. James Y. Wilson and Jason A. Krontz. Inside Bluetooth: Part I. *Dr. Dobb's Journal of Software Tools*, 25(3):62, 64–66, 68, 70, March 2000.

Engineering Event-Based Systems with Scopes

Ludger Fiege*, Mira Mezini, Gero Mühl*, and Alejandro P. Buchmann

Department of Computer Science
Darmstadt University of Technology, D-64283 Darmstadt
{fiege,gmuehl}@gkec.tu-darmstadt.de
{mezini,buchmann}@informatik.tu-darmstadt.de

Abstract. Event notification services enable loose coupling and they are therefore becoming an essential part of distributed systems' design. However, the development of event services follows the early stages of programming language evolution, disregarding the need for efficient mechanisms to structure event-based applications. In this paper, the well-known notion of scopes is introduced to event-based systems. We show that limiting the visibility of events is a simple yet powerful mechanism that allows to identify application structure and offers a module construct for the loosely coupled components in event-based systems. We are able to customize the semantics of scoped event notification services by binding meta-objects to the application structure that reify important aspects of notification delivery, like interface mappings and transmission policies. The scoping concept facilitates design and implementation by offering encapsulation and adaption of syntax and semantics of event-based systems.

1 Introduction

The focus of this paper is on abstractions for structuring event-based systems. The event-based architectural style has become prevalent for large-scale distributed applications [6] due to the inherent loose coupling of the participants. This loose coupling carries the potential for easy integration of autonomous, heterogeneous components into complex systems that are easy to evolve and scale. Traditional request/reply approaches, such as remote procedure calls (RPC), exhibit crucial scalability problems in data-centric environments [16]. The use of event-based dissemination as an alternative approach is superior in these scenarios [15].

The notion of event-based style used in this paper is basically the one defined in literature, e.g., [6]. In an event-based style components communicate by generating and receiving *event notifications*. An *event* is any transient occurrence of a happening of interest, i. e., a state change in some component. The affected component issues a notification that describes the event. An *event notification*

---

* Supported by the German National Science Foundation (DFG) as part of the PhD program "Enabling Technologies for Electronic Commerce" at Darmstadt University of Technology.

B. Magnusson (Ed.): ECOOP 2002, LNCS 2374, pp. 309–333, 2002.

service conveys the notifications between the components of an event-based system. A component in such a system can act both as producer and consumer of events.

Producers are components that publish notifications about internal events originating within that component. The output interface of a producer is described by advertisements specifying the kinds of notifications it will publish. A notification is not addressed to any specific (set of) receivers, it is rather distributed by the event service to consumers which have specified their interest in that kind of notification. *Consumers* issue subscriptions that describe the notifications they want to receive, i.e., their input interface. Hence, in the event-based cooperation model producers have no knowledge about any receivers—in particular, they do not anticipate any specific reaction on the receiver side.

A component's implementation in event-based systems is 'self-focused' in that it only publishes changes in its state and/or reacts on incoming notifications, resulting in a very loose coupling. However, it is mandatory to identify the role of an administrator[1] who assembles and orchestrates simple components. In the context of open systems, architecture references define a multitude of views of the system in addition to producers and consumers [23], including an administrator's role. It is her task to combine components in order to accomplish a common application functionality. Unfortunately, current work on event-based systems disregards this important role and do not provide any support therefor.

The potential of an event-based communication style has been recognized both in academia and industry. A number of event-based middleware infrastructures were developed [7,11,43,46] as well as the integration of corresponding services in modern component platforms based development such as CCM [35] and EJBs [44]. The prevalence of the event-based paradigm in the design of today's systems has not hindered, but rather encouraged, us in considering event-based systems from a critical point of view. The observation that we make is that while a considerable amount of work is done in the area of scalable event notification services, most effort is spent on implementation efficiency, thoroughly disregarding design, engineering and administration issues. Typical implementation techniques of publish/subscribe systems [38] concentrate on efficient notification dissemination algorithms and overlook the need for effective support of appropriate programming abstractions.

Software engineering research early identified information hiding and abstraction [39] as basic principles that have influenced the development of structured programming, modules, classes, and components, all of which provide mechanisms to structure software systems. While being an integral part of request/reply-based distributed systems, e.g., CORBA [34], comparable hierarchical structuring mechanisms are missing in event-based systems. As a result, event-based systems are generally characterized by a 'flat design space': Subscriptions select out of *all* published notifications without discriminating producers. Any further distinctions are necessarily hard-coded into the communicating compo-

---

[1] Currently, assemblers and administrators are not distinguished, like it is done in Sun's EJB model [44], for example.

nents, mixing application structure and component implementation. The very feature of event-based systems is thereby defeated: loose coupling.

What we are missing is the notion of a module for bundling several components into a higher-level component. Such a module construct would localize the relationships between components outside of the components themselves, playing a mediator role in the vein of Sullivan and Notkin [42]. The modules should themselves be first-class components, with their own input and output interfaces, so that they can be composed into higher-level modules much the same as objects can be composed into higher-level objects in an object-oriented system. This is to enable a hierarchical structuring of event-based systems.

In this paper, we analyze a set of engineering requirements for event-based systems and introduce the notion of scopes aimed at serving the needs. A scope bundles several components either (a) according to application structure, or (b) according to the structure of activities therein. The visibility of events is constrained in the sense that notifications are only delivered to consumers within the same scope but are a priori invisible otherwise. By being itself a component, a scope can recursively be composed into a larger scope. As a bundling unit and module, scopes represent application structure and are the appropriate location to refine and customize notification delivery semantics. In delimited parts of an application, syntax of the distributed notifications and even the semantics of delivery can be varied, while any modifications are encapsulated and do not interfere with the remaining system. Scopes provide a module construct as an abstraction for handling heterogeneity as well as for integrating security and transmission policies that deviate from the standard broadcast to all eligible consumers.

The remainder of this paper is organized as follows. In Section 2, design and engineering demands of event-based systems are discussed. Section 3 introduces the notion of scopes in event-based systems and describes their features with the help of a running example. An outline of implementation issues is given in Section 4. Related work is discussed in Section 5. The paper concludes with a summary and an outlook on future work.

2   Engineering Event-Based Systems

In this section, we discuss some requirements on engineering event-based systems and how they are supported by today's technology. Two main observations are made. The first is that event-based systems do not seem to imply other requirements for designing and engineering than those already known from engineering request/reply systems. The second observation is that while supporting abstractions are available for the latter they are missing for event-based systems. This makes them difficult to maintain, e.g., the effects of newly instantiated producers or of publishing a certain notification are not easy to determine, let alone control.

2.1 Illustrative Example

A stock trading application will be used as an illustrative example throughout the paper. This example shall not outline a perfect implementation but underline the requirements of engineering event-based applications.

Assume there is an Internet infrastructure which (also) utilizes events instead of the request/reply-oriented style of the Hypertext Transfer Protocol (HTTP) in order to facilitate the creation of the respective web-services and applications. Nearly all parts of a stock trading application are inherently event-based. The dissemination of stock quotes from the central trading floor (or its computerized equivalent) to the market participants is an accepted and plausible example of applying event notification services. The following components can be identified to constitute a stock market (see Fig. 1):

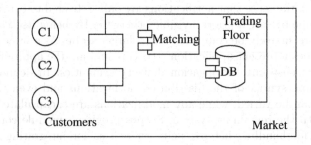

Fig. 1. An example stock trading application

- Customers monitoring quotes and issuing orders to buy or sell shares.
- A database logs the generated data to ensure consistency and persistence.
- A central matching engine implements the matching algorithm.

Database and matching engine are composed into the virtual trading floor, a component which consumes orders and publishes notifications carrying share prices of successfully executed trades.

2.2 Engineering Requirements

Four requirements posed by the engineering of event-based systems are identified: bundling of components, heterogeneity, flexible configurations, and support of activities.

Bundling Related Components

A fundamental requirement is that it should be possible to bundle individual components into higher-level syntactical and semantical units, offering higher levels of abstraction and reusability. From the syntactic point of view such a bundle should be a collection of existing components delimiting the visibility of the events produced by them. The bundling mechanism should be orthogonal to the subscription mechanisms so that the composed interfaces need not to be changed. This is important to support drawing event deliver localities not only based on the described interests of receivers but also on other criteria, such as the organizational and geographical constraints of a company or some other application-specific semantics.

From the semantical point of view, we require component bundles to be themselves components with well-defined interfaces and own semantics. That is, the bundles should not only delimit visibility, but also publish themselves events, resulting from notifications produced within the bundle that signify an important state change of the bundle as a whole, or consume events from the outside by further propagating them to their internal locality. This opens the possibility to recursively bundle component compositions into higher-level components, and hierarchically structure the design of an event-based system.

Locality, encapsulation, and composing existing units into higher-level units are well-known concepts for mastering complexity and support evolution [39]. These concepts are used in request/reply systems, but they are as important here and should therefore be available to the engineers of event-based systems as well. To motivate the requirement, consider our running example. The virtual trading floor in the stock trading application would be a first example of a component bundle. One can imagine a 'verbose' matching engine producing detailed notifications about the progress of the matching algorithm, of which the majority is only relevant for logging purposes (e.g., to support later traceability of the system operations) and only a few are relevant for customers. Hence, it makes sense to constrain the visibility of most of the events to the DB component and to allow only a few of them to pass the boundary of the trading floor bundle.

The next reasonable structuring step would be to bundle a trading floor and a set of customers (i.e., the participants in the market described in Fig. 1) into a higher-level syntactical and semantical market component. In this way multiple trading floors would be supported without having customers that observe quotes in a system with only a single trading floor receive duplicate and inconsistent quotes if an additional exchange is instantiated. Such duplication cannot be avoided in a flat design space where all components in the system are visible to each other. The absence of market bundles would require to encode knowledge about the market structure into the subscriptions of individual components, rendering them less reusable since more sensible to the structure of the application and changes to it.

Mastering Heterogeneity

A single uniform event notification service with uniform syntax and semantics will hardly be able to cope with the requirements of all parts of large distributed systems operating in heterogenous environments. An event service that, e.g., relies on some notion of a global naming scheme is not scalable and impedes system integration. Furthermore, the semantics of notifications will likely vary in heterogeneous environments [9]. In large distributed systems, there are inevitably different event models and representation schemes in use, ranging from hardware-dependent differences to application-dependent syntactical and semantical differences.

From the observations above, we draw the requirement that bundling of related components should not only encapsulate functionality but also delimit common syntax and semantics. This requires mechanisms to support adapting data crossing boundaries of component bundles by mapping event content and representation. To motivate the requirement consider again our running example. For efficiency reasons it would make sense in such a system to distinguish between low-volume external representations in XML versus more efficient, optimized internal representations. The matching and the database component may use such an internal representation in our example. Hence, mapping from an external XML representation to the efficient internal representation would be needed for notifications crossing the border of a virtual trading floor composite.

Flexible Configuration

Similar to the diverse requirements regarding data representation in heterogeneous environments, a static definition of notification transmission semantics is not adequate either. Application-specific needs often require that notifications are only delivered to a specific subset instead of the default broadcast to all eligible consumers. For example, an 1-of-n policy realizes load balancing features within a bundle of components in this way. In our stock application, the matching engine might be replicated to distribute processing load over multiple instances using a delivery policy that routes orders to instances dedicated to the respective share.

Furthermore, other delivery policies might be applicable and the whole event service is subject to customization: API, syntax and semantics of subscriptions, security policies, and implementation techniques of notification dissemination may vary to adapt to and fit differing needs in different parts of a complex system. For example, if the structure of the bundles are not static, some policy must control who is allowed to join. The trading floor component may be compromised if everyone is able to join and issue notifications which influence the matching engine; whereas getting prices of successfully executed trades need not to be controlled. Similarly, the implementation of the trading floor will likely use any broadcast features of a local area network while the dissemination of price information on the Internet has to use other techniques.

Supporting Sessions and Activities

The engineering of complex systems not only benefits from bundling related components according to application structure but also from identifying sessions of interdependent activities. This is especially important in event-based systems, where the identity of peers is unknown and communication is a priori stateless in the sense that consecutive notifications cannot be interrelated. By relating notifications, components are enabled to participate in multiple, distinguishable sessions and activities made up of interrelated notifications can be modeled as well-defined structures drawing on locality just as it is possible for application structure.

An example for the first goal is a stockbroker who listens to a specific share traded on two stock markets. Obviously, notifications distributed in one market must, generally, be invisible in the other. However, our broker should be able to observe and distinguish both. In abstract terms, the issue is that it should be possible for individual components to be simultaneously engaged in multiple sessions involving components from structurally disjoint application parts. Hence, it should be possible to identify such sessions and to delimit them from each other in order to support session state. Otherwise, a component involved in multiple sessions would only be able to maintain changes of its own state, not being able to sustain dependencies on other components.

The second requirement of supporting bundling of events in activities addresses the dynamic aspects of event-based systems in a similar way as the requirement for bundling components did in the previous discussion about the slowly changing structure of an application. In general terms, activities should be structured and it should itself be a component with well-defined semantics, determining when (parts of) the 'internal' notifications are to be made visible to the outside. This will help to prevent side-effects, to build structured, hierarchical sessions, and to customize and orchestrate them. An analogy to the activity concept from the world of request/reply-based systems would be a simplified version of the notion of transactions [20].

2.3   Engineering Support

In request/reply-based distributed systems, like the CORBA platform [34], solutions exists for all of the outlined requirements. Components and classes according to an object-oriented programming paradigm are used for decomposition, encapsulation and bundling of components. Heterogeneity is addressed by standardized interconnection protocols (e.g., CORBA-IIOP, SOAP [4] based on XML). Bundling of activities is facilitated by transaction services [37,2] and security services are available, e.g., Kerberos [32]. Appropriate support is easily provided since the identity of each component is known.

But how can the above mentioned requirements be realized in event services? Existing services recognizes and addresses them only partially. A first approach would be to build new features on top of the existing ones. For example, one could make use of content-based filtering mechanisms [30,8] to simulate a decomposition abstraction for event-based systems in which sets of components are bundled and delimited from each other. To achieve this goal, subscriptions of individual components have to be adapted to encode additional constraints on the decomposed structure.

This approach of modifying application components has a significant drawback. It disregards the administrator's role by compiling all configuration information into the components themselves. Knowledge about the application structure is put into the components, contradicting the idea of components being loosely coupled and self-focused. Furthermore, the structure is not explicitly enforced by the system and all components are eligible receivers if they have subscribed accordingly: 'hacked' filters may compromise security measures, and reflection, i.e., investigation and change [27], is restricted.

The following section will introduce a second approach of tackling the engineering requirements by introducing a scoping mechanism as an integral part of a design methodology and of an event service implementation.

3   Scoping in Event-Based Systems

In order to satisfy the requirements discussed in the previous section our approach introduces the concept of *scope* for decomposing event-based systems, a unifying concept to address the described requirements. A scope is *an abstraction that bundles a set of producers and consumers* and it can recursively be a member of other scopes. It offers a powerful structuring mechanism to group constituent components which belong together according to some criteria derived from the application structure and/or semantics. Vice versa, it defines locality that can be used to customize semantics in a discriminated part of the system and that provides an encapsulated module whose interaction with the remaining system can be explicitly controlled.

Formally, scoped event-based systems are modeled by a directed, acyclic graph $G = (C, E)$ (see Fig. 2) that describes the superscope/subscope relationship. The set of nodes C is comprised of simple components $\mathcal{C}$ and complex components $\mathcal{S}$, i.e., scopes. The edges E are a binary relation over C. An edge from node c_1 to c_2 in G stands for c_2 being a superscope of c_1. Next to being acyclic, the relation E must also satisfy the property that a simple component cannot be a superscope of any node in G.

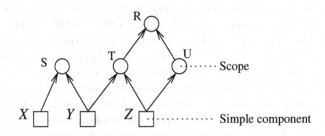

Fig. 2. A graph of components/scopes

The scope concept comes with three different flavors: *standard scopes* harnessing visibility and interfaces, *advanced scopes* that apply mappings and transmission policies, and *session scopes* which use the previous features. A more formal treatise on visibility, interfaces, and mappings is published in [14].

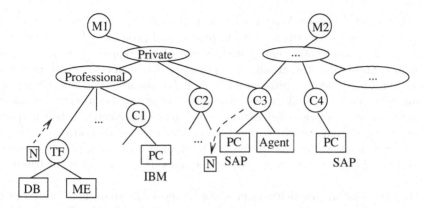

Fig. 3. The graph of the stock application

3.1 Controlling Visibility

Encapsulation is a prerequisite to system evolution [39] and the notion of visibility is widely used in software engineering as structuring technique in order to determine the impacts of changing parts of the system. The need for an equivalent notion for event-based systems was discussed in Section 2.2. The scope construct plays this role in our model in that the visibility of notifications published by a producer is confined to the consumers belonging to the same scope as the publisher.

Using the graph of scopes G given above, we define the *visibility* of components as a reflexive, symmetric relation v over C. Informally, component X is visible to Y iff X and Y have a common superscope. For a component X, let $super(X) = \{X' \mid (X, X') \in E\}$ denote the set of scopes that are direct superscopes of X. Formally, we recursively define

$$v(X, Y) \Leftrightarrow \quad X = Y$$
$$\lor \, v(Y, X)$$
$$\lor \, v(X', Y) \text{ with } X' \in super(X)$$

In the graph in Fig. 2, for example, $v(Y, U)$ holds but not $v(X, U)$.

A notification is delivered to a consumer if (a) the producer and the consumer are visible to each other, and (b) the notification matches one of the subscriptions previously issued by this consumer. Hence, the semantics of notification delivery is now not only based on the subscription mechanism but also on the visibility relation, with both dimensions being orthogonal in that they are employed independently of each other.

The visibility of notifications from different markets is restricted in a stock trade system designed with scopes (Fig. 3). The circles denote composed scopes in the figure, while rectangles represent simple components. There are two main scopes in which the simple components are organized, M1 and M2, denoting two different stock markets. Within each market customers are bundled into sub-scopes based on some criteria, e.g., in private and professional customers. Each customer is permanently represented by one of the scopes C1, C2, etc., which remain connected in the graph of scopes even if customers are not personally logged in. They group a customer's PCs, cellular phones, or agents running on a remote server. An example 'agent' would be a limit watcher which continuously monitors a share's price and issues a customized notification when a specific share deviates from the overall market performance. Newly and externally provided limit notifications can thereby be integrated into the application without changing existing components—one of the obvious benefits of event-based systems.

For the sake of simplicity, interest for at most one share is indicated in the figure below the rectangles representing the customers' PCs. The figure illustrates the scenario when the trading floor TF participates in the stock market M1 and issues a notification concerning SAP quotes. Although both consumers C3 and C4 have subscribed for notifications on SAP quotes, this notification will only reach C3, because C4 is not visible from the trading floor and C1 subscribed to a different share. On the other hand, consumer C3 listens to both markets and receives 'duplicate' SAP quotes (the implied problems are addressed in Sect. 3.6).

3.2   Interfaces

So far, visibility can be mapped to an only two-level hierarchy that is induced by the top-most superscopes of the graph G. Any two components are either able to see all of their published notifications or no at all. In order to overcome this problem and to improve the structuring ability, the basic mechanism provided by scopes is refined beyond the visibility relation by assigning input and output interfaces to scopes.

Input and *output interfaces* for simple components are defined by filters that determine the set of notifications allowed to cross a component's boundaries. A filter $F \in \mathcal{F} := \{f \mid f(e) = e \vee f(e) = \varepsilon\}$ is a mapping function over the set of all possible notifications $\mathcal{N}$ plus the empty notification ε. Often, filters are defined as boolean functions returning **true** if a notification matches. In our model, we use a generalized form of filters that are allowed to pass matched events in an unchanged form. A notification n is either mapped to itself or to ε, indicating that n is matched or blocked, respectively. Allowing filters to pass matched events in an unchanged form facilitates filter composition: $(F_1 \circ F_2)(e) = F_1(F_2(e))$.

A simple consumer component describes its input interface by issuing sub-scriptions that contain filters. A notification passes such a set of filters if it matches at least one of them. On the other hand, a producer has to issue *advertisements* that define the set of notifications it is able to publish. Advertisements also contain filters and serve as a specification of a component's output interface.

We associate similar sets of filters with the input and output interfaces of scopes, describing the set of notifications which are allowed to cross the scope boundary. Only those notifications matching one of the scope's output filters are forwarded up into its superscopes and only those that match at least one of its input filters are forwarded into the scope. Filters for scope interfaces are expressed in the language used for specifying subscriptions and advertisements for simple consumers and producers. With the introduction of interfaces for scopes, a notification is delivered only if producer and consumer are visible to each other, the notification is allowed to pass all interfaces along the path of visibility in the graph, and one of the receiver's subscriptions match.

Attaching interfaces to scopes allows to view scopes as ordinary producing and/or consuming components. The relationship between scopes and simple components is shown in the upper part of the UML class diagram in Fig. 4 which presents a simplified meta-model of our model.

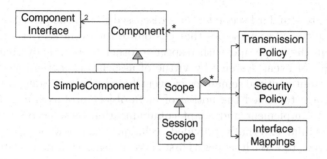

Fig. 4. The Meta-Model of the Scope Model

To illustrate how scope interfaces help in structuring event-based applications, let us consider the interfaces of the components in our running example as summarized in Table 1.

Table 1. Interfaces of the Components in the Example Application

Component	Description	Input	Output
M1, M2	The Stock Markets	–	–
Private	scope of all private customers	–	Trade
Prof	scope of all professionals	Order	Accept, Quote(delayed)
C_i	Customer representation	Accept	Order
TF	Trading Floor	Order	Accept, Quote
ME	Matching engine	Order	Accept, Quote OrderBook
DB	The logging database	Order, Quote	

Customers send out notifications of type *Order* which contain a share identification, the number to be sold or bought, and potential price limits. The trading floor TF listens to these orders, issues acceptance notification, and sends out *Quotes*, informing about successfully executed orders. The trading floor itself is composed of the matching engine ME and the database DB. The matching engine maintains a list of open orders and executes the matching algorithm, while the database logs all *Orders* and *Quotes*, and it issues acceptance notifications (*Accept*). Additionally, the matching engine publishes an orderbook summary with price and volume of the 10 best bid and ask orders. The summary is only visible within the trading floor, because the interface of TF prohibit further distribution. Based on this data, additional services may be integrated into the trading floor, like market makers ensuring that there is always at least one buy and one sell order open.

3.3   Advanced Features

In addition to standard scope features discussed so far, the presented model also supports advanced scope types that customize the event service's functionality, both within the scope and with respect to other scopes. They enable dynamic adaptability of event systems by virtue of associating meta-objects [24] which reify important runtime semantics of event-based systems. Software engineering research has established the notion of meta-object protocols as a very flexible technique to implement and adapt communication between objects. With our approach similar externally provided techniques can now be applied in event-based systems, too. With scopes as first class citizens, an administrator is enabled to easily group unmodified components and tailor the composed functionality with the help of such meta-objects.

The advanced features of the scope concept are shown on the right part of the meta-model shown in Fig. 4. Currently, the following aspects of the runtime semantics are reified. Other aspects of the runtime semantics might be reified as well, resulting in other types of scopes.

- Event reception and publication, allowing the administrator of an event-based system to attach event transformers at scope interfaces. This is aimed at coping with heterogeneity in event-based systems and is described in Sect. 3.4.
- Event transmission policies, allowing the administrator to configure each scope with a strategy to be used for traversing the scope hierarchy and for delivering notifications to consumers and superscopes (see Sect. 3.5).
- Security policies attached to a scope control membership management. Scopes are a proper place to implement these policies but we do not further investigate this issue here.

3.4   Event Mappings

In large systems, it is rather unlikely that a single uniform event model is used throughout the system. Different parts will use different representations and semantics of events. Constraining the visibility of notifications is the basis for dealing with heterogeneity issues and different administrative domains. Consequently, we extend the scoped event system model to include *event mappings* that

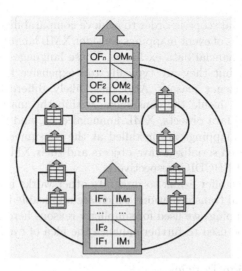

Fig. 5. Scopes with Event Mappings

transform notifications at scope boundaries. This extension clearly addresses the heterogeneity requirements stated in Section 2.2 and facilitates construction and maintenance of large systems. The structure of a scope with event mappings is schematically presented in Fig. 5.

Event mappings convert notifications from an external to an internal representation, and vice versa. They are attached to individual edges in the graph of scopes and are applied when a notification enters or leaves a scope, i.e., it travels down against or up along an edge, respectively. The mappings are a generalization of both the visibility $v(X, Y)$ and the scope interfaces [14] in that a published notification may be visible in a different, mapped representation, or not at all if it was blocked, i.e., mapped onto the empty notification ε. The set of filters F used for subscribing is a subset of the set of event mappings $\mathcal{M} \subseteq \{m \mid m : \mathcal{N}^* \to \mathcal{N}^*\}$ usable in the system. With this definition, a uniform way of filtering and transforming notifications is achieved, and conceptually, filters and general mappings can be concatenated at scope boundaries. Figure 4 distinguishes interfaces and mappings in order to emphasize their independence: interfaces and filters have to be declared in a language that depends on the underlying transmission technique while mappings are part of the scope implementation.

The interface of a scope is strictly separated from its implementation, i.e., its constituent components. Only boundary-crossing events are considered without interfering with internal communications. This separation offers great flexibility in controlling and adapting interface access at runtime. For example, by attaching mappings to individual edges in the graph, a scope may be visible with different interfaces in different superscopes.

Returning to the stock exchange example from the previous section, quotations are typically given in a local currency which need to be transformed at the boundary of the local scope in order to achieve comparability. As another example for the usefulness of event mappings consider XML languages like FIXML [33] that standardize financial data exchange. These languages are used to connect external partners, but they are typically too expensive for internal representations due to efficiency reasons. Also, most likely, different representations of events will be used inside the consumers, within the market, and within the trading floor, e.g., Java objects, XML financial data, and EBCDIC mainframe text fields. Event mappings are installed at the consumers and at the trading floor to map between serialized Java objects and their XML representation and between XML and EBCDIC, respectively.

Event mappings offer a link to integrate other works in the area of syntactical and semantical transformations which are applicable here [3,25] and which extend the 1:1 mappings we used for simplicity reasons here. Furthermore, event composition can be used to further enhance the idea of event mappings [26,47].

3.5   Transmission Policies

Following the arguments of Sect. 2.2, we suggest to allow refinement of delivery and dissemination semantics on a per scope basis. *Transmission policies* describe how notifications are forwarded and to which consumers. They refine the visibility definition both within a scope and with respect to its superscopes. We distinguish three different policies involved in notification transmission: delivery, traverse, and publishing policy.

Delivery policies affect deliverable notifications produced in a superscope or by some constituent subcomponent and determines which members of the scope are to receive the notification. An example is a 1-of-n policy which delivers only to one out of a group of possible receivers. The idea of meta object protocols of object-oriented programming languages is applied here [24] in order to offer the ability to order, queue, redirect, or transform incoming messages.

A *traverse policy* controls the downward path of incoming notifications in the graph of scopes. Actually, this policy allows a notification to deviate from a default path through the graph of scopes. In a top-down traverse policy eligible receivers, i.e., simple components with a matching subscription, are searched in the current scope first. A notification is forwarded to subscopes only when no-one is found. The bottom-up traverse policy starts the search in the deepest subscopes. Broadcast is the default policy which simply delivers to all components in a scope.

To make an analogy to the application of meta-object protocols in the area of object-oriented programming languages, multiple consumers of the same notification located along the inheritance/scope hierarchy can be considered to be implementing some form of generalized method overriding. Traditional programming languages like C++ and Java use only one, static policy to resolve calls to overridden methods. In a hierarchy of scopes, the traverse policies determines what kind of method lookup is used. The bottom-up policy resembles a virtual method call in C++ in that the implementation of the most derived class is used. Other policies are possible that implement other kinds of method lookups.

Policies can also be viewed in the opposite direction. A *publishing policy* controls publication into the direct superscopes. One may reject the idea of manually selecting where the data is published as contradicting with the event-based paradigm. However, this selection is part of the administrator's role and not interwoven with the application functionality in simple components. While event mappings provide the ability to support multiple interfaces, publishing policies operate on a per notification basis and might be used to delay notifications for a certain amount of time or until a condition becomes valid, for example.

To illustrate the usefulness of the advanced transmission policies, consider the categorization of the customer scopes in private and professional ones: private customers are bundled in the scope `Private` and professional traders in the scope `Professional`. Assume that the market strategy is such that *Quote* notifications should be notified to professionals first. It is because of the need to implement this application semantics that we have defined two different customer scopes and have made `Professional` an sub-scope of `Private`. By having `Professional` encapsulate `TF`, notifications from the trading floor will reach the professional scope first. In addition, the publishing policy of the professional scope is such that *Quotes* are forwarded to the `Private` superscope only after a delay of 15 minutes: a publishing policy puts all notifications in a queue and ensures the delay.

3.6   Sessions

The scoping model so far concentrated on application structure, but the discussion in Sect. 2.2 also identified the need to structure activities therein. In the following, we investigate the problems imposed by activities in event-based systems and give an outlook on how scopes can be used in solving the problem.

Dependent Notifications

The prevalent scenario of event-based applications are uni-directional flows of notifications from producers to consumers, like stock tickers and news feeds. So, it is simply about components lined up in chains. But in order to benefit from the loose coupling of event-based cooperation in other types of applications, it is necessary to support some form of stateful collaboration. Scopes offer this support to a certain extent since they build up structures of bilateral visibility. However, there is so far no explicit mechanism to identify interdependent notifications, which have a common cause and belong to the same activity.

This issue is aggravated by the fact that the graph of scopes is not a tree and a node may have multiple superscopes[2]. Consider the scopes S and T in Figure 2: notifications published in S are not visible in T, and vice versa. But an event in S which is consumed by Y may trigger an reaction in Y leading to the publication of a notification that is also visible in T. The delimitation imposed by scopes is

---

[2] Note that we do not address the important question of notification duplication in this paper.

diluted in this way since implications of an initially invisible event are diffused; an effect that is not always appropriate. For example, assume that Y is a security service that consumes, signs and republishes specific types of notifications so that S and T are able to publish signed notifications. Unfortunately, Y acts like a bridge and its reactions are visible in both superscopes. Obviously, it is not acceptable to publish these triggered signed data into both scopes.

One solution to this problem is to replicate the security service so that it is offered separately, but this is only feasible if the instances do not need to share a common state, i.e., they are independent. However, this solution does not work with components that cannot be instantiated but are deployed in a different administrative domain and are only accessible remotely, like web services on the Internet. Furthermore, the graph of scopes would be restricted to be a tree, resulting in a structure built from only a single point of view, even though it was corroborated that engineering of complex systems always benefits from facilitating multiple viewpoints [22].

Session Scopes

In order to support dependent notifications and solve the problem of diluting delimitation in multiple superscopes we define an extended type of scope which provides notification contexts. *Session scopes* group components and especially all of their published notifications. They are tagged scopes and the tag is appended to every notification published within. A tagged notification is processed like any other notification, but additionally, the hidden context containing the tag is maintained in every consumer by the event service. The context remains valid during a consumer's reaction to the delivery of a tagged notification. All notifications published while a valid context is available are only disseminated into that tagged session superscope from which the context originated. Forwarding into untagged scopes is not affected so that the application structure and its behavior is not influenced by the creation of session scopes.

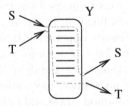

Fig. 6. Contexts of Multiple Superscopes

In our scenario, we would tag the scopes S and T, characterizing them to be *session scopes* (cf. Fig. 6). On delivery of a notification a previously registered processing function is invoked that computes the signature and publishes the result. The tag carried by the notification is maintained as hidden context during

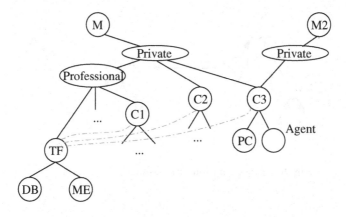

Fig. 7. The stock application with sessions

the execution of Y and any subsequent publication is transparently directed to the originating superscope. Note that the API of the event service needs not to be changed since calls to pub(*data*) are unmodified and any contexts are transparently maintained by the implementation of the API.

Session scopes are scopes that structure activities and allows components with multiple superscopes to distinguish multiple sessions. These scopes can be instantiated as first-class representatives of sessions, allowing to apply the other mentioned features of scopes and to integrate activities in the graph of scopes. One possible way of realizing sessions is pointed out, namely by using tagged scopes and transmission policies to add, strip, and enforce matching of tags. Obviously, the stated semantics of session scopes offer reasonable defaults but further investigation is necessary to explore other features.

In order to illustrate the use of session scopes, let us once again return to our running example. As already mentioned, customers send out notifications of type *Order*. However, the event-based order processing in this form is only feasible if the order data is only visible to the trading floor. For this purpose, customer scopes are tagged as session scopes and each scope also includes the trading floor, illustrated by the grey, dotted lines in Figure 7. The trading floor needs at least two interfaces, one for handling orders used for the customer scopes and one for publishing quotes into the professional market. Otherwise, the distinction between private and professional customers would be broken. The activity of putting an order is encapsulated in these session scopes so that an issued order is only forwarded to the trading floor and the resulting acceptance notification is only delivered back into the originating customer's scope.

4   Implementation Issues

Generally, scopes are not about efficiency but enable to utilize the provided constrained localities to consider efficient implementations. An implementation

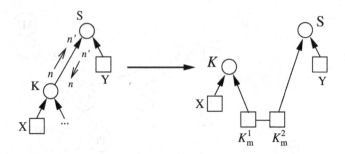

Fig. 8. Transformation of mappings into components.

of a given subgraph of scopes can draw on these locality in that it is tailored to the specific needs of the respective scopes and their constituents. For instance, a scope that groups components on a local area network will most likely use an implementation based on some broadcast mechanism, while the connections to its superscopes rely on point-to-point transmission.

The presented sketch of an implementation demonstrates feasibility in the sense that more efficient implementations may be applied in any part of the system. It is based on an event notification service that supports content-based filtering. Both are implemented in the REBECA project [13], but scopes can be based on other implementations, too. We first describe an implementation realizing scopes without interfaces and mappings. In a second step, full-featured scopes are based on top of a scoped event service.

The central idea of implementing scopes and the visibility $v(X, Y)$ is to transparently extend all subscriptions issued in the system to reflect the structure implied by the graph of scopes. This structure is orthogonal to any subscriptions issued by the components in the system and therefore the filter language must allow filter extension. For example, a filter F would be transformed to $F' = (F \wedge Scope = X)$, testing for a newly introduced name $Scope$. So, the scope in which a notification is published has to be appended to it. This is done transparently by an additional software layer between application code and the simple notification service, without influencing existing components or compromising loose coupling. Administration messages are sent when the graph of scopes is changed. This task is eased by using a simplification of the graph: According to the definition of the visibility $v(X, Y)$, it is sufficient to append to each notification the maximal elements, i.e., the root nodes of the graph which have no outgoing edges, that are visible to the publisher. All subscriptions are accordingly enhanced to filter on the visible maximal elements. For a detailed discussion, please refer to [14].

The second implementation realizes scopes with interfaces and mappings and relies on the previously described scoped event system; more efficient solutions with the same interface are usable, too. Figure 8 depicts the implementation idea. A scope graph with interfaces and mappings can be transformed into a graph without mappings by introducing additional components that implement

Table 2. Related Approaches

	Visibility	Activity	Flexibility	Heterogeneity
SIENA	o	–	–	o
Ready	+	–	o	+
CORBA	o	–	+	o
Information Bus	+	o	–	o
Mediators	+	–	+	–
Field	o	–	+	+
InfoBus	o	o	–	–
ActorSpace	o	–	o	–
Scopes	+	+	+	+

interface checks and event transformations. Such a component consists of two parts, one is registered in the superscope and one in the mapped scope. This is necessary in order to utilize the previously described scoped event system that delimits visibility according to the maximal elements, the roots in the graph. The depicted graph transformation creates a new root for every scope with an interface/event mapping. Although it is not the most efficient solution, it highlights the inherent problems and facilitates a modular implementation. A more efficient solution might explicitly instantiate a scope and integrate its implementation with the newly introduced components to form a 'scope manager' that transforms notifications, checks interfaces, applies delivery constraints, and controls security issues such as scope membership.

5   Related Work

In this section, we discuss related work and compare it with our model. An overview of the comparison with some of the discussed approaches is given in Table 2, with the sign '+' meaning 'supported', '–' meaning 'not supported', and 'o' meaning 'not appropriately supported'.

Scoping is a well-known concept which is widely used in programming languages and software engineering [39]. It is used in blocks, functions, classes, packages, and components, but the research literature on event-based systems often lack most of the basic ideas of these structuring mechanisms. The basic concept of visibility and the related problems are of fundamental nature and they are therefore identified and addressed in many publications. However, no other approach in the area of event-based systems is based on the notion of visibility.

Carzaniga et al. [8] describe the SIENA event notification service, which is a popular example of a service utilizing content-based filtering. A thorough presentation of filtering semantics and design choices is given, focusing on network bandwidth efficiency. As for all other content-based filtering approaches, the filters may be used to realize visibility constrains, but these issues are not explicitly addressed. Similar to other works on event services, the flat namespace of notification attributes inhibit scalability because globally unique names are assumed.

The Ready event notification service additionally offers event zones, partitioning components based on logical, administrative, or geographical boundaries [21] and delimiting the visibility of events. But a component belongs to exactly one zone so that there is no multi-level hierarchy, and the system is structured only based on one specific point of view, prohibiting composition and mixing of aspects [22]. It is only mentioned that concepts from group communication [40] may be applicable, offering the flexibility of changing notification delivery semantics. Boundary routers are able to connect event zones and apply transformations on crossing notifications. This work presents some scoping aspects, but they do not offer one basic concept that integrates the different aspects of visibility.

The event channels of the CORBA notification service [36] offer a structuring mechanism in that notifications are only visible within the channel in which they were published. Channels can be connected to compose the reachable components, facilitating visibility and composition. However, producers must explicitly publish notifications in a specific channel, moving information about application structure into the components and limiting dynamic system evolution.

In subject-based addressing schemes for notification delivery, a tree of subjects is used to partition and select notifications; the Information Bus [38] and the Java Message Service [43] are prominent examples of this addressing scheme and even a lot of commercial products are available, from Tibco [46] and others. But the simplicity of the model results in severe disadvantages. Similar to selecting event channels, producers have to select the appropriate subjects, and the predefined tree of subjects constrain the view onto the system, impeding composition in heterogeneous environments [22]. Nevertheless, the simplicity of the concept led to wide acceptance and a multitude of implementations, e.g., in Tibco Rendezvous the basic characteristics are extended to support additional features such as bridges connecting multiple busses, integration of transactional activities, and security considerations.

Sullivan and Notkin introduce mediators [42] in order to offer a design approach which explicitly instantiates and expresses integration relationships. An implicit invocation abstraction is used to bundle components and mediators, and, with its own interface, to compose new components. A similar approach regarding visibility is used as in our scoping model, but no default semantics is outlined so that they 'only' suggest a framework that facilitates design without identifying features that are attached to visibility: transmission policies, activities, security, etc.

The Field environment [41] is an early work on tool integration and it is built around a centralized server that distribute messages. Messages sent to the server were selectively re-broadcasted to receivers that registered patterns matching the message. The original approach realized content-based filtering in a flat space of notifications. With the Field Policy Tool, it was later possible to extend the semantics by introducing a mapping of any sent message to a set of message-receiver pairs. While this opened up Field to include any delivery semantics, it is a mechanism which is very hard to control because it is based on rule and trigger evaluation. An additional extension allowed to limit the visibility of messages to a set of receivers, but did not support composition and interfaces.

The InfoBus [10] is a small Java API which allows JavaBeans or cooperating applets on a Web page to communicate data to one another. Multiple instances of InfoBus might be manually connected with bridges, providing a limited means of structuring without any inherent interfaces or composition support. It is merely a mechanism to distribute change notifications and requests for data items. Matching of messages is done by names, i.e., string matching. Besides being limited to one virtual machine, it is a tool for connecting components not for composing new ones.

Research on coordination models is dominated by Linda-like systems [18], although it was criticized that race conditions are possible in Linda and its variants, resulting from the inherent concurrency of the model [1]. In comparison to Linda, event-based systems offer a more loose coupling of components, facilitating distributed deployment of independent components. A general difference between our approach and Linda-like systems is that we have identified the administrator role and the need for externally provided configuration mechanisms that do not change instantiated components. The need to specify names or identities of tuplespaces is a major characteristic of many works on multiple tuplespaces [19]. In this way, many of the considered ideas are relevant for event-based systems but the suggested solutions are not directly adoptable. There exist some work on Linda systems which establish structures on the components. Agha and Callsen propose actorSpaces to limit distribution of messages [1]. The basic drawback of their approach is that, even though previously unknown objects are intended to cooperate, senders have to specify destination addresses. The sketched implementation is rather limited. In [29], Merrick and Wood introduce scopes to limit the visibility of tuples in Linda, but again, senders have to specify destination scopes. Furthermore, nesting of scopes is restricted to two levels. LIME [31] realizes an transparent access to multiple tuplespaces, although the approach is limited to a three-level hierarchy bound to the physical layout of the system. It is focused on the intended application domain of mobile agents and do not offer a general solution.

Cardelli and Gordon propose a process calculus for mobile ambients [5]. It is used to describe the management of a tree of ambients whose intended purpose of grouping computation resembles our graph of scopes. The calculus might be used to model scope graph dynamics, but communication across ambients is only indirectly supported and destination identities must be known.

Ported objects [28] are objects which communicate by processing messages which arrive at ports. A port is a connector in a data stream which is not directed by the object. A compound ported object encapsulates a number of ported objects and hides the data flow inside. This resembles the idea of grouping producers and consumers in scopes, while all the other features are lacking.

Evans and Dickman defined 'zones' in order to support partial system evolution [12]. The meta object protocol [24] shows the relationship between OO programming languages and scoping in event-based systems. Controlling and modifying method calls is similar to the handling of notifications in transmission policies and event mappings presented in this paper.

Garlan and Scott presented delivery policies for implicit invocation systems [17]. Four different delivery policies are distinguished: full (broadcast) and single delivery (1-of-n, that is 'indirect invocation'), parameter-based selection (filter), and a state-based policy. The policies resembles our definition but does not include the other transmission policies.

6 Conclusion

Former work on event-based systems has concentrated on efficiency issues, neglecting to support the engineering of complex systems. We have applied the notion of scopes as a fundamental structuring mechanism for event-based systems. Following classical developments in software engineering, the scoping concept is based on the notion of visibility of components and notifications. A set of design requirements for engineering event-based systems is investigated showing that, similar to approaches in traditional request/reply-based systems, visibility is the main underlying principle here. Although many other earlier contributions tackled some of the involved problems the scoping concept offers a unified approach for event-based systems based on visibility.

From an engineering point of view, scopes offer a module construct for event-based systems, being an abstraction and encapsulation unit at the same time. As an abstraction unit, a scope provides the rest of the world with common higher-level input and output interfaces to the bundled subcomponents. As an encapsulation unit, a scope constrains the visibility of the notifications published by the grouped components. It hides the details of the composition implementation, such as the underlying data transmission mechanisms, the interface mappings that map between internal and external representations of notifications, security policies, transmission policies controlling the way notifications are forwarded, etc. The structure built thereby is orthogonal to the components' implementation, separating concerns of implementation and interaction. As defined in our model, scopes have the flavor of component frameworks in the sense of Szyperski [45]: they encode the interactions between components and can themselves act as components in higher-level frameworks. The ability to model, to integrate, and to realize dynamic sessions with this concept shows the flexibility of the presented scoping concept.

The main ideas presented in this paper have been implemented in a prototype of an event notification service as part of the REBECA project. We are currently evaluating the prototype with the help of the stock trading example used throughout this article and two other example applications dealing with Internet auctions and self-actualizing Web pages. This allows us to investigate the design of event-based systems and of the necessary infrastructure not only in theory but also in practice.

Future work will include a more detailed discussion of session scopes and their relation to traditional transactions, and engineering tools that allow to build and administer scoped event-based systems via a graphical user interface.

References

1. G. Agha and C. J. Callsen. ActorSpace: an open distributed programming paradigm. *ACM SIGPLAN Notices*, 28(7):23–32, July 1993.
2. P. A. Bernstein. Transaction processing monitors. *Communications of the ACM*, 33(11):75–86, Nov. 1990.
3. C. Bornhövd and A. Buchmann. A prototype for metadata-based integration of internet sources. In *11th International Conference on Advanced Information Systems Engineering (CAiSE'99)*, volume 1626 of *LNCS*, Heidelberg, Germany, June 1999. Springer-Verlag.
4. D. Box et al. Simple object access protocol (SOAP) 1.1. Technical report, W3C, 2000. http://www.w3.org/TR/SOAP/.
5. L. Cardelli and A. D. Gordon. Mobile ambients. In M. Nivat, editor, *Proceedings of Foundations of Software Science and Computation Structures (FoSSaCS)*, volume 1378 of *LNCS*, pages 140–155. Springer-Verlag, Berlin, Germany, 1998.
6. A. Carzaniga, E. Di Nitto, D. S. Rosenblum, and A. L. Wolf. Issues in supporting event-based architectural styles. In *ISAW '98: Proceedings of the Third International Workshop on Software Architecture*, pages 17–20, 1998.
7. A. Carzaniga, D. Rosenblum, and A. Wolf. Design of a scalable event notification service: Interface and architecture. Technical Report CU-CS-863-98, Department of Computer Science, Univ. of Colorado at Boulder, USA, 1998.
8. A. Carzaniga, D. S. Rosenblum, and A. L. Wolf. Design and evaluation of a wide-area event notification service. *ACM Transactions on Computer Systems*, 19(3):332–383, 2001.
9. M. Cilia, C. Bornhövd, and A. P. Buchmann. Moving active functionality from centralized to open distributed heterogeneous environments. In *Proceedings of the 6th International Conference on Cooperative Information Systems (CoopIS '01)*, volume 2172 of *LNCS*. Springer, 2001.
10. M. Colan. *InfoBus 1.2 Specification*. Lotus.
11. G. Cugola, E. Di Nitto, and A. Fuggetta. The JEDI event-based infrastructure and its application to the development of the opss wfms. *IEEE Transactions on Software Engineering*, 2001.
12. H. Evans and P. Dickman. DRASTIC: A run-time architecture for evolving, distributed, persistent systems. In M. Akşit and S. Matsuoka, editors, *European Conference for Object-Oriented Programming (ECOOP '97)*, volume 1241 of *LNCS*, pages 243–275. Springer-Verlag, 1997.
13. L. Fiege and G. Mühl. Rebeca Event-Based Electronic Commerce Architecture, 2000. http://www.gkec.informatik.tu-darmstadt.de/rebeca.
14. L. Fiege, G. Mühl, and F. C. Gärtner. A modular approach to build structured event-based systems. In *Proceedings of the 2002 ACM Symposium on Applied Computing (SAC'02)*, pages 385–392, Madrid, Spain, 2002. ACM Press.
15. M. J. Franklin and S. B. Zdonik. A framework for scalable dissemination-based systems. In *Proceedings of the 12th ACM Conference on Object-Oriented Programming Systems, Languages, and Applications (OOPSLA '97)*, Atlanta, Georgia, USA, Oct. 5–9, 1997.
16. M. J. Franklin and S. B. Zdonik. "Data In Your Face": Push Technology in Perspective. In L. M. Haas and A. Tiwary, editors, *SIGMOD 1998, Proceedings ACM SIGMOD International Conference on Management of Data, June 2-4, 1998, Seattle, Washington, USA*, pages 516–519. ACM Press, 1998.

17. D. Garlan and C. Scott. Adding implicit invocation to traditional programming languages. In *Proceedings of the 15th Intl. Conference on Software Engineering (ICSE '93)*, pages 447–455. IEEE Computer Society Press / ACM Press, 1993.

18. D. Gelernter. Generative communication in Linda. *ACM Transactions on Programming Languages and Systems*, 7(1):80–112, Jan. 1985.

19. D. Gelernter. Multiple tuple spaces in Linda. In E. Odijk, M. Rem, and J.-C. Syre, editors, *PARLE '89: Parallel Architectures and Languages Europe*, volume 366 of *Lecture Notes in Computer Science*, pages 20–27, 1989.

20. J. Gray and A. Reuter. *Transaction Processing: Concepts and Techniques*. Morgan Kaufmann, 1993.

21. R. Gruber, B. Krishnamurthy, and E. Panagos. The architecture of the READY event notification service. In *Proceedings of the 19th IEEE International Conference on Distributed Computing Systems Middleware Workshop*, Austin, Texas, USA, May 1999.

22. W. Harrison and H. Ossher. Subject-oriented programming (A critique of pure objects). In A. Paepcke, editor, *Proceedings of the 8th ACM Conference on Object-Oriented Programming Systems, Languages, and Applications (OOPSLA '93)*, pages 411–428, 1993.

23. ISO/IEC. Reference model of open distributed processing. Draft Standard, May 1995.

24. G. Kiczales, J. des Rivieres, and D.G. Bobrow. *The Art of the Meta-Object Protocol*. MIT Press, Cambridge, MA, USA, 1991.

25. O. Lassila and R. R. Swick. Resource description framework (RDF) model and syntax specification. W3C Recommendation, Feb. 1999. http://www.w3.org/TR/REC-rdf-syntax.

26. C. Liebig, M. Cilia, and A. Buchmann. Event Composition in Time-dependent Distributed Systems. In *Proceedings of the 4th Intl. Conference on Cooperative Information Systems (CoopIS '99)*, Sept. 1999.

27. P. Maes. Concepts and experiments in computational reflection. In N. Meyrowitz, editor, *Proceedings of the 2nd ACM Conference on Object-Oriented Programming Systems, Languages and Applications (OOPSLA '87)*, pages 147–155, Orlando, FL, USA, Oct. 1987. ACM Press.

28. J. McAffer. Meta-level programming with CodA. In W. Olthoff, editor, *European Conference for Object-Oriented Programming (ECOOP '95)*, volume 952 of *LNCS*, Aarhus, Denmark, 1995. Springer-Verlag.

29. I. Merrick and A. Wood. Coordination with scopes. In *Proceedings of the ACM Symposium on Applied Computing (SAC 2000)*, pages 210–217, Como, Italy, Mar. 2000.

30. G. Mühl. Generic constraints for content-based publish/subscribe systems. In *Proceedings of the 6th International Conference on Cooperative Information Systems (CoopIS '01)*, volume 2172 of *LNCS*, pages 211–225. Springer, 2001.

31. A. L. Murphy, G. P. Picco, and G.-C. Roman. Lime: A Middleware for Physical and Logical Mobility. In F. Golshani, P. Dasgupta, and W. Zhao, editors, *Proceedings of the 21st International Conference on Distributed Computing Systems (ICDCS-21)*, pages 524–533, May 2001.

32. B. C. Neuman and T. Ts'o. Kerberos: An authentication service for computer networks. *IEEE Communications Magazine*, 32(9):33–38, Sept. 1994.

33. Oasis. *FIXML - A Markup Language for the Financial Information eXchange (FIX) protocol*, July 2001. http://www.oasis-open.org/cover/fixml.html.

34. Object Management Group. *The Common Object Request Broker: Architecture and Specification*. Version 2.3. Object Management Group, Framingham, MA, USA, 1998.
35. Object Management Group. *CORBA Components*. OMG, Framingham, MA, USA, 1999. orbos/99-07-01.
36. Object Management Group. Corba notification service. OMG Document telecom/99-07-01, 1999.
37. Object Management Group. Corba transaction service v1.1. OMG Document formal/00-06-28, 2000.
38. B. Oki, M. Pfluegl, A. Siegel, and D. Skeen. The information bus—an architecture for extensible distributed systems. In B. Liskov, editor, *Proceedings of the 14th Symposium on Operating Systems Principles*, pages 58–68, New York, NY, USA, Dec. 1993. ACM Press.
39. D. L. Parnas. On the criteria to be used in decomposing systems into modules. *Communications of the ACM*, 15(12):1053–1058, Dec. 1972.
40. D. Powell. Group communication. *Communications of the ACM*, 39(4):50–53, Apr. 1996.
41. S. P. Reiss. Connecting tools using message passing in the Field environment. *IEEE Software*, 7(4):57–66, July 1990.
42. K. J. Sullivan and D. Notkin. Reconciling environment integration and software evolution. *ACM Transactions of Software Engineering and Methodology*, 1(3):229–269, July 1992.
43. Sun. Java message service specification 1.0.2, 1999.
44. Sun Microsystems, Inc. Enterprise javabeans specification, version 2.0. Proposed Final Draft, 2000. http://java.sun.com/products/ejb/index.html.
45. C. Szyperski. *Components Software, Beyond Object-Oriented Programming*. Addison-Wesley, 1997.
46. TIBCO, Inc. TIB/Rendezvous. White Paper, 1996. http://www.rv.tibco.com/.
47. S. Yang and S. Chakravarthy. Formal Semantics of Composite Events for Distributed Environments. In *Proceedings of the 15th International Conference on Data Engineering (ICDE '99)*, pages 400–407. IEEE Computer Society Press, 1999.

Architectural Reasoning in ArchJava

Jonathan Aldrich, Craig Chambers, and David Notkin

Department of Computer Science and Engineering
University of Washington
Box 352350
Seattle, WA 98195-2350 USA
+1 206 616-1846
{jonal,chambers,notkin}@cs.washington.edu

Abstract. Software architecture describes the structure of a system, enabling more effective design, program understanding, and formal analysis. However, existing approaches decouple implementation code from architecture, allowing inconsistencies that cause confusion, violate architectural properties, and inhibit software evolution. We are developing ArchJava, an extension to Java that seamlessly unifies software architecture with an object-oriented implementation. In this paper, we show how ArchJava's type system ensures that implementation code conforms to architectural constraints. A case study applying ArchJava to an Islamic tile design application demonstrates that ArchJava can express dynamically changing architectures effectively within implementation code, and suggests that the resulting program may be easier to understand and evolve.

1   Introduction

Software architecture [GS93,PW92] is the organization of a software system as a collection of components, connections between the components, and constraints on how the components interact. Describing architecture in a formal architecture description language (ADL) [MT00] can aid in the specification and analysis of high-level designs. Software architecture can also facilitate the implementation and evolution of large software systems. For example, a system's architecture can show which components a module may interact with, help identify the components involved in a change, and describe system invariants that should be respected during software evolution.

Existing ADLs, however, are loosely coupled to implementation languages, causing problems in the analysis, implementation, understanding, and evolution of software systems. Some ADLs [SDK+95,LV95] connect components that are implemented in a separate language. However, these languages do not guarantee that the implementation code obeys architectural constraints. Instead, they require developers to follow style guidelines that prohibit common programming idioms such as data sharing. Architectures described with more abstract ADLs [AG97,MQR95] must be implemented in an entirely different language. Thus, it may be difficult to trace architectural features to the implementation, and the implementation may become inconsistent with the

B. Magnusson (Ed.): ECOOP 2002, LNCS 2374, pp. 334–367, 2002.
© Springer-Verlag Berlin Heidelberg 2002

architecture as the program evolves. In summary, while architectural analysis in existing ADLs may reveal important architectural properties, these properties are not guaranteed to hold in the implementation.

In order to enable architectural reasoning about an implementation, the implementation must conform to its architecture. Luckham and Vera [LV95] identified three criteria for architectural conformance:

- *Decomposition*: For each component in the architecture, there should be a corresponding component in the implementation.
- *Interface Conformance*: Each component in the implementation must conform to its architectural interface.
- *Communication Integrity*: Each component in the implementation may only communication directly with the components to which it is connected in the architecture.

ADLs that provide tool support for skeleton code generation or component linking generally support the first two architectural conformance criteria: decomposition and interface conformance. However, existing ADLs cannot enforce communication integrity, seriously compromising the benefits of architecture during implementation, testing, and software evolution.

We are developing ArchJava [ACN02a], a small, backwards-compatible extension to Java that integrates software architecture smoothly with Java implementation code. ArchJava supports a flexible object-oriented programming style, allowing data sharing and supporting dynamic architectures where components are created and connected at run time. The unique feature of ArchJava is a type system that guarantees communication integrity between an architecture and its implementation, even in the presence of shared objects and run-time architecture configuration. In previous work [ACN02a] we introduced the ArchJava language and described our initial experience with the subset of ArchJava that supports static architectures.

This paper makes two novel contributions:

- A formalization of the language semantics as ArchFJ, a core language that integrates primitive object-oriented constructs with support for specifying dynamic software architectures. We outline a proof of type soundness and communication integrity for the core language.
- An evaluation of ArchJava in a case study specifying the dynamic architecture of Taprats, a 12,000-line application for designing Islamic tiling patterns.

The rest of this paper is organized as follows. After the next section's discussion of related work, section 3 describes the ArchJava language. Section 4 formalizes ArchJava as ArchFJ, and proves type soundness and communication integrity. Section 5 describes a case study in which we reengineered Taprats, using ArchJava to express a conceptual architecture drawn by the developer. Finally, section 6 concludes with a discussion of future work.

2   Previous Work

Architecture Description Languages. A number of architecture description languages (ADLs) have been defined to describe, model, check, and implement software architectures [MT00]. Many of these languages support sophisticated analysis and reasoning. For example, Wright [AG97] allows architects to specify temporal communication protocols and check properties such as deadlock freedom. SADL [MQR95] formalizes architectures in terms of theories, shows how generic refinement operations can be proved correct, and describes a number of flexible refinement patterns. Rapide [LV95] supports event-based behavioral specification and simulation of reactive architectures. ArchJava's architectural specifications are probably most similar to those of Darwin [MK96], an ADL designed to support dynamically evolving distributed architectures.

While Wright and SADL are pure design languages, other ADLs have supported implementation in a number of ways. UniCon's tools [SDK+95] generate code to connect components implemented in other languages, while C2 [MOR+96] provides runtime libraries in C++ and Java that connect components together. Rapide architectures can be given implementations in an executable sub-language or in languages such as C++ or Ada. More recently, the component-oriented programming languages ComponentJ [SC00] and ACOEL [Sre02] extend a Java-like base language to explicitly support component composition.

However, existing ADLs cannot enforce communication integrity. Instead, system implementers must follow *style guidelines* that ensure communication integrity. For example, the Rapide language manual suggests that components should only communicate with other components through their own interfaces, and interfaces should not include references to mutable types. These guidelines are not enforced automatically and are incompatible with common programming idioms such as shared mutable data structures.

Module Interconnection Languages. Module interconnection languages (MILs) support system composition from separate modules [PN86]. Jiazzi [MFH01] is a component infrastructure for Java, and a similar system, Knit, supports component-based programming in C. These tools are derived from research into advanced module systems, exemplified by MzScheme's Units [FF98] and ML's functors. ADLs differ from MILs in that the former make *connectors* explicit in order to describe *data and control flow* between components, while the latter focus on describing the *uses* relationship between modules [MT00]. Existing MILs cannot be used to describe dynamic architectures, where component object instances are created and linked together at run time.

Furthermore, MILs provide encapsulation by hiding names, which is insufficient to guarantee communication integrity in general. For example, first-class functions or objects can be passed from one module to another, and later used to communicate in ways that are not directly described in the MIL description. Thus, in these systems, programmers must follow a careful methodology to ensure that each module communicates only with the modules to which it is connected in the architecture.

CASE Tools. A number of computer-aided software engineering tools allow programmers to define a software architecture in a design language such as UML, UML-RT, ROOM, or SDL, and fill in the architecture with code in the same language or in C++ or Java. While these tools have powerful capabilities, they either do not enforce communication integrity or enforce it in a restricted language that is only applicable to certain domains. For example, the SDL embedded system language prohibits sharing objects between components. This restriction ensures communication integrity, but it also makes the language awkward for general-purpose programming. Many UML tools such as Rational Rose RealTime or I-Logix Rhapsody, in contrast, allow method implementations to be specified in a language like C++ or Java. This supports a great deal of flexibility, but since the C++ or Java code may communicate arbitrarily with other system components, there is no guarantee of communication integrity in the implementation code. The techniques described in this paper can be applied in tools such as Rational Rose RealTime to provide a static guarantee of communication integrity.

Other Tools. Tools such as Reflexion Models [MNS01] have been developed to show an engineer where an implementation is and is not consistent with an architectural view of a software system. Similar systems include Virtual Software Classifications [MW99] and Gestalt [SSW96]. Unlike ArchJava, these systems describe architectural components in terms of source code, not run-time component object instances, and the architectural descriptions must be updated separately as the code evolves.

Previous ArchJava Work. In previous work [ACN02a], we describe in detail a case study applying ArchJava to Aphyds, a 12,000-line circuit design application with a static architecture and little use of inheritance. The primary contributions of that paper are an informal description of the language and an empirical evaluation of ArchJava on the Aphyds application. In contrast, this paper contributes a formalization of the language design, and proofs of type soundness and communication integrity. This paper also presents a new case study applying ArchJava to Taprats, a second, contrasting application that exercises ArchJava's support for dynamic architectures and component inheritance.

3   The ArchJava Language

ArchJava is intended to investigate the benefits and drawbacks of a relatively unexplored part of the ADL design space. Our approach extends a practical object-oriented implementation language to incorporate architectural features and enforce communication integrity. Key benefits we hope to realize with this approach include better program understanding, reliable architectural reasoning about code, keeping architecture and code consistent as they evolve, and encouraging more developers to take advantage of software architecture. ArchJava's design also has some limitations, discussed below in section 3.5.

```
public component class Parser {
    public port in {
        provides void setInfo(Token symbol, SymTabEntry e);
        requires Token nextToken() throws ScanException;
    }
    public port out {
        provides SymTabEntry getInfo(Token t);
        requires void compile(AST ast);
    }

    public void parse() {
        Token tok = in.nextToken();
        AST ast = parseFile(tok);
        out.compile(ast);
    }

    AST parseFile(Token lookahead) { ... }
    void setInfo(Token t, SymTabEntry e) {...}
    SymTabEntry getInfo(Token t) { ... }
    ...
}
```

Fig. 1. A parser component in ArchJava. The `Parser` component class uses two ports to communicate with other components in a compiler. The parser's `in` port declares a required method that requests a token from the lexical analyzer, and a provided method that enters tokens into the symbol table. The `out` port requires a method that compiles an AST to object code, and provides a method that looks up tokens in the symbol table.

To allow programmers to describe software architecture, ArchJava adds new language constructs to support *components*, *connections*, and *ports*. The rest of this section reviews the language design [ACN02a], describing by example how to use these constructs to express software architectures. Throughout the discussion, we show how the constructs work together to enforce communication integrity. Reports on the ArchJava web site [Arc02] provide more information, including the complete language semantics.

3.1   Components and Ports

A *component* is a special kind of object that communicates with other components in a structured way. Components are instances of *component classes*, such as the `Parser` component class in Figure 1.

A component can only communicate with other components at its level in the architecture through explicitly declared ports—regular method calls between components are not allowed. A *port* represents a logical communication channel between a component and one or more components that it is connected to.

Ports declare three sets of methods, specified using the **requires**, **provides**, and **broadcasts** keywords. A *provided* method is implemented by the component and is available to be called by other components connected to this port. Conversely, each *required* method is provided by some other component connected to this port. A

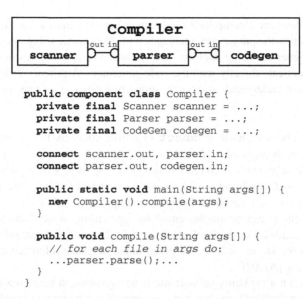

```
public component class Compiler {
    private final Scanner scanner = ...;
    private final Parser parser = ...;
    private final CodeGen codegen = ...;

    connect scanner.out, parser.in;
    connect parser.out, codegen.in;

    public static void main(String args[]) {
        new Compiler().compile(args);
    }

    public void compile(String args[]) {
        // for each file in args do:
        ...parser.parse();...
    }
}
```

Fig. 2. A graphical compiler architecture and its ArchJava representation. The Compiler component class contains three subcomponents—a Scanner, a Parser, and a CodeGen. This compiler architecture follows the well-known pipeline compiler design [GS93]. The scanner, parser, and codegen components are connected in a linear sequence, with the out port of one component connected to the in port of the next component.

component can invoke one of its required methods by sending a message to the port that defines the required method. For example, the parse method calls nextToken on the parser's in port. *Broadcast* methods are just like required methods, except that they can be connected to an unbounded number of implementations and must return **void**.

The goal of this port design is to specify both the services implemented by a component and the services a component needs to do its job. Required interfaces make dependencies explicit, reducing coupling between components and promoting understanding of components in isolation. Ports also make it easier to reason about a component's communication patterns.

3.2   Component Composition

In ArchJava, hierarchical software architecture is expressed with *composite components*, which are made up of a number of subcomponents connected together. A *subcomponent*[1] is a component instance nested within another component. Singleton subcomponents can be declared as **final** fields of component type.

---

[1] Note: the term *subcomponent* indicates composition, whereas the term *component subclass* would indicate inheritance.

Figure 2 shows how a compiler's architecture can be expressed in ArchJava. The example shows that the parser communicates with the scanner using one protocol, and with the code generator using another. The architecture also implies that the scanner does *not* communicate directly with the code generator. A primary goal of ArchJava is to ease program understanding tasks by supporting this kind of reasoning about program structure.

Connections. The symmetric **connect** primitive connects two or more ports together, binding each required method to a provided method with the same name and signature. The arguments to connect may be a component's own ports, or those of subcomponents in **final** fields. Connection consistency checks are performed to ensure that each required method is bound to a unique provided method.

Provided methods can be implemented by forwarding invocations to subcomponents or to the required methods of another port. The detailed semantics of method forwarding and broadcast methods are given in the language reference manual on the ArchJava web site [Arc02].

ArchJava does not explicitly support alternative connection semantics such as asynchronous communication; however, these semantics can be implemented in ArchJava by writing custom components that play the role of "smart connectors." The ArchJava release includes an example AsynchronousConnector component that caches required method calls in an internal worklist and then returns immediately, invoking the corresponding provided methods asynchronously from an internal thread.

Inheritance. Component classes can inherit from other component classes, or from class Object. The compiler's legacy mode also allows component classes to inherit from ordinary classes, at the cost of losing communication integrity guarantees for inherited methods, so that developers can use non-component-based legacy frameworks like the Java GUI libraries. Component subclasses inherit methods, ports, and connections from their superclasses. Component subclasses may also override method definitions and specify new methods and ports. However, component subclasses may not specify new required methods because this could break subtype substitutability.

ArchJava also supports architectural design with **abstract** components and ports, which allow an architect to specify and typecheck an ArchJava architecture before beginning program implementation.

3.3   Communication Integrity

The compiler architecture in Figure 2 shows that while the parser communicates with the scanner and code generator, the scanner and code generator do not directly communicate with each other. If the diagram in Figure 2 represented an abstract architecture to be implemented in Java code, it might be difficult to verify the correctness of this reasoning in the implementation. For example, if the scanner obtained a reference to the code generator, it could invoke any of the code generator's methods, violating the intuition communicated by the architecture. In contrast, programmers can have confidence that an ArchJava architecture accurately represents communication between components, because the language semantics enforce communication integrity.

Communication integrity in ArchJava means that components in an architecture can only call each other's methods along declared connections between ports. Each component in the architecture can use its ports to communicate with the components to which it is connected. However, a component may not directly invoke the methods of components other than its own subcomponents, because this communication may not be declared in the architecture, and thus may violate communication integrity. We define communication integrity more precisely in section 4.1.

3.4   Dynamic Architectures

The constructs described above express architecture as a static hierarchy of interacting component instances, which is sufficient for a large class of systems. However, some system architectures require creating and connecting together a dynamically determined number of components.

Dynamic Component Creation. Components can be dynamically instantiated using the same **new** syntax used to create ordinary objects. For example, Figure 2 shows the compiler's `main` method, which creates a `Compiler` component and calls its `compile` method. At creation time, each component records the component instance that created it as its *container component*. For components like `Compiler` that are instantiated outside the scope of any component instance, the container component is **null**.

Communication integrity places restrictions on the ways in which component instances can be used. Because only a component's container can invoke its methods directly, it is essential that typed references to subcomponents do not escape the scope of their container component. This requirement is enforced by prohibiting component types in the ports and public interfaces of components, and prohibiting ordinary classes from declaring arrays or fields of component type. Since a component instance can still be freely passed between components as an expression of type `Object`, a `ComponentCastException` is thrown if an expression is downcast to a component type outside the scope of its container component instance.

Connect Expressions. Dynamically created components can be connected together at run time using a *connect expression*. For instance, Figure 3 shows a web server architecture where a `Router` component receives incoming HTTP requests and passes them through connections to `Worker` components that serve the request. The `requestWorker` method of the web server dynamically creates a `Worker` component and then connects its `serve` port to the `workers` port on the `Router`.

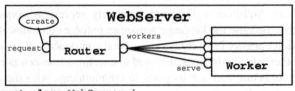

```
public component class WebServer {
  private final Router r = new Router();
  connect r.request, create;
  connect pattern Router.workers, Worker.serve;

  public void run() { r.listen(); }
  private port create {
    provides r.workers requestWorker() {
      final Worker newWorker = new Worker();
      r.workers connection = connect(r.workers, newWorker.serve);
      return connection;
    }
  }
}

public component class Router {
  public port interface workers {
    requires void httpRequest(InputStream in, OutputStream out);
  }
  public port request {
    requires this.workers requestWorker();
  }
  public void listen() {
    ServerSocket server = new ServerSocket(80);
    while (true) {
      Socket sock = server.accept();
      this.workers conn = request.requestWorker();
      conn.httpRequest(sock.getInputStream(), sock.getOutputStream());
    }
  }
}

public component class Worker extends Thread {
  public port serve {
    provides void httpRequest(InputStream in, OutputStream out) {
      this.in = in; this.out = out; start();
    }
  }
  public void run() {
    // gets requested file and sends it on the output stream
  }
}
```

Fig. 3. A web server architecture. The `Router` subcomponent accepts incoming HTTP requests and passes them on to a set of `Worker` components that respond. When a request comes in, the `Router` requests a new worker connection on its `request` port. The `WebServer` then creates a new worker and connects it to the `Router`. The `Router` assigns requests to `Workers` through its `workers` port.

Communication integrity requires each component to explicitly document the kinds of architectural interactions that are permitted between its subcomponents. A *connection pattern* is used to describe a set of connections that can be instantiated at run time

using connect expressions. For example, **connect pattern** Router
.workers, Worker.serve describes a set of connections between the Router
subcomponent and dynamically created Worker subcomponents.

Each connect expression must match a connection pattern declared in the enclosing
component. A connect expression *matches* a connection pattern if the connected ports
are identical and each connected component is an instance of the type specified in the
pattern. The connect expression in the web server example matches the corresponding
connection pattern because the r and newWorker components in the connect expression conform to the types Router and Worker that are declared in the connection
pattern.

Port Interfaces. Often a single component participates in several connections using
the same conceptual protocol. For example, the Router component in the web
server communicates with several Worker components, each through a different
connection. A *port interface* describes a port that can be instantiated several times to
communicate through different connections.

Each port interface defines a type that includes all of the required methods in that
port. A *port interface type* combines a port's required interface with an *instance expression* that indicates which component instance the port belongs to. For example, in
the Router component, the type **this**.workers refers to an instance of the
workers port of the current Router component. Similarly, in the WebServer,
the type r.workers refers to an instance of the workers port of the r subcomponent. Port interface types can be used in method signatures such as request-
Worker and in local variable declarations such as conn in the listen method. In
ArchJava, the required methods of a port can only be called by the component instance
the port belongs to. Therefore, required methods can only be invoked on expressions
of port interface type when the instance expression is **this**, as shown by the call to
httpRequest within Router.listen.

Port interfaces are instantiated by connect expressions. A connect expression returns a *connection object* that represents the connection. This connection object implements the port interfaces of all the connected ports. Thus, in Figure 3, the connection object connection implements the interfaces newWorker.serve and
r.workers, and can therefore be assigned to a variable of either type.

Provided methods use the **sender** keyword to obtain the connection object
through which they were invoked. The detailed semantics of **sender** and other language features are covered in the ArchJava language reference available on the
ArchJava web site [Arc02].

Removing Components and Connections. Just as Java does not provide a way to
explicitly delete objects, ArchJava does not provide a way to explicitly remove components and connections. Instead, components are garbage-collected when they are no
longer reachable through direct references, running threads, or architectural connections. For example, in Figure 3, a Worker component will be garbage collected
when the reference to the original worker (newWorker) and the references to its

connections (`connection` and `conn`) go out of scope, and the thread within `Worker` finishes execution.

3.5   Limitations of ArchJava

There are currently several limitations to the ArchJava approach. Our technique is presently only applicable to programs written in a single language and running on a single JVM, although the concepts may extend to a wider domain. Architectures in ArchJava are more concrete than architectures in ADLs such as Wright, restricting the ways in which a given architecture can be implemented—for example, inter-component connections must be implemented with method calls. Also, our design focuses on ensuring communication integrity, and does not yet support other types of architectural reasoning, such as reasoning about the temporal order of architectural events, or about component multiplicity.

ArchJava's definition of communication integrity supports reasoning about communication through method calls between components; however, components may still used shared data to communicate in ways that are not directly expressed in the architecture. Because existing ways to control communication through shared data involve significant restrictions on programming style, we chose to allow unrestricted data sharing. Future work includes developing ways to reason about communication through shared data while preserving expressiveness. Our preliminary experience with ArchJava [ACN02a] suggests that rigorous reasoning about architectural control flow can aid in program understanding and evolution, even in the presence of shared data structures.

3.6   Implementation

A prototype compiler for ArchJava is publicly available for download at the ArchJava web site [Arc02]. Our compiler is implemented on top of the Barat infrastructure [BS98]. The compiler accepts a list of ArchJava files (.archj), compiles each one down to Java source code, and invokes `javac` on the resulting .java files. Our compilation technique is incremental, so that when a source file is updated, only that file and the files that depend on it need to be recompiled.

The ArchJava compiler translates each component class to an ordinary class in Java, leaving the fields and method bodies substantially unchanged. We mangle the names of classes to ensure that code not compiled by our compiler will not accidentally misuse component classes; the `main` function is left in a class with the original name, so that ArchJava applications work smoothly on existing Java virtual machines. Each component class stores its container component and implements an interface that allows the container to be checked. All casts to a component class are compiled into calls to a generated cast method that verifies that the cast expression's container is the current component **this**, throwing a `ComponentCastException` if the check fails.

Each port and port interface in the ArchJava source code is compiled into an interface containing the required methods of the port. All variables of port interface type are compiled to variables of that port's interface type.

Each connection is compiled into a "connection class" that implements all of the interfaces of the connected ports. The connect expression returns a new connection object, passing the connected components to the connection object's constructor. The constructor assigns the connected components to internal fields. Whenever a required method is invoked on that connection, the connection object invokes the corresponding provided method on the appropriate component.

Although in ArchJava the source code is the canonical representation of the architecture, visual representations are also important for conveying architectural structure. Parts of this paper use hand-drawn diagrams to communicate architecture; however, we have also constructed a simple visualization tool that generates architectural diagrams automatically from ArchJava source code. In addition, we intend to provide an `archjavadoc` tool that would automatically construct graphical and textual web-based documentation for ArchJava architectures.

Performance. The main cost of our implementation technique is that calls through connections are routed through connection objects, adding a layer of indirection to the system. Our current compiler is a prototype and does not perform any optimizations; however, future implementations could use well-known techniques like specialization to eliminate this indirection in many cases.

Thus far, the only applications of significant size to which we have applied ArchJava are interactive, and thus it is difficult to benchmark their performance. An independent evaluation of ArchJava on a microbenchmark that exhibited a very fine-grained architecture measured an overhead of about 10% relative to Java code with a similar decomposition [AL02]. We expect that most realistic applications would use architectural features at a more coarse grain, and so this estimate is probably close to the worst case in practice.

4   ArchJava Formalization

In this section, we discuss the formal definition of communication integrity and ArchJava's semantics. The next subsection defines communication integrity in ArchJava. Subsection 4.2 gives the static and dynamic semantics of ArchFJ, a language incorporating the core features of ArchJava. Finally, subsection 4.3 outlines states type soundness theorems for ArchFJ, and subsection 4.4 outlines a proof of communication integrity.

4.1   Definition of Communication Integrity

Communication integrity is the key property of ArchJava that ensures that the implementation does not communicate in ways that could violate reasoning about control flow in the architecture. Intuitively, communication integrity in ArchJava means that a component instance A may not call the methods of another component instance B unless B is A's subcomponent, or A and B are sibling subcomponents of a common component instance that declares a connection or connection pattern between them.

We now precisely define communication integrity in ArchJava. We want to reason about not only the direct method calls made by a component instance c to a component instance b, but also indirect method calls made through non-component intermediary objects. To reason about these indirect calls, we define the *execution scope* of component instance c on the run-time stack, denoted *escope*(c), be any of c's executing methods and any of the object methods they transitively invoke.

Definition 1 [Dynamic Execution Scope]: Let c be a component instance, let mf range over method frames executing on the stack, and assume that the *caller* function returns the previous method frame on the stack. Then we can define the execution scope of c recursively as follows:

$$escope(c) \equiv \{ \; mf \mid (mf.\textbf{this} = c) \; \} \cup$$
$$\{ \; mf \mid !component(mf.\textbf{this}) \wedge caller(mf) \in escope(c) \; \}$$
$$escope(\textbf{null}) \equiv \{ \; mf \mid \forall c \neq \textbf{null} \; . \; mf \notin escope(c) \; \}$$

It is easy to show that each method frame mf is in the execution scope of either exactly one component or **null**.

Now we can define communication integrity. Let $<:$ be the subtyping relation over component classes (defined precisely in section 4.2, below). Let the function *container* return a component's container component (i.e., the component instance in whose scope it was created), or **null** if there is no such container. We use *class* to refer to the class of a component instance, and *requiredmethods* and *providedmethods* to refer to the set of required and provided methods in a port.

Definition 2 [Communication Integrity in ArchJava]: A program has communication integrity if, for all run-time method calls to a method m of a component instance b in an executing stack frame $mf \in escope(a)$:

1. For direct method calls, a = b or a = *container*(b)
2. For calls through connections, there exists a component instance c such that:
    *   c = a or c = *container*(a), and
    *   c = b or c = *container*(b), and
    *   **connect pattern** $P_1.z_1, \ldots, P_n.z_n \in class(c)$, and
    * $\exists i,j \in 1..n$. $class(a) <: P_i \wedge class(b) <: P_j \wedge$
        $m \in requiredmethods(p_i) \wedge m \in providedmethods(p_j)$

In the definition above, the first case represents direct method calls between components: the callee must either be the caller itself or one of the caller's subcomponents. The second case represents a method call along a connection between components: some component instance c that is equal to or contains a and b must have declared a connection pattern between a and b that matches the types of a and b and includes the

```
CL      ::= class C extends C {C̄ f̄; K̄ M̄} _ _       _         _ _ _
CP      ::= component class P extends E_{C̄ f̄; K̄ M̄ port z {R̄ M̄} X̄}
K       ::= E(C̄ f̄)_{super(f̄); this.f̄ = f̄;}
M       ::= T m(T̄ x̄) { return e; }
R       ::= requires T m(T̄ x̄)_ _
X       ::= connect pattern (P̄.z̄)

e       ::= v               _
        |   new E(ē)
        |   e.f _
        |   e.m(ē)
        |   (T)e
        |   θ ▷ e

v       ::= x
        |   ℓ             _ _
        |   connect(v̄.z̄)
        |   error

T,V     ::= E
        |   v.z _
        |   U(v.z)

S       ::= ℓ → E_ς(ℓ̄)
Γ       ::= x → T
Σ       ::= ℓ → T

ℓ,θ,ς   ∈ Locations
```

Fig. 4. ArchFJ Syntax

invoked method m. In section 4.4, we state and prove this communication integrity property for a core subset of ArchJava.

This definition has been simplified slightly in the interest of clarity. Calls to broadcast methods can be modeled as calls to multiple required methods, and static connections can be modeled with dynamic connections and connect pattern declarations.

4.2   Formalization as ArchFJ

We would like to use formal techniques to prove that the ArchJava language design guarantees communication integrity, and show that the language is type safe. A standard technique, exemplified by Featherweight Java [IPW99], is to formalize a core language that captures the key typing issues while ignoring complicating language details. We have formalized ArchJava as ArchFJ, a core language based on Featherweight Java (FJ).

Syntax. Figure 4 presents the syntax of ArchFJ. The metavariables C and D range over class names; E and F range over component and class names; T and V range over types; P and Q range over component classes; f and g range over fields; v ranges over values; d and e range over expressions; z ranges over port names; S ranges over stores; ℓ, θ, and ς range over locations in the store, where θ is typically used to represent the value of **this** and ς represents the container of an object, and M ranges over methods. As a shorthand, we use an overbar to represent a sequence. We assume a fixed class table CT mapping regular and component classes to their definitions. A program, then, is a pair $(CT,\ e)$ of a class table and an expression.

ArchFJ makes a number of simplifications relative to ArchJava. In ArchFJ, each component has exactly one port, defining a set of required and provided methods. For simplicity, we require that the same set of methods appear in the class body and in the port body. Static connections and component fields are left out, as they are subsumed by dynamically created connections and components. We also omit the **sender** keyword and broadcast methods. As in Featherweight Java (FJ), we omit interfaces, assignment, and some statement and expression forms. These changes make our type soundness proof shorter, but do not materially affect it otherwise.

ArchFJ extends FJ in several ways. Regular classes extend another class (which can be Object, a predefined class) and define a constructor K and a set of fields $\bar{f}$ and methods $\bar{M}$. Component classes can extend another component class, or Object. Component classes also define a single port that includes a set of required methods $\bar{R}$ and provided methods $\bar{M}$. Finally, component classes declare a set of connection patterns $\bar{x}$ between their subcomponents.

We need to reason about object identity (represented by a location ℓ) in order to verify communication integrity. A store S maps locations ℓ to their contents: the class of the object and the values stored in its fields. As in ArchJava, the store also keeps track of each object's container object (represented by a subscript on the class name) in order to check run time component casts properly. We will write S$[\ell]$ to denote the store entry for ℓ. Functional store updates are abbreviated S$[\ell{\rightarrow}E_\ell(\bar{\ell})]$. The function *container*(S,ℓ) looks up the container of ℓ in store S.

Expressions include object creation expressions, field lookup, method calls, and casts. Component creations and casts must refer to the current value of **this**, so our reduction rules keep track of the **this** reference as part of the executing context. We give a small-step reduction semantics, and so a program expression must represent a stack of executing methods, each with a potentially different receiver value **this**. Therefore, we use an expression $\theta \triangleright e$ to represent a method body e executing with a receiver θ.

Values represent irreducible computational results, and include locations and connections. ArchFJ represents failed casts with an explicit **error** value. We include variables as values because a variable may appear as the instance expression in a port interface type. The set of variables includes the distinguished variable **this** used to refer to the receiver of a method. Neither the **error** value, nor locations, nor $\theta \triangleright e$ expressions may appear in the source text of the program; these represent intermediate forms.

Types include class and component types (E), port interface types (v.z), and a union type that matches any one of a set of port interface types.

$$\frac{\ell \notin domain(S) \qquad S' = S\,[\ell \to E_\theta(\bar{\ell})\,]}{S, \theta \vdash \mathbf{new}\ E\,(\bar{\ell}) \to \ell,\ S'} \qquad \text{(R-New)}$$

$$\frac{S\,[\ell] = E_\varsigma(\bar{\ell}) \qquad fields(E) = \bar{C}\ \bar{f}}{S, \theta \vdash \ell.\,f_i \to \ell_i,\ S} \qquad \text{(R-Field)}$$

$$\frac{S\,[\ell] = F_\varsigma(\bar{\ell}) \qquad F <: E \qquad E\ a\ component \Rightarrow (\theta = \ell \lor \theta = container(S, \ell))}{S, \theta \vdash (E)\ell \to \ell,\ S} \qquad \text{(R-Cast)}$$

$$\frac{\ell.\,z \in \bar{\ell}.\bar{z}}{S, \theta \vdash (\ell.\,z)\,(\mathbf{connect}(\overline{\ell.z})\,) \to \mathbf{connect}(\overline{\ell.z}),\ S} \qquad \text{(R-ConnectCast)}$$

$$\frac{S\,[\ell] = E_\varsigma(\bar{\ell}) \qquad mbody(m, E) = (\bar{x}, e_0) \qquad e_b = [\bar{v}/\bar{x},\ \ell/\mathbf{this}]\,e_0}{S, \theta \vdash \ell.\,m\,(\bar{v}) \to \ell \rhd e_b,\ S} \qquad \text{(R-Invk)}$$

$$\frac{S\,[\bar{\ell}] = P_{\bar{\ell}_0}(...) \qquad mbody(m, \bar{P}) = (\bar{x}, e_0, i) \qquad e_b = [\bar{v}/\bar{x},\ \ell_i/\mathbf{this}]\,e_0}{S, \theta \vdash \mathbf{connect}(\overline{\ell.z})\,.m\,(\bar{v}) \to \ell_i \rhd e_b,\ S} \qquad \text{(R-ConnectInvk)}$$

$$S, \theta \vdash \ell \rhd v \to v,\ S \qquad \text{(R-Context)}$$

$$\frac{S, \ell \vdash e \to e',\ S'}{S, \theta \vdash \ell \rhd e \to \ell \rhd e',\ S'} \qquad \text{(RC-Context)}$$

Fig. 5. ArchFJ Evaluation Rules

Reduction Rules. The evaluation relation, defined by the reduction rules given in Figure 5, is of the form $S, \theta \vdash e \to e', S'$ read "In the context of store S and receiver θ, expression e reduces to expression e' in one step, producing the new store S'." We write $\to^*$ for the reflexive, transitive closure of $\to$. Most of the rules are standard; the interesting features are how they manipulate architectural constructs. The R-New rule reduces a new expression into a fresh location. The store is updated at that location to refer to a new object with its fields set to the values passed into the constructor, and with its container set to the current object θ (representing **this**). The field read rule looks up the receiver in the store and returns the location in the ith field.

The reduction rule for object casts looks up the actual type of the casted object in the store, and verifies that the actual type is a subtype of the type in the cast expression. In addition, if the cast is to a component class, the rule verifies that the current component θ is equal to either ℓ or ℓ's container. Similarly, the rule for casts to a port interface type verifies that the named port interface type is one of the ones in the actual connection. If any of the conditions on the cast fails, then the cast reduces to the **error** expression (the error rules are given in the companion technical report [ACN02b]).

The method invocation rule R-Invk looks up the receiver in the store, then uses the *mbody* helper function (defined in Figure 9) to determine the correct method body to

$$T <: T \qquad\qquad (S\text{-Reflex})$$

$$\frac{T <: T' \quad T' <: T''}{T' <: T''} \qquad\qquad (S\text{-Trans})$$

$$\frac{CT(\text{E}) = [\textbf{component}]\ \textbf{class}\ \text{E}\ \textbf{extends}\ \text{F}\ \{\ \ldots\ \}}{\text{E} <: \text{F}} \qquad\qquad (S\text{-Extends})$$

$$T <: \text{Object} \qquad\qquad (S\text{-Object})$$

$$\frac{\text{v.z} \in \overline{\text{v.z}}}{\bigcup(\overline{\text{v.z}}) <: \text{v.z}} \qquad\qquad (S\text{-Union})$$

Fig. 6. ArchFJ Subtyping

invoke. In the method body, all occurrences of the formal method parameters and **this** are replaced with the actual arguments and the receiver, respectively. Execution of the method body continues in the context of the receiver location. The rule for invocations on connections is similar, except that the *mbody* helper function also determines which of the connected components defines the invoked method. When a method expression reduces to a value, the R-CONTEXT rule propagates the value outside of its method context and into the surrounding method expression.

The full semantics of the language include a set of congruence rules (such as if e→e′ then e.f→e′.f) allow reduction to proceed in the order of evaluation defined by Java. We include the congruence rule RC-CONTEXT because it shows the semantics of the $\ell \triangleright$ e construct: evaluation of the expression e occurs in the context of the receiver ℓ instead of the receiver θ. The rest of the congruence rules are omitted here, but can be found in a companion technical report [ACN02b].

Subtyping Rules. ArchFJ's subtyping rules are given in Figure 6. Subtyping of classes and components is defined by the reflexive, transitive closure of the immediate subclass relation given by the extends clauses in *CT*. In the S-EXTENDS rule and elsewhere, the brackets and ellipses indicate optional syntax that does not affect the rule's semantics. We require that there are no cycles in the induced subtype relation. Every type is a subtype of Object, and a union type is a subtype of all its member types.

Typing Rules. Typing judgments, shown in Figure 7, are of the form $\Gamma, \Sigma, \text{E} \vdash \text{e:T}$, read "In the type environment Γ, store typing Σ, and class E, expression e has type T." The T-VAR rule looks up the type of a variable in Γ, and the T-LOC rule looks up the type of a location in Σ. The object creation rule verifies that the types of all the actual constructor argument types are subtypes of the declared constructor argument types. The connection rule assigns the connection a union type of all the connected ports. If the instance expressions in the connection are variables, then this is a connection in the source text, and so the connection must match a connect pattern declaration in the enclosing component. It is not necessary to perform this check once the variables in the

$$\Gamma, \Sigma, E \vdash \ell : \Sigma(\ell) \qquad\qquad (\text{T-Loc})$$

$$\Gamma, \Sigma, E \vdash x : \Gamma(x) \qquad\qquad (\text{T-Var})$$

$$\frac{\Gamma, \Sigma, F \vdash \bar{e} : \bar{C} \qquad \mathit{fields}(E) = \bar{D}\ \bar{f} \qquad \bar{C} <: \bar{D}}{\Gamma, \Sigma, F \vdash \textbf{new } E(\bar{e}) : E} \qquad (\text{T-New})$$

$$\frac{\Gamma, \Sigma, E \vdash \bar{v} : \bar{P} \qquad \bar{v} = \bar{x} \Rightarrow (E = P_{\text{this}} \wedge \textbf{connect pattern } \overline{Q.z} \in \mathit{connects}(P_{\text{this}}) \wedge \bar{P} <: \bar{Q})}{\Gamma, \Sigma, E \vdash \textbf{connect}(\bar{v.z}) : \bigcup(\overline{v.z})} \qquad (\text{T-Connect})$$

$$\frac{\Gamma, \Sigma, E \vdash e_0 : E_0 \qquad \mathit{fields}(E_0) = \bar{C}\ \bar{f}}{\Gamma, \Sigma, E \vdash e_0.f_i : C_i} \qquad (\text{T-Field})$$

$$\frac{\Gamma, \Sigma, E \vdash e : T_0 \qquad T \text{ is a component} \Rightarrow E \text{ is a component}}{\Gamma, \Sigma, E \vdash (T)e : T} \qquad (\text{T-Cast})$$

$$\frac{\begin{array}{c}\Gamma, \Sigma, E_{\text{this}} \vdash e_0 : T_0 \qquad \mathit{mtype}(m, T_0) = \bar{T} \to T \qquad \Gamma, \Sigma, E_{\text{this}} \vdash \bar{e} : \bar{V} \\ \bar{V} <: [e_0/\textbf{this}]\bar{T} \qquad T_R = [e_0/\textbf{this}]T \qquad T_0 = x.z \Rightarrow x = \textbf{this}\end{array}}{\Gamma, \Sigma, E_{\text{this}} \vdash e_0.m(\bar{e}) : T_R} \qquad (\text{T-Invk})$$

$$\frac{\Gamma, \Sigma, E \vdash \ell : F \qquad \Gamma, \Sigma, F \vdash e : T}{\Gamma, \Sigma, E \vdash \ell \rhd e : T} \qquad (\text{T-Context})$$

Fig. 7. ArchFJ Typechecking

connect expression have been replaced with locations. The rule for field reads looks up the declared type of the field using the *fields* function defined in Figure 9. Casts to a component class in ArchJava can only appear in methods of a component class; the cast rule for ArchFJ checks this constraint.

Rule T-INVK looks up the invoked method's type using the *mtype* function defined in Figure 9, and verifies that the actual argument types are subtypes of the method's argument types. Because **this** may appear as part of port interface types in the method's argument and result types, the rule substitutes any occurrences of **this** in the method's type with the actual receiver value. This substitution is undefined if the method's type contains **this** and the receiver is not a value. If the invocation is through a port interface type and the instance expression is a variable, then the instance expression must be **this**, as in ArchJava. Finally, the T-CONTEXT typing rule for an executing method checks the method's body in the context of the class of the **this** pointer.

Class and Store Typing. Figure 8 shows the rules for well-formed class definitions and stores. The rules for well-formed classes have the form "class declaration E is OK," and "method/port/connection X is OK in E." The class rules checks that the form of the constructor simply calls the superclass constructor, then assigns the values passed to the constructor to the corresponding fields. It also verifies that any methods, ports, and connections in the class are well-formed. Component classes may only inherit from other component classes, or from class Object.

$$\frac{\begin{array}{c} \text{K} = \text{F}(\overline{\text{D}}\ \overline{\text{g}},\ \overline{\text{C}}\ \overline{\text{f}})\ \{\textbf{super}(\overline{\text{g}})\,;\ \textbf{this}.\overline{\text{f}} = \overline{\text{f}};\} \qquad \textit{fields}(\text{E}) = \overline{\text{D}}\ \overline{\text{g}} \qquad \overline{\text{M}}\ \text{OK IN F} \\ \text{F}\ \textit{a component class} \Rightarrow (\,(\text{E}\ \textit{a component class}\ \vee\ \text{E} = \texttt{Object})\ \wedge\ \overline{\text{z}},\overline{\text{X}}\ \text{OK IN F}\,)\end{array}}{\text{[\textbf{component}]\ \textbf{class}\ F\ \textbf{extends}\ E\ \{\overline{\text{C}}\ \overline{\text{f}};\ \overline{\text{K}}\ \overline{\text{M}}\ [\textbf{port}\ \overline{\text{z}\{\overline{\text{R}}\ \overline{\text{M}}\}}\ \overline{\text{X}}]\,\}\ \text{OK}} \qquad \text{(T-Class)}$$

$$\frac{CT(\text{E}) = [\textbf{component}]\ \textbf{class}\ E\ \textbf{extends}\ F\ \{..\} \qquad \textit{override}(\text{m, F, }\overline{\text{T}}\to\text{T})}{\text{T m}(\overline{\text{T}}\ \overline{\text{x}})\ \{\ \textbf{return}\ \text{e; }\}\ \text{OK in E}} \qquad \text{(T-Meth)}$$

where $\{\overline{\text{x}}:\overline{\text{T}},\ \texttt{this}:\text{E}\},\varnothing,\text{E} \vdash \text{e:V} \qquad \text{V} <: \text{T} \qquad \text{T},\overline{\text{T}}\ \textit{not components}$

$$\frac{\begin{array}{c} \text{R}_i = \textbf{requires}\ \text{T}_i\ \text{m}(\overline{\text{T}_i}\ \overline{\text{x}_i})\,; \qquad \text{T}_i,\overline{\text{T}_i}\ \textit{not components} \\ CT(\text{P}) = \textbf{component}\ \textbf{class}\ P\ \textbf{extends}\ E\ \{..\} \\ \text{E} \neq \texttt{Object} \Rightarrow \textbf{port}\ \text{z}\ \{\ \overline{\text{R}}\ \overline{\text{M}}\ \} \in \text{E}\end{array}}{\textbf{port}\ \text{z}\ \{\ \overline{\text{R}}\ \overline{\text{M}}\ \}\ \text{OK in P}} \qquad \text{(T-Port)}$$

$$\frac{\begin{array}{c} \forall i\ (\textit{mtype}(\text{m},\text{z}_i) = \overline{\text{T}}\to\text{T}) \\ \Rightarrow (\exists j \neq i\ \textit{s.t.}\ \textit{mtype}(\text{m},\text{P}_j) = \overline{\text{T}}\to\text{T}\ \wedge\ \forall k \neq j\ \textit{mtype}(\text{m},\text{P}_k)\ \textit{not defined})\end{array}}{\textbf{connect}\ \textbf{pattern}(\overline{\text{P.z}})\ \text{OK IN Q}} \qquad \text{(T-Pattern)}$$

$$\frac{\textit{dom}(\Sigma) = \textit{dom}(\text{S}) \qquad \forall \ell \in \textit{dom}(\text{S})\ .\ (\text{S}[\ell] = \text{E}_\varsigma(\overline{\ell})\ \wedge\ \textit{fields}(\text{E}) = \overline{\text{C}}\ \overline{\text{f}} \Rightarrow \overline{\Sigma(\ell)} <: \overline{\text{C}})}{\Sigma \vdash \text{S}} \qquad \text{(T-Store)}$$

Fig. 8. Class, Method, Port, Connection, and Store Typing

The rule for methods checks that the method body is well typed, and uses the *override* function (defined in Figure 9) to verify that methods are overridden with a method of the same type. It also ensures that the signature of a component method does not include component types. For component classes, the port typing rule verifies that only subclasses of Object may define new required and provided methods. The rule for connect patterns verifies that each required method has a unique provided method with the right signature.

The store typing rules ensure that the form of the store is consistent with the Java's typing rules. The two clauses of the store typing rule are the usual well-formedness rules, requiring the store type Σ to type every location in S, and verifying that the types of objects in a field are compatible with the field's type.

Auxiliary Definitions. Most of the auxiliary definitions shown in Figure 9 are straightforward and are derived from FJ. The field and connection lookup rules return the list of fields and connections in a given class. ArchFJ follows Java's lookup rules for method types and method bodies, with straightforward extensions for port types and union types. The method body lookup rule *mbody* for connections chooses the component i providing the method. It is guaranteed to choose a unique component because the T-Pattern rule implies that only one of the components in a connection defines each method. It then computes the actual method body using the usual *mbody* rule. Finally, the *override* rule checks that overriding methods have the same type signatures as the methods they override.

Field lookup:

$$fields(\texttt{Object}) = \bullet$$

$$\frac{CT(\texttt{E}) = [\texttt{component}] \ \texttt{class} \ \texttt{E} \ \texttt{extends} \ \texttt{F} \ \{\overline{\texttt{C} \ \texttt{f}}; \ \overline{\texttt{K}} \ \overline{\texttt{M}} \ [\overline{\texttt{R} \ \texttt{X}}] \} \qquad fields(\texttt{F}) = \overline{\texttt{D} \ \texttt{g}}}{fields(\texttt{E}) = \overline{\texttt{D} \ \texttt{g}}, \ \overline{\texttt{C} \ \texttt{f}}}$$

Connection lookup:

$$connects(\texttt{Object}) = \bullet$$

$$\frac{CT(\texttt{P}) = \texttt{component} \ \texttt{class} \ \texttt{P} \ \texttt{extends} \ \texttt{E} \ \{\overline{\texttt{C} \ \texttt{f}}; \ \overline{\texttt{K}} \ \overline{\texttt{M}} \ \overline{\texttt{R}} \ \overline{\texttt{X}}\} \qquad connects(\texttt{E}) = \overline{\texttt{X}_0}}{connects(\texttt{P}) = \overline{\texttt{X}_0}, \ \overline{\texttt{X}}}$$

Method type lookup:

$$\frac{CT(\texttt{E}) = [\texttt{component}] \ \texttt{class} \ \texttt{E} \ \texttt{extends} \ \texttt{F} \ \{...\overline{\texttt{M}}...\} \qquad \texttt{T} \ \texttt{m} \ (\overline{\texttt{T} \ \texttt{x}}) \ \{ \ \texttt{return} \ \texttt{e}; \ \} \in \overline{\texttt{M}}}{mtype(\texttt{m},\texttt{E}) = \overline{\texttt{T}} \to \texttt{T}}$$

$$\frac{CT(\texttt{E}) = [\texttt{component}] \ \texttt{class} \ \texttt{E} \ \texttt{extends} \ \texttt{F} \ \{...\overline{\texttt{M}}...\} \qquad \texttt{m} \ \textit{is not defined in} \ \overline{\texttt{M}}}{mtype(\texttt{m},\texttt{E}) = mtype(\texttt{m},\texttt{F})}$$

$$\frac{\texttt{component} \ \texttt{class} \ \texttt{P} \ \texttt{extends} \ \texttt{E} \ \{...\texttt{port} \ \texttt{z} \ \{\overline{\texttt{R} \ \texttt{M}}\}...\} \in CT \qquad \texttt{requires} \ \texttt{T} \ \texttt{m} \ (\overline{\texttt{T} \ \texttt{x}}) \in \overline{\texttt{R}}}{mtype(\texttt{m},\texttt{z}) = \overline{\texttt{T}} \to \texttt{T}}$$

$$\frac{mtype(\texttt{m},\texttt{z}_i) = \overline{\texttt{T}} \to \texttt{T}}{mtype(\texttt{m}, \textstyle\bigcup(\texttt{v}.\texttt{z})) = \overline{\texttt{T}} \to \texttt{T}}$$

Method body lookup:

$$\frac{CT(\texttt{E}) = [\texttt{component}] \ \texttt{class} \ \texttt{E} \ \texttt{extends} \ \texttt{F} \ \{...\overline{\texttt{M}}...\} \qquad \texttt{T} \ \texttt{m} \ (\overline{\texttt{T} \ \texttt{x}}) \ \{ \ \texttt{return} \ \texttt{e}; \ \} \in \overline{\texttt{M}}}{mbody(\texttt{m},\texttt{E}) = (\overline{\texttt{x}},\texttt{e})}$$

$$\frac{CT(\texttt{E}) = [\texttt{component}] \ \texttt{class} \ \texttt{E} \ \texttt{extends} \ \texttt{F} \ \{...\overline{\texttt{M}}...\} \qquad \texttt{m} \ \textit{is not defined in} \ \overline{\texttt{M}}}{mbody(\texttt{m},\texttt{E}) = mbody(\texttt{m},\texttt{F})}$$

$$\frac{mbody(\texttt{m},\texttt{P}_i) = (\overline{\texttt{x}},\texttt{e}_0)}{mbody(\texttt{m},\texttt{P}) = (\overline{\texttt{x}},\texttt{e}_0,i)}$$

Valid method overriding:

$$\frac{mtype(\texttt{m}, \ \texttt{E}) = \overline{\texttt{T}} \to \texttt{T}_0 \ \Rightarrow \ \overline{\texttt{V}} = \overline{\texttt{T}} \ \wedge \ \texttt{V}_0 = \texttt{T}_0}{override(\texttt{m}, \ \texttt{E}, \ \overline{\texttt{V}} \to \texttt{V}_0)}$$

Fig. 9. ArchFJ Auxiliary Definitions

4.3   Type Soundness

Before proving communication integrity, we show that our type system is sound, i.e., execution of ArchFJ programs will not become stuck except due to failed casts. We frame type soundness with the usual theorems: Subject Reduction states that if a well-typed program reduces to another program in a single reduction step, the resulting program is either well-typed or contains an **error** subexpression from a failed cast. Progress states that a well-typed program is either an irreducible value or an expression to which one or more of the evaluation rules applies. Our presentation is modeled after that of Featherweight Java [IPW99]; the full details of the proofs can be found in the companion technical report [ACN02b].

Theorem [Subject Reduction]: If $\Gamma,\Sigma,E \vdash e:T$, $\Sigma(\theta) = E$, $\Sigma \vdash s$, and
$s,\theta \vdash e \rightarrow e',s'$ then either $\exists \Sigma' \supseteq \Sigma$, $T' <: T$ such that $\Gamma,\Sigma',E \vdash e':T'$ and $\Sigma' \vdash s'$, or else e' has an **error** subexpression.

Before proving the theorem, we define a term substitution lemma, necessary for the method invocation case in the proof. This enables us to show that substituting terms in a well-typed expression preserves the typing:

Lemma [Term Substitution]: If $\{\overline{x:T}, \mathtt{this}:E\}$, $\varnothing$, $E \vdash e:T$, $\varnothing,\Sigma,F \vdash \overline{\ell:V}$,
$\varnothing,\Sigma,F \vdash \ell:E'$, $\overline{V} <: [\ell/\mathtt{this}]\overline{T}$, and $E' <: E$, then $\varnothing,\Sigma,F \vdash \ell \triangleright [\overline{\ell/x},\ell/\mathtt{this}]e:T'$ for some $T' <: [\ell/\mathtt{this}]T$.

The proof is by induction over the structure of e, with a case analysis on the form of the outermost term.

Subject reduction is then proved by induction on the derivation of $s,\theta \vdash e \rightarrow e',s'$ with a case analysis on the last reduction rule used.   □

Theorem [Progress]: If $\varnothing,\Sigma,E \vdash e:T$, then either e is an irreducible value, or else $\forall s, \theta$ such that $\Sigma \vdash s$ and $\Sigma(\theta) = E$ we have $s,\theta \vdash e \rightarrow e',s'$.

The proof is by induction on the derivation of $\varnothing,\Sigma,E \vdash e:T$ with a case analysis on the last typing rule used.   □

4.4 Communication Integrity

Like the definition of communication integrity for ArchJava in section 4.1, communication integrity for ArchFJ has two parts: a theorem for direct method calls, and a theorem for method calls through a connection. The first theorem states that for all direct method invocations on a component, the receiver must be the current component **this** or one of its immediate subcomponents. The formal statement of the theorem is somewhat technical:

Theorem [Communication Integrity of Direct Calls]: Consider any method call $e'.n(\overline{e})$ in the body of another method m. We assume that the method body is well typed, so we have $T\ m(\overline{T\ x})\ \{\ \mathtt{return}\ e;\ \}$ OK in E with $e'.n(\overline{e})$ a subexpression of e. Consider a well-typed run time method call to m on an object θ, such that $s,\theta_o \vdash \theta.m(\overline{v}) \rightarrow \theta \triangleright e_b$, $s,\Gamma,\Sigma,F \vdash \theta \triangleright e_b:T$, and $\Sigma \vdash s$. Communication integrity means that if e' has a component type ($\Gamma, \Sigma, E \vdash e' : P$) and e' reduces to a location ℓ ($S, \theta \vdash e \rightarrow^* \ell, S'$), then the current component θ is either the receiver ℓ of the method call or the container of the receiver ($\theta = \ell$ or $\theta = container(S, \ell)$). This last condition corresponds to the first case of communication integrity given in section 4.1.

The theorem is proved by a case analysis on the form of expression e', followed by induction on the derivation of $S, \theta \vdash e \rightarrow^* \ell, S'$. For example, one of the more interesting cases occurs if e' is a cast to a component type. The last reduction rule used in the derivation of $S, \theta \vdash e \rightarrow^* \ell, S'$ must be R-CAST, which checks that $\theta = \ell$ or $\theta = container(S, \ell)$, ensuring that communication integrity holds for this case.   □

The second theorem states that for all method invocations on a connection, there exists a creating component that declared a matching connection pattern, and all components in the connection are either the creating component or one of its subcomponents. Furthermore, the current component **this** must be a part of the connection.

Theorem [Communication Integrity of Indirect Calls]: If an initial expression e evaluates to a well-typed expression e' ($\varnothing, \theta_o \vdash e \rightarrow^* e', S$, $\varnothing, \Sigma, \text{Object} \vdash e' : T$, $\Sigma \vdash S$), and $\text{connect}(\overline{\ell. z})$ is a subexpression of e' then there exists a component instance ℓ that declared a connection pattern (**connect pattern** $\overline{Q.z} \in connects(\Sigma(\ell))$) whose types match the connected components ($\Sigma(\overline{\ell}) <: \overline{Q}$), and all of the connected components are equal to or contained by ℓ ($\forall \ell_i \in \overline{\ell} . \ell = \ell_i \vee \ell = container(S, \ell_i)$). Furthermore, if a method is called on the connection ($S, \theta \vdash \text{connect}(\overline{\ell. z}).m(\overline{v}) \rightarrow \ell_i \rhd e_b, S$) then the current component $\theta \in \overline{\ell}$.

The proof is by induction on the derivation of $\varnothing, \theta_o \vdash e \rightarrow^* e', S$. Connect expressions may only be introduced into e' through method calls, and the T-CONNECT rule verifies that the appropriate connection pattern is present in the enclosing component class. A lemma similar to the communication integrity of direct calls theorem is used to show that $\forall \ell_i \in \overline{\ell} . \ell = \ell_i \vee \ell = container(S, \ell_i)$.

Finally, we show that $\theta \in \overline{\ell}$. The key insight is that rule T-INVK requires that any port interface type with a variable as the instance expression must be of the form **this**.z. When the method is called the variable **this** will be replace with the actual receiver θ, and so type soundness guarantees that the connect expression includes θ.   □

5   Experience

In previous work, we validated the basic design of ArchJava with a case study on Aphyds, a 12,000-line circuit-design program with a static architecture [ACN02a]. In this section, we describe a case study that evaluates ArchJava's support for dynamic architectures and component inheritance, and adds to our confidence in the application of ArchJava. In our case study, we attempt to answer the following experimental questions:

- Is ArchJava expressive enough to describe a real architecture that is dynamically evolving?
- How does the difficulty of reengineering a Java program in order to express its architecture vary with the program's characteristics?
- What might be the benefits of expressing a program's architecture in ArchJava?

5.1   Methodology

Our approach to answering these questions was to translate Taprats from Java into ArchJava, using the conceptual architecture provided by the program's developer as a guide. In the process of our Taprats case study, we refined the hypotheses formed in our initial case study, and made new hypotheses, outlined in bold below.

The case study participant was a graduate student with five years' experience of system programming in Java. Although the participant was the developer of the ArchJava compiler, he was unfamiliar with Taprats and had little experience writing user interfaces in Java. Thus, the study reflects the common reality of a programmer asked to evolve an unfamiliar system. The participant was one of us, and will be informally referred to as "we" in the following text.

We reengineered Taprats to express the conceptual architecture described by the developer. After browsing the code to determine which classes corresponded to the components in the developer's conceptual architecture, we converted these classes into ArchJava component classes.

The next four subsections describe the process of reengineering Taprats, a comparison to the earlier Aphyds case study, an analysis of what we learned about the ArchJava language, and a summary of the benefits of reengineering Taprats in ArchJava.

5.2   Reengineering Taprats

Taprats [Kap00] is an application for designing Islamic star patterns. The user first chooses a basic tiling pattern from a library, then defines the exact shapes used within the tiles, and finally renders the design in one of several styles. Different windows are provided for these tasks, and the user can simultaneously work on different variations of a single design.

The developer of Taprats (not one of us) is a computer science graduate student and an experienced Java programmer. Taprats won the grand prize in the 2000 ACM/IBM Quest for Java, and can thus be considered a model Java program with a quality design and implementation. The application is 12,540 lines of Java source code, as measured by the Unix wc (word count) program, not counting the Java libraries used.

We asked the developer to draw the conceptual architecture of Taprats, as shown in Figure 10. He drew two diagrams, one representing the user interface and one representing the internal data structures. The user interface is a pipeline architecture of four windows, each of which passes an increasingly detailed data structure to the next win-

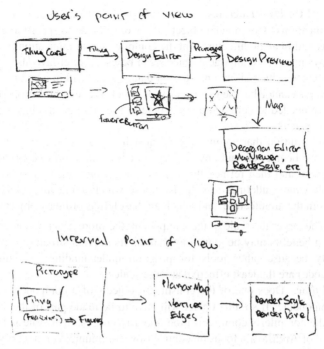

Fig. 10. The developer's drawing of Taprats' architecture. The drawing on the top shows the user's point of view, describing the four main user interface windows, what they look like on the screen, and what data structures are passed from one window to the next. The drawing on the bottom shows the internal data structures, beginning with a `Tiling` that is nested withing a `Prototype`, which first evolves into a `Map` and then has rendering style information added.

dow. The internal view shows how data structures are contained within and produced from each other.

Validating Taprats' Architecture. We began the study by examining the Taprats source code to try to determine how it corresponds to the developer's conceptual architecture. We discovered that the `main` method in the `Program` class created the first user interface window, and that each successive window spawned the next one in the action code for the appropriate button.

Although the conceptual architecture of the user interface showed a sequence of windows, the implementation structure was more like a nesting of window instances, where each window object is responsible for creating child window objects for the next tile design stage. Thus, our experience with Taprats supports a hypothesis from our previous case study:

> **Hypothesis 1: Developers have a conceptual model of their architecture that is mostly accurate, but this model may be a simplification of reality, and it is often not explicit in the code.**

Architectural Design Principles. ArchJava provides two kinds of objects with which to build applications. Component objects allow developers to specify the communication patterns within an architecture, but the compiler's communication integrity checks limit the ways in which component objects can be used. ArchJava also provides ordinary Java objects, which allow unrestricted data sharing within a component architecture, but which cannot be used to specify or check architectural properties. Design principles are needed to help determine where to use component objects and where to use ordinary objects.

Using the intuition that architecture is most important at the largest scales in the application, we began our study by creating a component representing the entire Taprats application, and then refined this architecture to increase its level of detail. We used the following guidelines to help us choose which application objects should be components in the architecture, and which are best left as ordinary objects:

- *Scale.* The larger the scale of the component, the more program understanding and evolution benefits may be gained by making its internal structure explicit. This is primarily because other tools for program understanding (including browsing source code) are the least effective at large scales.
- *Control flow.* Does one of the constituent objects of a component call back into that component? If so, that object will have to be made part of the architecture to satisfy the compiler's communication integrity checks. This rule is largely a consequence of ArchJava's focus on control flow communication integrity.
- *Sharing.* ArchJava supports a hierarchical view of software architecture, and therefore does not allow a component to be shared by two container components. Thus, structures that are shared between components should be left as ordinary objects, unless the sharing can be easily replaced with method calls through the container component's port.
- *Database objects.* Singleton objects that encapsulate information shared by multiple components are good component candidates, forming a repository architecture style. They may need to be promoted up a level in the component hierarchy to make the sharing explicit.
- *Data structures.* Small data structures that have many instances and are shared or passed between components are best left as ordinary objects. ArchJava's component mechanisms may be too "heavyweight" to use at these small application scales.
- *Cooperation.* If a set of objects communicate with each other in complex ways, making them component classes in an architecture may aid program understanding by making the communication patterns explicit as connections in the architecture.
- *Lack of communication.* ArchJava's architectural features can be used to document the invariant that a set of components do not communicate directly with one another.

These principles are not orthogonal; a designer must make tradeoffs based on the applicability of the different design criteria, and the specific nature of the application. We hope to refine these design principles based on future experience with ArchJava.

Architectural Design. Applying the design principles above, we initially focused on the architecture of the user interface, as shown in the top part of Figure 10. Our rationale was that the user interface is the highest level of *scale* in the application, and also that *control flow* originates in the user interface. Our experience suggests:

> **Hypothesis 2: Because ArchJava ensures control-flow communication integrity, it has a natural bias towards a UI-centric architecture in user-interface driven applications.**

This hypothesis is also supported by our previous case study, which also resulted in a UI-centric architecture. Our hypothesis suggests that in the future, we should apply ArchJava to systems applications that are not user-interface driven, to determine the effectiveness of the language in that domain.

As we reengineered Taprats, we used the architecture design guidelines to flesh out our initial architecture. Following the developer's conceptual architecture, we made each user interface window into a component. We then refined the architecture by making several window panes into subcomponents of their containing window, either because there was *control flow* from the pane back into the window, or because we wanted to document the fact that the panes were *unshared* and they *did not communicate* with other components. Ultimately, we decided not to encode the bottom part of Figure 10 in the architecture, because these are *data structures* that are passed along the user interface pipeline.

Parts of the user interface architecture made extensive use of inheritance, exercising ArchJava's support for component inheritance. For example, the user interface employs window panes of different classes depending on the tiling pattern chosen by the user. Taprats' design shows how inheritance can be useful in a component-based system.

Code Restructuring. As described above, each window in the user interface creates the next one, suggesting a series of nested windows rather than a pipeline of windows. In order to make the developer's conceptually linear architecture more explicit, we decided to make two structural changes to the application.

First, we made the windows siblings in the architecture instead of being nested within each other. Because components can only be created by their container component in ArchJava, this meant we had to move all the application's window-creation code into the `Program` class. This change complicated the application slightly, because each window had to call into the container component to create the next window. However, it has benefits as well: the new design shows the conceptual architecture more directly than the original design. This "factory pattern" design [GHJ+94] also decouples the different user interface windows, because each window no longer specifies exactly which window will be created next and how it will be created. This information is hidden within the container component, potentially allowing the interface to be modified at a smaller cost.

> **Hypothesis 3: Using ArchJava to express software architecture explicitly can aid information hiding by encouraging developers to reduce coupling between different components in their architecture.**

In a post-study interview, the Taprats developer said that this change made the ArchJava architecture appear more like his conceptual architecture, but thought that there should be some way to allow components to be constructed by their siblings in the architecture. We are considering how to address this limitation of the current ArchJava language design, perhaps by supporting constructor calls through ports.

Second, instead of passing tiling data from one window to the next via an argument to the latter window's constructor, we created explicit connections between the windows, along which the data could be passed. We made this change in order to express the developer's conceptual architecture as directly as possible, and the developer agreed that the new design helped to accomplish this goal. However, a serious drawback of the new design is that windows are not completely initialized when the constructor completes, but remain in a partially initialized state until the tiling data is passed via a separate method call. Because of this, the developer said that he would not have made this second architectural change. It is possible that allowing constructor calls through ports will enable us to express this type of connection directly without the drawbacks of our current implementation.

Reengineering Process. We performed our reengineering as a series of small refactoring steps, compiling the program and fixing introduced defects after every stage. Thus, we never went more than an hour without a correctly running program. This methodology was suggested in our previous case study, after we tried to make many changes at once and ended up introducing several hard-to-repair defects. We found that this methodology was effective at limiting defects in this study.

To help us understand the process of reengineering a program to make its architecture explicit with ArchJava, we recorded the major refactoring steps we performed, and categorized them into the following refactoring patterns:

- *Change class to component class*: When a class describes an object that is part of the architecture, change it into a component class. This may require applying other refactorings in order to pass communication integrity checks.

- *Move creation to container component*: When a component creates one of its sibling components in the architecture, create a port in the component and its container with a single method, `requestCreate`. The container component creates the sibling in `requestCreate`, connects it as appropriate in the architecture, and optionally returns a connected port to the original child component.

- *Change a field link into a connection*: When a component has a field that refers to a sibling component, replace the field with a port that contains all of the methods invoked on the sibling component. In the container component, connect the component's port to a corresponding port on its sibling, and then convert method invocations on the field into invocations on the appropriate port.

In addition to these major refactoring steps, we used several conventional refactoring patterns [FBB+99], as well as a few more minor refactoring patterns that are specific to ArchJava.

Reengineering Cost. We spent about 5½ developer hours reengineering Taprats, or about 30 minutes of work per KLOC. Of this time, approximately half was spent in design activity—understanding the structure of the original program, planning the conversion to ArchJava, considering architectural alternatives, and examining the final architecture for completeness at the end. Because the developer of Taprats had already put considerable effort into making a clean design and implementation, a relatively small amount of our time was spent actually implementing the architectural changes.

Our implementation time was divided roughly equally between modifying the source code to express the architecture, and repairing defects that were introduced in these refactoring steps. The final program code is 12693 lines long—only 153 lines longer than the original application. A total of 242 lines of code were added or changed in the process. Our experience supports a hypothesis from our previous study:

> **Hypothesis 4: Applications can be translated into ArchJava with a modest amount of effort, and without excessive code bloat.**

Code Characteristics. One particular code characteristic that stood out as we edited Taprats was the Law of Demeter [LH89], which states that objects should only communicate directly with their immediate neighbors in a system. The Law of Demeter can be thought of as the object-oriented analog of communication integrity, since ArchJava components may only communicate with the architectural "neighbors" to which they are connected in the architecture.

We discovered this connection by examining a violation of the Law of Demeter that forced us to restructure Taprats' code. After constructing a new window, the Taprats code called an accessor function to get a pane of that window, and then set the parameters of the pane's viewport directly—violating the Law of Demeter, since the pane was not an immediate neighbor of the original code. In our architecture, the pane was an internal component of the window component, and so this communication violated communication integrity. Therefore, we had to restructure the program to pass the viewport parameters to the enclosing window, which then passed them on to the pane. When shown the offending code, the developer agreed with our assessment and thought our solution was appropriate.

Despite this example, most of the Taprats code obeyed the Law of Demeter. This had a beneficial effect on our reengineering: when we converted an object into a component, the new component would often pass the compiler's communication integrity checks as soon as we converted direct method calls into calls on ports. Our experience suggests:

> **Hypothesis 5: It will be relatively easy to use ArchJava to express the software architecture of an object-oriented program whose source code obeys the Law of Demeter.**

```
public component class Program {

    // the tiling selector window subcomponent
    private final TilingSelector ts = new TilingSelector();

    // ports for creating windows
    private port createDesignEditor {
      provides ts.sendTiling requestEditor() {
        DesignEditor e = new DesignEditor();
        connect(createPreviewPanel, e.createNext);
        ts.sendTiling aPort = connect(ts.send, e.receive);
        return aPort;
      }
    }
    private port interface createPreviewPanel {
      provides Object requestPreview(Object edit) {
        DesignEditor e = (DesignEditor) edit;
        PreviewPanel p = new PreviewPanel();
        connect(createRenderPanel, p.createNext);
        return connect(e.send, p.receive);
      }
    }
    private port interface createRenderPanel {
      provides Object requestRender(Object prevw) {
        PreviewPanel p = (PreviewPanel) prevw;
        RenderPanel r = new RenderPanel();
        return connect(p.send, r.receive);
      }
    }

    // connections between the creation ports and the windows
    connect createDesignEditor, ts.createNext;
    connect pattern createPreviewPanel, DesignEditor.createNext;
    connect pattern createRenderPanel, PreviewPanel.createNext;

    // connections between the windows
    connect pattern TilingSelector.send, DesignEditor.receive;
    connect pattern DesignEditor.send, PreviewPanel.receive;
    connect pattern PreviewPanel.send, RenderPanel.receive;

    // the main methods of the program
    public void run() {
      Frame f = new Frame( "Taprats 0.3" );
      f.add( "Center", ts );
      // more code to finish setting up the window...
    }

    public static void main(String[] args) {
      new Program().run();
    }
}
```

Fig. 11. ArchJava code for the `Taprats` component.   The main application method creates a `Program` component and invokes `run` on it. The initial `TileSelector` window is created in the field initializer for `ts`, and the `run` method wraps it in a `Frame`. The three private ports contain methods that create and connect new window components.   Connect declarations show communication patterns between windows.

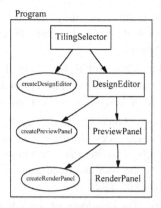

Fig. 12. A visualization of the Taprats architecture, automatically derived from the ArchJava source code. Boxes represent subcomponents, and arrows represent inter-component control flow. The ovals are internal ports of the program component, which are used by the first three window components to create the next window in the sequence.

Final Architecture. Figure 11 shows the ArchJava code that expresses the architecture of Taprats. The complete ArchJava source code for Taprats is available at the ArchJava web site [Arc02]. Compared to the developer's conceptual architecture, our final ArchJava architecture describes identical communication patterns between the user interface windows.

Figure 12 shows a visualization of the Taprats architecture automatically derived from the ArchJava source code using a visualization tool. We showed the developer this diagram, and he agreed that it captured his conceptual architecture well.

Alternative Architectural Choices. Our study was directed towards implementing the developer's conceptual architecture as directly as possible in ArchJava. However, an architect could have expressed alternative Taprats architectures using ArchJava. For example, we could have followed the original source code more closely, producing a nested hierarchy of components instead of a linear sequence of components. Although this architecture would not show all of the user interface components and connections within one composite component, it would express the constraint that the user interface window instances form a tree with each window spawning multiple windows on the next level. The architecture we chose does not eliminate the possibility that the windows form a dag, where data from two source windows might be combined into a later-stage window (this does not occur in practice, of course). ArchJava is flexible enough to express both architectures, depending on which the software architect deems more appropriate.

5.3   Comparison to Aphyds Case Study

We found that expressing the conceptual architecture of Taprats with ArchJava was straightforward when compared with our earlier case study. In all, we spent approximately five times less effort in this case study than in the Aphyds case study, despite the fact that the programs were of similar size. Several application characteristics may have contributed to this difference:

- *Architecture Style.* The pipeline architecture style of Taprats, where data is passed from one component to another, has simpler communication patterns than the repository architecture style of Aphyds, where components access a shared database.

- *Architectural Connectivity.* Once spawned, Taprats' user interface windows are completely independent: they access different data, and do not communicate in any way. In contrast, Aphyds' user interface windows show different views of the same data, and therefore the user interface architecture includes connections to pass updated data and window state.

- *Architecture Granularity.* The developer of Aphyds specified a fairly fine-grained architecture, and the control flow within the user interface encouraged us to make the architecture even more fine-grained than the developer specified. In contrast, the Taprats user interface architecture was more coarse-grained, consisting of only four windows and their window panes.

- *Architectural Mismatches.* The structure of Taprats was quite similar to the architecture we tried to express. In the Aphyds study, we chose to make some previously dynamic structures static, requiring us to restructure the code to support re-initialization where new objects had been created previously.

- *Code Interdependence.* As described above, Taprats had a well-factored codebase that generally followed the Law of Demeter, making the architectural reengineering easy. In contrast, the Aphyds codebase contained many dependencies across object structures. Its frequent violations of the Law of Demeter required many reengineering steps before the compiler's communication integrity checks were satisfied.

Our experience suggests that looking at these application characteristics may shed light on how much effort will be required to express an application's architecture with ArchJava.

5.4   Evaluation of the ArchJava Language

In general, our experience suggests that the ArchJava language design was adequate for expressing the architecture of Taprats. We were able to describe the conceptual architecture of the developer with minimal reengineering effort. The dynamic constructs of the language, which were largely untested in our earlier case study, were sufficient to express the dynamic nature of the Taprats user interface.

We also noticed areas in which the language design could be improved. As discussed before, it would be cleaner if each window in Taprats' user interface pipeline could create the next window in a more natural way, rather than requesting that the container component create the next window, as is done in the current solution. Also, in Figure 12, the creation ports (such as `createPreviewPanel`) that are connected to dynamically created child windows cannot accept an argument of component type telling them which window to connect, nor can they return a port with the correct type (as does the `createDesignEditor` port). Due to limitations in the current type system of ArchJava, two extra casts are required, one in the container component and one in the window component. We are considering ways to extend the ArchJava language design to handle these cases more smoothly.

5.5   Benefits of ArchJava

The ArchJava architecture has a number of advantages compared to the original, conceptual architecture of Taprats. ArchJava architectures are guaranteed to be complete, listing all method call communication between components. The ArchJava architecture is guaranteed to stay up-to-date as the code evolves with changing requirements, and architectural visualizations can be generated automatically. Finally, it is easy to examine the source code to look at the interior structure of an ArchJava component, determine what methods are in each port, or examine how the methods are implemented.

The process of reengineering Taprats to make its architecture explicit may also have made the code more maintainable and easier to change. For example, the compiler's communication integrity checks identified several violations of the Law of Demeter, enabling us to replace them with better-factored code. Because ports encapsulate all control-flow communication between components, the components are more loosely coupled in the final version of the code, making them easier to evolve as requirements change. More experience with evolving ArchJava programs is needed to determine if these potential benefits are realized in practice.

In summary, we were able to capture the conceptual architecture of Taprats effectively in ArchJava with a small amount of effort relative to the size of the program. Our experience demonstrates that the language is flexible enough to describe dynamically evolving software architectures, and suggests future improvements to the language design.

6   Conclusion and Future Work

ArchJava allows programmers to express architectural structure and then seamlessly fill in the implementation with Java code. At every stage of the software lifecycle, ArchJava ensures that the implementation conforms to the specified architecture. Our formalization of ArchJava gives us confidence in its type system's ability to enforce communication integrity. A case study suggests that ArchJava can be applied with relatively little effort to moderate-sized Java programs with dynamically evolving architectures, making the program's structure explicit and improving the maintainability of code. Thus, ArchJava helps to promote effective architecture-based design, implementation, program understanding, and evolution.

In future work, we intend to gather experience from outside users of ArchJava, and perform further case studies to see if the language can be successfully applied to programs larger than 100,000 lines of code. We will also investigate extending the language design to enable more advanced architectural reasoning, including temporal ordering constraints on component method invocations and constraints on data sharing between components.

Acknowledgements

We would like to thank David Garlan, Sorin Lerner, Vassily Litvinov, Vibha Sazawal, Todd Millstein, and Matthai Philipose for their comments and suggestions. We especially thank Craig Kaplan for his time and the Taprats program. This work was supported in part by NSF grant CCR-9970986, NSF Young Investigator Award CCR-945776, and gifts from Sun Microsystems and IBM.

References

[ACN02a] Jonathan Aldrich, Craig Chambers, and David Notkin. ArchJava: Connecting Software Architecture to Implementation. Proc. International Conference on Software Engineering, Orlando, Florida, May 2002.

[ACN02b] Jonathan Aldrich, Craig Chambers, and David Notkin. Architectural Reasoning in ArchJava. University of Washington Technical Report UW-CSE-02-04-01, available at http://www.archjava.org/, April 2002.

[AG97] Robert Allen and David Garlan. A Formal Basis for Architectural Connection. ACM Transactions on Software Engineering and Methodology, 6(3), July 1997.

[Arc02] ArchJava web site. http://www.archjava.org/

[AL02] Andrei Alexandrescu and Konrad Lorincz. ArchJava: An Evaluation. University of Washington CSE 503 class report, available at http://www.archjava.org/, February 2002.

[BS98] Boris Bokowski and André Spiegel. Barat—A Front-End for Java. Freie Universität Berlin Technical Report B-98-09, December 1998.

[FBB+99] Martin Fowler, Kent Beck, John Brant, William Opdyke, and Don Roberts. Refactoring: Improving the Design of Existing Code. Addison-Wesley, 1999.

[FF98] Matthew Flatt and Matthias Felleisen. Units: Cool modules for HOT languages. Proc. Programming Language Design and Implementation, Montreal, Canada, June 1998.

[GHJ+94] Erich Gamma, Richard Helm, Ralph Johnson and John Vlissides. Design Patterns: Elements of Reusable Object-Oriented Software. Addison-Wesley, 1994.

[GS93] David Garlan and Mary Shaw. An Introduction to Software Architecture. In Advances in Software Engineering and Knowledge Engineering, I (Ambriola V, Tortora G, Eds.) World Scientific Publishing Company, 1993.

[IPW99] Atsushi Igarashi, Benjamin Pierce, and Philip Wadler. Featherweight Java: A Minimal Core Calculus for Java and GJ. Proc. Object Oriented Programming Systems, Languages and Applications, Denver, Colorado, November 1999.

[Kap00] Craig S. Kaplan. Computer Generated Islamic Star Patterns. Proc. Bridges 2000: Mathematical Connections in Art, Music and Science, Winfield, Kansas, July 2000.

[LH89] Karl Lieberherr and Ian Holland. Assuring Good Style for Object-Oriented Programs. IEEE Software, Sept 1989.

[LV95] David C. Luckham and James Vera. An Event Based Architecture Definition Language. IEEE Trans. Software Engineering 21(9), September 1995.

[MFH01] Sean McDirmid, Matthew Flatt and Wilson C. Hsieh. Jiazzi: New-Age Components for Old-Fashioned Java. Proc. Object Oriented Programming Systems, Languages, and Applications, Tampa, Florida, October 2001.

[MK96] Jeff Magee and Jeff Kramer. Dynamic Structure in Software Architectures. Proc. Foundations of Software Engineering, San Francisco, California, October 1996.

[MNS01] Gail C. Murphy, David Notkin, and Kevin J. Sullivan. Software Reflexion Models: Bridging the Gap Between Design and Implementation. IEEE Trans. Software Engineering, 27(4), April 2001.

[MOR+96] Nenad Medvidovic, Peyman Oreizy, Jason E. Robbins, and Richard N. Taylor. Using Object-Oriented Typing to Support Architectural Design in the C2 Style. Proc. Foundations of Software Engineering, San Francisco, California, October 1996.

[MQR95] Mark Moriconi, Xiaolei Qian, and Robert A. Riemenschneider. Correct Architecture Refinement. IEEE Trans. Software Engineering, 21(4), April 1995.

[MT00] Nenad Medvidovic and Richard N. Taylor. A Classification and Comparison Framework for Software Architecture Description Languages. IEEE Trans. Software Engineering, 26(1), January 2000.

[MW99] Kim Mens and Roel Wuyts. Declaratively Codifying Software Architectures using Virtual Software Classifications. Proc. Technology of Object-Oriented Languages and Systems Europe, Nancy, France, June 1999.

[PN86] Ruben Prieto-Diaz and James Neighbors. Module Interconnection Languages. Journal of Systems and Software 6(4), April 1986.

[PW92] Dewayne E. Perry and Alexander L. Wolf. Foundations for the Study of Software Architecture. ACM SIGSOFT Software Engineering Notes, 17:40-52, October 1992.

[RN00] David S. Rosenblum and Rema Natarajan. Supporting Architectural Concerns in Component-Interoperability Standards. IEE Proceedings-Software 147(6), 2000.

[SC00] João C. Seco and Luís Caires. A Basic Model of Typed Components. Proc. European Conference on Object-Oriented Programming, Cannes, France 2000.

[SDK+95] Mary Shaw, Rob DeLine, Daniel V. Klein, Theodore L. Ross, David M. Young, and Gregory Zelesnik. Abstractions for Software Architecture and Tools to Support Them. IEEE Trans. Software Engineering, 21(4), April 1995.

[Sre02] Vugranam C. Sreedhar. Mixin' Up Components. Proc. International Conference on Software Engineering, Orlando, Florida, May 2002.

[SSW96] Robert W. Schwanke, Veronika A. Strack, and Thomas Werthmann-Auzinger. Industrial software architecture with Gestalt. Proc. International Workshop on Software Specification and Design, Paderborn, Germany, March 1996.

Patterns as Signs

James Noble and Robert Biddle

Computer Science
Victoria University of Wellington
New Zealand
kjx@mcs.vuw.ac.nz

Abstract. Object-oriented design patterns have been one of the most important and successful ideas in software design over the last ten years, and have been well adopted both in industry and academia. A number of open research problems remain regarding patterns, however, including the differences between patterns, variant forms of common patterns, the naming of patterns, the organisation of collections of patterns, and the relationships between patterns. We provide a semiotic account of design patterns, treating a pattern as a sign comprised of the programmers' intent and its realisation in the program. Considering patterns as signs can address many of these common questions regarding design patterns, to assist both programmers using patterns and authors writing them.

1 Introduction

An object-oriented design pattern is a "*description of communicating objects and classes that are customised to solve a general design problem in a particular context*" [44, p.3]. Designers can incorporate patterns into their program to address general problems in the structure of their programs' designs, in a similar way that algorithms or data structures are incorporated into programs to solve particular computational or storage problems. A growing body of literature catalogues patterns for object-oriented design, including reference texts such as *Design Patterns* [44] or *Pattern-Oriented Software Architecture* [17,70], and patterns compendia such as the *Pattern Languages of Program Design* series [28,78,57,48].

Unfortunately, there are a number of important open research problems regarding patterns. These include: what are the differences between outwardly similar patterns (such as Strategy and State); how can one pattern solve more than one problem (such as Proxy); have distinctly different variant forms (such as Adapter); how can several different patterns have the same name (such as Prototype); and how can the relationships between patterns best be characterised.

In this paper, we provide a semiotic account of design patterns. Semiotics is the study of signs in society, that investigates the way meaning is carried by communication, treating communication as an exchange of signs [35]. When semiotics began in the early years of the last century, most work was concerned with conventional signs — first speech, and then writing. Since then, the scope of semiotics has widened to cover all kinds of signs, to the point where semiotics underlies much of structuralist and post-structuralist literary theory, film studies, cultural studies, advertising, and even the

B. Magnusson (Ed.): ECOOP 2002, LNCS 2374, pp. 368–391, 2002.
© Springer-Verlag Berlin Heidelberg 2002

theory of popular music and studies of communications between animals (zoosemiotics) and within them (biosemiotics) [71]. One of the avowed values of the design patterns movement is to treat "patterns as literature" [51,24]; our semiotic approach builds on this idea by applying techniques from the study of literature and culture to programs and patterns.

This paper is organised as follows. Section 2 briefly reviews object-oriented design patterns and the major constituents of the pattern form, and section 3 provides a brief introduction to semiotics and the structure of signs. Next, section 4 presents our semiotic model of design patterns, and then section 5 addresses a number of open questions in the analysis of design patterns, showing how the semiotic approach can cast some light upon these problems. Section 6 discusses the ramifications of our approach more broadly, section 7 places this approach in the context of other work organising and theorising patterns, and other work on the semiotics of information processing, and finally, section 8 concludes the paper and draws out some possible future directions for a semiotic approach.

2   Object-Oriented Design Patterns

A pattern is an abstraction from a concrete recurring solution that solves a problem in a certain context [44,17]. Patterns were developed by an architect, Christopher Alexander [54], to describe techniques for town planning, architectural designs, and building construction techniques, and described in Alexander's *A Pattern Language* • *Towns, Buildings, Construction* [4,3,5]. Design patterns were first applied to software by Kent Beck and Ward Cunningham to describe user interface design techniques [14,51], and were then popularised by the *Design Patterns* catalogue, which described twenty-three patterns for general purpose object-oriented design. Since *Design Patterns'* publication, a large number of other patterns have been identified and published. More recently, different types of patterns have been identified, including Composite or Compound Patterns [63,77].

A design pattern is written in *pattern form*, that is, in one of a family of literary styles designed to make patterns easy to apply [23,58,66]. A design pattern has a name to facilitate communication about programs in terms of patterns, a description of the problems for which the pattern is applicable, an analysis of the *forces* (important concerns) addressed by the pattern, and the important considerations and consequences of using the pattern, a sample implementation of the pattern's solution, and references to known uses of the pattern and to other patterns to which it is related.

Moreso than other forms of writing about software, patterns are self-consciously *"literature"* about software. The patterns "PLoP" conference series, for example, has modelled itself on some parts of the creative writing community. At PLoP conferences, for example, papers are workshopped to improve their *expression* (as against than their *content*), rather than being presented to a passive audience [26]. The patterns movement catchphrase *"the aggressive disregard for innovation"*[1] again encapsulates this idea: the focus is on the literary expression of existing tested ideas, rather than the advocacy of new idiosyncrasies.

---

[1] Attributed to Thomas J. "Tad" Peckish by Brian Foote [41].

The patterns movement's focus on literature has partly inspired our interest in applying semiotics to patterns. Semiotics is the foundation of structuralist and post-structuralist literary theory, so if patterns are indeed literature, and a *critical* literature in particular, they should be amenable to study using the same tools as other forms of literature or culture.

3   Semiotics

Semiotics as defined by Saussure [32] is the study of signs in society; where a *sign* is *"something standing for something else"* [35]. Saussure was a linguist, so we will mostly use examples from language in this section, although semiotics has now been applied to a wide range of different kind of signs.

The key idea underlying semiotics is the *sign*, shown in Fig. 1.

Fig. 1. Saussure's Sign

A sign is a two-part relationship between a *signifier* and a *signified* — a computer scientist might write "sign = signifier + signified". The signifier (or *expression* of the sign) is some phenomenon that an individual can see, hear, sense, or imagine; and the signified (or *content*) is the mental concept that the signifier produces. For example, consider the English colour name purple as a sign. The spoken or written word "purple" is the signifier while the resulting concept of the colour purple is the signified[2].

One important principle from Saussure is the *"arbitrariness of the sign"*, that is, that the relationship between signifier and signified can be an arbitrary one. There is no compelling reason why the colour red should be associated with the signifier (name) "red" rather than the signifier "yellow" or signifier "blue". Yellow, for example, could be just as well be expressed by "jaune" or "gelb" or "glonko", provided all participants in the communication knew that this was the signifier for yellow.

The arbitrariness of signs is compounded because signifiers and signifieds are not defined absolutely: rather they are only distinguishable relatively by *difference* from each other. Saussure defines a value (such as a five franc piece) as something which can be *exchanged* for something *different* (a loaf of bread) or *compared* with something *similar* (a ten franc piece). In this way, a signifier may be compared with another signifier, or a signified with a signified, or a signifier may be exchanged with a signified when taken as a sign.

In spoken English, for example, there are no absolute definitions of the way the signifiers "rid", "red", and "reed" should be pronounced: the pronunciations blend into

---

[2] Following Charles Peirce, American semiotics takes a sign as a three-part relationship, including an *object* or *referent*, as well as the signifier (called a *representamen*) and signified (*interpretant*). We use Saussure's binary sign in this paper as it suffices for our analysis [35].

one another and what is "red" pronounced with one accent may be "rid" with another. Other spoken languages function in this way. Furthermore, any utterance (*token* is the semiotic term) of a given word will differ slightly from any other utterance, even from the same speaker, although all will be understood as the same word (or *type*). This is also true for signifieds: the colours pink, red, and brown, for example, differ according to their saturation, but we can't say for sure where pink ends and red begins — or rather, such definitions are relative and arbitrary. Another affect of the arbitrariness of signs is that signifiers and signifieds are not uniquely related: signs are individual, rather than their component parts. So in spoken English for example, the same signifier is part of the sign for the colour red and the past tense of verb "to read", and some particular instance of the colour red could also be spoken of by words such as "maroon", "crimson", or even "orange" or "brown".

Signs carry meaning in communication because the participants understand the structures of the signs that make up the messages exchanged between them — that is, the relations of difference between signifiers and between signifieds. Saussure introduces the term *langue* to signify the entire underlying abstract structure of a system of signs — a repertoire of possibilities (or differences) from which a language community can construct messages. Every participant in a communication tacitly shares the same *langue*. In contrast to the overarching langue, the speech acts or sign instances making up a particular communication (the subset of the langue actually used in any given message) is termed the *parole*. A *text* — a given instance of *parole* — a single utterance, a sentence, a conference paper — will be made up of a series of signs taken from the *langue*, according to the rules by which it operates: the meaning of the whole message is produced by the interdependencies between the meanings of the individual signs.

This section has provided only a brief introduction to semiotics, which is capable of much more complex and subtle analyses than those we have presented here [35,7,18]. We have kept this presentation to the minimum necessary to support our account of design patterns. For similar reasons, most of our examples of object-oriented patterns are taken from Gamma et. al.'s *Design Patterns* [44] because this is the best known collection of patterns, although our approach is applicable to other kinds of patterns.

4   Patterns as Signs

In the classic definition, a pattern is a *"solution to a problem in a context"* [54,49]. A object-oriented design pattern, for example, is a description of a piece of knowledge about object-oriented programming or design phrased as a solution to a problem; an architectural pattern (as in *A Pattern Language* [3]) is a description of a piece of knowledge about architectural design. We call the descriptive part of a pattern a *pattern-description*. Patterns have a secondary function (emphasised more by *Design Patterns* than Alexander) of providing a working vocabulary with which designers can communicate. This section begins by modelling pattern descriptions as signs, and then considers how those pattern descriptions are named.

4.1   Pattern Descriptions

The *solution* is the core of a pattern description. An average pattern in *Design Patterns* is about ten pages long, and eight of these pages are taken up with a description of the solution of the pattern. This description is quite concrete: it is both graphical (using class and sequence diagrams) and textual (with descriptions of participants in the pattern, possible implementations, annotated example source code, and descriptions of known uses). In a program which uses the pattern, the elements corresponding to the pattern's solution can literally be pointed to in a listing of the programs source code or on a diagram showing the program's classes — a pattern describes a *type* of solution, and a particular solution embodied in a program is a *token* of that type.

A similarly concrete solution is also at the core of each of Alexander's architectural patterns: the elements of the pattern's solution can literally be touched inside a building that incorporates the pattern, or pointed out on the building's plan. Alexander insists that each pattern should be accompanied by a sketch, diagram, or photograph, presumably to ensure the pattern describes a concrete solution.

Note that although the description of a pattern's solution must be concrete, capable of being incorporated into a program or building, this incorporation is not necessarily straightforward — just as the same person can never pronounce the same word twice exactly the same way, a pattern will never be incorporated into a program twice in the same way. The names used in a design pattern description can be changed in the actual program, for example, or the dimensions of architectural features altered to suit the building being built.

The other main parts of a pattern, the problem, context, discussion of forces and so on, are much more abstract than the concrete solution. The problem and context are tightly interrelated in that they present a qualitative analysis of the solution, and should comprise a convincing argument that the solution proposed by the pattern does in fact resolve the problem. The problem statement is typically a brief and pithy statement of the problem the pattern sets out to solve, while the context can be an extended description of a general area or kind of design, and may enumerate important issues (forces) to be resolved, or discuss why obvious or naive candidate solutions would not solve the problem satisfactorily.

When reading a program or wandering around a building, we can see the concrete features of patterns: however, we understand those patterns as being more than just their concrete features. For example, when we see a door under a set of stairs on the ground floor, we don't just think *"Oh, there's a door under the stairs on the ground floor"*. Rather, we think *"Oh, there's a **Cupboard Under The Stairs**"* — where CUPBOARD UNDER THE STAIRS [68] is one of Alexander's patterns and we have recognised a particular token of that general type.

In the same way, when a programmer sees a class diagram sketched in a notebook or on a whiteboard (such as Fig. 2) or when they read a program's source code, they can see only the concrete structure —- an inheritance hierarchy where a subclass has a one-to-many relationship back to its own superclass.

If the programmer understands patterns well, they could recognise this diagram as an application of the Composite pattern, and thus bring their knowledge of that pattern to bear without having to work it out from first principles — so, for example, they will immediately appreciate that:

- The program implements a recursive tree structure of Quote objects.
- A single quote or tree of quotes can be accessed uniformly via the common Quote interface.

Fig. 2. A sketch of a class diagram for part of a sales quotation system.

- Whenever client code expects a Quote object, a CompositeQuote can be supplied instead.
- Client code is simplified, as it doesn't need to know whether it is dealing with primitive or composite Quotes.
- New kinds of Quotes can be added easily.
- Leaf nodes in the recursive composite all inherit from the SimpleQuote class
- Similar designs have been used in Interviews, ET++, Smalltalk, and many other systems since [44].

Both of these examples, recognising the cupboard under the stairs and recognising the Composite pattern, involve signs. In each case, we see concrete features (signifiers such as doors, handles, classes, relationships) and then imagine abstract concepts (signifieds such as cupboards and Composite patterns) to make sense of those concrete features.

This, then, leads us to the key point of this paper:

> **A pattern-description** *is a sign, where the* **signifier** *is the pattern's solution and the* **signified** *is the pattern's* **intent***, that is, its problem, context, known uses, and rationale.*

The structure of this sign is illustrated in Fig. 3.

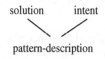

Fig. 3. A pattern description as a sign.

Reading a program (or "reading" a building) is an example of semiosis, of sign exchange, in this case, producing meaning by exchanging the concrete signifiers for the abstract signifieds. Writing a program using patterns is also a process of sign exchange, producing a text of signifiers which are the concrete parts of the signs whose signifieds capture the meanings we need to embed into the program. Technically, patterns describe general *types* of problems and solutions; in reading or writing patterns we apprehend particular *tokens* of these *types*.

Patterns are not the *only* signs in a program: the lexical elements of a programming language can be considered as signs, as can algorithms, data structures, idioms, programming styles, and so on. We cannot construct the meaning of a whole program by considering each sign in isolation (as we have been doing here for the sake of a simple presentation): the meaning of a program (or a building or a novel or a movie) is produced by the combination of a large range of signs, where any particular sign's meaning can be influenced and altered by its context, and by other signs in the text — for a simple example the signifier ! in a Boolean expression in a C++ program forms a sign which negates signs in its subexpression.

4.2 A Discourse of Patterns

Representing pieces of knowledge about programming is not the only function of patterns. Patterns exist within a social context, where they provide a shared language with a common vocabulary that programmers can use to talk about design [54,44,23,58]. Were a team of programmers working on the quotation system shown in Fig. 2, they would not just talk about the advantages of the pattern-based design versus other alternatives. Rather, every pattern has a *name* that programmers can use to refer to it: by saying "we could use Composite here", for example, one programmer can communicate all the essential details of the design in Fig. 2 — both the basic shape of the final implementation and the underlying abstract intent, rationale, design tradeoffs that are part of the pattern.

This is another instance of semiosis — a word in a language signifying an abstract concept. In this case, the language is the human language spoken by the programmers, and the abstract concept is the pattern, that is, both the abstract concept of the pattern and a description of the concrete implementation. A pattern name is the signifier of a second sign of which the pattern-description is the signified.

This gives the second key point of this paper:

> *A* **pattern** *is a* **sign,** *where the* **signifier** *is the* **pattern's** **name** *and the* **signified** *is the* **pattern-description.**

The resulting second-order semiotic system is shown in Fig. 4. This is a second-order system because it is composed of two signs, in such a way that one sign is a component of the other. It is a *denotative* system because the second-order sign names the first-order sign[3] [18].

---

[3] This is in contrast to many other semiotic systems, where a (denotative) first-order sign is the signifier of a (connotative) second-order sign. Here the first-order sign is the signified, so the second-order sign is denotative; we briefly address connotative (third-order) signification in patterns in section 6.3.

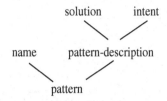

Fig. 4. A pattern as a second-order sign

The second-order sign can also be "read" to produce meaning — when a pattern name is written or spoken, a reader or listener can construct the pattern-description as the meaning of that signifier; similarly, a pattern latent in a program can be named by the signified. This is a second order process because, say, reading a program for patterns involves two stages of semiosis: first, the concrete implementation is exchanged for the pattern's abstract intent, and second, this sign as a whole is exchanged for the name of the whole pattern. Similarly, hearing a pattern name as part of a conversation also invokes a two-stage process to construct its meaning: first, the pattern name must be exchanged for the first (pattern-description) sign, then the signified of that sign can be exchanged for the intent.

5   Questions about Patterns

The are a number of quite basic open questions regarding design patterns. Some of these questions are posed by novices to patterns, perhaps during their first reading of *Design Patterns*: other questions are more subtle, and arise only after more considered study, or experience attempting to write patterns.

In this section we show how a number of these questions can be addressed using our semiotic approach — beginning with questions of pattern descriptions, then pattern names, and finally considering the relationships between patterns.

In the spirit of the patterns movement, our proposed *answers* to these questions are not necessarily novel. The contribution of this paper is in the semiotic explanation of the answers to these questions.

5.1   Questions of Pattern Descriptions

We begin by considering questions relating to patterns' intents and designs — that is, questions of pattern-descriptions.

How can two patterns have the same implementation?   One common question asked about patterns is "What's the difference between the Strategy and State patterns?" Both these patterns have almost identical structure diagrams, that is, solutions — Fig. 5 shows the two structure diagrams from *Design Patterns*. How, then, can they be different patterns? Would we not be better of with a single pattern encompassing both State and Strategy? [1].

In terms of our semiotic approach to patterns, we can see this question as symptomatic of a misunderstanding about the nature of patterns: confusing signifiers and signs. One

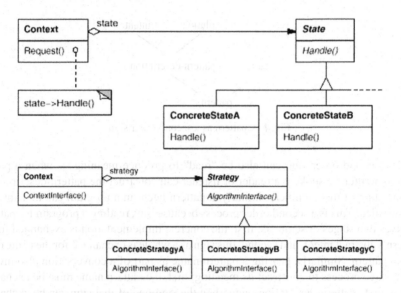

Fig. 5. *Design Patterns* State and Strategy pattern structure diagrams [44].

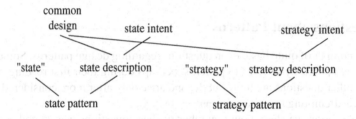

Fig. 6. State and Strategy Patterns

signifier can form more than one sign, just as the English pronunciation "red" can signify both the colour red and the past tense of the verb "to read". In the same way, a pattern description is a sign, not just a signifier, so the same signifier (the same implementation) can form part of more than one pattern description. In other words, a pattern is a solution to a problem, not just a solution. Fig. 6 shows the semiotic structure of these two patterns, each sharing a solution but with different intents and names.

How can one pattern have more than one implementation? Sometimes the text of a pattern describes more than one implementation. For example, the Adaptor pattern describes four separate kinds of Adaptors — Class Adaptors that use (multiple) inheritance, Object Adaptors that use delegation, Two-Way Adaptors that again use multiple inheritance, and Pluggable Adaptors where adaption is built in to the adaptee classes. Each of these implementations have different advantages and disadvantages that are discussed in the consequences and implementation sections of the pattern.

In terms of our semiotic model, we can see that each of these variants is effectively a different pattern-description (the first-order sign) — a different abstract concept (signified) with different consequences and tradeoffs, and obviously with a different design (signifier) — with, presumably, the same name at the second-order sign. This is not a problem *per se*, as multiple signs with the same signifiers are common in sign systems: a sign is not just a signified, but a relationship between signified and signifier. Technically, a signifier forming multiple signs is called *polysemy* [18]; the semiotic approach at least lets us analyse this cleanly (see Fig. 7).

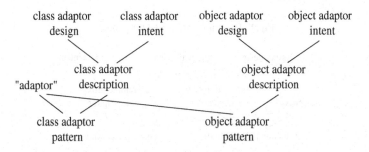

Fig. 7. Polysemy in the Adaptor pattern

In terms of the language used to communicate about patterns this causes certain practical difficulties: each of these different designs leads to a different sign (a different pattern) with the same name. These names can be disambiguated as necessary by other components of the message of which the polysemic signifier forms part, or by negotiation (*"Do you mean a Class Adaptor or an Object Adaptor?"*) [36]. A closer analysis shows that the text *Design Patterns* does this in practice, explicitly introducing extra disambiguating signs as we have done in this discussion. *Design Patterns* introduces particular names for the more radical variants: in the text, the phrases "pluggable adaptor" and "two-way adaptor" are printed in boldface, which is a sign that these phrases are important.

This gives an alternative interpretation in our model, where each adaptor variant is again a separate sign, but where the second-order signs differ not only in their signified but also their signifiers. In conventional pattern terminology, this can be expressed as each variant design giving rise to a separate "first class" pattern, each with its own name: Class Adaptor, Object Adaptor, Two-Way Adaptor, Pluggable Adaptor (Fig. 8 shows the first two patterns).

How can one pattern solve two or more problems? Complementing those patterns which have multiple solutions, some patterns are described as solving multiple problems with a single design. The best example here is the Proxy pattern: the *Design Patterns* Proxy is presented as solving four different problems (protection, loading on-demand, remote access, pointer dereference), while *Pattern-Oriented Software Architecture* describes seven different problems which can be solved by the proxy pattern.

In terms of our semiotic model, this means that each pattern-description will be a different (first order) sign with the same signifier (the same design) but different signified,

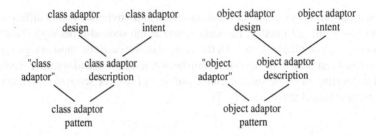

Fig. 8. Disambiguated Adaptor patterns

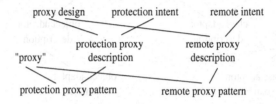

Fig. 9. Multipurpose patterns

because the purpose of the pattern is part of its signified. In terms of the second order sign, often all these patterns have the same name (Fig. 9).

This is similar to the situation described above where one pattern has multiple designs, except here the fundamental difference between each pattern is in the intent (first order signified), rather than the design (first order signifier): the pattern name (second order signifier) is again polysemic. If each separate problem is in fact a separate sign, then each separate problem gives rise to a separate pattern: this would certainly follow naively from a pattern being defined as *"a solution to a problem in a context"*: here, although the solutions (and names) may be the same, the problems are certainly different.

Again, both *Design Patterns* and *Pattern-Oriented Software Architecture* tend towards resolving the ambiguity of the pattern names by introducing more specialised names for each particular problem. Thus there are Protection Proxies, Virtual Proxies, Remote Proxies, and so on, where each different pattern has a different name.

5.2   Questions of Pattern Names

As well as questions primarily related to pattern descriptions, there are also a number of questions relating to pattern names.

How can one pattern have more than one name? Every pattern form ensures that each pattern has a name. Most large-scale pattern forms, however, allow a number of alternative names — synonyms for each pattern. In terms of the semiotic model, we must treat each as a separate second-order sign because the signifiers (names) are different, even though the first-order signs are the same. Fig. 10 illustrates this for Decorator and its synonym Wrapper.

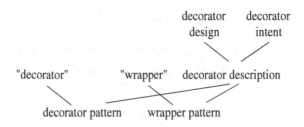

Fig. 10. Patterns with synonyms

What is interesting here is the way that names evolve to reflect different shades of meaning: treating each name as producing a separate (second-order) sign allows us to consider this evolution explicitly. For example, part of what it has meant for the *Design Patterns* book to become widely accepted is that the pattern names it proposes have themselves become the canonical names for the pattern-descriptions in the book, and almost all of the alternative names (even those proposed in *Design Patterns*) have fallen out of use. So, for example the alternative name "Kit" for "Abstract Factory" is no longer used; "Bridge" has replaced "Handle/Body" (although "Handle/Body is arguably a more descriptive name for the pattern);"Factory Method" has replaced "Virtual Constructor"; "Iterator" has replaced "Cursor", and so on.

One case where this has not happened has been with the name "Wrapper". *Design Patterns* gives both the Adapter and Decorator patterns the synonym "Wrapper"; however the name "Wrapper" is still in general use both for Adapters, Decorators, and also for Proxies. All these patterns are quite closely related; in particular, their implementations can be identical in many cases. The pattern-name Wrapper may be acting as a signifier for a more basic pattern describing the solution, where the intent is simply to "wrap" another object for whatever reason, and the other patterns — Adaptor, Decorator, and Proxy — could be (special kinds of) Wrappers used to solve more specific problems.

How can many different pattern-descriptions share the same name? The complementary problem to one pattern having many different names is where one name is used for many different patterns[4]. For example, in the *Patterns Almanac* [67] there are a number of patterns with the name "Prototype" — the Prototype pattern from *Design Patterns*; Prototype from Coplien's *Generative Development-Process Pattern Language* [22]; a similar pattern from Cockburn's *Surviving Object-Oriented Projects* [20]: the almanac also lists at least three other patterns named as some variation on "Prototype", and no doubt more have been published subsequently. Similarly, a recent J2EE textbook [30] includes a pattern named "Value Object" which is quite different from existing patterns called "Value Object" [42,52].

In the patterns community, control of pattern names is an important issue, and a significant part of a crucial problem: how to index and identify patterns. The *Patterns Almanac* [67] is the most successful attempt at building such an index so far, but it suffers from many duplicate named patterns. Some of these duplicates may be almost unrelated ("Prototype-Based Object System" and "Prototype And Reality") while others may be

---

[4] This problem was identified by Linda Rising.

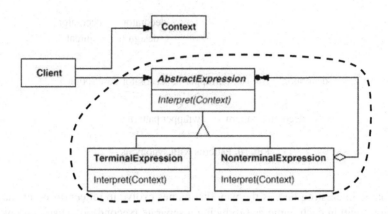

Fig. 11. *Design Patterns* Interpreter structure showing Composite substructure [44]

very closely related, as in Coplien and Cockburn's Prototype pattern. Furthermore, a single "pattern" can be described in a number of different versions — very similar Proxy patterns have been published in both *Design Patterns* and *Pattern-Oriented Software Architecture*.

In terms of the semiotic approach, we can see this as each pattern being a separate sign; however, the two second order signs each share the same signifier (the same structure as Fig. 7) — in much the same way the spoken English word "red" can form part of two signs. In general conversation, we can distinguish the intended pattern according to context — disambiguating via other signifiers in the message containing the term "prototype" and explicit bibliographic references if necessary. Rather than attempting to privilege one final "best" description, the semiotic approach can facilitate negotiation and discussion, highlighting relationships and differences between several patterns.

5.3 Relationships between Patterns

Semiotics, being fundamentally concerned with the difference between signifiers, signifieds, and signs, can also help define the relationships between patterns [81,58,60]. Some pairs of patterns will fundamentally be different: that is, both their signifier (design) and signified (intent) will be mutually unrelated. More interesting cases arise when one (or both) of the parts of a pattern are *similar*, yet the pattern-descriptions as a whole differ.

Uses. The primary relationship between patterns is that one pattern may use another pattern in its implementation. "Uses" is also known by longer names, including "requires", "completes", or "follows", (although "follows" can also mean that one pattern is printed after another pattern in an Alexandrian pattern language). The key to this relationship is that you must apply one pattern as part of applying the other pattern — for this reason, the larger pattern is often called a *compound* pattern [63,77].

The classic example from *Design Patterns* is the relationship between Composite and Interpreter: as part of applying the Interpreter pattern, you must apply the Composite pattern to represent the language being interpreted (Fig. 11).

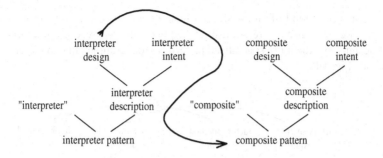

Fig. 12. Composite and Interpreter Patterns

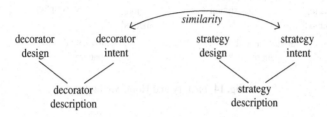

Fig. 13. Decorator and Strategy Patterns

In our semiotic approach, we recognise this relationship where two patterns have a different intent (Composite models recursive structures, Interpreter interprets a language), but where the implementation of the larger pattern is related to the pattern it uses, as Interpreter's implementation is related to the whole Composite pattern; see Fig. 12.

Alternative. A second relationship between patterns is that two patterns can be alternatives, that is, they provide different implementations to address (some of) the same problems. *Design Patterns*, for example, discusses how Decorator and Strategy provide alternative designs to address problems of adding and changing responsibilities of objects, possibly dynamically. A Decorator changes the "skin" of an object, changing it from the outside by adding a transparent wrapper, while a Strategy changes the "guts" of an object, possibility requiring the object to be changed to be aware of the extension [44, p. 180]. Both Strategy and Decorator are applicable to a wide range of common problems, such as adding graphical decorations (title bars, close buttons) to windows, or adjusting event-handling behaviour, but both clearly present different designs and have some different consequences.

In our semiotic approach, we recognise this relationship where two patterns have a similar intent (both Decorator and Strategy allow programmers to change objects), but where the designs that support these intents are different (Figure 13).

Specialisation. The third primary relationship between patterns is that one pattern can be a specialisation of another (conversely, the second pattern can be a generalisation of the first). *Design Patterns* again provides several examples, for example, a Factory

Method is a special kind of Hook Method that creates objects. In our semiotic model of patterns, we recognise this relationship when two patterns present similar intents and similar designs, but the more specialised pattern is more complex than the more general pattern (see Fig. 14).

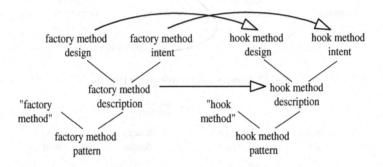

Fig. 14. Factory and Hook Methods

For example, considering intent, both Factory Method and Hook Method allow subclasses to modify behaviour defined in their superclasses (similar intent), however Factory Methods modify this behaviour to change the type of object created (changing a particular kind of behaviour). Considering implementation, both Factory Method and Hook Method are typically implemented by specially-named abstract (C++ pure virtual) methods that must be redefined in subclasses, however a Factory Method must return an object which is in some sense "new", whereas the behaviour of a Hook Method (qua Hook Method) is undefined.

Figure 14 shows how specialisation occurs primarily between first-order signs. Especially after disambiguating variants, the names of a specialised pattern may be related to a more general pattern (a "Protection Proxy" is a special kind of "Proxy") so there may also be a specialisation relationship in the second-order sign.

6 Discussion

In this section we discuss further aspects of the semiotics of patterns and outline some future directions for this work.

6.1 Misinterpreting Patterns

One of the biggest challenges in documenting patterns is to avoid their misinterpretation[5] — that is, that someone reading a description of a pattern will not understand (or understand imperfectly) the solution and the intent of the pattern being described. When reading a program (or inspecting a building), we can similarly misunderstand the

---

[5] This observation is due to Frank Buschmann.

patterns we find — the "cupboard" under the stairs is really a staircase to the basement office, the door we expect to push must be pulled, and the code we think is the Observer pattern is actually using Mediator, or is just a random bad design, and so on.

Our semiotic approach encompasses misinterpretation by making the possibility explicit. While signifiers, by their nature, are concrete, tangible, and therefore public, signifieds are abstract, intangible, and private mental concepts — when reading a program or exploring a building, each of us alone constructs signifieds of any signs we encounter. Due to this, it is perfectly possible to produce an "incorrect" mental image of a signified for which a given signifier stands.

For example, upon reading some code or seeing a messy sketch like Fig. 2, we could misinterpret the design as supporting the Decorator pattern (by missing the scribbled asterisk for the many-to-one relationship); the Proxy pattern (by a more general confusion); or even as the Prototype pattern (through ignorance, through weakness, or through our own deliberate fault).

Semiotics makes clear that these kinds of misunderstandings can happen whenever you use signs, so it should not be surprising that such misunderstandings arise with patterns. Eco [35] describes semiotics as "the theory of the lie" precisely because these misunderstandings are possible: we may construct a different signified to that intended by the author of the signifier (especially when signifiers are polysemic); an incorrect signifier can be maliciously presented or chosen in error; we could accidently interpret something as a signifier when it is merely decoration; and so on.

In practice, Eco argues, we negotiate to clarify communication, repeatedly exchanging our private concepts and eventually converging on an agreed shared public "meaning" [36] — "red" means red (or "observer" means Observer) because the speakers of the language tacitly agree on this sign. In programming language design, attention has been recently called to the need for secondary notation, such as comments, even in novel visual forms for programming [61]. In the patterns community, the shepherding and workshopping of patterns at PLoP conferences provides an explicit forum for these negotiations, and thus helps to manage misinterpretation of patterns [26].

6.2 Patterns and Pattern Languages

Alexander's architectural patterns are contained within a larger structure of patterns known as a *pattern language* [4,3] — a tree or directed graph of patterns, similar in structure to a formal grammar. Each individual pattern provides a single solution to a single problem, and then, like a production rule in a grammar, uses (*leads to* or *contains*) other patterns which address subproblems raised by that solution. The language begins with an *initial pattern* (like a grammar's start symbol) addressing a large scale problem — how to organise all of human habitation — of which all the other patterns transitively form subparts. The key advantage Alexander claims for this structure is that it guides the reader through the process of design: beginning at the initial pattern, *A Pattern Language* provides complete instructions from large scale town planning down to decorating the edges of windowsills [3].

This is a fundamentally different structure from that used in "catalogues" or "systems" of patterns such as *Design Patterns* or *Pattern-Oriented Software Architecture*, which are primarily collections of individual patterns. This difference gives rise to questions such as *"How can a collection of patterns be transformed into an Alexander-style pattern language?"*[6].

Given the structural differences between a pattern collection and a pattern language, converting a collection into a language would require a major refactoring of the collection [70]. To ensure one pattern relates one problem to one solution, we would need to "normalise" the patterns — ensuring each pattern describes a single solution to single problem, splitting problem variants (like the multiple uses of Proxy) and solution variants (like the multiple designs for Adaptor) into separate smaller patterns. Then, many more patterns would have to be written to meet the structural constraints of a pattern language: the *Design Patterns*, say, are nowhere near a complete prescription for producing whole programs, as there is no initial pattern (presumably describing how to build any kind of system) of which all the other patterns eventually form subparts.

The semiotic approach offers an alternative organisation for collections of patterns. While grammars are useful for describing which sentences are correct, they do not describe the semantics of those sentences: rather, dictionaries and encyclopædia describe the vocabulary of languages in terms of the semantics of signs and the relationships between them [19,35,36]. Indeed, most pattern books are structured this way, to a greater or lesser extent (*Design Patterns* even describes itself as an "encyclopedia" (sic) [44, p.357]) . Compared with a pattern language, an encyclopædia admits a richer description of the relationships between patterns, with not just the uses relationship, but also alternative, specialisation, and arguably many secondary relationships as well [60].

An encyclopædia can be very similar to a pattern language in places. Where one compound pattern uses another pattern (as with Composite and Interpreter in section 5.3) a structure like a pattern language is created in a localised part of the pattern collection, as and when it makes sense. Unlike a pattern language, this structure does not have to encompass the whole encyclopædia, so a pattern author is not required to provide an initial pattern describing a single large-scale problem, to ensure all patterns are subparts of the initial pattern, or to omit patterns that do not fit.

Our semiotic approach allows us to describe a common vocabulary of patterns that evolves over time, facilitated by negotiation involving its users, and so allowing an evolutionary, rather than prescriptive, form of progress. New patterns can be added to the vocabulary (or old patterns removed) without affecting its underlying structure, in the same way that entries can be added or removed from a encyclopædia without affecting the integrity of the encyclopædia. Several later patterns (such as Null Object [79], Value Object [52,12,42], and Role Object [13]) have effectively been added to the vocabulary originated by *Design Patterns* while some (such as Builder or Interpreter) have almost fallen out of common use.

6.3   A More Detailed Semiotics of Patterns

The two-level semiotics we have presented (Fig. 4) is sufficient to address questions of the structures, names, and relationships between object-oriented design patterns, and also applies to other kind of patterns — we chose examples from *Design Patterns* simply because it is the best known software patterns collection. We plan to analyse the semiotic

---

[6] This question was posted to the design patterns mailing list by Mark Ratjens on 2 July 2001.

structure of object-oriented designs and design patterns in more detail. For example, patterns' designs are partially presented using *class diagrams* (amongst other diagrams and notations); these diagrams are themselves signs, relating a *graphical design* (signifier) to some *class structure* (signified).

We can also consider the pattern itself as participating in further semiosis — patterns are actually written up as book chapters or web pages, so we can consider a *pattern-writeup* as a sign, where the *text of the pattern* from the book is the signifier and a *pattern* is the signified. The discussion of a pattern within a social context illustrates another way a pattern can be treated as a sign: when a pattern is discussed it raises other connotations in participants in the conversation ("Observer? that's always too slow!").

Finally, patterns are not alone as forms of knowledge about programming. Although we have not yet considered them in depth, data structures and algorithms have a very similar semiotic structure to that we have described for patterns in this paper: an algorithm is a named description of a concrete signifier (typically code or pseudocode) together with the analysis of the algorithm as its signified. Idioms and style rules, architectures, idioms, and cliches may all be amenable to description within this kind of semiotic framework.

7   Related Work

On patterns and the patterns community. Since the publication of *Design Patterns* [44], patterns have become an accepted part of the literature of software engineering. A number of other large-scale patterns texts have been published, some deriving directly from *Design Patterns*, others describing new patterns for the technical design of systems, and still others describing patterns for methodologies or development processes. Yet more individual patterns, or small collections of related patterns have been published in the *Pattern Languages of Program Design* book series [28,78,48,57] or have been presented at various patterns conferences.

Probably the most important documents shaping and recording the development of the patterns "community" are Coplien's *Software Patterns* [23] and *Pattern Language for Writer's Workshops* [26]; Meszaros and Doble's *Pattern Language for Pattern Writing* [58] (which neatly sidesteps social restrictions on patterns criticism by employing the pattern form to that end); and the virtual records on the WikiWikiWeb [31]. Gabriel's *Patterns of Software* [43] and Lea's *Christopher Alexander: An Introduction* [54] also provide exegeses of Alexander, including an introduction to some of his more recent theorising [11]. In as much as any theory of patterns is presented in these works, it follows Alexander explicitly — the patterns conferences are named "*Pattern Languages of Programming*" (our emphasis) for just this reason.

On analysis of relationships between patterns. Given this flood of primary material there has been surprisingly little analysis of patterns — partly due to an explicit value of the patterns movement to eschew reflexion in favour of action [21]. Zimmer provided some early analysis on the relationships between patterns latent within *Design Patterns* [81]. Many authors of patterns collections proceeded to develop individual schemes of pattern relationships: we have surveyed many of these in previous work [60]. These schemes are generally either based upon Alexander-style pattern languages, or are variations of the relationships we analyse in section 5.3.

Although there have been no complete attempts at restructuring *Design Patterns*, Schmidt et. al. [70, p.509] and Coplien [25] have attempted to convert smaller collections of patterns into pattern languages, and Dyson and Anderson have converted the State pattern into a fragment of a pattern language [33].

A more original (and less Alexandrian) analysis of design patterns are the compound (or composite) patterns investigated by Riehle and Vlissides [63,77]. Riehle shows how complex patterns such as Bureaucracy [65] can be composed from simpler patterns using a role analysis similar to OORAM [62] — essentially the "uses" relationship between patterns. This role analysis also formed the theoretical basis of a catalogue of patterns [64]. Compared to our work, the role analysis gives more insight into the solutions provided by more complex patterns, but does not address the intents or names of patterns, and is not situated with any conceptual framework.

Tichy produced an early classification of many of the patterns from *Design Patterns* and *Pattern-Oriented Software Architecture* [75]. More recently the *Patterns Almanac* [67] catalogues many patterns published in book form. The classifications underlying these catalogues are generally coarse-grained, and designed to help programmers rather than being based on an underlying theory.

Agerbow and Cornlis [1] analysed the *Design Patterns* to determine how many patterns were artifacts of programming language, that is, given a sufficiently powerful language how many patterns could be expressed using language features directly, and Gil and Lorenz have developed a similar taxonomy [45]. Coplien and Zhao recently analysed the interactions between patterns and programming languages, in particular where programming language features are not orthogonal ("asymmetrical" in their terminology) [29,27], and have analysed this using group theory [80]. Meanwhile, a separate branch of research has focused on applying theory from functional programming to patterns, often focusing on the recursive combination of patterns such as Visitor, [52,55,76]. While this work may explain many of the subtleties of implementations of individual patterns, it does not address programmers' use of patterns to produce and communicate designs, that is, the semiotic aspects of patterns.

On pattern tools and formalisms. Rather than analyse patterns per se, some work on describing, categorising or recognising patterns has been carried out in order to build tools that support patterns or formalisms that describe them. The earliest work here involved systems that generated code for particular patterns [15,73]; more recently some support for patterns has been incorporated into experimental CASE tools or programming environments [37,40,56,16]. Several design notations for patterns have also been proposed — the UML standard now supports patterns by way of parameterised collaborations [69] and a number of more powerful visual techniques have been developed [53,74]. While several of these systems are useful in practice, in terms of underlying theories of patterns this work has often been completely ad-hoc (e.g. generating whatever code seemed to be required at the time) or has generalised constructs from object-oriented design to represent patterns. The catch is that such approaches miss much of the articulation revealed by our semiotic model: subtleties such as the way the same implementation could support either the Strategy or Decorator pattern, or the multiple implementations of the Adaptor pattern, cannot be captured by these approaches.

Formalisms (generally based upon logic rather than grammars or semiotics) have also been employed to describe patterns. LePUS, for example, describes patterns in the context of a multi-level object model framework [38]; other work has used a variety of formal models to capture designs and patterns (e.g. [59]). Again, inasmuch as this work is based on any underlying rationale, they are extensions of concepts drawn from object-oriented design, or naively justified as obviously correct for patterns.

Pattern-Lint performs static and dynamic analyses of programs to check that they comply with higher level models [72], ArchJava can similarly relate a program's structure to its implementation [2], and Jacobsen, Nowack, and Kristensen have applied conceptual modelling to software artifacts and development processes [50]. Although this work is not strictly related to patterns, nor explicitly semiotic, it does take account of the "possibility of lie" [35], that is, it accepts that a design not the same thing as a program, but a (possibly incorrect) signifier.

On semiotics. Although semiotics has adapted to study many areas of cultural practice from high culture to comics, there has been surprisingly little work in the direct application of semiotics to computer science. Peter Bøgh Andersen has completed the most work in this area, establishing a sub-field of Computer Semiotics focusing on human-computer interaction and the programming required to support user interfaces and pervasive computing, but also addressing a broader background [7,9,8,10]. Andersen also argued for a semiotic approach to information systems, rather than relying solely upon generative grammars or logic [6]. Gougen has established Algebraic Semiotics, also primarily concerned with user interface design [47] and design notations [46], focusing on formal systems.

Regarding semiotics more generally, *Semiotics for Beginners* is quite approachable (with many pictures!) [19] and a variety of readers and companions are often intelligible even to readers with technical backgrounds [34,39,18]. The semiotics used in this paper is a very small part of that proposed by Eco [35].

8 Conclusion

In this paper, we have described how object-oriented design patterns can be analysed as signs. A pattern-description is a sign where a pattern's solution is the signifier and the intent is the signified. Then, a pattern is a second order sign where a name is a signifier and a pattern-description is the signified.

Treating patterns as signs provides us with an analytic framework that is based on semiotics, rather than logic, mathematics, mysticism, or a metaphor without a name. Using this framework, we have addressed a number of common questions about patterns — explicating patterns that propose similar designs or have similar intents, that have many names or share names, and clarifying the relationships between patterns. Semiotics also allows us to analyse misinterpretations of patterns, and the role of patterns in creating an evolving common vocabulary of program design.

We hope that this framework can provide a platform for future progress in the research and application of design patterns.

Acknowlegements

Thanks to Frank Buschmann, Mary Lynn Manns, Palle Nowack, and Ewan Tempero for their comments on various drafts, to Charles Weir for being around as many of these ideas germinated, and to the anonymous reviewers for their encyclopædic comments.

References

1. Ellen Agerbo and Aino Cornils. How to preserve the benefits of design patterns. In *OOPSLA Proceedings*, pages 134–143. ACM, 1998.
2. Jonathan Aldrich, Craig Chambers, and David Notkin. Component-oriented programming in ArchJava. In *OOPSLA'01 Workshop on on Language Mechanisms for Software Components*. ACM Press, Tampa, Florida, October 2001.
3. Christopher Alexander. *A Pattern Language*. Oxford University Press, 1977.
4. Christopher Alexander. *The Timeless Way of Building*. Oxford University Press, 1979.
5. Christopher Alexander. The origins of pattern theory: The future of the theory, and the generation of a living world. *IEEE Software*, 16(5):71–82, September 1999.
6. Peter Bøgh Andersen. Computer semiotics. *Scandinavian Journal of Information Systems*, 4:3–30, 1992.
7. Peter Bøgh Andersen. *A Theory of Computer Semiotics*. Cambridge University Press, second edition, 1997.
8. Peter Bøgh Andersen, Per Hasle, and Per Aage Brandt. Machine semiosis. In Roland Posner, Klaus Robering, and Thomas A. Sebeok, editors, *Semiotics: a Handbook about the Sign-Theoretic Foundations of Nature and Culture*, volume 1, pages 548–570. Walter de Gruyter, 1997.
9. Peter Bøgh Andersen, Berit Holmqvist, and Jens F. Jensen, editors. *The Computer As Medium*. Learning in doing: Social, cognitive and computational perspectives. Cambridge University Press, 1993.
10. Peter Bøgh Andersen and Palle Nowack. Tangible objects: Connecting informational and physical spac. In L. Qvortrup, editor, *Virtual Space: The Spatiality of Virtual Inhabited 3D Worlds*, volume 2. Springer-Verlag, 2002.
11. Brad Appleton. On the nature of the nature of order. Notes on a Presentation given by James O. Coplien to the Chicago Patterns Group.
http://www.enteract.com/~bradapp/docs/NoNoO.html, August 1997.
12. Dirk Bäumer, Dirk Riehle, Wolf Siberski, Carola Lilienthal, Daniel Megert, Karl-Heinz Sylla, and Heinz Züllighoven. Values in object systems. Technical Report Technical Report 98.10.1, Ubilab, Zurich, Switzerland, 1998.
13. Dirk Bäumer, Dirk Riehle, Wolf Siberski, and Martina Wulf. Role object. In Harrison et al. [48].
14. Kent Beck and Ward Cunningham. Using pattern languages for object-oriented programs. Technical report, Tektronix, Inc., 1987. Presented at the OOPSLA-87 Workshop on Specification and Design for Object-Oriented Programming.
15. F. J. Budinsky, M. A. Finnie, J. M. Vlissides, and P. S. Yu. Automatic code generation from design patterns. *IBM Systems Journal*, 35(2):151–171, 1996.

16. Andy Bulka. Design pattern automation. In James Noble and Paul Taylor, editors, *Proceedings of KoalaPlop 2002*, To Appear in Conferences in Research and Practice in Information Technology. Australian Computer Society, 2002.

17. Frank Buschmann, Regine Meunier, Hans Rohnert, Peter Sommerlad, and Michael Stal. *Pattern-Oriented Software Architecture*. John Wiley & Sons, 1996.

18. Paul Cobley, editor. *The Routledge Companion to Semiotics and Linguistics*. Routledge, New Fetter Lane, London, 2001.

19. Paul Cobley and Litza Jansz. *Semiotics for Beginners*. Icon Books, Cambridge, England, 1997.

20. Alistair Cockburn. *Surviving Object-Oriented Projects: A Manager's Guide*. Addison-Wesley, 1998.

21. James O. Coplien. Pattern value system. `http://www.c2.com/cgi/wiki?PatternValueSystem`.

22. James O. Coplien. A generative development-process pattern language. In *Pattern Languages of Program Design*. Addison-Wesley, 1994.

23. James O. Coplien. *Software Patterns*. SIGS Management Briefings. SIGS Press, 1996.

24. James O. Coplien. Idioms and patterns as architectural literature. *IEEE Software*, 14(1):36–42, January 1997.

25. James O. Coplien. C++ idioms. In Harrison et al. [48], chapter 10.

26. James O. Coplien. A pattern language for writer's workshops. In Harrison et al. [48].

27. James O. Coplien. The future of language: Symmetry or broken symmetry? In *Proceedings of VS Live 2001*, San Francison, California, January 2001.

28. James O. Coplien and Douglas C. Schmidt, editors. *Pattern Languages of Program Design*. Addison-Wesley, 1995.

29. James O. Coplien and Liping Zhao. Symmetry and symmetry breaking in software patterns. In *Proceedings Second International Symposium on Generative and Component Based Software Engineering (GCSE2000)*, pages 373–398, 2000.

30. John Crupi, Deepak Alur, and Dan Malks. *Core J2EE Patterns*. Prentice Hall PTR, 2001.

31. Ward Cunningham. The wikiwikiweb. `http://www.c2.com/cgi/wiki`.

32. Ferdinand de Saussure. *Cours de linguistique générale*. V.C. Bally and A. Sechehaye (eds.), Paris/Lausanne, 1916.

33. Paul Dyson and Bruce Anderson. State objects. In Martin et al. [57].

34. Anthony Easthope and Kate McGowan, editors. *A Critical And Cultural Theory Reader*. Allen & Unwin, 1992.

35. Umberto Eco. *A Theory of Semiotics*. Indiana University Press, 1976.

36. Umberto Eco. *Kant and the Platypus*. Random House, 1997.

37. A. H. Eden, A. Yehudai, and G. Gil. Precise specification and automatic application of design patterns. In *1997 International Conference on Automated Software Engineering (ASE'97)*, 1997.

38. Amnon H. Eden. LePUS: A visual formalism for object-oriented architectures. In *Sixth World Conference on Integrated Design and Process Technologies*. Society for Design and Process Science, June 2002.

39. Andrew Edgar and Peter Sedgwick, editors. *Key Concepts in Curtural Theory*. Routledge, New Fetter Lane, London, 1999.

40. Gert Florijn, Marco Meijers, and Pieter van Winsen. Tool support for object-oriented patterns. In *ECOOP Proceedings*, pages 472–468, 1997.

41. Brian Foote. Hybrid vigor and footprints in the snow. In Robert Martin, Dirk Riehle, and Frank Buschmann, editors, *Pattern Languages of Program Design 3*. Addison-Wesley, 1998.

42. Martin Fowler. Value object. `http://www.martinfowler.org`, 2001.

43. Richard P. Gabriel. *Patterns of Software: Tales from the Software Community*. Oxford University Press, 1996.

44. Erich Gamma, Richard Helm, Ralph E. Johnson, and John Vlissides. *Design Patterns*. Addison-Wesley, 1994.
45. Joseph (Yossi) Gil and David H. Lorenz. Design patterns and language design. *IEEE Computer*, 31(3):118–120, March 1998.
46. Joseph Gougen. On notation. In *TOOLS 10: Technology of Object-Oriented Languages and Systems*, pages 5–10, 1993.
47. Joseph Gougen. An introduction to algebraic semiotics, with applications to user interface design. In Chrystopher Nehaniv, editor, *Computation for Metaphor, Analogy and Agents*, volume 1562 of *LNAI*, pages 242–291. Springer-Verlag, 1999.
48. Neil Harrison, Brian Foote, and Hans Rohnert, editors. *Pattern Languages of Program Design*, volume 4. Addison-Wesley, 2000.
49. Hillside Inc. Patterns homepage. http://www.hillside.net, 2001.
50. Eydun Eli Jacobsen, Bent Bruun Kristensen, and Palle Nowack. Architecture = abstractions over software. In *TOOLS Pacific*, 2000.
51. Norman L. Kerth and Ward Cunningham. Using patterns to improve our architectural vision. *IEEE Software*, 14(1):53–59, January 1997.
52. Thomas Kühne. *A Functional Pattern System for Object-Oriented Design*, volume 47 of *Forschungsergbnisse zur Informatik*. Verlag Dr. Kovač, 1999.
53. Anthony Lander and Stuart Kent. Precise visual specification of design patterns. In *ECOOP Proceedings*, pages 114–134, 1998.
54. Doug Lea. Christopher alexander: An introduction for object-oriented designers. *ACM Software Engineering Notes*, January 1994.
55. David H. Lorenz. Tiling design patterns — a case study. In *OOPSLA Proceedings*, 1997.
56. D. Mapelsden, J. Hosking, and J. Grundy. Design pattern modelling and instantiation using DPML. In James Noble and John Potter, editors, *In Proc. Fortieth International Conference on Technology of Object-Oriented Languages and Systems (TOOLS Pacific 2002)*, Conferences in Research and Practice in Information Technology. Australian Computer Society, 2002.
57. Robert C. Martin, Dirk Riehle, and Frank Buschmann, editors. *Pattern Languages of Program Design*, volume 3. Addison-Wesley, 1998.
58. Gerard Meszaros and Jim Doble. A pattern language for pattern writing. In Martin et al. [57].
59. Tommi Mikkonen. Formalizing design patterns. In *International Conference on Software Engineering (ICSE)*, pages 115–124, 1998.
60. James Noble. Classifying relationships between object-oriented design patterns. In *Australian Software Engineering Conference (ASWEC)*, pages 98–107, 1998.
61. M. Petre., A. F. Blackwell, and T.R.G. Green. Cognitive questions in software visualisation. In John Stasko, John B. Domingue, Blaine A. Price, and Marc Brown, editors, *Software Visualization: Programming as a Multimedia Experience*. M.I.T. Press, 1997.
62. Trygve Reenskaug. *Working with Objects: The OOram Software Engineering Method*. Manning Publications, 1996.
63. Dirk Riehle. Composite design patterns. In *ECOOP Proceedings*, 1997.
64. Dirk Riehle. A role based design pattern catalog of atomic and composite patterns structured by pattern purpose. Technical Report 97-1-1, UbiLabs, 1997.
65. Dirk Riehle. Bureaucracy. In Martin et al. [57].
66. Dirk Riehle and Heinz Züllighoven. Understanding and using patterns in software development. *Theory and Practice of Object Systems*, 2(1):3–13, 1996.
67. Linda Rising. *The Pattern Almanac 2000*. Addison-Wesley, 1999.
68. J. K. Rowling. *Harry Potter and the Philospher's Stone*. Bloomsbury, 1997.
69. James Rumbaugh, Ivar Jacobson, and Grady Booch. *The Unified Modeling Language Reference Manual*. Addison-Wesley, 1998.

70. Douglas Schmidt, Michael Stal, Hans Rohnert, and Frank Buschmann. *Pattern-Oriented Software Architecture: Patterns for Concurrent and Networked Objects*, volume 2. John Wiley & Sons, 2000.
71. Thomas A. Sebeok. Nonverbal communication. In Cobley [18], chapter 1.
72. Mohlalefi Sefika, A. Sane, and R. H. Campbell. Monitoring compliance of a software system with its high-level design models. In *Proceedings of the 18th Int'l Conf. on Software Eng., (ICSE-18)*, 1996.
73. Jiri Soukup. *Taming C++: Pattern Classes and Persistence for Large Projects*. Addison-Wesley, 1994.
74. Gerson Sunyé, Alain Le Guennec, and Jean-Marc Jézéquel. Design pattern application in UML. In *ECOOP Proceedings*, 2000.
75. Walter F. Tichy. A catalogue of general-purpose software design patterns. In *TOOLS USA 1997*, 1997.
76. Joost Visser. Visitor combination and traversal control. In *OOPSLA Proceedings*, pages 270–282, 2001.
77. John Vlissides, editor. *Pattern Hatching: Design Patterns Applied*. Addison-Wesley, 1998.
78. John M. Vlissides, James O. Coplien, and Norman L. Kerth, editors. *Pattern Languages of Program Design*, volume 2. Addison-Wesley, 1996.
79. Bobby Woolf. Null object. In Martin et al. [57].
80. Liping Zhao and James O. Coplien. Symmetry in class and type hierarchy. In James Noble and John Potter, editors, *In Proc. Fortieth International Conference on Technology of Object-Oriented Languages and Systems (TOOLS Pacific 2002)*, Conferences in Research and Practice in Information Technology. Australian Computer Society, 2002.
81. Walter Zimmer. Relationships between design patterns. In *Pattern Languages of Program Design*. Addison-Wesley, 1994.

Pattern-Based Design and Implementation of an XML and RDF Parser and Interpreter: A Case Study

Gustaf Neumann[1] and Uwe Zdun[2]

[1] Department of Information Systems, Vienna University of Economics, Austria
gustaf.neumann@wu-wien.ac.at
[2] Specification of Software Systems, Institute for Computer Science,
University of Essen, Germany
zdun@acm.org

Abstract. Software patterns have been widely promoted as a means of conveying practical design knowledge in a reusable fashion. Several approaches for providing better implementation variants of certain patterns have been presented. These approaches promise great advantages for flexibility, traceability, and reusability of pattern implementations. However, there are only a few larger practical case studies of these concepts available. In this paper we will present a case study of a component framework for flexible processing of markup languages in the object-oriented scripting language XOTcl. The language offers high-level means and architectural support for component integration ("component glueing"), introspection, language dynamics, and message interception techniques. These language constructs enable developers to extend the language with pattern implementations, and so to provide language support for certain pattern fragments. As a case study domain we discuss an extensible and flexible framework for XML/RDF parsing and interpretation that was developed and evolved over a period of three years and is now in use in numerous applications.

1   Introduction

Object-oriented design with patterns and programming language support for design patterns is proposed in several works. One direction proposes code generation for patterns (see for instance [6,4]). Other approaches target on language constructs implementing pattern parts at runtime, as in [23,22,9,19]. But virtually no larger practical case studies of systems, built with these ideas, are available that are actually used in non-trivial applications.

In this paper we present the design and implementation of a parsing and interpretation framework for the Extensible Markup Language (XML) [5] and the Resource Description Framework (RDF) [20]. The case is well suited to demonstrate pattern implementation and variation in an object-oriented scripting languages because it is of a reasonable size, yet comprehensible, and has diverse requirements. These include high flexibility in interpretation of markup and meta-data, on the one hand, and efficient text parsing facilities, on the other. Parsing of XML text does not need to be highly customizable, but it has to be

B. Magnusson (Ed.): ECOOP 2002, LNCS 2374, pp. 392–414, 2002.
© Springer-Verlag Berlin Heidelberg 2002

efficient and reliable. Several fast parsers for XML exist which can be reused as off-the-shelf components. The interpretation of the data in the web context is highly application-dependent. It is very likely to frequently change and must provide considerable customizability, depending on the application needs. XML and RDF have been developed to represent data from a diversity of domains. This flexibility of the data representation demands a high flexibility in the application frameworks as well.

An XML and RDF interpretation framework has to provide flexible means of interpretation, suitable for a variety of different application contexts. Typical applications will extract information from the XML and RDF representation, modify it, and create (or recreate) XML and RDF markup from their internal representation. In this case study, the required flexibility is achieved through usage of "high-level," object-oriented scripting in XOTcl [26] and patterns in the "hot spots" of the framework architecture. We will discuss the new pattern implementation variants on top of XOTcl's language constructs briefly to illustrate how partially language supported patterns can be reused and flexibly adapted to the application context. However, we will not focus on language support for patterns here, but on the component-based use of such constructs.

In our case study different programming languages (here: C, Tcl, and XOTcl) are combined to fulfill the application requirements. We generally argue that different expression resources, such as software paradigms, programming language, markup, and pattern languages, have to co-exist for different types of applications, and also within larger application systems. The application developer has to choose proper expression resources for implementing a particular task. For example, for the text parsing task, system languages, such as C or C++, are very useful because of their efficiency. Scripting languages are more appropriate for the semantic part of parsing (parse tree generation) and for the task of interpretation, because they provide powerful string manipulation facilities and flexible language resources for rapid adaptability and customization. However, the two parts have to be integrated properly.

Note that the applicability of these concepts is not limited to their use in the XOTcl language. In [34,14,12,13] we present an architectural pattern language enabling the introduction of the core concepts of XOTcl into languages such as C, C++ or Java. In [14,15] an industrial case study of this pattern language is presented. However, XOTcl directly supports these concepts as language elements; therefore, in XOTcl they do not have to be implemented and maintained by application developers.

In this paper we briefly summarize the application domain of XML and RDF text parsing and interpretation as a motivation (readers familiar with XML and RDF may skip this section). Then we introduce the idea of using patterns in the hot spots of an application, together with dynamic and introspective language constructs that were used for the pattern implementation. These language resources are reused later on. In the remainder of the paper, several crucial excerpts from the actual design of the XML/RDF framework are presented to demonstrate these ideas in a non-trivial case study. Finally, we discuss the results.

2   Case Synopsis: XML and RDF Parsing

In this section, we give a brief overview of the domain of our case study: parsing
and interpreting of XML and RDF. First we briefly introduce XML and RDF.
Secondly, we discuss requirements of parsing and interpreting XML and RDF. In
our experience similar requirements for interpretational flexibility are recurring
in many business applications that are based on XML (or other generic content
formats).

2.1   XML and RDF

The Extensible Markup Language (XML) [5] is a simple, extensible language for
structuring documents and data. It is primarily designed for Internet usage. XML
provides content-oriented ("semantic") markup of data. XML is a standardized
language for the notation of markup languages. It provides a meta-grammar
for the structure of the application documents, given in a Schema or DTD.
An important property of XML is its suitability as a language- and platform-
independent intermediate data representation in a distributed environment.

The Resource Description Framework (RDF) [20] is a formal model for describing meta-data. Its primary application domain is the description of web resources. An RDF model [20] represents a set of RDF statements. RDF statements
are used to assign named properties to web resources and to define associations
between resources. In the RDF terminology a resource is every web element with
a Uniform Resource Identifier (URI); that is, an element addressable over the
web, such as an HTML or XML document or a part of it. An RDF data model
is a directed graph with two kinds of nodes: resources (represented by ovals)
and property values (represented by rectangles). The nodes are connected by
directed arcs. These are labeled with the property names.

An RDF statement is a triple consisting of a specific resource (*subject*), a
property name (*predicate*) and a property value (*object*). The property name
is always an atomic name, while the property value can be a resource as well.
An RDF model can be represented in XML markup (see [20]) to provide a
standardized data exchange for RDF.

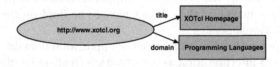

Fig. 1. Simple Example RDF Graph: One resource with two properties.

Figure 1 presents a simple RDF model consisting of two statements: A certain
HTML document (the subject, denoted by the URL) has the properties named
title and *domain* with associated values. The linearization of Figure 1 in XML
is:

```
<?xml version="1.0"?>
<rdf:RDF
   xmlns:rdf="http://www.w3.org/1999/02/22-rdf-syntax-ns#"
   xmlns:wp="http://www.xotcl.org/schema/web-page/">
  <rdf:Description about="http://www.xotcl.org/">
    <wp:title> XOTcl Homepage </wp:title>
    <wp:domain> Programming Languages </wp:domain>
  </rdf:Description>
</rdf:RDF>
```

The first line of this example states that the content of the document is XML markup. The `rdf:RDF` tag indicates that RDF markup follows. XML uses namespace prefixing to avoid name clashes between different schemata and to support reusable schemata. The example uses two XML namespaces, denoted by the prefixes `rdf` and `wp`. To obtain the full predicate names, the prefixes can be replaced by the corresponding, unambiguous schema-URI, given by `xmlns` namespace declarations. A `Description` bundles statements about a resource that is named by the `about` attribute.

To provide further structuring, RDF provides containers. They refer to a collection of resources or literals. RDF defines three different kinds of containers, as follows:

- *Bag:* Unordered List, to be used when processing order does not matter. Duplicates are permitted.
- *Sequence:* Ordered List, to be used when processing order does matter. Duplicates are permitted.
- *Alternative:* List representing a set of alternatives for a single value of a property.

Every container must contain a statement declaring its type (`rdf:Bag`, `rdf:Seq` or `rdf:Alt`) and a number of members. These are automatically named `rdf:_1`, `rdf:_2`, ... by the parser, in their order of appearance in the XML text.

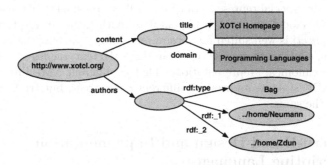

Fig. 2. Bag Example: Resource with two anonymous resources. One is a bag with two members.

In Figure 2 the earlier example is enhanced with a bag containing the authors of the web page as resources. To serialize the bag we have to add a new property `authors` to the inner description of the preceding example:

```
...
<wp:authors>
  <rdf:Bag>
    <rdf:li resource="../home/Neumann"/>
    <rdf:li resource="../home/Zdun"/>
  </rdf:Bag>
</wp:authors>
...
```

2.2   Parsing and Interpreting XML and RDF

In this section we will summarize a few requirements from the domain of markup processing to demonstrate that an XML/RDF interpretation framework must provide high extensibility and flexibility.

Parsed XML markup can be used in different data representations. For example, XML text can be seen as an event flow with events of three types: *start*, *pcdata*, and *end*. Examples for event-based APIs are the SAX API [21] or the Expat API [8]. Sometimes such event flows are parsed into a node tree, like a DOM [32] tree. The tree can be used for further processing.

Different data representations for parsed XML markup have specific benefits and drawbacks, and so it makes sense to choose the most appropriate representation for a given task. The event stream representation has the advantage of potentially high efficiency and low memory consumption. Moreover, it is well suited for incremental parsing. This is especially important for documents that are too large to fit into memory. In a node tree representation, information can be accessed apart from the event stream, random access to the data is possible, and introspection of the tree structure allows for navigation through the tree. If we know where the targeted information is located in the document, a tree representation can be very valuable for reducing search times.

Besides the token event stream and the parse tree, the RDF specification [20] defines two special representations for RDF: a so-called triple representation and the RDF model graph. A triple database with triples of the form ⟨*subject, predicate, object*⟩ is well suited for several reasoning tasks over the whole model. Moreover, in contrast to a parse tree from the XML text, triples and RDF model graphs are "canonical" representations. That is, different XML linearizations of the same RDF statements produce different parse trees, but triples and model graphs are the same.

3   Pattern-Based Design and Implementation in Scripting Languages

In this section we will firstly motivate pattern-based design in scripting languages as a way to find flexible and maintainable architectures, as they are required by the XML and RDF parsing domain. Secondly, we will briefly introduce the object-oriented scripting language XOTcl that we have used to implement the XML/RDF parser and interpreter.

3.1 Flexible and Reusable Pattern Implementations

Design patterns provide abstractions from reusable designs. They can typically be found in the "hot spots" or centers of software architectures. A pattern describes a recurring *solution* to a *problem* in a *context* balancing a set of *forces*. Patterns cover the problem that expertise is hard to convey. They work by describing frequently used solutions that have proven their inherent capability to be fitted to the environment of numerous applications successfully.

Very often several patterns can be used on the same design problem, and several pattern parts are mutually dependent. A general problem is that of composition based on patterns. Pattern parts resemble architectural roles rather than classes; that is, architectural fragments in patterns enrich the design repository of the developer with elements, mostly of different granularity than classes. Such elements can be reused as architectural roles, which are orthogonal extensions to class composition. In other words, one class in a framework often plays various roles in several different design patterns at once. Alexander's original ideas on patterns [1] suggest using them in a pattern language which defines the correlations between the patterns used; that is, no pattern is used in isolation, but as an element of a language.

To date, there is little or no support in traditional, mainstream programming languages for implementing and using patterns. This implies several problems for the usage of patterns. Recurring pattern implementations cannot be reused, but have to be programmed again for each usage. The architectural fragments in the pattern are conceptual entities of the design repository, but they are split into several entities of the implementation language, like several classes or objects. Missing introspection facilities mean that patterns are neither traceable at runtime nor in the code. Many pattern implementations in mainstream languages have considerable implementation overhead, e.g., for unnecessary forwarding of messages and other recurring tasks (these problems of pattern usage are discussed more deeply in [23,24]).

3.2 The Object-Oriented Scripting Language 'Extended Object Tcl' (XOTcl)

In this section, we give a brief overview of the XOTcl language and its use for pattern implementation. XOTcl [26] (pronounced *exotickle*) is a value-added replacement of OTcl [33]. Both XOTcl and OTcl are object-oriented flavors of the scripting language Tcl (Tool Command Language [27]). Tcl offers a dynamic type system with automatic conversion, is extensible with components and is equipped with read/write introspection. In the remainder of this section we briefly describe XOTcl's language concepts.

In XOTcl, all inter-object and inter-class relationships are fully dynamic and can be changed at runtime. Each dynamic language functionality can be introspected. Classes are also objects; therefore, all methods applicable for objects can be applied to class-objects as well. Since a class is a special (managing) kind of object it is itself managed by a special class called a "meta-class." New user-defined meta-classes can be derived to restrict or enhance the abilities of certain classes.

The XOTcl extensions focus on complexity, flexibility, and adaptability in object-oriented systems. Moreover, XOTcl gives architectural support for component glueing and the implementation of larger architectural fragments. In particular, the following language constructs are supported:

- *Dynamic Object Aggregation* supports the 'part-of' relationship [25]. Children are automatically destroyed when the parent is destroyed. With introspection options on child and parent, we can automatically retrieve the current parent and the current list of children. The relation is completely dynamic and can be restructured using deep copy and move operations. We will use the language construct in the XML/RDF case study to implement a "canonical" dynamic object tree representation of the parsed XML data.
- *Nested Classes* reduce the interference of independently developed program structures by letting classes aggregate dependent class descriptions.
- *Assertions* let us provide formal and informal conditions for documenting (and checking) program invariants.
- *Per-Class/Per-Object Mixins* are classes that are dynamically attached to or detached from a class or object. They intercept every message to a class or to an object and can handle the message before/after the original receiver. They are ordered in a chain and inherit from super-classes [22].
- *Per-Class/Per-Object Filters* are special instance methods which are dynamically registered or deregistered for a class hierarchy or an object. Every time an instance of this class hierarchy or this object receives a message, the filter is invoked automatically and intercepts this message. Filters are also ordered in chains and inherited [23].
- *Dynamic Component Loading and Wrapping* allows XOTcl, Tcl, C, and C++ components to be loaded and integrated using the same basic mechanisms, as discussed in [11]. In this work we use the mechanism to load third-party XML parsers (implemented in Tcl and C) and reusable pattern implementations from external components dynamically at runtime.

The XOTcl language constructs are designed to help in the implementation and use of patterns. Filters [23] and mixin classes [22,24] are interception techniques for messages. That is, messages sent to an object, a class, or a class hierarchy are intercepted before they reach the original receiver. The interceptor can adapt the message to another receiver, handle it directly or decorate it with arbitrary behavior before/after the original receiver gets it. Filters are used to implement entities and concerns cutting across an entity as a whole, whereas mixins only intercept certain message calls. Both, filters and mixins, primarily implement extensions to an object or a class hierarchy. Mixins may be used to compose several filters that form a semantic unit in a reusable component. This way, concerns cutting across several instances or class hierarchies, as targeted by aspect-oriented programming [18], can be modeled as well.

By intercepting the calls to a pattern structure, we can implement the recurring pattern parts as separate and reusable entities. These parts can be placed in a component and dynamically loaded at runtime. Language dynamics and introspection can be used to adapt and change the pattern implementation to the current context. In this paper we assume that such pattern implementations are available as components. Note that the XOTcl distribution contains all used pattern components. They are dynamically loaded into the framework and can be reused as if they were native XOTcl language constructs.

3.3   Approaches for Pattern Implementation

In this paper we will present a case study combining scripting languages, high-level language constructs, and design patterns. Much other work has been done on the combination of high-level language constructs and patterns, but unfortunately there are only a few case studies showing the validity of these approaches available. We will discuss some other approaches in this section.

A classic approach to code generation for patterns can be found in [6]. There are several subsequent approaches, some of them with notable similarities to the filter. Bosch, for example, uses static layer definitions [4] to intercept messages to a pattern fragment. Besides several differences of detail, the general difference between our approach for pattern reuse and code generation is dynamics. A pattern is not a reusable entity per se, but a reusable design solution in a context. It therefore has to be fitted to the current implementation and application context. (Static) code generation mechanisms offer no language means for this customization step. Consequently, pattern reuse through code generation seems to be rather rigid. In some sense this contradicts the idea of wholeness often associated with patterns, because in many cases it is hard to produce a flexible and elegant piece of design (and code) from a rigid, pre-fabricated building block.

Some approaches, such as component connectors [9], introduce additional runtime means to represent patterns. These split the pattern, as one conceptual entity, into several runtime entities. In contrast to the interception techniques filter and mixin class, component connectors are not transparent for the client.

A role (as proposed in [19]) is used to express extrinsic properties of a design entity. In this concept a role can be dynamically taken and abandoned. The approach does not provide an abstraction at a broader structural level, as does a per-class filter and per-class mixin. Using roles, a pattern can be implemented as a dynamic composition of its architectural fragments. That means that, by inspecting roles, patterns may be more traceable than in an implementation scattered over classes.

Several patterns express concerns cutting across different design entities. Aspect-oriented programming [18] targets such cross-cutting concerns. There are different approaches for implementing aspects; here, we will compare with the concepts of AspectJ [17]. In AspectJ, so-called pointcut designators let us specify certain events in the message flow. These events are called join points. Before, after, and around advice let us specify behavior to run when a specified join point is reached. The general idea resembles the message interceptors in XOTcl. Thus most concerns in this paper may be implemented using aspects. However, in contrast to the approach presented, AspectJ does not allow for language extension in a component-oriented sense. In other words, aspects cannot be dynamically introduced as language extensions. Instead, an aspect weaver, a kind of generative compiler, is used. Hence AspectJ does not allow for dynamic runtime changes. Aspects are given as non-local extensions to the targeted design units. Since the pattern examples presented in this paper require knowledge about the extended class and runtime callstack information, it is rather unwieldy to implement them with aspects. However, concerns cutting across several entities of the program can be better expressed using aspects, since it may take several mixins with filters to express one complex aspect.

4   Component Framework Design

In this section we will present several crucial excerpts from our XML/RDF component framework design. By "crucial" we mean that these framework hot spots are critical for reusability, flexibility, and runtime efficiency of the framework. Before we give the design excerpts in detail, we will present an overview of the baseline architecture of the component framework.

4.1   Baseline Architecture

Of several available XML parsers we decided to re-use the C written parser Expat [8] and the Tcl written parser TclXML [3]. Both can be used as Tcl components with the same interface for parsing. In the framework presented here, an object-oriented XML parser wraps these third-party parsers. It forms an abstraction integrating procedural parsers implemented in other languages (here C and Tcl). Those parsers are encapsulated in a distinct layer and are thus exchangeable with other implementations.

The XML information elements form an aggregation tree, in which children have an "is part-of" relationship to their parents. These nodes represent the grammar of XML and RDF in our framework's information architecture. Data and attributes will be treated as properties of nodes.

As a requirement, it should be possible to flexibly extend and change the grammar, so that future changes of the XML/RDF specifications can be easily incorporated. Since XML and RDF are very general data models, it is a requirement of the framework to interpret the representation in different ways and to possibly add new interpretation forms. A factory component for nodes abstracts object creation, thereby enabling extensible node creation. Since there are several node classes having a set of features in common, another goal was to create the node classes automatically.

The basic architecture described applies to both the xoXML and xoRDF components. XML, RDF, and the reused parser part are additionally structured in layers (see Figure 3), as in the Layers architectural pattern [7]. The pattern couples similar responsibilities in a distinct layer. Thus it decomposes complex aspects of the system. The three layers of Figure 3 are the basic components of xoXML/xoRDF.

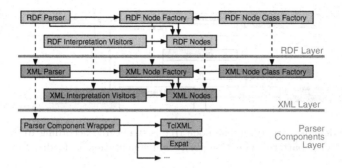

Fig. 3. The xoXML and xoRDF Layers: The RDF layer specializes the sub-components of the XML layer. Basic text parsing is handled by a procedural parser, e.g., in C or Tcl. It is wrapped by a generic interface. Different layers are depicted in different color.

4.2   Nodes of the Parse Tree

RDF provides a relatively simple, formally defined grammar. The central problem of the design is how to build an object-oriented structure from the RDF graph expressed by the XML linearization. There are several options for mapping the XML elements to a computational representation. Following the line set out in Section 2, we first create a dynamic object aggregation tree; other representations can then be retrieved from the tree.

To provide an XML/RDF interpretation of the node tree, we used the Interpreter pattern [10]. It defines an object-oriented structure for a language grammar, along with an Interpreter. Clients use an abstract interface for node interpretation and, thereby, abstract node implementation details. At runtime node objects form an abstract syntax tree. Terminal nodes, like literals in RDF, terminate the tree structure, while non-terminals are able to aggregate an arbitrary number of nodes. As a consequence of the usage of the pattern, the language represented can be exchanged and extended by object-oriented means, since new node classes are very similar to existing ones.

We will use the common implementation variant of the Interpreter pattern to build the abstract syntax tree: a Composite structure [10]. Composites arrange objects in trees with two kinds of nodes: Leafs terminate the tree, and Composites forward registered Composite operations to all children of the Composite. We have used XOTcl filters to handle the recurring tasks of the Composite pattern, such as forwarding messages through the hierarchy [23]. The pattern implementation is loaded from a pattern component *Ordered Composite* that uses the *dynamic object aggregation* language construct of XOTcl to handle the aggregation structure of the pattern automatically.

As shown in Figure 4, we define a class `AbstractNode` with the meta-class `OrderedComposite`. Each meta-class inherits the ability to define classes from the most general meta-class `Class`. On `AbstractNode` we define a core set of abstract operations, common to all node classes. These let us parse data, as well as starting and ending node tags, and allow them to be printed. Methods for

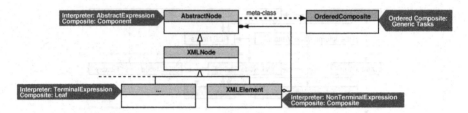

Fig. 4. Node Tree Structure: The node tree is structured according to the Interpreter and Composite pattern. The Composite implementation is loaded from a separate component.

interpretation on concrete classes will be registered as Composite operations. Registration is handled by the registration methods of the `OrderedComposite` class, called `addOperations` and `addAfterOperations`. The pattern implementation will ensure that the Composite operations work recursively on the tree. The XOTcl code for loading of the Composite and definition of the abstract node class is:

```
package require OrderedComposite
...
OrderedComposite AbstractNode
AbstractNode abstract instproc parseStart {name attrList}
AbstractNode abstract instproc parseData {text}
AbstractNode abstract instproc parseEnd {name}
AbstractNode abstract instproc print {}


Class XMLNode -superclass AbstractNode
```

First, the `OrderedComposite` component is loaded. Then an abstract node with abstract methods is defined as a general node interface. Finally, a special node class, the general `XMLNode`, inherits from `AbstractNode`.

4.3   XML Namespaces

XML and RDF nodes may contain namespace declarations starting with `xmlns`. Often namespaces are declared within the top node, but it is also possible to declare namespaces within inner nodes. These overlap the namespace declarations of outer nodes, and they are only valid for the current node and its inner nodes. A direct coupling between namespaces and connected nodes would cause the namespace objects to store unnecessary information. A new namespace would be difficult to add in applications with a dynamically changing node tree. A better solution is an indirection to a namespace handler; that is, each node must be connected to one responsible namespace handler. The namespace handler knows its successor in a Chain of Responsibility [10]. If a namespace handler cannot resolve a namespace it delegates the task to its successor.

The Chain of Responsibility pattern is implemented as a reusable component. We add operations to the general `Namespace` class for adding a namespace and for

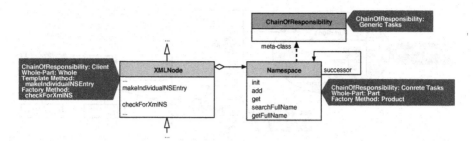

Fig. 5. XML Namespaces: Namespaces are part-of their node and are structured in a Chain of Responsibility

determining a namespace's full name from the prefix, as well as two operations, `searchPrefix` and `searchFullName`, for retrieval of a namespace object from a handler by prefix and full name. The two retrieval operations act on a single handler. To automatically act recursively on the chain, they must be registered as chained operations with `addChainedOperation`:

```
package require ChainOfResponsibility
...
ChainOfResponsibility Namespace
Namespace instproc add {prefix ns} {...}
Namespace instproc searchPrefix {prefix} {...}
Namespace instproc searchFullName fname {...}
Namespace instproc getFullName fname {...}
Namespace addChainedOperation searchPrefix {}
Namespace addChainedOperation searchFullName {}
```

A chained operation returns a value indicating whether the operation was successful or not. If not, the next namespace in the chain is tried. This way the chain is searched until the last namespace in the chain is reached.

Namespace declarations are closely coupled to the nodes, and their lifetime is determined by the surrounding node; therefore, the node aggregates its namespaces in a Whole-Part pattern [7]. Moreover, the namespace chain is integrated in the Composite structure of the nodes. Note that this combination of Composite and Chain of Responsibility is a quite typical design for cases in which responsibilities have to be delegated up the tree.

4.4   Wrapping the Parser Component

Different XML parsers exist that perform the same task but have no common interface. Since applications should be portable to different components performing the same task, direct invocations of these components should be avoided. Instead an object-oriented interface can encapsulate the functions of the third-party parser components, as in the Wrapper Facade pattern [30]. A Wrapper Facade provides an interface for client objects. It forwards methods to the functions (or procedures) of the procedural (legacy) components. The pattern Component Wrapper [34] integrates different techniques to access foreign language

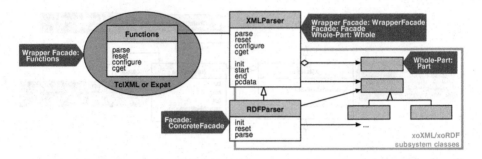

Fig. 6. Parser Design: The reused parser is wrapped behind an object-oriented interface. It forms a Facade to the sub-system for clients.

and paradigm components as black-boxes. Here, Wrapper Facade is used as a part of a Component Wrapper.

We define a Wrapper Facade XMLParser to incorporate the interface of TclXML or Expat as object-oriented methods (see Figure 6). The method configure sets the parser configuration, cget queries a configuration option, parse invokes the parsing of XML text, and reset cleans up the parser. This generic interface may also be used with other parsers, e.g., by using the Adapter pattern [10]. It is also reusable in a component-based fashion [23]. To make the interface more generic we add three methods: start, end, and pcdata. These will be called when the start or end of an XML node or XML data is reached.

As another role of the parser, we define a Facade [10] for the xoXML and xoRDF sub-system. Facades unify the interfaces of a sub-system into one interface. They thus ease access to the sub-system, because client objects have to access a smaller number of interfaces and are more strongly decoupled from the sub-system's implementation details.

As another architectural role, the parser has to serve as a central access point for the namespace chain introduced previously, and for the Node Factory presented in the next section. The parser aggregates both of these roles as parts in a Whole-Part structure.

4.5   Node Object Factory

Node creation is a hot spot of the framework; that is, variation requirements can be foreseen in these spots. Let us consider a collective change for all node creations, such as introducing the Flyweight pattern [10] for sharing literal nodes. In XOTcl Flyweights are reusable in a component-based way; for one creation process only three lines of additional code are necessary to load and use the Flyweight component. Integration of the Flyweight into the creation processes of every single literal node class would represent a significant implementation overhead. Node creations may well be scattered throughout the code, and would have to be searched to introduce collective changes. Furthermore, these creations are often located in code of clients of the node classes. A strong coupling between client code and node classes would exist, making all future changes problematic. Since changes in node creations are foreseeable, e.g., in situations where the XML/RDF specifications change, control of all creation processes from a central point is a superior solution.

Factory patterns, like Abstract Factory and Factory Method [10], provide us with a central access point to creations of related or dependent objects (called *products*). To create a node factory, we firstly create the Abstract Factory with a method getNode. It returns a newly created node:

```
Class AbstractNodeFactory
AbstractNodeFactory abstract instproc getNode {keyCl objName}
```

Now we concretize the factory with a simple node factory, whose function is to create every requested node.

```
Class NodeFactory -superclass AbstractNodeFactory
NodeFactory instproc getNode {keyCl objName} {
  ...
  return [$keyCl create $objName]
}
```

4.6   Node Class Factory

One major benefit of using the Interpreter pattern lies in the similarities between node classes. New node classes can be added rapidly. A trivial way of adding similar classes is to copy the classes' code and change it slightly. Since changes must be propagated throughout the code, changeability may suffer, because for each change all dependent places in the code have to be searched and updated. Replicated parts of the code are an implementation overhead, and so this solution is inelegant and error-prone. Using code generation or putting recurring parts into superclasses minimizes these problems. But the object creational problems sketched in the previous section also occur with class creation.

Central control of the adaptation of newly created classes to the application context and domain let the programmer implement changes on several classes at once. As XOTcl supports meta-classes and dynamics in class-structures, a solution similar to the Abstract Factory pattern can be provided in a meta-class. Each XOTcl class is a runtime object; therefore, there are the same benefits and liabilities as for ordinary object Factories. Our main concerns for applying the pattern for class creation purposes is that the node class configuration tends to change, as the architecture evolves and new requirements for the parsing framework emerge. During the Class Factory's creation process we can introduce interdependent constraints, such as the possible compositions of RDF nodes, in a central place. In XOTcl a meta-class is defined by specifying the most general meta-class Class as superclass. Afterwards we create a class for the XML element type dynamically:

```
Class XMLNodeClassFactory -superclass Class
XMLNodeClassFactory create XMLElement -superclass XMLNode
```

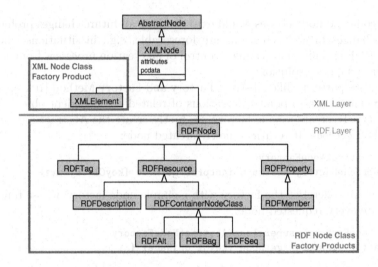

Fig. 7. Node Class Hierarchy: RDF node classes are specialized, but through their generic superclasses they form a dynamic node tree.

For the RDF node tree we specialize the Class Factory, because RDF nodes define the constraints of nodes they may nest in or be attributed to at creation time. We add these initializations to the `create` method of the node class object.

```
Class RDFNodeClassFactory -superclass XMLNodeClassFactory
...
RDFNodeClassFactory proc create args {
  set name [next]          ;# create the class
  ...                      ;# perform initializations
}
```

Subsequently, all types of RDF nodes are defined in a loop. All classes are automatically placed at the right point in the class hierarchy, and all initializations are performed during creation. The loop creates the hierarchy in Figure 7:

```
foreach {name sc content attributeList} {
  RDFTag        RDFNode                RDF          {}
  RDFBag        RDFContainerNodeClass  Bag          {ID}
  RDFSeq        RDFContainerNodeClass  Seq          {ID}
  RDFAlt        RDFContainerNodeClass  Alt          {ID}
  RDFProperty   RDFNode                ""           {bagID ID resource parseType}
  RDFMember     RDFProperty            li           {resource parseType}
  RDFDescription RDFResource           Description  {ID bagID about type
    aboutEach aboutEachPrefix}
} {
  RDFNodeClassFactory create $name -superclass $sc \
    -content $content -attributeList $attributeList \
}
```

It is quite common for XML interpretation frameworks to have constraints for node nesting and node attributes, because usually the information architecture reflects the XML structure. The pattern Generic Content Format [31] describes such structural interdependencies in the area of web engineering architectures. Composite and Leaf classes represent each information element type used in the XML documents. As business requirements, standards, or other interpretation requirements change, both, the XML structure and the class hierarchy have to be changed accordingly. These forces can be observed for our RDF framework as well; here, the changes are mainly introduced by the changing RDF standard and the interpretation requirements of our applications.

In our framework, changes of the class hierarchy and its constraints can be rapidly performed in the central place provided by the Class Factory. Introspection options can be used to find out these interdependencies at runtime.

4.7 Generic Interpretation with Visitors

In our implementation of the XML/RDF processor we have chosen to provide both an event stream model and a tree structure model. In a first step, the RDF structure is parsed from the event stream into a node object tree. The event stream can be used by applications, if required. Next the tree is interpreted according to the application domain and context. One implementation option would be to insert the interpretation code into the node classes. This is a bad choice when different or multiple interpretations of the node tree are needed. As another drawback, interpretations cannot be changed without making changes to every node class. Parsing cannot be adapted without checking all dependencies against interpretation code.

An interpretation facility is required for abstracting implementation details of the node tree and for supporting several different interpretation forms. The Visitor pattern [10] provides such a facility. Visitors perform operations on all parts of an object structure separated from the object classes. An abstract Visitor declares an interface that can be attached to a given object structure. Concrete Visitors are used for visiting each element of the structure. The elements implement `accept` operations that take a Visitor as an argument and return themselves in the concrete implementations to the concrete Visitor. The concrete Visitor performs the interpretation task on the concrete element.

In the case of the XML/RDF parser the nodes are used as elements for the Visitor. So we attach a new architectural role to the abstract node class. It becomes a Visitor's abstract element, while the concrete nodes become concrete elements. We use interpretation to reconstruct the start and end of a node by adding two operations to the abstract node's definition. In conventional implementations both operations would have to propagate `accept` calls to their children. Here, this is handled automatically by the Composite pattern implementation:

```
Abstract Node abstract instproc accept {visitor}
AbstractNode abstract instproc acceptEnd {visitor}
AbstractNode addOperations {accept accept}
AbstractNode addAfterOperations {accept acceptEnd}
```

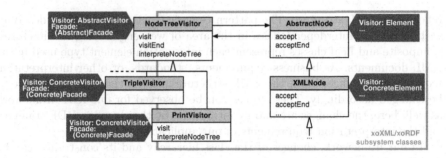

Fig. 8. Node Tree Visitor: Interpretations tasks are decomposed from the node tree. Customized visitors can be added by sub-classing.

Now, `accept` is a Composite operation; that is, before the operation `accept` is performed on the node, an `accept` call is performed on each child. `acceptEnd` is performed on the child after the return from the parent operation. Both concrete operations on `XMLNode` merely call the appropriate Visitor with a self-reference as argument:

```
XMLNode instproc accept {visitor} {
  $visitor visit [self]
}
XMLNode instproc acceptEnd {visitor} {
  $visitor visitEnd [self]
}
```

These operations can be specialized to more sophisticated `accept` handling in subclasses. An abstract Visitor is defined with operations for visiting, and an operation starting the interpretation of a node tree. `visitEnd` is not defined as abstract but as an empty method, because it may remain unspecified in concrete Visitors:

```
Class NodeTreeVisitor
NodeTreeVisitor abstract instproc visit objName
NodeTreeVisitor instproc visitEnd objName {;}
NodeTreeVisitor abstract instproc interpretNodeTree n
```

Shown below is the implementation of a simple `PrintVisitor`, using only the node's `print` operation. Each node prints its content to the standard output. Calling the Visitor's `interpretNodeTree` operation on the top node outputs the whole hierarchy.

```
Class PrintVisitor -superclass NodeTreeVisitor
PrintVisitor instproc visit objName {
  puts [$objName print]
}
PrintVisitor instproc interpretNodeTree node {
  $node accept [self]
}
```

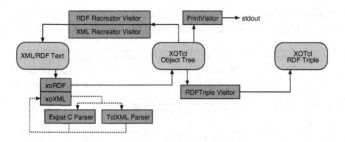

Fig. 9. Components and Data Representations in the xoXML/xoRDF Framework: From the XML/RDF text either an object aggregation tree or a triple database or both is produced.

The xoXML/xoRDF framework contains several Visitors for different interpretation tasks, including one for building up an RDF triple database from the node tree, Visitors for recreation of XML/RDF text from the nodes, and Visitors for pretty-printing of the object tree. These features can be found in the XOTcl distribution. Since they are, from an architectural point of view, similar to the Visitor presented above, we do not discuss them in detail here.

4.8 Framework Overview

Figure 9 shows the different components and data representations in the xoXML/xoRDF framework. Arrows indicate the data flows between components, and conversion between data representations. XML/RDF text can be processed by different parsers that are wrapped by the object-oriented parser components. An intermediate object tree representation is created, on which interpretations are performed. Each individual interpretation is implemented as a Visitor. In many applications we provide domain-specific Visitors that extract the required information.

With the same Visitor architecture we can also derive other representation of the information contained in the object tree. In our framework, we have implemented a Visitor for creating RDF triples. Another component recreates XML and RDF text from the object tree.

5 Speed Comparison

In this section we discuss the speed penalties of using high-level XOTcl language constructs, such as patterns and object-oriented scripting, relative to C- and Java-based single-purpose implementations. We provide speed comparisons with the W3C reference implementation SiRPAC [29] 1.14. SiRPAC uses an external parser: we used IBM's XML4J [16] version 3.0.1 in the Xerces-J [2] variant. In addition, we compared with the pure C implementation HTRdf [28]. All speed comparisons were performed on an Intel Pentium III 500 Mhz single processor

Table 1. Speed Comparison: Different xoXML/xoRDF Setups Compared to the HTRdf/Expat C Implementation and the SiRPAC/Xerces-J Java Implementation

Filename/Description	SiRPAC/ Xerces-J (Java)	HTRdf/ Expat (pure C)	xoRDF/ Expat (only tree)	xoRDF/ Expat (tree & triples)	xoRDF/ TclXML (only tree)	xoRDF/ TclXML (tree & triples)
example1.rdf Nested Description	273 ms	17 ms	28 ms	44 ms	44 ms	57 ms
example2.rdf Two Descriptions	284 ms	27 ms	27 ms	49 ms	40 ms	63 ms
example3.rdf Bag & aboutEach	274 ms	23 ms	28 ms	43 ms	40 ms	56 ms
example4.rdf Resource Property	282 ms	19 ms	26 ms	42 ms	35 ms	51 ms
pics.rdf 2 BagIDs & aboutEachs	366 ms	116 ms	67 ms	165 ms	81 ms	180 ms
dc.rdf Larger Dublin Core Example	1183 ms	131 ms	215 ms	363 ms	277 ms	429 ms
Sum: Whole Test Suite	2389 ms	316 ms	363 ms	662 ms	473 ms	779 ms
Comparison to HTRdf (in %)	+656 %	0 %	+15 %	+109 %	+49 %	+149 %

machine running RedHat Linux 6.1 with 128 MB RAM. The version of XOTcl and the xoXML/xoRDF components used was 0.84.

For each setup we tested each test case 20 times, and used the best result achieved (note that the average results were almost identical; therefore we omit those figures here for space reasons). Finally, we summed the results and calculated the percentage difference between each sum and the figure for HTRdf, as the fastest implementation in the test.

For the comparisons we used example RDF files from the SiRPAC distribution and from the W3C site. For all tests we measured the overall time for instantiating the parser, reading the file and parsing the text. Since xoXML/xoRDF offers different setups, we provide figures for different combinations of parser and created representation. For xoXML/xoRDF the most common variant is to create the object aggregation tree representation with the Expat C Parser. As discussed above, xoXML/xoRDF generates the triples via an object tree representation. Our measurements contain figures for the tree and triple generation. Finally we performed both tests with the Tcl-only parser TclXML as parser back-end. TclXML has a similar interface to Expat and can be plugged into the system by specifying a single configuration parameter.

Even though a comparison of such results is quite hard and subjective, the performance measurements (summarized in Table 1) are very encouraging for the scripting approach with patterns. In all cases the implementation in the scripting language is substantially faster than SiRPAC, despite all high level constructs, patterns and indirections. Even the Tcl-only, but platform-independent, parser and triple generation from the tree still operate at a useful performance level. Of course, the scripting implementation is slower than an efficient, pure C implementation. xoRDF is, as expected, 0.14-1.46 times slower than HTRdf in our tests, but HTRdf only builds triples.

The performance comparison indicates that the xoXML and xoRDF implementation can be used in practical applications, when considerable control and customization is needed. Nevertheless, the speed comparisons are still unsatisfactory if the task is merely to create triples. Since we argue for the component reuse aspect, we can provide a wrapper for HTRdf (or another C implementation), enabling HTRdf to directly create triples. In this case, construction of the object tree representation is skipped.

6 Conclusion

In this paper we have presented an extensible design of an XML/RDF parser and interpreter framework. The case is non-trivial, yet of a comprehensible size. The design presented has evolved over three years and, during this time period, we had to cope with diverse new requirements, such as higher performance demands, less memory consumption, simplification of interfaces, and changes in the RDF standard (and its interpretation). The use of patterns and high-level constructs in crucial parts of the design has allowed us to easily adapt the design to new, unexpected situations. Despite considerable new requirements, the original design core is still stable.

Flexible glueing of components, combined with the Component Wrapper pattern, has given us the opportunity to reuse existing parser implementations in a manner transparent to the object-oriented implementation. The high level language constructs of XOTcl, such as filters, mixins, and dynamic object aggregations provide flexible means of adapting and supporting higher-level design constructs, say, certain design patterns, roles, or Whole-Part structures. Several examples have demonstrated how patterns and high-level constructs interact, and how this interaction produces pattern variations. For example, we have discussed the language-supported Composite pattern and the Ordered Composite variant. Variants often can be derived by runtime language means. The idea of the Class Factory came from combining that of the Abstract Factory pattern and the class object and dynamic classes language constructs of XOTcl.

Our approach does not force developers to use XOTcl as the implementation language of the whole system, since components can be integrated with little effort in any C or C++ program. Moreover, the concepts can be introduced into almost any procedural and object-oriented language with the pattern language from [34,14,12,13]. Thus, the ideas can be used independently of the concrete XOTcl implementation, and the case study discussed here can be seen as an example of a usage of this pattern language with XOTcl. To a certain extent, other implementation languages, such as AspectJ, can be used. Our experiments with AspectJ and other Java-based AOP approaches indicate that current implementations have similar liabilities as our approach in respect to speed penalties, but, as generative approaches, they do not allow for runtime changes. XOTcl is completely implemented in C and heavily optimized for runtime performance.

Therefore, we believe, future implementations of dynamic message interception techniques in Java or C++ will have similar consequences as using XOTcl together with C or C++ components.

The benefits of our approach are only useful for applications requiring high flexibility and component glueing. There are also some drawbacks in the approach discussed. Scripting languages are slower than system programming languages, such as C or C++, because of dynamic conversions and method lookup. We can minimize these problems by using C components wherever high flexibility is not required. If the tasks performed in the scripting language are not even required by the application, however, the performance penalty becomes significant. For example, if an application only needs a triple representation of an RDF structure, the creation of an intermediate object tree is unnecessary.

It may be hard for application developers, not used to the scripting language, to understand the "new" language. Similarly, the patterns and their relations have to be understood and cannot simply be used "out-of-the-box," but they require usage experience and knowledge of possible implementation variants. In our experience, usage experience and understanding of patterns is especially relevant to inexperienced programmers who want to *extend* the framework (as for instance observed in student projects). Here, our approach helps novices to trace the patterns as design units in the code. However, for modifications and customizations of the design, the intent, the effects on quality attributes, and the structure of the used patterns have to be fully understood. The component-oriented structuring hides the patterns from users writing applications that only *use* the framework; therefore, for merely using the framework its internal design has not to be fully understood but only the component interfaces. If the pattern language from [34,14,12,13] is used instead of XOTcl, the implementations of the wrapping and indirection mechanisms have to be maintained by the development organization.

In general, our case study shows that the choice of the expression resources used for programming, such as programming languages, patterns, paradigms, etc., has to deal with conflicting forces. These can be at least partially resolved by a glueing approach. We have introduced component glueing as a wrapping technique for combining several languages and paradigms properly. Note that some of the glued components were XOTcl components for implementing recurring pattern variants. Thus the component glueing concept has allowed us to extend XOTcl with the concerns implemented in pattern components. These components implement a variant of the pattern that can be further customized to the application context by different dynamic language resources. The patterns have extended the XOTcl language dynamically with new language elements that are as well elements of the design repository. The loaded language element, implementing the pattern variant, uses the standard XOTcl syntax, and it is dynamic, introspectible, and traceable as a runtime entity of the language like all other XOTcl language elements.

XOTcl and the XML/RDF components are freely available from:
http://www.xotcl.org.

References

1. C. Alexander. *The Timeless Way of Building.* Oxford Univ. Press, 1979.
2. Apache XML Project. The Apache XML project. http://xml.apache.org/, 2000.
3. S. Ball. XML support for Tcl. In *Proc. of the Sixth Tcl/Tk Conference*, San Diego, CA, USA, September 1998.
4. J. Bosch. Design patterns as language constructs. *Journal of Object Oriented Programming*, 11(2), 1998.
5. T. Bray, J. Paoli, and C. Sperberg-McQueen. Extensible markup language (XML) 1.0. http://www.w3.org/TR/1998/REC-xml-19980210, 1998.
6. F. Budinsky, M. Finnie, P. Yu, and J. Vlissides. Automatic code generation from design patterns. *IBM Systems Journal*, 35(2), 1996.
7. F. Buschmann, R. Meunier, H. Rohnert, P. Sommerlad, and M. Stal. *Pattern-orinented Software Architecture - A System of Patterns.* J. Wiley and Sons Ltd., 1996.
8. J. Clark. Expat - XML parser toolkit. http://www.jclark.com/xml/expat.html, 1998.
9. S. Ducasse. Message passing abstractions as elementary bricks for design pattern implementation. In *Proceeding of ECOOP Workshop on Language Support for Design Patterns and Frameworks*, Jyväskylä, Finland, 1997.
10. E. Gamma, R. Helm, R. Johnson, and J. Vlissides. *Design Patterns: Elements of Reusable Object-Oriented Software.* Addison-Wesley, 1994.
11. M. Goedicke, G. Neumann, and U. Zdun. Design and implementation constructs for the development of flexible, component-oriented software architectures. In *Proc. of Second International Symposium on Generative and Component-Based Software Engineering (GCSE'2000)*, Erfurt, Germany, Oct 2000.
12. M. Goedicke, G. Neumann, and U. Zdun. Object system layer. In *Proceeding of EuroPlop 2000*, Irsee, Germany, July 2000.
13. M. Goedicke, G. Neumann, and U. Zdun. Message redirector. In *Proceeding of EuroPlop 2001*, Irsee, Germany, July 2001.
14. M. Goedicke and U. Zdun. Piecemeal legacy migrating with an architectural pattern language: A case study. Accepted for publication in Journal of Software Maintenance: Research and Practice, 2001.
15. M. Goedicke and U. Zdun. Piecemeal migration of a document archive system with an architectural pattern language. In *5th European Conference on Software Maintenance and Reengineering (CSMR'01)*, Lisbon, Portugal, Mar 2001.
16. IBM. XML4J, Version 3.0.1. http://www.alphaworks.ibm.com/, 2000.
17. G. Kiczales, E. Hilsdale, J. Hugunin, M. Kersten, J. Palm, and W. G. Griswold. Getting started with AspectJ. *Communications of the ACM*, October 2001.
18. G. Kiczales, J. Lamping, A. Mendhekar, C. Maeda, C. Lopes, J. Loingtier, and J. Irwin. Aspect-oriented programming. In *Proceedings of the European Conference on Object-Oriented Programming (ECOOP'97)*, LNCS 1241. Springer-Verlag, 1997.
19. B. B. Kristensen and K. Østerbye. Roles: Conceptual abstraction theory & practical language issues. *Theory and Practice of Object Systems*, 2:143–160, 1996.
20. O. Lassila and R. R. Swick. Resource description framework (RDF): Model and syntax specification. http://www.w3.org/TR/WD-rdf-syntax/, 1999.
21. D. Megginson. SAX 2.0: The simple API for XML. http://www.megginson.com/SAX/index.html, 1999.
22. G. Neumann and U. Zdun. Enhancing object-based system composition through per-object mixins. In *Proceedings of Asia-Pacific Software Engineering Conference (APSEC)*, Takamatsu, Japan, December 1999.

23. G. Neumann and U. Zdun. Filters as a language support for design patterns in object-oriented scripting languages. In *Proceedings of COOTS'99, 5th Conference on Object-Oriented Technologies and Systems*, San Diego, California, USA, May 1999.
24. G. Neumann and U. Zdun. Implementing object-specific design patterns using per-object mixins. In *Proceedings of NOSA'99, Second Nordic Workshop on Software Architecture*, Ronneby, Sweden, August 1999.
25. G. Neumann and U. Zdun. Towards the usage of dynamic object aggregation as a foundation for composition. In *Proceedings of Symposium of Applied Computing (SAC'00)*, Como, Italy, March 2000.
26. G. Neumann and U. Zdun. XOTCL, an object-oriented scripting language. In *Proceedings of Tcl2k: The 7th USENIX Tcl/Tk Conference*, Austin, Texas, USA, February 2000.
27. J. K. Ousterhout. TCL: An embeddable command language. In *Proc. of the 1990 Winter USENIX Conference*, January 1990.
28. J. Punin. W3C sample code library libwww RDF parser. http://www.w3.org/Library/src/HTRDF, 1998.
29. J. Saarela. SiRPAC - simple RDF parser & compiler. http://www.w3.org/RDF/Implementations/SiRPAC/, 1998.
30. D. C. Schmidt. Wrapper facade: A structural pattern for encapsulating functions within classes. *C++ Report, SIGS*, 11(2), February 1999.
31. O. Vogel and U. Zdun. Dynamic content conversion and generation on the web: A pattern language. submitted to EuroPlop 2002, 2002.
32. W3C. Document object model. http://www.w3.org/DOM/, 2000.
33. D. Wetherall and C. J. Lindblad. Extending TCL for dynamic object-oriented programming. In *Proc. of the Tcl/Tk Workshop '95*, Toronto, July 1995.
34. U. Zdun. *Language Support for Dynamic and Evolving Software Architectures*. PhD thesis, University of Essen, Germany, January 2002.

Modern Concurrency Abstractions for C#

Nick Benton, Luca Cardelli, and Cédric Fournet

Microsoft Research

Abstract. Polyphonic C# is an extension of the C# language with new
asynchronous concurrency constructs, based on the join calculus. We describe the design and implementation of the language and give examples
of its use in addressing a range of concurrent programming problems.

1 Introduction

1.1 Languages and Concurrency

Concurrency is an important factor in the behaviour and performance of modern
code: concurrent programs are difficult to design, write, reason about, debug,
and tune. Concurrency can significantly affect the meaning of virtually every
other construct in the language (beginning with the atomicity of assignment),
and can affect the ability to invoke libraries. Yet, most popular programming
languages treat concurrency not as a language feature, but as a collection of
external libraries that are often underspecified.

Considerable attention has been given, after the fact, to the specification of
important concurrency libraries [4,15,14,9] to the point where one can usually
determine what their behaviour should be under any implementation. Yet, even
when the concurrency libraries are satisfactorily specified, the simple fact that
they are libraries, and not features of the language, has undesirable consequences.

Many features can be provided, in principle, either as language features or as
libraries: typical examples are memory management and exceptions. The advantage of having such features "in the language" is that the compiler can analyze
them, and can therefore produce better code and warn programmers of potential
and actual problems. In particular, the compiler can check for syntactically embedded invariants which would be difficult to extract from a collection of library
calls. Moreover, programmers can more reliably state their intentions through a
clear syntax, and tools other than the compiler can more easily determine the
programmers' intentions. Domain Specific Languages [29,20] are an extreme example of this linguistic approach: new ad-hoc languages are routinely proposed
not to replace general-purpose language, but to facilitate domain-specific code
analysis by the simple fact of expressing domain-related features as primitive
language constructs.

We believe that concurrency should be a language feature and a part of
language specifications. Serious attempts in this direction were made beginning

---

* An earlier version of this work was presented at the FOOL9 workshop in January
 2002 Portland, Oregon.

B. Magnusson (Ed.): ECOOP 2002, LNCS 2374, pp. 415–440, 2002.
© Springer-Verlag Berlin Heidelberg 2002

in the 1970's with the concept of monitors [16] and the Occam language [19] (based on Hoare's Communicating Sequential Processes [17]). The general notion of monitors has become very popular, particularly in its current object-oriented form of threads and object-bound mutexes, but it has been provided at most as a veneer of syntactic sugar for optionally locking objects on method calls.

Many things have changed in concurrency since monitors were introduced. Communication has become more asynchronous, and concurrent computations have to be "orchestrated" on a larger scale. The concern is not as much in the efficient implementation and use of locks on a single processor or multiprocessor, but on the ability to handle asynchronous events without unnecessarily blocking clients for long periods, and without deadlocking. In other words, the concern is shifting from shared-memory concurrency to message- or event-oriented concurrency.

These new requirements deserve programming constructs that can handle well asynchronous communications and that are not shackled to the shared-memory approach. Despite the development of a large collection of design patterns [22] and of many concurrent languages [2,28,1], only monitors have gained widespread acceptance as programming constructs.

An interesting new linguistic approach has emerged recently with Fournet and Gonthier's *join calculus* [11,12], a process calculus well-suited to direct implementation in a distributed setting. Other languages, such as JoCaml [8] and Funnel [27], combine similar ideas with the functional programming model. Here we propose an adaptation of join calculus ideas to an object-oriented language that already has an existing threads-and-locks concurrency model.

1.2   Asynchronous Programming

Asynchronous events and message passing are increasingly used at all levels of software systems. At the lowest level, device drivers have to respond promptly to asynchronous device events, while being parsimonious on resource use. At the Graphical User Interface level, code and programming models are notoriously complex because of the asynchronous nature of user events; at the same time, users hate being blocked unnecessarily. At the wide-area network level, e.g. in collaborative applications, distributed workflow or web services, we are now experiencing similar problems and complexity because of the asynchronous nature and latencies of global communication.

All these areas naturally lead to situations where there are many asynchronous messages to be handled concurrently, and where many threads are used to handle them. Threads are still an expensive resource on most systems. However, if we can somewhat hide the use of messages and threads behind a language mechanism, then many options become possible. A compiler may transform some patterns of concurrency into state machines, optimize the use of queues, use lightweight threads when possible, avoid forking threads when not necessary, and use thread pools. All this is really possible only if one has a handle on the spectrum of "things that can happen": this handle can be given by a syntax for concurrent operations that can both hide and enable multiple implementation techniques.

Therefore, we aim to promote abstractions for asynchronous programming that are high-level, from the point of view of a programmer, and that enable multiple low-level optimizations, from the point of view of a compiler and run-time systems. We propose an extension of the C$^\sharp$ language with modern concurrency abstraction for asynchronous programming. In tune with the musical spirit of C$^\sharp$ and with the "orchestration" of concurrent activities, we call this language Polyphonic C$^\sharp$ [1].

1.3   C$^\sharp$ and .NET

C$^\sharp$ is a modern, type-safe, object-oriented programming language recently introduced by Microsoft as part of Visual Studio.NET [10]. C$^\sharp$ programs run on top of the .NET Framework, which includes a multilanguage execution engine and a rich collection of class libraries.

The .NET execution engine provides a multithreaded execution environment with synchronization based on locks potentially associated with each heap-allocated object. The C$^\sharp$ language includes a **lock** statement, which obtains the mutex associated with a given object during the execution of a block. In addition, the .NET libraries implement many traditional concurrency control primitives such as semaphores, mutexes and reader/writer locks, as well as an asynchronous programming model based on delegates[2]. The .NET Framework also provides higher-level infrastructure for building distributed applications and services, such as SOAP-based messaging and remote method call.

The concurrency and distribution mechanisms of the .NET Framework are powerful, but they are also undeniably complex. Quite apart from the bewildering array of primitives which are more or less 'baked in' to the infrastructure, there is something of a mismatch between the 1970s model of concurrency on a single machine (shared memory, threads, synchronization based on mutual exclusion) and the asynchronous, message-based style which one uses for programming web-based applications and services. C$^\sharp$ therefore seems an ideal testbed for our ideas on language support for concurrency in mainstream languages.

2   Polyphonic C$^\sharp$ Language Overview

This section describes the syntax and semantics of the new constructs in Polyphonic C$^\sharp$ and then gives a more precise, though still informal, specification of the syntax.

---

[1] *Polyphony* is musical composition that uses simultaneous, largely independent, melodic parts, lines, or voices (Encarta World English Dictionary, Microsoft Corporation, 2001).

[2] An instance of a delegate class encapsulates an object and a method on that object with a particular signature. So a delegate is more than a C-style function pointer, but slightly less than a closure.

2.1   The Basic Idea

To C$^\sharp$'s fairly conventional object-oriented programming model, Polyphonic C$^\sharp$ adds just two new concepts: *asynchronous methods* and *chords*.

Asynchronous Methods. Conventional methods are synchronous, in the sense that the caller makes no progress until the callee completes. In Polyphonic C$^\sharp$, if a method is declared *asynchronous* then any call to it is guaranteed to return (essentially) immediately. Asynchronous methods never return a result and are declared by using the **async** keyword instead of **void**. Calling an asynchronous method is much like sending a message, or posting an event.

Since asynchronous methods have to return immediately, the behaviour of a method such as

```
async postEvent(EventInfo data) {
    // large method body
}
```

is the only thing it could reasonably be: the call returns immediately and 'large method body' is scheduled for execution in a different thread (either a new one spawned to service this call, or a worker from some pool). However, this kind of definition is actually rather rare in Polyphonic C$^\sharp$. More commonly, asynchronous methods are defined using chords, as described below, and do not necessarily require new threads.

Chords. A *chord* (also called a 'synchronization pattern', or 'join pattern') consists of a header and a body. The header is a set of method declarations separated by '&'. The body is only executed once *all* the methods in the header have been called. Method calls are implicitly queued up until/unless there is a matching chord. Consider for example

```
class Buffer {
    string Get() & async Put(string s) {
        return s;
    }
}
```

The code above defines a class *Buffer* declaring two instance methods which are defined together in a single chord. The first method **string** *Get*() is a synchronous method taking no arguments and returning a **string**. The second method **async** *Put*(**string** *s*) is asynchronous (so returns no result) and takes a **string** argument.

If *buff* is a instance of *Buffer* and one calls the synchronous method *buff* . *Get*() then there are two possibilities:

– If there has previously been an unmatched call to *buff*.*Put*(*s*) (for some string *s*) then there is now a match, so the pending *Put*(*s*) is de-queued and the body of the chord runs, returning *s* to the caller of *buff* . *Get*().

- If there are no previous unmatched calls to *buff*.*Put*(.) then the call to *buff*.*Get*() blocks until another thread supplies a matching *Put*(.).

Conversely, on a call to the asynchronous method *buff*.*Put*(*s*), the caller will never wait but there are two possible behaviours with regard to other threads:

- If there has previously been an unmatched call to *buff*.*Get*() then there is now a match, so the pending call is de-queued and its associated blocked thread is awakened to run the body of the chord, which will return *s*.
- If there are no pending calls to *buff*.*Get*() then the call to *buff*.*Put*(*s*) is simply queued up until one arrives.

Exactly *which* pairs of calls will be matched up is unspecified, so even a single-threaded program such as

```
Buffer buff = new Buffer();
buff.Put("blue");
buff.Put("sky");
Console.Write(buff.Get() + buff.Get());
```

is non-deterministic (printing either "bluesky" or "skyblue")[3].

Note that the implementation of *Buffer* does not involve spawning any threads – whenever the body of the chord runs, it does so in a preexisting thread (viz. the one which called *Get*()). The reader may at this point wonder what the rules are for deciding in which thread a body runs, or how we know to which method call the final value computed by the body will be returned. The answer is that in any given chord, at most one method may be synchronous. If there is such a method, then the body runs in the thread associated with, and the value is returned to, the call to that method. If there is no such method (i.e. all the methods in the chord are asynchronous) then the body runs in a new thread and there is no value to return.

It should also be pointed out that the *Buffer* code, trivial though it is, is unconditionally thread-safe. The locking that is required (for example to prevent the argument to a single *Put* being returned to two distinct *Get*s) is generated automatically by the compiler. More precisely, deciding whether any chord is enabled by a call and, if so, removing the other pending calls from the queues and scheduling the body for execution is an atomic operation. There is, however, no mutual exclusion between chord bodies beyond that which is explicitly provided by the synchronization in the headers.

The *Buffer* example uses a single chord to define two methods. It is also possible (and common) to have multiple chords involving a given method. For example:

---

[3] Of course, in any real implementation the nondeterminism in this very simple example will be resolved statically, so different executions will always produce the same result, but this is not part of the official semantics.

```
class Buffer {
  int Get() & async Put(int n) {
    return n;
  }

  string Get() & async Put(int n) {
    return n.ToString();
  }
}
```

Now we have defined a method for putting integers into the buffer, but two methods for getting them out (which happen to be distinguished by type rather than name). A call to *Put()* can synchronize with a call to either of the *Get()* methods. If there are pending calls to both *Get()*s, then which one synchronizes with a subsequent *Put()* is unspecified.

3 Informal Specification

3.1 Grammar

The syntactic extensions to the C$^\sharp$ grammar [10, Appendix C] are very minor. We add a new keyword, **async**, and add it as an alternative *return-type*:

$$return\text{-}type \quad ::= \quad type \mid \textbf{void} \mid \textbf{async}$$

This allows methods, delegates and interface methods to be declared asynchronous. In *class-member-declarations*, we replace *method-declaration* with *chord-declaration*:

> *chord-declaration* ::=
>   *method-header* [& *method-header*]* *body*
> *method-header* ::=
>   *attributes modifiers return-type member-name(formals)*

We call a chord declaration *trivial* if it declares a single, synchronous method (i.e. it is a standard C$^\sharp$ method declaration).

3.2 Well-Formedness

Extended classes are subject to a number of well-formedness conditions:

– Within a single *method-header*:
  1. If *return-type* is **async** then the formal parameter list *formals* may not contain any **ref** or **out** parameter modifier[4].

---

[4] Neither **ref** nor **out** parameters make sense for asynchronous messages, since they are both passed as addresses of locals in a stack frame which may have disappeared when the message is processed.

- Within a single *chord-declaration*:
  2. At most one *method-header* may have a non-**async** *return-type*.
  3. If the chord has a *method-header* with *return-type type*, then *body* may use **return** statements with *type* expressions, otherwise *body* may use empty **return** statements.
  4. All the *formals* appearing in *method-headers* must have distinct identifiers.
  5. Two *method-headers* may not have both the same *member-name* and the same argument type signature.
  6. The *method-headers* must either all declare instance methods or all declare static methods.
- Within a particular class:
  7. All *method-headers* with the same *member-name* and argument type signature must have the same *return-type* and identical sets of *attributes* and *modifiers*.
  8. If it is a value class (**struct**), then only static methods may appear in non-trivial chords.
  9. If any *chord-declaration* includes a virtual method m with the **override** modifier[5], then any method n which appears in a chord with m *in the superclass containing the overridden definition of* m must also be overridden in the subclass.

Most of these conditions are fairly straightforward, though Conditions 2 and 9 deserve some further comment.

Condition 9 provides a conservative, but simple, sanity check when refining a class that contains chords since, in general, implementation inheritance and concurrency do not mix well [24]. Our approach is to enforce a separation of these two concerns: a series of chords must be syntactically local to a class or a subclass declaration; when methods are overridden, all their chords must also be completely overridden. If one takes the view that the implementation of a given method consists of all the synchronization and bodies of all the chords in which it appears then our inheritance restriction seems not unreasonable, since in (illegal) code such as

```
class C {
    virtual void f() & virtual async g() { /* body1 */ }
    virtual void f() & virtual async h() { /* body2 */ }
}

class D : C {
    override async g() { /* body3 */ }
}
```

one would, by overriding $g()$, have also 'half' overridden $f()$.

---

[5] In C♯, methods which are intended to be overridable in subclasses are explicitly marked as such by use of the **virtual** modifier, whilst methods which are intended to override ones inherited from a superclass must explicitly say so with the **override** modifier.

More pragmatically, removing the restriction on inheritance makes it all too easy to introduce inadvertent deadlock (or 'async leakage'). If the above code were legal, then code written to expect instances of class C which makes matching calls to $f()$ and $g()$ would fail to work when passed an instance of D – all the calls to $g()$ would cause *body3* to run and all the calls to $f()$ would deadlock.

Note that the inheritance restriction means that code such as

class C {
   virtual void $f()$ & **private async** $g()$ { /* body1 */ }
}

is incorrect: declaring just one of $f()$ and $g()$ to be **virtual** makes no sense, as overriding one requires the other to be overridden too. It is also worth observing that there is a transitive closure operation implicit in our inheritance restriction: if $f()$ is overridden and joined with $g()$ then because $g()$ must be overridden, so must any method $h()$ which is joined with $g()$ and so on.

It is possible to devise more complex and permissive rules for overriding. Our current rule has the advantage of simplicity, but we refer the reader to [13] for a more thorough study of inheritance in the join calculus, including more advanced type systems for its control.

Well-formedness Condition 2 above is also justified by a potentially bad interaction between existing $C^\sharp$ features and the pure join calculus. Allowing more than one synchronous call to appear in a single chord would give a potentially useful *rendez-vous* facility (provided one also added syntax allowing results to be returned to particular calls). But one would then have to decide in which of the blocked threads the body ran, and this choice is observable. If this were simply because thread identities can be obtained and checked for equality, the problem would be fairly academic. However, since reentrant locks are associated with threads, the choice of thread could make a significant difference to the synchronization behaviour of the program, thus making & 'very' non-commutative.

Of course, it is not hard to program a rendez-vous explicitly in Polyphonic $C^\sharp$. In the following example, calls from different threads of the methods f and g will wait for each other and then exchange arguments before proceeding.

```
class RendezVous {
  public int f(int i) & async gotj(int j) {
    goti(i); return j;
  }

  public int g(int j) {
    gotj(j); return waitfori();
  }

  int waitfori() & async goti(int i) {
    return i;
  }
}
```

3.3   Typing Issues

We treat **async** as a subtype of **void** and allow 'covariant return types' just in the case of these two (pseudo)types. Thus

- an **async** method may override a **void** one,
- a **void** delegate may be created from an **async** method, and
- an **async** method may implement a **void** method in an interface

but not conversely. This design makes intuitive sense (an **async** method *is* a **void** one, but has the extra property of returning 'immediately') and also maximises compatibility with existing code (superclasses, interfaces and delegate definitions) which makes use of **void**.

4   Programming in Polyphonic C♯

Having introduced the language, we now show how it may be used to address a range of concurrent programming problems.

4.1   A Simple Cell Class

We start with an implementation of a simple one-place cell class. Cells have two public synchronous methods: **void** *Put*(*Object o*) and *Object Get*(). A call to *Put* blocks until the cell is empty and then fills the cell with its argument. A call to *Get* blocks until the cell is full and then removes and returns its contents:

```
class OneCell {
   public OneCell() {
      empty();
   }

   public void Put(Object o) & async empty() {
      contains(o);
   }

   public Object Get() & async contains(Object o) {
      empty();
      return o;
   }
}
```

In addition to the two public methods, the class uses two private asynchronous methods, *empty*() and *contains*(*Object o*), to carry the state of cells. There is a simple declarative reading of the constructor and the two chords which explains how this works:

constructor: When a cell is created, it is initially *empty*().

put-chord: If we *Put* an *Object o* into a cell which is *empty*() then the cell *contains*(*o*).

get-chord: If we *Get*() the contents of a cell which *contains* an *Object o* then afterwards the cell is *empty*() and the returned value is *o*.

implicitly: In all other cases, *Put*s and *Get*s wait.

The technique of using private asynchronous methods (rather than fields) to carry state is very common in Polyphonic C♯. Observe that the constructor establishes, and every body in class *OneCell* preserves, a simple and easily verified invariant:

> There is always exactly one pending asynchronous method call: either an *empty*() or a *contains*(*o*), for some *Object o*.

(In contrast there may be an arbitrary number of client threads blocked with pending calls to *Put* or *Get*, or even concurrently running statement **return** *o* within the last body.) Hence one can also read the class definition as a direct specification of an automaton:

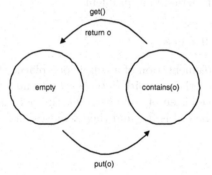

4.2   Reader-Writer Locks

As a more realistic example of the use of asynchronous methods to carry state and chords to synchronize access to that state, we now consider the classic problem of protecting a shared mutable resource with a multiple-reader, single-writer lock. Clients each request, and then release, either shared access or exclusive access, using the corresponding public methods *Shared*, *ReleaseShared*, *Exclusive*, and *ReleaseExclusive*. Requests for shared access block until no other client has exclusive access, whilst requests for exclusive access block until no other client has any access. A canonical solution to this problem using traditional concurrency primitives in Modula 3 may be found in [5]; using Polyphonic C♯, it can be written with just five chords:

class *ReaderWriter*
{
  ReaderWriter() { *Idle*(); }

```
public void Shared() & async Idle() { S(1); }
public void Shared() & async S(int n) { S(n+1); }
public void ReleaseShared() & async S(int n) {
   if (n == 1) Idle(); else S(n−1);
}
public void Exclusive() & async Idle() {}
public void ReleaseExclusive() { Idle(); }
}
```

Provided that every release follows the corresponding request, the invariant is that the state of the lock (no message, a single message $Idle()$, or a single message $Shared(n)$ with $n > 0$) matches the kind and number of threads currently holding the lock (an exclusive thread, no thread, or n sharing threads).

It is a matter of choice whether to use private fields or parameters in private messages. In the example above, n makes sense only when there is an S message present. Nonetheless, we could write instead the following equivalent code:

```
class ReaderWriterPrivate
{
   ReaderWriter() { Idle(); }
   private int n; // protected by S()

   public void Shared() & async Idle() { n=1; S(); }
   public void Shared() & async S() { n++; S(); }
   public void ReleaseShared() & async S() {
      if (−−n == 0) Idle(); else S();
   }
   public void Exclusive() & async Idle() {}
   public void ReleaseExclusive() { Idle(); }
}
```

Our model of concurrency provides basic fairness properties. In cases when some application-specific fairness is required, one can supplement it with programmed fairness. For instance, we could further refine our code to implement some fairness between readers and writers, by adding extra shared states, $T()$, when we don't accept new readers, and $IdleExclusive()$, when we provide the exclusive lock to a previously-selected thread.

```
class ReaderWriterFair
{
   ... // same content as above, plus:

   public void ReleaseShared() & async T() {
      if (−−n == 0) IdleExclusive(); else T();
   }
   public void Exclusive() & async S() { T(); wait(); }
   void wait() & async IdleExclusive() {}
}
```

4.3   Combining Asynchronous Messages

The external interface of a server which uses message-passing will typically consist of asynchronous methods, each of which takes as arguments both the parameters for a request *and* somewhere to send the final result or notification that the request has been serviced. For example, using delegates as callbacks, a service taking a string argument and returning an integer might look like:

delegate async *IntCallback*(**int** *result*);

```
class Service {
  public async Request(string arg, IntCallback cb) {
    int r;
    // do some work
    ...
    cb(r); // send the result back
  }
}
```

A common client-side pattern then involves making several concurrent asynchronous requests and later blocking until *all* of them have completed. This may be programmed as follows:

```
class Join2 {
  public void wait(out int i, out int j)
  & public async first(int fst)
  & public async second(int snd) {
    i = fst; j = snd;
  }
}
  // Client code...
  int i,j;
  Join2 x = new Join2();
  service1.Request(arg1,new IntCallback(x.first));
  service2.Request(arg2,new IntCallback(x.second));
  // do something useful in the meantime...
  // now wait for both results to come back
  x.wait(i,j);
  // and do something with i and j
```

The call to $x.wait(i,j)$ will block until/unless both of the services have replied by invoking their respective callbacks on x. Once that has happened, the two results will be assigned to i and j and the client will proceed. Generalising *Join2* to an arbitrary number of simultaneous calls, or defining classes which wait for conditions such as 'at least 3 out of 5 calls have completed' is straightforward.

4.4   Active Objects

Some concurrent object oriented languages take as primitive the notion of *active objects*. These have an independent thread of control associated with each instance which is used to process (typically sequentially) messages sent (typically asynchronously) from other objects. One way to express this pattern in Polyphonic C$^\sharp$ is via inheritance from an abstract base class:

```
public abstract class ActiveObject {
  protected bool done;

  abstract protected void ProcessMessage();

  public ActiveObject () {
    done = false;
    mainLoop();
  }

  async mainLoop() {
    while (!done) {
      ProcessMessage();
    }
  }
}
```

The constructor of *ActiveObject* calls the asynchronous method *mainLoop()* which spawns a new message-handling thread for that object. Subclasses of *ActiveObject* then define chords for each message to synchronize with a call to *ProcessMessage()*. Here, for example, is a skeleton of an active object which multicasts stock quote messages to a list of clients:

```
public class StockServer : ActiveObject {
  private ArrayList clients;

  public async AddClient(Client c) // add new client
  & void ProcessMessage() {
    clients . Add(c);
  }

  public async WireQuote(Quote q) // new quote off wire
  & void ProcessMessage() {
    foreach (Client c in clients ) {
      c.UpdateQuote(q);   // and send to all  clients
    }
  }

  public async CloseDown() // request to terminate
  & void ProcessMessage() {
    done = true;
  }
}
```

Interestingly, one cannot move the *CloseDown*() chord to the superclass (to share it amongst all *ActiveObjects*) since that would violate the restriction on combining overriding with synchronization which we described in Section 3.2.

4.5 Custom Schedulers

In Polyphonic C$^\sharp$, we have to both coexist with and build upon the existing threading model. Because these threads are relatively expensive, and are the holders of locks, C$^\sharp$ programmers often need explicit control over thread usage. In such cases, Polyphonic C$^\sharp$ is a convenient way to write what amount to custom schedulers for a particular application.

To illustrate this point, we present an example in which we dynamically schedule series of related calls in large batches, to favour locality. (This is loosely related to what is sometimes called 'staged' or 'pipelined' computation [21].) The two following classes model such batch computations, represented as *Heavy* objects that have large startup costs and limited concurrency. Pragmatically, those costs may be due to a large code and data footprint. The helper class *Token* enables us to limit the number of active *Heavy* objects, here 2.

```
class Token {
    public void Grab() & public async Release() {}
    public Token(int n) { for (int i = 0; i < n; i++) Release(); }
}
class Heavy {
    static Token tk = new Token(2); // limits parallelism
    public Heavy (int q) { tk.Grab (); ...; }  // rather slow
    public int Work(int p) { return ...; } // rather fast
    public void Close() { tk.Release(); }
}
```

The class below implements our scheduler. To each task, *Burst* provides a front-end that attempts to organise calls into long series that share the startup cost. A burst can be in two states, represented by either *idle*() or *open*(). The state is initially idle. When a first thread tries to access the resource, the state becomes open, then this thread proceeds with the potentially-blocking *Heavy*(q) call. As long as the state is open, subsequent callers are queued-up. When the first thread completes its own task, and before releasing the *Heavy* resource, it also processes the tasks for all pending calls and resumes their threads with the respective results. Meanwhile, the state is still open, and new threads may be queued-up, so the process is repeated until no other thread is present. Eventually, the state becomes idle again. The helper class *Thunk* is used to block each queued-up thread and resume it with the result r, in asynchronous message-passing style.

```
class Burst {
    int others = 0; int q;
    public Burst(int q) { this.q = q; idle (); }

    public int Work(int p) & async idle() {
        open();
        Heavy h = new Heavy(q);
        int r = h.Work(p);
        helpful (h); // any delayed threads?
        h.Close();
        return r;
    }
    public int Work(int p) & async open() {
        others++; open();
        Thunk t = new Thunk(); delayed(t,p);
        return t.Wait(); // usually blocking
    }
    void helpful(Heavy h) & async open() {
        if ( others == 0) idle();
        else {
            int batch = others; others = 0;
            open();
            while(batch-- > 0) extraWork(h);
            helpful (h); // newly-delayed threads?
        }
    }
    void extraWork(Heavy h) & async delayed(Thunk t,int p) {
        t.Done(h.Work(p));
    }
}
class Thunk {
    public int Wait() & public async Done(int r) {
        return r;
    }
}
```

We omit the code that allocates an array of *Burst* objects to be shared by all threads, and some performance test code, which unsurprisingly exhibits a large speedup when concurrent threads call *Burst* rather than directly calling *Heavy*.

5 Implementation

This section describes the implementation of chords using lower-level concurrency primitives. The compilation process is best explained as a translation from a polyphonic class to a plain C$^\sharp$ class. The resulting class has the same name and signature as the source class, and also has private state and methods to deal with synchronization.

5.1   Synchronization and State Automata

In the implementation of a polyphonic class, each method body combines two kinds of code, corresponding to the synchronization of polyphonic method calls (generated from the chord headers) and to their actual computation (copied from the chord bodies), respectively.

We now describe how the synchronization code is generated from a set of chords. Since synchronization is statically defined by those chords, we can efficiently compile it down to a state automaton. This is the approach initially described in [23], though our implementation does not construct explicit state machines.

The *synchronization state* consists of pending calls for any method that occurs in a chord, that is, threads for regular methods and messages for asynchronous methods. However, synchronization effectively depends on a much simpler state that records only the presence of pending calls; the actual parameters and the calling contexts become relevant only after a chord is fired. Hence, the whole synchronization state can be summarized in a word, with a single bit that records the presence of (one or more) pending calls, for every method appearing in a least a chord. Accordingly, every chord declaration is represented as a constant word with a bit set for every method appearing in that chord, and the synchronization code checks whether a chord can be fired by comparing the synchronization word with these precomputed bitmasks.

Performance Considerations. The cost of polyphonic method calls should be similar to the cost of regular method calls unless a synchronized method call blocks waiting for **async** messages—in that case, we cannot avoid paying the rather high cost of dynamic thread scheduling.

When an asynchronous method is called, it performs a bounded amount of computation on the caller thread before returning.

When a regular, synchronized method is called, the critical path to optimize is the one in which, for at least one chord, all complementary asynchronous messages are already present. In that case, the synchronization code retrieves the content of the complementary messages, updates the synchronization state, and immediately proceeds with the method body. Conversely, when there is no such chord, the thread must be suspended, and the cost of running our synchronization code is likely to be small as compared to lower-level context-switching and scheduling.

Firing a completely asynchronous chord is always comparatively expensive since it involves spawning a new thread. Hence, when an asynchronous message arrives, it makes sense to check for matches with synchronous chords first. We also lower the cost of asynchronous chords by using .NET's *thread pool* mechanism rather than simply spawning a fresh operating system thread every time. The scheduling policy of the thread pool is not optimal for all applications, however, so we may use attributes to allow programmer control over thread creation policy.

Low-Level Concurrency. The code handling the chords must be unconditionally thread-safe, for all source code in the class. To this end, we use a single, auxiliary lock to protect our private synchronization state. (We actually use the regular object lock for one of the queues.) Locking occurs only for short periods of time, for each incoming call that goes through the chords, so hopefully the lock will nearly always be available.

This lock is independent of the regular object lock, which may be used as usual to protect the rest of the state and prevent race conditions.

5.2   The Translation

We now present, by means of a simple example, the details of the translation of Polyphonic C$^\sharp$ into ordinary C$^\sharp$. The translation presented here is actually an abstraction of that which we have implemented. For didactic purposes, we modularise the translated code by introducing auxiliary classes for queues and bitmasks, whereas our current implementation effectively inlines the code contained in these classes.

Supporting Classes. The following value class (structure) provides operations on bitmasks:

```
struct BitMask {
    private int v; // = 0;
    public void set(int m) { v |= m; }
    public void clear(int m) { v &= ~m; }
    public bool match(int m) { return (~v & m)==0; }
}
```

Next, we define the classes that represent message queues. To every asynchronous method, the compiler associates a message-queue that stores pending messages for that method, with an *empty* property for testing its state and two methods *add* and *get* for adding an element to the queue and getting an element back (when asserting that the queue is not empty). The implementation of each queue depends on the message contents (and, potentially, on compiler-deduced invariants); it does not necessarily use an actual queue.

A simple case is that of single-argument asynchronous messages (here, **int** messages); these generate a thin wrapper on top of the standard queue library:

```
class intQ {
    private Queue q;
    public intQ() {q = new Queue(); }
    public void add(int i) { q.Enqueue(i); }
    public int get() {return (int) q.Dequeue(); }
    public bool empty {get{return q.Count == 0;}}
}
```

Another important case of message-queue deals with empty (no argument) messages. It is implemented as a single message counter.

```
class voidQ {
  private int n;
  public voidQ() { n = 0; }
  public void add() { n++; }
  public void get() { n--; }
  public bool empty {get{ return n==0; }}
}
```

Finally, for synchronous methods, we need classes implementing queues of waiting threads. As with message queues, there is a uniform interface and a choice of several implementations.

Method *yield* is called to store the current thread in the queue and awaits for additional messages; it assumes the thread holds some private lock on a polyphonic object, and releases that lock while waiting. Conversely, method *wakeup* is called to wake up a thread in the queue; it immediately returns and does not otherwise affect the caller thread.

The code below implements synchronization using *monitors*, the low-level interface to object locks in $C^\sharp$.

```
class threadQ {
  private Queue q;
  public threadQ() { q = new Queue(); }
  public bool empty {get{ return (q.Count == 0); }}
  public void yield(object myCurrentLock) {
    q.Enqueue(Thread.CurrentThread);
    Monitor.Exit(myCurrentLock);
    try {
      Thread.Sleep(Timeout.Infinite);
    }
    catch (ThreadInterruptedException) {}
    Monitor.Enter(myCurrentLock);
    q.Dequeue();
  }
  public void wakeup() {((Thread) q.Peek()).Interrupt();}
}
```

(The specification of monitors guarantees that an interrupt on a non-sleeping thread does not happen until the thread actually does call *Thread.Sleep*, hence it *is* correct to release the lock before entering the **try catch** statement.)

As the thread awakens in the **catch** clause, it first reacquires the lock, which might block the thread again; we expect this case to be uncommon. The thread which is then de-queued and discarded is always the current thread.

Generated Synchronization Code. Figure 1 shows a simple polyphonic class *Token* (from Section 4.5, though with the addition of a parameter (rather pointlessly) passed to and returned from the *Grab* method) and its translation into ordinary $C^\sharp$, making use of the auxiliary classes defined above. *Token* imple-

```
class Token {
  public Token(int initial_tokens) {
    for (int i = 0; i < initial_tokens ; i++) Release();
  }
  public int Grab(int id) & public async Release() {
    return id;
  }
}
```

```
class Token {
  private const int mGrab = 1 << 0;
  private const int mRelease = 1 << 1;
  private threadQ GrabQ = new threadQ();
  private voidQ ReleaseQ = new voidQ();

  private const int mGrabRelease = mGrab | mRelease;
  private BitMask s = new BitMask();
  private object mlock = GrabQ;

  private void scan() {
    if (s.match(mGrabRelease)) GrabQ.wakeup();
  }
  public Token(int initial_tokens) {
    for (int i = 0; i < initial_tokens ; i++) Release();
  }
  [OneWay] public void Release() {
    lock(mlock) {
      ReleaseQ.add();
      if (! s.match(mRelease)) {
        s.set(mRelease);
        scan(); }}
  }
  public int Grab(int id) {
    Monitor.Enter(mlock);
    if (! s.match(mGrab)) goto now;
  later :
    GrabQ.yield(mlock); if (GrabQ.empty) s.clear(mGrab);
  now:
    if (s.match(mRelease)) {
      ReleaseQ.get(); if (ReleaseQ.empty) s.clear(mRelease);
      scan();
      Monitor.Exit(mlock);
      {
        return id; // source code for the chord
      }
    }else{
      s.set(mGrab); goto later; }}
}
```

Fig. 1. The *Token* class and its translation

ments an n-token lock. It has a regular synchronous method, an asynchronous method, and a single chord that synchronizes the two.

We now describe what is happening in the translations of the two methods:

Code for *Release*. After taking the chord lock, we add the message to the queue and, unless they were already messages stored in *ReleaseQ*, we update the mask and scan for active chords.

In a larger class with chords that do not involve *Release*, the *scan*() statement could be usefully inlined and specialized: we only need to test patterns where **async** *Release*() appears; besides, we know that the *mRelease* bit is set.

The Use of OneWay. The reader unfamiliar with C$^\sharp$ may wonder why the translation of the *Release*() method is prefixed with '[**OneWay**]'. This is a C$^\sharp$ attribute[6] which indicates to the .NET infrastructure that where appropriate (e.g. when calling between different machines) calls of *Release*() should be genuinely non-blocking. The translation adds this attribute to all asynchronous methods.

Code for *Grab*. After taking the chord lock, we first check whether there are already deferred *Grab*s stored in *GrabQ*. If so, this call cannot proceed for now so we enqueue the current thread and will retry later.

Otherwise, we check whether there is at least one pending *Release* message to complete the chord **int** *Grab*(**int** *id*) & **async** *Release*(). If so, we select this chord for immediate execution; otherwise we update the mask to record the presence of deferred *Grab*s, enqueue the current thread and will retry later. (In classes with multiple patterns for *Grab*, we would perform a series of tests for each potential chord.) Notice that it is always safe to retry, independently of the synchronization state.

Once a chord is selected, we still have to update *ReleaseQ* and the mask. (Here, we don't have asynchronous parameters; more generally, we would read them from the queue and bind them to local variables.) At least in some cases, we must check whether there are still enough messages to awaken another thread; this is achieved by *scan*(). Finally, we release the lock and enter the block associated with the selected chord.

Why Rescanning? One may wonder why we systematically call *scan*() after selecting a chord for immediate execution (just before releasing the lock and executing the guarded block). In our simple example, this is unnecessary whenever we already know that this was the last *scan*() call or the last *Release*() message. In general, however, this may be required to prevent deadlocks. Consider for instance the polyphonic class

---

[6] Attributes are a standardized, declarative way of adding custom metadata to .NET programs. Code-manipulating tools and libraries, such as compilers, debuggers or the object serialization libraries can then use attribute information to vary their behaviour.

```
class Foo {
  void m1() & async s() & async t() {...}
  void m2() & async s() {...}
  void m3() & async t() {...}
}
```

and the following global execution trace, with four threads:

Thread 1 calls $m1()$ and blocks.
Thread 2: calls $m2()$ and blocks.
Thread 0: calls $t()$ then $s()$, awaking Thread 1
Thread 3: calls $m3()$ and succeeds, consuming $t()$.
Thread 1: retries $m1()$ and blocks again.

With this scheduling, Thread 3 preempts Thread 1 and "steals" its message $t()$. Although Thread 1 blocks again, the remaining message $s()$ suffices to run Thread 2. But if neither Thread 3 nor Thread 1 awakes Thread 2, we have a race condition leading to a deadlock.

Accordingly, in our implementation, the synchronization code in Thread 3 performs an additional $scan()$ that awakes Thread 2 in such unfortunate cases.

In many special cases, the final $scan()$ could safely be omitted, but identifying these cases would complicate the translation unnecessarily.

Deadlock Freedom. Next, we sketch a proof that our translation does not introduce deadlocks. (Of course, calls involving a chord that is never fired may be deadlocked, and our translation must implement those deadlocks.)

We say that an object is *active* when there are enough calls in the queues to trigger one of its patterns; assuming a fair scheduling of running processes, we show that active states are transient. We prove the invariant: *when an object is active, at least one thread on top of a queue is scheduled for execution and can succeed.*

- After $scan()$, the invariant always holds.
- An object becomes active when an asynchronous message is received, and this always triggers a scan.
- A thread whose polyphonic call succeeds (and thus consumes asynchronous messages) also triggers a scan.

When the algorithm awakes a thread, it is guaranteed that this thread may succeed if immediately scheduled, but not that it will necessarily succeed.

Fully Asynchronous Chords. To complete the description of our implementation, we explain the compilation of fully asynchronous chords. When such chords are fired, there is no thread at hand to execute their body, so a new thread must be created.

To illustrate this case, assume the class *Token* also contains the asynchronous method declaration

```
public async live(string s,int id) {
   Grab(id); Release ();
   Console.WriteLine(s);
}
```

The generated code is messy but straightforward:

```
private class liveArgs {
  public string s; public int id;
  public liveArgs(string s, int id) {
    this.s = s; this.id = id;
  }
}
private void liveBody(object o) {
  liveArgs  a = (liveArgs)o;
  string s = a.s; int id = a.id;
    Grab(id); Release ();   // async chord body code
    Console.WriteLine(s);
}
[OneWay]
public void live(string s,int id) {
  liveArgs  a = new liveArgs(s,id);
  WaitCallback  c = new  WaitCallback(liveBody);
  ThreadPool.QueueUserWorkItem(c,a);
}
}
```

We use an auxiliary class *liveArgs* to pass the parameters to the new thread, and a delegate to the host object's *liveBody* method to resume execution within the same object context.

More generally, for a chord containing several asynchronous methods, the code in the *live* method above would occur instead of $mQ.wakeup()$ to fire the pattern in method *scan*().

6   Current Status and Future Work

We have two prototype implementations of Polyphonic C$^\sharp$. The first is a modified version of the 'official' C$^\sharp$ compiler, which is written in C++, whilst the second is a simpler source-to-source translator written in ML. The latter has proven invaluable in explaining the language to others and is also considerably more straightforward to modify and maintain, though it does not cope with the full language. As our initial experiences using Polyphonic C$^\sharp$ have been positive, we are building a more robust, full-featured and maintainable implementation using an 'experimentation-friendly' C$^\sharp$-in-C$^\sharp$ compiler written by another group within Microsoft Research.

We have written a number of non-trivial samples in Polyphonic C$^\sharp$, including some web combinators along the lines of [6], an animated version of the dining philosophers, a distributed stock-dealing simulation built on .NET's remoting infrastructure[7] and a multithreaded client for the TerraServer [3] web service [25].

Amongst the other areas for further work on Polyphonic C♯ which we think are particularly interesting are:

Concurrency Types. As suggested in our examples, it is relatively easy to state and verify invariants in polyphonic classes, often from the shape of the chords and the visibility of their methods.

Several type systems and other static analyses have been developed in similar settings to automate the process, and check (or even infer) at compile time some behavioural properties such as

1. There is one, or at most one, pending message for this asynchronous method, or for this set of methods.
2. Calls to this method are always eventually processed (partial deadlock-freedom).

The potential benefits are obvious: the compiler can catch more programming errors, and otherwise produce more efficient code. While these tools are still rather complex, this is a very active area of research in concurrency [26,18,7]. (Needless to say, it would be much more difficult to check those properties on a code that directly uses threads and locks instead of chords.)

Timeouts and Priorities. In terms of expressiveness, it is tempting to supplement the syntax for chords with some declarative support for priorities or timeouts and, more generally, to provide a finer control over dynamic scheduling. We have a plausible-looking design for a timeout mechanism which we plan to implement and evaluate soon.

Optimizations. There are many opportunities for optimizing the simple-minded implementation described here. Some of these require proper static analysis, whereas others could usefully be implemented on the basis of more naive compile-time checks:

- Lock optimization. There are situations when we could safely 'fuse' successive critical sections which are protected by the same lock, for example when a bounded series of asynchronous messages are sent to the same object, or when a chord body sends messages to **this**.
- Queue optimization. 'Affine' methods, for which it can be determined that there can be at most one pending call on a particular object, may be compiled without queues.
- Thread optimization. Purely asynchronous chords which only perform very brief terminating computations (such as sending other messages) can also be compiled to run in the invoking thread, rather than a new one. This is a very

---

[7] Remoting provides remote method call over TCP (binary) or HTTP (SOAP).

desirable optimization, since it is not uncommon to have a public method which arguably *should* be asynchronous but which is only used to synchronize with, and then send, other (typically private) asynchronous messages. In such cases, one usually prefers not to pay the cost of thread startup and so defines the method as **void** rather than **async**, although this damages compositionality, for example by preventing one from instantiating an **async** delegate with the method. Concrete examples of this situation are provided by the *ReleaseShared* and *ReleaseExclusive* methods of the *ReaderWriter* class from Section 4.2 – although the potentially-blocking calls to *obtain* the lock clearly have to be synchronous, the methods for the *relinquishing* it could safely and neatly be made asynchronous were it not for the fact that they would then be handled by an expensive new threadpool task. Unfortunately, using static analysis to detect that a non-trivial chord body will always terminate 'quickly' is rather hard, so it may be that programmer annotation is a better s olution to this problem.

Pattern-Matching. There are situations in which it would be convenient to specify chords which are only enabled if the *values* passed as arguments to the methods satisfy additional constraints. For example, one might wish to correlate related messages using code something like this:

```
async Sell(string item, Client seller)
& async Buy (string item, Client buyer) {
    // match them up...
}
```

in which the *item* parameters passed to the two calls are required to be equal for the pattern to match. An alternative syntax for the above might be to use 'guards':

```
async Sell(string sellitem, Client seller)
& async Buy (string buyitem, Client buyer)
& (sellitem == buyitem) {
    // match them up...
}
```

One could even imagine allowing richer conditions (e.g. *sellprice* $<=$ *buyprice*) in guards, though it would be a very bad idea to allow guard expressions to call methods (including accessing properties) since they might have arbitrary side-effects, be evaluated an unpredictable number of times and have arbitrary semantics (there is no guarantee that implementations of *Equals* define equivalence relations, for example). For these reasons we intend to add only rather restricted matching to the language.

7   Conclusions

Asynchronous concurrent programming is becoming more important and widespread but is still extremely hard. We have designed and implemented a join-based extension of C$^\sharp$ which is simple, expressive, and can be efficiently implemented. In our experience, writing correct concurrent programs is considerably less difficult in Polyphonic C$^\sharp$ than in ordinary C$^\sharp$ (though we would certainly not go so far as to claim that it is *easy*...).

The integration of the join-calculus constructs with objects and the existing platform support for concurrency is not entirely straightforward – our implementation is slightly constrained by the threads and locks model and some uses of existing libraries and frameworks require a little 'impedence matching'. Nevertheless, the new constructs seem to work very well in practice.

Acknowledgements

Thanks to Mark Shinwell, who did the initial implementation work on the Polyphonic C$^\sharp$ compiler during an internship at Microsoft Research.

References

1. G. Agha, P. Wegner, and A. Yonezawa. *Research Directions in Concurrent Object-Oriented Programming*. MIT Press, 1993.
2. P. America. Issues in the design of a parallel object-oriented language. *Formal Aspects of Computing*, 1(4):366–411, 1989.
3. T. Barclay, J. Gray, and D. Slutz. Microsoft TerraServer: A spatial data warehouse. In *Proceedings of ACM SIGMOD*, May 2000. Also Microsoft Research Tech Report MS-TR-99-29.
4. A. D. Birrell, J. V. Guttag, J. J. Horning, and R. Levin. Synchronization primitives for a multiprocessor: A formal specification. Research Report 20, DEC SRC, August 1987.
5. A. D. Birrell. An introduction to programming with threads. Research Report 35, DEC SRC, January 1989.
6. L. Cardelli and R. Davies. Service combinators for web computing. *Software Engineering*, 25(3):309–316, 1999.
7. S. Chaki, S. K. Rajamani, and J. Rehof. Types as models: Model checking message-passing programs. In *Proceedings of the 29th Annual ACM SIGPLAN-SIGACT Symposium on Principles of Programming Languages*. ACM, 2002.
8. S. Conchon and F. Le Fessant. Jocaml: Mobile agents for Objective-Caml. In *First International Symposium on Agent Systems and Applications (ASA'99)/Third International Symposium on Mobile Agents (MA'99)*, pages 22–29. IEEE Computer Society, October 1999. Software and documentation available from `http://pauillac.inria.fr/jocaml`.
9. D. L. Detlefs, K. R. M. Leino, G. Nelson, and J. B. Saxe. Extended static checking. Research Report 159, DEC SRC, December 1998.
10. ECMA. Standard ECMA-334: C$^\sharp$ Language Specification, December 2001.
11. C. Fournet and G. Gonthier. The reflexive chemical abstract machine and the join-calculus. In *Proc. POPL'96*, pages 372–385. ACM, January 1996.
12. C. Fournet and G. Gonthier. The join calculus: a language for distributed mobile programming. In *Proceedings of the Applied Semantics Summer School (APPSEM), Caminha, September 2000*. To appear. Draft available from `http://research.microsoft.com/~fournet`.

13. C. Fournet, C. Laneve, L. Maranget, and D. Rémy. Inheritance in the join-calculus (extended abstract). In *FST TCS 2000: Foundations of Software Technology and Theoretical Computer Science*, volume 1974 of *LNCS*, pages 397–408, New Delhi, India, December 2000. Springer-Verlag. Full version available from http://research.microsoft.com/~fournet.

14. J. Gosling, B. Joy, and G. Steele. Threads and locks. In *The Java Language Specification*, chapter 17. Addison Wesley, 1996.

15. Y. Gurevich, W. Schulte, and C. Wallace. Investigating Java concurrency using abstract state machines. In Y. Gurevich, P. Kutter, M. Odersky, and L. Thiele, editors, *Abstract State Machines: Theory and Applications*, volume 1912 of *Lecture Notes in Computer Science*, pages 151–176. Springer, 2000.

16. C. A. R. Hoare. Monitors: An operating system structuring concept. *Communications of the ACM*, 17(10):549–557, October 1974.

17. C. A. R. Hoare. *Communicating Sequential Processes*. Prentice-Hall, 1985.

18. A. Igarashi and N. Kobayashi. A generic type system for the Pi-Calculus. In *Proceedings of the 28th Annual ACM SIGPLAN-SIGACT Symposium on Principles of Programming Languages*. ACM, 2001.

19. INMOS Limited. *Occam Programming Manual*. Prentice-Hall Int., 1984.

20. S. Kamin, editor. *Proceedings of the First ACM-SIGPLAN Workshop on Domain-Specific Languages*, Paris, France, January 1997.

21. J. R. Larus and M. Parkes. Using cohort scheduling to enhance server performance. Technical Report MSR-TR-2001-39, Microsoft Research, March 2001.

22. D. Lea. *Concurrent Programming in Java: Design Principles and Patterns*. Addison-Wesley, second edition edition, 1999.

23. F. Le Fessant and L. Maranget. Compiling join-patterns. In U. Nestmann and B. C. Pierce, editors, *HLCL '98: High-Level Concurrent Languages*, volume 16(3) of *Electronic Notes in Theoretical Computer Science*. Elsevier Science Publishers, September 1998.

24. S. Matsuoka and A. Yonezawa. Analysis of inheritance anomaly in object-oriented concurrent programming languages. In AghaWegnerYonezawa [1], chapter 4, pages 107–150.

25. Microsoft Corporation. Terraservice. http://terraserver.microsoft.net/.

26. H. R. Nielson and F. Nielson. Higher-order concurrent programs with finite communication topology. In *Proceedings of the 21st Annual ACM SIGPLAN-SIGACT Symposium on Principles of Programming Languages*. ACM, 1994.

27. M. Odersky. Functional nets. In *Proc. European Symposium on Programming*, volume 1782 of *LNCS*, pages 1–25. Springer Verlag, 2000.

28. M. Philippsen. Imperative concurrent object-oriented languages: An annotated bibliography. Technical Report TR-95-049, International Computer Science Institute, Berkeley, CA, 1995.

29. J. C. Ramming, editor. *Proceedings of the First USENIX Conference on Domain-Specific Languages*, Santa Barbara, California, October 1997.

On Variance-Based Subtyping
for Parametric Types

Atsushi Igarashi[1] and Mirko Viroli[2]

[1] Graduate School of Informatics, Kyoto University
Yoshida-Honmachi, Sakyo-ku, Kyoto 606-8501, Japan
igarashi@kuis.kyoto-u.ac.jp
[2] DEIS, Università degli Studi di Bologna
via Rasi e Spinelli 176, 47023 Cesena (FC), Italy
mviroli@deis.unibo.it

Abstract. We develop the mechanism of *variant parametric types*, inspired by *structural virtual types* by Thorup and Torgersen, as a means
to enhance synergy between parametric and inclusive polymorphism in
object-oriented languages. Variant parametric types are used to control both subtyping between different instantiations of one generic class
and the visibility of their fields and methods. On one hand, one parametric class can be used as either covariant, contravariant, or bivariant by attaching a variance annotation—which can be either +, -, or
*, respectively—to a type argument. On the other hand, the type sys-
tem prohibits certain method/field accesses through variant parametric
types, when those accesses can otherwise make the program unsafe. By
exploiting variant parametric types, a programmer can write generic code
abstractions working on a wide range of parametric types in a safe way.
For instance, a method that only reads the elements of a container of
strings can be easily modified so that it can accept containers of any
subtype of string.
The theoretical issues are studied by extending Featherweight GJ—an
existing core calculus for Java with generics—with variant parametric types. By exploiting the intuitive connection to bounded existential
types, we develop a sound type system for the extended calculus.

1 Introduction

The recent development of high-level constructs for object-oriented languages
is witnessing renewed interest in the design, implementation, and applications
of parametric polymorphism. For instance, Java's designers initially decided to
avoid generic features, and to provide programmers only with the inclusive polymorphism supported by inheritance. However, as Java was used to build large-
scale applications, it became clear that the introduction of parametric polymorphism would have significantly enhanced programmers' productivity, as well as
the readability, maintainability, and safety of programs. In response to Sun's
call for proposals for adding generics to the Java programming language [29]
many extensions have been proposed ([5,13,36,25,1] to cite some); finally, Bracha,

B. Magnusson (Ed.): ECOOP 2002, LNCS 2374, pp. 441–469, 2002.
© Springer-Verlag Berlin Heidelberg 2002

Stoutamire, Odersky, and Wadler's GJ [5] has been chosen as the reference implementation technique for the first upcoming release of Java with generics. More recently, an extension of Microsoft's .NET Common Language Runtime [26] (CLR) with generics has been studied [30]. Such an extension not only provides $C^\#$ with generic classes and methods but also has a potential impact to promote genericity as a key paradigm in the whole CLR framework, because, in principle, *all* the languages supported by CLR can be extended with generic features. In this scenario, it is clear that studying language constructs related to genericity is likely to play a key role in increasing the expressiveness of modern high-level languages such as Java and $C^\#$.

Following this research direction, we explore a technique to enhance the synergy between inclusive and parametric polymorphism, with the goal of increasing expressiveness and reuse in object-oriented languages supporting generics.

In most current object-oriented languages—such as Java, C++, and $C^\#$—inclusive polymorphism is supported only through inheritance. Their extensions with generics allow a generic class to extend from another generic class [20], and introduce *pointwise* subtyping: for instance, provided that class Stack<X> is a subclass of Vector<X> (where X is a type parameter) a parametric type Stack<String> is a subtype of Vector<String>.

Historically, most of well-known attempts to introduce another subtyping scheme for generics were based on the notion of *variance*, which is used to define a subtype relation between different instantiations of the same generic class. Basically, a generic class C<X> is said to be *covariant* with respect to X if S <: T implies C<S> <: C<T> (where <: denotes the subtyping relation), and conversely, C<X> is said to be *contravariant* with respect to X, if S <: T implies C<T> <: C<S>. Also, C<X> is said to be *invariant* when C<S> <: C<T> is derived only if S = T. For the resulting type system to be sound, covariance and contravariance can be permitted under some constraints on the occurrences of type variable X within C<X>'s signature. For example, consider a generic collection class whose element type is abstracted as a type parameter. Typically, it can be covariant only if it is read-only, while it can be contravariant only if write-only. Thus, to make use of variance, one has to be more careful about the design of classes.

Recently, Thorup and Torgensen [33] briefly sketched how some flavors of programming with *structural virtual types*, which support safe covariance, can be simulated by an extension of parametric classes. The idea is to specify the variance of each type parameter when the type is *used*, rather than when the class is *declared*. For any type argument T, a parametric class C<X> induces two types: C<T>, which is invariant, and C<+T>, which is covariant; in exchange for covariance, certain (potentially unsafe) member accesses through C<+T> are forbidden. Thus, it is expected that class designers are released from the burden of taking variance into account, and moreover class reuse is promoted. Unfortunately, it has not been rigorously discussed how this idea works in a full-blown language design.

Our contribution is to generalize this approach, and develop it into the mechanism of *variant parametric types* for possible application to widely disseminated languages such as Java and C#. In particular, we study their basic design and usefulness. Moreover, in order to discuss their fundamental concepts and subtleties rigorously, we introduce a core language based on Featherweight GJ, a generic version of Featherweight Java [20], with a formalization of its syntax, type system, and operational semantics, along with a proof of type soundness.

Variant parametric types are a new form of parametric types, in which any type parameter can come with one of the following variance annotation symbols: + for covariance, - for contravariance, and * for *bivariance*—C<*T> is a subtype of C<*R> whatever T and R are. The type argument without an annotation is considered invariant[1]. While types that are invariant in every type argument are used for run-time types of objects, variant parametric types are used for field types, method (argument and return) types, and local variable types.

Roughly speaking, a variant parametric type can be viewed as a set of run-time types: for instance, type Vector<+Number> is the type of all those vectors whose elements can be given type Number, including Vector<Number>, Vector<Float>, Vector<Integer>, and so on. Thus, both subtype relations Vector<Number> <: Vector<+Number> and Vector<Float> <: Vector<+Number> hold (note that Vector<Float> is *not* a subtype of Vector<Number>). On the other hand, since no hypothesis can be made on what kinds of elements can be stored in a vector of type Vector<+Number>, the invocation of methods inserting elements in the vector is statically forbidden. With this language construct, for example, the applicability of those methods accepting an argument of type Vector<Number> and only reading its elements can be safely widened by extending the argument type to Vector<+Number>, enabling the method to accept generic vectors instantiated with any subtype of Number. As a result, while standard variance is (typically) constrained to read-only and write-only generic collection classes, variant parametric types are available for every class; they provide uniform views of different instantiations of a generic class and can be exploited by those code abstractions that access a collection only by reading or by writing its elements.

We also show how some technical subtleties come in, especially when variant parametric types are arbitrarily nested. It seems that in previous work on variance such as [14], such cases are not systematically addressed even though they often arise in practice, making the whole safety argument not very convincing. The key intuition to tackle the subtleties is similarity between variant parametric types and bounded existential types [12]. In the above example of Vector<+Number>, the element type is only known to be *some* subtype of Number. In this sense, Vector<+Number> would correspond to type $\exists X <: Number . Vector<X>$. In fact, this intuitive connection is exploited in the whole design of a sound type system for variant parametric types.

---

[1] In [14], the term "bivariant" was used to mean what here we refer to as "invariant." We decide to adopt the term invariant since we believe it is standard and more appropriate to denote the cases where type arguments cannot be different for an instantiation to be a subtype of another.

The remainder of the paper is organized as follows. In Section 2, the classical approach to variance of parametric types is briefly outlined. Section 3 informally presents the language construct of variant parametric types, and addresses its design issues. Section 4 discusses the applicability and usefulness of these types, comparing their expressiveness to that of parametric methods in conjunction with bounded polymorphism. Section 5 elaborates the interpretation of variant parametric types as a form of bounded existential types, discussing the subtleties of our language extension. Section 6 presents the core calculus for variant parametric types and provides a sound type system for it. Section 7 discusses related work and section 8 presents concluding remarks and perspectives on future work. For brevity, a detailed proof of type soundness is omitted in this paper; interested readers are referred to a full version of this paper, which will be available at http://www.sato.kuis.kyoto-u.ac.jp/~igarashi/papers.html.

2   Classical Approach to Variance for Parametric Classes

Historically, one main approach to flexible inclusive polymorphism for generics was through the mechanism called *variance*, which is briefly reviewed in this section. The limitation of the approach is also discussed along with a proposed solution, which inspired us to develop our variant parametric types.

A generic class C<X> is said to be *covariant* in the type parameter X when the subtype relation C<R> <: C<S> holds if R <: S. Conversely, C<X> is said to be *contravariant* in X when C<R> <: C<S> holds if S <: R. Less general notions of *bivariance* and *invariance* can be defined as well. C<X> is said to be *bivariant* in X when C<R> <: C<S> for any R and S. C<X> is said to be *invariant* in X when C<R> <: C<S> holds only when R = S. Since variance is a property of each type parameter of a generic class, all these definitions can be easily extended to generic classes with more than one type parameter.

However, not every class can be safely given a variance property, as the array types in Java show us. Java arrays can be considered a generic class from which the element type is abstracted out as a type parameter; moreover, the array types are covariant in that type—e.g., String[] is a subtype of Object[]. However, since arrays provide the operation to update their content, this can lead to a run-time error, as the following Java code shows:

```
Object[] o=new String[]{"1","2","3"};
o[0]=new Integer(1);   // Exception thrown
```

The former statement is permitted because of covariance. The latter is also statically accepted, because Integer is a subtype of Object. However, when the code is executed an exception java.lang.ArrayStoreException is thrown: at run time, the bytecode interpreter tries to insert an Integer instance to where a String instance is actually expected.

To recover safety, previous work [14,2,3] proposed to pose restriction on how a type variable can appear in a class definition, according to its variance. In the case of a class covariant in the type parameter X, for instance, X should not

appear as type of a public (and writable) field or as an argument type of any
public method. Conversely, in the contravariant case, X should not appear as
type of a public (and readable) field or as return type of any public method. For
example, the following class (written in a GJ-like language [5])

```
class Pair<X extends Object, Y extends Object> extends Object{
    private X fst;
    private Y snd;
    Pair(X fst,Y snd){ this.fst=fst; this.snd=snd; }
    void setFst(X fst){ this.fst=fst; }
    Y getSnd(){ return snd; }
}
```

can be safely considered covariant in type variable Y and contravariant in type
variable X, since X appears as the argument type in setFst and Y appears as the
return type in getSnd. It is easy to see that any type Pair<R,S> can be safely
considered a subtype of Pair<String,Number> when R is a supertype of String
and S is a subtype of Number, as the following code reveals.

```
Number getAndSet(Pair<String,Number> c, String s){
    c.setFst(s);
    return c.getSnd();
}
...
Number n=getAndSet(
         new Pair<Object,Integer>(null, new Integer(1)),"1");
```

In fact, the invocation of getAndSet causes the string "1" to be safely passed to
setFst, which expected an Object, and an Integer object to be returned by
getSnd, whose return type is Number.

However, as claimed e.g. in [15], the applicability of this mechanism is considered not very wide, since type variables typically occur in such positions that
forbid both covariance and contravariance. In fact, consider the usual application
of generics as collection classes, and their typical signature schema with methods
for getting and setting elements, as is shown in the following class Vector<X>:

```
class Vector<X>{
    private X[] ar;
    Vector(int size){ ar=new X[size];}
    int size(){ return ar.length; }
    X getElementAt(int i){ return ar[i];}
    // Reading elements disallows contravariance
    void setElementAt(X t,int i){ ar[i]=t;}
    // Writing elements disallows covariance
}
```

Typically, the type variable occurs as a method return type when the method is
used to extract some element of the collection, while the type variable occurs as
a method argument type when the method is used to insert new elements into
the collection. As a result, a generic collection class can be considered covariant

only if it represents read-only collections, and contravariant only if it represents write-only collections. Bivariance is even more useless since it would be safely applied only to collections whose content is neither readable nor writable. As a result, class designers have to be responsible for the tradeoff between variance and available functionality of a class.

More recently, Thorup and Torgersen [33] have briefly sketched a possible solution to the applicability limitations of this classical approach. The idea is to let a programmer specify within parametric types whether he/she wants the type argument to be invariant or covariant: for the latter case, the + symbol is inserted before the (actual) type argument, e.g. writing `Vector<⁺Object>`, which behaves similarly to the structural virtual type `Vector[X<:Object]` and prohibits write access to the vector of that type. With this syntax, the choice of the variance property can be deferred from when a class is defined to when a class is used to derive a type. It seems that two advantages arise from this approach: the applicability of the mechanisms is widened—e.g., from read-only containers to read-write ones—and the designers of libraries are generally released from the burden of making decisions about the tradeoff mentioned above. Unfortunately, aside from the fact that they dealt with only covariance, the informal idea has been not fully explored so far. So, we generalize this idea to include contravariance and bivariance, and investigate how it works in a full-fledged language design.

3   Variant Parametric Types

Now, based on the idea sketched in [33], we introduce the notion of *variant parametric types* and their basic aspects.

Variant parametric types are a generalization of standard parametric (or generic) types where each type parameter may be associated with a *variance annotation*, either +, -, or *, respectively referred to as the *covariance, contravariance,* or *bivariance annotation symbol*. Syntactically, a variance annotation symbol precedes the type parameter it refers to and introduces the corresponding variance to the argument position: for example, `Vector<+String>` is a subtype of `Vector<+Object>`. Similarly to the case of generic types, the type parameter of a variant parametric type can be either a variant parametric type or a type variable, as in `Vector<+String>`, `Pair<+String,-Integer>`, and `Vector<Vector<*X>>`. A parametric type where no (outermost) type argument has a variance annotation is called a *fully invariant type* (or just an invariant type). `Vector<String>` and `Pair<Vector<+String>,Integer>` are examples of invariant types. Since the type argument following * does not really matter, due to bivariance, it is often omitted by simply writing e.g. `Vector<*>`, which is also the syntax we propose for an actual language extension.

Unlike the standard mechanism of variance, described in the previous section, programmers derive covariant, contravariant, and bivariant types from one generic class. Safety is achieved by restricting accesses to fields and methods, instead of constraining their declarations. For example, even when `setElementAt`

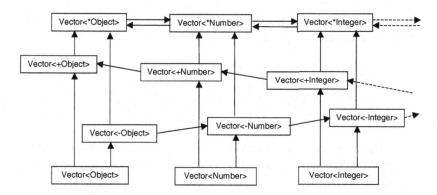

Fig. 1. Subtyping graph of variant parametric types

is declared in `Vector`, `Vector<+Number>` can be used in a program; the type system just forbids accessing the method `setElementAt` through the covariant type `Vector<+Number>`.

A simple interpretation of variant parametric types is given as a set of invariant types. A type `C<+T>` can be interpreted as the set of all invariant types of the form `C<S>` where `S` is a subtype of `T`; a type `C<-T>` can be interpreted as the set of all invariant types of the form `C<S>` where `S` is a supertype of `T`; and, a type `C<*T>` can be interpreted as the set of all invariant types of the form `C<S>`. Hence, `Vector<+Integer>` <: `Vector<+Number>` directly follows as an inclusion of the set they denote. Moreover, it is easy to derive subtyping between types that differ only in variance annotations: since an invariant type would correspond to a singleton, `Vector<Integer>` <: `Vector<+Integer>` and `Vector<Integer>` <: `Vector<-Integer>` hold. Similarly, `Vector<+Integer>` <: `Vector<*Integer>` and `Vector<-Integer>` <: `Vector<*Integer>` hold as well. In summary, Figure 1 shows the subtyping relation for the class `Vector` and type arguments `Object`, `Number`, and `Integer` (under the usual subtyping relation: `Integer` <: `Number` <: `Object`.)

More generally, subtyping for variant parametric types is defined as follows. Suppose `C` is a generic class that takes n type arguments, and `S`, and `T` (possibly with subscripts) are types.

- The following subtype relations hold that involve variant parametric types differing just in the variance annotation symbol on one type parameter[2]:

$$C<\ldots,\ T,\ldots> \ <: \ C<\ldots,+T,\ldots>$$
$$C<\ldots,\ T,\ldots> \ <: \ C<\ldots,-T,\ldots>$$
$$C<\ldots,+T,\ldots> \ <: \ C<\ldots,*T,\ldots>$$
$$C<\ldots,-T,\ldots> \ <: \ C<\ldots,*T,\ldots>$$

---

[2] More precisely, e.g. the first relation means that for any types $T_1, T_2, \ldots, T_n$ we have $C<T_1,\ldots,T_{i-1},T,T_{i+1},\ldots,T_n> \ <: \ C<T_1,\ldots,T_{i-1},+T,T_{i+1},\ldots,T_n>$, and similarly for the others.

– The following relations hold that involve variant parametric types differing in the instantiation of just one type parameter:

$$C<\ldots, S, \ldots> <: C<\ldots, T, \ldots> \text{ if } S <: T \text{ and } T <: S$$
$$C<\ldots, +S, \ldots> <: C<\ldots, +T, \ldots> \text{ if } S <: T$$
$$C<\ldots, -S, \ldots> <: C<\ldots, -T, \ldots> \text{ if } T <: S$$
$$C<\ldots, *S, \ldots> <: C<\ldots, *T, \ldots> \forall S, T$$

(Note that the subtyping relation is *not* anti-symmetric: `Vector<*Object>` and `Vector<*Integer>` are subtypes of each other but not (syntactically) equal.)

– Other cases of subtyping between different instantiations of the same generic class can be obtained by the above ones through transitivity.

Subtyping of variant parametric types which are instantiations of different generic classes—that is, involving inheritance—is more subtle than it might have been expected, and is discussed in Section 5.

Objects are created from generic classes through an expression of the form new $C<T_1, \ldots, T_n>(\ldots)$, without specifying any variant annotation in the (outermost) type arguments (variance annotations can appear inside T_i.) Objects created through this expression are given the corresponding invariant parametric type $C<T_1, \ldots, T_n>$. While an invariant parametric type denotes a singleton set and is used for the run-time type of an object, a variant parametric type can be generally used as a common supertype for many different instantiations of the same generic class.

A more refined view of variant parametric types is given as a correspondence to bounded existential types [12], originally used for modeling partially abstract types. Actually, this view, exploited throughout the development of the type system, explains how access restriction is achieved. Intuitively, the covariant type `Vector<+Number>` would correspond to the existential type $\exists X<:Number.Vector<X>$, read "`Vector<X>` for *some* X which is a subtype of Number." Then, an invocation of `setElementAt` on an expression of type `Vector<+Number>` is forbidden because the first argument type is X, which is known as some unknown subtype of Number, but the actual argument cannot be given a subtype of X. Similarly, `Vector<-Number>` would correspond to $\exists X:>Number.Vector<X>$, where only the lower bound of the element type is known. Thus, invocation of `getElementAt` is not allowed because its return type would be an abstract type X, which cannot be promoted to a concrete type. Finally, `Vector<*>` would correspond to the unbounded existential type $\exists X.Vector<X>$, which prevents both `getElementAt` and `setElementAt` from being invoked. Actually, if the type structure over which type variables range has the "top" type (for example, `Object` is a supertype of any reference type in Java), it is possible to allow `getElementAt` to be invoked on `Vector<-T>` or `Vector<*>`, giving the result the top type. However, we decided to disallow it so that member access restrictions and method/field typing becomes much the same as expected for the classical approach, discussed in the previous section.

The intuitive connection is further explored in Section 5 to deal with more complicated use of type variables, in particular when they appear inside parametric types, and to deal with inheritance-based subtyping—type variables naturally appear inside the type specified as the superclass in the extends clause.

In summary, variant parametric types provide uniform views over different instantiations of the same generic class. Unlike the standard mechanism reviewed in the previous section, variant parametric types are just a means for static access control, so there is no additional constraints on how classes are declared.

4   On Applicability and Usefulness

In this section, the usefulness of variant parametric types is studied by focusing on those generic classes representing collections—such as classes Pair<X,Y> (completed with methods setSnd and getFst), and Vector<X> defined in previous sections—which actually form one of the basic and significant application cases for generic classes.

4.1   Covariance

As discussed in the previous section, type Vector<+T> is a supertype of any type Vector<R> if R as a subtype of T, and can be interpreted as the type of all those vectors whose extracted elements can be given type T. Hence, the invocation of method setElementAt is forbidden on an object with type Vector<+T>, while method getElementAt can be invoked that returns an object of type T. As a first application, consider the following method fillFrom for class Vector:

```
class Vector<X extends Object>{
    ...
    void fillFrom(Vector<+X> v, int start){
        // Here no methods with X as argument type are invoked on v
        for (int i=0;i<v.size() && i+start<size();i++)
            setElementAt(v.getElementAt(i),i+start);
} }
    ...
Vector<Number> vn = new Vector<Number>(20);
Vector<Integer> vi = new Vector<Integer>(10); ...
Vector<Float> vf = new Vector<Float>(10); ...
vn.fillFrom(vi,0); // Permitted for Vector<Integer> <: Vector<+Number>
vn.fillFrom(vf,10);// Permitted for Vector<Float> <: Vector<+Number>
```

Here the method fillFrom accepts a vector which is meant to be only read, and whose elements are expected to be given type X. As a result, instead of simply declaring formal argument v to have type Vector<X>, it is more convenient to use type Vector<+X>. The corresponding method execution is always safe since the only method invoked on v is getElementAt, and even more, the applicability of fillFrom is extended to a wider set of vectors. In the code above a vector of numbers is filled with elements of vectors of integers and floats. So, in general, the

covariant parameterization structure can be exploited to widen the applicability
of methods that take a collection and simply read its elements.

Now that we have a mechanism to deal with different instantiations of the
same generic class in a uniform way, one may be willing to rely on nested parameterizations so as to further exploit the flavors of collections classes, as in
the following method `fillFromVector`:

```
class Vector<X extends Object>{
    ...
    void fillFromVector(Vector<+Vector<+X>> vv){
        int pos=0;
        for (int i=0;i<vv.size();i++){
            Vector<+X> v = vv.getElementAt(i);
            if (pos+v.size()>=size()) break;
            fillFrom(v,pos);
            pos += v.size();
} } }
    ...
Vector<Number> vn = new Vector<Number>(20);
Vector<Integer> vi = new Vector<Integer>(10);
Vector<Float> vf = new Vector<Float>(10);
Vector<Vector<+Number>> vvn = new Vector<Vector<+Number>>(2);
vvn.setElementAt(vi,0);
vvn.setElementAt(vf,1);
vn.fillFromVector(vvn);
```

The method `fillFromVector` takes a vector of vectors and puts its inner-level
elements into the vector on which the method is invoked. Since neither the
outer vector nor the inner vectors are updated, the argument can be given type
`Vector<+Vector<+X>>`. The inner +, which means that the inner vectors are
read-only, allows different inner vectors to be mixed in one vector: as in the code
above, a vector of integers and a vector of floats are put in one vector vvn. The
outer +, which means that the outer vector is also read-only, allows inner vectors
passed to `fillFromVector` to extend class `Vector`, as in the following code:

```
class MyVector<X extends Object> extends Vector<X> { ... }
    ...
Vector<MyVector<+Number>> mvv = ...;
vn.fillFromVector(mvv);
```

4.2 Contravariance

Contravariance has a dual kind of use. Type `Vector<-T>` is a supertype of any
type `Vector<R>` if T is a subtype of R, and can be interpreted as the type of all
those vectors which is safe to fill with elements of type T. Hence, the invocation
of method `getElementAt` on an object of type `Vector<-T>` is forbidden, while
method `setElementAt` can be invoked passing an object of type T. The following
method `fillTo` provides an example similar to the one shown for the covariance
case:

```
class Vector<X extends Object>{
    ...
    void fillTo(Vector<-X> v,int start){
        // Here no methods with X as return type are invoked on v
        for (int i=0;i<size() && i+start()<v.size();i++)
            v.setElementAt(getElementAt(i),i+start);
} }
    ...
Vector<Number> vn = new Vector<Number>(20);
Vector<Integer> vi = new Vector<Integer>(10);
Vector<Float> vf = new Vector<Float>(10);
vi.fillTo(vn,0); // Permitted for Vector<Number> <: Vector<-Integer>
vf.fillTo(vn,10);// Permitted for Vector<Number> <: Vector<-Float>
```

Mixed variance parameterizations can be useful as well. For instance, consider a method fillToVector that inserts elements of the receiver vector this into a structure of the kind Vector<Vector<X>> provided as input—which is a dual case with respect to the method fillFromVector. In this case, the method's formal argument vv should be safely given type Vector<+Vector<-X>>. There, the outer vector is just used to access its elements through method getElementAt—hence it can be safely declared covariant—while the inner vectors may only be updated through method setElementAt—so they can be safely declared contravariant.

4.3   Bivariance

From a conceptual point of view, the construct of bivariant parametric types comes for free once covariance and contravariance are defined. In fact, for the same reason why one may need to denote by Vector<+T> the supertype of each Vector<R> with R <: T, and conversely for contravariance, then it may also be the case to explicitly denote the supertype of both Vector<+T> and Vector<-T>, which is represented here by Vector<*T>—or more concisely, by Vector<*>.

No methods that contain the type variable X in their signature can be invoked on an expression of Vector<*>, so Vector<*> is meant to represent a sort of "frozen" vector, which can be neither read nor written. For instance, bivariance can be exploited to build a method that sums the sizes of a vector of vectors, as follows:

```
int countVector(Vector<+Vector<*>> vv){
    int sz=0;
    for (int i=0;i<vv.size();i++){
        sz+=vv.getElementAt(i).size();
    return sz;
}
```

More useful are those cases where a generic class involves more than one type parameter. Consider the following method:

```
class Vector<X>{
  void fillFromFirst(Vector<+Pair<+X,*>> vp,int start){
    for (int i=0;i<vp.size() && i+start<size();i++)
      setElementAt(vp.getElementAt(i).getFst(),i+start);
} }
```

Since method `fillFromFirst` does not actually read or write the second element in each pair, its type can be any type, so annotation symbol * can be used in place of it. This example suggests an interesting application for bivariance as a mechanism providing a parametric type's partial instantiation.

4.4   Comparison with Parametric Methods

One may wonder if parametric methods with bounded polymorphism can be used for the examples shown above; indeed, some of them can be easily handled with parametric methods. For instance, the method `fillFrom` can be implemented as follows:

```
class Vector<X extends Object>{
  ...
  <Y extends X> void fillFrom(Vector<Y> v, int start){
    for (int i=0;i<v.size() && i+start<size();i++)
      setElementAt(v.getElementAt(i), i+start);
} }
...
Vector<Number> vn = new Vector<Number>(20);
Vector<Integer> vi = new Vector<Integer>(10);
Vector<Float> vf = new Vector<Float>(10);
vn.fillFrom<Integer>(vi,0);
vn.fillFrom<Float>(vf,10);
```

Here, the definition of `fillFrom` is parameterized by a type variable Y, bounded by an upper bound X and the actual type arguments are explicitly given (inside <>) at method invocations. Similarly, `fillTo` can be expressed by using a *lower bound* of a type parameter:

```
class Vector<X extends Object>{
  ...
  <Y extendedby X> void fillTo(Vector<Y> v,int start){
    for (int i=0;i<size() && i+start<v.size();i++)
      v.setElementAt(getElementAt(i),i+start);
} }
```

Here, the keyword **extendedby** means that the type parameter Y must be a *supertype* of X. In general, it seems that a method taking arguments of variant parametric types can be easily rewritten to a parametric methods.

Although they can be used almost interchangeably for some cases, we think variant parametric types and parametric methods are complementary mechanisms. On one hand, variant parametric types provides a uniform viewpoint over different instantiations of the same generic classes, making it possible to mix different types in one data structure, as we have seen in `Vector<+Vector<+X>>` and `Vector<+Vector<-X>>`. On the other hand, parametric methods can better express type dependency among method arguments and results, as in the two methods below:

```
// swapping pos-th element in v1 and v2
<X> void swapElementAt(Vector<X> v1,Vector<X> v2,int pos){...}

// a database-like join operation on tables v1 and v2.
<X,Y,Z> Vector<Pair<X,Z>> join(Vector<Pair<X,Y>> v1,
                               Vector<Pair<Y,Z>> v2){...}
```

The method `swapElementAt` requires the arguments to be vectors carrying the same type of elements, while in method `join` variables X, Y, and Z are used to express dependency among the inputs and outputs. In both cases, such dependencies cannot be expressed by variant parametric types.

As shown above, simulating contravariance with parametric methods requires type parameters with lower bounds. However, their theory has not been well studied and it is not very clear whether or not basic implementation techniques such as type-erasure [5] can be extended to parametric methods with lower bounds. One may argue that the features provided by the methods `fillTo` and `fillFrom` are much the same, so one can easily find the covariant version of any method that uses contravariance, and then implement it using a parametric method only with upper bounds. However, in general, this will force programmers to always write that kind of methods in the container class receiving elements instead of in the class producing them. We believe that hampering that freedom would lead to poor programming practice.

Also, we believe that a language with generics should enjoy the combination of both constructs so as to achieve even more power and expressiveness. For instance, the following example shows potential benefits of the combination:

```
<X> Vector<X> unzipleft(Vector<+Pair<+X,*>> vp){
    Vector<X> v=new Vector<X>(vp.size());
    for (int i=0;i<vp.size();i++)
        v.addElementAt(vp.getElementAt(i).getFst(),i);
    return v;
}
```

Method `unzipleft` creates a `Vector<X>` element by unzipping the argument and projecting on the left side. The use of variance widens its applicability, *(i)* abstracting from the type of the right side, *(ii)* allowing the left side to be a subtype of the expected type X, and *(iii)* also allowing subclasses of `Pair` to be used for zipping. We leave further studies on the combination of parametric methods and variance for future work.

5   Variant Parametric Types and Existential Types

In this section, we further investigate the informal connection between variant parametric types and (bounded) existential types [12], used to describe partially abstract types. The basic intuition was that, for example, `Vector<+Nm>` (in what follows, `Number` is often abbreviated to `Nm` for conciseness) would correspond to the bounded existential type `∃X<:Nm.Vector<X>`. Since only the upper bound `Nm` of `X` is known and its identity is unknown, a method that takes `X` as an argument cannot be invoked, while the field of type `X` can be accessed and given type `Nm`. Similarly, the type `Vector<*T>`—abbreviated to `Vector<*>`—would correspond to the unbounded existential type `∃X.Vector<X>`, and the type `Vector<-Nm>` to the bounded existential type `∃X:>Nm.Vector<X>`, where the abstract type `X` has a *lower* bound. For a nested parametric type, the existential quantifier comes inside, too: for example, `Vector<+Vector<+Nm>>` would correspond to `∃X<:(∃Y<:Nm.Vector<Y>).Vector<X>`.

5.1   Existential Types *à la* Mitchell and Plotkin

We first begin with reviewing the standard formulation of (bounded) existential types [27]. A value of an existential type `∃X<:S.T` is considered an ADT package, consisting of a pair of a hidden witness (or implementation) type `U`, which is a subtype of `S`, and an ADT implementation `v` of type `[U/X]T`. The expression `pack [U,v]` as `∃X<:S.T` creates such a package; the expression `open o as [X,x]` in `b` unpacks a package `o` and binds the type variable `X` and the value variable `x` to the witness type and the implementation, where their scope is `b`. The typing rules for those expressions are informally written as follows:

$$\frac{\vdash U <: S \qquad \vdash v \in [U/X]T}{\vdash (\texttt{pack } [U,v] \texttt{ as } \exists X{<:}S.T) \in \exists X{<:}S.T}$$

$$\frac{\vdash o \in \exists X{<:}S.T \qquad X{<:}S, x{:}T \vdash b \in U \qquad X \notin FV(U)}{\texttt{open } o \texttt{ as } [X,x] \texttt{ in } b \in U}$$

Note that the side condition requires `X` not to be a free variable of `U`; otherwise the hidden type `X` would escape the abstraction. The following rule describes subtyping between bounded existential types[3]:

$$\frac{\vdash S_1 <: S_2 \qquad X{<:}S_1 \vdash T_1 <: T_2}{\vdash \exists X{<:}S_1.T_1 <: \exists X{<:}S_2.T_2}$$

---

[3] This rule is known as one for the full variant of System $F_{\leq}$, in which subtyping is undecidable. Subtyping of variant parametric types, though, is easily shown to be decidable: they correspond to rather restricted forms of bounded existential types.

5.2   Variant Parametric Types as Existential Types

Variant parametric types can be explained in terms of the formulation above. For example, covariant and contravariant subtyping directly corresponds to subtyping mentioned above. On the other hand, when a variance annotation is introduced, as in Vector<Nm> <: Vector<+Nm>, it is considered a packing pack [Nm,v] as ∃X<:Number.Vector<X>.

When an operation (a field access or a method invocation) is performed on a variant parametric type, it is considered as if **open** were implicitly inserted. Consider the following class

```
class Pair<X extends Object, Y extends Object> {
  X fst; Y snd;
  Pair(X fst,Y snd){ this.fst=fst; this.snd=snd; }

  X getFst(){ return this.fst; }
  Y getSnd(){ return this.snd; }
  void setFst(X x){ this.fst=x; }
  void setSnd(Y y){ this.snd=y; }
  void copyFst(Pair<+X,*> p) { setFst(p.getFst()); }
  Pair<Y,X> reverse() {
    return new Pair<Y,X>(this.getSnd(), this.getFst());
  }
  Pair<Pair<X,Y>, Pair<X,Y>> dup () {
    return new Pair<Pair<X,Y>,Pair<X,Y>>(this, this);
  }
}
```

and assume x is given type Pair<+Nm,-Nm>, which corresponds to ∃X<:Nm,Y:>Nm.Pair<X,Y>. Then, for example, x.setFst(e) corresponds to open x as [Z,W,y] in y.setFst(e). Inside open, method/field types can be easily obtained by simply replacing the type parameters of a class with the actual type arguments of the opened type. For example, the argument type of setFst is Z, that of setSnd is W, and that of copyFst is Pair<Z,+Object>. Similarly, the result type of getFst is Z, that of getSnd is W, that of reverse is Pair<W,Z>, and that of dup is Pair<Pair<Z,W>, Pair<Z,W>>. Now, it turns out that open x as [Z,W,y] in y.setFst(e) is not well typed for any expression e: the argument type of setFst is Z, which is constrained by Z<:Nm, but the type of e cannot be a subtype of Z [4]. On the other hand, setSnd can be invoked with an argument of type Nm (or its subtype) because if T is a subtype of Nm, it is the case that T <: W. Thus, + and - can be used to protect particular fields from being written or read. For much the same reason as setFst, the method call p.copyFst(new Pair<Integer,Float>(...)) is not allowed because the argument type of copyFst would be Pair<Z,*>, which is not a super type of Pair<Integer,Float>. Actually, it *should not* be allowed because p may be bound to new Pair<Float,Object> and executing the expression above

---

[4] One exception could be null, which could be given the bottom type, which is a subtype of *any* type (even of unknown abstract type).

will assign an `Integer` to the field that holds `Float`. This example shows that a method type cannot be obtained by naively substituting for X the type argument `+Nm` together with a variance annotation; it would lead to a wrong argument type `Pair<+Nm,+Object>`, a supertype of `Pair<Integer,Float>`. In the next section, we formalize transformation from variant parametric types to invariant types with constrained abstract types as the operation *open*: for example, `Pair<+Nm,-Nm>` is opened to `Pair<Z,W>` with `Z<:Nm` and `W:>Nm`.

If a type of a body of unpacking includes the abstract type variables, the type of the whole expression has to be promoted to the least supertype without them, in order for abstract types not to escape from their scope. When such promotion is not possible, the expression is not typed. For example, consider `p.getFst()`, whose return type is Z with a constraint `Z<:Nm`. The type of the whole expression is the least supertype of Z without mentioning Z, i.e., its upper bound `Nm`. On the other hand, `p.getSnd` is not typeable because the return type W cannot be promoted to a supertype without W. Similarly, the return type of `p.reverse()` is `Pair<W,Z>`, which can be promoted to a supertype `Pair<-Nm,+Nm>` by exploiting the fact that Z is a subtype of `Nm` and W is a supertype of `Nm`.

It looks as if the type arguments and variances `+Nm` and `-Nm` were substituted for X and Y, respectively, but this naive view is wrong as we will see in the next example `p.dup()`. The return type of this method invocation is `Pair<Pair<Z,W>,Pair<Z,W>>`. However, the type we obtain by the naive substitution—that is, `Pair<Pair<+Nm,-Nm>,Pair<+Nm,-Nm>>`—is *not* a supertype of `Pair<Pair<Z,W>,Pair<Z,W>>`! That's because the two inner occurrences of `Pair` are invariant. So, as long as `Pair<Z,W>` and `Pair<+Nm,-Nm>` are different, those two types are not in the subtype relation. If it were a supertype, another pair could be assigned to the outer pair, making the two first elements of the inner pairs have different types. The correct supertype is a covariant type `Pair<+Pair<+Nm,-Nm>,+Pair<+Nm,-Nm>>`; in general, `+` is attached to everywhere the type argument is changed by promotion. So, naive substitution of an actual type argument with its variance for a type variable does not work, again. In the next section, we will formalize this operation for obtaining an abstract-type-free supertype as the operation called *close*. A similar operation is found in a type system for bounded existential types with minimal typing property [17]; it was introduced to omit a type annotation for the open expression.

The notions of opening and closing are also used for deriving inheritance-based subtyping. Suppose we declare two subclasses of `Pair`.

```
class PairX<X extends Object> extends Pair<X,X> { ... }
class PP<X extends Object, Y extends Object>
      extends Pair<Pair<X,Y>, Pair<X,Y>> { ... }
```

As in GJ, inheritance-based subtyping for invariant types is simple. A supertype is obtained by substituting the type arguments for type variables in the type after `extends`: for example,

```
PairX<Integer> <: Pair<Integer,Integer>
```

and

```
PP<Integer,String> <: Pair<Pair<Integer,String>,Pair<Integer,String>>.
```

Subtyping for other non-invariant types involves opening and closing, similarly to field and method accesses. For example, `PairX<+Nm>` is a subtype of `Pair<+Nm,+Nm>` because the open operation introduces `PairX<Z>` where `Z<:Nm` and a supertype of `PairX<Z>` is `Pair<Z,Z>`, which obtained by substitution of Z for X and closes to `Pair<+Nm,+Nm>`. Similarly, `PP<+Nm,-Nm>` is a subtype of `Pair<+Pair<+Nm,-Nm>,+Pair<+Nm,-Nm>>` (note that + before the inner occurrences of `Pair`).

5.3   Comparison with Explicit Use of Existential Types

As a last remark, it would be interesting to see the full power of existential types. By using unpacking appropriately, more expressions are typeable. For example, suppose x is given type $\exists X.\texttt{Vector<X>}$ and a programmer wants to get an element from x and put it to x. Actually, the expression

```
open x as [Y,y] in y.setElementAt(y.getElementAt(0), 1)
```

would be well-typed (if y is read-only) since inside **open**, the elements are all given an identical type Y. On the other hand, in our language,

```
x.setElementAt(x.getElementAt(0),1)
```

is not typeable since this expression would correspond to

```
open x as [Y,y] in
  y.setElementAt(open x as [Z,z] in z.getElementAt(0), 1)
```

which introduces two **open**s, and Y and Z are distinguished. Although there is an advantage when using existential types explicitly, we think that allowing programmers to directly insert **open** operations can easily turn programming into a cumbersome task.

6   Core Calculus for Variant Parametric Types

We introduce a core calculus for class-based object-oriented languages with variant parametric types. Our calculus is considered a variant of Featherweight GJ (FGJ for short) by Igarashi, Pierce, and Wadler [20], originally proposed to formally investigate properties of the type system and compilation scheme of GJ [5]. Like FGJ, our extended calculus is functional and supports only minimal features including top-level parametric classes with variant parametric types, object instantiation, field access, method invocation, and typecasts. For simplicity, polymorphic methods, found in FGJ, are omitted so as to focus on the basic mechanism of variant parametric types.

N ::= C<$\overline{\text{vT}}$>	variant parametric types
T ::= X | N	types
v ::= o | + | - | *	variance annotations
L ::= class C<$\overline{\text{X}}$◁$\overline{\text{N}}$>◁D<$\overline{\text{S}}$> { $\overline{\text{T}}$ $\overline{\text{f}}$; $\overline{\text{M}}$ }	class definitions
M ::= T m($\overline{\text{T}}$ $\overline{\text{x}}$){ return e; }	method definitions
e ::= x	variables
| e.f	field access
| e.m($\overline{\text{e}}$)	method invocation
| new C<$\overline{\text{T}}$>($\overline{\text{e}}$)	object instantiation
| (T)e	typecasts

Fig. 2. Syntax

6.1   Syntax

The metavariables A, B, C, D, and E range over class names; S, T, U, and V range over types; X, Y, and Z range type variables; N, P, and Q range over variant types; L ranges over class declarations; M ranges over method declarations; v and w range over variance annotations; f and g range over field names; m ranges over method names; x ranges over variables; and e and d range over expressions. The abstract syntax of types, class declarations, method declarations, and expressions is given in Figure 2.

We write $\overline{\text{f}}$ as shorthand for a possibly empty sequence $f_1,\dots,f_n$ (and similarly for $\overline{\text{C}}$, $\overline{\text{x}}$, $\overline{\text{e}}$, etc.) and write $\overline{\text{M}}$ as shorthand for $M_1\dots M_n$ (with no commas). We write the empty sequence as • and denote concatenation of sequences using a comma. The length of a sequence $\overline{\text{x}}$ is written $|\overline{\text{x}}|$. We abbreviate operations on pairs of sequences in the obvious way, writing "$\overline{\text{C}}$ $\overline{\text{f}}$" as shorthand for "C_1 $f_1,\dots,C_n$ f_n" and "$\overline{\text{C}}$ $\overline{\text{f}}$;" as shorthand for "C_1 $f_1;\dots C_n$ f_n;", "<$\overline{\text{X}}$◁$\overline{\text{N}}$>" as shorthand for "<X_1◁$N_1,\dots,X_n$◁N_n>", and "C<$\overline{\text{vT}}$>" for "C<$v_1T_1,\dots,v_nT_n$>". Sequences of field declarations, parameter names, type variables, and method declarations are assumed to contain no duplicate names. The empty brackets <> are often omitted for conciseness. We denote by m $\notin \overline{\text{M}}$ that a method of the name m is not included in $\overline{\text{M}}$. We introduce another variance annotation o to denote invariant, which would be regarded as default and omitted in the surface language. Then, a partial order $\leq$ on variance annotations is defined: formally, $\leq$ is the least partial order satisfying o $\leq$ + $\leq$ * and o $\leq$ - $\leq$ *. We write $v_1 \vee v_2$ for the least upper bound of v_1 and v_2. If every v_i is o in a variant type C<$\overline{\text{vT}}$>, we call it an *invariant type* and abbreviates to C<$\overline{\text{T}}$>.

A class declaration consists of its name (class C), type parameters ($\overline{\text{X}}$) with their (upper) bounds ($\overline{\text{N}}$), fields ($\overline{\text{T}}$ $\overline{\text{f}}$), and methods ($\overline{\text{M}}$)[5]; moreover, every class

---

[5] We assume that each class has a trivial constructor that takes the initial (and also final) values of each fields of the class and assigns them to the corresponding fields. In FGJ, such constructors have to be declared explicitly, in order to retain compatibility with GJ. We omit them because they play no other significant role.

must explicitly declare its supertype D<$\overline{\text{S}}$> with ◁ (read **extends**) even if it is
Object. Note that only an invariant type is allowed as a supertype, just as in
object instantiation. Since our language supports F-bounded polymorphism [11],
the bounds $\overline{\text{N}}$ of type variables $\overline{\text{X}}$ can contain $\overline{\text{X}}$ in them. A body of a method just
returns an expression, which is either a variable, field access, method invocation,
object instantiation, or typecasts. As we have already mentioned, the type used
for an instantiation must be an invariant type, hence C<$\overline{\text{T}}$>. For the sake of generality, we allow the target type T of a typecast expression (T)e to be any type,
including a type variable. Thus, we will need an implementation technique where
instantiation of type parameters are kept at run-time, such as the framework of
LM [36]. Should it be implemented with the type-erasure technique as in GJ, T
has to be a non-variable type and a special care will be needed for downcasts
(see [5] for more details). We treat this in method bodies as a variable, rather
than a keyword, and so require no special syntax. As we will see later, the typing
rules prohibit this from appearing as a method parameter name.

A class table CT is a mapping from class names C to class declarations L; a
program is a pair (CT, e) of a class table and an expression. Object is treated
specially in every program: the definition of Object class never appears in the
class table and the auxiliary functions to look up field and method declarations
in the class table are equipped with special cases for Object that return the
empty sequence of fields and the empty set of methods. (As we will see later,
method lookup for Object is just undefined.) To lighten the notation in what
follows, we always assume a *fixed* class table CT.

The given class table is assumed to satisfy some sanity conditions: (1)
$CT(\text{C}) = $ class C... for every C $\in dom(CT)$; (2) Object $\notin dom(CT)$; (3)
for every class name C (except Object) appearing anywhere in CT, we have
C $\in dom(CT)$; and (4) there are no cycles in the reflexive and transitive closure of the relation between class names induced by ◁ clauses in CT. By the
condition (1), we can identify a class table with a sequence of class declarations
in an obvious way; so, in the rules below, we just write class C ... to state
$CT(\text{C}) = $ class C ..., for conciseness.

6.2   Type System

For the typing, we need a few auxiliary definitions to look up the field and method
types of an invariant type, which are shown in Figure 3. As we discussed in the
previous section, we never attempt to determine the field or method types of
non-invariant types.

The fields of an invariant type C<$\overline{\text{T}}$>, written *fields*(C<$\overline{\text{T}}$>), are a sequence of
corresponding types and field names, $\overline{\text{S}}$ $\overline{\text{f}}$. In what follows, we use the notation
$[\overline{\text{T}}/\overline{\text{X}}]$ for a substitution of T_i for X_i. The type of the method invocation m at an
invariant type C<$\overline{\text{T}}$>, written *mtype*(m, C<$\overline{\text{T}}$>), returns a pair $\overline{\text{U}}$->U_0 of argument
types $\overline{\text{U}}$, and a result type U_0.

A *type environment* Δ is a finite mapping from type variables to pairs of a
variance except o (that is, either +, -, or *) and a type. We write $dom(\Delta)$ for the
domain of Δ. When X $\notin dom(\Delta)$, we write $\Delta, \text{X} : (\text{v}, \text{T})$ for the type environment

Field lookup:

$$fields(\texttt{Object}) = \bullet$$

$$\frac{\texttt{class C<}\overline{\texttt{X}}\triangleleft\overline{\texttt{N}}\texttt{>}\triangleleft\texttt{D<}\overline{\texttt{U}}\texttt{> \{}\overline{\texttt{S}}\ \overline{\texttt{f}}\texttt{;}\ \overline{\texttt{M}}\texttt{\}}\qquad fields([\overline{\texttt{T}}/\overline{\texttt{X}}]\texttt{D<}\overline{\texttt{U}}\texttt{>}) = \overline{\texttt{V}}\ \overline{\texttt{g}}}{fields(\texttt{C<}\overline{\texttt{T}}\texttt{>}) = \overline{\texttt{V}}\ \overline{\texttt{g}}, [\overline{\texttt{T}}/\overline{\texttt{X}}]\overline{\texttt{S}}\ \overline{\texttt{f}}}$$

Method type lookup:

$$\frac{\texttt{class C<}\overline{\texttt{X}}\triangleleft\overline{\texttt{N}}\texttt{>}\triangleleft\texttt{D<}\overline{\texttt{S}}\texttt{> \{}\ldots\ \overline{\texttt{M}}\texttt{\}}\qquad \texttt{U}_0\ \texttt{m(}\overline{\texttt{U}}\ \overline{\texttt{x}}\texttt{)\{ return e; \}} \in \overline{\texttt{M}}}{mtype(\texttt{m}, \texttt{C<}\overline{\texttt{T}}\texttt{>}) = [\overline{\texttt{T}}/\overline{\texttt{X}}](\overline{\texttt{U}}\texttt{->}\texttt{U}_0)}$$

$$\frac{\texttt{class C<}\overline{\texttt{X}}\triangleleft\overline{\texttt{N}}\texttt{>}\triangleleft\texttt{D<}\overline{\texttt{S}}\texttt{> \{}\ldots\ \overline{\texttt{M}}\texttt{\}}\qquad \texttt{m}\notin\overline{\texttt{M}}}{mtype(\texttt{m}, \texttt{C<}\overline{\texttt{T}}\texttt{>}) = mtype(\texttt{m}, [\overline{\texttt{T}}/\overline{\texttt{X}}]\texttt{D<}\overline{\texttt{S}}\texttt{>})}$$

Open:

if $(\texttt{v}_i, \texttt{T}_i) \neq (\texttt{w}_i, \texttt{U}_i)$, then

$$\frac{\texttt{w}_i = \texttt{o}\qquad \texttt{U}_i = \texttt{X}_i \notin dom(\Delta) \cup \{\overline{\texttt{U}}\} \setminus \{\texttt{U}_i\}\qquad \Delta'(\texttt{X}_i) = (\texttt{v}_i, \texttt{T}_i)}{\Delta \vdash \texttt{C<}\overline{\texttt{vT}}\texttt{>} \Uparrow^{\Delta'} \texttt{C<}\overline{\texttt{wU}}\texttt{>}}$$

Close:

$$\frac{\Delta(\texttt{X}) = (\texttt{+}, \texttt{T})}{\texttt{X} \Downarrow_\Delta \texttt{T}}\qquad\frac{\texttt{X} \notin dom(\Delta)}{\texttt{X} \Downarrow_\Delta \texttt{X}}\qquad\frac{\overline{\texttt{T}} \Downarrow_\Delta \overline{\texttt{T}}'\qquad \texttt{w}_i = \begin{cases}\texttt{v}_i & \text{if } \texttt{T}_i = \texttt{T}'_i\\ \texttt{+}\vee\texttt{v}_i & \text{otherwise}\end{cases}}{\texttt{C<}\overline{\texttt{vT}}\texttt{>} \Downarrow_\Delta \texttt{C<}\overline{\texttt{wT}'}\texttt{>}}$$

Subtyping:

$$\Delta \vdash \texttt{T} <: \texttt{T}\qquad\frac{\Delta \vdash \texttt{S} <: \texttt{T}\qquad \Delta \vdash \texttt{T} <: \texttt{U}}{\Delta \vdash \texttt{S} <: \texttt{U}}\qquad\frac{\Delta(\texttt{X}) = (\texttt{+}, \texttt{T})}{\Delta \vdash \texttt{X} <: \texttt{T}}\qquad\frac{\Delta(\texttt{X}) = (\texttt{-}, \texttt{T})}{\Delta \vdash \texttt{T} <: \texttt{X}}$$

$$\frac{\texttt{class C<}\overline{\texttt{X}}\triangleleft\overline{\texttt{N}}\texttt{>}\triangleleft\texttt{D<}\overline{\texttt{S}}\texttt{> \{}\ldots\texttt{\}}\qquad \Delta \vdash \texttt{C<}\overline{\texttt{vT}}\texttt{>} \Uparrow^{\Delta'} \texttt{C<}\overline{\texttt{U}}\texttt{>}\qquad ([\overline{\texttt{U}}/\overline{\texttt{X}}]\texttt{D<}\overline{\texttt{S}}\texttt{>}) \Downarrow_{\Delta'} \texttt{T}}{\Delta \vdash \texttt{C<}\overline{\texttt{vT}}\texttt{>} <: \texttt{T}}$$

$$\frac{\overline{\texttt{v}} \leq \overline{\texttt{w}}\qquad \text{if } \texttt{w}_i \leq \texttt{-}, \text{then } \Delta \vdash \texttt{T}_i <: \texttt{S}_i\qquad \text{if } \texttt{w}_i \leq \texttt{+}, \text{then } \Delta \vdash \texttt{S}_i <: \texttt{T}_i}{\Delta \vdash \texttt{C<}\overline{\texttt{vS}}\texttt{>} <: \texttt{C<}\overline{\texttt{wT}}\texttt{>}}$$

Type Well-formedness:

$$\Delta \vdash \texttt{Object ok}\qquad\frac{\texttt{X} \in dom(\Delta)}{\Delta \vdash \texttt{X ok}}\qquad\frac{\texttt{class C<}\overline{\texttt{X}}\triangleleft\overline{\texttt{N}}\texttt{>}\triangleleft\texttt{D<}\overline{\texttt{S}}\texttt{> \{}\ldots\texttt{\}}\qquad \Delta \vdash \overline{\texttt{T}}\texttt{ ok}\qquad \Delta \vdash \overline{\texttt{T}} <: [\overline{\texttt{T}}/\overline{\texttt{X}}]\overline{\texttt{N}}}{\Delta \vdash \texttt{C<}\overline{\texttt{vT}}\texttt{> ok}}$$

Fig. 3. Auxiliary Definitions for Typing

Δ' such that $dom(\Delta') = dom(\Delta) \cup \{X\}$ and $\Delta'(X) = (v, T)$ and $\Delta'(Y) = \Delta(Y)$ if $X \neq Y$. We often write X<:T for X : (+, T) and X:>T for X : (-, T).

The type system consists of five forms of judgments: $\Delta \vdash N \Uparrow^{\Delta'} P$ for opening a variant parametric type to an invariant type; $N \Downarrow_\Delta P$ for closing an invariant type with some free constrained type variables to a variant parametric type without them; $\Delta \vdash S <: T$ for subtyping; $\Delta \vdash T$ ok for type well-formedness; and $\Delta; \Gamma \vdash e \in T$ for typing, where Γ, called an *environment*, is a finite mapping from variables to types, written $\bar{x}:\bar{T}$. We abbreviate a sequence of judgments, writing $\Gamma \vdash \bar{S} <: \bar{T}$ as shorthand for $\Gamma \vdash S_1 <: T_1, \ldots, \Gamma \vdash S_n <: T_n$, $\Gamma \vdash \bar{T}$ ok as shorthand for $\Gamma \vdash T_1$ ok$, \ldots, \Gamma \vdash T_n$ ok, and $\Delta; \Gamma \vdash \bar{e} \in \bar{T}$ as shorthand for $\Delta; \Gamma \vdash e_1 \in T_1, \ldots, \Delta; \Gamma \vdash e_n \in T_n$.

Open and Close. As already mentioned, variant parametric types are essentially bounded existential types in disguised forms and so any operations on variant parametric types have to "open" the existential type first. A judgement of the open operation $\Delta \vdash N \Uparrow^{\Delta'} P$ is read "under Δ, N is opened to P and constraints Δ'." The open operation introduces fresh type variables to represent abstract types and replace non-invariant type arguments with the type variables: for example, List<+Integer> is opened to List<X> with the constraint X<:Integer, written $\vdash$ List<+Integer> $\Uparrow^{X<:Integer}$ List<X>.

When the result of an operation involves the abstract types (type variables under constraints) introduced by open, it needs to be "closed" so that the abstract types do not escape; a judgment of the close operation $N \Downarrow_\Delta P$ is read "N with abstract types in Δ closes to P." The close operation computes the least supertype without mentioning the abstract types. The first rule means that, if X's upper bound is known, X can be promoted to its bound. (When $\Delta(X) = (-, T)$, on the other hand, it cannot be promoted since an upper bound is unknown.) The second rule means that a type variable not bound in Δ remains the same. The third rule is explained as follows. In order to close C<$\bar{v}\bar{T}$>, the type arguments $\bar{T}$ have to be closed to $\bar{T}'$ first; when T_i is closed to a proper supertype $\bar{T}_i'$ (i.e. $T_i \neq T_i'$), the resulting type must be covariant in that argument, thus the least upper bound of + and v_i is attached. For example, under X<:Integer, X closes to Integer, List<X> to List<+Integer>, and List<List<X>> to List<+List<+Integer>> (not to List<List<+Integer>>).

Subtyping. A judgment for subtyping $\Delta \vdash S <: T$ is read "S is a subtype of T under Δ." As usual, the subtyping relation includes the reflexive and transitive closure of the relation induced by $\lhd$ clauses. When an upper or lower bound of a type variable is recorded in Δ, the type variable is a subtype or supertype of the bound, respectively (the third and fourth rules). The next rule is for subtyping based on subclassing. When C<$\bar{X}$> is declared to extend another type D<$\bar{S}$>, any (invariant) instantiation C<$\bar{T}$> is a subtype of D<$[\bar{T}/\bar{X}]\bar{S}$>. A supertype of a non-invariant type is obtained by opening it and closing the supertype of the opened type. Finally, the last rule deals with variance. The first conditional premise means that, if a variance annotation v_i for X_i is either contravariant or invariant, the corresponding type arguments S_i and T_i must satisfy $\Delta \vdash T_i <: S_i$; similarly for the second one.

Type Well-Formedness. A judgment for type well-formedness is of the form $\Delta \vdash$ T ok, read "T is a well-formed type under Δ". The rules for type well-formedness are straightforward: (1) Object is always well formed; (2) a type variable is well formed if it is in the domain of Δ; and (3) a variant parametric type C<$\overline{vT}$> is well-formed if the type arguments $\overline{T}$ are lower than their bounds, respectively. Note that variance annotations can be any.

Typing. The typing rules for expressions are syntax directed, with one rule for each form of expression, shown in Figure 4. In what follows, we use $bound_\Delta$(T) defined by: $bound_\Delta$(X) = S if Δ(X) = (+, S) and $bound_\Delta$(N) = N. Most rules are straightforward. When a field or method is accessed, the type on which the operation is performed is opened and the result type is closed. The typing rules for constructor/method invocations check that the type of each actual parameter is a subtype of the corresponding formal.

Typing for methods requires the auxiliary predicate *override* to check correct method overriding. *override*(m, N, $\overline{T}$->T_0) holds if and only if a method of the same name m is defined in the supertype N and has the same argument and return types (it would be safe to extend the rule to handle overriding of the result type covariantly, as allowed in GJ). The method body should be given a subtype of the declared result type under the assumption that the formal parameters are given the declared types and this is given type C<$\overline{X}$>. The environment prohibits this from occurring as a parameter name since name duplication in the domain of an environment is not allowed. Finally, a class declaration is well typed if all the methods are well typed.

6.3   Properties

Type soundness (Theorem 3) is shown through subject reduction and progress properties [37], after defining the reduction relation e $\longrightarrow$ e', read "expression e reduces to expression e' in one step." The definiton of the reduction relation and proofs of type soundness are found in the full version of the paper[6]. To state type soundness, we require the notion of values, defined by:
$v ::=$ new C<$\overline{T}$>$(v_1, \ldots, v_n)$ (n may be 0).

Theorem 1 (Subject Reduction). *If* $\Delta; \Gamma \vdash$ e $\in$ T *and* e $\longrightarrow$ e', *then* $\Delta; \Gamma \vdash$ e' $\in$ S *and* $\Delta \vdash$ S <: T *for some* S.

Theorem 2 (Progress). *Suppose* e *is a well-typed expression.*

1. *If* e *includes* new C<$\overline{T}$>$(\overline{e})$.f *as a subexpression, then* $fields$(C<$\overline{T}$>) = $\overline{U}$ $\overline{f}$ *and* f = f_i.
2. *If* e *includes* new C<$\overline{T}$>$(\overline{e})$.m$(\overline{d})$ *as a subexpression, then* $mbody$(m, C<$\overline{T}$>) = $\overline{x}.e_0$ *and* $|\overline{x}| = |\overline{d}|$.

---

[6] Strictly speaking, for run-time expressions, we would need another typing rule for stupid casts [20]—that is, casts that turn out to fail in the course of execution; we have omitted it just for brevity.

Expression Typing:

$$\Delta; \Gamma \vdash \mathtt{x} \in \Gamma(\mathtt{x})$$

$$\frac{\Delta; \Gamma \vdash \mathtt{e}_0 \in \mathtt{T}_0 \qquad \Delta \vdash \mathit{bound}_\Delta(\mathtt{T}_0) \Uparrow^{\Delta'} \mathtt{C}\mathtt{<}\overline{\mathtt{T}}\mathtt{>} \qquad \mathit{fields}(\mathtt{C}\mathtt{<}\overline{\mathtt{T}}\mathtt{>}) = \overline{\mathtt{S}} \ \overline{\mathtt{f}} \qquad \mathtt{S}_i \Downarrow_{\Delta'} \mathtt{T}}{\Delta; \Gamma \vdash \mathtt{e}_0.\mathtt{f}_i \in \mathtt{T}}$$

$$\frac{\Delta; \Gamma \vdash \mathtt{e}_0 \in \mathtt{T}_0 \qquad \Delta \vdash \mathit{bound}_\Delta(\mathtt{T}_0) \Uparrow^{\Delta'} \mathtt{C}\mathtt{<}\overline{\mathtt{T}}\mathtt{>} \qquad \mathit{mtype}(\mathtt{m}, \mathtt{C}\mathtt{<}\overline{\mathtt{T}}\mathtt{>}) = \overline{\mathtt{U}}\mathtt{->}\mathtt{U}_0 \\ \Delta; \Gamma \vdash \overline{\mathtt{e}} \in \overline{\mathtt{S}} \qquad \Delta \vdash \overline{\mathtt{S}} \mathrel{<:} \overline{\mathtt{U}} \qquad \mathtt{U}_0 \Downarrow_{\Delta'} \mathtt{T}}{\Delta; \Gamma \vdash \mathtt{e}_0.\mathtt{m}(\overline{\mathtt{e}}) \in \mathtt{T}}$$

$$\frac{\Delta \vdash \mathtt{C}\mathtt{<}\overline{\mathtt{T}}\mathtt{>} \ \mathrm{ok} \qquad \mathit{fields}(\mathtt{C}\mathtt{<}\overline{\mathtt{T}}\mathtt{>}) = \overline{\mathtt{U}} \ \overline{\mathtt{f}} \qquad \Delta; \Gamma \vdash \overline{\mathtt{e}} \in \overline{\mathtt{S}} \qquad \Delta \vdash \overline{\mathtt{S}} \mathrel{<:} \overline{\mathtt{U}}}{\Delta; \Gamma \vdash \mathtt{new} \ \mathtt{C}\mathtt{<}\overline{\mathtt{T}}\mathtt{>}(\overline{\mathtt{e}}) \in \mathtt{C}\mathtt{<}\overline{\mathtt{T}}\mathtt{>}}$$

$$\frac{\Delta; \Gamma \vdash \mathtt{e}_0 \in \mathtt{T}_0 \\ \Delta \vdash \mathit{bound}_\Delta(\mathtt{T}_0) \mathrel{<:} \mathit{bound}_\Delta(\mathtt{T}) \quad \mathrm{or} \quad \Delta \vdash \mathit{bound}_\Delta(\mathtt{T}) \mathrel{<:} \mathit{bound}_\Delta(\mathtt{T}_0)}{\Delta; \Gamma \vdash (\mathtt{T})\mathtt{e}_0 \in \mathtt{T}}$$

Method Typing:

$$\frac{\mathit{mtype}(\mathtt{m}, \mathtt{N}) = \overline{\mathtt{U}}\mathtt{->}\mathtt{U}_0 \ \text{implies} \ \overline{\mathtt{U}}, \mathtt{U}_0 = \overline{\mathtt{T}}, \mathtt{T}_0}{\mathit{override}(\mathtt{m}, \mathtt{N}, \overline{\mathtt{T}}\mathtt{->}\mathtt{T}_0)}$$

$$\frac{\Delta = \overline{\mathtt{X}}\mathtt{<:}\overline{\mathtt{N}} \qquad \Delta \vdash \overline{\mathtt{T}}, \mathtt{T}_0 \ \mathrm{ok} \qquad \Delta; \overline{\mathtt{x}} : \overline{\mathtt{T}}, \mathtt{this} : \mathtt{C}\mathtt{<}\overline{\mathtt{X}}\mathtt{>} \vdash \mathtt{e}_0 \in \mathtt{S}_0 \qquad \Delta \vdash \mathtt{S}_0 \mathrel{<:} \mathtt{T}_0 \\ \mathtt{class} \ \mathtt{C}\mathtt{<}\overline{\mathtt{X}} \vartriangleleft \overline{\mathtt{N}}\mathtt{>} \vartriangleleft \mathtt{D}\mathtt{<}\overline{\mathtt{S}}\mathtt{>} \ \{\ldots\} \qquad \mathit{override}(\mathtt{m}, \mathtt{D}\mathtt{<}\overline{\mathtt{S}}\mathtt{>}, \overline{\mathtt{T}}\mathtt{->}\mathtt{T}_0)}{\mathtt{T}_0 \ \mathtt{m}(\overline{\mathtt{T}} \ \overline{\mathtt{x}})\{\mathtt{return} \ \mathtt{e}_0;\} \ \mathtt{OK \ IN} \ \mathtt{C}\mathtt{<}\overline{\mathtt{X}} \vartriangleleft \overline{\mathtt{N}}\mathtt{>}}$$

Class Typing:

$$\frac{\overline{\mathtt{X}}\mathtt{<:}\overline{\mathtt{N}} \vdash \overline{\mathtt{N}}, \mathtt{D}\mathtt{<}\overline{\mathtt{S}}\mathtt{>}, \overline{\mathtt{T}} \ \mathrm{ok} \qquad \overline{\mathtt{M}} \ \mathtt{OK \ IN} \ \mathtt{C}\mathtt{<}\overline{\mathtt{X}} \vartriangleleft \overline{\mathtt{N}}\mathtt{>}}{\mathtt{class} \ \mathtt{C}\mathtt{<}\overline{\mathtt{X}} \vartriangleleft \overline{\mathtt{N}}\mathtt{>} \vartriangleleft \mathtt{D}\mathtt{<}\overline{\mathtt{S}}\mathtt{>} \ \{\overline{\mathtt{T}} \ \overline{\mathtt{f}}; \ \overline{\mathtt{M}}\} \ \mathtt{OK}}$$

Fig. 4. Typing

Theorem 3 (Type Soundness). *If* $\emptyset; \emptyset \vdash \mathtt{e} \in \mathtt{T}$ *and* $\mathtt{e} \longrightarrow^* \mathtt{e}'$ *being a normal form, then* $\mathtt{e}'$ *is either a value* v *such that* $\Delta; \Gamma \vdash v \in \mathtt{S}$ *and* $\emptyset \vdash \mathtt{S} \mathrel{<:} \mathtt{T}$ *for some* $\mathtt{S}$ *or an expression that includes* $(\mathtt{T})\mathtt{new} \ \mathtt{C}\mathtt{<}\overline{\mathtt{T}}\mathtt{>}(\overline{\mathtt{e}})$ *where* $\emptyset \vdash \mathtt{C}\mathtt{<}\overline{\mathtt{T}}\mathtt{>} \not\mathrel{<:} \mathtt{T}$.

7   Related Work

Parametric Classes and Variance. There have been several languages, such as POOL [2] and Strongtalk [4,3], that support variance for parametric classes; more recently, Cartwright and Steele [13] have discussed the possibility of the introduction of variance to NextGen—a proposal for extending Java with generics. The approach there is different from ours in that variance is a property of *classes*, rather than *types*. In these languages, the variance annotation is attached to the declaration of a type parameter so that a *designer* of a class can express his/her intent about all the parametric types derived from the class. Then, the system can statically check whether the variance declaration is correct: for example, if X is declared to be covariant in a parametric class C<X> but used in a method argument type or (writable) field type, the compiler will reject the class. Thus, in order to enhance reusability with variance, library designers must take great care to structure the API, casting a heavy burden on them. Day et al. [15] even argued that this restriction was too severe and, after all, they have decided to drop variance from the their language Theta. On the contrary, in our system, *users* of a parametric class can choose a variance: a class C<X>, for example, can have arbitrary occurrences of X and induces four different types C<T>, C<+T>, C<-T>, and C<*T> with one concrete type argument T. We believe that moving annotations to the use site provides much more flexibility.

In an early design of Eiffel, every parametric type was unsoundly assumed to be covariant. To remedy the problem, Cook [14] proposed to *infer*, rather than *declare*, variance of type parameters of a given class without annotations. For example, if X in the class C<X> appears only in a method return type, the type C<T> is automatically regarded as covariant, and similarly for contravariant. This proposal is not adopted in the current design, in which every parametric class is regarded as invariant [16].

Virtual Types. As we have already mentioned, the idea of variant parametric types has emerged from structural virtual types proposed by Thorup and Torgersen [33]. In a language with virtual types [24,32], a type can be declared as a member of a class, just as well as fields and methods, and the virtual type member can be overridden in subclasses. For example, a generic bag class Bag has a virtual type member ElmTy, which is bound to Object; specific bags can be obtained by declaring a subclass of Bag, overriding ElmTy by their concrete element types.

Since the original proposals of virtual types were unsafe and required runtime checks, Torgersen [34] developed a safe type system for virtual types by exploiting two kinds of type binding: open and final. An open type member is overridable but the identity of the type member is made abstract, prohibiting unsafe accesses such as putting elements into a bag whose element type is unknown; a final type member cannot be overridden in subclasses but the identity of the type member is manifest, making concrete bags. In a pseudo Java-like language, a generic bag class and concrete bag classes can be written as follows.

```
class Bag {
    type ElmTy <: Object; // open binding
    ElmTy get() { ... }
    void put(ElmTy e) { ... }
    // No element can be put into a Bag.
}
```

```
class StringBag extends Bag {
  type ElmTy == String; // final binding
  // Strings can be put into a String Bag.
}
class IntegerBag extends Bag { type ElmTy == Integer; }
```

One criticism on this approach was that it was often the case that concrete bags were obtained only by overriding the type member, making lots of small subclasses of a bag. Structural virtual types are proposed to remedy this problem: type bindings can be described in a type expression and a number of concrete types are derived from one class. For example, a programmer can instantiate Bag[ElmTy==Integer] to make an integer bag, where the [] clause describes a type binding. In addition, Bag[ElmTy==Integer] <: Bag[ElmTy<:Object] and Bag[ElmTy==String] <: Bag[ElmTy<:Object] hold as is expected.

In their paper [33], it is briefly (and informally) discussed how structural virtual types can be imported to parametric classes, the idea on which our development is based. The above programming is achieved by making ElmTy a type parameter to the class Bag, rather than a member of a class.

```
class Bag<ElmTy extends Object> extends Object {
  ElmTy get() { ... }
  void put(ElmTy e) { ... }
}
```

Then, an integer bag is obtained by new Bag<Integer>() and Bag<Integer> <: Bag<+Object> holds. In other words, the type Bag<Integer> corresponds to Bag[ElmTy==Integer] and Bag<+Object> to Bag[ElmTy<:Object]. This similarity is not just superficial: as in [19], programming with virtual types is shown to be simulated (to some degree) by exploiting bounded and manifest existential types [18,22], on which our formal type system is also partly based.

Thus, our variant parametric types can be considered a generalization of the idea above with contravariance and bivariance. Other differences are as follows. On one hand, virtual types seem more suitable for programming with extensible mutually recursive classes/interfaces [7,33,10]. On the other hand, our system allows a (partially) instantiated parametric class to be extended: as we have already discussed, a programmer can declare a subclass PP<X,Y> that inherits from Pair<Pair<X,Y>,Pair<X,Y>>. It is not very clear (at least, from their paper [33]) how to encode such programming in structural virtual types. More rigorous comparisons are interesting but left for future work.

Existential types in object-oriented languages. The idea of existential types can actually be seen in several mechanisms for object-oriented languages, often in disguised (and limited) forms.

In the language $\mathcal{LOOM}$ [8], subtyping is dropped in favor of matching [6,9], thus losing subsumption. To recover the flexibility of subsumption to some degree, they introduced the notion of the "hash" type #T, which stands for the set of types that match T. As is pointed out in [8], #T is considered a "match-bounded" existential type $\exists X$<#T.X, where X<#T stands for "X matches T."

The notion of exact types [7] is introduced in a proposal of a Java-like language with both parametric classes and virtual types. In that language, a class of the name C induces two types C and @C; the type C denotes a set of objects created only from the class C, while @C does a set of objects created from C or its subclasses. In this sense, @C can be considered the existential type ∃X<:C,X, where <: denotes subclassing[7].

Raw types [5] of GJ are also close to bounded existential types [21]. In GJ, the class Vector<X>, for example, induces the raw type Vector as well as parametric types including Vector<Integer> and Vector<String>. The raw type Vector is typically used by legacy classes written in monomorphic Java, making it smooth to importing old Java code into GJ. Vector is considered a supertype of every parametric type Vector<T> and behaves somehow like ∃X<:Object.Vector<X>. One significant difference is that certain unsafe operations putting elements into a raw vector are permitted with a compiler warning.

8   Conclusions and Future Work

In this paper, we have presented a language construct based on *variant parametric types* as an extension to common object-oriented languages with support for generic classes. Variant parametric types are used to exploit inclusive polymorphism for generic types, namely, providing a uniform view over different instantiations of a generic class.

Variant parametric types generally make it possible to widen the applicability of methods accessing a subset of a generic instance's members—e.g., when a method only reads the elements of a generic collection passed as argument. Furthermore, variant parametric types seem to increase the expressiveness in declaring more complex parameterizations, featuring nesting variant parametric types and partial instantiations through the bivariance symbol *. For a rigorous argument of type soundness, we have developed a core calculus of variant parametric types, based on Featherweight GJ [20]. A key idea in the development of the type system is to exploit similarity between variant parametric types and bounded existential types.

Implementation issues are not addressed in this paper which are likely to be a subject of future work. It is worth noting, however, that existing implementation techniques seem to allow for straightforward extensions providing variant parametric types. For instance, the type-erasure technique—which is one of the basic implementation approaches for generics, in both Java (GJ [5]) and the .NET CLR ([30])—can be directly exploited for dealing with variant parametric types, for they can be simply erased in the translated code just as standard parametric types. (The language would be constrained due to the lack of run-time

---

[7] A similar idea can be found in an old version of the type system of Sather [23], where the symbol $ replaces @ and is used to enable efficient method dispatching. In the current design of Sather [31], $ is used for names of abstract classes, from which subclasses can be derived, while names without the leading $ are used for concrete classes, from which objects can be instantiated but subclasses cannot be derived.

type arguments, though: for example, the target of typecasts cannot be a type variable.) Other advanced translation techniques where exact generic types are maintained at run time, such as LM translator [36,35], can be extended as well. In this case, variant parametric types can be supported by simply implementing a subtyping strategy in which variance-based subtyping is taken into account. Since the current design allows run-time type arguments to be variant parametric types, it will be important to estimate extra overhead to manage information on variance annotations. In general, one of the basic implementation issues would be to find an optimized algorithm for subtyping variant parametric types. For example, the approach presented in [28] may be worth investigating.

Other future work includes the further evaluation of the variant parametric type's expressiveness through large-scale applications and more rigorous comparisons with related constructs such as virtual types [33].

References

1. Ole Agesen, Stephen N. Freund, and John C. Mitchell. Adding type parameterization to the Java language. In *Proc. of ACM OOPSLA*, pages 49–65, Atlanta, GA, October 1997.
2. Pierre America and Frank van der Linden. A parallel object-oriented language with inheritance and subtyping. In *Proc. of OOPSLA/ECOOP*, pages 161–168, Ottawa, Canada, October 1990.
3. Gilad Bracha. The Strongtalk type system for Smalltalk. In *Proc. of the OOPSLA96 Workshop on Extending the Smalltalk Language*, 1996. Also available electronically through http://java.sun.com/people/gbracha/nwst.html.
4. Gilad Bracha and David Griswold. Strongtalk: Typechecking Smalltalk in a production environment. In *Proc. of ACM OOPSLA*, pages 215–230, Washington, DC, October 1993.
5. Gilad Bracha, Martin Odersky, David Stoutamire, and Philip Wadler. Making the future safe for the past: Adding genericity to the Java programming language. In *Proc. of ACM OOPSLA*, pages 183–200, Vancouver, BC, October 1998.
6. Kim B. Bruce. A paradigmatic object-oriented programming language: Design, static typing and semantics. *Journal of Functional Programming*, 4(2), April 1994. Preliminary version in POPL 1993, under the title "Safe type checking in a statically typed object-oriented programming language".
7. Kim B. Bruce, Martin Odersky, and Philip Wadler. A statically safe alternative to virtual types. In *Proc. of the 12th ECOOP*, LNCS 1445, pages 523–549, Brussels, Belgium, July 1998. Springer-Verlag.
8. Kim B. Bruce, Leaf Petersen, and Adrian Fiech. Subtyping is not a good "match" for object-oriented languages. In *Proc. of the 11th European Conference on Object-Oriented Programming (ECOOP'97)*, LNCS 1241, pages 104–127, Jyväskylä, Finland, June 1997. Springer-Verlag.
9. Kim B. Bruce, Angela Schuett, and Robert van Gent. PolyTOIL: A type-safe polymorphic object-oriented language. In W. Olthoff, editor, *Proc. of ECOOP*, LNCS 952, pages 27–51, Aarhus, Denmark, August 1995. Springer-Verlag.
10. Kim B. Bruce and Joseph C. Vanderwaart. Semantics-driven language design: Statically type-safe virtual types in object-oriented languages. In *Proc. of the 15th*

Conference on the Mathematical Foundations of Programming Semantics (MFPS XV), volume 20 of *Electronic Notes in Theoretical Computer Science*, New Orleans, LA, April 1999. Elsevier. Available through http://www.elsevier.nl/locate/entcs/volume20.html.

11. Peter Canning, William Cook, Walter Hill, Walter Olthoff, and John Mitchell. F-bounded quantification for object-oriented programming. In *Proc. of ACM FPCA*, pages 273–280, September 1989.

12. Luca Cardelli and Peter Wegner. On understanding types, data abstraction, and polymorphism. *Computing Surveys*, 17(4):471–522, December 1985.

13. Robert Cartwright and Guy L. Steele Jr. Compatible genericity with run-time types for the Java programming language. In *Proc. of ACM OOPSLA*, pages 201–215, Vancouver, BC, October 1998.

14. William Cook. A proposal for making Eiffel type-safe. In *Proc. of the 3rd ECOOP*, pages 57–70, Nottingham, England, July 1989. Cambridge University Press.

15. Mark Day, Robert Gruber, Barbara Liskov, and Andrew C. Meyers. Subtypes vs. where clauses: Constraining parametric polymorphism. In *Proc. of ACM OOPSLA*, pages 156–168, Austin, TX, October 1995.

16. Interactive Software Engineering. An Eiffel tutorial. Available through http://www.eiffel.com/doc/online/eiffel50/intro/language/tutorial-00.html, 2001.

17. Giorgio Ghelli and Benjamin Pierce. Bounded existentials and minimal typing. *Theoretical Computer Science*, 193:75–96, 1998.

18. Robert Harper and Mark Lillibridge. A type-theoretic approach to higher-order modules with sharing. In *Proc. of ACM POPL*, pages 123–137, Portland, OR, January 1994.

19. Atsushi Igarashi and Benjamin C. Pierce. Foundations for virtual types. *Information and Computation*, 2002. An earlier version in *Proc. of the 13th ECOOP*, Springer LNCS 1628, pages 161–185, 1999.

20. Atsushi Igarashi, Benjamin C. Pierce, and Philip Wadler. Featherweight Java: A minimal core calculus for Java and GJ. *ACM Transactions on Programming Languages and Systems*, 23(3):396–450, May 2001. A preliminary summary appeared in *proc. of OOPSLA'99*, pages 132–146, Denver, CO, October 1999.

21. Atsushi Igarashi, Benjamin C. Pierce, and Philip Wadler. A recipe for raw types. In *Informal Proc. of the 8th International Workshop on Foundations of Object-Oriented Languages (FOOL8)*, London, England, January 2001. Available through http://www.cs.williams.edu/~kim/FOOL/FOOL8.html.

22. Xavier Leroy. Manifest types, modules and separate compilation. In *Proc. of ACM POPL*, pages 109–122, Portland, OR, January 1994.

23. Chu-Cheow Lim and A. Stolcke. Sather language design and performance evaluation. Technical Report TR-91-034, International Computer Science Institute, University of California, Berkeley, May 1991.

24. Ole Lehrmann Madsen and Birger Møller-Pedersen. Virtual classes: A powerful mechanism in object-oriented programming. In *Proc. of ACM OOPSLA*, pages 397–406, New Orleans, LA, 1989.

25. Andrew C. Meyers, Joseph A. Bank, and Barbara Liskov. Parameterized types for Java. In *Proc. of ACM POPL*, pages 132–145. ACM, 1997.

26. Microsoft Corporation. The .NET Common Language Runtime. Information available through http://msdn.microsoft.com/net/, 2001.

27. John C. Mitchell and Gordon D. Plotkin. Abstract types have existential types. *ACM Transactions on Programming Languages and Systems*, 10(3):470–502, 1988. Preliminary version appeared in *Proc. of the 12th ACM POPL*, 1985.

28. Olivier Raynaund and Eric Thierry. A quasi optimal bit-vector encoding of tree hierarchies. application to efficient type inclusion tests. In *Proc. of the 15th ECOOP*, LNCS 2072, pages 165–180. Springer-Verlag, June 2001.

29. Sun Microsystems. Adding generic types to the Java programming language. Java Specification Request JSR-000014, http://jcp.org/jsr/detail/014.jsp, 1998.

30. Don Syme and Andrew Kennedy. Design and implementation of generics for the .NET Common Language Runtime. In *Proc. of ACM PLDI*. ACM, June 2001.

31. Clemens Szyperski, Stephen Omohundro, and Stephan Murer. Engineering a programming language: The type and class system of Sather. In Jurg Gutknecht, editor, *Programming Languages and System Architectures*, LNCS 782, pages 208–227. Springer-Verlag, November 1993.

32. Kresten Krab Thorup. Genericity in Java with virtual types. In *Proc. of the 11th ECOOP*, LNCS 1241, pages 444–471, Jyväskylä, Finland, June 1997. Springer-Verlag.

33. Kresten Krab Thorup and Mads Torgersen. Unifying genericity: Combining the benefits of virtual types and parameterized classes. In *Proc. of the 13th ECOOP*, LNCS 1628, pages 186–204, Lisbon, Portugal, June 1999. Springer-Verlag.

34. Mads Torgersen. Virtual types are statically safe. In *Proc. of the 5th Workshop on Foundations of Object-Oriented Languages (FOOL)*, San Diego, CA, January 1998. Available through http://www.cs.williams.edu/~kim/FOOL/FOOL5.html.

35. Mirko Viroli. Parametric polymorphism in Java: an efficient implementation for parametric methods. In *Proc. of the ACM Symposium on Applied Computing*, pages 610–619, March 2001.

36. Mirko Viroli and Antonio Natali. Parametric polymorphism in Java: an approach to translation based on reflective features. In *Proc. of ACM OOPSLA*, pages 146–165, Oct 2000.

37. Andrew K. Wright and Matthias Felleisen. A syntactic approach to type soundness. *Information and Computation*, 115(1):38–94, November 1994.

Type-Safe Prototype-Based
Component Evolution

Matthias Zenger

École Polytechnique Fédérale de Lausanne
INR Ecublens, 1015 Lausanne, Switzerland
matthias.zenger@epfl.ch

Abstract. Component-based programming is currently carried out using mainstream object-oriented languages. These languages have to be used in a highly disciplined way to guarantee flexible component composition and extensibility. This paper investigates abstractions for component-oriented programming on the programming language level. We propose a simple prototype-based model for first-class components on top of a class-based object-oriented language. The model is formalized as an extension of *Featherweight Java*. Our calculus includes a minimal set of primitives to dynamically build, extend, and compose software components, while supporting features like explicit context dependencies, late composition, unanticipated component extensibility, and strong encapsulation. We present a type system for our calculus that ensures type-safe component definition, composition, and evolution.

1 Introduction

Component-based software development techniques gain increasing attention in industry and research. Component technology is driven by the promise of software reuse and plug-and-play programming. This promise poses high demands on the implementation platform.

Currently, component-based programming is carried out using mainstream object-oriented languages. Object-oriented languages seem to promote component-based programming well: They support encapsulation of state and behavior, inheritance and overriding enable extensibility, and subtype polymorphism and late binding allow flexible reuse of objects and classes. Unfortunately, object-oriented techniques alone are not powerful enough to provide flexible and type-safe component composition and evolution mechanisms.

Therefore, industrial component models like *CORBA* [27], *COM* [46], or *JavaBeans* [33] rely on additional concepts, namely component frameworks and meta-programming. They provide a class framework for modeling components and component interactions together with an informal set of implementation rules. Components are composed using meta-programming technology like reflection. This ad-hoc approach yields a dynamic and flexible composition mechanism, but often does not guarantee any static type security. Furthermore, the

B. Magnusson (Ed.): ECOOP 2002, LNCS 2374, pp. 470–497, 2002.
© Springer-Verlag Berlin Heidelberg 2002

degree of extensibility depends on the framework or the meta-programming tools. In general, it has to be planned ahead, for instance by using suitable design patterns typically derived from the *AbstractFactory* pattern [22]. This lack of unanticipated extensibility hinders a smooth software evolution process substantially.

Another issue was recently pointed out by Aldrich and Chambers [2]. They observe that implementation languages are only loosely coupled to architectural descriptions. As a consequence, specifications of software architectures [44,50] formally expressed in architecture description languages [40] are often quite different from the actual object-oriented implementations. This makes it difficult to trace architectural properties in the implementation, which would allow to verify that an implementation is consistent with the corresponding architecture [2].

This is why recently various proposals have been put forward to integrate concepts known from architecture description languages into object-oriented programming languages [49,52,2]. These so-called component-oriented programming languages offer linguistic facilities for programming software components, for defining component interactions, and for composing software from components. Their promise is to do that in a type-safe way, ruling out illegal interaction patterns.

In this paper we study linguistic abstractions for component-oriented programming in the context of object-oriented programming languages. We describe the notion of prototype-based components. Our prototype-based component model is designed to support plug-and-play programming. It features lightweight components that can be dynamically manufactured and composed in a type-safe way. We emphasize the necessity for a smooth component adaption and evolution process. In particular, we allow to derive refined components from existing components without sacrificing consistency and type-safety. We present a formalization of our prototype-based component model as an extension of *Featherweight Java* [32,45]. Our typed calculus includes a minimal set of primitives to build, extend, and compose software components, while supporting principles like explicit context dependencies, late composition, unanticipated component extensibility, and strong encapsulation of component services.

We proceed by motivating the design principles of our component model. Section 2 emphasizes the importance of software adaptability, extensibility, and software evolution in general. Section 3 introduces prototype-based components by example, presenting the various component refinement primitives. A formalization of the model is presented in Section 4 in form of a core component calculus. We present a type system and prove that this system is sound with respect to the given operational semantics. A summary of the main features together with a discussion of related work is given in Section 5.2. Section 6 concludes.

2   Motivation

In this section we motivate specific design principles of our prototype-based component model. The main features of the model include:

1. Components are first-class core language abstractions,
2. composition operators enable coarse-grained component composition,
3. components can be manufactured and composed dynamically (late composition),
4. components are extensible, promoting component reuse, adaptability, and evolution.

Furthermore, our model adopts principles common among component-oriented languages, like explicit context dependencies (external linking), cyclic component linking, and strong encapsulation. Component manufacturing, composition, and refinement are type-safe. Our type system supports subtype polymorphism for components and component instances.

2.1 Language Integration

The introduction motivated already the need for specific component abstractions, directly integrated into the core of programming languages. With an explicit language construct for components, a programmer can implement architecture descriptions directly without the need for finding a suitable representation in a particular programming language.

2.2 Coarse-Grained Composition

Existing proposals for component abstractions on the programming language level like *ComponentJ* [49], *ACOEL* [52], and *ArchJava* [2] directly adopt common concepts and principles of architecture description languages. They provide constructs for manufacturing components with required and provided services. A service associates a port name with a type. Components are composed by linking ports with explicit plug instructions. The type system ensures that all ports are linked and that links are established only between compatible ports or service providers.

This approach does not scale, since for linking a component with n services, we have to issue n explicit plug instructions specifying the wiring of the component. For large-scale components with a lot of services involved, linking the component is a tedious and error-prone task. Furthermore, the sequence of plug instructions rather obscures the architecture of the system instead of making it explicit. Therefore, McDirmid, Flatt, and Hsieh argue that component systems should offer the possibility to connect many required and provided services at once [39].

We address this requirement by simplifying the interface of components and by providing means to infer the wiring of components to be linked together. Components can be composed with simple operators and without explicitly plugging ports. We also support incremental linking; i.e. we allow that components get only partially linked. For instance, components can be sent around in a distributed system and only the services available at a specific location get linked until in the end we have a fully linked component that can be instantiated.

2.3   Dynamic Manufacturing and Composition

Software component technology distinguishes two main tasks: component manufacturing and component composition. It is often explained that both tasks are separate steps being performed one after the other. But in practice, both tasks coincide when new components are built by composing other components. This form of component manufacturing is called *hierarchical component composition*.

Often it is assumed that component manufacturing is done statically before component composition takes place. Component composition itself cannot always be performed statically in cases where components are only known at runtime. Therefore component-based systems have to support some form of *dynamic linking*.

This observation implies that we also have to be able to manufacture software components dynamically, since component linking and manufacturing coincide in hierarchical component compositions. Thus, it makes no sense to assume that both manufacturing and composition are atomic tasks that are performed consecutively. In highly dynamic systems, component manufacturing and composition is rather an interleaved process in which components are created and linked incrementally.

2.4   Reuse, Adaption, Evolution and Extension

When using components from external vendors, it is quite unlikely that the interfaces of these third-party components fit to the required interfaces off-the-shelf. It is often necessary to adapt components before they can be used in a particular system [30,43]. As Section 2.3 already pointed out, components might only be supplied at runtime, therefore it is even more necessary that components can be adapted dynamically on-the-fly.

In a prototype-based component model, new components can only be created by refining an already existing component. As a consequence, we can derive two different components from a single base component. By doing this, we factor out potential reusable pieces, avoiding duplicated programming effort. In addition, this technique supports software evolution. Software evolution includes the maintenance and extension of component features and interfaces. Supporting software evolution is important, since components and component systems are architectural building blocks and as such, subject to continuous changes.

Extensibility of components [53] is not only required for a smooth component evolution. It is even more desired for enabling the development of families of software applications and product-lines in general. Traditionally, components are static black-boxes emphasizing encapsulation over extensibility. Features can be added to components only by creating a new component that forwards all existing services to the old version in addition to the new services. This is a cumbersome and error-prone procedure that duplicates programming efforts and complicates maintenance.

3   Introduction to Prototype-Based Components

In this section we describe prototype-based components in the context of a small, statically typed, object-oriented *Java*-like base language. Our component model relies on a nominal type system [45] of the base language. In nominal type systems, two types with the same structure but a different name are considered to be different, as opposed to structural type systems that match the structure and not the name. Prototype-based components do not rely on other base language features like inheritance or even classes, even though we present them here in a class-based context. Therefore it should be straightforward to add prototype-based components to other object-oriented languages with nominal object types.

3.1   Components and Component Instances

In our model, a component is a unit of computation that can be accessed through a well-defined interface. A component is a first-class citizen. Its interface specifies the services it provides to allow other components to interact with it. The interface also specifies the services a component requires from other components to be able to provide the own services.

Our component model is prototype-based; i.e. the only way to create a new component is by refining an already existing prototypical component. For bootstrapping purposes, we have a single predefined component that does not provide or require any services. This empty component is denoted by the keyword component.

We strictly distinguish components from component instances. A component describes a template for possibly multiple component instances. It is the component instances that provide the actual services. Services are described by object types, e.g. types defined by classes or interfaces. Objects serve as service providers. They usually get created at component instantiation time. Therefore, components can be seen as organizational units with well-defined interfaces that structure object interdependencies. Components have neither a unique identity, nor an observable state. They come to life through objects at the time they get instantiated.

In the remainder of this section we introduce prototype-based components by example. We derive some simple software components that could be used, for instance, in online retail stores to manage stock and clients.

3.2   Service Provision

We start by manufacturing a software component that provides access to a customer database. We want every customer to have a unique client number. A service that maps customer names to client numbers could be described by the following interface definition:

```
interface CustomerIDs {
    int lookupId(String name);
}
```

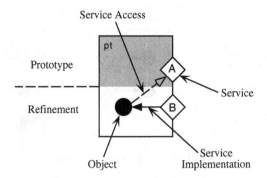

Fig. 1. Schematic notation for prototype-based components

The *CustomerIDs* interface consists of a single method *lookupId*. Given a customer's name, this method tries to find the corresponding client number. If there is no client number yet for this customer, a new number will be issued and returned by *lookupId*. Imagine we have the following implementation of the *CustomerIDs* interface:

```
class MyCustomerIDs implements CustomerIDs {
    MyCustomerIDs() { ... }
    int lookupId(String name) { ... }
    ...
}
```

With this implementation we are able to manufacture a software component that provides a *CustomerIDs* service. Since we can only create new components by refining existing ones, we have to take the empty component as a prototype and refine it such that it provides a *CustomerIDs* service. In our calculus, this is done with the **provides** primitive:

$c0 =$ **component**
        provides *CustomerIDs* **as** *This* **with new** *MyCustomerIDs();*

The clause d **provides** $\overline{C}$ **as** x **with** e returns a new component that refines component d by providing some possibly new services $\overline{C}$. These services are implemented by an object specified with expression e. Note that we are extending a component here. Therefore, expression e only gets evaluated at component instantiation time. x is a variable that gets bound to the own component instance. In object-oriented languages this self reference corresponds to variable *this* or *self* referring to the own object. Only expression e is in the scope of x. Typically, expression e refers to other services of the own component instance via x.

We use a graphical notation to illustrate the structure of components. Figure 1 gives an overview. Here, a component is represented by a box. The gray part corresponds to the prototype of the component, the white part specifies the refinement. In our graphical notation, services are symbolized by diamonds. Objects are simply black dots. An arrow from a service to an object expresses

Component c0:   Component c1:   Component c2:

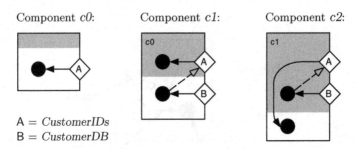

A = CustomerIDs
B = CustomerDB

Fig. 2. Component evolution

that this object implements the service. We also have outlined arrows that depict service dependencies. These dependencies are not explicit in our calculus. If an object refers to other services, for instance via the self reference, then every such dependency is specified with an outlined arrow. Figure 2 shows the structure of our previously defined component c0.

3.3   Component Instantiation

We already pointed out that components have to be instantiated before services can be accessed. In our component calculus, a component gets instantiated with the new primitive.

$i0 = $ **new** $c0;$

The services of a component instance like $i0$ get accessed via the service selection operator ::. The expression $e :: C$ selects a service C from component instance e. C is a type name that identifies a service and at the same time describes the service's interface. Other component models refer to services via named ports. In these models it is possible to have two distinct ports with the same interface type but different port names. In programming languages with nominal type systems like *Java* [26] or $C^\#$ [28], types do not only define structural object properties like available methods or fields. They also stand for semantic specifications [14], and as such, they are well-suited for specifying roles. In those type systems it is possible to have two distinct types with the same interface description but different type names. Therefore, it is no restriction to describe a service only by its type without having a port name in addition. This simplifies the definition of components and the service access in general significantly. It also acts as a standardization of port names. One only has to know a service's type in order to access it from a component instance. It is not necessary to lookup the port name in the component specification. We will see later in Section 3.7 that this standardization of component port names has another advantage: it promotes automatic composition mechanisms. Of course, in the few cases where two ports could share a type, we have to create new type names and in the worst case use wrappers to adapt existing objects.

Here is an example demonstrating the usage of the component *i0*. In this example we call the *lookupId* method of the *CustomerIDs* service provided by component instance *i0*.

i0 :: CustomerIDs.lookupId("John_Smith");

3.4   Component Refinement

Now imagine the requirements for our customer administration component *c0* are changing and we also need the capability to store customer names and addresses. We can describe this new database service with the following interface:

```
interface CustomerDB {
    void enter(String name, String address);
    String lookupName(int id);
    String lookupAddr(int id);
}
```

Method *enter* stores a new address in the database. Whenever a new customer is entered, a new client number will automatically be assigned to this new customer. The methods *lookupName* and *lookupAddr* find a name or address for a given client number. The following class implements *CustomerDB*. It depends on a component instance that provides a *CustomerIDs* service. This component instance is passed as a parameter to the constructor. Following [49], we use the notation $[S_1, ..., S_n]$ to specify the type for component instances supporting at least the services S_1 to S_n.

```
class MyCustomerDB implements CustomerDB {
    [CustomerIDs] This;
    MyCustomerDB([CustomerIDs] This) {
        this.This = This;
    }
    ... This::CustomerIDs.lookupId(name) ...
}
```

We already mentioned that prototype-based components offer a smooth component evolution mechanism. For creating an extended version of a component, we just have to interpret the old component as a prototype. In our example, the new refined component evolves out of the old one simply by an application of the provides primitive. The following code refines component *c0* by additionally providing the service *CustomerDB*.

*c1 = c0 **provides** CustomerDB **as** This **with new** MyCustomerDB(This);*

The provides primitive can also be used to refine a component by defining a new service implementation for an already provided service. In this case we *override* the old implementation. Here is the definition of component *c2* that refines *c1* by using, for instance, a more efficient client numbering service.

*c2 = c1 **provides** CustomerIDs **as** This **with new** EfficientCustomerIDs();*

Component $c3$:

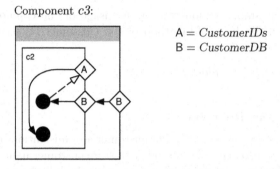

$A = CustomerIDs$
$B = CustomerDB$

Fig. 3. Service forwarding

The service implementation for *CustomerDB*, specified already in the prototype of $c2$, now automatically refers to this new numbering service implementation. A graphical illustration of components $c1$ and $c2$ can be found in Figure 2.

3.5   Service Forwarding

Until now, we are only able to develop new components by adding new services or by overriding existing service implementations of a prototypical component. Every service we add gets exported automatically; i.e. it can be accessed from outside the component. This *white-box approach* is necessary to keep the component extensible, because it allows us to override service implementations and to add new service implementations that refer to already existing services. But often we do not want to publish internally used services. Being able to hide internal interfaces is an important feature of component-oriented programming. Our component calculus supports this form of encapsulation with the component projection operator **forwards**. The clause d **forwards** $\overline{C}$ **as** x **to** e extends component prototype d with the services $\overline{C}$. The new component forwards accesses of these services to the component instance e. Expression e can refer to other services of the own component instance via the self reference x. This primitive is primarily used for hierarchical component compositions. In the following example it is specifically used to hide services and service interconnections. Thus, it turns a "white-box" into a "black-box" by wrapping the original component.

> $c3 =$ **component**
> **forwards** *CustomerDB* **as** *This* **to new** $c2;$

In this example we create a new component $c3$ that only provides a single service *CustomerDB* by forwarding calls to a component instance of $c2$. Thus, we hide the *CustomerIDs* service of component $c2$. We say, an instance of $c2$ is nested inside every instance of component $c3$. We call the hidden *CustomerIDs* service an internal service of component $c3$. An illustration of $c3$ instances can be found in Figure 3. Here, the instance of component $c2$ that is contained in $c3$ is depicted by a nested box. Service implementations are now arrows pointing from external services to internal services of nested component instances.

3.6   Service Abstraction

The previous sections showed how to evolve a component by incrementally adding new services either by a new service implementation or by forwarding services to a nested component instance. In both cases we introduced new services and implementations for these services at the same time. This approach does not allow us to write components that depend on services provided by other components. Furthermore, we are not even able to define two services where service implementations depend mutually on each other, because we introduce services linearly, one after the other.

We tackle both problems with a service abstraction facility. Before going into detail, we proceed by manufacturing a new component for handling orders of a shop. The service for placing orders is described by the following interface:

```
interface OrderDB {
    void order(int id, String article, int num);
}
```

With method *order*, new orders can be placed. Orders consists of a client number, an article descriptor and the number of items to deliver. If possible, this method tries to execute the order immediately. Therefore it needs access to a stock database service specified by the following interface:

```
interface StockDB {
    void enter(String article, int num);
    void remove(String article, int num);
    int available(String article);
}
```

Method *order* checks if the articles are available. If this is the case, it removes them from the stock database and sends the articles to the customer's address. Therefore, service implementations of *OrderDB* like *MyOrderDB* also need access to the *CustomerDB* service. Thus, the constructor of the following class expects a component instance providing *StockDB* and *CustomerDB* services.

```
class MyOrderDB implements OrderDB {
    [StockDB, CustomerDB] This;
    MyOrderDB([StockDB, CustomerDB] This) {
        this.This = This;
    }
    ...
}
```

Since we do not want our order system component to already commit to a specific service implementation for the *StockDB* and the *CustomerDB* service, we have to factor out these two services. In order to make use of the component later, we then either have to provide the missing service implementations from outside at composition time, or we further refine the component and provide service implementations from inside the component.

Component $d0$:   Component $e0$:

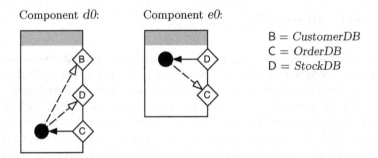

B = *CustomerDB*
C = *OrderDB*
D = *StockDB*

Fig. 4. Service abstraction

In our component calculus, services are factored out with the service abstraction primitive **requires**. The **requires** primitive allows to define services that are required for implementing other services without the need for specifying a concrete service implementation. We make use of this abstraction facility in the following implementation of component $d0$ which requires two services *CustomerDB* and *StockDB* and provides a *OrderDB* service. Figure 4 contains an illustration of component $d0$.

> $d0 =$ **component**
> **requires** *CustomerDB*
> **requires** *StockDB*
> **provides** *OrderDB* **as** *This* **with new** *MyOrderDB(This)*;

The expression d **requires** C takes a prototypical component d and returns a refined version with a service C that has to be provided before the component can be instantiated. Other service implementations can refer to this service, even though there is no implementation known yet. This is why in the example above, self reference *This* has type [*CustomerDB, StockDB, OrderDB*] and thus is a legal parameter for the constructor of *MyOrderDB*. Components have a type of the form $(R_1, \ldots, R_n \Rightarrow P_1, \ldots, P_m)$ where R_1 to R_n are services required by the component, and P_1 to P_m are the provided services. Thus, the type of component $d0$ is (*CustomerDB, StockDB $\Rightarrow$ OrderDB*). As already mentioned before, component $d0$ cannot be instantiated, since not all service provisions are resolved yet. We first have to derive a new component that specifies implementations for all required services before we can actually create component instances.

We continue in our example by defining a new component $e0$ that provides an implementation for a *StockDB* service.

> $e0 =$ **component**
> **requires** *OrderDB*
> **provides** *StockDB* **as** *This* **with new** *MyStockDB(This)*;

The implementation of service *StockDB* makes use of an externally supplied *OrderDB* service. This is, because in cases where new stock arrives and orders are still pending, it would trigger the process of sending out the articles. The type of component $e0$ is (*OrderDB $\Rightarrow$ StockDB*).

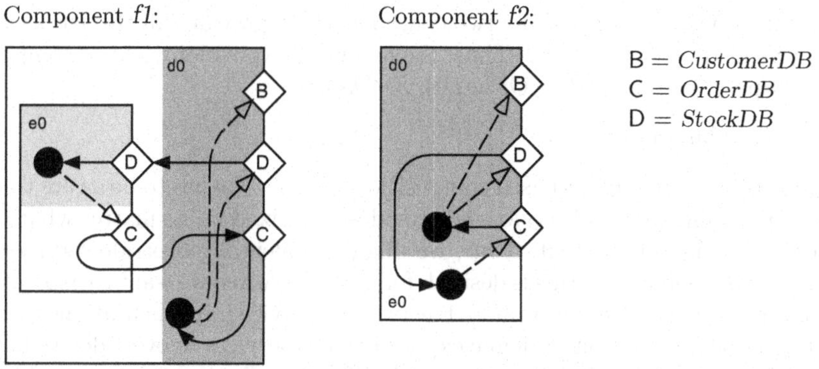

Component *f1*:   Component *f2*:

B = *CustomerDB*
C = *OrderDB*
D = *StockDB*

Fig. 5. Component composition

3.7   Component Composition

In the previous section we defined two components *d0* and *e0* that mutually refer to each other; i.e. the service provided by one component is required by the other one. We would now like to link these two components together yielding a component which only requires a *CustomerDB* service and provides both a *OrderDB* and a *StockDB* service. The simplest way to achieve this is to refine component *d0* with an implementation for service *StockDB*. This service is provided by a refined version of *e0* that refers back to the *OrderDB* service provided by the enclosing *d0* prototype.

> *f0* = *d0* **provides** *StockDB* **as** *This* **with**
>   (**new** (*e0* **provides** *OrderDB* **as** *Me* **with** *This::OrderDB*))*::StockDB*

This technique does not work for components where more than two services depend mutual recursively on each other. For such cases we have to use the forwards primitive in order to link the components together. A graphical illustration of the resulting component *f1* can be found in Figure 5.

> *f1* = *d0* **forwards** *StockDB* **as** *This* **to**
>   **new** (*e0* **provides** *OrderDB* **as** *Me* **with** *This::OrderDB*)

The previously discussed composition schemes use service forwarding where the nested component instance refers back to services provided by the enclosing component being defined. Our component calculus offers an alternative to this rather complicated composition pattern. With the mixin operator it is possible to create a new component by mixing in the services provided by another component. The expression *e* mixin *d* refines the prototypical component *e* with component *d*; i.e. *e* gets refined by including all the services provided by component *d*. Services that are already present in *e* are automatically overridden by the corresponding services of *d*. This operation identifies the self references of both components *e* and *d* by binding it to the resulting merged component. The resulting component requires services that are either required by *e* or *d* and that are not provided by any of the two components. It provides all the services that are provided by either e or d. Thus, the following expression yields a component $f2$ of type ($CustomerDB \Rightarrow OrderDB, StockDB$).

$f2 = d0$ **mixin** $e0$

When using such a mixin-based composition scheme, one has to be aware that for the expression above, all services $e0$ provides get mixed in, no matter what static type $e0$ has in this context. Thus, we might accidentally override services provided by $d0$. Sometimes this is desired, for instance, when we want to express that $e0$ has got the more recent or more trustworthy service implementations than $d0$. For cases where we want to define explicitly what services to override, we have to use a forwarding-based composition scheme instead. For instance, we could write $d0$ forwards $StockDB$ as $This$ to new ($e0$ forwards $OrderDB$ as Me to $This$).

All three components defined in this section are equivalent in the sense that they provide and require the same services and that services are implemented by the same objects. Though, Figure 5 reveals that the internal structure of components manufactured using the forwarding and the mixin technique are quite different. Therefore, they may behave differently when it comes to refinements of both components. In the given example, this is not the case. But one might imagine a bigger nested component instance where overriding a service of the enclosing component does not have any effect on the formerly forwarded service of the nested component, while it would have an effect on the mixin-based approach.

We finish this section by manufacturing a component that permits access to customer related services only; i.e. $CustomerDB$ and $OrderDB$. We do this by first linking together the customer management component $c2$ and the stock management component $f2$. The linked component $c2$ mixin $f2$ provides all the various services introduced in this section. Since we want to restrict the access to customer related services, we have to project the resulting component to a new component $g0$ offering only the desired services.

$g0 =$ **component**
    forwards $CustomerDB, OrderDB$ **as** $This$ **to new** ($c2$ **mixin** $f2$)

$g0$ has type ($\Rightarrow CustomerDB, OrderDB$); thus, it is possible to instantiate this component. The structure of an instance of our final component $g0$ is presented in Figure 6. Leaving out some intermediate steps, we could have composed $g0$ out of three essential components: $c2$ which administers clients, $d0$ which handles orders, and $e0$ which manages the stock.

$g0 =$ **component**
    forwards $CustomerDB, OrderDB$ **as** $This$ **to new** ($c2$ **mixin** $d0$ **mixin** $e0$)

This short expression demonstrates how concise component manufacturing and linking is in our model. Furthermore it outlines how components are typically deployed. The sub-expression $c2$ mixin $d0$ mixin $e0$[1] first links components $c2$,

---

[1] Please note that the mixin operator is associative.

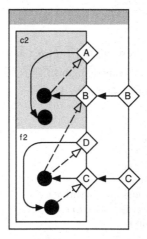

Fig. 6. The final component *g0*

d0, and *e0*, yielding a single extensible component. This component exposes internal interfaces. We might want that, for instance to use this component as a basis for further refinements. But before instantiating (or even selling) it, we should hide the internals by wrapping the component in a black-box only offering specific functionality with restricted support for extensibility. In the example above, this is done using the component projection primitive forwards.

4   Component Calculus

In this section we present a formalization of our prototype-based component model for a functional subset of *Java*. Our calculus is built on top of *Featherweight Java (FJ)* [32]. We omit type casts from the original calculus since type casts are irrelevant for our application and complicate the formal treatment unnecessarily.

4.1   Syntax

The syntax of the calculus is presented in Figure 7. Like in *FJ*, a program consists of a collection of class declarations plus an expression to be evaluated. The syntax of classes, constructors, and methods is identical to *FJ*. We only extend the set of expressions with the primitives introduced in Section 3. In particular, we add an empty component, a service abstraction and implementation primitive, a component projection primitive as well as a component mixin operator. In addition, we have a construct for instantiating components and a service selection operator for accessing services from a component instance. In our calculus, a service is characterized by a class name.

Opposed to the presentation in Section 3.2, the calculus only supports a provides primitive that introduces a single service. This is no restriction since we

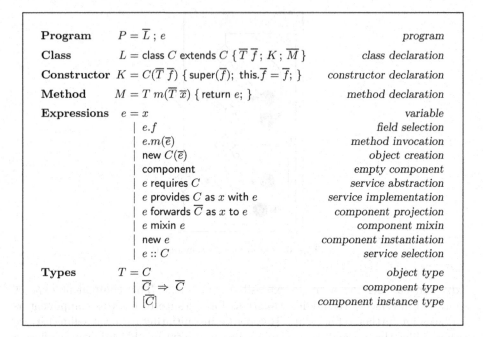

Fig. 7. Syntax

can easily model the former semantics by using the more general forwards construct in combination with a nested component that implements several services with a single object.

FJ's types only consist of class names. For simplicity, *Java*'s interface types are not modeled. For working with components and component instances we also need syntactical forms for expressing component and component instance types. Please note that compared to the explanations in Section 3.6, we use a slightly simplified syntax for component types without enclosing parenthesis. As in *FJ*, we write $\overline{T}$ as a shortcut for $T_1, \ldots, T_n$. We use similar shorthands for sequences like $\overline{C}, \overline{f}, \overline{e}$, etc. as well as for pairs of sequences like $\overline{T}\,\overline{f}$. Such a pair of sequences is a shorthand for $T_1\,f_1, \ldots, T_n\,f_n$.

We assume that sequences of field declarations, parameter names, and method declarations do not contain duplicate names. Furthermore, the service implementation and the component projection operators always introduce fresh names for their self reference variable. For the presentation of the operational semantics in the next section we assume to apply alpha-renaming whenever necessary to avoid name capture.

4.2   Semantics

The semantics of our calculus are formalized in Figure 8 as a small-step operational semantics. The reduction relation has the form $e \longrightarrow e'$ which expresses that expression e evaluates to expression e' in a single step.

$$(\text{R-FLD}) \ \frac{\text{fields}(C) = \overline{T}\,\overline{f}}{\text{new } C(\overline{e}).f_i \ \longrightarrow \ e_i} \qquad\qquad (\text{R-SERV}) \ \frac{\text{service}(\text{new } e, e, C) = e'}{\text{new } e :: C \ \longrightarrow \ e'}$$

$$(\text{R-INV}) \ \frac{\text{mbody}(m, C) = (\overline{x}, e_0)}{\text{new } C(\overline{e}).m(\overline{d}) \ \longrightarrow \ [\overline{d}/\overline{x}, \text{new } C(\overline{e})/\text{this}]\, e_0}$$

$$(\text{R-REQ}) \ \ e \text{ requires } C \ \longrightarrow \ e \qquad (\text{R-MIXC}) \ \ e \text{ mixin component} \ \longrightarrow \ e$$

$$(\text{R-MIXP}) \ \ e \text{ mixin } (e_0 \text{ provides } C \text{ as } x \text{ with } d) \ \longrightarrow \ (e \text{ mixin } e_0) \text{ provides } C \text{ as } x \text{ with } d$$

$$(\text{R-MIXF}) \ \ e \text{ mixin } (e_0 \text{ forwards } \overline{C} \text{ as } x \text{ to } d) \ \longrightarrow \ (e \text{ mixin } e_0) \text{ forwards } \overline{C} \text{ as } x \text{ to } d$$

$$(\text{RC-FLD}) \ \frac{e \longrightarrow e'}{e.f \longrightarrow e'.f} \qquad\qquad (\text{RC-INVR}) \ \frac{e \longrightarrow e'}{e.m(\overline{d}) \longrightarrow e'.m(\overline{d})}$$

$$(\text{RC-INVA}) \ \frac{e_i \longrightarrow e_i'}{d.m(\ldots, e_i, \ldots) \longrightarrow d.m(\ldots, e_i', \ldots)}$$

$$(\text{RC-NEWA}) \ \frac{e_i \longrightarrow e_i'}{\text{new } C(\ldots, e_i, \ldots) \longrightarrow \text{new } C(\ldots, e_i', \ldots)}$$

$$(\text{RC-INST}) \ \frac{e \longrightarrow e'}{\text{new } e \longrightarrow \text{new } e'} \qquad\qquad (\text{RC-SERV}) \ \frac{e \longrightarrow e'}{e :: C \longrightarrow e' :: C}$$

$$(\text{RC-PRV}) \ \frac{e \longrightarrow e'}{e \text{ provides } C \text{ as } x \text{ with } d \ \longrightarrow \ e' \text{ provides } C \text{ as } x \text{ with } d}$$

$$(\text{RC-FWD}) \ \frac{e \longrightarrow e'}{e \text{ forwards } \overline{C} \text{ as } x \text{ to } d \ \longrightarrow \ e' \text{ forwards } \overline{C} \text{ as } x \text{ to } d}$$

$$(\text{RC-MIXL}) \ \frac{e \longrightarrow e'}{e \text{ mixin } d \longrightarrow e' \text{ mixin } d} \qquad (\text{RC-MIXR}) \ \frac{d \longrightarrow d'}{e \text{ mixin } d \longrightarrow e \text{ mixin } d'}$$

Fig. 8. Operational semantics

We adopt all reduction rules from *FJ* and define various new rules for our new syntactical constructs. Service abstractions simply reduce to the prototype component, so they do not have any computational effect. The semantics of mixins are described by three reduction rules, depending on the form of the right operand. Mixing in the empty component results in the same component. For service implementations and component projections we mix the prototype of the right operand into the left operand and apply the component refinement on that new component. Thus, we incrementally combine the two operands into a single component where service definitions of the right operand override definitions of the left operand.

The reduction rule for service selections relies on an auxiliary function $\text{service}(e', e, C)$ which searches the component definition e of component instance

---

Field lookup

$$\text{fields}(\text{Object}) = \emptyset$$

$$\frac{CT(C) = \text{class } C \text{ extends } D \{ \overline{T}\,\overline{f}\,;\, K\,;\, \overline{M} \} \qquad \text{fields}(D) = \overline{U}\,\overline{g}}{\text{fields}(C) = \overline{U}\,\overline{g}, \overline{T}\,\overline{f}}$$

Method body lookup

$$\frac{CT(C) = \text{class } C \text{ extends } D \{ \overline{U}\,\overline{f}\,;\, K\,;\, \overline{M} \} \qquad T'\, m(\overline{T}\,\overline{x}) \{ \text{ return } e;\ \} \in \overline{M}}{\text{mbody}(m, C) = (\overline{x}, e)}$$

$$\frac{CT(C) = \text{class } C \text{ extends } D \{ \overline{T}\,\overline{f}\,;\, K\,;\, \overline{M} \} \qquad m \text{ not defined in } \overline{M}}{\text{mbody}(m, C) = \text{mbody}(m, D)}$$

Service lookup

$$\text{service}(e,\, e_0 \text{ provides } C \text{ as } x \text{ with } d, C) = [e/x]\, d$$

$$\text{service}(e,\, e_0 \text{ forwards } \overline{C} \text{ as } x \text{ to } d, C_i) = [e/x]\, d :: C_i$$

$$\frac{D \neq C}{\text{service}(e,\, e_0 \text{ provides } C \text{ as } x \text{ with } d, D) = \text{service}(e, e_0, D)}$$

$$\frac{D \notin \overline{C}}{\text{service}(e,\, e_0 \text{ forwards } \overline{C} \text{ as } x \text{ to } d, D) = \text{service}(e, e_0, D)}$$

Fig. 9. Auxiliary definitions for evaluation

e' for a service C. Note that the service lookup performed by $\text{service}(e', e, C)$ is only defined on service implementation and component projection terms. Thus, even for cases where e provides a service C, evaluation of $\text{service}(e', e, C)$ may not be well-defined if e has not been evaluated far enough. In such a case, we first have to apply rules (RC-Inst) and (RC-Serv) to further evaluate the component before making use of the actual service selection rule (R-Serv). An overview of all auxiliary definitions used by the operational semantics of Figure 8 are given in Figure 9.

4.3   Type System

We have three different forms of types: object types, component types and component instance types. An object type is simply denoted by a class name C. An object type is well-formed if the class name appears in the domain of the class table CT. The class table is a mapping from class names to class declarations. As in the presentation of FJ, we assume that we have a fixed class table to simplify the notation. Otherwise we would have to parameterize all typing rules with CT. It is assumed that CT satisfies some sanity conditions: $Object \notin \text{dom}(CT)$, all

---

Well-formed types

Object wf $\dfrac{CT(C) = \text{class } C \text{ extends } D\,\{\ldots\}}{C \text{ wf}}$ $\dfrac{\overline{C},\overline{C'} \text{ wf} \quad \overline{C} \cap \overline{C'} = \emptyset}{\overline{C} \Rightarrow \overline{C'} \text{ wf}}$ $\dfrac{\overline{C} \text{ wf}}{[\overline{C}] \text{ wf}}$

Subtyping

$C <: C$ $\dfrac{C <: D \qquad D <: E}{C <: E}$ $\dfrac{CT(C) = \text{class } C \text{ extends } D\,\{\ldots\}}{C <: D}$

$\dfrac{\overline{C} \subseteq \overline{D} \quad \overline{D'} \subseteq \overline{C'}}{\overline{C} \Rightarrow \overline{C'} <: \overline{D} \Rightarrow \overline{D'}}$ $\dfrac{\overline{D} \subseteq \overline{C}}{[\overline{C}] <: [\overline{D}]}$

Fig. 10. Well-formed types and subtyping

types appearing explicitly in CT are well-formed, and there are no cycles in the subtype relation induced by CT.

Component types have the form $\overline{C} \Rightarrow \overline{C'}$ where $\overline{C}$ specifies the services required by the component and $\overline{C'}$ specifies the provided services. Services are described by object types. A component type is only well-formed if the sets of the provided and required services are disjoint. $[\overline{C}]$ types a component instance that provides the services $\overline{C}$. Figure 10 summarizes the well-formedness criteria on types.

Method types cannot be written explicitly. In the type system, we use the notation $\overline{T} \to T'$ for a method with the argument types $\overline{T}$ and the result type T'. Note that depending on the context, $\overline{T}$ denotes either a sequence of types $(T_1, \ldots, T_n)$ or a set of types $\{T_1, \ldots, T_n\}$. We use shorthands of the form $\overline{C} \cup D$ for expressing $\overline{C} \cup \{D\}$.

Figure 10 also defines a subtype relation $T <: T'$ between two types T and T'. Subtyping of object types is identical to *FJ*. A component instance type is a subtype of another component instance type if the services provided by the supertype constitute a subset of the subtype's provided services. A component type $\tau_1 = \overline{C} \Rightarrow \overline{C'}$ is a subtype of component type $\tau_2 = \overline{D} \Rightarrow \overline{D'}$, if τ_1 requires less and provides more services than τ_2; i.e. $\overline{C} \subseteq \overline{D}$ and $\overline{D'} \subseteq \overline{C'}$. This corresponds to the typical co/contravariant subtyping rule for function types [17] adopted already by related approaches to component subtyping [20,49,25]. In Section 4.6 we discuss an alternative subtyping rule.

The type system is presented in Figure 11. We have three different typing judgment forms. The one for classes has the form "L ok" meaning that class declaration L is type correct. The judgment for method declarations has the form "M ok in C", expressing that the method declaration M typechecks as a declaration of class C. Both rules are directly taken from *FJ*. The judgment for expressions $\Gamma \vdash e : T$ relates a type T to an expression e. Most typing rules for expressions are straightforward. (T-Prv) and (T-Fwd) are among the interesting rules. Here, the service provision expression is typed under an extended

Expression typing

$$(\text{T-Var}) \quad \Gamma \vdash x : \Gamma(x) \qquad\qquad (\text{T-Fld}) \; \frac{\Gamma \vdash e : C \qquad \text{fields}(C) = \overline{T}\,\overline{f}}{\Gamma \vdash e.f_i : T_i}$$

$$(\text{T-Inv}) \; \frac{\Gamma \vdash d : C \qquad \text{mtype}(m, C) = \overline{T} \to T' \qquad \Gamma \vdash \overline{e} : \overline{U} \qquad \overline{U} <: \overline{T}}{\Gamma \vdash d.m(\overline{e}) : T'}$$

$$(\text{T-New}) \; \frac{\text{fields}(C) = \overline{T}\,\overline{f} \qquad \Gamma \vdash \overline{e} : \overline{U} \qquad \overline{U} <: \overline{T}}{\Gamma \vdash \text{new } C(\overline{e}) : C}$$

$$(\text{T-Inst}) \; \frac{\Gamma \vdash e : \emptyset \Rightarrow \overline{C}}{\Gamma \vdash \text{new } e : [\overline{C}]} \qquad\qquad (\text{T-Serv}) \; \frac{\Gamma \vdash e : [\overline{C}]}{\Gamma \vdash e :: C_i : C_i}$$

$$(\text{T-Com}) \quad \Gamma \vdash \text{component} : \emptyset \Rightarrow \emptyset$$

$$(\text{T-Mix}) \; \frac{\Gamma \vdash e : \overline{C} \Rightarrow \overline{C'} \qquad \Gamma \vdash d : \overline{D} \Rightarrow \overline{D'}}{\Gamma \vdash e \text{ mixin } d : (\overline{C} \cup \overline{D}) \backslash (\overline{C'} \cup \overline{D'}) \Rightarrow \overline{C'} \cup \overline{D'}}$$

$$(\text{T-Req}) \; \frac{C \text{ wf} \qquad \Gamma \vdash e : \overline{D} \Rightarrow \overline{D'}}{\Gamma \vdash e \text{ requires } C : \overline{D} \cup C \Rightarrow \overline{D'} \backslash C}$$

$$(\text{T-Prv}) \; \frac{C \text{ wf} \qquad \Gamma \vdash e : \overline{D} \Rightarrow \overline{D'} \qquad \Gamma, x : [\overline{D} \cup \overline{D'} \cup C] \vdash d : B \qquad B <: C}{\Gamma \vdash e \text{ provides } C \text{ as } x \text{ with } d : \overline{D} \backslash C \Rightarrow \overline{D'} \cup C}$$

$$(\text{T-Fwd}) \; \frac{\overline{C} \text{ wf} \qquad \Gamma \vdash e : \overline{D} \Rightarrow \overline{D'} \qquad \Gamma, x : [\overline{D} \cup \overline{D'} \cup \overline{C}] \vdash d : [\overline{B}] \qquad \overline{C} \subseteq \overline{B}}{\Gamma \vdash e \text{ forwards } \overline{C} \text{ as } x \text{ to } d : \overline{D} \backslash \overline{C} \Rightarrow \overline{D'} \cup \overline{C}}$$

Method and class typing

$$(\text{T-Meth}) \; \frac{\begin{array}{c}\overline{T} \text{ wf} \qquad T' \text{ wf} \qquad \overline{x} : \overline{T}, \text{this} : C \vdash e : U \qquad U <: T' \\ CT(C) = \text{class } C \text{ extends } D\,\{\ldots\} \qquad \text{override}(m, D, \overline{T} \to T')\end{array}}{T'm(\overline{T}\,\overline{x})\,\{\,\text{return } e;\,\} \text{ ok in } C}$$

$$(\text{T-Class}) \; \frac{\begin{array}{c}D \text{ wf} \qquad \overline{T} \text{ wf} \qquad K = C(\overline{U}\,\overline{g}, \overline{T}\,\overline{f})\,\{\,\text{super}(\overline{g}); \text{ this}.\overline{f} = \overline{f};\,\} \\ \text{fields}(D) = \overline{U}\,\overline{g} \qquad \overline{M} \text{ ok in } C\end{array}}{\text{class } C \text{ extends } D\,\{\overline{T}\,\overline{f}; \; K; \; \overline{M}\,\} \text{ ok}}$$

Fig. 11. Type system

environment, including the self reference to the own component instance. We assume that the type of the self reference variable is a component instance type offering both, the services that are required and provided by the component being refined. The auxiliary definitions used for typing field and method selections as well as object creations are directly adopted from *FJ* and summarized in Figure 12.

Method type lookup

$$\frac{CT(C) = \mathsf{class}\ C\ \mathsf{extends}\ D\,\{\,\overline{U}\ \overline{f}\,;\,K\,;\,\overline{M}\,\}\qquad T'm(\overline{T}\ \overline{x})\,\{\,\mathsf{return}\ e;\,\}\ \in \overline{M}}{\mathrm{mtype}(m,C) = \overline{T} \to T'}$$

$$\frac{CT(C) = \mathsf{class}\ C\ \mathsf{extends}\ D\,\{\,\overline{T}\ \overline{f}\,;\,K\,;\,\overline{M}\,\}\qquad m\ \mathrm{not\ defined\ in}\ \overline{M}}{\mathrm{mtype}(m,C) = \mathrm{mtype}(m,D)}$$

Valid method overriding

$$\frac{\mathrm{mtype}(m,C) = \overline{U} \to U'\ \mathrm{implies}\ \overline{U} = \overline{T}\ \mathrm{and}\ U' = T'}{\mathrm{override}(m,C,\overline{T} \to T')}$$

Fig. 12. Auxiliary definitions for typing

4.4 Type Soundness

For proving type soundness, we weaken the typing rules for provides and forwards terms. We use the following two rules (T-Prv') and (T-Fwd') instead:

$$(\text{T-Prv'})\ \frac{C\ \mathrm{wf}\qquad \Gamma \vdash e : \overline{D} \Rightarrow \overline{D'}\qquad \Gamma, x : [\overline{D''}] \vdash d : B\qquad B <: C}{\Gamma \vdash e\ \mathsf{provides}\ C\ \mathsf{as}\ x\ \mathsf{with}\ d : (\overline{D} \cup \overline{D''})\backslash(\overline{D'} \cup C) \Rightarrow \overline{D'} \cup C}$$

$$(\text{T-Fwd'})\ \frac{\overline{C}\ \mathrm{wf}\qquad \Gamma \vdash e : \overline{D} \Rightarrow \overline{D'}\qquad \Gamma, x : [\overline{D''}] \vdash d : [\overline{B}]\qquad \overline{C} \subseteq \overline{B}}{\Gamma \vdash e\ \mathsf{forwards}\ \overline{C}\ \mathsf{as}\ x\ \mathsf{to}\ d : (\overline{D} \cup \overline{D''})\backslash(\overline{D'} \cup \overline{C}) \Rightarrow \overline{D'} \cup \overline{C}}$$

In this weaker system we allow that provides and forwards primitives introduce service abstractions in a non-deterministic way. We show type soundness for this weaker type system. As a consequence, the type system with the stronger typing rules, presented in Figure 11, is sound as well. This system has the advantage that typings are deterministic. Furthermore, its design follows the principle that service abstractions have to be declared explicitly. Weakening the type system was necessary for subject reduction to hold. We present the type soundness results for our weaker type system in the style of Wright and Felleisen [56]. The proof can be found in [57].

Theorem 4.1 (Subject reduction) If all types in Γ are well-formed, $\Gamma \vdash e : T$ and $e \longrightarrow e'$, then $\Gamma \vdash e' : T'$ for some $T' <: T$.

For a well-typed term which can be reduced to a second term, Theorem 4.1 states that this second term is also well-typed. Furthermore, the type of the second term is a subtype of the type of the first term.

In addition to that we can show that the evaluation of every well-typed term does not get stuck. To formalize this, we introduce a term subset denoting values.

Value	$v = c$
	$\mid$ new c
	$\mid$ new $C(\overline{v})$
Component value	$c =$ component
	$\mid$ c provides C as x with e
	$\mid$ c forwards $\overline{C}$ as x to e

A value is either a component, a component instance or an object. For component values we have three different constructors. One denotes the empty component, one adds a new service to an existing component value, and a third one adds services by forwarding them to another component instance. Note that during evaluation, service abstractions are eliminated in expressions with reduction rule (R-Req). Therefore, the definition of component values does not include the requires primitive.

Theorem 4.2 states that every well-typed term is either a value or it can be reduced to another term. In other words, evaluation does not get stuck for well-typed terms.

Theorem 4.2 (Progress) If $\vdash e : T$ then e is either a value or $e \longrightarrow e'$ for some e'.

4.5   Component Instantiation Evaluation

The operational semantics presented in Figure 8 formalize an evaluation strategy that does not allow to reduce service implementation expressions inside of component instances. At component instantiation time, in fact none of these terms get evaluated. A term specifying a service implementation, for example in provides or forwards primitives, only gets evaluated when the service is accessed via the :: operator. Evaluating a service implementation expression more than once does no cause any problems in our calculus, since we only have functional objects without any side-effects. In real-world systems, this form of *lazy* evaluation can be efficiently implemented using a memoization technique, so that for multiple accesses to the same service, the service implementation expression will be evaluated only once.

We decided to have this restriction in our calculus for several reasons. First, it keeps the calculus simple. But lazy evaluation also constitutes a reasonable evaluation strategy for service implementations. A *strict* evaluation order would be difficult to define. For instance we could evaluate the service implementations in the order the component evolution primitives introduce a service. But this would be a completely arbitrary choice, since services can be introduced using the requires primitive in any order, not implying any dependencies.

With any fixed strict evaluation order one risks to access a not yet initialized service from the service implementation that is currently being evaluated. With a lazy service evaluation strategy one still faces this problem, but only for recursive service references. With our operational semantics, such recursive dependencies could possibly lead to infinite computations. We avoided this problem in the examples of the previous sections by not accessing services of the own component instance in service provision expressions directly. Instead, objects that implement a service access other services of the same component instance only at the time a method of the other service actually has to be called, which happens typically after the component got instantiated.

In [57] we present an extension of the operational semantics that supports the reduction of service provision expressions at component instantiation time.

4.6   Component Subtyping

The subtyping rule presented so far only supports *width*-subtyping for component types; i.e. subtypes provide more and require less services. We could relax this rules easily by additionally supporting a form of *depth*-subtyping which incorporates subtyping of service interface types. Here, $\tau_1 <: \tau_2$ would hold for two component types τ_1 and τ_2, if the required service types of τ_1 are supertypes of the required service types of τ_2. Similarly, the provided service types of τ_1 are supposed to be subtypes of the provided service types of τ_2. Exactly this is expressed by the following alternative subtyping rule:

$$\frac{\forall i \exists j : D_j <: C_i \qquad \forall i \exists j : C'_j <: D'_i}{\overline{C} \Rightarrow \overline{C'} <: \overline{D} \Rightarrow \overline{D'}}$$

To make use of such a rule in our type system, we would also have to update the subtyping rule for component instances together with the typing rules (T-Mix), (T-Req), (T-Prv), and (T-Fwd). Furthermore, the service lookup function would have to be modified to reflect the fact that we can now override a service by introducing a new service with a refined type.

5   Discussion and Related Work

Before concluding, we finally review the main ingredients of our component model, explain design decisions, and compare the constructs with related work.

5.1   Prototype-Based Components Revisited

In our model, components are first-class abstractions that have neither state nor identity. Components define the structure of component instances in the same way as classes define the structure of objects. In most class-based languages, classes are either not first-class, or they are specified using meta-classes. For simplicity, and in order to avoid such a meta-regress [55], our first-class components are prototype-based [1]. Thus, instead of instantiating components from meta-component descriptions, new components are derived from prototypical components by a set of refinement primitives. Since components are stateless, we do not need a cloning operation known from object-based programming languages [18,55]. This approach emphasizes the reuse of components in the creation of new, extended components by refinement. In fact, even component composition, which is mostly regarded as the only form of component reuse, is explained in terms of component refinement.

Components specify implementations for a set of provided services. These implementations may rely on services provided by other components. Thus, component types are characterized by a set of required and provided services. Services are described by nominal object types. In Section 3.3 we explained already why this approach does not constitute a restriction compared to component models with named ports [49,52,2]. Our service abstraction does not only allow us to conveniently refer to an aggregate of functionality, opposed to individual methods, for instance. It also facilitates to override an aggregate of functionality consistently and promotes distinct, non-interfering views of components. Service specifications that are solely based on nominal object types were inspired by *COM* [46,31].

Services are added to a component using the service abstraction and service implementation primitives. For composing components, two mechanisms are supported: forwarding and mixin-based composition. Forwarding delegates the implementation of a set of services to another, possibly nested component instance. The significance of the forwarding primitive is two-fold: On the one hand it enables hierarchical component compositions, on the other hand, it is used to hide internal services of encapsulated components.

Opposed to forwarding, the mixin-based approach merges two components by refining one component with the services provided by another component and by rebinding the self reference to the merged component. Compared with the approach based on forwarding where the services of the nested component cannot be overridden and are therefore statically linked, component composition based on mixins yields a fully extensible component where it is possible to redefine service implementations by overriding. On the other hand, forwarding allows us to specify exactly what services to include, opposed to the mixin-based approach which always mixes in all provided services. As mentioned already in Section 3.7, this may lead to accidental overrides. This weakness of our type system could be addressed, for example, by making overriding explicit and by including negative information in component types. Discussions about forwarding versus delegation (object-based inheritance), which can be seen as an implementation technique for mixins, can be found, for instance, in [54,34,15]. Support for dynamic object-based inheritance in a class-based context is provided by Büchi's and Weck's *generic wrappers* [15] and Kniesel's object model *Darwin* [34].

Mixins were first identified as linguistic abstractions for generalizing inheritance by Bracha and Cook [11]. It was also Bracha who observed that inheritance can be seen as a mechanism for modular program composition [13]. With his work on the programming language *Jigsaw* [10], he lifts the notion of class-based inheritance and overriding to the level of modules.

A formal account of mixins and mixin-based inheritance is given in [9,21,4]. In particular, Bono, Patel, and Shmatikov's calculus of first-class classes and mixins is similar to our work [9]. Bono's mixins correspond to components in our model.

Classes correspond roughly to components without required services. Based on the same framework, Bettini, Bono, and Venneri recently showed that mixins are a suitable abstraction for mobile software components [8]. Opposed to the work by Bono *et al.*, the programming language *Scala* [42] does not distinguish between classes and mixins. It only has the notion of classes that are interpreted as mixins when used in mixin-based class compositions (inheritance). This is identical to the way we interpret components. Scala's mixins were inspired by *Strongtalk* [12], an extension of the programming language *Smalltalk*.

5.2   Related Work

Our work is strongly related to alternative proposals for component abstractions on the level of programming languages. Seco and Caires describe *ComponentJ*, a simple typed imperative core calculus for first-class components in the context of inheritance-free object-oriented programming [49]. *ComponentJ* completely avoids inheritance in favor of object composition. Components are closed blackboxes that can be dynamically composed.

ACOEL has a similar component model [52]. Interaction points of *ACOEL* components are in- and out-ports. The language is class-based and supports a restricted form of inheritance. Like in *ComponentJ*, ports are connected explicitly. Opposed to *ComponentJ*, the design of *ACOEL* does not allow to check that all ports are connected. *ACOEL* supports a richer form of component subtyping, including other constraints, specified in *CORAL*, a language for abstracting and specifying *ACOEL* components [51].

ArchJava is an extension of *Java* that tries to unify the software architecture of a system with its implementation [2]. It introduces direct support for components, connections and ports. Components are implemented using extensible component classes. *ArchJava* does not distinguish between required and provided ports. Instead, a port declares required and provided methods. Ports are again connected explicitly. Like the previous two languages, *ArchJava* allows component composition only via nesting of subcomponents. A distinct feature of the *ArchJava* type system is to guarantee communication integrity [41].

Ibrahim formalizes *COM* by introducing a small programming language *COMEL* [31]. Similar to our approach, *COMEL* does not have named ports. Services are specified solely by type names. In the spirit of *COM*, *COMEL* emphasizes aggregation and does not support implementation inheritance. *COMEL* components have to be self-contained, not having any context dependencies. This is a severe restriction that contradicts the aim to modularize software into small components that have to depend on their deployment context in order to be flexibly reusable.

Most concepts of component-oriented programming languages originate from notions of architectural description languages (ADLs) like *ACME* [24], *Aesop* [23], *Darwin* [37], *Rapide* [35], *Wright* [3] etc. ADLs are used to specify a software architecture formally. A software architecture describes the organizational structure of a software system in terms of a collection of components and relationships among them [44,50]. Typically, a specification of a software architecture contains information about the participating software components, the connections between these components and constraints on the interactions [54]. By using ADLs, the details of a design get explicit and more precise, enabling formal analysis techniques. Furthermore, they can help in understanding the structure of a system, its implementation and reuse. A comparison of ADLs is given in [40].

Advanced module linking [16,25] and component systems that are built on top of a programming language can be used to model component systems as well. Module systems with external linking facilities include *SML*'s *functors* [36] and *MzScheme*'s *units* [20]. Opposed to our components, *SML functors* are neither first-class nor higher-order. Consequently, they cannot be used to dynamically manufacture modules. Furthermore, they are not extensible, which makes it difficult to perform adaptations. An extension of *SML* with first-class modules was recently proposed by Russo [47,48].

Unlike *SML* modules, *units* offer better support for component-oriented programming [20,19]. They provide first-class module abstractions and linking facilities to compose modules hierarchically. Like all the component-oriented languages mentioned before, *units* are linked by explicitly connecting provided with required ports. Since port descriptions of *units* are relatively fine-grained — they are, in fact, just variable definitions —, this can be a tedious task. For this reason, *MzScheme* supports *signed units* that support bundles of variables, called signatures, being connected in one step [19]. Even thought superficially similar to services in our component model, signatures are merely syntactic sugar and are flattened to a linear list of variables. *Jiazzi* [38] is a working enhancement of *Java* with support for large-scale software components based on *MzScheme*'s *units*. *Jiazzi*'s units are conceptually containers of compiled *Java* classes with support for well-defined connections, specified by a number of imported and exported classes.

A comparable module system for *Java*-like programming languages was proposed by Ancona and Zucca [7]. This system is based on *CMS* [5,6], a simple but expressive calculus of modules which can be instantiated over an arbitrary core calculus. The calculus supports a large variety of module composition mechanisms including mixin module composition with overriding. Recently, Hirschowitz and Leroy adapted the type system of *CMS* to a call-by-value setting [29].

6   Conclusion

In this paper, we presented a component model that was designed to support the implementation and evolution of lightweight, extensible components in object-oriented programming languages. The model supports dynamic component manufacturing and composition in a type-safe way through a minimal set of component refinement primitives. Opposed to other approaches, we do not need to link services of components explicitly. Instead, components are composed using high-level composition operators. We formalized the component model as an extension of *Featherweight Java* and prove our type system to be sound with respect to the operational semantics. Currently, we are investigating how to integrate our component model into a full programming language.

Acknowledgments

I am grateful to Martin Odersky for valuable discussions about related topics. I would also like to thank Christoph Zenger and Martin Sulzmann for their comments about the type soundness proof.

References

1. M. Abadi and L. Cardelli. *A Theory of Objects*. Monographs in Computer Science. Springer Verlag, 1996.
2. J. Aldrich, C. Chambers, and D. Notkin. Architectural reasoning in ArchJava. In *Proceedings of the 16th European Conference on Object-Oriented Programming*, Málaga, Spain, June 2002.
3. R. Allen. *A Formal Approach to Software Architecture*. PhD thesis, Carnegie Mellon University, Pittsburgh, PA, May 1997.
4. D. Ancona and E. Zucca. A theory of mixin modules: basic and derived operators. *Mathematical Structures in Computer Science*, 8(4):401–446, 1998.
5. D. Ancona and E. Zucca. A primitive calculus for module systems. In *Principles and Practice of Declarative Programming*, LNCS 1702. Springer-Verlag, 1999.
6. D. Ancona and E. Zucca. A calculus of module systems. *Journal of Functional Programming*, 2001.
7. D. Ancona and E. Zucca. True modules for Java-like languages. In *Proceedings of European Conference on Object-Oriented Programming*, LNCS 2072. Springer-Verlag, 2001.
8. L. Bettini, V. Bono, and B. Venneri. Coordinating mobile object-oriented code. In *Proceedings of Coordination 2002*, York, UK, April 2002.
9. V. Bono, A. Patel, and V. Shmatikov. A core calculus of classes and mixins. In *Proceedings of the 13th European Conference on Object-Oriented Programming*, pages 43–66, Lisbon, Portugal, 1999.
10. G. Bracha. *The Programming Language Jigsaw: Mixins, Modularity and Multiple Inheritance*. PhD thesis, University of Utah, 1992.
11. G. Bracha and W. Cook. Mixin-based inheritance. In N. Meyrowitz, editor, *Proceedings of the Conference on Object-Oriented Programming: Systems, Languages, and Applications*, pages 303–311, Ottawa, Canada, 1990. ACM Press.
12. G. Bracha and D. Griswold. Extending Smalltalk with mixins. In *OOPSLA '96 Workshop on Extending the Smalltalk Language*, April 1996.
13. G. Bracha and G. Lindstrom. Modularity meets inheritance. In *Proceedings of the IEEE Computer Society International Conference on Computer Languages*, pages 282–290, Washington, DC, 1992. IEEE Computer Society.
14. M. Büchi and W. Weck. Compound types for Java. In *Proceedings of OOPSLA 1998*, pages 362–373, October 1998.
15. M. Büchi and W. Weck. Generic wrappers. In *Proceedings of the 14th European Conference on Object-Oriented Programming*, pages 201–225, June 2000.

16. L. Cardelli. Program fragments, linking, and modularization. In *Proceedings of the 24th ACM SIGPLAN-SIGACT Symposium on Principles of Programming Languages*, pages 266–277, Paris, France, January 1997.

17. L. Cardelli and P. Wegner. On understanding types, data abstraction, and polymorphism. *Computing Surveys*, 17(4):471–522, December 1985.

18. C. Chambers and C. Team. The Cecil language, specification and rationale, December 1998.

19. M. Flatt. *Programming Languages for Reusable Software Components*. PhD thesis, Rice University, Department of Computer Science, June 1999.

20. M. Flatt and M. Felleisen. Units: Cool modules for HOT languages. In *Proceedings of the ACM Conference on Programming Language Design and Implementation*, pages 236–248, 1998.

21. M. Flatt, S. Krishnamurthi, and M. Felleisen. Classes and mixins. In *Proceedings of the 25th ACM Symposium on Principles of Programming Languages*, pages 171–183, San Diego, California, 1998.

22. E. Gamma, R. Helm, R. Johnson, and J. Vlissides. *Design Patterns: Elements of Reusable Object-Oriented Software*. Addison-Wesley, 1994.

23. D. Garlan, R. Allen, and J. Ockerbloom. Exploiting style in architectural design environments. In *Proceedings of SIGSOFT '94: Foundations of Software Engineering*, pages 175–188, New Orleans, Louisiana, USA, December 1994.

24. D. Garlan, R. Monroe, and D. Wile. ACME: An architecture description interchange language. In *Proceedings of CASCON '97*, November 1997.

25. N. Glew and G. Morrisett. Type-safe linking and modular assembly language. In *Conference Record of the 26th ACM SIGPLAN-SIGACT Symposium on Principles of Programming Languages*, pages 250–261, San Antonio, Texas, 1999.

26. J. Gosling, B. Joy, G. Steele, and G. Bracha. *The Java Language Specification*. Java Series, Sun Microsystems, second edition, 2000. ISBN 0-201-31008-2.

27. O. M. Group. The Common Object Request Broker: Architecture and specification, revision 2.0, February 1997.

28. A. Hejlsberg and S. Wiltamuth. C# language specification. Microsoft Corporation, 2000.

29. T. Hirschowitz and X. Leroy. Mixin modules in a call-by-value setting. In *Proceedings of the European Symposium on Programming*, Grenoble, France, April 2002.

30. U. Hölzle. Integrating independently-developed components in object-oriented languages. In *Proceedings of the European Conference on Object-Oriented Programming*, pages 36–56, 1993.

31. R. Ibrahim. COMEL: A formal model for COM. Technical report, Queensland University of Technology, Brisbane, Australia, 1998.

32. A. Igarashi, B. Pierce, and P. Wadler. Featherweight Java: A minimal core calculus for Java and GJ. In *Proceedings of the Conference on Object-Oriented Programming, Systems, Languages & Applications*, volume 34(10), pages 132–146, 1999.

33. JavaSoft. JavaBeans™. http://java.sun.com/beans, December 1996.

34. G. Kniesel. Type-safe delegation for run-time component adaptation. In *Proceedings of the 13th European Conference on Object-Oriented Programming*, pages 351–366, Lisbon, Portugal, 1999.

35. D. Luckham, L. Augustin, J. Kenney, J. Vera, D. Bryan, and W. Mann. Specification and analysis of system architecture using Rapide. In *IEEE Transactions on Software Engineering*, April 1995.

36. D. MacQueen. Modules for Standard ML. In *Conference Record of the 1984 ACM Symposium on Lisp and Functional Programming*, pages 198–207, New York, August 1984.

37. J. Magee, N. Dulay, S. Eisenbach, and J. Kramer. Specifying distributed software architectures. In *Proceedings of the 5th European Software Engineering Conference*, Barcelona, Spain, September 1995.

38. S. McDirmid, M. Flatt, and W. Hsieh. Jiazzi: New-age components for old-fashioned Java. In *Proceedings of the 2001 ACM SIGPLAN Conference on Object-Oriented Programming, Systems, Languages & Applications*, October 2001.

39. S. McDirmid, M. Flatt, and W. C. Hsieh. Mixing COP and OOP. In *OOPSLA Workshop on Language Mechanisms for Programming Software Components*, pages 29–32. Technical Report NU-CCS-01-06, Northeastern University, Boston, MA, October 2001.

40. N. Medvidovic and R. N. Taylor. A classification and comparison framework for software architecture description languages. In *IEEE Transactions on Software Engineering*, volume 26, pages 70–93, January 2000.

41. M. Moriconi, X. Quian, and A. Riemenschneider. Correct architecture refinement. In *IEEE Transactions on Software Engineering*, volume 21, April 1995.

42. M. Odersky. Report on the programming language Scala. École Polytechnique Fédérale de Lausanne, Switzerland, 2002. http://lamp.epfl.ch/~odersky/scala.

43. M. Odersky. Objects + views = components? In *Proceedings of Abstract State Machines 2000*, March 2000.

44. D. E. Perry and A. L. Wolf. Foundations for the study of software architecture. In *ACM SIGSOFT Software Engineering Notes*, volume 17, pages 40–52, October 1992.

45. B. C. Pierce. *Types and Programming Languages*. MIT Press, February 2002. ISBN 0-262-16209-1.

46. D. Rogerson. *Inside COM: Microsoft's Component Object Model*. Microsoft Press, 1997.

47. C. Russo. *Types for Modules*. PhD thesis, University of Edinburgh, 1998.

48. C. Russo. First-class structures for Standard ML. In *Proceedings of the 9th European Symposium on Programming*, pages 336–350, Berlin, Germany, 2000.

49. J. C. Seco and L. Caires. A basic model of typed components. In *Proceedings of the 14th European Conference on Object-Oriented Programming*, pages 108–128, 2000.

50. M. Shaw and D. Garlan. *Software Architecture: Perspectives on an Emerging Discipline*. Prentice Hall, 1996.

51. V. C. Sreedhar. ACOEL on CORAL: A component requirement and abstraction language. In *OOPSLA Workshop on Specification and Verification of Component-Based Systems*, October 2001.

52. V. C. Sreedhar. Programming software components using ACOEL. Unpublished manuscript, IBM T.J. Watson Research Center, 2002.

53. C. Szyperski. Independently extensible systems – software engineering potential and challenges. In *Proceedings of the 19th Australian Computer Science Conference*, Melbourne, Australia, 1996.

54. C. Szyperski. *Component Software: Beyond Object-Oriented Programming*. Addison Wesley / ACM Press, New York, 1998. ISBN 0-201-17888-5.

55. D. Ungar and R. B. Smith. Self: The power of simplicity. *Lisp and Symbolic Computation*, March 1991.

56. A. K. Wright and M. Felleisen. A syntactic approach to type soundness. *Information and Computation*, 115, 1994.

57. M. Zenger. Type-safe prototype-based component evolution. Technical report, École Polytechnique Fédérale de Lausanne, Switzerland, April 2002.

Thin Guards:
A Simple and Effective Technique for
Reducing the Penalty of Dynamic Class Loading*

Matthew Arnold[1,2] and Barbara G. Ryder[1]

[1] Department of Computer Science, Rutgers University, Piscataway NJ 08855, USA
{marnold,ryder}@cs.rutgers.edu
[2] IBM T.J. Watson Research Center, Hawthorne, NY, 10532, USA

Abstract. Dynamic class loading is an integral part of the Java[TM] programming language, offering a number of advantages such as lazy class
loading and dynamic installation of software components. Unfortunately,
these advantages often come at the cost of decreased performance because certain optimizations become more difficult to perform when an
optimizing compiler cannot assume that it has seen the whole program.
This paper introduces *thin guards*, a simple but effective technique that
uses lightweight runtime tests to identify regions of code within which
speculative optimizations can be performed. One application of thin
guards is described in detail, demonstrating how they can be used to
perform speculative inlining in the presence of dynamic class loading.
Our experimental evaluation shows that when used in combination with
other traditional compiler optimizations, thin guards can eliminate most
of the penalty of dynamic class loading. Performance improvements of
up to 27% are observed, eliminating up to 92% of the penalty imposed
by dynamic class loading.

1 Introduction

Dynamic class loading [20] is an integral part of the Java programming language,
offering a number of advantages such as lazy class loading and dynamic installation of software components. Unfortunately, these advantages often come at
the cost of decreased performance because certain optimizations become more
difficult to perform when an optimizing compiler cannot assume that it has seen
the whole program.

Object-oriented languages encourage data encapsulation through the use of
methods, resulting in frequent method invocations. Additionally, object-oriented
languages support dynamically dispatched (virtual) calls, where the method
called depends on the runtime type of the receiver object. Efficient implementations of virtual dispatch [15,12] help reduce the direct overhead of virtual method
invocation, however, *method inlining* remains an important optimization for effective implementation of object-oriented languages.

---

* Funded, in part, by NSF grant CCR-9808607.

B. Magnusson (Ed.): ECOOP 2002, LNCS 2374, pp. 498–524, 2002.

One technique for performing inlining at potentially polymorphic call sites is *guarded inlining* [17, 6, 14, 18] (also called *receiver class prediction* [14] and *guarded devirtualization* [18]), where a runtime test is inserted to check whether is safe to execute the inlined code; if not, a full virtual dispatch is invoked. Guarded inlining allows *some* of the benefits of direct inlining, but not all. The two main disadvantages are 1) executing the guard incurs runtime overhead, and 2) optimization of the caller method is restricted because of the possibility that the default virtual dispatch will be executed. Code patching [24,8] is a technique that removes the overhead of executing the guard itself, but does not address the second problem of restricted optimization.

Interprocedural analysis, such as *class hierarchy analysis* (CHA) [10,13], can help eliminate guards by identifying call sites that are provably monomorphic (have only one possible target method) and therefore can be directly inlined without a guard. However, dynamic class loading precludes the use of traditional interprocedural analysis because classes loaded in the future may cause the result of the analysis to become incorrect. Call sites will be referred to as *currently-monomorphic* if traditional analysis identifies them as monomorphic, but dynamic class loading may cause them to become polymorphic in the future.

Several existing techniques have addressed the goal of allowing direct inlining of currently-monomorphic call sites in presence of dynamic class loading. Such techniques include on-stack replacement [16], preexistence-based inlining [11], code patching [24,8], and extant analysis [23]. As discussed further in Sections 2 and 9, these techniques either 1) do not completely remove the penalty of dynamic class loading, or 2) have implementation complexities that limit their use in mainstream JVMs. The latter is made evident by the fact that many VM's [1,24,11,8] continue to perform guarded inlining at currently-monomorphic call sites.

This paper introduces *thin guards*, a simple but effective technique that uses lightweight runtime tests to identify regions of code within which speculative optimizations can be performed, even without the ability to perform on-stack replacement. One application of thin guards is described in detail, demonstrating how they can be used to perform speculative inlining in the presence of dynamic class loading. Thin guards are almost as easy to implement as traditional guarded inlining, yet offer two substantial advantages: thin guards are 1) more efficient (generally one machine load) and 2) test a more general condition, making it easier to guard multiple inlined call sites with a single test. Our experimental evaluation shows that when used in combination with other traditional compiler optimizations, such as control flow graph splitting [6], thin guards can eliminate most of the penalty of dynamic class loading.

The remainder of this paper is organized as follows. Section 2 reviews existing techniques for inlining in the presence of dynamic class loading. Section 3 presents a motivating example demonstrating the benefits of thin guards. Section 4 describes thin guards in full generality, while Section 5 shows one application of thin guards using class hierarchy analysis. Sections 6 and 7 describe our implementation and experimental results using the Jikes Research Virtual

Machine[1]. Section 8 describes applications of thin guards other than inlining in the presence of dynamic class loading. Sections 9 and 10 describe related work and conclusions.

2   Background: Dynamic Class Loading

Dynamic languages such as Self [6] and the Java programming language make it difficult, or even impossible, to determine the set of components that comprise the whole program. For example in Java, `Class.forName` can be used to load a class whose name is computed at runtime. Optimizations performed in the presence of such semantics must be conservative to ensure that all code produced will execute properly regardless of what classes are loaded in the future.

In practice, however, programs may execute for long periods of time without performing dynamic class loading. There may be many applications for which class loading occurs during program startup, and then either 1) never occurs again, 2) occurs only infrequently during software updates, 3) occurs frequently, but affects only a portion of the class hierarchy. For these types of programs it can be profitable to optimize *speculatively* (or *optimistically*) to obtain maximum performance, and rely on potentially expensive invalidation mechanisms to ensure safety when class loading occurs. Direct inlining at currently-monomorphic call sites is an example of such an optimization.

One approach for invalidation is to simply recompile any methods that contain unsafe code after class loading occurs. Although this will ensure that all future calls execute safely, currently running methods may be executing unsafe code, and may continue to do so indefinitely. Therefore, without a technique such as *on-stack replacement* to allow recompilation of currently executing methods, optimizations must be conservative to ensure safety in the presence of dynamic class loading.

The remainder of this section describes existing techniques for safely performing inlining of currently-monomorphic call sites.

2.1   Guarded Inlining

Guarded inlining is one solution for safely inlining currently-monomorphic call sites. It is relatively easy to implement and is used by many systems to avoid incorrect execution in the presence of dynamic class loading [18,1,8,11].

There are two common types of guards. A *class test* [14,6] checks the type of the receiver object, while *method test* [11] checks which method will be called by the receiver. The advantages and disadvantages of each are discussed further in Section 3.1.

---

[1] Jikes RVM is an open source version of the Jalapeño Research Virtual Machine [1,3]. Documentation and source code are available at
http://www.ibm.com/developerworks/oss/jikesrvm

2.2   On-stack Replacement

On-stack replacement or *dynamic deoptimization* [16] is a technique that allows a currently executing method (i.e., on the activation stack) to be stopped and replaced by another version of that method, presumably optimized in a different manner, or possibly not optimized at all. By allowing currently executing methods to be deoptimized, on-stack replacement is an effective mechanism for performing invalidation of unsafe code. In fact, Hotspot [21] uses on-stack replacement to allow direct inlining of currently-monomorphic methods.

However, there are disadvantages associated with on-stack replacement. It is a fairly complex technique that can require space consuming data structures [16,7]. Additionally, optimizations may need to be restricted to maintain the ability to later perform on-stack replacement [7]. The bottom line is that few JVMs today perform on-stack replacement; to our knowledge, Hotspot [21] is the only publicly described JVM to do so. An implementation of on-stack replacement in Jikes RVM is currently underway, although not yet complete.

2.3   Preexistence-Based Inlining

Preexistence-based inlining [11] is a technique that enables direct inlining at *some* currently-monomorphic call sites, without requiring on-stack replacement. The goal of preexistence is to identify call sites at which the receiver object must have been created before the caller method was invoked; thus the receiver object *preexists* the method invocation. If the receiver of a currently-monomorphic call site is guaranteed to preexist the method invocation, the call site can be directly inlined.

When dynamic class loading occurs, all invalid methods are recompiled so new calls to those methods execute safely. Currently executing methods are safe because receiver objects at directly inlined call sites preexist their caller's invocation. This implies that the receiver object also preexists the dynamic class loading that occurred, ensuring that the type of the receiver object cannot be one of the newly loaded classes.

Preexistence is a simple and effective technique for identifying candidates for direct inlining, and is complementary to the work presented here. The main limitations of preexistence-based inlining is that it is effective for only a subset of the currently-monomorphic call sites. As discussed further in Section 7.5, substantial performance can be gained by directly inlining the remaining call sites not covered by preexistence. Additionally, we show that the effectiveness of preexistence is reduced as more aggressive inlining techniques are applied.

2.4   Code Patching

Code patching [24, 8] is a technique used to eliminate the runtime overhead of executing guards. Inlining is performed just like traditional guarded inlining, where a guard is inserted during optimization and a backup virtual dispatch is

```
class A {

  public int bar() {
    A a = getSomeA_or_B();
    B b = getSomeB();
    return a.getX() + b.getY();
  }

  public int getX() { return 99; }
  public int getY() { return 100; }
}

class B extends A {
}
```

Fig. 1. Example program fragment. Assume no classes override classes A or B.

included in case the guard should fail. However, with code patching the instructions to implement the guard are not included in the final generated code and the inlined body executes unconditionally. If the inlining decision is later invalidated by dynamic class loading, the first instruction of the inlined code is dynamically overwritten with an unconditional jump to the backup virtual dispatch.

Code patching is more efficient than traditional guarded inlining because it eliminates the overhead of executing the guards themselves. However, code patching does not address the restrictions placed on optimization by the presence of the backup virtual dispatch. As discussed in the next section, the performance penalty caused by restricted optimization can be as great, or greater than the penalty imposed by executing guards.

3   Motivating Example

This section presents a motivating example to convey the basic idea behind thin guards. Consider the partial program shown in Figure 1. Assume that currently there are no subclasses of A or B. Methods getX() and getY() are not private or final so dynamic class loading could cause them to be overridden at some point in the future; therefore, these methods cannot be inlined directly in method bar(). Even though they are currently-monomorphic, the directly inlined code could become incorrect if either method is overridden in the future.

Figure 2 shows how method bar() would be optimized using traditional guarded inlining. A method test is used to guard the inlined body of getX() because the receiver (a) could be of type A or B. A class test is used to guard the inlined body of getY() because the only possible type for the receiver (b) is B. Neither guard can be identified as redundant and eliminated because each method is dispatched on a different receiver object. Preexistence-based inlining would not help because the objects referenced by a and b may have been created after method bar() was invoked.

```
void bar() {
    a = ...;
    b = ...;
    if ( METHOD_TEST(a,getX()) )
        t1 = 99;      // Inlined body
    else
        t1 = a.getX();
    if ( CLASS_TEST(b,B) )
        t2 = 100;     // Inlined body
    else
        t2 = b.getY();
    return t1 + t2;
}
```

Fig. 2. Method `bar()` from Figure 1 optimized using traditional guards (method and class tests).

```
void bar() {
    a = ...;
    b = ...;
    if (noClassLoadingHasOccured)
        return  199;
    else
        return a.getX() + b.getY();
}
```

Fig. 3. Method `bar()` from Figure 1 optimized using thin guards.

However, as long as no class loading occurs, directly inlining these calls would be safe; therefore, both guards in `bar()` could be replaced by a single test that checks whether any class loading has occured since `bar()` was compiled, as shown in Figure 3. This simple example illustrates the key idea behind *thin guards*: using a boolean condition bit to represent program-wide conditions. This technique decreases the overhead of the guards themselves, and also allows more optimization to occur because a larger area of code can be covered by a single guard.

3.1   Comparison of Guards

Table 1 summarizes the relative strengths and weaknesses of thin guards compared to class tests and method tests. The first advantage of thin guards is the efficiency of the guard itself. Checking a condition bit can be performed with a single load, whereas methods tests typically require two [11] or three [2] loads, depending on the implementation[2]. Similarly, class tests typically require one or two loads.

---

[2] An additional load is necessary in Jikes RVM because the *type information block* (TIB) can potentially be moved by a copying garbage collector. See [2] for more details on dynamic type checking in Jikes RVM.

Table 1. Comparison of the advantages and disadvantages of each guarded inlining technique. The code in the column "Example" assumes the class hierarchy from Figure 1, and that variables a and b are of static type A and B respectively.

Characteristic	Example	Class Test	Method Test	Thin Guard
Runtime overhead of typical implementation (# loads)	—	1 (or 2)	2 (or 3)	1
Can one guard cover multiple call sites dispatching different methods on the same receiver object?	b.getX() b.getY()	Yes	No	Yes
Can one guard be used at call sites where multiple receiver types are possible, but call the same method?	a.getX()	No	Yes	Yes
Can one guard cover multiple call sites dispatched on different receiver objects?	a.getX() b.getY()	No	No	Yes
Effective for polymorphic call sites (assuming distribution is peaked).	—	Yes	Yes	No

Choosing between a class test or a method test involves balancing tradeoffs because each has limitations. Class tests offer the advantage that multiple dispatches on the same receiver object can be guarded by a single test, even if the calls are to different methods; this is not true for method tests. However, a single method test can be used for call sites where multiple receiver types are possible, as long as all of these types result in a call to the same method; this is not the case for class tests, which would need to test each potential type individually.

Thin guards will handle both of the these scenarios with a single guard. Furthermore, thin guards can allow multiple calls to be covered by a single test *even if the calls are dispatched from different receiver objects*, as demonstrated in Figure 3 where the two calls on receiver objects a and b are both guarded by a single test.

The main disadvantage of thin guards (as discussed later in Section 4) is that they are effective only for currently-monomorphic call sites. Class and method tests can be effective for polymorphic call sites because they examine the receiver object of each dispatch. Thin guards, however, test whether a condition is true for *all possible receivers*, and therefore cannot be used to distinguish receivers at polymorphic call sites. It is for this reason that thin guards are most effective for infrequently changing, program-wide conditions, such as dynamic class loading.

3.2   Effect of Code Patching

Code patching [18,8] (see Section 2.4) is a technique that can be used to reduce the overhead of executing the guards, and is orthogonal to the particular guard implementation being used. Code patching can be used with all of the guards shown in Table 1, including thin guards. Augmenting each guard type with code patching would reduce the runtime overhead (the first row of Table 1) to zero.

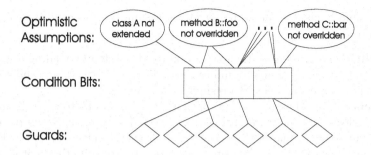

Fig. 4. The general structure of thin guards. Optimistic assumptions are mapped to condition bits, which are referenced by guards throughout the application.

However, code patching does not relax any of the restrictions that guards place on optimization, and thus does not affect the other characteristics shown in Table 1.

4   Thin Guards

Thin guards are lightweight runtime tests designed to efficiently monitor *optimistic assumptions* about the executing program. For the purpose of this paper, an optimistic assumption is some fact about the executing program that 1) is currently true, 2) is unlikely to change in the near future, and 3) enables additional optimization to be performed. For example, "Method `A::getX()` is not overridden" is an optimistic assumption. By providing a mechanism to efficiently verify optimistic assumptions, thin guards can be used to create regions of code within which these assumptions can be relied upon to perform more aggressive optimization.

The general structure of thin guards is shown in Figure 4. Optimistic assumptions are mapped to some number of *condition bits* that are used to record whether the optimistic assumptions are still true[3]. There may be more optimistic assumptions than condition bits, so multiple assumptions may map to the same bit. A condition bit is true only if *all* of its optimistic assumptions are true. A condition bit must be set to false if any of its optimistic assumptions become false.

During compilation, optimizations that may benefit from relying on an optimistic assumption can be performed as long as the region of code is guarded by a test that checks a condition bit associated with that optimistic assumption. The guards in Figure 4 represent conditional tests compiled into code throughout the application. Each of these guards tests a single condition bit to determine whether the optimistic assumptions mapped to that bit are still true.

---

[3] Although referred throughout the paper as *condition bits*, the notion of a *bit* is abstract. The actual implementation of the conditions could use any representation that is most convenient and efficient.

This mechanism of mapping optimistic assumptions to condition bits serves two purposes.

1. **Efficiency.** An optimistic assumption can be tested by reading a single bit. Because there is a small number of condition bits, checking a bit can most likely be implemented with a single load.
2. **Generality.** Mapping several optimistic assumptions to a single condition bit allows multiple assumptions to be tested with a single guard, reducing the number of guards that need to be executed. The example in Figure 3 demonstrated this by using single condition bit to verify that neither method (`A::getX()` nor `A::getY()`) was overridden.

The main disadvantage of thin guards is that they are effective only for assumptions that can be mapped to a condition bit. Program-wide characteristics that change infrequently fit most naturally into this model. Dynamic class loading is the primary application discussed in this paper, however, other potential applications are presented in Section 8.

4.1   When Optimistic Assumptions Change

After a program has executed for some time, optimistic assumptions may change. When they do, all condition bits associated with the false optimistic assumptions must be set to false. Guards testing these condition bits will fail so execution will continue safely, but more slowly. To recover performance, the VM can choose to recompile all methods necessary to remove failing guards. Such an approach is not specific to thin guards. A system using traditional guarded inlining would likely choose to recompile certain methods after class loading occurs, to remove method or class tests that have begun failing.

However, thin guards introduce additional complexity because multiple optimistic assumptions may be hashed to the same condition bit. A guard G that reads a condition bit B becomes dependent on all B's optimistic assumptions, even if G was originally inserted to test only a subset of those assumptions. For example, the code from Figure 3 used a single bit (`classLoadingHasNotOccured`) to cover all inlined call sites. If some obscure class Q is loaded that does not extend A or B, the guard in `bar()` will begin failing even though the inlined code is still valid.

For ease of reference, some terminology will be established. A guard G is *intentionally-dependent* on an optimistic assumptions O if G was inserted specifically to test O. G is *unintentionally-dependent* on O if G was not inserted to test O, but becomes dependent on O only because multiple assumptions map to the same condition bit.

When a condition bit becomes false, guards reading that bit can be classified into two categories

1. A guard is *permanently-disabled* if it is intentionally-dependent on an optimistic assumption that has become false. Permanently-disabled guards must never succeed or invalid code would be executed.

2. A guard is *temporarily-disabled* if it is *not* permanently-disabled, but is reading a false condition bit. Temporarily-disabled guards are safe to succeed at any time, but fail because of an unfortunate mapping to the condition bit.

Additionally, any method that contains a permanently-disabled guard will be referred to as an *unsafe method*. The false condition bit cannot be reset to true while unsafe methods are executing, otherwise permanently-disabled guards could succeed and incorrect execution may result.

In terms of regaining performance it is desirable to re-enable the condition bit as soon as possible so that temporarily-disabled guards can begin succeeding again. There are several possible strategies that could used to recover performance. Below we discuss a recompilation-based approach, as well as a code patching approach.

Recompilation. A failing condition bit can be re-enabled once all permanently-disabled guards dependent on that bit have been eliminated. To accomplish this, the VM could eliminate all unsafe methods as follows:

1. Recompile all unsafe methods to remove permanently-disabled guards so that new calls to these methods go to safe code. Alternatively, unsafe methods could be marked for lazy compilation [19] so that future calls trigger a new compilation of that method.
2. Wait for all currently executing unsafe methods to exit. This could be implemented in a variety of ways, one of which is to periodically scan the stack (possibly during garbage collection when the stack is already scanned) to see if unsafe methods are still active.

Once no unsafe method can possibly execute, the condition bit can be re-enabled; temporarily-disabled guards will begin succeeding again and performance will no longer be degraded. However, it may be the case that unsafe methods continue executing for a long period of time. During this time, temporarily-disabled guards throughout the application must fail to ensure safety. If the unsafe methods continue executing for an unacceptable period of time, the VM can use a backup plan to recover performance. A new condition bit could be introduced that tests only those optimistic assumptions that are still true; all methods that contain temporarily-disabled guards can then be recompiled to take advantage of the new condition bit[4]. This strategy is undesirable in the case that the unsafe methods exit quickly (because then the additional recompilation is not necessary), but can be used to prevent performance from being degraded indefinitely in extreme cases.

Code Patching. Although the previous section presented a recompilation-only strategy for recovering performance, code patching can be used to simplify the process. When a condition bit becomes false, code patching can be used to replace

---

[4] The previous condition bit can remain false indefinitely, or potentially be reused if the unsafe methods ever exit.

all permanently-disabled guards with an unconditional jump to the backup path. Once the patching occurs, the condition bit can be reset so that the temporarily-disabled guards succeed once again.

In fact, code patching can also be used in combination with thin-guards to remove the guards altogether, similar to traditional code patching as described in Section 2.4. The combination of thin-guards and code patching would yield higher (peak) performance than either technique used in isolation: code patching eliminates the direct overhead of executing guards, while the thin guards approach of mapping multiple optimistic assumptions to a single guard creates larger regions of check-free code, thus reducing the indirect overhead overhead due to restricted optimization. When optimistic assumptions change, permanently-disabled guards would be be patched to be unconditionally false, while temporarily-disabled guards would be left alone (and thus would remain unconditionally true).

5   Example Application: Inlining

This section describes one particular application of thin guards, showing how they can be used to allow more effective inlining in the presence of dynamic class loading. The goal is reduce the overhead introduced by dynamic class loading, allowing performance to approach that which could be obtained if dynamic class loading did not exist.

5.1   Using Thin Guards with CHA

For our example application, class hierarchy analysis (CHA) [10] is used to identify currently-monomorphic call sites. Inlining at such call sites is guarded using thin guards to ensure proper execution if the class hierarchy should change in the future.

For simplicity, a single condition bit is used to represent all optimistic assumptions, similar to the example from Figure 3. However, using a single condition bit does not imply that the bit must represent *all possible* class loading (like the noClassLoadingHasOccurred bit did in Figure 3). Instead, optimistic assumptions can be selected carefully to minimize the chance of invalidation. Only parts of the class hierarchy that are relatively stable (i.e., have not been extended for some amount of time) should be associated with the condition bit. Methods in classes that are extended frequently can still be inlined with traditional techniques. Using this selective approach, even applications that perform frequent class loading can benefit from thin guards as long as some portion of the class hierarchy is stable.

The following steps can be followed during optimization, and when class loading occurs, to safely achieve the benefits of thin guards.

During Optimization. During compilation the optimizing compiler can make optimistic assumptions about call sites using class hierarchy analysis. To inline a call to method `A::foo()` using thin guards, the compiler needs to perform the following steps.

1. Use class hierarchy analysis to confirm that the call to `A::foo()` is currently-monomorphic and therefore a candidate for direct inlining.
2. Let O represent the optimistic assumption "`A::foo()` is not overridden". If O is already mapped to the condition bit, goto step 5.
3. Decide whether class `A`, or more specifically method `A::foo()`, is stable enough to justify using a thin-guard (i.e., has not been extended for a sufficient amount of time). If this is not the case, use traditional guarded inlining and skip steps 4–6.
4. Insert O into the set of optimistic assumptions mapped to the condition bit. If class loading later violates O, then the condition bit must be set to false.
5. Record that the method being compiled (M) contains a guard that is intentionally-dependent on the optimistic assumption O. This allows M to be identified as an unsafe method if O should become false.
6. Guard the inlined code with a conditional that tests the condition bit.

At this stage, a separate guard is inserted for each call site, with the assumption that redundant checks can be eliminated at a later stage. Section 5.2 describes techniques for increasing the amount of code covered by each guard.

During Class Loading. When class loading occurs, the following steps must be performed before the loaded class is made available.

1. Compute the set of optimistic assumptions that were violated by the classes that were loaded. If no assumptions were violated, no further action is necessary.
2. For each optimistic assumption that is now false, compute the set of unsafe methods. This is just a lookup of the information recorded in step 3 during optimization. If there are no unsafe methods, no further action is necessary.
3. Change the condition bit to false so that all thin guards begin to fail.

At this point, the loaded class can be made available and execution will continue safely, but with degraded performance because guards will be failing. Performance can be regained using the techniques described in Section 4.1.

5.2   Eliminating Redundant Guards

One of the main advantages of thin guards is that they test more general conditions than traditional guards, allowing a larger region of code to be covered by a single guard. The algorithm described in 5.1 placed one guard per call site. This section describes how to safely identify guards that are redundant and can be removed.

Guard removal becomes slightly more complex in a multi-threaded environment, so the single-threaded case is considered first. In a single-threaded environment, redundant guards can be eliminated by using a slight variant of conditional constant propagation [25] to forward propagate condition bit values. The value of the condition bit can be assumed to be true along the "true" path after being tested by a thin guard, and false along the "false" path. These values can be propagated forward and guards that can be proven to test a constant condition can be removed.

The only special treatment necessary is to account for the fact that class loading may change the value of any condition bit; therefore, the analysis needs to ensure that all instructions that may cause dynamic class loading, either directly or indirectly, kill the condition bit values being propagated. In our implementation (as discussed further in Section 6.2) calls are among the instructions that act as thin guard barriers because interprocedural analysis is not performed to identify methods that are guaranteed not to perform class loading.

Multiple threads. In a multi-threaded environment removing guards becomes more difficult because while one thread (T1) is executing, a second thread T2 could load classes at any time. In such a scenario, none of the guards in T1 can safely be removed.

Fortunately, this problem can be solved by adding logic to the class loader. Section 5.1 described the actions taken by the class loader to trigger invalidation. In a multi-threaded environment a 4th step can be performed by the class loader before making the loaded classes available:

4. Wait for all threads to exit any region of code that is guarded by a false condition bit.

With this addition, guards can be removed as in the single-threaded case; by the time the newly loaded class is made available, all execution will have exited the unsafe regions, and unsafe regions cannot be re-entered because the condition bit has been set to false.

The question is how can this 4th step be implemented? It is actually quit easy in any system that uses some variation of *safe points* such as *interrupt points* in Self [16], or *yieldpoints* in Jikes RVM [1]. Safe points are simply program locations at which the VM can preempt the currently executing thread; they are typically placed on method entries and loop backedges to ensure that only a finite amount of execution can occur between them. Given such safe points, step 4 can be implemented by

- During redundant guard elimination, ensure that guards are not eliminated across safe points (i.e., safe points kill during the propagation of condition bit values).
- During class loading, wait for all threads to reach a safe point before making the newly loaded class available.

Together, these two conditions ensure that all threads will have existed unsafe code by reaching a safe point, therefore class loading can continue. Making safe points barriers to guard elimination may increase the number of guards executed; however, if safe points are placed at method entries and loop backedges, guard removal can still be quite liberal. The entire body of a loop, or the entire body of a loop-free method can potentially be covered by one guard (assuming the loop or method does not contain other barriers to guard elimination).

Increasing Opportunities for Guard Elimination. Although the previous section described how to identify guards that are redundant and can be eliminated, it is easy to construct simple code fragments containing guards that cannot be eliminated. For example, consider the code fragment from Figure 2. Even if the method test and class test are replaced by thin guards, the second guard cannot automatically be removed. The true and false paths of the first guard merge before reaching the second guard, therefore the condition bit must be retested. However, several well known transformations can help increase the opportunities for removing redundant guards.

Splitting. Splitting [6] is a transformation originally designed to reduce the overhead of message sends in Self. Splitting exposes optimization opportunities by specializing sections of code within a method. Specialization is achieved by performing tail-duplication of conditional control flow to eliminating control flow merges where data flow information would have been lost.

For the example from Figure 2, splitting can be used to duplicate the second guard (along with the code it protects) by placing a copy along each path of the first guard. After splitting, both copies of the second guard can be identified as redundant, producing the code in Figure 3. Splitting is effective for exposing a variety of optimization opportunities, but is particularly effective for thin guards, as discussed further in Section 7.4.

Inlining. Calls are likely to be barriers for guard elimination; eliminating guards across a call would require interprocedural analysis to prove that the dynamic class loading could not occur during at any point during the call. Aggressive inlining will reduce the number of (non-inlined) call sites, thus reducing interference with guard removal.

Loop transformations. Loop transformations, such as loop cloning [6], or loop unrolling, can be used to expose opportunities for removing redundant guards. Consider a tight loop that executes only a single call site that is inlined with a guard. The guard cannot simply be removed; the condition bit must be tested at some point to ensure that class loading has not occured. However, by unrolling the loop N times it may be possible for guards 2–N to be identified as redundant on the first guard.

5.3   Multiple Condition Bits

Our example application uses a single condition bit to represent all optimistic assumptions. This approach has advantages besides that of simplicity. Having all guards test the same condition bit maximizes the number of guards that can be identified as redundant and eliminated. As long as class loading does not occur, a single condition bit offers the highest possible performance.

The disadvantage of using a single condition bit is recovery cost, because all thin guards in the program will begin failing when any optimistic assumptions become false. Performance is not recovered until the temporarily-disabled guards can be re-enabled as described in Section 4.1. Invalidation is expected to occur infrequently, although it could be the case that this potential temporary performance degradation is undesirable or even unacceptable.

However, in scenarios where temporary performance degradation is unacceptable, it is likely that on-stack replacement is also not a viable solution. With on-stack replacement the program must *stop completely* until all unsafe methods have been recompiled and replaced on the stack. With thin guards, the failing guards allow execution to continue safely, but more slowly, until the unsafe code has been recompiled and is no longer executing. Better yet, if code patching is used in combination with thin guards (see Section 4.1) then the only cost of recovery is the time needed to patch the permanently-disabled guards[5].

However, in cases where code patching is not being used *and* the potential performance degradation associated with using a single condition bit is too high, multiple bits could be used to reduce the number of guards that become temporarily-disabled when class loading occurs. There are many possible ways to incorporate multiple condition bits, each of which has its own advantages and disadvantages. We mention only a few examples below.

One possibility is to allocate one condition bit per optimistic assumption. This would ensure that guards are never temporarily-disabled because guards would fail only if their own optimistic assumption becomes false. Unfortunately, this approach reduces the opportunity for identifying and eliminating redundant guards; guards that were previously identified as redundant may now be testing different condition bits.

Another extreme is to allocate a separate bit for each method that is compiled. All optimistic assumptions relied upon during compilation of a method could be mapped to the condition bit for that method. This ensures that guards within a method all test the same condition bit, maximizing the possibility of removing redundant guards within the method. Additionally, each method has its own condition bit, so class loading will disable guards only in methods that are legitimately affected. However, the disadvantage of this approach is that increasing the number of condition bits will eventually degrade performance due to decreased cache behavior of reading the bits.

A more practical strategy would be to use a fixed number of bits that is small enough to provide desirable cache behavior, yet large enough to help reduce the performance penalty incurred when classes are loaded. Such a scenario creates many new potential strategies for deciding which optimistic assumptions map to which condition bits, with the goal of maximizing guard removal. However, we

---

[5] Methods containing permanently-disabled guards (which have been patched to be permanently false) will not regain their performance until they are recompiled and re-entered, but all other methods will execute at full speed once the patching completes.

did not explore this approach because combining code patching with thin guards is a simpler, yet effective option. By using code patching, temporarily-disabled guards are no longer an issue, so the recovery performance and scalability concerns associated with the single bit strategy are no longer a concern.

6   Implementation

To validate the ideas presented in this work, we implemented thin guards in the Jikes Research Virtual Machine. Section 6.1 provides a brief overview of Jikes RVM and Section 6.2 describes details of the implementation.

6.1   Jikes RVM

Jikes RVM [1] is an open source Research Virtual Machine developed at IBM T.J. Watson Research Center. Jikes RVM is written almost entirely in Java, and takes a compile only approach (no interpreter). Methods are compiled with a non-optimizing compiler upon their first execution, and an aggressive optimizing compiler [5] is applied selectively by the adaptive optimization system [3]. Although not a fully complete JVM, the performance of Jikes RVM has been shown to be competitive with that of commercial JVMs on the PowerPC platform.

Jikes RVM has the ability to perform inlining based on static heuristics, as well as adaptive inlining based on a call-edge profile collected via time-based sampling [3]. Direct inlining (without a guard) is performed when inlining monomorphic `private` and `final` `methods`, as well as for call sites proven monomorphic by local type propagation. Preexistence-based inlining [11] based on *invariant argument analysis* [11] is also performed to eliminate guards when possible. All other inlined methods are guarded with either a class test or method test.

Our version of Jikes RVM also performs some optimizations not yet available in the open source version, including feedback-directed splitting [4] and loop unrolling.

6.2   Thin Guards Implementation

Our thin guards implementation is the example application described in Section 5.1; class hierarchy analysis is used to identify candidates for direct inlining, and a single condition bit is used to represent all optimistic assumptions regarding dynamic class loading. To prevent invalidation from occurring unnecessarily, our implementation does not insert thin guards until a method has reached the highest level of optimization ("O2" in Jikes RVM). Traditional guards are used for all lower levels of optimization. This approach allows the application to execute for some time before any optimistic assumptions are made. Using this technique, no invalidation occurred for any of the benchmarks used in this study.

Redundant Guard Elimination. To identify and eliminate redundant thin guards, a separate optimization pass was added to the Jikes RVM optimizing compiler. The elimination pass is not performed until after inlining, splitting, and loop unrolling have been performed, to allow the elimination to benefit from the effects of those transformations. However, the elimination is performed fairly early in the optimization process to allow the remaining optimizations to benefit from the simplified control flow.

Jikes RVM's *yieldpoints* were used as the mechanism to ensure safety in a multi-threaded environment, as described in Section 5.2. Jikes RVM's yieldpoints are simply a small sequence of instructions that checks a timer-set bit to determine whether the currently executing thread should yield to the thread scheduler. Yieldpoints are placed on all method entries and backedges to ensure that only a finite amount of execution can occur before a yieldpoint is executed[6].

Yieldpoints act as a barrier to guard elimination to ensure safety in a multi-threaded environment, as described in Section 5.2. Additionally, all instructions that can potentially cause dynamic class loading also act as a barrier to guard elimination[7]; this includes all calls, because interprocedural analysis is not performed to identify methods that are guaranteed not to perform dynamic class loading.

Class Loader Modifications. When class loading causes an optimistic assumption to be violated, the newly loaded class is not made available until all threads have executed at least one yieldpoint (see Section 5.2). In Jikes RVM this is achieved by stopping all threads at the next executed yieldpoint[8]. After all threads have stopped, the thin guard condition bit is set to false and execution continues.

All unsafe methods are marked for recompilation to remove all permanently-disabled guards. Our current implementation does not have the capability to identify when all active unsafe methods have finished executing (are no longer on the stack), although this functionality is currently being implemented. Therefore, to safely recover performance after class loading, our current implementation immediately employs the "backup" mechanism described in Section 4.1; a new condition bit is introduced and all methods containing temporarily-disabled guards are marked for lazy compilation so they will be recompiled on their next invocation. As mentioned previously, invalidation never occurs during the execution of our benchmarks, although the invalidation mechanism and recovery process is fully implemented.

---

[6] Jikes RVM also places yieldpoints on method epilogues to improve the accuracy of the time-based samples collected by the adaptive optimization system. This placement is not necessary for correctness.

[7] The following bytecode instructions have the potential to cause a class to be loaded: anewarray, checkcast, getfield, getstatic, instanceof, invokeinterface, invokespecial, invokestatic, invokevirtual, multianewarray, new, putfield, and putstatic. However, in many cases it can be identified that class loading cannot occur. For example, getstatic cannot cause class loading once the class of the static field being accessed has been loaded.

[8] The current implementation simply triggers a garbage collection, which automatically stops all threads the next yieldpoint when using one of Jikes RVM's *stop-the-world* collectors.

7 Experimental Evaluation

This section describes our experimental evaluation of the thin guards implementation described in Section 6.

7.1 Methodology

Our experimental evaluation investigates the effect of thin guards on the SPECjvm98 benchmarks suite [9]. A standard *autorun* execution of the SPECjvm98 benchmarks consists of n executions of each benchmark in the same JVM. For our experiments, n was chosen separately for each benchmark to allow all benchmarks to run for approximately 4 minutes (using the size 100 inputs). This experimental setup was used to ensure that each benchmark executed long enough for the adaptive optimization system to approach a steady state. The time for the best run was chosen as the representative time for each autorun sequence. The goal of this study is to evaluate inlining effectiveness, so the startup performance of Jikes RVM is of no particular interest.

The Jikes RVM adaptive optimization system is nondeterministic, and sometimes this nondeterminism causes visible performance differences, even when comparing two runs of the same configuration. To eliminate noise, the final time used for each benchmark was computed by collecting 10 representative times (described above) and taking the median.

All experiments were performed on a 500 MHz 6 processor IBM RS/6000 Model S80 with 4 GB of RAM running IBM AIX 4.3.2. Jikes RVM was run using 1 processor and a 400 MB heap.

7.2 Benchmark Characterization

Figure 5 characterizes these benchmarks by showing the rate at which they execute virtual call sites (`invokevirtual` bytecodes). All call sites (both inlined and not inlined) were instrumented to record dynamic execution frequencies. These execution frequencies were then divided by the running time of the benchmark to compute executions per second. Call sites were divided into 5 categories.

1. Non-inlined virtual dispatch.
2. Guarded inlining of call site that CHA identifies as potentially polymorphic[9].
3. Guarded inlining of a call site that CHA identifies as monomorphic.
4. Direct inlining performed using preexistence.
5. Direct inlining performed without needing preexistence (callee was `private`, `final`, or belongs to a `final` class).

Our thin guards implementation can affect only the third category, shown in white in Figure 5. _201_compress _213_javac and _222_mpegaudio have virtually no such dynamic calls; therefore, it can be expected that thin guards will

---

[9] These call sites must have been inlined by the profile-driven adaptive inlining because the static heuristics inline only call sites that are monomorphic according to CHA.

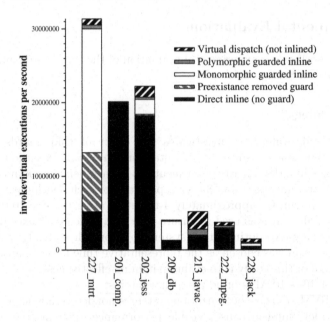

Fig. 5. Execution rate of invokevirtual call sites (both inlined and not inlined).

have no effect for these benchmarks. Many of the benchmarks have a large portion of their call sites directly inlined (the solid black bar). As an experiment, the benchmarks were also included in the study in a modified form, where the `private` and `final` modifiers were removed from all methods[10]. This creates the most challenging scenario possible for the optimizing compiler because all methods in the program may potentially be extended.

This is clearly a somewhat artifical modification because the `private` and `final` are language constructs that can be used to enforce information hiding and avoid undesirable software updates. However, programmers are often afraid of the overhead associated with data encapsulation, and specify methods `private` or `final` solely for the purpose of improving performance (allowing them to be directly inlined by the optimizing compiler), or even worse, avoid using data encapsulation altogether. This practice defeats the point of having dynamic class loading as part of the language, and would occur less frequently if programmers trusted their optimizing compiler to provide more competitive performance. Our goal for evaluating the modified benchmarks is simply to see how much these language constructs affect performance, and how much of this performance penalty can be regained by using our technique.

---

[10] For benchmarks whose source was not available, Jikes RVM was modified to ignore the `final` and `private` modifiers when making inlining decisions. This will not catch all cases because the Java to bytecode compiler may have performed direct inlining while compiling the bytecodes.

7.3   Effectiveness of Thin Guards

To evaluate the effectiveness of thin guards, timings were collected using the following 3 configurations of Jikes RVM:

1. **Base**: This configuration is the original Jikes RVM performing its full suite of optimizations [1,5]. Guarded inlining is performed using traditional method tests and class tests. Relevant optimizations performed include preexistence-based inlining and local type propagation (to eliminate guards whenever possible), adaptive inlining [3], feedback directed splitting [4] and loop unrolling.
2. **Thin guards**: Identical to Base but thin guards are used for currently-monomorphic call sites when methods reach the highest optimization level (O2).
3. **Ideal**: Guards are removed (unsafely) from all inlined call sites that are currently-monomorphic, thus representing the performance that could be achieved if dynamic class loading did not exist[11]. Incorrect execution can occur if classes are dynamically loaded.

Figure 6 shows the performance of these three configurations. The black bar shows the performance improvement of Thin guards over Base (higher bar means more improvement over Base), and the full height of the bar represents the upper bound on performance using the Ideal configuration. The number above each bar represents the percentage of the Ideal improvement that is achieved by using thin guards. This number is not meaningful (and thus not reported) for benchmarks with Ideal performance less than 2%.

The benchmarks showing the most substantial Ideal improvements are _227_mtrt (in its original form) and the modified version of _201_compress. _202_jess and _209_db show reasonable improvement, particularly _202_jess in its modified form. These improvements are mostly consistent with the breakdown of invocation types previously shown in Figure 5.

The total performance obtained by Ideal is *not* a contribution of this paper; it is simply an observation of the potential performance that could be obtained using well-known techniques, assuming dynamic class loading did not exist. The contribution of this paper is the percentage of Ideal performance that is obtained using thin guards. For _227_mtrt and the modified _201_compress, thin guards achieved 92% and 88% of the Ideal performance. _202_jess and _209_db showed reasonable performance, achieving over 70% of the possible Ideal win. The authors were pleasantly surprised by the substantial fraction of Ideal performance that could be obtained by using thin guards, and that such a simple technique could eliminate the majority of the penalty imposed by dynamic class loading.

---

[11] It should not be assumed that a JVM implementing on-stack replacement (see Section 2.2) would safely achieve the performance of Ideal. Optimization may need to be restricted to support on-stack replacement, resulting in degraded performance relative to Ideal. There is currently little published data quantifying the degree to which these potential optimization restrictions affect performance in practice.

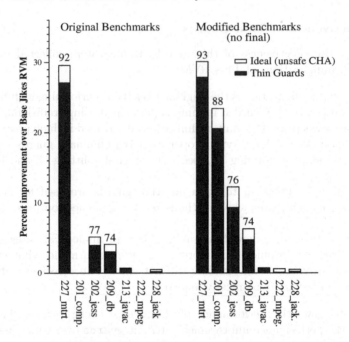

Fig. 6. Performance improvement of thin guards. The full bar shows the `Ideal` improvement using (unsafe) class hierarchy analysis. The black bar shows the performance improvement obtained safely using thin guards. The number above each bar shows the percent of the `Ideal` improvement that was achieved using thin guards.

7.4   Importance of Splitting

The results of Figure 6 were achieved using a system that performs feedback-directed splitting of intraprocedural control flow paths. As discussed in Section 5.2, splitting exposes optimization opportunities allowing additional guards to be identified as fully redundant and removed. This section takes a closer look at the interactions between thin guards and splitting. To evaluate the importance of splitting, the experiments of the previous section were repeated using the identical version of Jikes RVM, but with splitting disabled. The results are shown in Figure 7. Splitting was disabled for all 3 configurations shown in Figure 7, so the results show how much performance improvement can be expected when thin guards are added to a system that does not perform splitting.

Thin guards are clearly less effective when splitting is not performed, achieving roughly 50% of the `Ideal` win in most cases. It may be tempting to conclude from this data that thin guards did not actually provide the performance improvements previously reported in Figure 6, but that splitting is responsible instead; however, this is not the case. Recall that splitting was used in *all three* configurations of Figure 6, including the base configuration. Traditional guards often cannot be eliminated because of the limitations discussed in Section 3, *even when splitting is applied.* It is the synergy between splitting and the more general

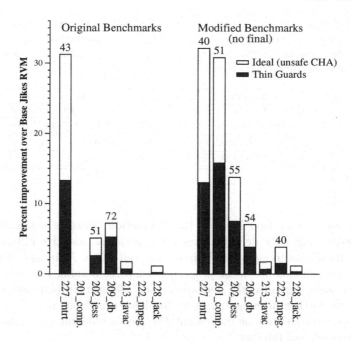

Fig. 7. Performance of thin guards in VM that does not perform splitting. Data is collected identically to that of Figure 6, but all 3 configurations (`Base`, `Thin guards`, and `Ideal`) were run with splitting disabled.

condition tested by thin guards that accounts for the increased performance of Figure 6.

Clearly, thin guards provide increased motivation for incorporating some form of splitting into the optimizing compiler. However, even without splitting the performance improvements offered by thin guards can be substantial (13.5% for _227_mtrt and 17% for the modified version of _201_compress), particularly given the implementation simplicity of thin guards.

7.5   Effectiveness of Preexistence

Preexistence-based inlining is implemented in Jikes RVM and was included in the `Base` configuration for our experiments. This section makes two observations about the effectiveness of preexistence when used without thin guards.

The first observation involves the bottom line effectiveness of preexistence-based inlining. The first row of Table 2 (labeled "Orig. RVM") shows the effect of preexistence (based on invariant argument analysis) on the _227_mtrt benchmark. The runtime is improved from 10.3 seconds to 8.6 seconds, a 16.2% improvement. However, the ideal performance is 5.9 seconds, meaning that preexistence achieved roughly a third of the ideal win (42.2%), leaving plenty of performance opportunity remaining for techniques such as thin guards.

Table 2. Effectiveness of preexistence-based inlining for _227_mtrt, both with and without aggressive adaptive inlining. "Orig. RVM" is an unmodified version of Jikes RVM. "No A.I." stands for "No Adaptive inlining", and represents a version of Jikes RVM with adaptive inlining disabled.

	Performance (seconds)			Dynamic Counts (millions)		
	Without Preexistence	Argument Preexistence	Ideal (unsafe CHA)	Guarded Inlined	Unguarded Non-Preex	Inlined Preex
Orig. RVM	10.3	8.6 (-16.2%)	5.9 (-42.2%)	643	83	532
No A.I.	10.6	8.5 (-19.2%)	7.0 (-34.0%)	500	27	706
Difference	—	—	—	-143	-56	+147

Our second observation involves the interaction between aggressive inlining and preexistence. By default, Jikes RVM performs adaptive inlining using profiling information to aggressively inline hot call edges. Although effective at improving performance for most programs, adaptive inlining has consistently, and mysteriously, degraded the performance of _227_mtrt (previously reported in [3]). Upon further investigation, the problem turned out not to be a deficiency of the adaptive inlining implementation, but a fundamental characteristic of preexistence-based inlining.

Preexistence relies on method boundaries as a mechanism for performing invalidation of unsafe code without the need for on-stack replacement. As more aggressive inlining is performed, methods become larger and method invocations become less frequent; the result is that fewer objects preexist the most recent method invocation, and preexistence-based inlining becomes less effective[12]. Consider an extreme example where the entire program is inlined into main(). The call to main() will be the only call executed during the program, so no objects can preexist this call[13]. therefore, no inlined call sites will be candidates for direct inlining based on preexistence.

To confirm that this effect occurs in practice, the row labeled "No A.I." in Table 2 repeats the measurements from the previous row but using a version of Jikes RVM with adaptive inlining disabled. Adaptive inlining improves performance in both scenarios where preexistence was *not* used (columns "Without preexistence" and "Ideal"), but degrades performance when preexistence is used (column "Argument preexistence").

The final three columns of the table provide dynamic inlining counts to confirm our hypothesis. The first of the three columns reports the dynamic number of call sites that were executed with a guard, while the remaining two columns represent call sites that were inlined directly. The directly inlined call sites are broken into two categories to distinguish whether or not the guard was removed by preexistence.

As expected, disabling adaptive inlining for _227_mtrt decreased the number of guarded inline sites (-143 million) and also decreased the number of call

---

[12] True for preexistence in general, not just invariant argument preexistence.

[13] Except possibly objects created by static initializers.

sites directly inlined for reasons other than preexistence (-56 million). However, disabling adaptive inlining *increased* the dynamic number of call sites that were directly inlined due to preexistence (+147 million), confirming that preexistence was hindered by adaptive inlining.

These observations are not meant to suggest that preexistence-based inlining is not an effective technique for improving performance. Preexistence is a simple idea that offers large speedups in many cases. Even though adaptive inlining's negative effect on _227_mtrt is related to preexistence, both configurations *with* preexistence are much faster than either configuration *without* preexistence. Our goal is only to argue that preexistence cannot be relied upon to eliminate all of the performance penalty of dynamic class loading, particularly in systems that perform aggressive inlining.

8 Other Applications

Although this paper focused on performing inlining in the presence of dynamic class loading, thin guards are general mechanism for allowing speculative optimizations to be performed safely without the need for on-stack replacement. One obvious extension is to use analyses other than class hierarchy analysis to identify currently-monomorphic call sites. The only requirement for incorporating analyses with thin guards is the ability to identify the set of call sites that become invalid after a class has been loaded.

Thin guards also have potential for testing other infrequently changing conditions not related to dynamic class loading. For example, thin guards could be used to reduce the performance penalty of non-final static fields. Guards could be inserted to create regions of code within which optimizations can exploit the values of infrequently changing static fields. Any code modifying the value of such fields would need to trigger invalidation. Other examples include using thin guards to remove synchronization for single-threaded programs by testing whether more than one application thread has been created. Similarly, thin guards could be used to keep track of whether reflection has been used; if not, then it is safe to apply optimizations that take advantage of private fields (which can be modified using reflection).

9 Additional Related Work

Sreedhar et al. [23] describe *extant analysis*, an offline, interprocedural static analysis that operates on a predefined set of classes that are defined to be the *closed world*. The goal of extant analysis is to categorize references into two categories, 1) *unconditionally extant* references guaranteed to remain in the closed world, and 2) *conditionally extant* references *not* guaranteed to stay in the closed world. For the first category, optimizations such as inlining can be directly applied. For the second category, runtime tests called *extant safety tests* can be used to create regions of code within which direct optimizations can be applied.

As described, extant analysis is an offline analysis that would be non-trivial to incorporate into an online JVM. The extant safety test proposed in their work examines the receiver of the method being dispatched, and therefore is more expensive and offers less opportunity for guard elimination than thin guards. The importance of optimizing extant safety tests (to minimize the dynamic number of tests executed) is discussed in their work, but no algorithm for doing so is presented; other variants of extant safety tests are mentioned but not thoroughly discussed. Thin guards could be considered to be one particular kind of extant safety test that is simple, yet effective in practice. Finally, their experimental evaluation admittedly relied on several unsafe assumptions about entry points into the closed world; our experimental evaluation makes no unsafe assumptions.

Pechtchanski and Sarkar [22] present a framework for performing optimistic interprocedural analysis. Their work describes a general dependency tracking mechanism for speculative optimizations, and presents an optimistic interprocedural type analysis as an application of their framework. Although addressing a similar problem, there are significant differences between their work and ours. Their framework is designed for systems that have on-stack replacement available as a mechanism for invalidation; the goal of our work is to avoid the need for on-stack replacement. Additionally, because on-stack replacement was not available in their system, the potential restrictions on optimization it imposes were not present in their experimental evaluation. Our evaluation used a complete implementation that ensures correct execution when class loading occurs. For some benchmarks, thin guards based on class hierarchy analysis offered speedups larger than those reported for their interprocedural type analysis.

Sealed calls [26] take advantage of *sealed packages* to identify additional methods that can not be overridden, even if these methods are not `final`. Such methods can be inlined directly without a guard.

10   Conclusions and Future Work

Dynamic class loading is important aspect of the Java programming language, although it complicates many optimizations such as inlining. Thin guards are a simple technique that can be used to reduce the performance penalty imposed by dynamic class loading. They are almost as easy to implement as traditional guards, but offer two advantages: they are 1) more efficient and 2) test a more general condition, allowing a larger region of code to be covered by a single guard.

For the benchmarks used in our study, thin guards were able to eliminate the majority of the penalty imposed by dynamic class loading. For the _227_mtrt benchmark, thin guards improved performance by 27% achieving 92% of ideal performance. Intraprocedural path splitting was shown to substantially improve the effectiveness of thin guards, although even without splitting, thin guards yielded reasonable performance improvements (13.5% for _227_mtrt).

For future work we are planning to evaluate the effectiveness of combining code patching and thin guards, to further improve performance. We intend to move our implementation into the open source release of Jikes RVM, as well as continue exploring the effectiveness of our technique on a larger suite of benchmarks. We hope to experiment with benchmarks that perform enough class loading to trigger invalidation; such benchmarks will allow us to evaluate the performance penalty incurred by failing guards, as well as evaluate various recovery strategies.

Acknowledgments

We would like to thank IBM Research and the entire Jikes RVM team for providing the infrastructure to make this research possible. We would also like to thank David Grove, Michael Hind, and Stephen Fink for helpful discussions and feedback on an earlier draft of this paper. Finally, we thank Michael Hind and Vivek Sarkar for their support of this work.

References

1. B. Alpern, C. R. Attanasio, J. J. Barton, M. G. Burke, P. Cheng, J.-D. Choi, A. Cocchi, S. J. Fink, D. Grove, M. Hind, S. F. Hummel, D. Lieber, V. Litvinov, M. F. Mergen, T. Ngo, J. R. Russell, V. Sarkar, M. J. Serrano, J. C. Shepherd, S. E. Smith, V. C. Sreedhar, H. Srinivasan, and J. Whaley. The Jalapeño virtual machine. *IBM Systems Journal*, 39(1), 2000.
2. B. Alpern, A. Cocchi, and D. Grove. Dynamic typechecking in Jalapeño. In *Usenix Java Virtual Machine Research and Technology Symposium (JVM'01)*, Apr. 2001.
3. M. Arnold, S. Fink, D. Grove, M. Hind, and P. Sweeney. Adaptive optimization in the Jalapeño JVM. In *ACM Conference on Object-Oriented Programming Systems, Languages, and Applications*, Oct. 2000.
4. M. Arnold. Online instrumentation and feedback-directed optimization of Java. Technical Report DCS-TR-469, Department of Computer Science, Rutgers University, 2001.
5. M. G. Burke, J.-D. Choi, S. Fink, D. Grove, M. Hind, V. Sarkar, M. J. Serrano, V. C. Sreedhar, H. Srinivasan, and J. Whaley. The Jalapeño dynamic optimizing compiler for Java. In *ACM 1999 Java Grande Conference*, pages 129–141, June 1999.
6. C. Chambers and D. Ungar. Making pure object-oriented languages practical. In *ACM Conference on Object-Oriented Programming Systems, Languages, and Applications*, pages 1–15, Nov. 1991. *SIGPLAN Notices* 26(11).
7. C. Chambers. *The Design and Implementation of the SELF Compiler, an Optimizing Comiler for Object-Oriented Programming Languages*. PhD thesis, Stanford University, 1992.
8. M. Cierniak, G.-Y. Lueh, and J. M. Stichnoth. Practicing JUDO: Java Under Dynamic Optimizations. In *SIGPLAN 2000 Conference on Programming Language Design and Implementation*, June 2000.
9. T. S. P. E. Corporation. SPEC JVM98 Benchmarks. http://www.spec.org/osg/jvm98/, 1998.
10. J. Dean, D. Grove, and C. Chambers. Optimization of object-oriented programs using static class hierarchy analysis. In *9th European Conference on Object-Oriented Programming*, 1995.

11. D. Detlefs and O. Agesen. Inlining of virtual methods. In *13th European Conference on Object-Oriented Programming*, 1999.
12. K. Driesen and U. Hoelzle. Minimizing row displacement dispatch tables. *ACM SIGPLAN Notices*, 30(10):141–155, Oct. 1995.
13. M. Fernandez. Simple and effective link-time optimizations of modula-3 programs. In *SIGPLAN '95 Conference on Programming Language Design and Implementation*, 1995.
14. D. Grove, J. Dean, C. Garrett, and C. Chambers. Profile-guided receiver class prediction. In *ACM Conference on Object-Oriented Programming Systems, Languages, and Applications*, pages 108–123, Oct. 1995.
15. U. Hölzle, C. Chambers, and D. Ungar. Optimizing dynamically-typed object-oriented languages with polymorphic inline caches. In P. America, editor, *Proceedings ECOOP '91*, LNCS 512, pages 21–38, Geneva, Switzerland, July 15-19 1991. Springer-Verlag.
16. U. Hölzle, C. Chambers, and D. Ungar. Debugging optimized code with dynamic deoptimization. In *Proceedings of the ACM SIGPLAN '92 Conference on Programming Language Design and Implementation*, pages 32–43, June 1992.
17. U. Hölzle and D. Ungar. Optimizing dynamically-dispatched calls with run-time type feedback. In *Proceedings of the ACM SIGPLAN'94 Conference on Programming Language Design and Implementation (PLDI)*, pages 326–336, Orlando, Florida, 20–24 June 1994. *SIGPLAN Notices* 29(6), June 1994.
18. K. Ishizaki, M. Kawahito, T. Yasue, H. Komatsu, and T. Nakatani. A study of devirtualization techniques for a Java Just-In-Time compiler. In *ACM Conference on Object-Oriented Programming Systems, Languages, and Applications*, Oct. 2000.
19. C. Krintz, D. Grove, D. Lieber, V. Sarkar, and B. Calder. Reducing the overhead of dynamic compilation. *Software – Practice and Experience*, 31(8):717–738, Dec. 2000.
20. S. Liang and G. Bracha. Dynamic class loading in the Java virtual machine. In *Conference on Object-oriented programming, systems, languages, and applications (OOPSLA'98)*, pages 36–44, 1998.
21. M. Paleczny, C. Vic, and C. Click. The Java Hotspot(tm) server compiler. In *USENIX Java Virtual Machine Research and Technology Symposium*, 2001.
22. I. Pechtchanski and V. Sarkar. Dynamic optimistic whole program analysis: a framework and an application. In *ACM Conference on Object-Oriented Programming Systems, Languages, and Applications*, Oct. 2001.
23. V. C. Sreedhar, M. Burke, and J.-D. Choi. A framework for interprocedural optimization in the presence of dynamic class loading. In *SIGPLAN 2000 Conference on Programming Language Design and Implementation*, June 2000.
24. T. Suganuma, T. Yasue, M. Kawahito, H. Komatsu, and T. Nakatani. A dynamic optimization framework for a Java just-in-time compiler. In *ACM Conference on Object-Oriented Programming Systems, Languages, and Applications*, Oct. 2001.
25. M. N. Wegman and F. K. Zadeck. Constant propagation with conditional branches. *ACM Transactions on Programming Languages and Systems*, 13(2):181–210, 1991.
26. A. Zaks, V. Feldman, and N. Aizikowitz. Sealed calls in Java packages. In *Conference on Object-oriented programming, systems, languages, and applications (OOPSLA'00)*, pages 83–92, 2000.

Type-Safe Method Inlining

Neal Glew[1] and Jens Palsberg[2]

[1] aglew@acm.org
[2] Purdue University, Dept of Computer Science, W Lafayette, IN 47907, USA
palsberg@cs.purdue.edu

Abstract. In a typed language such as Java, inlining of virtual methods does not always preserve typability. The best known solution to this problem is to insert type casts, which may hurt performance. This paper presents a solution that never hurts performance. The solution is based on a transformation that modifies static type annotations and changes some virtual calls into static calls, which can then be safely inlined. The transformation is parameterised by a flow analysis, and for any analysis that satisfies certain conditions, the transformation is correct and idempotent. The paper presents the transformation, the conditions on the flow analysis, and proves the correctness properties; all in the context of a variant of Featherweight Java.

1 Introduction

1.1 Background

A number of recent compilers use typed intermediate languages (*e.g.*, [11, 12, 21, 6]) to obtain debugging and optimisation benefits [11, 19]. Such compilers require transformations that are typability preserving, that is, transformations that produce output that type checks. This paper is concerned with one such transformation, that of inlining of method calls in a statically-typed object-oriented language. While there has been substantial previous work on method inlining (*e.g.*, [2, 3]), the known approaches are either for an untyped language, or have to rely on adding type casts or extra types, as we explain next.

Consider the following well-typed Java program:

```
class B {                      // a code snippet:
  B m() { return this; }       B x = new C();
}                              x = x.m();
                               x = ((B)new C()).m();
class C extends B {
  C f;
  B m() {
    return this.f;
  }
}
```

B. Magnusson (Ed.): ECOOP 2002, LNCS 2374, pp. 525–544, 2002.

Both of the method calls x.m() and ((B)new C()).m() have a unique target method that is a small code fragment, so it makes sense to inline these calls.

In both cases, a compiler could inline by taking the body of m and replacing this with the actual receiver expression to get:

```
x = x.f;                    // does not type check
x = ((B)new C()).f          // does not type check
```

These two assignments do not type check. The reason is that while this in class C has static type C, both x and (B)new C() have static type B. Hence, both x.f and ((B)new C()).f will yield the compile-time error that there is no f-field in either x or (B)new C().

The problem can be solved by inserting type casts. In their Java compiler, Wright et al. [21] insert type casts (in the form of a typecase expression) of this in all translated method bodies. Applying this idea to our example program produces the following declaration for method m in class C:

```
B m() {
    return ((C)this).f;
}
```

After inlining, the two assignments type check:

```
x = ((C)x).f;                  // type checks
x = ((C)((B)new C())).f;       // type checks
```

A different approach was taken by Gagnon et al. [5] who first compile Java to an untyped representation of Java bytecode, and then infer types to regain static type annotations. Their results show that this works well for a substantial suite of benchmark programs. In general, however, their algorithm for type inference may fail, and in such cases they revert to inserting type casts.

A third approach, which does not require type casts at all, is to add new types to the program. Knoblock and Rehof [10] demonstrated how to do that automatically in such a way that type inference will succeed for all verifiable Java bytecode programs.

In general, inserting type casts may hurt performance, and adding new types may not be acceptable. Since these type casts and types are not added in the untyped setting, they are there just for the purposes of satisfying the type system. It is intellectually unsatisfying that we cannot just use the untyped techniques. Until now, it has remained an open problem to devise a scheme for supporting typability-preserving method inlining in a way that does not require the insertion of type casts or new types.

1.2   Our Result

We present an approach to typability-preserving method inlining that never hurts performance, and does not require the insertion of type casts or new types. Our approach is based on a transformation that modifies static type annotations and changes some virtual calls into static calls, which can then be safely inlined. The transformation is parameterised by a flow analysis, and for any analysis that satisfies certain conditions, the transformation is correct and idempotent. We present the transformation, the conditions on the flow analysis, and prove the correctness properties; all in the context of a variant of Featherweight Java. It is straightforward to extend our approach to full Java.

Note that our transformation, like most previous work, is a whole-program transformation. By making suitable conservative assumptions it could be used to transform separate program fragments. How effective this might be is beyond the scope of this paper. We also leave open the question of how suitable the transformation might be to a just-in-time compiler.

The flow analysis approximates the results of evaluating expressions. For each expression, it determines a set of classes such that every possible result of evaluating the expression is an instance of one of those classes. Given such a set the transformation can use the least upper bound as the new explicit type information. For our example program, the best flow set for both receiver expressions in the program is {C}, and the least upper bound for this set is C. Therefore, in the transformed program the code snippet is as follows—and it type checks:

```
C x = new C();        // the type of x has been changed to C
x = x.m();
x = ((C)new C()).m(); // the type cast has been changed to C
```

Inlining then produces the following well-typed code snippet:

```
C x = new C();
x = x.f;              // type checks
x = ((C)new C()).f;   // type checks
```

One result of our study is the need to align the flow analysis with the type system, and this is crucial to our proofs. In particular, there were several aspects of Java's type system that lead to unusual conditions on the flow analysis. One example is Java's lack of a bottom type leading to a nonemptyness condition on flow sets. Another example is the mixed use of subset [1, 14] and equality constraints [4]. (An idea also studied by Fähndrich and Aiken [4].) We were lead to this mixture by well known results about aligning flow analyses with type systems [16, 7, 15, 17, 10], and in particular that subset constraints correspond to subtyping. The Java type system allows the use of subtyping in some places but not in others. Thus, our flow analyses must satisfy subset constraints in some places and equality constraints in others.

Our approach does method inlining in two steps:

1. change some dynamic method invocations to static method invocations (and change the type annotations and the classes used in type casts) and
2. inline the static method invocations.

The idea is, as in previous work, that in a dynamic method dispatch e.m(e$_1$, ..., e$_n$), if all the objects that e could evaluate to are instances of classes which inherit m from a fixed class D, then the dynamic dispatch can be transformed to a static dispatch $e.D::m(e_1, \ldots, e_n)$. (The expression $e.D::m(e_1, \ldots, e_n)$ invokes D's version of m on e with e_1 through e_n as arguments.) A static dispatch $e.D::m(e_1, \ldots, e_n)$ can be inlined to $e'\{this, x_1, \ldots, x_n := e, e_1, \ldots, e_n\}$ where D has for method m, body e' and parameters x_1 through x_n. This is nothing other than applying a nonstandard reduction rule at compile time, and it is straightforward to show that the rule is typability preserving.

The following section presents our variant of Featherweight Java, Section 3 presents the constraints flow analyses must satisfy, and Section 4 presents the program transformation. The proofs of the correctness theorems are presented in three appendices.

2   The Language

We formalise our results in Featherweight Java [8] (FJ) extended with a static dispatch construct, a language we call FJS. The language and its presentation follow the original FJ paper as closely as possible.

As in FJ, an FJS program is a list of class definitions and an expression to be evaluated. Each class definition is in a stylised form. Every class extends another, top level classes extend Object. Every class has exactly one constructor. This constructor has one parameter for each of the fields of the class, with the same names and in the same order. It first calls the superclass constructor with the parameters that correspond to the superclass's fields. Then it uses the remaining parameters to initialise the fields declared in the class. Constructors are the only place where super or = appear in an FJS program. The receiver of a field access or method invocation is always explicit, this is used to refer to an object's fields and methods. FJS is functional, so a method body consists just of a return statement with an expression and there is no void type. There are just six forms of expressions: variables, field access, object constructors, dynamic casts, dynamic method invocation, and static method invocation. Although FJS does not have super, static method invocation can be used to call a superclass's methods. The remainder of this section formalises the language.

2.1   Syntax and Semantics

The syntax of FJS is:

$$P ::= (\overline{CD}, e)$$
$$CD ::= class\ C\ extends\ C\ \{\overline{C}\ f^\ell;\ K\ \overline{M}\}$$
$$K ::= C(\overline{C}\ \overline{f})\ \{super(\overline{f});\ this.\overline{f} = \overline{f};\}$$
$$M ::= C\ m(\overline{C}\ \overline{x^\ell})\ \{return^\ell e;\}$$
$$e ::= x^\ell \mid e.f^\ell \mid new^\ell\ C(\overline{e}) \mid (C)^\ell e \mid e.m(\overline{e})^\ell \mid e.C::m(\overline{e})^\ell$$

The metavariables A, B, C, D, and E range over class names; f and g range over field names; m ranges over method names; x ranges over variables; d and e range over expressions; M ranges over method definitions; K ranges over constructors; CD ranges over class definitions; and P ranges over programs. Object is a class name, but no program may give it a definition; this is a variable, but no program may use it as a parameter. The over bar notation denotes sequences, so $\overline{\mathtt{f}}$ abbreviates $\mathtt{f}_1, \ldots, \mathtt{f}_n$. This notation also denotes pairs of sequences in an obvious way—$\overline{\mathtt{C}}$ $\overline{\mathtt{f}^\ell}$ abbreviates $\mathtt{C}_1 \; \mathtt{f}_1^{\ell_1}, \ldots, \mathtt{C}_n \; \mathtt{f}_n^{\ell_n}$, $\overline{\mathtt{C}} \; \overline{\mathtt{f}^\ell}$; abbreviates $\mathtt{C}_1 \; \mathtt{f}_1^{\ell_1}; \; \cdots; \; \mathtt{C}_n \; \mathtt{f}_n^{\ell_n};$, and this.$\overline{\mathtt{f}}$=$\overline{\mathtt{f}}$ abbreviates this.$\mathtt{f}_1$=$\mathtt{f}_1$; $\cdots$; this.$\mathtt{f}_n$=$\mathtt{f}_n$. The empty sequence is •, and comma concatenates sequences. Sequences of class definitions, field declarations, method definitions, and parameter declarations may not contain duplicate names. We abuse notation and consider a sequence of class definitions to also be a mapping from class names to class definitions, and write $\overline{\mathtt{CD}}(\mathtt{C})$ to mean the definition of C under the map corresponding to $\overline{\mathtt{CD}}$. Any class name C except Object appearing in a program must be given a definition by that program, and the **extends** clauses of a program must be acyclic.

Class definition **class** C **extends** D $\{\overline{\mathtt{C}} \; \overline{\mathtt{f}^\ell};$ K $\overline{\mathtt{M}}\}$ declares class C a subclass of D. In addition to the fields of its superclass, C has fields $\overline{\mathtt{f}^\ell}$ of types $\overline{\mathtt{C}}$. K is the constructor for the class, and has the stylised form described above. $\overline{\mathtt{M}}$ are the methods declared by C, they may be new methods or might override those of D. C also inherits all methods of D that it does not override. Method declaration C $\mathtt{m}(\overline{\mathtt{C}} \; \overline{\mathtt{x}^\ell})$ {**return**$^\ell$e;} declares a method m with return type C, with parameters $\overline{\mathtt{x}^\ell}$ of types $\overline{\mathtt{C}}$, and that when invoked evaluates expression e and returns it as the result of the invocation.

As mentioned above, there are six forms of expression: variables x, field selection e.$\mathtt{f}^\ell$, object constructors new$^\ell$ C$(\overline{\mathtt{e}})$, casts (C)$^\ell$e, dynamic method invocations e.$\mathtt{m}(\overline{\mathtt{e}})^\ell$, and static method invocations e.C::$\mathtt{m}(\overline{\mathtt{e}})^\ell$. The latter invokes C's version of method m on object e, which should be in C or one of its subclasses.

Metavariable ℓ ranges over a set of labels. Notice that there is a label associated with all expressions, fields, method returns, and formal arguments; these labels are assumed to be unique. For a program P, *labels*(P) denotes the set of labels used in P. To simplify the technical definitions later, all the field names and argument names must be distinct. Furthermore, the label on any variable occurrence must be the same as the label on its declaration, and any two occurrences of this in a class must have the same label. Any well-typed program can easily be transformed to satisfy these conditions. Function *lab* maps an expression, a field name, or an argument name to its label.

Some auxiliary definitions that are used in the rest of the paper appear in Figure 1. Unlike the FJ paper, we do not make the list of class declarations global, but have them appear explicitly as parameters to functions, predicates, and rules. Function *fields*$(\overline{\mathtt{CD}}, \mathtt{C})$ returns a list of C's fields and their types; *mtype*$(\overline{\mathtt{CD}}, \mathtt{C}, \mathtt{m})$ returns the type of method m in class C, this type has the form $\overline{\mathtt{C}} \to \mathtt{C}$ where C is the return type and $\overline{\mathtt{C}}$ are the argument types; *mbody*$(\overline{\mathtt{CD}}, \mathtt{C}, \mathtt{m})$ returns the body of method m in class C, this has the form $(\ell, \overline{\mathtt{x}}, \mathtt{e})$ where ℓ is the label of the return statement, e is the expression to evaluate, and $\overline{\mathtt{x}}$ are the parameter names; *impl*$(\overline{\mathtt{CD}}, \mathtt{C}, \mathtt{m})$ returns the class from which class C inherits method m (this might be C itself if C declares m), this has the form D::m where D is the class. Predicate *override*$(\overline{\mathtt{CD}}, \mathtt{D}, \mathtt{m}, \overline{\mathtt{C}} \to \mathtt{C})$ is true when method m of type $\overline{\mathtt{C}} \to \mathtt{C}$ may be

Field Lookup:

$$fields(\overline{\texttt{CD}}, \texttt{Object}) = \bullet \tag{1}$$

$$\frac{\overline{\texttt{CD}}(\texttt{C}) = \texttt{class C extends D } \{\overline{\texttt{C}}\ \overline{\texttt{f}^\ell};\ \texttt{K } \overline{\texttt{M}}\} \qquad fields(\overline{\texttt{CD}}, \texttt{D}) = \overline{\texttt{D}}\ \overline{\texttt{g}}}{fields(\overline{\texttt{CD}}, \texttt{C}) = \overline{\texttt{D}}\ \overline{\texttt{g}}, \overline{\texttt{C}}\ \overline{\texttt{f}}} \tag{2}$$

Method Type Lookup:

$$\frac{\overline{\texttt{CD}}(\texttt{C}) = \texttt{class C extends D } \{\overline{\texttt{C}}\ \overline{\texttt{f}^{\ell_1}};\ \texttt{K } \overline{\texttt{M}}\} \qquad \texttt{B}_0\ \texttt{m}(\overline{\texttt{B}}\ \overline{\texttt{x}^{\ell_2}})\ \{\texttt{return}^\ell\texttt{e};\} \in \overline{\texttt{M}}}{mtype(\overline{\texttt{CD}}, \texttt{C}, \texttt{m}) = \overline{\texttt{B}} \to \texttt{B}_0} \tag{3}$$

$$\frac{\overline{\texttt{CD}}(\texttt{C}) = \texttt{class C extends D } \{\overline{\texttt{C}}\ \overline{\texttt{f}^\ell};\ \texttt{K } \overline{\texttt{M}}\} \qquad \texttt{m not defined in } \overline{\texttt{M}}}{mtype(\overline{\texttt{CD}}, \texttt{C}, \texttt{m}) = mtype(\overline{\texttt{CD}}, \texttt{D}, \texttt{m})} \tag{4}$$

Method Body Lookup:

$$\frac{\overline{\texttt{CD}}(\texttt{C}) = \texttt{class C extends D } \{\overline{\texttt{C}}\ \overline{\texttt{f}^{\ell_1}};\ \texttt{K } \overline{\texttt{M}}\} \qquad \texttt{B}_0\ \texttt{m}(\overline{\texttt{B}}\ \overline{\texttt{x}^{\ell_2}})\ \{\texttt{return}^\ell\texttt{e};\} \in \overline{\texttt{M}}}{mbody(\overline{\texttt{CD}}, \texttt{C}, \texttt{m}) = (\ell, \overline{\texttt{x}}, \texttt{e})} \tag{5}$$

$$\frac{\overline{\texttt{CD}}(\texttt{C}) = \texttt{class C extends D } \{\overline{\texttt{C}}\ \overline{\texttt{f}^\ell};\ \texttt{K } \overline{\texttt{M}}\} \qquad \texttt{m not defined in } \overline{\texttt{M}}}{mbody(\overline{\texttt{CD}}, \texttt{C}, \texttt{m}) = mbody(\overline{\texttt{CD}}, \texttt{D}, \texttt{m})} \tag{6}$$

Class of Method Lookup:

$$\frac{\overline{\texttt{CD}}(\texttt{C}) = \texttt{class C extends D } \{\overline{\texttt{C}}\ \overline{\texttt{f}^{\ell_1}};\ \texttt{K } \overline{\texttt{M}}\} \qquad \texttt{B}_0\ \texttt{m}(\overline{\texttt{B}}\ \overline{\texttt{x}^{\ell_2}})\ \{\texttt{return}^\ell\texttt{e};\} \in \overline{\texttt{M}}}{impl(\overline{\texttt{CD}}, \texttt{C}, \texttt{m}) = \texttt{C}::\texttt{m}} \tag{7}$$

$$\frac{\overline{\texttt{CD}}(\texttt{C}) = \texttt{class C extends D } \{\overline{\texttt{C}}\ \overline{\texttt{f}^\ell};\ \texttt{K } \overline{\texttt{M}}\} \qquad \texttt{m not defined in } \overline{\texttt{M}}}{impl(\overline{\texttt{CD}}, \texttt{C}, \texttt{m}) = impl(\overline{\texttt{CD}}, \texttt{D}, \texttt{m})} \tag{8}$$

Valid Method Overriding:

$$\frac{mtype(\overline{\texttt{CD}}, \texttt{D}, \texttt{m}) = \overline{\texttt{D}} \to \texttt{D}_0 \text{ implies } \overline{\texttt{C}} = \overline{\texttt{D}} \text{ and } \texttt{C}_0 = \texttt{D}_0}{override(\overline{\texttt{CD}}, \texttt{D}, \texttt{m}, \overline{\texttt{C}} \to \texttt{C}_0)} \tag{9}$$

Fig. 1. Auxiliary Definitions

declared in a subclass of D. It checks that if D declares or inherits m then it has the same type, as required by Java's type system. The more general rule with contravariant argument types and covariant result types could be used, and the results of this paper would still hold (the definition of acceptable flow would change slightly).

The operational semantics of the language appear in Figure 2. Metavariable X ranges over evaluation contexts, which are expressions with exactly one hole; $X\langle e \rangle$ denotes the expression formed by replacing the hole in X by the expression e. Unlike the FJ paper, in addition to making the list of class declarations explicit in the rules we make the evaluation context explicit as well.

Because the language is functional and each class has exactly one constructor of a particular form, the values of the language, which are all objects, can be represented using object constructors $\texttt{new}^\ell\ \texttt{C}(\overline{\texttt{e}})$. Field access reduces to the

$$\frac{\mathit{fields}(\overline{\text{CD}}, \text{C}) = \overline{\text{C}} \ \overline{\text{f}}}{(\overline{\text{CD}}, \text{X}\langle \text{new}^{\ell_1} \ \text{C}(\overline{\text{e}}).\text{f}_i{}^{\ell_2}\rangle) \mapsto (\overline{\text{CD}}, \text{X}\langle \text{e}_i\rangle)} \tag{10}$$

$$\frac{\overline{\text{CD}} \vdash \text{C} <: \text{D}}{(\overline{\text{CD}}, \text{X}\langle(\text{D})^{\ell_1}\text{new}^{\ell_2} \ \text{C}(\overline{\text{e}})\rangle) \mapsto (\overline{\text{CD}}, \text{X}\langle\text{new}^{\ell_2} \ \text{C}(\overline{\text{e}})\rangle)} \tag{11}$$

$$\frac{\mathit{mbody}(\overline{\text{CD}}, \text{C}, \text{m}) = (\ell, \overline{\text{x}}, \text{e}_0)}{(\overline{\text{CD}}, \text{X}\langle\text{new}^{\ell_1} \ \text{C}(\overline{\text{e}}).\text{m}(\overline{\text{d}})^{\ell_2}\rangle) \mapsto (\overline{\text{CD}}, \text{X}\langle\text{e}_0\{\text{this}, \overline{\text{x}} := \text{new}^{\ell_1} \ \text{C}(\overline{\text{e}}), \overline{\text{d}}\}\rangle)} \tag{12}$$

$$\frac{\mathit{mbody}(\overline{\text{CD}}, \text{D}, \text{m}) = (\ell, \overline{\text{x}}, \text{e}_0)}{(\overline{\text{CD}}, \text{X}\langle\text{new}^{\ell_1} \ \text{C}(\overline{\text{e}}).\text{D}::\text{m}(\overline{\text{d}})^{\ell_2}\rangle) \mapsto (\overline{\text{CD}}, \text{X}\langle\text{e}_0\{\text{this}, \overline{\text{x}} := \text{new}^{\ell_1} \ \text{C}(\overline{\text{e}}), \overline{\text{d}}\}\rangle)} \tag{13}$$

Fig. 2. Operational Semantics

appropriate element of $\overline{\text{e}}$. The cast $(\text{C})^{\ell_1}\text{new}^{\ell_2} \ \text{D}(\overline{\text{e}})$ reduces to the object new^{ℓ_2} $\text{D}(\overline{\text{e}})$ if D is a subclass of C. If D is not a subclass of C then the cast is irreducible representing that the cast fails as a checked run-time error. The reduction rule for method invocation $\text{new}^{\ell_1} \ \text{C}(\overline{\text{e}}).\text{m}(\overline{\text{d}})^{\ell_2}$ looks up the method body of m in C, if this is $(\ell, \overline{\text{x}}, \text{e}_0)$ then the reduced expression is the body e_0 with the actuals $\overline{\text{d}}$ substituted for the formals $\overline{\text{x}}$ and the object $\text{new}^{\ell_1} \ \text{C}(\overline{\text{e}})$ substituted for this. Static method invocation $\text{new}^{\ell_1} \ \text{C}(\overline{\text{e}}).\text{D}::\text{m}(\overline{\text{d}})^\ell$ reduces similarly except that the method is looked up in D not C. Note that this method lookup can be done at compile time and a static method invocation can be implemented as a direct call rather than an indirect call through a virtual-dispatch table.

An irreducible expression is *stuck* if it is of the form $\text{X}\langle\text{e}.\text{f}^\ell\rangle$, $\text{X}\langle\text{e}.\text{m}(\overline{\text{e}})^\ell\rangle$, or $\text{X}\langle\text{e}.\text{D}::\text{m}(\overline{\text{e}})^\ell\rangle$. The type system prevents stuck expressions from occurring during execution of a program. Irreducible expressions that are not stuck are of the form $\text{v}::=\text{new}^\ell \ \text{C}(\overline{\text{v}})$ or $\text{X}\langle(\text{C})^{\ell_1}\text{new}^{\ell_2} \ \text{D}(\overline{\text{e}})\rangle$ where D is not a subclass of C; the former represents normal termination with a fully evaluated object, the latter represents a failed cast.

2.2 Type System

The type system consists of the following judgements:

Judgement	Meaning
$\overline{\text{CD}} \vdash \text{C} <: \text{D}$	C is a subtype of D
$\overline{\text{CD}}; \varGamma \vdash \text{e} \in \text{C}$	e is well formed and of type C
$\overline{\text{CD}} \vdash \text{M OK in C}$	M is well formed in class C
$\overline{\text{CD}} \vdash \text{CD OK}$	CD is well formed
$\vdash \text{P} \in \text{C}$	P is well formed and of type C

A typing context $\varGamma$ has the form $\overline{\text{x}}:\overline{\text{C}}$ where there are no duplicate variable names. The only types are the names of classes, and such a type includes all instances of that class and its subclasses. The rules appear in Figure 3. The bar notation denotes sequences of typing judgements, so $\overline{\text{CD}}; \varGamma \vdash \overline{\text{e}} \in \overline{\text{C}}$ abbreviates $\overline{\text{CD}}; \varGamma \vdash \text{e}_1 \in \text{C}_1, \ldots, \overline{\text{CD}}; \varGamma \vdash \text{e}_n \in \text{C}_n$.

Subtyping:

$$\overline{\text{CD}} \vdash \text{C} <: \text{C} \tag{14}$$

$$\frac{\overline{\text{CD}} \vdash \text{C} <: \text{D} \qquad \overline{\text{CD}} \vdash \text{D} <: \text{E}}{\overline{\text{CD}} \vdash \text{C} <: \text{E}} \tag{15}$$

$$\frac{\overline{\text{CD}}(\text{C}) = \texttt{class C extends D \{...\}}}{\overline{\text{CD}} \vdash \text{C} <: \text{D}} \tag{16}$$

Expression Typing:

$$\overline{\text{CD}}; \Gamma \vdash \text{x}^\ell \in \Gamma(\text{x}) \tag{17}$$

$$\frac{\overline{\text{CD}}; \Gamma \vdash \text{e}_0 \in \text{C}_0 \qquad \textit{fields}(\overline{\text{CD}}, \text{C}_0) = \overline{\text{C}} \ \overline{\text{f}}}{\overline{\text{CD}}; \Gamma \vdash \text{e}_0.\text{f}_i^\ell \in \text{C}_i} \tag{18}$$

$$\frac{\textit{fields}(\overline{\text{CD}}, \text{C}) = \overline{\text{D}} \ \overline{\text{f}} \qquad \overline{\text{CD}}; \Gamma \vdash \overline{\text{e}} \in \overline{\text{E}} \qquad \overline{\text{CD}} \vdash \overline{\text{E}} <: \overline{\text{D}}}{\overline{\text{CD}}; \Gamma \vdash \texttt{new}^\ell \ \text{C}(\overline{\text{e}}) \in \text{C}} \tag{19}$$

$$\frac{\overline{\text{CD}}; \Gamma \vdash \text{e}_0 \in \text{D}}{\overline{\text{CD}}; \Gamma \vdash (\text{C})^\ell \text{e}_0 \in \text{C}} \tag{20}$$

$$\frac{\overline{\text{CD}}; \Gamma \vdash \text{e}_0 \in \text{C}_0 \qquad \textit{mtype}(\overline{\text{CD}}, \text{C}_0, \text{m}) = \overline{\text{D}} \rightarrow \text{C} \qquad \overline{\text{CD}}; \Gamma \vdash \overline{\text{e}} \in \overline{\text{C}} \qquad \overline{\text{CD}} \vdash \overline{\text{C}} <: \overline{\text{D}}}{\overline{\text{CD}}; \Gamma \vdash \text{e}_0.\text{m}(\overline{\text{e}})^\ell \in \text{C}} \tag{21}$$

$$\frac{\begin{array}{l} \overline{\text{CD}}; \Gamma \vdash \text{e}_0 \in \text{C}_0 \\ \overline{\text{CD}} \vdash \text{C}_0 <: \text{D} \\ \textit{mtype}(\overline{\text{CD}}, \text{D}, \text{m}) = \overline{\text{E}} \rightarrow \text{E}_0 \\ \overline{\text{CD}}; \Gamma \vdash \overline{\text{e}} \in \overline{\text{C}} \\ \overline{\text{CD}} \vdash \overline{\text{C}} <: \overline{\text{E}} \end{array}}{\overline{\text{CD}}; \Gamma \vdash \text{e}_0.\text{D}\texttt{::}\text{m}(\overline{\text{e}})^\ell \in \text{E}_0} \tag{22}$$

Method Typing:

$$\frac{\begin{array}{l} \overline{\text{CD}}; \texttt{this} : \text{C}, \overline{\text{x}} : \overline{\text{C}} \vdash \text{e}_0 \in \text{E}_0 \\ \overline{\text{CD}} \vdash \text{E}_0 <: \text{C}_0 \\ \overline{\text{CD}}(\text{C}) = \texttt{class C extends D \{...\}} \\ \textit{override}(\overline{\text{CD}}, \text{D}, \text{m}, \overline{\text{C}} \rightarrow \text{C}_0) \end{array}}{\overline{\text{CD}} \vdash \text{C}_0 \ \text{m}(\overline{\text{C}} \ \overline{\text{x}^\ell}) \ \{\texttt{return}^\ell \text{e}_0\texttt{;}\} \ \text{OK in C}} \tag{23}$$

Class Typing:

$$\frac{\overline{\text{CD}} \vdash \overline{\text{M}} \text{ OK in C} \qquad \textit{fields}(\overline{\text{CD}}, \text{D}) = \overline{\text{D}} \ \overline{\text{g}} \qquad \text{K} = \text{C}(\overline{\text{D}} \ \overline{\text{g}}, \ \overline{\text{C}} \ \overline{\text{f}}) \ \{\texttt{super}(\overline{\text{g}})\texttt{;} \ \texttt{this}.\overline{\text{f}}{=}\overline{\text{f}}\texttt{;}\}}{\overline{\text{CD}} \vdash \texttt{class C extends D} \ \{\overline{\text{C}} \ \overline{\text{f}^\ell}\texttt{;} \ \text{K} \ \overline{\text{M}}\} \ \text{OK}} \tag{24}$$

Program Typing:

$$\frac{\overline{\text{CD}} \vdash \overline{\text{CD}} \text{ OK} \qquad \overline{\text{CD}}; \bullet \vdash \text{e} \in \text{C}}{\vdash (\overline{\text{CD}}, \text{e}) \in \text{C}} \tag{25}$$

Fig. 3. Typing Rules

The rules for constructors and method invocation check that each actual has a subtype of the corresponding formal. The typing rule for dynamic method dispatch looks up the type of the method in the class of the receiver. The typing rule for static method dispatch $\text{e}.\text{D}\texttt{::}\text{m}(\overline{\text{e}})^\ell$ requires that e has some subtype of D and looks up the type of the method in D. As in FJ, the typing rules allow *stupid casts*, such as $(C)^{\ell_1} \text{new}^{\ell_2} D(\bar{e})$ where D is not a subclass of C and the cast will always fail. Allowing stupid casts is needed to prove type preservation. Unlike in FJ, FJS has only one rule for casts, which just requires the expression being cast to have some type. This rule is equivalent to FJ's three rules except that it does not issue stupid-cast warnings. The type system is sound, that is, well-typed programs never get stuck. This fact is stated in the following theorem, which can be proved by standard methods [13, 20, 8].

Theorem 1 (Type Soundness). *If* $\vdash P \in C$ *then* P *does not reduce to a program with a stuck expression.*

The rules are syntax directed, with the exception of the rules for subtyping. So, disregarding the details of how subtyping judgments are derived, for any program there is exactly one derivation possible. Thus for a program P and any ℓ, which can be the label of a field, method parameter, method return, or expression appearing in P, there is a uniquely determined static type for the program point labeled ℓ, written *static-type*(ℓ, P).

3 Flow Analysis

A flow analysis approximates the results of evaluating expressions. In our setting, flow information for an expression is a set of classes such that the expression will evaluate to an instance of one of those classes.

For a program P, *classes*(P) denotes the set of class names declared in P, *flow*(P) is the powerset of *classes*(P); *subclasses*(P, C) is the set of subclasses of C (including C). Flow information for P is a member of *flow-information*(P) = *labels*(P) → *flow*(P). Metavariables S and T range over *flow*(P) and φ ranges over *flow-information*(P). We order *flow-information*(P) such that $\varphi_1 \leq \varphi_2$ if and only if $\varphi_1(\ell) \subseteq \varphi_2(\ell)$ for every $\ell \in$ *labels*(P). In *flow-information*(P), the least element is $\lambda\ell.\emptyset$ and the greatest element is $\lambda\ell.classes(P)$.

Some members of *flow-information*(P) are not valid approximations of the results of evaluating expressions in P, and do not support our program transformation. The flow analyses with the desired properties are the ones that are both *acceptable* and *type respecting*. (The term "type respecting" was coined by Jagannathan *et al.* [9].) Intuitively, an acceptable analysis contains sets that are *big* enough, in that it correctly approximates the results of evaluating expressions. A type-respecting analysis contains sets that are *small* enough, in that it is at least as precise as the static type system, that is, each flow only contains classes that are subclasses of the corresponding static type. For a program P, we define:

$$acceptable(P) = \{\ \varphi \in \textit{flow-information}(P)\ |$$
$$\varphi \text{ satisfies the conditions listed in Figure 4 }\}$$
$$\textit{type-respecting}(P) = \{\ \varphi \in \textit{flow-information}(P)\ |$$
$$\forall \ell \in \textit{labels}(P) : \varphi(\ell) \subseteq \textit{subclasses}(P, \textit{static-type}(\ell, P))\ \}$$
$$\textit{flow-analysis}(P) = \textit{acceptable}(P) \cap \textit{type-respecting}(P).$$

The conditions in Figure 4 for a flow analysis to be acceptable are somewhat unusual. The design of those conditions is influenced by the way the program transformation will use flow information to change type annotations: for a program point with label ℓ, the transformation uses the least upper bound of $\varphi(\ell)$, written $\sqcup\varphi(\ell)$, as the new type annotation. With that in mind, here is a closer look at the rules in Figure (4).

First, notice that Rule (40) ensures that least upper bounds are of a nonempty set. Rules (26)–(37) are related to one way of specifying 0-CFA [18, 14, 15]. The unusual aspect of them is that they are a mixture of subset constraints [14] and equality constraints [15]. If the sole purpose were to approximate the results of evaluating expressions, then all of the equality constraints can be relaxed to be subset constraints. The reason for using equality constraints in some cases is to align the flow analysis with the type system. The type system does not have a general subsumption rule that allows subtyping to be used everywhere. Rather, in the type rules in Figure 3, subtyping is used in four places: Rule (19) for new-expressions, Rule (21) for calls, Rule (22) for static calls, and Rule (23) for method typing. In each case, there is a subset constraint in the corresponding rule for acceptable flow analyses in Figure 4: Rule (27) for new-expressions, Rule (30) for dynamic method invocations, Rule (33) for static method invocations, and Rule (37) for method typing. In contrast, Rule (18) for field selection requires the type of the field to equal the type of the field-selection expression; this is matched by the equality constraint in Rule (26). A similar comment applies to Rules (31) and (34). Rules (29), (32), and (35) have no counterparts in the type system and are needed to ensure that the flow analysis approximates the results of evaluating expressions. Rule (36) is rather conservative: it says that the **this** object always can be an object of the class in which **this** occurs. The rule is needed because of Rule (23) for method typing, which asserts that **this** has type C. Finally, Rules (38) and (39) ensure that the signature of a method and the signature of an overriding method are the same.

A variant of Class Hierarchy Analysis [2] (CHA) can be defined as follows:

$$CHA(\mathrm{P}) = \lambda\ell.subclasses(\mathrm{P}, static\text{-}type(\ell, \mathrm{P})).$$

It is straightforward to show that $CHA(\mathrm{P})$ is the coarsest flow analysis of P, as stated in the following theorem.

Theorem 2. (CHA) $CHA(\mathrm{P})$ *is the greatest element of flow-analysis*(P).

Note that *flow-analysis*(P) does not have a least element. This is due to Rule (40) that requires all flows to be nonempty. If Java had a bottom type, then this type could be used as the least upper bound of the empty set and Rule (40) would not be needed. Then *flow-analysis*(P) would be a meet semilattice with both a greatest and least element. However, Java does not have a bottom type, so we have kept this constraint.

The property of being a flow analysis is preserved during computation, as stated in the following theorem, which is proved in Appendix A. (Palsberg [14] proved a similar result for the λ-calculus.)

– for each $e.f^\ell$ in P:

$$\varphi(lab(f)) = \varphi(\ell) \tag{26}$$

– for each new^ℓ $D(\bar{e})$ in P, where $fields(\overline{CD}, D) = \bar{E}\ \bar{f}$:

$$\varphi(lab(\bar{e})) \subseteq \varphi(lab(\bar{f})) \tag{27}$$

$$D \in \varphi(\ell) \tag{28}$$

– for each $(D)^\ell e$ in P:

$$\varphi(lab(e)) \cap subclasses(P, D) = \varphi(\ell) \tag{29}$$

– for each $e.m(\bar{e})^\ell$ in P and each class D in P, where $mbody(\overline{CD}, D, m) = (\ell', \bar{x}, e')$, $impl(\overline{CD}, D, m) = E::m$, and ℓ'' is the label for E's **this** occurrences:

$$D \in \varphi(lab(e)) \Rightarrow \varphi(lab(\bar{e})) \subseteq \varphi(lab(\bar{x})) \tag{30}$$

$$D \in \varphi(lab(e)) \Rightarrow \varphi(\ell') = \varphi(\ell) \tag{31}$$

$$\varphi(lab(e)) \subseteq \varphi(\ell'') \tag{32}$$

– for each $e.D::m(\bar{e})^\ell$ in P, where $mbody(\overline{CD}, D, m) = (\ell', \bar{x}, e')$, $impl(\overline{CD}, D, m) = E::m$, and ℓ'' is the label for E's **this** occurrences

$$\varphi(lab(\bar{e})) \subseteq \varphi(lab(\bar{x})) \tag{33}$$

$$\varphi(\ell') = \varphi(\ell) \tag{34}$$

$$\varphi(lab(e)) \subseteq \varphi(\ell'') \tag{35}$$

– for each class C in P, where ℓ is the label for C's **this** occurrences:

$$C \in \varphi(\ell) \tag{36}$$

– for each method in P, with body $\{return^\ell e_0;\}$

$$\varphi(lab(e_0)) \subseteq \varphi(\ell) \tag{37}$$

– for each method name m declared or inherited in class C of P, if

$$\overline{CD}(C) = class\ C\ extends\ D\ \{\bar{C}\ \bar{f};\ K\ \bar{M}\}$$
$$mbody(\overline{CD}, C, m) = (\ell_1, \bar{x}_1, e_1)$$
$$mbody(\overline{CD}, D, m) = (\ell_2, \bar{x}_2, e_2)$$

then

$$\varphi(lab(\bar{x}_1)) = \varphi(lab(\bar{x}_2)) \tag{38}$$

$$\varphi(\ell_1) = \varphi(\ell_2) \tag{39}$$

– for each $\ell \in labels(P)$:

$$\varphi(\ell) \neq \emptyset \tag{40}$$

Fig. 4. Requirements for an acceptable flow analyses φ of a program $P = (\overline{CD}, e)$.

Theorem 3 (Flow Preservation). *If* $\varphi \in$ *flow-analysis*(P_1) *and* $P_1 \mapsto P_2$, *then* $\varphi \in$ *flow-analysis*(P_2).

It is straightforward to compute $CHA(P)$. However, since $CHA(P)$ is the greatest element of *flow-analysis*(P), it is the most conservative choice of flow analysis and will lead to the least number of inlinings. This raises the question of whether other polynomial-time algorithms could do better. The main difficulty is that *flow-analysis*(P) does not have a least element so there is not a unique best choice of flow analysis that improves on $CHA(P)$.

To illustrate that indeed there is a better polynomial time algorithm, we now define a flow analysis with mixed constraints and nonempty sets; the analysis is called $MN(P)$ (for Mixed and Nonempty). First, the notion of *lifting* a flow analysis is:

$$lift(\varphi) \;:\; \textit{flow-information}(P) \rightarrow \textit{flow-information}(P)$$
$$lift(\varphi) = \lambda \ell. \begin{cases} \varphi(\ell) & \text{if } \sqcup \varphi(\ell) \text{ exists} \\ \{\; static\text{-}type(\ell, P) \;\} & \text{otherwise} \end{cases}$$

Notice that $lift(\varphi)(\ell) \neq \emptyset$ for all $\ell \in labels(P)$. For Featherweight Java and FJS, $\sqcup\varphi(\ell)$ exists for all nonempty sets $\varphi(\ell)$. The full Java type system enables multiple subtyping among interfaces which can lead to nonempty flows without a least upper bound.

Second, the definition of $MN(P)$ is:

$\varphi_0 =$ the least flow analysis satisfying Rules (26)–(39)

$MN(P) =$ the least flow analysis greater than $lift(\varphi_0)$ satisfying Rules (26)–(39)

This algorithm is polynomial time: φ_0 takes polynomial time to compute using the technique of Fähndrich and Aiken [4], which intuitively is a fixed-point computation with $\lambda\ell.\emptyset$ as the starting point. Lifting clearly takes polynomial time, and $MN(P)$ takes polynomial time to compute by using the Fähndrich-Aiken algorithm again, but this time with $lift(\varphi_0)$ as the starting point for the fixed-point computation. This two-step procedure makes $\sqcup MN(P)(\ell)$ equal to $static\text{-}type(\ell, P)$ for any $\ell \in labels(P)$ such that $\varphi_0(\ell) = \emptyset$. Thus the program transformation based on $MN(P)$ will not change the type annotation for the program points labeled by such ℓ.

There might be worthwhile elements of *flow-analysis*(P) other than $CHA(P)$ and $MN(P)$. Any element of *flow-analysis*(P) can be used as an argument to the program transformation, which we present next.

4   Program Transformation

The program transformation is parameterized by a flow analysis, and it operates on program fragments and type environments in a compositional fashion. It transforms each program fragment into a similar program fragment with the same label, and it transforms each type environment into a type environment which defines the same variables. The changes made by the transformation are that:

- it changes some dynamic method invocations to static method invocations,
- it changes the type annotations, and
- it changes the classes used in type casts.

In each case, the change is made on the basis of the supplied flow analysis. Specifically, (1) a dynamic call is changed to a static call when the flow analysis determines that there is a unique target method and (2) a type annotation and the class in a type cast are changed to the least upper bound of the classes in the corresponding flow. Taking the least upper bound of the classes in a flow is justified because the transformation is restricted to flow analyses that are acceptable and type respecting, so: (i) all flows are nonempty, (ii) nonempty sets of classes admit least upper bounds because FJS is a single-inheritance language, and (iii) the property of being type respecting implies that the new types (that is, the least upper bounds) can only more refined than the old ones.

The transformation consists of the following cases:

Transformation	Meaning
$[\![P]\!]_\varphi$	the transformation of P using φ
$[\![CD]\!]_\varphi^{\overline{CD}}$	the transformation of CD using φ and $\overline{CD}$
$[\![K]\!]_\varphi$	the transformation of K using φ
$[\![M]\!]_\varphi^{\overline{CD}}$	the transformation of M using φ and $\overline{CD}$
$[\![e]\!]_\varphi^{\overline{CD}}$	the transformation of e using φ and $\overline{CD}$
$[\![\Gamma]\!]_\varphi$	the transformation of Γ using φ

The definition of the transformation appears in Figure 5.

We now present four correctness theorems: the transformation preserves typability, the transformation is operationally correct, a flow analysis of the original program is also a flow analysis of the transformed program, and the transformation is idempotent. First our main result, which is proved in Appendix B.

Theorem 4 (Typability Preservation). *Suppose* $\varphi \in$ *flow-analysis*(P) *and* $P = (\overline{CD}, e)$. *If* $\vdash P \in C$ *then* $\vdash [\![P]\!]_\varphi \in \sqcup\varphi(lab(e))$.

The transformation is also operationally correct, in that the transformed program simulates the original program step for step and vice versa, as stated in the following theorem, which is proved in Appendix C. Operational correctness for a multistep computation follows from Theorems 3 and 5.

Theorem 5 (Operational Correctness). *If* $\varphi \in$ *flow-analysis*(P$_1$) *then:* P$_1 \mapsto$ P$_2$ *if and only if* $[\![P_1]\!]_\varphi \mapsto [\![P_2]\!]_\varphi$.

It is straightforward to prove that a flow analysis of a program is also a flow analysis of the transformed program, as stated in the following theorem.

Theorem 6 (Analysis Preservation). *If* $\varphi \in$ *flow-analysis*(P), *then* $\varphi \in$ *flow-analysis*($[\![P]\!]_\varphi$).

$$[\![(\overline{CD},e)]\!]_\varphi = ([\![\overline{CD}]\!]_\varphi^{\overline{CD}}, [\![e]\!]_\varphi^{\overline{CD}})$$

$$[\![\texttt{class C extends D } \{\overline{C}\ \overline{f}^\ell;\ K\ \overline{M}\}]\!]_\varphi^{\overline{CD}} = \texttt{class C extends D } \{$$
$$\sqcup\varphi(\overline{\ell})\ \overline{f}^\ell;\ [\![K]\!]_\varphi\ [\![\overline{M}]\!]_\varphi^{\overline{CD}}\}$$

$$[\![\texttt{C(}\overline{D}\ \overline{f}\texttt{) }\{\texttt{super(}\overline{f1}\texttt{); this.}\overline{f2=f2}\}]\!]_\varphi = \texttt{C(}\sqcup\varphi(lab(\overline{f}))\ \overline{f}\texttt{)}$$
$$\{\texttt{super(}\overline{f1}\texttt{); this.}\overline{f2=f2}\}$$

$$[\![\texttt{D m(}\overline{E}\ \overline{x}^\ell\texttt{) }\{\texttt{return}^\ell e;\}]\!]_\varphi^{\overline{CD}} = \sqcup\varphi(\ell)\ \texttt{m(}\sqcup\varphi(\overline{\ell})\ \overline{x}^\ell\texttt{)}\{\texttt{return}^\ell [\![e]\!]_\varphi^{\overline{CD}};\}$$

$$[\![x^\ell]\!]_\varphi^{\overline{CD}} = x^\ell$$

$$[\![\texttt{e.f}^\ell]\!]_\varphi^{\overline{CD}} = [\![e]\!]_\varphi^{\overline{CD}}.\texttt{f}^\ell$$

$$[\![\texttt{new}^\ell\ \texttt{D(}\overline{e}\texttt{)}]\!]_\varphi^{\overline{CD}} = \texttt{new}^\ell\ \texttt{D(}[\![\overline{e}]\!]_\varphi^{\overline{CD}}\texttt{)}$$

$$[\![\texttt{(D)}^\ell e]\!]_\varphi^{\overline{CD}} = (\sqcup\varphi(\ell))^\ell [\![e]\!]_\varphi^{\overline{CD}}$$

$$[\![\texttt{e.m(}\overline{e}\texttt{)}^\ell]\!]_\varphi^{\overline{CD}} = [\![e]\!]_\varphi^{\overline{CD}}.\texttt{D::m(}[\![\overline{e}]\!]_\varphi^{\overline{CD}}\texttt{)}^\ell$$
$$\text{where } \forall E \in \varphi(lab(e)) : impl(\overline{CD}, E, m) = \texttt{D::m}$$

$$[\![\texttt{e.m(}\overline{e}\texttt{)}^\ell]\!]_\varphi^{\overline{CD}} = [\![e]\!]_\varphi^{\overline{CD}}.\texttt{m(}[\![\overline{e}]\!]_\varphi^{\overline{CD}}\texttt{)}^\ell$$
$$\text{otherwise}$$

$$[\![\texttt{e.D::m(}\overline{e}\texttt{)}^\ell]\!]_\varphi^{\overline{CD}} = [\![e]\!]_\varphi^{\overline{CD}}.\texttt{D::m(}[\![\overline{e}]\!]_\varphi^{\overline{CD}}\texttt{)}^\ell$$

$$[\![x_1 : C_1, \ldots, x_n : C_n]\!]_\varphi = x_1 : \sqcup\varphi(lab(x_1)), \ldots, x_n : \sqcup\varphi(lab(x_n))$$

Fig. 5. The Transformation of Dynamic to Static Dispatch

Given a flow analysis, it is sufficient to apply the transformation only once; applying it again will not lead to any further change. We can state this as the following idempotence property of the transformation, which is straightforward to prove.

Theorem 7 (Idempotence). *If* $\varphi \in$ *flow-information*(P) *then* $[\![[\![P]\!]_\varphi]\!]_\varphi = [\![P]\!]_\varphi$.

5   Conclusion

Type-safe method inlining can be done for a single-inheritance language without resorting to the insertion of type casts or new types. Our approach is based on flow analysis, and our experience is that it is tricky to get the requirements for the flow analysis right. During the process of proving correctness, we discovered the need for flow constraints that would not usually be used in a flow analysis, e.g., Rule (36). The requirement that all flow sets must be nonempty is unusual, and it entails that there is no unique best analysis that satisfies the requirements. While Class Hierarchy Analysis and our own *MN* analysis satisfy requirements, more work in needed to investigate alternatives. Future work includes implementing and experimenting with our approach in the context of Java.

Acknowledgements

We thank the 84 students who took Palsberg's graduate course on programming languages in 1999-2001 and tried, as a homework, to find and implement a solution to the problem of type-safe method inlining for a subset of Java. Only

10 of the implementations seemed not to have errors, leading to the realization that the problem is considerably harder than flow-directed inlining for an untyped language. We thank Mayur Naik and the anonymous referees for helpful comments on a draft of the paper.

Palsberg is supported by a National Science Foundation Faculty Early Career Development Award, CCR–9734265.

A   Proof of Theorem 3

First, observe that $labels(P_2) \subseteq labels(P_1)$ so φ (restricted to $labels(P_2)$) is a flow analysis of P_2. Let $P_i = (\overline{CD}, X\langle e_i \rangle)$ where e_1 and e_2 are as in the rules of Figure 2. Since P_1 and P_2 differ only in e_1 and e_2, φ satisfies the conditions for acceptability and type respecting for P_2 except for the conditions on e_2 and its subexpressions that are not subexpressions of e_1, and on the expression that e_1 appears immediately within. The last condition will hold if $\varphi(lab(e_2)) \subseteq \varphi(lab(e_1))$. Thus, we need just to show the latter and that φ satisfies the conditions for e_2 and its subexpressions that are not subexpressions of e_1. Consider the various cases for the reduction rule.

field selection: In this case $e_1 = \text{new}^{\ell_1} \ C(\overline{e}).f_i^{\ell_2}$, $e_2 = e_i$, and $fields(\overline{CD}, C) = \overline{C} \ \overline{f}$. Thus, e_2 is a subexpression of e_1. By the conditions for acceptability, $\varphi(lab(e_i)) \subseteq \varphi(lab(f_i))$ and $\varphi(lab(f_i)) = (\ell_2)$. By transitivity, $\varphi(e_2) = \varphi(lab(e_i)) \subseteq \varphi(\ell_2) = \varphi(lab(e_1))$.

cast: In this case $e_1 = (C)^{\ell_1} \ \text{new}^{\ell_2} \ D(\overline{e})$, $e_2 = \text{new}^{\ell_1} \ D(\overline{e})$, and $\overline{CD} \vdash D \mathrel{<:} C$. The only subexpressions of e_2 that are not subexpressions of e_1 is e_2 itself. For acceptability, it must be that $D \in \varphi(\ell_1)$ and $\varphi(lab(\overline{e})) \subseteq \varphi(\overline{f})$ where $fields(\overline{CD}, D) = \overline{C} \ \overline{f}$. The latter follows by the acceptability conditions for e_1. The same conditions also give that $D \in \varphi(\ell_2)$ and $\varphi(\ell_2) \cap subclasses(P_1, C) = \varphi(\ell_1)$. Since D is a subclass of C, $D \in \varphi(\ell_1)$ as required. For type respecting, it must be that $\overline{CD} \vdash E \mathrel{<:} D$ for each $E \in \varphi(\ell_1)$ (*). By type respecting for $lab(e_1)$, $\overline{CD} \vdash E \mathrel{<:} D$ for each $E \in \varphi(\ell_2)$. Since $\varphi(\ell_1) = \varphi(\ell_2) \cap subclasses(P_1, C)$, (*) holds. Finally, $\varphi(lab(e_2)) = \varphi(\ell_1) = \varphi(lab(e_2))$.

dynamic method invocation: In this case $e_1 = \text{new}^{\ell_1} \ C(\overline{e}).m(\overline{d})^{\ell_2}$ and $e_2 = e\{\text{this}, \overline{x} := \text{new}^{\ell_1} \ C(\overline{e}), \overline{d}\}$ where $mbody(\overline{CD}, C, m) = (\ell', \overline{x}, e)$. By the conditions for acceptability $\varphi(lab(\overline{d})) \subseteq \varphi(lab(\overline{x}))$ and $\varphi(\ell_1) \subseteq \varphi(lab(\text{this}))$. By Lemma 1, φ satisfies the conditions for acceptability and type respecting for e_2 and all its subexpressions. Also by the conditions for acceptability $\varphi(\ell') = \varphi(\ell_2)$ and $\varphi(lab(e)) \subseteq \varphi(\ell')$. Thus $\varphi(lab(e_2)) = \varphi(lab(e)) \subseteq \varphi(\ell_2) = \varphi(lab(e_1))$.

static method invocation: In this case $e_1 = \text{new}^{\ell_1} \ C(\overline{e}).D::m(\overline{d})^{\ell_2}$ and $e_2 = e\{\text{this}, \overline{x} := \text{new}^{\ell_1} \ C(\overline{e}), \overline{d}\}$ where $mbody(\overline{CD}, D, m) = (\ell', \overline{x}, e)$. By the conditions for acceptability $\varphi(lab(\overline{d})) \subseteq \varphi(lab(\overline{x}))$ and $\varphi(\ell_1) \subseteq \varphi(lab(\text{this}))$. By Lemma 1, φ satisfies the conditions for acceptability and type respecting for e_2 and all its subexpressions. Also by the conditions for acceptability $\varphi(\ell') = \varphi(\ell_2)$ and $\varphi(lab(e)) \subseteq \varphi(\ell')$. Thus $\varphi(lab(e_2)) = \varphi(lab(e)) \subseteq \varphi(\ell_2) = \varphi(lab(e_1))$.

Lemma 1. *If φ satisfies the conditions for acceptability and type respecting for all labels in $\mathbf{e}$ and $\overline{\mathbf{d}}$ and if $\varphi(lab(\overline{\mathbf{d}})) \subseteq \varphi(lab(\overline{\mathbf{x}}))$ then φ satisfies the conditions for acceptability and type respecting for all labels in $\mathbf{e}\{\overline{\mathbf{x}} := \overline{\mathbf{d}}\}$.*

Proof. Straightforward.

B   Proof of Theorem 4

Theorem 4 follows immediately from Rule (25), and from Lemma 2 and Lemma 4, as stated and proved below.

Lemma 2. *Suppose $\varphi \in acceptable(\mathrm{P}) \cap type\text{-}respecting(\mathrm{P})$, and $\mathrm{P} = (\overline{\mathrm{CD}}, \mathbf{e}_0)$. If $\overline{\mathrm{CD}} \vdash \overline{\mathrm{CD}}$ OK, then $[\![\overline{\mathrm{CD}}]\!]_\varphi^{\overline{\mathrm{CD}}} \vdash [\![\overline{\mathrm{CD}}]\!]_\varphi^{\overline{\mathrm{CD}}}$ OK.*

Proof. Immediate from Lemma 3 and Lemma 7, using Rule (24).

Lemma 3. *Suppose $\varphi \in acceptable(\mathrm{P}) \cap type\text{-}respecting(\mathrm{P})$, and $\mathrm{P} = (\overline{\mathrm{CD}}, \mathbf{e}_0)$. If $\overline{\mathrm{CD}} \vdash \overline{\mathrm{M}}$ OK in C, then $[\![\overline{\mathrm{CD}}]\!]_\varphi^{\overline{\mathrm{CD}}} \vdash [\![\overline{\mathrm{M}}]\!]_\varphi^{\overline{\mathrm{CD}}}$ OK in C.*

Proof. Straightforward from Lemmas 4, 5, 8, 9, using Rules (17), (23), (36), (37).

Lemma 4. *Suppose $\varphi \in acceptable(\mathrm{P}) \cap type\text{-}respecting(\mathrm{P})$, and $\mathrm{P} = (\overline{\mathrm{CD}}, \mathbf{e}_0)$. If $\overline{\mathrm{CD}}; \Gamma \vdash \mathbf{e} \in \mathrm{D}$, then $[\![\overline{\mathrm{CD}}]\!]_\varphi^{\overline{\mathrm{CD}}}; [\![\Gamma]\!]_\varphi \vdash [\![\mathbf{e}]\!]_\varphi^{\overline{\mathrm{CD}}} \in \sqcup\varphi(lab(\mathbf{e}))$.*

Proof. We proceed by induction on the structure of the derivation of $\overline{\mathrm{CD}}; \Gamma \vdash \mathbf{e} \in \mathrm{D}$. There are six cases, depending on which one of Rules (17)–(22) was the last one to be used to derive $\overline{\mathrm{CD}}; \Gamma \vdash \mathbf{e} \in \mathrm{D}$.

- (17) $\mathbf{e} \equiv \mathbf{x}^\ell$. We have $[\![\mathbf{x}^\ell]\!]_\varphi^{\overline{\mathrm{CD}}} = \mathbf{x}^\ell$ and $[\![\Gamma]\!]_\varphi(\mathbf{x}) = \sqcup\varphi(\ell)$, so we can derive, using Rule (17), $[\![\overline{\mathrm{CD}}]\!]_\varphi^{\overline{\mathrm{CD}}}; [\![\Gamma]\!]_\varphi \vdash [\![\mathbf{e}]\!]_\varphi^{\overline{\mathrm{CD}}} \in \sqcup\varphi(\ell)$, as desired.

- (18) $\mathbf{e} \equiv \mathbf{e}_0.\mathbf{f}_i^{\;\ell}$. We have $\overline{\mathrm{CD}}; \Gamma \vdash \mathbf{e}_0 \in \mathrm{C}_0$ and $fields(\overline{\mathrm{CD}}, \mathrm{C}_0) = \overline{\mathrm{C}}\ \overline{\mathbf{f}}$, where $\mathbf{f}_i$ occurs in $\overline{\mathbf{f}}$. From the induction hypothesis we have $[\![\overline{\mathrm{CD}}]\!]_\varphi^{\overline{\mathrm{CD}}}; [\![\Gamma]\!]_\varphi \vdash [\![\mathbf{e}_0]\!]_\varphi^{\overline{\mathrm{CD}}} \in \sqcup\varphi(lab(\mathbf{e}_0))$. From $\varphi \in type\text{-}respecting(\mathrm{P})$ we have $\overline{\mathrm{CD}} \vdash \sqcup\varphi(lab(\mathbf{e}_0)) <: \mathrm{C}_0$ so $fields(\overline{\mathrm{CD}}, \sqcup\varphi(lab(\mathbf{e}_0))) = \overline{\mathrm{D}}\ \overline{\mathbf{g}}\ \overline{\mathrm{C}}\ \overline{\mathbf{f}}$. Hence, from Lemma 7, we have $fields([\![\overline{\mathrm{CD}}]\!]_\varphi^{\overline{\mathrm{CD}}}, \sqcup\varphi(lab(\mathbf{e}_0))) = \sqcup\varphi(lab(\overline{\mathbf{g}}))\ \overline{\mathbf{g}}\ \sqcup\varphi(lab(\overline{\mathbf{f}}))\ \overline{\mathbf{f}}$. From Rule (26) we have $\varphi(lab(\mathbf{f}_i)) = \varphi(\ell)$, so $\sqcup\varphi(lab(\mathbf{f}_i)) = \sqcup\varphi(\ell)$, so we can derive, using Rule (18), that $[\![\overline{\mathrm{CD}}]\!]_\varphi^{\overline{\mathrm{CD}}}; [\![\Gamma]\!]_\varphi \vdash [\![\mathbf{e}]\!]_\varphi^{\overline{\mathrm{CD}}} \in \sqcup\varphi(\ell)$, as desired.

- (19) $\mathbf{e} \equiv \mathbf{new}^\ell\ \mathrm{C}(\overline{\mathbf{e}})$. We have $fields(\overline{\mathrm{CD}}, \mathrm{C}) = \overline{\mathrm{D}}\ \overline{\mathbf{f}}$, and $\overline{\mathrm{CD}}; \Gamma \vdash \overline{\mathbf{e}} \in \overline{\mathrm{E}}$, and $\overline{\mathrm{CD}} \vdash \overline{\mathrm{E}} <: \overline{\mathrm{D}}$. From Lemma 7 we have $fields([\![\overline{\mathrm{CD}}]\!]_\varphi^{\overline{\mathrm{CD}}}, \mathrm{C}) = \sqcup\varphi(lab(\overline{\mathbf{f}}))\ \overline{\mathbf{f}}$. From the induction hypothesis we have $[\![\overline{\mathrm{CD}}]\!]_\varphi^{\overline{\mathrm{CD}}}; [\![\Gamma]\!]_\varphi \vdash [\![\overline{\mathbf{e}}]\!]_\varphi^{\overline{\mathrm{CD}}} \in \sqcup\varphi(lab(\overline{\mathbf{e}}))$. From Rule (27), we have $\varphi(lab(\overline{\mathbf{e}})) \subseteq \varphi(lab(\overline{\mathbf{f}}))$, so from Lemma 9 we have $\overline{\mathrm{CD}} \vdash \sqcup\varphi(lab(\overline{\mathbf{e}})) <: \sqcup\varphi(lab(\overline{\mathbf{f}}))$, and so from Lemma 8 we have $[\![\overline{\mathrm{CD}}]\!]_\varphi^{\overline{\mathrm{CD}}} \vdash \sqcup\varphi(lab(\overline{\mathbf{e}})) <: \sqcup\varphi(lab(\overline{\mathbf{f}}))$. Finally we have from Rule (28) that $\mathrm{C} \in \varphi(\ell)$, and since $\mathbf{new}^\ell\ \mathrm{C}(\overline{\mathbf{e}})$ has static type C and $\varphi \in type\text{-}respecting(\mathrm{P})$, we have $\sqcup\varphi(\ell) = \mathrm{C}$. We conclude, using Rule (19), that we have $[\![\overline{\mathrm{CD}}]\!]_\varphi^{\overline{\mathrm{CD}}}; [\![\Gamma]\!]_\varphi \vdash \mathbf{new}^\ell\ \mathrm{C}([\![\overline{\mathbf{e}}]\!]_\varphi^{\overline{\mathrm{CD}}}) \in \mathrm{C}$.

– (20) $e \equiv (C)^{\ell}e_0$. We have $\overline{CD}; \Gamma \vdash e_0 \in D$. From the induction hypothesis we have $[\![\overline{CD}]\!]_{\varphi}^{\overline{CD}}; [\![\Gamma]\!]_{\varphi} \vdash [\![e_0]\!]_{\varphi}^{\overline{CD}} \in \sqcup\varphi(lab(e_0))$. From Rule (20) we have that we can derive $[\![\overline{CD}]\!]_{\varphi}^{\overline{CD}}; [\![\Gamma]\!]_{\varphi} \vdash (\sqcup\varphi(\ell))^{\ell}[\![e_0]\!]_{\varphi}^{\overline{CD}} \in \sqcup\varphi(\ell)$.

– (21) $e \equiv e_0.m(\overline{e})^{\ell}$. There are two cases. First, assume that there is a class D in P such that $\forall E \in \varphi(lab(e_0)) : impl(\overline{CD}, E, m) = D::m$. We have

$$\overline{CD}; \Gamma \vdash e_0 \in C_0 \tag{41}$$

$$mtype(\overline{CD}, C_0, m) = \overline{D} \to C \tag{42}$$

$$\overline{CD}; \Gamma \vdash \overline{e} \in \overline{C} \tag{43}$$

From (41), (43), and the induction hypothesis, we have

$$[\![\overline{CD}]\!]_{\varphi}^{\overline{CD}}; [\![\Gamma]\!]_{\varphi} \vdash [\![e_0]\!]_{\varphi}^{\overline{CD}} \in \sqcup\varphi(lab(e_0)) \tag{44}$$

$$[\![\overline{CD}]\!]_{\varphi}^{\overline{CD}}; [\![\Gamma]\!]_{\varphi} \vdash [\![\overline{e}]\!]_{\varphi}^{\overline{CD}} \in \sqcup\varphi(lab(\overline{e})) \tag{45}$$

We have $\overline{CD} \vdash \sqcup\varphi(lab(e_0)) <: D$, so from Lemma 8, we have

$$[\![\overline{CD}]\!]_{\varphi}^{\overline{CD}} \vdash \sqcup\varphi(lab(e_0)) <: D, \tag{46}$$

and together with (42), we have $mtype(\overline{CD}, D, m) = \overline{D} \to C$. Suppose also $mbody(\overline{CD}, D, m) = (\ell', \overline{x}, e')$, From Lemma 6 we have

$$mtype([\![\overline{CD}]\!]_{\varphi}^{\overline{CD}}, D, m) = (\sqcup\varphi(lab(\overline{x}))) \to (\sqcup\varphi(\ell')). \tag{47}$$

From Rule (40) we have $\varphi(lab(e_0)) \neq \emptyset$, so suppose $E_0 \in \varphi(lab(e_0))$. Suppose also $mbody(\overline{CD}, E_0, m) = (\ell'', \overline{x''}, e'')$, From Rules (30)–(31) we have

$$\varphi(lab(\overline{e})) \subseteq \varphi(lab(\overline{x''}))$$
$$\varphi(\ell'') = \varphi(\ell).$$

Finally, from Rules (38)–(39) we have

$$\varphi(lab(\overline{x})) \subseteq \varphi(lab(\overline{x''}))$$
$$\varphi(\ell') = \varphi(\ell''),$$

so

$$\varphi(lab(\overline{e})) \subseteq \varphi(lab(\overline{x})) \tag{48}$$
$$\varphi(\ell') = \varphi(\ell). \tag{49}$$

Thus, from Rule (22), and from (44)–(49), we have that we can derive

$$[\![\overline{CD}]\!]_{\varphi}^{\overline{CD}}; [\![\Gamma]\!]_{\varphi} \vdash [\![e_0]\!]_{\varphi}^{\overline{CD}}.D::m([\![\overline{e}]\!]_{\varphi}^{\overline{CD}})^{\ell} \in \sqcup\varphi(\ell)$$

as desired.

Second, suppose we have the "otherwise" case from the definition of the transformation of a method call. The proof of this case is similar to the first case, we omit the details.

– (22) $e \equiv e_0.D::m(\bar{e})^\ell$. The proof of this case is similar to the previous case, we omit the details.

Lemma 5. *Suppose* $\varphi \in acceptable(P) \cap type\text{-}respecting(P)$, *and* $P = (\overline{CD}, e_0)$. *If* $override(\overline{CD}, D, m, \overline{C} \rightarrow C_0)$, $\overline{CD} \vdash C <: D$, *and* $mbody(\overline{CD}, C, m) = (\ell, \bar{x}, e)$, *then*

$$override(\llbracket \overline{CD} \rrbracket_\varphi^{\overline{CD}}, D, m, (\sqcup\varphi(lab(\bar{x}))) \rightarrow (\sqcup\varphi(\ell))).$$

Proof. Immediate from Lemma 6, using Rule (9), (14)–(16).

Lemma 6. *Suppose* $\varphi \in acceptable(P) \cap type\text{-}respecting(P)$, *and* $P = (\overline{CD}, e_0)$. *If* $mtype(\overline{CD}, D, m) = \overline{D} \rightarrow D_0$, $\overline{CD} \vdash C <: D$, *and* $mbody(\overline{CD}, C, m) = (\ell, \bar{x}, e)$, *then*

$$mtype(\llbracket \overline{CD} \rrbracket_\varphi^{\overline{CD}}, D, m) = (\sqcup\varphi(lab(\bar{x}))) \rightarrow (\sqcup\varphi(\ell)).$$

Proof. Straightforward, using the rules Rules (3)–(6), (14)–(16), (38)–(39).

Lemma 7. *Suppose* $\varphi \in acceptable(P) \cap type\text{-}respecting(P)$, *and* $P = (\overline{CD}, e_0)$. *If* $fields(\overline{CD}, D) = \overline{D}\ \bar{g}$, *then* $fields(\llbracket \overline{CD} \rrbracket_\varphi^{\overline{CD}}, D) = \sqcup\varphi(lab(\bar{g}))\ \bar{g}$.

Proof. Straightforward, by induction on the structure of the derivation of the judgment $fields(\overline{CD}, D) = \overline{D}\ \bar{g}$, using Rules (1)–(2).

Lemma 8. *If* $\overline{CD} \vdash C <: D$, *then* $\llbracket \overline{CD} \rrbracket_\varphi^{\overline{CD}} \vdash C <: D$.

Proof. Immediate from the definition of subtyping, that is, Rules (14)–(16).

Lemma 9. *Suppose* $S, T \in flow(P) \setminus \emptyset$. *If* $S \subseteq T$, *then* $\overline{CD} \vdash \sqcup S <: \sqcup T$.

Proof. Immediate from the observation that the subtyping order forms a tree and therefore admits least upper bounds of nonempty sets.

C   Proof of Theorem 5

$(\Rightarrow)$ Let $P_1 = (\overline{CD}, X\langle e_1\rangle)$ and $P_2 = (\overline{CD}, X\langle e_2\rangle)$ where e_1 and e_2 are given by one of the rules in Figure 2. Clearly $\llbracket P_i \rrbracket_\varphi = (\llbracket \overline{CD} \rrbracket_\varphi^{\overline{CD}}, \llbracket X \rrbracket_\varphi^{\overline{CD}}\langle \llbracket e_i \rrbracket_\varphi^{\overline{CD}}\rangle)$, so it remains to show that $\llbracket e_1 \rrbracket_\varphi^{\overline{CD}} \mapsto \llbracket e_2 \rrbracket_\varphi^{\overline{CD}}$. The interesting cases are when e_1 is a cast and when e_1 is a dynamic method invocation that is transformed to a static method invocation. Case 1, $e_1 = (C)^{\ell_1}new^{\ell_2}\ D(\bar{e})$: In this case $e_2 = new^{\ell_1}$ $D(\bar{e})$, $\llbracket e_1 \rrbracket_\varphi^{\overline{CD}} = (\sqcup\varphi(\ell_1))^{\ell_1}new^{\ell_2}\ D(\llbracket \bar{e} \rrbracket_\varphi^{\overline{CD}})$, and $\overline{CD} \vdash D <: C$. By the acceptability of φ, $D \in \varphi(\ell_2)$ and $\varphi(\ell_2) \cap subclasses(P_1, C) \subseteq \varphi(\ell_1)$. Thus $D \in \varphi(\ell_1)$, so $\overline{CD} \vdash D <: \sqcup\varphi(\ell_1)$. By the reduction rules $\llbracket e_1 \rrbracket_\varphi^{\overline{CD}} \mapsto new^{\ell_1}\ D(\llbracket \bar{e} \rrbracket_\varphi^{\overline{CD}}) = \llbracket e_2 \rrbracket_\varphi^{\overline{CD}}$. Case 2, $e_1 = new^{\ell_1}\ C(\bar{e}).m(\bar{d})^{\ell_2}$ and $\llbracket e_1 \rrbracket_\varphi^{\overline{CD}} = new^{\ell_1}\ C(\llbracket \bar{e} \rrbracket_\varphi^{\overline{CD}}).D::m(\llbracket \bar{d} \rrbracket_\varphi^{\overline{CD}})^{\ell_2}$: In this case, $\forall E \in \varphi(\ell_1) : impl(\overline{CD}, E, m) = D::m$ and $e_2 = e\{this, \bar{x} := new^{\ell_1}\ C(\bar{e}), \bar{d}\}$ where $mbody(\overline{CD}, C, m) = (\ell, \bar{x}, e)$. By the acceptability of φ, $C \in \varphi(\ell_1)$. So

$impl(\overline{\text{CD}}, \text{C}, \text{m}) = \text{D}::\text{m}$. By inspecting the definitions, $mbody(\overline{\text{CD}}, \text{D}, \text{m}) = (\ell, \overline{\text{x}}, \text{e})$. Thus:

$$\llbracket e_1 \rrbracket_\varphi^{\overline{\text{CD}}} = \text{new}^{\ell_1}\ \text{C}(\llbracket \overline{e} \rrbracket_\varphi^{\overline{\text{CD}}}).\text{D}::\text{m}(\llbracket \overline{d} \rrbracket_\varphi^{\overline{\text{CD}}})^{\ell_2}$$

$$\mapsto \llbracket e \rrbracket_\varphi^{\overline{\text{CD}}}\{\text{this}, \overline{\text{x}} := \text{new}^{\ell_1}\ \text{C}(\llbracket \overline{e} \rrbracket_\varphi^{\overline{\text{CD}}}), \llbracket \overline{d} \rrbracket_\varphi^{\overline{\text{CD}}}\}$$

$$= \llbracket e_2 \rrbracket_\varphi^{\overline{\text{CD}}}$$

($\Leftarrow$) If $\llbracket P_1 \rrbracket_\varphi$ takes any step then it is easy to see that P_1 has the form $(\overline{\text{CD}}, \text{X}\langle e_1 \rangle)$ and that $\llbracket P_1 \rrbracket_\varphi \mapsto (\llbracket \overline{\text{CD}} \rrbracket_\varphi^{\overline{\text{CD}}}, \llbracket \text{X} \rrbracket_\varphi^{\overline{\text{CD}}}\langle e' \rangle)$ for $\llbracket e_1 \rrbracket_\varphi^{\overline{\text{CD}}}$ and e' as in the rules in Figure 2. It remains to show that $e_1 \mapsto e_2$ and $\llbracket e_2 \rrbracket_\varphi^{\overline{\text{CD}}} = e'$. The interesting cases are when e_1 is a cast and when e_1 is a dynamic method invocation that is transformed to a static method invocation. Case 1, $e_1 = (\text{C})^{\ell_1}\text{new}^{\ell_2}\ \text{D}(\overline{e})$: In this case $\llbracket e_1 \rrbracket_\varphi^{\overline{\text{CD}}} = (\sqcup\varphi(\ell_1))^{\ell_1}\text{new}^{\ell_2}\ \text{D}(\llbracket \overline{e} \rrbracket_\varphi^{\overline{\text{CD}}})$, $e' = \text{new}^{\ell_1}\ \text{D}(\llbracket \overline{e} \rrbracket_\varphi^{\overline{\text{CD}}})$, and $\overline{\text{CD}} \vdash \text{D} <: \sqcup\varphi(\ell_1)$. Since φ is type respecting $\overline{\text{CD}} \vdash \sqcup\varphi(\ell_1) <: \text{C}$. By transitivity of subtyping, $\overline{\text{CD}} \vdash \text{D} <: \text{C}$. Letting e_2 be $\text{new}^{\ell_1}\ \text{D}(\overline{e})$ then $e_1 \mapsto e_2$ and $\llbracket e_2 \rrbracket_\varphi^{\overline{\text{CD}}} = e'$. Case 2, $e_1 = \text{new}^{\ell_1}\ \text{C}(\overline{e}).\text{m}(\overline{d})^{\ell_2}$ and $\llbracket e_1 \rrbracket_\varphi^{\overline{\text{CD}}} = \text{new}^{\ell_1}\ \text{C}(\llbracket \overline{e} \rrbracket_\varphi^{\overline{\text{CD}}}).\text{D}::\text{m}(\llbracket \overline{d} \rrbracket_\varphi^{\overline{\text{CD}}})^{\ell_2}$: In this case, $\forall \text{E} \in \varphi(\ell_1) : impl(\overline{\text{CD}}, \text{E}, \text{m}) = \text{D}::\text{m}$ and $e' = \llbracket e \rrbracket_\varphi^{\overline{\text{CD}}}\{\text{this}, \overline{\text{x}} := \text{new}^{\ell_1}\ \text{C}(\llbracket \overline{e} \rrbracket_\varphi^{\overline{\text{CD}}}), \llbracket \overline{d} \rrbracket_\varphi^{\overline{\text{CD}}}\}$ where $mbody(\overline{\text{CD}}, \text{D}, \text{m}) = (\ell, \overline{\text{x}}, \text{e})$. By the acceptability of φ, $\text{C} \in \varphi(\ell_1)$. So $impl(\overline{\text{CD}}, \text{C}, \text{m}) = \text{D}::\text{m}$. By examination of the auxiliary definitions, $mbody(\overline{\text{CD}}, \text{C}, \text{m}) = (\ell, \overline{\text{x}}, \text{e})$. Letting e_2 be $\text{e}\{\text{this}, \overline{\text{x}} := \text{new}^{\ell_1}\ \text{C}(\overline{e}), \overline{d}\}$ then $e_1 \mapsto e_2$ and $\llbracket e_2 \rrbracket_\varphi^{\overline{\text{CD}}} = e'$.

References

1. Lars Ole Andersen. Self-applicable C program specialization. In *Proceedings of PEPM'92, Workshop on Partial Evaluation and Semantics-Based Program Manipulation*, pages 54–61, June 1992. (Technical Report YALEU/DCS/RR-909, Yale University).

2. Jeffrey Dean, David Grove, and Craig Chambers. Optimization of object-oriented programs using static class hierarchy analysis. In *Proceedings of European Conference on Object-Oriented Programming*, pages 77–101, Aarhus, Denmark, August 1995. Springer-Verlag (*LNCS 952*).

3. David Detlefs and Ole Agesen. Inlining of virtual methods. In *Proceedings of ECOOP'99*, pages 258–278. Springer-Verlag (LNCS 1628), 1999.

4. Manuel Fähndrich and Alexander Aiken. Program analysis using mixed term and set constraints. In *Proceedings of SAS'97, International Static Analysis Symposium*, pages 114–126. Springer-Verlag (*LNCS*), 1997.

5. Etienne M. Gagnon, Laurie J. Hendren, and Guillaume Marceau. Efficient inference of static types for Java bytecode. In *Proceedings of SAS'00, International Static Analysis Symposium*, pages 199–219. Springer-Verlag (*LNCS* 1824), 2000.

6. Neal Glew. An efficient class and object encoding. In *Proceedings of OOPSLA'00, ACM SIGPLAN Conference on Object-Oriented Programming Systems, Languages and Applications*, pages 311–324, Minneapolis, Minnesota, October 2000.

7. Nevin Heintze. Control-flow analysis and type systems. In *Proceedings of SAS'95, International Static Analysis Symposium*, pages 189–206. Springer-Verlag (*LNCS* 983), Glasgow, Scotland, September 1995.

8. Atsushi Igarashi, Benjamion Pierce, and Philip Wadler. Featherweight Java: A minimal core calculus for Java and GJ. In *ACM SIGPLAN Conference on Object-Oriented Programming, Systems, Languages, and Applications*, pages 132–146, Denver, CO, USA, October 1999.

9. Suresh Jagannathan, Andrew Wright, and Stephen Weeks. Type-directed flow analysis for typed intermediate languages. In *Proceedings of SAS'97, International Static Analysis Symposium*. Springer-Verlag (*LNCS*), 1997.

10. Todd Knoblock and Jakob Rehof. Type elaboration and subtype completion for Java Bytecode. *ACM Transactions on Programming Languages and Systems*, 23(2):243–272, March 2001.

11. Greg Morrisett, David Tarditi, Perry Cheng, Christopher Stone, Robert Harper, and Peter Lee. The TIL/ML compiler: Performance and safety through types. In *ACM SIGPLAN Workshop on Compiler Support for System Software*, Tucson, AZ, USA, February 1996.

12. Greg Morrisett, David Walker, Karl Crary, and Neal Glew. From System F to typed assembly language. *ACM Transactions on Progamming Languages and Systems*, 21(3):528–569, May 1999.

13. Flemming Nielson. The typed lambda-calculus with first-class processes. In *Proceedings of PARLE*, pages 357–373, April 1989.

14. Jens Palsberg. Closure analysis in constraint form. *ACM Transactions on Programming Languages and Systems*, 17(1):47–62, January 1995. Preliminary version in Proceedings of CAAP'94, Colloquium on Trees in Algebra and Programming, Springer-Verlag (*LNCS* 787), pages 276–290, Edinburgh, Scotland, April 1994.

15. Jens Palsberg. Equality-based flow analysis versus recursive types. *ACM Transactions on Programming Languages and Systems*, 20(6):1251–1264, 1998.

16. Jens Palsberg and Patrick M. O'Keefe. A type system equivalent to flow analysis. *ACM Transactions on Programming Languages and Systems*, 17(4):576–599, July 1995. Preliminary version in Proceedings of POPL'95, 22nd Annual SIGPLAN–SIGACT Symposium on Principles of Programming Languages, pages 367–378, San Francisco, California, January 1995.

17. Jens Palsberg and Christina Pavlopoulou. From polyvariant flow information to intersection and union types. *Journal of Functional Programming*, 11(3):263–317, May 2001. Preliminary version in Proceedings of POPL'98, 25th Annual SIGPLAN–SIGACT Symposium on Principles of Programming Languages, pages 197–208, San Diego, California, January 1998.

18. Jens Palsberg and Michael I. Schwartzbach. *Object-Oriented Type Systems*. John Wiley & Sons, 1994.

19. David Tarditi, Greg Morrisett, Perry Cheng, Christopher Stone, Robert Harper, and Peter Lee. TIL: A type-directed optimizing compiler for ML. In *1996 ACM SIGPLAN Conference on Programming Language Design and Implementation*, pages 181–192, Philadelphia, PA, USA, May 1996. ACM Press.

20. Andrew Wright and Matthias Felleisen. A syntactic approach to type soundness. *Information and Computation*, 115(1):38–94, 1994.

21. Andrew Wright, Suresh Jagannathan, Cristian Ungureanu, and Aaron Hertzmann. Compiling Java to a typed lambda-calculus: A preliminary report. In *ACM Workshop on Types in Compilation*, Kyoto, Japan, March 1998.

Polychotomic Encoding: A Better Quasi-Optimal Bit-Vector Encoding of Tree Hierarchies

Robert E. Filman

Research Institute for Advanced Computer Science
NASA Ames Research Center MS/269-2
Moffett Field, CA 94025 USA
rfilman@mail.arc.nasa.gov

Abstract. Polychotomic Encoding is an algorithm for producing bit vector encodings of trees. Polychotomic Encoding is an extension of the Dichotomic Encoding algorithm of Raynaud and Thierry. Polychotomic and Dichotomic Encodings are both examples of hierarchical encoding algorithms, where each node in the tree is given a *gene*—a subset of $\{1, \ldots, n\}$. The encoding of each node is then the union of that node's gene with the genes of its ancestors. Reachability in the tree can then be determined by subset testing on the encodings.

Dichotomic Encoding restructures the given tree into a binary tree, and then assigns two bit, incompatible (chotomic) "genes" to each of the two children of a node. Polychotomic Encoding substitutes a multibit encoding for the children of a node when the restructuring operation of Dichotomic Encoding would produce a new heaviest child (child requiring the most bits to represent a tree of its children) for that node. The paper includes a proof that Polychotomic Encoding never produces an encoding using more bits than Dichotomic Encoding. Experimentally, Polychotomic Encoding produces a space savings of up to 15% on examples of naturally occurring hierarchies, and 25% on trees in the randomly generated test set.

1 Introduction

Bit-vectors encodings are a popular mechanism for quickly determining reachability in a directed graph. Let the reachability relation be $\prec\!\!\prec$. A bit-vector encoding is a function, γ, from the nodes of the graph to a subset of $\{1, \ldots, n\}$. With a bit-vector encoding, $x \prec\!\!\prec y \iff \gamma(y) \subseteq \gamma(x)$. Figure 1 shows a bit-vector encoding of a simple tree. Since subsets of integers can be represented by bit vectors and bit-vector subset testing requires only a few instructions on most hardware, bit vector encodings can be both a time and space efficient way of testing reachability. Reachability is important for object-oriented programming languages, as determining if an element of direct class X can be safely cast to class Y is frequently required. Similarly, method dispatch in object-oriented languages requires dynamic subclass testing [2,7,8,10]. Membership testing is also found in many AI applications [6,13]. Directed graph reachability is a common problem throughout Computer Science.

B. Magnusson (Ed.): ECOOP 2002, LNCS 2374, pp. 545–561, 2002.
© Springer-Verlag Berlin Heidelberg 2002

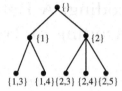

Fig. 1. A bit-vector encoding

Bit-vector encodings have been a subject of much research. Good algorithms quickly determine an encoding for a graph using as few as bits as possible. Bit-vector encoding algorithms divide into algorithms over trees versus all acyclic graphs, and algorithms that demand the entire graph before deciding the encoding (static algorithms) versus algorithms that can incrementally modify the encoding on the addition of new nodes and relations (dynamic algorithms).

Here we are concerned with algorithms encoding static trees. This paper describes the *Polychotomic Encoding* (PE) algorithm. Polychotomic Encoding combines elements of both the Dichotomic Encoding (DE) encoding of Raynaud and Thierry [11] and the 2-dimensional (multibit) encoding of Caseau et al. [4] (CHNR). Succinctly, Polychotomic Encoding performs Dichotomic Encoding of a node's children until doing so would create a new heaviest child (child requiring the most bits to represent a tree of its children), and then uses a multibit encoding to encode the remaining children. Polychotomic Encoding has the same time and space complexity as Dichotomic Encoding. Section 8 contains a proof that Polychotomic Encoding never produces an encoding requiring more bits than Dichotomic Encoding. Experimentally, Polychotomic Encoding produces a savings of up to 15% over Dichotomic Encoding on naturally occurring examples of hierarchies, and up to 25% on some randomly generated trees.

2   Hierarchies

A hierarchy, H is a set T and a transitive, reflexive and anti-symmetric relation $\twoheadleftarrow$, $H = (T, \twoheadleftarrow)$. The *transitive reduction* of H, $x \prec y$, is defined as $x \twoheadleftarrow y, x \neq y$, and $\neg \exists z. x \twoheadleftarrow z \twoheadleftarrow y, x \neq z \neq y$. Often, given T and the various $\prec$ relationships, one infers $\twoheadleftarrow$ by closing over $\prec$ (extended with $x \twoheadleftarrow x$). A common example of a hierarchy is subclass relationships in object-oriented languages, where $\prec$ is the parent-child relation.

The computational problem is to build a representation and algorithm that can answer the question $x \stackrel{?}{\twoheadleftarrow} y$. The developer of such an algorithm can perform tradeoffs about the time taken to build the representation, the space required by the representation, the time needed to perform the test, and the cost of modifying the representation dynamically if new elements of T or new $\prec$ relationships are asserted. Some algorithms apply to arbitrary partial orders (multiple inheritance, or MI), while others are restricted to trees (single inheritance, or SI).

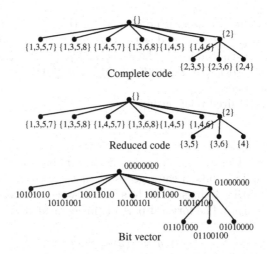

Fig. 2. Three representations of bit-vector encoding

Hierarchies are important in object-oriented systems technology, because object types over subclass form a hierarchy, and the $\preceq$ test is used to determine if one object can be viewed as an instance of another class. For this reason, this is sometimes called the *subtyping problem*, though the results are clearly applicable to any partial order. Subtyping is a frequent operation in the compiled code of object systems. Zibin and Gil provide a good discussion of the space of tradeoffs and the impact of the performance of the subclassing test in OO systems [17].

3   Encodings

In a bit-vector encoding, the root of the tree is assigned the null set. Every other node in the hierarchy has some non-null subset of $\{1, \ldots, n\}$ (its *gene*) associated with that node. The encoding of a node (γ) is the union of the gene of the node with the encoding of its parents. Thus, the encoding of a node is the union of the gene of a node with genes of its ancestors. Such a coding scheme is called a hierarchical encoding.

Figure 2, adapted from [11], shows three different representations of a bit-vector encoding. The *complete code* lists the elements of the set $\{1, \ldots, n\}$ used to encode each node. Since the code is hierarchical, the encoding can also be represented in the *reduced code* as just the gene of the node. The complete code can be obtained by taking the union this gene with the genes of its ancestors. The *bit-vector* encoding is obtained by associating a one in a vector of bits with the corresponding elements of the complete code. The three are equivalent representations: each can be straightforwardly derived from any other. This close correspondence between the bit-vector encoding and the numeric encodings leads us to refer to individual numbers in an encoding as *bits*.

A set of genes are *chotomic* if no element of the set is a subset of another. The genes $\{1\}$ and $\{2\}$ (represented as the two bit bit-vectors [10] and [01]) are a two-element, two bit chotomic set; the genes $\{1, 2\}$, $\{1, 3\}$, $\{1, 4\}$, $\{2, 3\}$, $\{2, 4\}$, and $\{3, 4\}$ ([1100], [1010], [1001], [0110], [0101], and [0011]) represent a set of six four-bit chotomic genes.

In general, our desired relationship

$$x \twoheadleftarrow y \iff \gamma(y) \subseteq \gamma(x)$$

is always true of a hierarchical encoding if the sibling nodes in the tree have chotomic genes, and the bits of these genes are not reused in the genes of any of the descendants of the siblings. (The bits can, however, be safely reused in the cousins of the siblings.) The forward part of this equivalence:

$$x \twoheadleftarrow y \Rightarrow \gamma(y) \subseteq \gamma(x)$$

is true by the definition of a hierarchical encoding—since $\gamma(x)$ includes all the bits of its ancestors, γ of any ancestor, y, is a subset of $\gamma(x)$. The reverse part of the equivalence

$$\gamma(y) \subseteq \gamma(x) \Rightarrow x \twoheadleftarrow y$$

can be seen to be true by a proof by contradiction. Assume that in our tree, $\gamma(y) \subseteq \gamma(x)$ and y is not an ancestor of x. (x cannot be a proper ancestor of y, as each level of the tree extends γ by a non-null gene.) Since this is a tree, y and x have a least common ancestor, z, and each of y and x have ancestors (or y or x itself) y' and x' that are siblings and children of z. The genes of $\gamma(y')$ and $\gamma(x')$ are chotomic—neither is a subset of the other, and the gene of each is not included in its sibling's descendants. Hence, there is at least one bit, b, of the gene of y' that is not in the gene of x'. Since the genes of chotomic siblings can't be the genes of their descendants, this number, b, is not in $\gamma(x)$. But this contradicts our assumption that $\gamma(y) \subseteq \gamma(x)$.

4   Prior Work

The naive approach to bit vector encoding associates a unique single bit gene with each type (node). This then requires $|T|^2$ space—a vector of $|T|$ bits for each of the $|T|$ nodes. While in the worst case (a tree of single-child nodes), this space complexity is unavoidable, several researchers have developed algorithms that are usually considerably more space efficient.

Aït-Kaci et al. [1] proposed a modulation algorithm, which started by assigning a unique single-bit gene to each node of the tree and then applied a repeated binary splitting and dichotomic coding to the recursive subtrees.

Another early study of bit vector encodings for MI hierarchies was Caseau [3]. That work used single bit genes. Caseau's algorithm was based on embedding the partial order in a lattice, determining which nodes have incompatible encodings, and parceling out gene assignments as a search process, where failure can prompt a change in earlier decisions. Unfortunately, completing the lattice from a partial order can take exponential time.

Vitek, Horspool and Krall [14] extended this approach. Like Caseau, they constructed a conflict graph and colored this graph, using one bit for each gene. However, to get a better encoding, they preceded this step by "balancing" the original hierarchy. One of the results that came out of this work was the recognition that that the gene allocation problem can be expressed as a graph coloring problem. Thus, the literature of graph-coloring algorithms is applicable to the bit-vector encoding problem.

Caseau et al presented a method [4] centered on conflict graphs, but also included an algorithm for trees. The key idea of that work was to use multi-bit genes for distinguishing the children of a node.

Most relevant to the current paper is the work of Raynaud and Thierry on Dichotomic Encoding [11]. Dichotomic Encoding performs a quick balancing that experimentally often produces shorter encodings. Dichotomic Encoding is discussed in detail in Section 5.

There are also many non–bit-vector approaches to the subtyping problem. The most straightforward way of computing $\overset{\scriptscriptstyle 2}{\twoheadleftarrow}$ is to literally represent the relation in a binary matrix. This requires space proportional to $|T|^2$ and provides access in constant time. At the opposite extreme is the graph encoding, where only the $\prec$ relations are stored and the system dynamically searches to establish the path at each request. This requires space only proportional to the number of links (in an SI system, $|T|$), but work at runtime(in SI systems) proportional to the height of the graph for each $\overset{\scriptscriptstyle 2}{\twoheadleftarrow}$ test.

Algorithms for efficiently minimizing the space needed to represent inheritance hierarchies have been a fertile area for research. For SI hierarchies, *relative numbering* (Schubert numbering) [12] associates with each node of the tree, a, its index, i_a in a preorder traversal. Relative numbering also stores its upper bound, u_a, the maximum index of its descendants (nodes for which $x \twoheadleftarrow a$ is true). With Schubert numbering,

$$x \twoheadleftarrow a \iff i_a \leq i_x \leq u_a.$$

Cohen's algorithm [5], for a tree of height h, stored for each node, a, both its depth in the hierarchy (distance from the root), d_a, and an array, p_a of h elements. It stored each of its ancestors in this array, putting an ancestor x at the d_x element of this array. For this algorithm,

$$a \twoheadleftarrow x \iff p_a[d_x] = x.$$

Vitek, Horspool and Krall [14] generalized Cohen's algorithm to Bit-Packed Encoding (BPE) which handled multiple inheritance by slicing, partitioning T into chunks. Recently, Zibin and Gil [17] extended the ideas of BPE with a more efficient slicing algorithm based on PQ-trees.

```
chotomic(node x, int nextFreeBit)
{
    int neededBits = cHat (x.children.size);
    for child in x.children
     as c in code (nextFreeBit, neededBits)
    {
        child.gene = c;
        chotomic (child, nextFreeBit + neededBits);
    }
}
```

Fig. 3. Chotomic encoding algorithm.

5   Dichotomic Encoding

At the last ECOOP, Raynaud and Thierry [11] presented *Dichotomic Encoding*, a quick (linear in $|T|$ times $k \log k$ in the branching factor of the tree) algorithm for creating a bit vector encoding. Dichotomic Encoding transforms the initial hierarchy into a binary tree by introducing new nodes, and giving 2-bit, chotomic (that is, dichotomic) genes to the children in the transformed tree. The transformation is driven by the goal of balancing the binary tree, so that the number of bits required to represent the two children of a node are both relatively low and equal.

In general, chotomic encoding algorithms are given a node, x, and a value, *nextFreeBit* of the next free integer for assignment. The algorithm determines the number of bits needed to code the number of children of x (cHat), which we call *neededBits*. It then assigns chotomic genes to its children using the values *nextFreeBit*, *nextFreeBit* + 1, ..., *nextFreeBit* + *neededBits* − 1, and then recursively encodes its children starting at *nextFreeBit* + *neededBits*. Figure 3 illustrates this is pseudo-code, where code(n, k) returns chotomic sets of k elements based at n.

CHNR is a chotomic algorithm that works on the original tree and uses as many bits as needed to distinguish the children of a node. Dichotomic Encoding relies on restructuring the tree into a binary tree before applying the chotomic algorithm, with the goal of reducing the number of bits needed. For a node x with children $[a, b, ...]$, the algorithm first (recursively) computes the weight (number of bits needed to represent) of each child. Nodes with no children have weight 0. Nodes with one child, weigh 1 more than that child. Nodes with two children weigh 2 more than the heavier child. For a node with more than two children, the algorithm sorts the children by weight and selects the two "lightest" children, call them a (the lightest) and b (the second lightest). It then constructs a new node y (of weight $b + 2$), changes the parentage of a and b to be y, and inserts y into the child-set of x in their place. The algorithm iterates this process until x has only two children. The algorithm then uses the chotomic encoding algorithm (Figure 3) to assign the actual genes. Thus, the tree is a binary tree; except for the root, every node has one bit of two in its gene; and the genes of

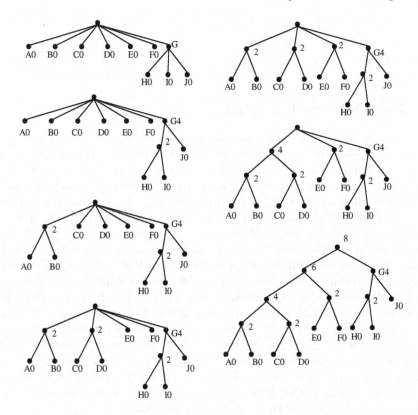

Fig. 4. Dichotomic Encoding with weights

siblings are chotomic, hence, Dichotomic Encoding. The encoding of a node is then the union of its gene with the genes of its ancestors.

Figure 4 illustrates the Dichotomic Encoding process. That figure shows the emerging binary tree with the computed weights of the nodes. In their ECOOP paper, Raynaud and Thierry proved that this algorithm produces the minimal size dichotomic encoding. Dichotomic encoding has the virtues of being fast, easy to code, and of producing reasonably compact encodings. Raynaud and Thierry report that on benchmark OO hierarchies, Dichotomic Encoding produced a 13–36% improvement over the previously best algorithm, VHK.

In the discussion that follows, the elements of a bag S are $[x_1, \ldots, x_n]$, where the x_i are sorted. Thus, x_1 of a bag is the smallest element of that bag; the x_2 is the second smallest. The rightmost element of a bag is the largest. The use of two ellipses (e.g., $[x_1, \ldots x_i \ldots x_n]$) indicates that we can't specify where an element goes in the bag's sort. The cardinality of S is $|S|$. All logarithms are in base 2.

More formally, the behavior of Dichotomic Encoding is illuminated by defining $\mathcal{D}(S)$, the function that takes a bag of child weights and computes the weight of a node. $\mathcal{D}(S)$ is computed as

$$\mathcal{D}(S) = \begin{cases} 0 & |S| = 0 \\ 1 + x_1 & |S| = 1 \\ 2 + x_2 & |S| = 2 \\ \mathcal{D}([x_3, \ldots, x_2 + 2, \ldots, x_n]) & |S| > 2 \end{cases}$$

6   Polychotomic Encoding

For some graphs, Dichotomic Encoding is strikingly inefficient. For example, a parent with, say, ten equal weight children requires 8 bits in Dichotomic Encoding to differentiate its children. The multiple-bit encoding of CHNR needs only 5. Dichotomic is particularly clever when a node has a child that weighs a lot more than its other children—it efficiently combines these other children into a subtree. When the weight of that subtree is dwarfed by the weight of the heaviest child, the weight of the parent is just two more than that heaviest child's weight. On the other hand, Dichotomic Encoding gets into trouble with nodes that have more than a few equally heavy child nodes—it tends to find itself in an escalation of biggest child weights as it combines its children.

Polychotomic Encoding ameliorates this problem. It behaves like Dichotomic Encoding for nodes with zero, one or two children. Before performing the joining step of Dichotomic, where the two smallest children are combined into a single node of weight two more than the heavier, it checks to make sure that doing so would not create a new heaviest child. If it doesn't, like Dichotomic Encoding, it builds the new node and iterates. If it would, it stops joining children and uses a multi-bit, chotomic (CHNR) encoding for all the remaining children. Figure 5 illustrates the behavior of the Polychotomic algorithm.

The function $\mathcal{C}$ defines the number of different chotomic genes using n bits:

$$\mathcal{C}(n) = \binom{n}{\lfloor n/2 \rfloor} = 2^{\lfloor n/2 \rfloor} \prod_{1 \le i \le \lceil n/2 \rceil} (2i - 1)/i$$

Note that adding two bits to a multibit encoding covers three to four times as many cases:

$$\forall n. 3\mathcal{C}(n) \le \mathcal{C}(n + 2) \le 4\mathcal{C}(n).$$

The function $\hat{c}(n)$ is the "inverse" of $\mathcal{C}$—the number of bits needed to create n different chotomic genes.

$$\hat{c}(n) = \text{the smallest } k \text{ such that } \mathcal{C}(k) \ge n.$$

Thus, $\hat{c}(9) = \hat{c}(10) = 5; \hat{c}(11) = 6$.

Once again, the structure of the algorithm is revealed in its weight function, $\mathcal{P}(S)$. The Polychotomic Encoding weight function is

$$\mathcal{P}(S) = \begin{cases} 0 & |S| = 0 \\ 1 + x_1 & |S| = 1 \\ 2 + x_2 & |S| = 2 \\ \mathcal{P}([x_3, \ldots, x_2 + 2, \ldots, x_n]) & |S| > 2, x_2 + 2 \le x_n \\ x_n + \hat{c}(n) & |S| > 2, x_2 + 2 > x_n \end{cases}$$

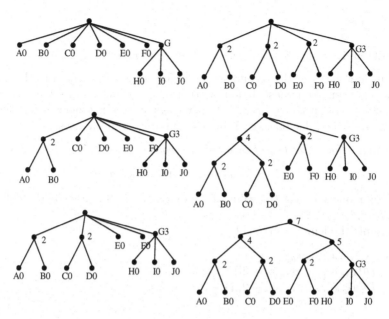

Fig. 5. Polychotomic Encoding

7 Computational Complexity

The computational complexity of Polychotomic Encoding is the same as that of Dichotomic Encoding. Each algorithm requires work proportional to $|T|$; the sorting step implies that for a tree with a largest branching factor of k, $k \log k$ additional steps may be needed at each node. (The actual assignment of bits to each gene can be done in time proportional to k; memoization can be used to pay this charge only once for each value of k.) That the worst case behavior of Polychotomic Encoding is the same as Dichotomic Encoding is not surprising, as Polychotomic Encoding algorithm is just a pruning of some of the work done under Dichotomic Encoding. The pruning is itself inexpensive (just a comparison at each split step), and for some trees, no pruning takes place at all.

In the worst case, for a "straight line" hierarchy composed single-child nodes, bit vector encoding needs one bit for each node except the root. Thus, the worst case space complexity of all bit vector encoding algorithms is proportional to $|T|^2$. In practice, the required space seems more on the scale of $|T| \log(|T|)$.

8 Polychotomic Encoding Is Never Worse Than Dichotomic Encoding

This Section is a proof that Polychotomic Encoding never produces an encoding using more bits than Dichotomic Encoding. (Of course, it often produces one that uses fewer.) This is equivalent to showing that for bags of child weights, S,

$$\forall S.\mathcal{P}(S) \le \mathcal{D}(S).$$

Definition 1. *A* flat bag *is a bag in which* $x_2 = x_n$ *or* $x_2 = x_n - 1$.

That is, in a flat bag, the second smallest element is either equal to the largest, or one less than the largest. It follows that all the elements of a flat bag except the smallest are either x_n or $x_n - 1$. Flat bags are the key place where PE and DE differ: for non-flat bags, each builds a subnode and recurses.

Lemma 1. *For a flat bag of cardinality a power of 2,* $S = [x_1, \ldots, x_n], n = 2^z$

$$\mathcal{D}(S) = x_n + 2z = x_n + 2\log n.$$

Proof by induction over the value of z. For $z = 1, S = [x_1, x_2]$, by the definition of $\mathcal{D}, \mathcal{D}(S) = x_2 + 2$.

Assume the lemma is true of $(z-1)$.

$$
\begin{aligned}
\mathcal{D}([x_1, x_2, &\ldots, x_{n-1}, x_n]) \\
&= \mathcal{D}([x_3, x_4, \ldots, x_n, x_2 + 2]) \\
&= \mathcal{D}([x_5, x_6, \ldots, x_n, x_2 + 2, x_4 + 2]) \\
&\qquad\qquad \vdots \qquad\qquad\qquad\quad \text{After } n/2 \text{ steps} \\
&= \mathcal{D}([x_2 + 2, x_4 + 2, \ldots, x_{n-2} + 2, x_n + 2]) \quad \text{A bag of size } 2^{z-1} \\
&= (x_n + 2) + 2\log(n/2) \qquad\qquad\qquad\qquad \text{Induction assumption} \\
&= x_n + 2\log n
\end{aligned}
$$

Lemma 2. *For a flat bag* $S = [x_1, \ldots, x_n], n \ge 3$,

$$\mathcal{D}(S) = x_{2(n - 2^{\lfloor \log(n-1) \rfloor})} + 2\lceil \log n \rceil$$

Proof, by strong induction, over the size of the bag S.

For a flat bag of size 3,

$$
\begin{aligned}
\mathcal{D}([x_1, x_2, x_3]) &= \mathcal{D}([x_3, x_2 + 2]) \\
&= x_2 + 4 \\
&= x_2 + 2\lceil \log 3 \rceil \\
&= x_{2(3 - 2^{\lfloor \log(3-1) \rfloor})} + 2\lceil \log 3 \rceil
\end{aligned}
$$

Assume the theorem is true for all flat bags up to size $n - 1$. We have three cases: (1) even n that is a power of 2, (2) even n not a power of two, and (3) odd n.

Case 1. Even n that is a power of 2

$$
\begin{aligned}
\mathcal{D}([x_1, x_2, &\ldots, x_{n-1}, x_n]) \\
&= x_n + 2\log n \qquad\qquad\quad \text{Lemma 1} \\
&= x_n + 2\lceil \log n \rceil \qquad\quad \text{For powers of 2, } \lceil \log n \rceil = \log n \\
&= x_{2(n-n/2)} + 2\lceil \log n \rceil \\
&= x_{2(n - 2^{\lfloor \log(n-1) \rfloor})} + 2\lceil \log n \rceil
\end{aligned}
$$

For cases 2 and 3, after $\lfloor n/2 \rfloor$ recursions, the argument bag is once again flat, allowing application of the induction assumption.

Case 2. Even n, not a power of 2

$$
\begin{aligned}
\mathcal{D}([x_1, x_2, \ldots, x_{n-1}, x_n]) \\
= \mathcal{D}([x_3, x_4, \ldots, x_n, x_2 + 2]) \\
= \mathcal{D}([x_5, x_6, \ldots, x_n, x_2 + 2, x_4 + 2]) \\
\vdots \\
= \mathcal{D}([x_2 + 2, x_4 + 2, \ldots, x_{n-2} + 2, x_n + 2]) \\
= x_{2 \cdot 2(n/2 - 2^{\lfloor \log(n/2 - 1) \rfloor})} + 2 + 2\lceil \log(n/2) \rceil \\
= x_{2(n - 2^1 \cdot 2^{\lfloor \log(n/2 - 1) \rfloor})} + 2 + 2\lceil \log(n/2) \rceil \\
= x_{2(n - 2^1 \cdot 2^{\lfloor \log(n - 1) \rfloor - 1})} + 2 + 2\lceil \log(n/2) \rceil \\
= x_{2(n - 2^{\lfloor \log(n - 1) \rfloor})} + 2\lceil \log(n) \rceil
\end{aligned}
$$

After $n/2$ steps, A flat bag of $n/2$ elts. Induction, as the kth elt. of this set is x_{2k}

Case 3. Odd n

$$
\begin{aligned}
\mathcal{D}([x_1, x_2, \ldots, x_{n-1}, x_n]) \\
= \mathcal{D}([x_3, x_4, \ldots, x_n, x_2 + 2]) \\
= \mathcal{D}([x_5, x_6, \ldots, x_n, x_2 + 2, x_4 + 2]) \\
\vdots \\
= \mathcal{D}([x_n, x_2 + 2, \ldots, x_{n-3} + 2, x_{n-1} + 2]) \\
= x_{2 \cdot 2((n+1)/2 - 2^{\lfloor \log((n+1)/2 - 1) \rfloor}) - 2} + 2 + 2\lceil \log((n + 1)/2) \rceil \\
= x_{2((n+1) - 2 \cdot 2^{\lfloor \log((n+1)/2 - 1) \rfloor} - 1)} + 2 + 2\lceil \log((n + 1)/2) \rceil \\
= x_{2(n - 2 \cdot 2^{\lfloor \log((n+1)/2 - 1) \rfloor})} + 2\lceil \log n \rceil \\
= x_{2(n - 2^{\lfloor \log(n - 1) \rfloor})} + 2\lceil \log n \rceil
\end{aligned}
$$

After $\lfloor n/2 \rfloor$ steps A flat bag of $n/2 + 1$ elements. Induction, as for $k \geq 2$, the kth elt. of this set is x_{2k-2}

Lemma 3.

$$
x_n - 1 + 2\lceil \log n \rceil \leq \mathcal{D}([x_1, \ldots, x_n]) \leq x_n + 2\lceil \log n \rceil
$$

This follows from Lemma 2, as $n - 2^{\lfloor \log(n-1) \rfloor} \geq 1$, and for flat bags, $\forall i.i \geq 2 \Rightarrow x_n - 1 \leq x_i \leq x_n$.

Theorem 1. $\forall S.\mathcal{P}(S) \leq \mathcal{D}(S)$

Proof by induction.
For $|S| \leq 2, \mathcal{P}(S) = \mathcal{D}(S)$.

Table 1. Dichotomic and Polychotomic Encoding for small flat bags

Bag Size	DE	PE	Bag Size	DE	PE
2	x_2+2	x_2+2	10	x_4+8	$x_{10}+5$
3	x_2+4	x_3+3	11	x_6+8	$x_{11}+6$
4	x_4+4	x_4+4	12	x_8+8	$x_{12}+6$
5	x_2+6	x_5+4	13	$x_{10}+8$	$x_{13}+6$
6	x_4+6	x_6+4	14	$x_{12}+8$	$x_{14}+6$
7	x_6+6	x_7+5	15	$x_{14}+8$	$x_{15}+6$
8	x_8+6	x_8+5	16	$x_{16}+8$	$x_{16}+6$
9	x_2+8	x_9+5	17	x_2+10	$x_{17}+6$

For $|S| = 3$, we have the bag $S = [x_1, x_2, x_3]$. If $x_2 + 2 \leq x_3, \mathcal{P}(S) = \mathcal{D}(S)$. If $x_2 + 2 > x_3$,

$$\mathcal{D}(S) = \mathcal{D}([x_3, x_2 + 2]) = x_2 + 4$$
$$\mathcal{P}(S) = x_3 + \hat{c}(3) = x_3 + 3$$

If $x_2 + 2 > x_3$, then $x_2 + 4 > x_3 + 2$, and (since we're dealing with integers here), $x_2 + 4 \geq x_3 + 3$. So for bags of cardinality 3, $\mathcal{P}(S) \leq \mathcal{D}(S)$. Table 1 shows the results of $\mathcal{D}$ and $\mathcal{P}$ for flat bags of size up to 17. Keep in mind that for $i \geq 2, x_i$ is at most one less than x_n.

Assume the theorem is true for bags of size up to $n - 1$. There are two possibilities, either S is not flat, or flat. If S is not flat, $\mathcal{D}(S) = \mathcal{D}([x_3, \ldots, x_2 + 2, \ldots, x_n])$ and $\mathcal{P}(S) = ([x_3, \ldots, x_2 + 2, \ldots, x_n])$. We've reduced the problem to comparing $\mathcal{P}$ and $\mathcal{D}$ on the same bag of size $n-1$, so by the induction assumption, the theorem follows.

If S is flat, from Lemma 3, $\mathcal{D}(S) \geq x_n - 1 + 2\lceil \log n \rceil$ and $\mathcal{P}(S) = x_n + \hat{c}(n)$. Table 1 shows that by bags of size 16, $\mathcal{P}$ is already two bits smaller than $\mathcal{D}$. For larger bags, where $\mathcal{D}$ is more than a couple of bits larger than $\hat{c}$, with each additional 2 bits, $\mathcal{D}$ allows us to cover twice as many elements. However, with an additional 2 bits, $\hat{c}$ allows us to cover $2(2i-1)/i$ (or between three and four times as many) elements. On flat bags, $\mathcal{D}$ is thus larger. In the limit, $\mathcal{D}(S) = 2\mathcal{P}(S)$; for large flat bags, $\mathcal{D}$ uses almost twice as many bits.

9   Greedy Polychotomic Encoding

Polychotomic Encoding is based on the idea of doing Dichotomic Encoding until it would create a new heaviest child, and then switching to a multi-bit encoding. But consider the tree of Figure 2. Dichotomic Encoding requires 8 bits; Polychotomic Encoding 7 bits, and CHNR (pure multibit encoding) also 7. However, multibit encoding the six single leaves and then dichotomically combining the resulting node with the multibit encoding of the rightmost node yields a 6 bit code (Figure 6). This suggests the Greedy Polychotomic Encoding (GPE) algorithm: combine as many small children as possible using a multi-bit encoding until doing so would create a new heaviest child, and then use a multibit encoding on the remainder. Experiments with variations on this theme—splitting

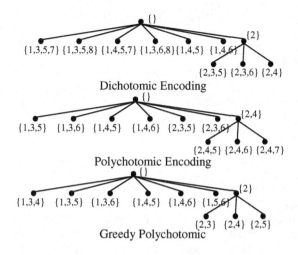

Fig. 6. Alternative encodings

some of the children of a node into a subtree for multibit encoding, then recursively processing the child set—failed to find any algorithm that was consistently better than PE. While we can not recommend greedy PE algorithms, we include GPE in the results of Section 10 for the sake of comparison.

10   Experimental Results

There are three ways to experimentally evaluate algorithms: by examining their results on "natural" hierarchies, consistent structures (for example, complete trees of a given branching factor and depth), and by their performance on random trees. Natural hierarchies occur in the class structures of object-oriented programs, in the hierarchies of AI systems that attempt to model the world, in databases, and in other computer applications. This experiment compared the CHNR, Dichotomic Encoding, Polychotomic Encoding and Greedy Polychotomic Encoding algorithms. For programming class hierarchies, five examples are shown: VisualWorks2 and Digitalk3, SMALLTALK-80 class libraries; types extracted from the NextStep libraries; the ET++ graphical user interface; and the Java 1.3 class library. The first four of these are the benchmarks of [14]. As an example of an AI hierarchy, the algorithms were applied to the biological taxonomy of Mammalia (see [16], after correcting for the inconsistent indentation.)

As an example of a database system, we used the DARWIN wind-tunnel system [15]. Wind tunnel test data are hierarchical. The set of measurements about a model are a *test*. A given test can be checked for different *configurations* (e.g., orientation of the model or arrangements of sensors), a given configuration can be checked for a specific *run*, and for a run, data is collected at *points* (temporal instants). Thus, tests contain configurations which contain runs which contain points. Rather than having a single table of point data, where each line is

Table 2. Tree Parameters

	Nodes	INodes	MaxB	MeanB	SDB	MaxH	MeanH	SDH
Program classes								
NextStep	311	65	142	4.76	17.578	7	2.93	1.156
ET	371	82	87	4.51	11.131	8	3.29	1.935
Digitalk3	1357	434	142	3.12	9.873	13	5.39	2.190
Java 1.3 classes	1478	307	572	4.81	32.804	7	2.47	1.502
VisualWorks2	1957	625	181	3.12	10.400	15	6.39	2.905
Real classes								
Mammals	6059	1431	151	4.23	8.682	7	4.99	1.130
Databases								
Darwin	66991	1770	529	37.84	27.306	4	3.97	0.170
File directories								
Java 1.3 directory	1980	99	173	19.98	27.962	8	4.85	1.016
010725 C Drive	33130	1707	3139	19.40	122.338	13	6.01	2.021
010725 F Drive	114598	7286	1724	15.72	54.455	15	7.18	1.865
Complete trees								
Depth 4, width 6	1555	259	6	6.00	0.000	4	3.80	0.486
Depth 6, width 4	5461	1365	4	4.00	0.000	6	5.66	0.664

Key:: Nodes = Nodes in tree. INodes = interior (non-leaf) nodes. MaxB = maximum branching factor. MeanB = average Inode branching factor. SDB = standard deviation, branching factor. MaxH = maximum height. MeanH = mean height. STD = standard deviation, heights.

a (fairly redundant) quadruple, the database stores this information in separate tables for each kind of data. Because access control is also hierarchical, it can be important to quickly determine if a given data element is a piece of something to which a user has access. A bit-vector encoding, at each data point, could be used to vet access.

As examples of other "naturally occurring" "computational" hierarchies, the algorithms were run on the file structure trees of the Java 1.3 distribution, and the file/directory trees of my C and F drives on July 25, 2001. I also considered two "Complete trees," one of branching factor 4 and depth 6, and other of branching factor 6 and depth 4.

Table 2 presents the structural statistics on these trees; Table 3 the number of bits each of the four algorithms requires for that tree. These examples suggest that Polychotomic Encoding is almost always better than Dichotomic Encoding, though how much better can vary considerably.

Running PE and DE on random trees enabled a better understanding of the algorithms' relative strengths[1]. The "jar graph" of Figure 7 shows the results

---

[1] For this experiment, the random tree generator $\mathcal{G}$ was parameterized by the number of nodes to be generated, a mean branching factor, and a standard deviation of the branching factor. ($\mathcal{G}(n, m, sd)$). When $n = 0$ the algorithm would just generate a leaf node. Otherwise, a Gaussian random number generator would be repeatedly invoked with the given mean and standard deviation until it returned a positive number, b. If $b \leq n$, the node received n leaf children. If not, the allocation of $n - b$ nodes was randomly divided among the children by picking dividing points at random, and $\mathcal{G}$ recursively invoked to generate the child trees.

Table 3. Algorithm results

	CHNR	DE	PE	GPE
Program classes				
Java 1.3 classes	36	23	21	21
Digitalk3	52	29	28	30
ET	41	20	20	22
NextStep	28	20	19	18
VisualWorks2	58	33	31	35
Real classes				
Mammals	41	30	26	29
Databases				
Darwin	30	36	28	27
File directories				
Java 1.3 directory	40	27	23	23
010725 C Drive	60	38	33	36
010725 F Drive	73	43	38	40
Complete trees				
Depth 6, width 4	24	24	24	24
Depth 4, width 6	16	24	16	16

Key:: CHNR = Multi-bit encoding. DE = Dichotomic Encoding. PE = Polychotomic Encoding. GPE = Greedy Polychotomic Encoding.

of running DE and PE on such random trees. For each experimental point, 30 trees were generated, $\mathcal{D}$ and $\mathcal{P}$ calculated and averaged. The experiment was run with tree sizes of 200, 2,000, 20,000, and 200,000; mean branching factors of 2, 8, 32, and 128 nodes, and standard deviations that varied from one half the mean (the narrow jars), the mean (the medium jars) and twice the mean (the fat jars). The upper number on each jar is the average number of bits needed for Dichotomic Encoding; the lower number, the average number of bits needed for Polychotomic Encoding. Visually, each jar is as "full" as the ratio of these two numbers.

The increasing white space in the jars as one moves to the right suggests that PE has greater advantage when dealing with trees with higher branching factors, that this advantage is relatively independent of the tree size, and that greater variance in the branching factor produces only a minor boost to the performance of PE, perhaps as wider nodes are more likely to be in the tree.

11 Discussion

This paper described the Polychotomic Encoding algorithm, an improvement to the Dichotomic Encoding algorithm of Raynaud and Thierry. Polychotomic Encoding, like its predecessor, is near-linear in execution and produces good (but not optimal) bit-vector encodings. (The problem of taking an arbitrary directed acyclic graph finding the minimal encoding is NP-hard [9]. The difficulty of trees is an open question.) An open research question suggested by this work is how

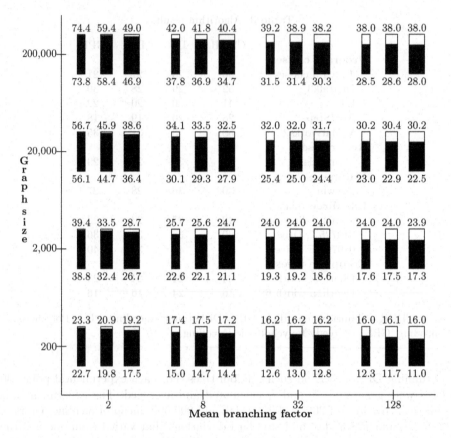

Fig. 7. Dichotomic and Polychotomic performance on random trees. Each bar shows the portion of the number of bits required by DE used by PE. The three jars in each entry show the test run with different standard deviations of the branching factor (half the mean, the mean, and twice the mean.)

best to apply hierarchical encoding algorithms to multiple inheritance graphs. A promising direction is to partition the hierarchy into slices, each of which could be quickly encoded with a different bit-set. The recent work of Zibin and Gil on PQ-trees [17] suggests a possible approach to the partitioning problem.

Acknowledgments

My thanks to Cecilia Aragon, Diana Lee, Barry Leiner, Tarang Patel, Olivier Raynaud, Eric Thierry, and Rajkumar Thirumalainambi for discussions and comments on the drafts of this paper, and to Louise Chan for help with the DARWIN database.

References

1. Aït-Kaci, H., Boyer, R., Lincoln, P., and Nasr, R.. Efficient implementation of lattice operations. *TOPLAS 11*, 1 (Jan. 1989), 115–146.
2. Baker, H. A Decision Procedure for Common Lisp's SUBTYPEP Predicate. *J. Lisp and Symbolic Computation 5*, (Sept. 1992), 157–190.
3. Caseau, Y. Efficient handling of multiple inheritance hierarchies. In *Proc. OOPSLA-93*, (Washington, D.C., 1993), 271–287.
4. Caseau, Y., Habib, M., Nourine, L., and Raynaud, O. Encoding of multiple inheritance hierarchies and partial orders. *Computational Intelligence 15*, 1 (1999), 50–62.
5. Cohen, N. H. Type-extension tests can be performed in constant time. *TOPLAS 13* (1991), 626–629.
6. Fikes, R., and Kehler, T. The role of frame-based representation in reasoning. *CACM, 28*, 9 (September 1985), 904–920.
7. Goldberg, A., and Robson, D. *SmallTalk-80: The Language and its Implementation.* Addison-Wesley, Reading, MA. (1980).
8. Gosling, J., Joy, B., Steele, G., and Bracha, G. *The Java Language Specification, 2nd Edition.* Addison-Wesley, Reading, MA, (2000).
9. Habib, M., and Nourine, L., Bit-vector encoding for partially ordered sets, *ORDAL'94*, LNCS No 831, Springer-Verlag, Berlin (1994), 1–12.
10. Keene, S. E. *Object-Oriented Programming in Common Lisp: A Programmer's Guide to CLOS.* Addison-Wesley, Reading, Massachusetts (1989).
11. Raynaud, O. and Thierry, E. A quasi optimal bit-vector encoding of tree hierarchies. Application to efficient type inclusion tests. In *Proc. ECOOP 2001.* LNCS 2072, Berlin: Springer-Verlag, (2001), 165–180.
12. Schubert, L. K., Papalaskaris, M. A., and Taugher, L. Determining type, part, color, and time relationships. *IEEE Computer 16*, 10 (October 1983), 53–60.
13. Stickel, M. E. Automatic deduction by theory resolution. In *Proc. IJCAI-85.* Los Angeles, Morgan Kauffman, Los Altos, CA (1985), 1181–1186.
14. Vitek, J., Horspool, R. N., and Krall, A. Efficient type inclusion tests. In *Proc. OOPSLA-97*, Atlanta, (October 1997), 142–157.
15. Walton, J., Filman, R. E., and Korsmeyer, D. J. The evolution of the DARWIN system. In *Proc. ACM Symposium on Applied Computing*, Como, Italy, (March 2000), 971–977.
16. Wilson, D. E., and Reeder, D. M. (Eds.). *Mammal Species of the World.* Smithsonian Institution Press, Washington, D.C., 1993.
    gopher://nmnhgoph.si.edu/00/.docs/mammals_data/list
17. Zibin, Y. and Gil, J. Efficient subtyping tests with PQ-Encoding. In *Proc. OOPSLA-2001*, Tampa, Florida (October 2001), 96–106.

Semantics-Based Composition
of Class Hierarchies

Gregor Snelting[1] and Frank Tip[2]

[1] Universität Passau, Lehrstuhl für Softwaresysteme
Innstr. 33, 94032 Passau, Germany
snelting@fmi.uni-passau.de
[2] IBM T.J. Watson Research Center
P.O. Box 704, Yorktown Heights, NY 10598, USA
tip@watson.ibm.com

Abstract. Class hierarchy composition aims at constructing software systems by *composing* a set of class hierarchies into an executable system. Current composition algorithms cannot provide semantic guarantees. We present a composition algorithm, together with an interference criterion and its correctness proof, which guarantees that behavior of the original hierarchies is preserved for interference-free compositions. In case of interference, an impact analysis can determine the consequences of integration. The method is based on existing program analysis technology and is illustrated by various examples.

1 Introduction

Class hierarchy composition aims at constructing software systems by *composing* the code associated with a set of class hierarchies into an executable system [5,19], or by weaving separately written aspects into a class hierarchy [8,22]. Advocates of composition argue that, by putting the functionality associated with each system feature in a separate hierarchy, a better separation of concerns is achieved, resulting in code that is easier to understand, maintain, and change.

Although considerable amounts of work have been devoted to developing specification formalisms for software composition, and on the methodological aspects of compositional software development, current techniques and tools for hierarchy composition operate on a purely syntactical basis and cannot provide any semantic guarantees about the behavior of the composed hierarchy. It is thus our aim to develop a semantically well-founded notion of composition that enables reasoning about the behavior of composed class hierarchies. We have opted for the following approach:

- We define notions of *static interference* and *dynamic interference* that capture how features in one hierarchy may impact the behavior of code in another. The former notion captures behavioral impact at composition-time, whereas the latter is concerned with run-time changes in program behavior.

B. Magnusson (Ed.): ECOOP 2002, LNCS 2374, pp. 562–584, 2002.

- We consider two kinds of compositions. *Basic compositions* involve hierarchies that do not statically interfere. *Overriding compositions* rely on a mechanism by which a user can explicitly resolve static interference.
- In cases where interference is found, an *impact analysis* (similar to the one of [16]) is performed that determines a set of methods in the composed hierarchy for which preservation of behavior cannot be guaranteed.

Hence, our techniques allow a developer to quickly determine if a proposed composition may result in behavioral changes, and—if so—report precisely which parts of the program may be affected. In the longer term, we hope to incorporate these techniques in a system such as Hyper/J [19] in the form of a tool that performs various sanity checks on compositions.

In order to illustrate our techniques, Figure 1 shows three hierarchies that model a number of aspects of university life. $\mathcal{H}_1$ defines classes `Course`, `Person`, `Student`, and `Professor`, and provides functionality for enrolling students in courses, for associating professors with courses, and for professors to approve the graduation of students (method `Professor.approveGraduation()`). This latter operation requires the approval of the courses taken by a student, modeled using a method `approveCourses()`. We have omitted the details of `approveCourses()`, but one can easily imagine adding functionality for keeping track of a student's course load and grades which would be checked by the professor to base his decision on. Class `Driver1` contains a small test driver that exercises the functionality of hierarchy $\mathcal{H}_1$.

Hierarchy $\mathcal{H}_2$ is concerned with employment and advisory relationships. A student can designate a professor as his/her advisor (method `Student.set Advisor()`, and a professor can hire a student as a teaching assistant using method `Professor.hireAssistant()`. Class `Driver2` exercises the functionality in this hierarchy.

Hierarchy $\mathcal{H}_3$ shows a slightly more elaborate model, where a distinction is made between (undergraduate) `Student`s and `PhDStudent`s. This impacts the approval of graduations, because `PhDStudent`s are also required to produce a thesis of sufficient quality (modeled by method `Professor.approvePhDThesis()`). Due to space limitations, we have omitted the details of this method.

Let us now consider the composition of $\mathcal{H}_1$ and $\mathcal{H}_2$. These hierarchies are not disjoint, since they contain the same classes. However, since there are no "syntactic collisions" between members in $\mathcal{H}_1$ and $\mathcal{H}_2$ (i.e., $\mathcal{H}_1$ and $\mathcal{H}_2$ do not contain methods with the same name and signatures, but with different bodies), one can simply construct a hierarchy that contains the union of the classes in $\mathcal{H}_1$ and $\mathcal{H}_2$, where each class in the combined hierarchy contains the union of the methods/fields that occur in the corresponding class(es) in $\mathcal{H}_1$ and $\mathcal{H}_2$. The resulting hierarchy is shown in Figure 2. What can be said about the behavior of $\mathcal{H}_1 \oplus \mathcal{H}_2$? In this case, our interference check guarantees that the behavior of the client applications of these hierarchies (modeled by `Driver1.main()` and `Driver2.main()`) are unaffected by the composition. For this specific composition, we can even provide the stronger guarantee that the behavior of *any* client of $\mathcal{H}_1$ and $\mathcal{H}_2$ is preserved. As we shall see shortly, this is not always the case.

$$\mathcal{H}_1$$

```
class Course {
  Course(Professor p, String name){
    prof = p; courseName = name;
    students = new HashSet();
  }
  String toString(){ return courseName; }
  void enroll(Student s){
    if (!students.contains(s)){
      students.add(s);
      s.coursesTaken.add(this); }
  }
  void assign(Professor p){
    prof = p;
    p.coursesGiven.add(this);}
  Set students; Professor prof;
  String courseName;
}
class Person {
  Person(String n, String a){
    name = n; address = a;
  }
  String name; String address; }
class Student extends Person {
  Student(String n, String a){
    super(n, a);
    coursesTaken = new HashSet(); }
  String toString(){
    return "student "+name+" takes "+
      coursesTaken+"\n"; }
  Set coursesTaken;
}
class Professor extends Person {
  Professor(String n, String a){
    super(n, a);
    coursesGiven = new HashSet(); }
  String toString(){
    return "prof. "+name+" teaches "+
      coursesGiven+"\n"; }
  boolean approveGraduation(Student s){
    return approveCourses(s); }
  boolean approveCourses(Student s){
    return true; // details omitted
  }
  Set coursesGiven;
}
class Driver1 {
  void main(){
    Professor p1 =
      new Professor("prof1","padd1"); P1
    Student s1 =
      new Student("stu1","sadd1"); S1
    Course c1 = new Course(p1, "CS121");
    c1.enroll(s1); c1.assign(p1);
    boolean b = p1.approveGraduation(s1);
  }
}
```

$$\mathcal{H}_2$$

```
class Person { ... } // as in H1
class Student {
  Student(String n, String a){
    ... // as in H1
  }
}
```

```
  void setAdvisor(Professor p){
    advisor = p; }
  Set coursesTaken; Professor advisor;
}
class Professor {
  Professor(String n, String a){
    ... // as in H1
  }
  void hireAssistant(Student s){
    assistant = s; }
  Set coursesGiven; Student assistant;
}
class Driver2 {
  void main(){
    Professor p2 =
      new Professor("prof2","padd2"); P2
    Student s2 =
      new Student("stu2","sadd2"); S2
    s2.setAdvisor(p2);p2.hireAssistant(s2);
  }
}
```

$$\mathcal{H}_3$$

```
class Person { ... } // as in H1
class Student {
  Student(String n,String a){
    ... // as in H1
  }
  Set coursesTaken;
}
class PhDStudent extends Student {
  PhDStudent(String n,String a){
    super(n,a);
  }
}
class Professor {
  Professor(String n,String a){
    ... // as in H1
  }
  boolean approveGraduation(Student s){
    boolean approved = approveCourses(s);
    if (s instanceof PhDStudent){
      approved = approved &&
        approveThesis((PhDStudent)s);
    }
    return approved;
  }
  boolean approveCourses(Student s){
    ... // as in H1
  }
  boolean approveThesis(PhDStudent s){
    /* details omitted */
  }
  Set coursesGiven;
}
class Driver3 {
  void main(){
    Professor p3 =
      new Professor("prof3","padd3"); P3
    PhDStudent s3 =
      new PhDStudent("stu3","sadd3"); S3
    p3.approveGraduation(s3);
  }
}
```

Fig. 1. Example hierarchies concerned with different aspects of university life. Allocation sites are labeled (shown in boxes).

```
class Course { ⋯ }                               // as in H₁
class Person { ⋯ }                               // as in H₁ and H₂
class Student extends Person {
  Student(String n, String a){ ⋯ }               // as in H₁ and H₂
  String toString(){ ⋯ }                         // as in H₁
  void setAdvisor(Professor p){ ⋯ }              // as in H₂
  Set coursesTaken;
  Professor advisor;
}
class Professor extends Person {
  Professor(String n, String a){ ⋯ }             // as in H₁ and H₂
  String toString(){ ⋯ }                         // as in H₁
  boolean approveGraduation(Student s){ ⋯ }      // as in H₁
  boolean approveCourses(Student s){ ⋯ }         // as in H₁
  void hireAssistant(Student s){ ⋯ }             // as in H₂
  Set coursesGiven;
  Student assistant;
}
class Driver1 { ⋯ }                              // as in H₁
class Driver2 { ⋯ }                              // as in H₂
```

Fig. 2. A basic composition: $\mathcal{H}_1 \oplus \mathcal{H}_2$.

Now consider composing $\mathcal{H}_1$ and $\mathcal{H}_3$, which contain different methods `Professor.approveGraduation()`, an example of static interference. Method `approveGraduation()` in $\mathcal{H}_3$ is "more general" than `approveGraduation()` in $\mathcal{H}_1$. In constructing $\mathcal{H}_1 \oplus \mathcal{H}_3$ (see Figure 3), we have assumed that the user specified that the definition of `approveGraduation()` in $\mathcal{H}_3$ should be preferred over that in $\mathcal{H}_1$. In this case, our techniques report dynamic interference, i.e., preservation of behavior for clients of the original hierarchies cannot be guaranteed. Impact analysis reports that `Driver3.main()` is not affected by the composition, but that the behavior of `Driver1.main()` may have changed.

2   Composition of Hierarchies

One of the first issues that arises when composing two class hierarchies is the question which classes and methods in the input hierarchies correspond. The Hyper/J composition system [19] relies on a specification language to express these correspondences. For example, one can specify "merge-by-name" compositions in which two classes in different input hierarchies are matched if they have the same name, and one can explicitly specify pairs of matching classes (with different names) using an "equate" construct.

In order to simplify the presentation in this paper, we will assume that classes are matched "by name" only. Compositions that are not name-based can be modeled using an additional preprocessing step in which classes and methods are renamed appropriately. In particular, manually established relations between

```
class Course { ··· }                              // as in H₁
class Person { ··· }                              // as in H₁ and H₃
class Student extends Person {
  Student(String n, String a){ ··· }              // as in H₁ and H₃
  String toString(){ ··· }                        // as in H₁
  Set coursesTaken;
}
class PhDStudent extends Student { ··· }          // as in H₃
class Professor extends Person {
  Professor(String n, String a){ ··· }            // as in H₁ and H₃
  String toString(){ ··· }                        // as in H₁
  boolean approveGraduation(Student s){ ··· }     // as in H₃
  boolean approveCourses(Student s){ ··· }        // as in H₁ and H₃
  boolean approveThesis(PhDStudent s){ ··· }      // as in H₃
  Set coursesGiven;
}
class Driver1 { ··· }                             // as in H₁
class Driver3 { ··· }                             // as in H₃
```

Fig. 3. An overriding composition: $\mathcal{H}_1 \oplus \mathcal{H}_3$.

entities in the two hierarchies are assumed to be modeled by appropriate renaming.

2.1   Class Hierarchies

Definition 1 defines the notion of a class hierarchy. To keep our definitions simple, we assume that fields and abstract methods have undefined bodies ($body(m) = \bot$), and that fields and abstract methods cannot have the same name.

Definition 1 (class hierarchy). *A class hierarchy $\mathcal{H}$ is a set of classes together with an inheritance relation: $\mathcal{H} = (\mathcal{C}, \leq)$. For a class $C \in \mathcal{C}$ we also write $C \in \mathcal{H}$. A class $C \in \mathcal{H}$ has a name and contains a set of members[1]: $C = (n, M)$, where $name(C) = n$, $members(C) = M$. A member $m \in members(C)$ is characterized by its name, its signature and its body: $m = (f, \sigma, B)$ where $\sigma \in \mathcal{C}^* \times \mathcal{C}$. We will use $namesig(m)$ to denote the combination $\langle f, \sigma \rangle$ that together uniquely identify a member within a class, and $body(m)$ to denote the body B of member m.*

2.2   Classes and Inheritance Relations in the Composed Hierarchy

Semantically sound composition requires that the original inheritance relations can be order-embedded into the composed hierarchy. That is, a relationship A instanceof B that holds in an input hierarchy should also hold in the composed hierarchy. In general, one cannot simply compute the union of the inheritance

---

[1] According to this definition, *members(C)* does not contain inherited members that are declared in superclasses of C.

relations in the input hierarchies because the resulting hierarchy may contain cycles. We therefore use a well-known factorization technique (see, e.g., [3]) that produces an acyclic hierarchy. This construction has the advantage that hierarchies can be composed even if there are cycles in the union of the original inheritance relations – which might sometimes be useful in practice.

Given two input hierarchies $\mathcal{H}_1$ and $\mathcal{H}_2$, their composition is denoted $\mathcal{H}_1 \oplus \mathcal{H}_2$. The construction of $\mathcal{H}_1 \oplus \mathcal{H}_2$ is given in Definition 2. This involves: creating a set of pairs of the form $\langle$ class, hierarchy $\rangle$ (step 1), determining the "union" of the inheritance relations in the input hierarchies (assuming that classes are matched by name) (2), determining cycles in the transitive closure of these inheritance relations, and constructing a set of equivalence classes[2] $\mathcal{E}$ corresponding to these cycles (3-5), creation of a class in the composed hierarchy for each equivalence class in $\mathcal{E}$ (6), associating a name and a set of members (7) with each class, and creation of the inheritance relations in the composed hierarchy (8).

Definition 2 (hierarchy composition). *Let $\mathcal{H}_1 = (\mathcal{C}_1, \leq_1)$ and $\mathcal{H}_2 = (\mathcal{C}_2, \leq_2)$ be two class hierarchies. Then, $\mathcal{H}_1 \oplus \mathcal{H}_2 = (\mathcal{C}, \leq)$, which is defined as follows:*

1. $S = \{ \langle C_1, \mathcal{H}_1 \rangle \mid C_1 \in \mathcal{C}_1 \} \cup \{ \langle C_2, \mathcal{H}_2 \rangle \mid C_2 \in \mathcal{C}_2 \}$,
2. $\langle C_1, \mathcal{H}_1 \rangle \leq' \langle C_2, \mathcal{H}_1 \rangle \Leftarrow C_1 \leq_1 C_2$, $\langle C_1, \mathcal{H}_2 \rangle \leq' \langle C_2, \mathcal{H}_2 \rangle \Leftarrow C_1 \leq_2 C_2$,
   $\langle C_1, \mathcal{H}_i \rangle \leq' \langle C_2, \mathcal{H}_j \rangle \Leftarrow \text{name}(C_1) = \text{name}(C_2), \ (i, j \in \{ 1, 2 \})$
3. $x \, \rho \, y \iff x \leq'^* y \wedge y \leq'^* x$,
4. $\leq \ = \ \leq'^* / \rho$,
5. $\mathcal{E} = \{ [x]_\rho \mid x \in S \}$,
6. $\mathcal{C} = \{ \text{class}([x]_\rho) \mid [x]_\rho \in \mathcal{E} \}$,
7. $\text{class}([x]_\rho) = \langle \text{name}([x]_\rho), \text{members}([x]_\rho) \rangle$, *and*
8. $\text{class}([x]_\rho) \leq \text{class}([y]_\rho) \iff [x]_\rho \leq [y]_\rho$

The name *function determines the name of the composed class from the names of the classes in equivalence class $[C]_\rho$ and will not be formally defined here (some examples will be given below). Note that the members of a composed class do not include inherited members from the original classes, but only the members defined locally in the original classes. Different* members *operators will be presented for different kinds of compositions in Definitions 4 and 6 below.*

Note that $\leq'$ is not necessarily transitive, hence the use of the closure operator. As usual, $[x]_\rho$ consists of all classes ρ-equivalent to x, and $[x]_\rho \leq [y]_\rho \iff x \leq' y$; we assume that $\leq$ is the smallest partial order satisfying the conditions from the definition. We will use $\mathcal{E}$ to denote the set of all equivalence classes $[\langle C, \mathcal{H} \rangle]_\rho$, for any $\langle C, \mathcal{H} \rangle \in S$. Moreover, we define a partial order on $\mathcal{E}$ by: $\langle C, \mathcal{H} \rangle \leq' \langle C', \mathcal{H}' \rangle \iff [\langle C, \mathcal{H} \rangle]_\rho \leq [\langle C', \mathcal{H}' \rangle]_\rho$. Intuitively, one can imagine this order as the directed acyclic graph of all strongly connected components of the union of the two input hierarchies.

---

[2] Unfortunately, the term "class" as in "equivalence class" is different from "class" as in "class hierarchy"; we use this "overloading" in order to be compatible with both mathematical and computer science conventions.

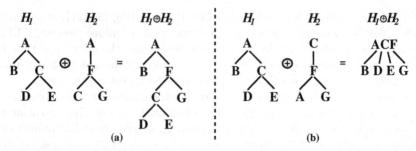

Fig. 4. Hierarchy composition without class merging(a), and with class merging (b).

Example 1. In the hierarchy of Figure 4(a), the transitive closure of $\leq_1$ and $\leq_2$ does not contain any cycles. Hence, we have: $\mathcal{E} = \{ \{\langle A, \mathcal{H}_1 \rangle, \langle A, \mathcal{H}_2, \rangle\}, \{\langle B, \mathcal{H}_1 \rangle\},$ $\{\langle C, \mathcal{H}_1 \rangle, \langle C, \mathcal{H}_2, \rangle\}, \{\langle D, \mathcal{H}_1 \rangle\}, \{\langle E, \mathcal{H}_1 \rangle\}, \{\langle F, \mathcal{H}_2, \rangle\}, \{\langle G, \mathcal{H}_2, \rangle\} \}$. Consequently, the following inheritance relations are constructed: $B < A, F < A, C < F, G < F, D < C, E < C$. Here, class names in the composed hierarchy are generated from the names of the classes in the corresponding equivalence sets (e.g., class A corresponds to $\{ \langle A, \mathcal{H}_1 \rangle, \langle A, \mathcal{H}_2 \rangle \}$). Note that *immediate* subclass/superclass relations need not be preserved: F is now between A and C. □

Example 2. For the slightly more interesting example of Figure 4(b), we have: $\mathcal{E} = \{ \{\langle A, \mathcal{H}_1 \rangle, \langle A, \mathcal{H}_2 \rangle, \langle C, \mathcal{H}_1 \rangle, \langle C, \mathcal{H}_2 \rangle, \langle F, \mathcal{H}_2 \rangle\}, \{\langle B, \mathcal{H}_1 \rangle\}, \{\langle D, \mathcal{H}_1 \rangle\}, \{\langle E, \mathcal{H}_1 \rangle\},$ $\{\langle G, \mathcal{H}_2, \rangle\} \}$. The composed hierarchy contains a class for each of these equivalence classes (for the purposes of this example, we assume that the *name* function constructs a class name by concatenating the names of elements in the equivalence class). There is an inheritance relation $X < Y$ if the equivalence class corresponding to X contains a class x, and the equivalence class corresponding to Y contains a class y such that x inherits from y in one or both of the input hierarchies. For example, class B inherits from ACF because $\langle B, \mathcal{H}_1 \rangle$ is part of equivalence class $\{ \langle B, \mathcal{H}_1 \rangle \}$, $\langle A, \mathcal{H}_1 \rangle$ is part of equivalence class $\{ \langle A, \mathcal{H}_1 \rangle, \langle A, \mathcal{H}_2 \rangle, \langle C, \mathcal{H}_1 \rangle, \langle C, \mathcal{H}_2 \rangle, \langle F, \mathcal{H}_2 \rangle \}$, and class B inherits from class A in $\mathcal{H}_1$. Again, *immediate* subclass/superclass relations need not be preserved: some immediate relations (e.g., $F < C$) have been collapsed. □

In case classes have been merged, new class names have been introduced as well (e.g., ACF in the above example). Thus any client code must be transformed accordingly: any occurrence of the old class name x must be replaced by $name([x]_\rho)$. In the example, any occurrence of class names A, C, or F in client code must be replaced by ACF.

A final issue to note is that the composed inheritance relation may contain multiple inheritance. This may cause problems in languages such as Java that do not support general multiple inheritance. We consider this issue to be outside the scope of this paper, and plan to pursue an approach in which multiple inheritance is automatically transformed into delegation, along the lines of [20].

2.3   Basic Composition

In defining the set of members in the composed hierarchy, the question arises of what to do when two or more classes in an equivalence class $[x]_\rho$ define the same member. We will refer to such cases as *static interference*. The easiest approach of dealing with this issue is to simply disallow composition if static interference occurs. We will refer to this scenario as *basic composition*. As we shall see shortly, the absence of static interference does not guarantee preservation of behavior.

Definition 3 defines basic static interference. Note that it *does* allow situations where an equivalence class $[x]_\rho$ contains two elements $\langle C_1, \mathcal{H}_1 \rangle$ and $\langle C_2, \mathcal{H}_2 \rangle$ such that C_1 and C_2 each contain a member m, provided that (i) $body(m) = \bot$ holds for at least one of these m's, or (ii) that the two m's have the same body.

Definition 3 (basic static interference). $\mathcal{E}$ *contains basic static interference if there is an equivalence class* $[x]_\rho \in \mathcal{E}$ *such that for some* $\langle C_1, \mathcal{H} \rangle, \langle C_2, \mathcal{H}' \rangle \in [x]_\rho$, $C_1 \neq C_2$, $m_1 \in members(C_1)$, $m_2 \in members(C_2)$, $namesig(m_1) = namesig(m_2)$ *we have that:* $body(m_1) \neq \bot$, $body(m_2) \neq \bot$, *and* $body(m_1) \neq body(m_2)$.

Definition 4 defines the set of members in the composed hierarchy. Note that, in cases where the classes in an equivalence class contain multiple methods with the same name and signature, the unique method with a non-$\bot$ body is selected.

Definition 4 (members). *Let* $\mathcal{E}$ *be free of basic static interference, and let* $[x]_\rho \in \mathcal{E}$ *be an equivalence class. Define:*

$$members([x]_\rho) = \quad \{\, m \mid \langle C, \mathcal{H} \rangle \in [x]_\rho, \ m \in members(C),$$
$$(\langle C', \mathcal{H}' \rangle \in [x]_\rho, \ C' \neq C, \ m' \in members(C'),$$
$$namesig(m) = namesig(m') \implies body(m') = \bot) \,\}$$

Example 3. The transitive closure of the inheritance relations in $\mathcal{H}_1$ and $\mathcal{H}_2$ of Figure 1 does not contain any cycles. Hence, the construction of Definition 2 produces a hierarchy with classes Course, Person, Student, Professor, Driver1, and Driver2, with inheritance relations Student $<$ Person and Professor $<$ Person. The equivalence classes constructed are: $S_1 = \{\, \langle Course, \mathcal{H}_1 \rangle \,\}$, $S_2 = \{\, \langle Person, \mathcal{H}_1 \rangle \,\}$, $S_3 = \{\, \langle Student, \mathcal{H}_1 \rangle, \langle Student, \mathcal{H}_2 \rangle \,\}$, $S_4 = \{\, \langle Professor, \mathcal{H}_1 \rangle, \langle Professor, \mathcal{H}_2 \rangle \,\}$, $S_5 = \{\, \langle Driver1, \mathcal{H}_1 \rangle \,\}$, and $S_6 = \{\, \langle Driver2, \mathcal{H}_2 \rangle \,\}$. Definition 3 states that there is basic static interference if an equivalence class S contains multiple methods with the same name but different bodies. Singleton equivalence classes such as S_1, S_2, S_5, and S_6 cannot give rise to interference because a class can contain only one method with a given name and signature. S_3 and S_4 do not give rise to interference either because Student and Professor in $\mathcal{H}_1$ and $\mathcal{H}_2$ do not contain conflicting methods. Hence, there is no basic static interference. Figure 2 shows the composed hierarchy.   □

Example 4. Consider composing the class hierarchies $\mathcal{H}_1$ and $\mathcal{H}_3$ of Figure 1. The set equivalence classes $\mathcal{E}$ constructed according to Definition 2 contains, among others, the element $S = \{ \langle \text{Professor}, \mathcal{H}_1 \rangle, \langle \text{Professor}, \mathcal{H}_3 \rangle \}$. $\mathcal{E}$ exhibits basic static interference because both elements of S contain a member `Professor.approveGraduation(Student)` and the bodies of these methods are different. Hence, basic composition cannot be applied to $\mathcal{H}_1$ and $\mathcal{H}_3$.   □

2.4 Overriding Composition

As we have seen in Figure 3, basic static interference is not necessarily an unwanted phenomenon. Often, a method from $\mathcal{H}_2$ is an "improved" or "generalized" version of a method in $\mathcal{H}_1$. To address such cases, we augment basic composition with a mechanism that allows one to express conditions such as "member $B.m$ in $\mathcal{H}'$ has precedence over member $A.m$ in $\mathcal{H}$". This is captured by a precedence relation $\ll$ containing elements $\langle \mathcal{H}, m_1 \rangle \ll \langle \mathcal{H}', m_2 \rangle$ indicating that method m_2 of hierarchy $\mathcal{H}'$ has precedence over method m_1 of hierarchy $\mathcal{H}$. Note that it may be the case that $\mathcal{H} = \mathcal{H}'$. It is assumed that '$\ll$' is a partial order.

The static interference notion of Definition 3 only requires minor modifications to allow situations where an equivalence class contains two classes C_1 and C_2 originating from hierarchies $\mathcal{H}_1$ and $\mathcal{H}_2$, respectively, such that $\langle \mathcal{H}_1, m_1 \rangle$ and $\langle \mathcal{H}_2, m_2 \rangle$ are $\ll$-ordered. Definition 5 shows the resulting definition.

Definition 5 (overriding static interference). $\mathcal{E}$ *contains overriding static interference w.r.t. '$\ll$' if there is an equivalence class* $[x]_\rho \in \mathcal{E}$ *such that for some* $\langle C_1, \mathcal{H} \rangle, \langle C_2, \mathcal{H}' \rangle \in [x]_\rho$, $C_1 \neq C_2$, $m_1 \in members(C_1)$, $m_2 \in members(C_2)$, *and* $namesig(m_1) = namesig(m_2)$ *we have that:* $body(m_1) \neq \bot$, $body(m_2) \neq \bot$, $body(m_1) \neq body(m_2)$, $\langle \mathcal{H}, m_1 \rangle \not\ll \langle \mathcal{H}', m_2 \rangle$, *and* $\langle \mathcal{H}', m_2 \rangle \not\ll \langle \mathcal{H}, m_1 \rangle$.

Definition 6 shows the *members* function for overriding compositions. In the sequel, we will often say "$\mathcal{H}_1 \oplus \mathcal{H}_2$ is free of overriding syntactic interference" if it is obvious which ordering '$\ll$' is used.

Definition 6 (members). *Let* $\mathcal{E}$ *be free of overriding static interference w.r.t. '$\ll$', and let* $[x]_\rho \in \mathcal{E}$ *be an equivalence class. Define:*

$$members([x]_\rho) = \{m_1 \mid \langle C_1, \mathcal{H}_1 \rangle \in [x]_\rho, m_1 \in members(C_1),$$
$$(\langle C_2, \mathcal{H}_2 \rangle \in [x]_\rho, C_2 \neq C_1, m_2 \in members(C_2),$$
$$namesig(m_1) = namesig(m_2)) \implies$$
$$body(m_2) = \bot \vee \langle \mathcal{H}_2, m_2 \rangle \ll \langle \mathcal{H}_1, m_1 \rangle \}$$

Example 5. Consider an overriding composition of hierarchies $\mathcal{H}_1$ and $\mathcal{H}_3$ of Figure 1 using $\langle \text{Professor.approveGraduation(Student)}, \mathcal{H}_1 \rangle \ll \langle \text{Professor} \text{.approveGraduation(Student)}, \mathcal{H}_3 \rangle$. Then, the set of equivalence classes $\mathcal{E}$ constructed by Definition 2 is: $S_1 = \{ \langle \text{Course}, \mathcal{H}_1 \rangle \}$, $S_2 = \{ \langle \text{Person}, \mathcal{H}_1 \rangle \}$, $S_3 = \{ \langle \text{Student}, \mathcal{H}_1 \rangle \}$, $S_4 = \{ \langle \text{Professor}, \mathcal{H}_1 \rangle, \langle \text{Professor}, \mathcal{H}_3 \rangle \}$, $S_5 = \{ \langle \text{Driver1}, \mathcal{H}_1 \rangle \}$, $S_6 = \{ \langle \text{PhDStudent}, \mathcal{H}_3 \rangle \}$, and $S_7 = \{ \langle \text{Driver3}, \mathcal{H}_3 \rangle \}$. Since singleton sets never give rise to interference, we only need to verify that S_4 does not cause overriding static interference. This is the case because the only method that occurs in both `Professor` classes is `approveGraduation()`, and these methods are $\ll$-ordered. The composed hierarchy can now be constructed using Definition 6, and was shown earlier in Figure 3.   □

2.5   Type Correctness

A class hierarchy is type correct if: (1) any member access $e.m(\cdots)$ refers to a declared member definition, and (2) for any assignment $x = y$, the type of x is a superclass of the type of y. As a first step towards providing semantic guarantees about the composed class hierarchy, we demonstrate that the composed hierarchy is type correct. Due to space limitations, we only demonstrate these properties for basic compositions. The arguments for overriding compositions are similar.

Definition 7 (type correctness). *Let $\mathcal{H}$ be a hierarchy.*

1. *The static type of an object or object reference o in a hierarchy is denoted TypeOf($\mathcal{H}, o$). For convenience, we use TypeOf($\mathcal{H}_{1,2}, o$) $= C$ as an abbreviation for TypeOf($\mathcal{H}_1, o$) $= C \vee$ TypeOf($\mathcal{H}_2, o$) $= C$.*
2. *For a class $C \in \mathcal{H}$ and $m \in members(C)$, we define StaticLookup($\mathcal{H}, C,$ m) $= m'$, where $m' \in members(C')$ for some class C' such that $C \leq C'$, namesig(m) $=$ namesig(m'), and there is no class C'' such that $C \leq C'' \leq C'$, $m'' \in members(C'')$, namesig(m) $=$ namesig(m''). We will use StaticLookup($\mathcal{H}_{1,2}, C, m$) $= m'$ as a shorthand for StaticLookup($\mathcal{H}_1, C,$ m) $= m' \vee$ StaticLookup($\mathcal{H}_2, C, m$) $= m'$.*
3. *A hierarchy $\mathcal{H}$ is type correct if for all assignments $x = y \in \mathcal{H}$ we have that TypeOf($\mathcal{H}, x$) $\geq$ TypeOf($\mathcal{H}, y$), and for all member accesses $o.m(\cdots) \in \mathcal{H}$ we have that: StaticLookup($\mathcal{H}$, TypeOf($\mathcal{H}, o$), m) $\neq \perp$.*

Note that if TypeOf($\mathcal{H}_{1,2}, o$) $= C$, then by construction TypeOf($\mathcal{H}_1 \oplus \mathcal{H}_2$, o) $= class([C]_\rho)$. As an example, consider Figure 4, and assume that v is a variable such that TypeOf($\mathcal{H}_1, v$) $= A$. Then, in Figure 4(a) we have that TypeOf $(\mathcal{H}_1 \oplus \mathcal{H}_2, v) = A$ and in Figure 4(b) that TypeOf($\mathcal{H}_1 \oplus \mathcal{H}_2, v$) $= ACF$. The latter case demonstrates that sometimes new class names are introduced, and member declarations must be changed accordingly. In particular, whenever $name([C]_\rho) \neq name(C)$, all declarations containing class name C must be updated to reflect the new class name $name([C]_\rho)$. This will only happen if classes have been merged due to cycles in the transitive inheritance relations of the input hierarchies.

The following two lemmas show that assignments and member lookups in the composed hierarchy remain type correct. Note that this includes assignments due to parameter-passing in method calls, and implicit assignments to this-pointers.

Lemma 1 (assignment correctness). *Let $x = y$ be an assignment in $\mathcal{H}_{1,2}$. Then, this assignment is still type correct in $\mathcal{H}_1 \oplus \mathcal{H}_2$.*

Proof. Without loss of generality, let $x = y \in \mathcal{H}_1$. Then, TypeOf($\mathcal{H}_1, x$) $\geq_1$ TypeOf($\mathcal{H}_1, y$). By construction, TypeOf($\mathcal{H}_1 \oplus \mathcal{H}_2, x$) $= class([$TypeOf($\mathcal{H}_1, x$)$]_\rho) \geq class([$TypeOf($\mathcal{H}_1, y$)$]_\rho) =$ TypeOf($\mathcal{H}_1 \oplus \mathcal{H}_2, y$). $\qquad \square$

Lemma 2 (member access correctness). *If $\mathcal{H}_1$ and $\mathcal{H}_2$ are type correct and without basic static interference, then StaticLookup($\mathcal{H}_{1,2}$, TypeOf($\mathcal{H}_{1,2}, o$), m) $\neq$ $\perp \implies$ StaticLookup($\mathcal{H}_1 \oplus \mathcal{H}_2$, TypeOf($\mathcal{H}_1 \oplus \mathcal{H}_2, o$), m) $\neq \perp$*

```
class A {                class A {                      class A {
  void foo(){ ··· }        void foo(){ /* same as H1 */ }  void foo(){ ··· }
}                        }                              }
class B extends A {      class B extends A {            class B extends A {
  /* no foo() */           void foo(){ ··· }              void foo(){ /* from H2 */ }
}                        }                              }
class C {                                               class C {
  static void main(){                                    static void main(){
    A o = new B();  B1                                      A o = new B();  B1
    o.foo();                                                o.foo();
  }                                                      }
}                                                      }
           H1                      H2                          H1 ⊕ H2
```

Fig. 5. Dynamic interference in a basic composition.

Proof. Without loss of generality, let $C = TypeOf(\mathcal{H}_1, o)$, and let D be the class which contains $m' = StaticLookup(\mathcal{H}_1, TypeOf(\mathcal{H}_1, o), m)$. Then, we have $C \leq_1 D$, $m \in members(D)$ and by construction $m \in members(class([D]_\rho))$ as there is no static interference. Furthermore, $class([C]_\rho) \leq class([D]_\rho)$ and $TypeOf$ $(\mathcal{H}_1 \oplus \mathcal{H}_2, o) = class([C]_\rho)$. m could also occur in a subclass of $class([D]_\rho)$ in $\mathcal{H}_1 \oplus \mathcal{H}_2$, but for class D' which contains $m'' = StaticLookup(\mathcal{H}_1 \oplus \mathcal{H}_2, TypeOf$ $(\mathcal{H}_1 \oplus \mathcal{H}_2, o), m)$, we have in any case that $D' \leq class([D]_\rho)$, hence $StaticLookup$ $(\mathcal{H}_1 \oplus \mathcal{H}_2, TypeOf(\mathcal{H}_1 \oplus \mathcal{H}_2, o), m) \neq \bot$. □

Corollary 1. *For hierarchies $\mathcal{H}_1$ and $\mathcal{H}_2$ without static interference, $\mathcal{H}_1 \oplus \mathcal{H}_2$ is type correct.*

3   Dynamic Interference

3.1   Motivating Examples

Even basic composition (which makes the strongest assumptions about static noninterference) does not guarantee preservation of client behavior. This can be seen in the basic composition of Figure 5, which does not exhibit static interference. However, $\mathcal{H}_1 \oplus \mathcal{H}_2$ contains an overriding definition of foo() in class B, hence the call to foo() in C.main() binds to B.foo() instead of A.foo() as it did in $\mathcal{H}_1$. Hence, behavior of $\mathcal{H}_1$'s client C.main() is not preserved.

Figure 6 shows an overriding composition (constructed using $\langle \mathcal{H}_1, A.foo() \rangle \ll$ $\langle \mathcal{H}_2, A.foo() \rangle$) that is free of overriding static interference. However, in the composed hierarchy, variable x is bound to a B-object instead of an A-object. Thus, the call x.bar() suddenly resolves to B.bar() instead of A.bar() as in $\mathcal{H}_1$.

3.2   Dynamic Interference

We will use the term *dynamic interference* to refer to run-time behavioral changes such as the ones in the above examples. Some additional definitions are required to make this notion precise. To this end, we will use an operational semantics, where the effect of statement execution is described as a state transformation.

```
class A {                    class A {                  class A {
  static A x;                  void foo(){                static A x;
                                 x = new B();  B2         void foo(){
  void foo(){ x = new A(); } A1  }                          x = new B();  B2
  void bar(){ ··· }          }                            }
}                                                         void bar(){ ··· }
class B extends A {                                     }
  void bar(){ ··· }                                    class B extends A {
}                                                        void bar(){ ··· }
class C {                                              }
  static void main(){                                  class C {
                                                         static void main(){
    A a = new B();  B1
    a.foo(); A.x.bar();                                    A a = new B();  B1
  }                                                        a.foo(); A.x.bar();
}                                                        }
                                                       }
```

$$\mathcal{H}_1 \qquad\qquad\qquad \mathcal{H}_2 \qquad\qquad\qquad \mathcal{H}_1 \oplus \mathcal{H}_2$$

Fig. 6. Dynamic interference in an overriding composition.

Definition 8 (state, state transformation).

1. *A program state maps variables to values:* $\sigma \in \Sigma = Var \to Value$.
2. *The effect of executing a statement S is a state transformation:* $\sigma \xrightarrow{S} \sigma'$.

Details of *Var* and *Value* are left unspecified, as they are not important for our purposes. The reader may consult [7,13] for complete operational semantics of relevant Java subsets. *Var* includes local variables, parameters, and this-pointers in method invocation stack frames—note that the domain of *Var* may change as execution proceeds. *Value* comprises primitive values (e.g., integers) and objects in the heap. In order to model reference-typed fields, we assume that *Var* also contains an element for each field f of an object o, where o is an object in *Value* whose type contains a field f (either directly or through inheritance).

Now let us assume that we have a hierarchy $\mathcal{H}$ together with some client code K which is type correct with respect to $\mathcal{H}$. We define:

Definition 9 (execution sequence).

1. *An execution sequence of a hierarchy $\mathcal{H}$ is the (finite or infinite) sequence of statements $E(\mathcal{H}, K, I, \sigma_0) = S_1, S_2, S_3, \ldots$ which results from executing the client code K of $\mathcal{H}$ with input I in initial state σ_0. The corresponding sequence of program states is $\Sigma(\mathcal{H}, K, I, \sigma_0) = \sigma_0 \to \sigma_1 \to \sigma_2 \to \sigma_3 \ldots$.*
2. *The statement subsequence of $S_1, S_2 \ldots$ consisting only of member accesses (data member accesses or method calls) is denoted $M(\mathcal{H}, K, I, \sigma_0) = S_{\nu_1}, S_{\nu_2}, \ldots$ where $S_{\nu_i} = S_j \in E(\mathcal{H}, K, I, \sigma_0)$. The corresponding sequence of invoked target methods is denoted $T(\mathcal{H}, K, I, \sigma_0) = t_{\nu_1}, t_{\nu_2}, \ldots$ where each t_{ν_i} is the method that is actually invoked at run-time.*

Definition 10 states that two hierarchies $\mathcal{H}$ and $\mathcal{H}'$ are behaviorally equivalent if the same sequence of statements is executed using the two hierarchies, for all given clients of $\mathcal{H}$ with appropriate inputs and initial states. Definition 11 states that a composed hierarchy $\mathcal{H}_1 \oplus \mathcal{H}_2$ exhibits *dynamic interference* if $\mathcal{H}_1$ and $\mathcal{H}_1 \oplus \mathcal{H}_2$ are not behaviorally equivalent (for some client of $\mathcal{H}_1$ with associated input and initial state), or if $\mathcal{H}_2$ and $\mathcal{H}_1 \oplus \mathcal{H}_2$ are not behaviorally equivalent (for some client of $\mathcal{H}_2$ with associated input and initial state).

Definition 10 (behavioral equivalence). *Two hierarchies $\mathcal{H}$, $\mathcal{H}'$ are behaviorally equivalent iff for all clients K of $\mathcal{H}$ with appropriate inputs and initial states I, σ_0 we have that $E(\mathcal{H}, K, I, \sigma_0) = E(\mathcal{H}', K, I, \sigma_0)$.*

Definition 11 (dynamic interference). *$\mathcal{H}_1 \oplus \mathcal{H}_2$ contains dynamic interference, if (for some $\mathcal{H}_1$-client K with associated I, σ_0) $\mathcal{H}_1$ and $\mathcal{H}_1 \oplus \mathcal{H}_2$ are not behaviorally equivalent, or if (for some $\mathcal{H}_2$-client K with associated I, σ_0) $\mathcal{H}_2$ and $\mathcal{H}_1 \oplus \mathcal{H}_2$ are not behaviorally equivalent.*

Remark. From an observational point of view, $E(\mathcal{H}_1, K, I, \sigma_0) = E(\mathcal{H}_1 \oplus \mathcal{H}_2, K, I, \sigma_0)$ is not a necessary condition for behavioral equivalence, because a modified sequence of statements might still produce the same visible effects. However, we are not interested in cases where the observable behavior of a client of a composed hierarchy is *accidentally* identical to its original behavior.

3.3   Checking for Dynamic Interference

We would like to *verify* whether or not a certain composition exhibits dynamic interference. In general, determining whether or not two arbitrary programs will execute the same statement sequences for all possible inputs is undecidable of course. However, for the compositions studied in this paper, the situation is not hopeless. Our approach will be to develop a *noninterference criterion* that implies $E(\mathcal{H}_1, K, I, \sigma_0) = E(\mathcal{H}_1 \oplus \mathcal{H}_2, K, I, \sigma_0)$ that is based on static analysis information. This approach is also used in our earlier work on semantics-preserving class hierarchy transformations [17,18]. Being a sufficient, but not a necessary condition, our criterion may occasionally generate false alarms. However, we believe that the impact analysis of Section 4 will provide the user with sufficient information to determine whether reported interferences can occur in practice.

Definition 12 defines a function *srcHierarchy* that defines the class hierarchy that a program construct originated from. The *srcHierarchy* of an object is defined as the *srcHierarchy* of the statement that created it. Definition 13 uses *srcHierarchy* to define the *projection* of a state onto a hierarchy.

Definition 12 (srcHierarchy). *For $\mathcal{H} = (\mathcal{C}, \leq)$, $C = \langle c, M \rangle \in \mathcal{H}$, $m \in M$, and a statement s in $body(m)$, we write srcHierarchy$(C) =$ srcHierarchy$(m) =$ srcHierarchy$(s) = \mathcal{H}$. Moreover, let $s \equiv$ **new** $C(\cdots)$ be an object creation site, and let object $o \in Value$ be an instance of C created by s at run-time. Then, srcHierarchy$(o) =$ srcHierarchy(s). Further, for any $x \in Var$, we define srcHierarchy$(x) =$ srcHierarchy(s), where s is the static program part responsible for the creation of x at run-time.*

Definition 13 (state projection). *The projection of a program state σ onto a hierarchy $\mathcal{H}$ is defined as $\sigma|\mathcal{H} = \{x \mapsto v \mid x \mapsto v \in \sigma, \text{srcHierarchy}(x) = \mathcal{H}\}$.*

Moreover, we extend the projection operator to apply to a sequence of program states as follows: $\Sigma(\mathcal{H}_1 \oplus \mathcal{H}_2, K, I, \sigma_0)|\mathcal{H}_1 = \sigma_0|\mathcal{H}_1 \rightarrow \sigma_1|\mathcal{H}_1 \rightarrow \sigma_2|\mathcal{H}_1 \rightarrow \cdots,$ *where* $\Sigma(\mathcal{H}_1 \oplus \mathcal{H}_2, K, I, \sigma_0) = \sigma_0 \rightarrow \sigma_1 \rightarrow \sigma_2 \rightarrow \cdots.$

The noninterference criterion relies on information produced by a *points-to* analysis [1]. A points-to analysis computes for each reference-typed variable the set of objects that it may point to. Definitions 14 and 15 define appropriate notions *ObjectRefs* of object references and *Objects* of objects.

Definition 14 (object reference). *Let* $\mathcal{H}$ *be a hierarchy. Then, ObjectRefs* $(\mathcal{H}) \subseteq Var$ *is the set of all object references in* $\mathcal{H}$. *This includes class-typed local variables, method parameters, fields, static variables, and* **this** *pointers of methods.*

Definition 15 (object). *Let* $\mathcal{H}$ *be a hierarchy. Then, Objects*$(\mathcal{H})$ *is the set of all object creation sites in* $\mathcal{H}$, *that is, all statements* $S \equiv new\ C(...);$ *occurring in some method body. Moreover, for* $o \in Objects(\mathcal{H})$, $o \equiv new\ C(...)$, *we define* TypeOf$(\mathcal{H}, o) = C$.

Object creation sites in *Objects*$(\mathcal{H})$ should not be confused with run-time objects in *Value*. Finally, Definition 16 formalizes the notion of points-to sets. We do not make any assumptions about the specific algorithm used to compute these points-to sets. Any method suitable for object-oriented languages will do (e.g., [11,14]).

Definition 16 (points-to sets). *Let* $\mathcal{H}$ *be a hierarchy, and let* $p \in ObjectRefs$ $(\mathcal{H})$. *Then, PointsTo*$(\mathcal{H}, p) \subseteq Objects(\mathcal{H})$ *is the set of all objects (represented by creation sites) that object reference* p *might point to at run-time.*

The noninterference criterion (Definition 17) states that the method invoked by a virtual method call $p.m(\cdots)$ (as determined by applying *StaticLookup* on the receiver object) in $\mathcal{H}_1 \oplus \mathcal{H}_2$ is the same as it was in $\mathcal{H}_1$. Note that the condition does not say anything about $\mathcal{H}_2$ objects. While the points-to sets in the composed hierarchy may also contain $\mathcal{H}_2$ objects, these objects are never created by clients of $\mathcal{H}_1$, and therefore need not be considered.

Definition 17 (noninterference criterion). *A composition* $\mathcal{H}_1 \oplus \mathcal{H}_2$ *meets the noninterference criterion if for all* $p \in ObjectRefs(\mathcal{H}_1)$, *for all method calls* $p.m(\cdots)$ *in* $\mathcal{H}_1$, *and for all* $o \in PointsTo(\mathcal{H}_1 \oplus \mathcal{H}_2, p) \cap Objects(\mathcal{H}_1)$ *we have that StaticLookup*$(\mathcal{H}_1, T, m) = StaticLookup(\mathcal{H}_1 \oplus \mathcal{H}_2, T', m)$ *where* $T = TypeOf$ $(\mathcal{H}_1, o)$, *and* $T' = TypeOf(\mathcal{H}_1 \oplus \mathcal{H}_2, o)$.

The use of points-to information deserves a few more comments. First, one might wonder about the consequences of using imprecise points-to information (i.e., overly large points-to sets). In this case, the "for all o" in the noninterference criterion runs over a larger scope than necessary, making the criterion stronger than necessary, and spurious interference may be reported. However, the criterion is safe in the sense that it will never erroneously report non-interference.

Note also that the criterion is much more precise than the static checks from Section 2. To see this, consider again the examples of Figures 5 and 6. One could argue that the simple interferences in these examples are not really dynamic. In fact, one could report *static interference* in the examples of of Figures 5 and 6 by modifying *members*(C) to also include members in superclasses of C (as opposed to only the members defined locally in C). So why use the more complex criterion of Definition 17? The reason is that, for large programs, the suggested modified static interference check will report interference even if the class exhibiting the changed behavior is never used in the program. In Definition 17, the scope of the key condition

$$StaticLookup(\mathcal{H}_1 \oplus \mathcal{H}_2, T, m) = StaticLookup(\mathcal{H}_1, T', m)$$

is limited by the size of the points-to set associated with the receiver of the method call. This effectively restricts the condition to method calls that are actually reachable, and to many fewer calling relationships than those that are possible, resulting in many fewer spurious interferences being reported.

Most points-to analysis algorithms compute information that is valid for a specific client K. This has the advantage that the points-to sets are more precise, reducing the number of false alarms. However, in this case the noninterference criterion only holds for the client K. To compute results that are safe for *any* client, one could employ algorithms such as [15] that are capable of analyzing incomplete programs.

Concerning the complexity of the interference test, it is dominated by the computation of points-to information, as the test itself just performs two static lookups per member access, which is linear in the program size. Various points-to algorithms of various precision are known, ranging from Steensgaard's almost linear algorithm (which scales to millions of LOC) to Andersen' cubic algorithm which has recently been scaled to a million-line C-program [6] by using a new approach for dynamically computing transitive closures. The performance of this algorithm on object-oriented applications is still unknown, as far as we know.

3.4 Justification

We will now demonstrate that the noninterference criterion of Definition 17 ensures that the behavior of client K of $\mathcal{H}_1$ is preserved. The analogous argument for $\mathcal{H}_2$ is completely symmetrical.

Lemma 3 states that it is sufficient to demonstrate that the sequence of call targets in $\mathcal{H}_1$ does not change after composition.

Lemma 3. *For all K, I and σ_0, we have that:* $T(\mathcal{H}_1, K, I, \sigma_0) = T(\mathcal{H}_1 \oplus \mathcal{H}_2, K, I, \sigma_0)$ $\implies$ $E(\mathcal{H}_1, K, I, \sigma_0) = E(\mathcal{H}_1 \oplus \mathcal{H}_2, K, I, \sigma_0)$ *and therefore:* $T(\mathcal{H}_1, K, I, \sigma_0) = T(\mathcal{H}_1 \oplus \mathcal{H}_2, K, I, \sigma_0) \implies \Sigma(\mathcal{H}_1, K, I, \sigma_0) = \Sigma(\mathcal{H}_1 \oplus \mathcal{H}_2, K, I, \sigma_0)|\mathcal{H}_1$

Proof. The proof is by induction on the length n of sequence $E(\mathcal{H}_1, K, I, \sigma_0)$. For $n = 0$, the statement is trivial, as both hierarchies start in state σ_0. Now consider statement S_n in $E(\mathcal{H}_1, K, I, \sigma_0)$. By induction, the previously executed statements $S_1, S_2, \ldots S_{n-1}$ are the same in both $E(\mathcal{H}_1, K, I, \sigma_0)$ and $E(\mathcal{H}_1 \oplus \mathcal{H}_2, K, I, \sigma_0)$, and lead to corresponding states σ_{n-1} and $\sigma_{n-1}|\mathcal{H}_1$, respectively.

Now, S_n is a statement at some position π in some method m_1 of $\mathcal{H}_1$. By assumption, the sequence of executed method bodies is the same in $\mathcal{H}_1 \oplus \mathcal{H}_2$. Since there is no static interference, we may conclude that we are at the same position π in some method m_2 in $\mathcal{H}_1 \oplus \mathcal{H}_2$, for which $body(m_1) = body(m_2)$. Hence, S_n is also the next statement to be executed in $E(\mathcal{H}_1 \oplus \mathcal{H}_2, K, I, \sigma_0)$.

Now there are two cases. 1) S_n is a method call $p.m(\cdots)$. Then, by assumption, this call resolves to the same target t_{ν_i} which is executed in the same state σ_{n-1}. Thus, after execution of the method body, both hierarchies are in the same state σ_n at the same position π' in the same method bodies m_1 and m_2. 2) S_n is not a method call. Then, it must be the same in m_1 and m_2 due to the absence of static interference. Hence, after execution, the same state σ_n is reached. $\square$

Theorem 1 (correctness of criterion). *Let $\mathcal{H}_1 \oplus \mathcal{H}_2$ be a composition that meets the noninterference criterion of Definition 17. Then, we have that: $E(\mathcal{H}_1, K, I, \sigma_0) = E(\mathcal{H}_1 \oplus \mathcal{H}_2, K, I, \sigma_0)$ and $\Sigma(\mathcal{H}_1, K, I, \sigma_0) = \Sigma(\mathcal{H}_1 \oplus \mathcal{H}_2, K, I, \sigma_0)|\mathcal{H}_1$, for all K, I, σ_0.*

Proof. Again the proof is by induction on n. For $n = 0$ the statement is trivial, as both hierarchies start in state σ_0. Now consider statement S_n in $E(\mathcal{H}_1, K, I, \sigma_0)$. By induction, the previously executed statements $S_1, S_2, \ldots S_{n-1}$ are the same in both $E(\mathcal{H}_1, K, I, \sigma_0)$ and $E(\mathcal{H}_1 \oplus \mathcal{H}_2, K, I, \sigma_0)$ and lead to corresponding states σ_{n-1} and $\sigma_{n-1}|\mathcal{H}_1$, respectively. As in the previous lemma, we may conclude that S_n is the same in both execution sequences. (This time the necessary fact that the previous call targets have been the same is not by assumption, but by induction: if $S_1, S_2, \ldots$ are the same in both $E(\mathcal{H}_1, K, I, \sigma_0)$ and $E(\mathcal{H}_1 \oplus \mathcal{H}_2, K, I, \sigma_0)$, so are $S_{\nu_1}, S_{\nu_2}, \ldots$ and $t_{\nu_1}, t_{\nu_2}, \ldots$).

Now there are two cases. If S_n is not a method call or data member access, we may conclude that the corresponding states σ_n and $\sigma_n|\mathcal{H}_1$ are produced in $\Sigma(\mathcal{H}_1, K, I, \sigma_0)$ and $\Sigma(\mathcal{H}_1 \oplus \mathcal{H}_2, K, I, \sigma_0)|\mathcal{H}_1$, respectively. In case $S_n = p.m(x)$, we know $\sigma_{n-1}(p) \in PointsTo(\mathcal{H}_1 \oplus \mathcal{H}_2, p)$ (remember that σ_{n-1} was reached in both $\mathcal{H}_1$ and $\mathcal{H}_1 \oplus \mathcal{H}_2$). Furthermore, $\sigma_{n-1}(p) \in Objects(\mathcal{H}_1)$, as $\sigma_{n-1}|\mathcal{H}_1 \in \Sigma(\mathcal{H}_1, K, I, \sigma_0)$, and $\mathcal{H}_1$ does not contain $\mathcal{H}_2$ objects. We know $StaticLookup(\mathcal{H}_1, TypeOf(\mathcal{H}_1, o), m) \neq \bot$ and by the type correctness lemma thus $StaticLookup(\mathcal{H}_1 \oplus \mathcal{H}_2, TypeOf(\mathcal{H}_1 \oplus \mathcal{H}_2, o), m) \neq \bot$. By the static noninterference criterion, both static lookups must compute the same result, namely method definition (resp. data member) m. After execution of m's body (resp. access to m's value in state σ_{n-1}), we may as in the above lemma conclude that execution of both hierarchies is in the same state σ_n. $\square$

Example 6. For the example of Figure 5, we have $PointsTo(\mathcal{H}_1, o) = PointsTo(\mathcal{H}_1 \oplus \mathcal{H}_2, o) = \{B1\}$. For the method call `o.foo()`, we obtain $StaticLookup(\mathcal{H}_1, TypeOf(\mathcal{H}_1, B1), foo()) = StaticLookup(\mathcal{H}_1, B, foo()) = $ `A.foo()`, but $StaticLookup(\mathcal{H}_1 \oplus \mathcal{H}_2, TypeOf(\mathcal{H}_1 \oplus \mathcal{H}_2, B1), foo()) = StaticLookup(\mathcal{H}_1 \oplus \mathcal{H}_2, B, foo()) = $ `B.foo()`. Hence, dynamic interference is reported. $\square$

In Example 7 and in subsequent examples, we use the labels shown in boxes in Figure 1 to identify object creation sites.

Example 7. For client `Driver1.main()` in Figure 2, we obtain *PointsTo* $(\mathcal{H}_1 \oplus \mathcal{H}_2, \mathtt{c1}) \cap Objects(\mathcal{H}_1) = \{ \mathtt{C1} \}$, *PointsTo*$(\mathcal{H}_1 \oplus \mathcal{H}_2, \mathtt{p1}) \cap Objects(\mathcal{H}_1) = \{ \mathtt{P1} \}$. Hence, *StaticLookup*$(\mathcal{H}_1, TypeOf(\mathcal{H}_1, \mathtt{C1}), \mathtt{enroll}()) = \mathtt{Course.enroll}()$ $= StaticLookup(\mathcal{H}_1 \oplus \mathcal{H}_2, TypeOf(\mathcal{H}_1 \oplus \mathcal{H}_2, \mathtt{C1}), \mathtt{enroll}())$. Moreover, we have that *StaticLookup*$(\mathcal{H}_1, TypeOf(\mathcal{H}_1, \mathtt{C1}), \mathtt{assign}()) = \mathtt{Course.assign}() = $ *StaticLookup*$(\mathcal{H}_1 \oplus \mathcal{H}_2, TypeOf(\mathcal{H}_1 \oplus \mathcal{H}_2, \mathtt{C1}), \mathtt{assign}())$, and that *StaticLookup* $(\mathcal{H}_1, TypeOf(\mathcal{H}_1, \mathtt{P1}), \mathtt{approveGraduation}()) = \mathtt{Professor.approveGraduation}$ $() = StaticLookup(\mathcal{H}_1 \oplus \mathcal{H}_2, TypeOf(\mathcal{H}_1 \oplus \mathcal{H}_2, \mathtt{P1}), \mathtt{Professor.approve}$ `Graduation()`). Similar arguments can be made for all other method calls in Figure 2. Hence, the behavior of `Driver1.main()` in $\mathcal{H}_1$ is preserved in $\mathcal{H}_1 \oplus \mathcal{H}_2$. $\square$

In fact, the basic composition in Figure 2 preserves the behavior of *any* possible client. Potential clients may introduce arbitrary allocation sites and arbitrary points-to relationships. A conservative approximation must therefore assume that for any member access $p.m(\cdots) \in \mathcal{H}_1$, *PointsTo*$(\mathcal{H}_1 \oplus \mathcal{H}_2, p) \cap$ *Objects*$(\mathcal{H}_1)$ contains all allocation sites $S \in Objects(\mathcal{H}_1)$ where $TypeOf(\mathcal{H}_1 \oplus \mathcal{H}_2, S) \le TypeOf(\mathcal{H}_1 \oplus \mathcal{H}_2, p)$. Nevertheless, *StaticLookup*$(\mathcal{H}_1, TypeOf(\mathcal{H}_1, S), m) = StaticLookup(\mathcal{H}_1 \oplus \mathcal{H}_2, TypeOf(\mathcal{H}_1 \oplus \mathcal{H}_2, S), m)$, because in the example the methods from $\mathcal{H}_1$ and $\mathcal{H}_2$ are either disjoint or identical.

3.5   Overriding Compositions

The noninterference criterion was designed for basic compositions. It can be applied to overriding compositions as well, but will report failure as soon as a method call $p.m(\cdots)$ resolves to methods that have different bodies in $\mathcal{H}_1$ and $\mathcal{H}_1 \oplus \mathcal{H}_2$. Nevertheless, interference checks may still succeed if the overridden methods are not reachable from client code. Constructing an interference check for overriding compositions that ignores conflicts that users are aware of (via the $\ll$-ordering) is a topic for future research.

Example 8. Let us apply the criterion to Figure 6. We have *PointsTo*$(\mathcal{H}_1,$ $\mathtt{a}) = PointsTo(\mathcal{H}_1 \oplus \mathcal{H}_2, \mathtt{a}) = \{ \mathtt{B1} \}$, but due to the overriding, *StaticLookup* $(\mathcal{H}_1, TypeOf(\mathcal{H}_1, \mathtt{B1}), \mathtt{foo}()) = \mathtt{A.foo}()_{\mathcal{H}_1} \ne \mathtt{A.foo}()_{\mathcal{H}_2} = StaticLookup(\mathcal{H}_1 \oplus \mathcal{H}_2,$ $TypeOf(\mathcal{H}_1 \oplus \mathcal{H}_2, \mathtt{B1}), \mathtt{foo}())$. Here, we use subscripts $\mathcal{H}_1$ and $\mathcal{H}_2$ to indicate the hierarchies that the different methods `A.foo()` originate from. Hence, the behavior of call `a.foo()` is not preserved. For call `x.bar()`, we obtain *PointsTo* $(\mathcal{H}_1 \oplus \mathcal{H}_2, \mathtt{x}) = \{ \mathtt{B2} \}$, hence *PointsTo*$(\mathcal{H}_1 \oplus \mathcal{H}_2, \mathtt{x}) \cap Objects(\mathcal{H}_1) = \emptyset$. Thus the criterion is trivially satisfied for `x.bar()`. $\square$

Remark: In Example 8, one might wonder why the criterion is satisfied for `x.bar()` despite the fact that the behavior of this call obviously changed: We have that `B.bar()` is called in $\mathcal{H}_1 \oplus \mathcal{H}_2$ whereas `A.bar()` was called in $\mathcal{H}_1$. This *secondary* behavioral change is caused by another change in behavior (in this case, the changed behavior of call `a.foo()`, which causes x to be bound to an object of type B). While the noninterference criterion does not necessarily detect secondary behavioral changes, it *does* find all primary changes, which suffices to guarantee behavioral equivalence. We plan to use impact analysis to obtain a more precise understanding of where behavioral changes occur, as will be discussed in Section 4.

4   Impact Analysis

When the purpose of composition is to add functionality that is not completely orthogonal to the system's existing functionality, changes in behavior are often unavoidable. The interference check of Section 3 determines whether the behavior of a specific client K is affected. In principle, one could manually apply the interference check to successively smaller clients to determine the impact of the composition. However, such a non-automated process is tedious and labor-intensive, and problematic in cases where it is not possible to partition the code in K. In order to provide a less labor-intensive approach, we plan to adapt the change impact analysis of [16] in order to automatically determine the set of program constructs affected by a composition. The remainder of this section presents some preliminary ideas on how this can be accomplished.

4.1   Change Impact Analysis

We begin with a brief review of the change impact analysis of [16]. In this work, it is assumed that a program is covered by a set of regression test drivers $\mathcal{T} = t_1, \cdots, t_n$. Each test driver is assumed to consist of a separate `main` routine from which methods in the application are called. Prior to the editing session, a *call graph* G_i is built for each t_i. Any of several existing call graph construction algorithms can be used. We plan to employ an algorithm that has been demonstrated to scale to large applications [21].

After the user has ended the editing session, the edits are decomposed into a set $\mathcal{A}$ of atomic changes. $\mathcal{A}$ consists of (i) a set **AC** of (empty) classes that have been added, (ii) a set **DC** of classes that have been deleted, (iii) a set **AM** of methods that have been added, (iv) a set **DM** of methods that have been deleted, (v) a set **CM** of methods whose body contains one or more changed statements, (vi) a set **AF** of fields that have been added, (vii) a set **DF** of fields that have been deleted, and (viii) a set **LC** of elements of the form $\langle T, C.m() \rangle$, indicating that the dispatch behavior for a call to $C.m()$ on an object of type T has changed. In general, a simple user edit can imply several atomic changes. For example, addition of a method may involve the addition of an empty method (in **AM**), a change in dispatch behavior (in **LC**) of existing call sites in cases where the added method overrides an existing method, and a change of a method body (in **CM**).

By analyzing the call graphs G_i and the set of atomic changes $\mathcal{A}$, a subset of *affected tests* $\mathcal{T}' \subseteq \mathcal{T}$ is determined. Figure 7 shows how correlating the nodes

$$AffectedTests(\mathcal{T}, \mathcal{A}) = \{\, t_i \mid t_i \in \mathcal{T},\ Nodes(P, t_i) \cap (\mathbf{CM} \cup \mathbf{DM})) \neq \emptyset \,\} \cup$$
$$\{\, t_i \mid t_i \in \mathcal{T},\ n \in Nodes(P, t_i),\ n \rightarrow_B A.m \in Edges(P, t_i),$$
$$\langle B, X.m() \rangle \in \mathbf{LC},\ B <^* A \leq^* X \,\}$$

Fig. 7. Definition of *AffectedTests* (taken from [16]).

and edges in the call graphs for the test drivers with the **CM**, **DM**, and **LC** changes leads to the identification of a set of affected tests t_i. Here, $Nodes(P, t_i)$ and $Edges(P, t_i)$ denote the set of nodes resp. edges in the call graph for test driver t_i. Informally, the formula shown in the figure states that a test driver t_i is potentially affected if a node in the call graph for t_i corresponds to a deleted or changed method (line 1), or if one of the edges in the call graph for t_i corresponds to a dispatch relation that has been changed (lines 2 3).

Any test driver that is not in $\mathcal{T}'$ is guaranteed to have the same behavior as before. If a test driver t_i occurs in $\mathcal{T}$, the user can run this test to determine if the new behavior of the test meets his expectations. If this is not the case, an additional analysis (also based on call graphs) determines a *subset* of atomic changes $\mathcal{A}' \subseteq \mathcal{A}$ that contribute to t_i's altered behavior. The user can apply successively larger subsets of $\mathcal{A}'$ to identify the change that "broke" test driver t_i. Alternatively, divide-and-conquer strategies similar to the ones in [23] can be applied to quickly narrow down the search space.

4.2 Impact Analysis for Composition

We plan to adapt the analysis of [16] to determine the impact of a composition $\mathcal{H}_1 \oplus \mathcal{H}_2$ on a set of test drivers $\mathcal{T} = t_1, \cdots, t_k$ associated with hierarchy $\mathcal{H}_i$ by interpreting a composition as a set of changes w.r.t $\mathcal{H}_i$. To do so, we need to establish a relationship between classes/members in $\mathcal{H}_1 \oplus \mathcal{H}_2$, and the classes/members in $\mathcal{H}_1$ and $\mathcal{H}_2$ that these classes/members originate from. This is expressed by Definition 18 below.

Definition 18 (origin). *Let $\mathcal{H}_1 = (\mathcal{C}_1, \leq_1)$ and $\mathcal{H}_2 = (\mathcal{C}_2, \leq_2)$ be two class hierarchies, let $\mathcal{H} = \mathcal{H}_1 \oplus \mathcal{H}_2 = (\mathcal{C}, \leq)$, and let $\mathcal{E}$ be the set of equivalence classes constructed by Definition 2. Furthermore, let C be a class in $\mathcal{C}$, and let $m \in members(C)$. Define:*

$$origin(C) = \{\, \langle C', \mathcal{H} \rangle \mid S \in \mathcal{E},\ name(S) = name(C),\ \langle C', \mathcal{H} \rangle \in S \,\}$$
$$origin(m) = \{\, \langle C', m', \mathcal{H} \rangle \mid \langle C', \mathcal{H} \rangle \in origin(C),\ m' \in members(C'),$$
$$namesig(m) = namesig(m'),\ body(m) = body(m')$$

Definition 18 defines the origin of a class C in $\mathcal{C}$ as the set of (class,hierarchy) pairs in its equivalence class, and the origin of a method m in C is the set of methods in each such class with the same name and body as m. Note that these definitions work with both of the *members* definitions given earlier.

Example 9. For hierarchy $\mathcal{H} = \mathcal{H}_1 \oplus \mathcal{H}_3$ of Figure 3 we have $origin(\texttt{Professor}) = \{\, \langle \texttt{Professor}, \mathcal{H}_1 \rangle,\ \langle \texttt{Professor}, \mathcal{H}_3 \rangle \,\}$ and $origin(\texttt{Professor.approveGraduation}) = \{\, \langle \texttt{Professor}, \texttt{approveGraduation}, \mathcal{H}_3 \rangle \,\}$. $\square$

It is now straightforward to construct the sets of atomic changes w.r.t. one of the original hierarchies. For example, for the composition $\mathcal{H} = \mathcal{H}_1 \oplus \mathcal{H}_3$, where $\mathcal{H} = \langle \mathcal{C}, \leq \rangle$, $\mathcal{H}_1 = \langle \mathcal{C}_1, \leq_1 \rangle$, and $\mathcal{H}_3 = \langle \mathcal{C}_4, \leq_4 \rangle$, the sets **AC** and **CM** w.r.t. $\mathcal{H}_1$ may be computed as:

$$AC = \{ C' \mid \langle C', \mathcal{H}' \rangle \in origin(C), C \in \mathcal{C}, \mathcal{H}' \neq \mathcal{H}_1 \}$$
$$CM = \{ m' \mid \langle C', \mathcal{H}_1 \rangle \in origin(C), C \in \mathcal{C}, m' \in members(C),$$
$$origin(m') = \emptyset, \not\exists m \text{ in } members(C') \text{ s.t.}$$
$$namesig(m) = namesig(m') \text{ and } body(m) = body(m') \}$$

The other sets of atomic changes are computed similarly. We can now apply the analysis of [16] to determine the impact of the composition.

Example 10. Consider the overriding composition of Figure 3, for which we previously found that behavior could not be preserved (see Example 8). We will now apply impact analysis to obtain a more precise understanding of where the interferences occur. Interpreting $\mathcal{H}_1 \oplus \mathcal{H}_3$ as a set of changes w.r.t. $\mathcal{H}_1$, we find that `Driver1.main()` is affected, because **CM** contains method `Professor.approveGraduation()`, which occurs in the call graph for `Driver1.main()`. Moreover, interpreting $\mathcal{H}_1 \oplus \mathcal{H}_3$ as a set of changes w.r.t. $\mathcal{H}_3$, we find that `Driver3.main()` is not affected, because the call graph for `Driver3.main()` does not contain any added, changed, or deleted methods, or any edges corresponding to a changed dispatch behavior.

Thus far, we have computed the impact of a composition on a set of test drivers. In order to obtain more fine-grained information, one could construct a separate call graph for each method m in hierarchy $\mathcal{H}_1$ (using appropriate conservative assumptions about the run-time types of parameters and accessed fields), and proceed as before. Then, impact could be reported as the set of methods whose behavior might have changed. For example, if separate call graphs are constructed for all methods of $\mathcal{H}_1$ in the overriding composition $\mathcal{H} \oplus \mathcal{H}_3$ of Figure 3, we can report that only the behavior of methods `Driver1.main()` and `Professor.approveGraduation()` is impacted by the composition because these are the only methods that transitively call methods whose behavior may have changed. Space limitations prevent us from providing more details.

5   Related Work

Research on aspect-oriented software development has been gaining in popularity recently [24]. In essence, the goal of this field is to obtain more extensible and reusable designs by distributing unrelated functionality over disjoint hierarchies or aspects. To achieve this, a mechanism for *composing* these functionalities into executable code is needed. In our setting, this is accomplished by composing hierarchies. Aspect-oriented languages such as AspectJ [8] have language constructs that allow one to specify the conditions under which a piece of *advice* is "woven in" at a *joint point*. Until recently, there has been very little work on the semantic foundations of composition.

The work most closely related to ours is the Aspect Sandbox (ASB) project by Wand et al. [22], who incorporate several key aspect-oriented language constructs such as join points, pointcut designators, and advice into a simple language with procedures, classes, and objects. Wand et al. formalize the semantics of this language using a denotational semantices. Wand et al. do not provide any guarantees about the noninterference of aspects, nor do they determine the semantic impact of "weaving in" an aspect.

Ernst presented a class hierarchy composition system, where the composition operator is built into the syntax of the programming language gbeta [4]. Explicitly specified compositions may trigger propagation of implicit compositions, for example an explicit combination of methods or classes may trigger implicit composition of other (e.g. auxiliary) methods or classes. Ernst showed that his composition system and propagation mechanism preserve static type correctness, but nothing is said about preservation of dynamic client behaviour.

Our approach is similar in spirit to the work by Binkley et al. [2] on the integration of C programs that are variations of a common base, by analyzing and merging their program dependence graphs. Similar to our work, Binkley et al. use an interference test, which is a sufficient criterion for noninterference. The main differences between [2] and our work is that [2] operates at the statement level, whereas our techniques operate on calling relationships between methods. Binkley et al. do not consider object-oriented language features.

Composition of object-oriented programs has been studied by other authors in the context of component-based systems (see [12] for a collection of relevant articles). One approach is concerned with the dynamic interaction of concurrent objects, and the goal is to create new behavior as a composition of given behavior. Our approach aims to preserve old behavior while combining given behavior. Another line of research has investigated the composition of systems from components, where the components are treated as black boxes and come with some interface specification, usually in the form of a type system.

We already discussed how our impact analysis is a derivative of the change impact analysis of [16]. Offutt and Li [10,9] also presented a change impact analysis for object-oriented programs, which only relies on structural relationships between classes and members (e.g., containment), and is therefore much less precise than approaches such as [16] that rely on static analysis.

6   Future Work

The work presented in this paper represents a first step in an ongoing effort to provide better semantic support for composition-based software development. We plan to implement the compositions and interference check of this paper, and gain practical experience with the approach. Other future work includes:

- The current paper abstracts away from peculiarities of specific programming languages. Programming languages such as Java contain several features that require further thought (e.g., exception handling).

- We plan to explore more complex compositions such as "merging" compositions, in which two interfering methods m_1 and m_2 are "merged" in some user-specified way (e.g., by constructing a new method that first executes the body of m_1 and then that of m_2).
- We plan to investigate more sophisticated interference tests can that can provide behavioral guarantees even in the presence of dynamic interference, by taking into account those conflicts that users have explicitly resolved.
- We have outlined how the impact analysis of [16] can be used to obtain a more detailed view of where behavioral interferences occur. We consider this to be a topic that needs much further thought.
- In practice, class hierarchy compositions are often performed with the intention of changing program behavior. We consider methods for distinguishing behavioral changes expected by the user from unanticipated behavioral changes to be an important research topic. Such methods could be used to filter the information produced by the impact analysis.

Acknowledgments

We are grateful to Charles Barton, Harold Ossher, and Max Störzer for comments on a draft of this paper. We would also like to thank the anonymous ECOOP referees for their detailed feedback.

References

1. L. O. Andersen. *Program Analysis and Specialization for the C Programming Language*. PhD thesis, DIKU, Univ. of Copenhagen, May 1994. DIKU report 94/19.
2. David Binkley, Susan Horwitz, and Thomas Reps. Program integration for languages with procedure calls. *ACM Transactions on Software Engineering and Methodology*, pages 3–35, January 1995.
3. B. A. Davey and H. A. Priestley. *Introduction to Lattices and Order*. Cambridge University Press, 1990.
4. Erik Ernst. Propagating class and method combination. In *Proc. European Conference on Object-Oriented programming (ECOOP99)*, pages 67–91, Lisboa, 1999.
5. William Harrison and Harold Ossher. Subject-oriented programming (a critique of pure objects). In *Proceedings of the Conference on Object-Oriented Programming Systems, Languages, and Applications*, pages 411–428, 1993.
6. Nevin Heintze and Oliver Tardieu. Ultra-fast alias analysis using CLA. In *Proc. ACM SIGPLAN Symposium on Programming Language Design and Implementation (PLDI01)*, pages 254–263, Snowbird, Utah, 2001.
7. Atshushi Igarashi, Benjamin Pierce, and Philip Wadler. Featherweight Java: A minimal core calculus for Java and GJ. In *Proc. SIGPLAN/ Conference an Onject-Oriented Programmin, Systems, Languages and Applications (OOPSLA'99)*, pages 132–146. ACM, November 1999.
8. Gregor Kiczales, Erik Hilsdale, Jim Hugunin, Mik Kersten, Jeffrey Palm, and William G. Griswold. An overview of AspectJ. In *Proc. 15th European Conf. on Object-Oriented Programming (ECOOP'01)*, Budapest, Hungary, June 2001.

 9. Michelle L. Lee. *Change Impact Analysis of Object-Oriented Software*. PhD thesis, George Mason University, 1998.
10. Michelle Lee and A. Jefferson Offutt. Algorithmic analysis of the impact of changes to object-oriented software. In *IEEE International Conference on Software Maintenance*, pages 171–184, Monterey, CA, November 1996.
11. Donglin Liang, Maikel Pennings, and Mary Jean Harrold. Extending and evaluating flow-insensitive and context-insensitive points-to analyses for Java. In *Proc. ACM SIGPLAN/SIGSOFT Workshop on on Program Analysis for Software Tools and Engineering (PASTE'01)*, pages 73–79, Snowbird, Utah, 2001.
12. Oscar Nierstrasz and Dennis Tsichritzis (ed.). *Object-Oriented Software Composition*. Prentice Hall, 1995.
13. Tobias Nipkow and David von Oheimb. Java$_{light}$ is type safe - definitely. In *Proc. SIGPLAN/SIGACT Symposium on Principles of Program Languages (POPL'98)*, pages 161–170. ACM, January 1998.
14. Atanas Rountev, Ana Milanova, and Barbara G. Ryder. Points-to analysis for Java using annotated constraints. In *Proc. ACM SIGPLAN Conf. on Object-Oriented Programming Systems, Languages, and Applications (OOPSLA'01)*, Tampa, FL, 2001.
15. Atanas Rountev, Barbara G. Ryder, and William Landi. Data-flow analysis of program fragments. In *Proceedings of Symposium on the Foundations of Software Engineering (FSE 1999)*, pages 235–252, Toulouse, France, 1999.
16. Barbara G. Ryder and Frank Tip. Change impact analysis for object-oriented programs. In *Proceedings of the ACM SIGPLAN-SIGSOFT Workshop on Program Analysis for Software Tools and Engineering (PASTE'01)*, pages 46–53, Snowbird, UT, June 2001.
17. Gregor Snelting and Frank Tip. Reengineering class hierarchies using concept analysis. In *Proc. ACM SIGSOFT Symposium on the Foundations of Software Engineering*, pages 99–110, Orlando, FL, November 1998.
18. G. Snelting and F. Tip. Understanding class hierarchies using concept analysis. *ACM Trans. on Programming Languages and Systems*, pages 540–582, May 2000.
19. Peri Tarr, Harold Ossher, William Harrison, and Stanley M. Sutton, Jr. *N* degrees of separation: Multi-dimensional separation of concerns. In *Proceedings of the 1999 International Conference on Software Engineering*, pages 107–119. IEEE Computer Society Press / ACM Press, May 1999.
20. Krishnaprasad Thirunarayan, Günter Kniesel, and Haripriyan Hampapuram. Simulating multiple inheritance and generics in Java. *Computer Languages*, 25:189–210, 1999.
21. Frank Tip and Jens Palsberg. Scalable propagation-based call graph construction algorithms. In *Proc. ACM SIGPLAN Conf. on Object-Oriented Programming Systems, Languages, and Applications (OOPSLA'00)*, pages 281–293, Minneapolis, MN, 2000. *SIGPLAN Notices* 35(10).
22. Mitchell Wand, Gregor Kiczales, and Christopher Dutchyn. A semantics for advice and dynamic join points in aspect-oriented programming. October 2001.
23. Andreas Zeller. Yesterday my program worked. Today, it does not. Why? In *Proc. of the 7th European Software Engineering Conf./7th ACM SIGSOFT Symp. on the Foundations of Software Engineering (ESEC/FSE'99)*, pages 253–267, Toulouse, France, 1999.
24. Communications of the ACM. 44(10), October 2001. Special issue on Aspect-Oriented Programming.

Behavioral Compatibility
of Self-Typed Theories*

Suad Alagić[1] and Svetlana Kouznetsova[2]

[1] Department of Computer Science, University of Southern Maine,
96 Falmouth Street, Portland, ME 04104-9300, USA
alagic@cs.usm.maine.edu
http://www.cs.usm.maine.edu/~alagic/
[2] Department of Computer Science, Wichita State University,
1845 Fairmount Avenue, Wichita, KS 67260-0083, USA
svkouzne@cs.twsu.edu

Abstract. The notion of self-typing is extended with the semantic constraints expressed as sentences. Specifying these behavioral properties is far beyond the expressiveness of type systems. The cornerstone of the approach is the view of classes as theories. The inheritance of class constraints is viewed as a theory morphism. The validity of the results across various possible logics for expressing class constraints is based on the object-oriented view of the notion of an institution. This view ties together the inheritance of class constraints and semantically correct object substitutability. The developed formal system is termed behavioral matching and it is proved to be an institution. Implications of this result are also analyzed.

1 Introduction

This paper is addressing the semantic compatibility problems in object-oriented paradigms that are based on self typing. A well-established notion of behavioral subtyping [31] does not apply because the conditions for subtyping are typically not satisfied. Hence the problem of specifying the behavioral compatibility conditions for more flexible typing notions, such as matching ([13], [2]), is actually open. This problem is in the focus of this paper.

There are two distinctive features of the approach to behavioral compatibility developed in the paper. The first one is the view of classes as theories. The second one is the object-oriented view of the notion of an institution [18] which is proved to be essential for addressing the problems of behavioral compatibility.

The view of a class as a theory is based on the notion of the class interface which consists of the signatures of the public methods of the class. Most importantly, a class as a theory also includes the class constraints expressed in some

---

* This material is based upon work supported in part by the NSF grant number IIS-9811452, and in part by the U.S. Army Research Office under grant number DAAH04-96-1-0192.

B. Magnusson (Ed.): ECOOP 2002, LNCS 2374, pp. 585–608, 2002.

logic-based language. These constraints specify (some of) the semantics of the public methods of the class. The level of expressiveness of the underlying logic determines to what extent the semantics of methods is captured by the class constraints.

There are two aspects of behavioral compatibility. One of them is the inheritance of constraints which is expressed by the notion of a theory morphism. The other is behaviorally compatible substitution of objects of a subclass where an object of a superclass is expected. When these two notions are tied to each other, we obtain the *Satisfaction Condition*, a fundamental component of the notion of an institution [18]. This is a key observation in this paper which makes it significantly different from other published results on behavioral compatibility for the object-oriented paradigm.

With this model-theoretic approach to behavioral compatibility the notion of behavioral matching is introduced. It is established that the formal system underlying behavioral matching is an institution. The subtle point is proving that the Satisfaction Condition holds. This is in fact the core result of this paper.

A variety of logics may be used for expressing class constraints. But the results on behavioral compatibility should be independent of the choice of a particular logical system for specifying the constraints. This paper shows that the object-oriented view of the notion of an institution [18] provides such a general framework.

The paper is organized as follows. In section 2 the notion of a class as a theory is introduced, as well as the notions of models and satisfaction. Theories, models, and their morphisms are introduced in sections 3 and 4. Matching and behavioral matching are defined and their properties proved in sections 5 and 6. Institutions are introduced in section 7. The notions of behavioral compatibility and preservation of semantics are also presented in this section, along with the most important results of this paper. The implications of these results are discussed in sections 8 and 9. The conclusions are given in section 10.

2   Classes as Theories

Self typing ([13], [2]) is accomplished by a distinguished type variable, denoted *thisType* in this paper. *thisType* stands for the class in which it occurs. In a subclass, *thisType* thus changes its interpretation, and stands for the subclass. An example of a class interface in which both self typing and constraints are used is given below:

Example 1 *(Self typing and constraints)*

```
class Collection {
    boolean belongs(Object a);
    boolean insert(Object a);
    boolean delete(Object a);
    thisType copy();
```

constraints:
   forAll thisType this; Object x require
   (this.belongs(x) ← this.insert(x)),
   (this.copy().belongs(x) ← this.belongs(x))
}

class *Set* **extends** *Collection* {
   thisType union(thisType S);
   thisType intersect(thisType S);
constraints:
   forAll thisType this, S; Object x require
   (this.union(S).belongs(x) ← this.belongs(x)),
   (this.union(S).belongs(x) ← S.belongs(x)),
   (this.intersect(S).belongs(x) ← this.belongs(x), S.belongs(x))
}

The above example is based on a particularly simple logic: Horn clause logic. A more sophisticated logic such as a temporal Horn clause logic that appears in section 8 is much better suited for the object-oriented paradigm because it can express constraints on sequences of object states. This means that the effects of mutating the object state may be specified as well. With Horn clause logic as used in the above example a constraint is necessarily evaluated in a single object state. So for example, in the constraint $this.belongs(x) \leftarrow this.insert(x)$, both $this.insert(x)$ and $this.belongs(x)$ are evaluated in the object state after completion of the insert method. The ability to deal with a variety of logics is a particularly distinctive feature of this model theory as explained in sections 7 and 8.

A class interface consists of the signatures of the public methods of the class. This standard idea is defined below in the notion of a class signature.

Definition 1 *(Class signature Σ)*
   The signature Σ_A of a class A consists of

- *A finite set of sorts S_A. S_A necessarily includes A as well as boolean.*
- *A finite set of method signatures of the form $C\ m(C_1\ x_1, C_2\ x_2, \ldots, C_n\ x_n)$ where $C \in S_A$ and $C_i \in S_A$ for $i = 1, 2, \ldots, n$. (m is the method name, C is the return type, and C_i is the type of parameter x_i).*

Class constraints are expressed as sentences whose syntax is defined below:

Definition 2 *(Σ terms and atoms)*
   Let S_A be the set of sorts of a signature Σ_A, as in the definition 1. For each sort $C \in S_A$

- *A constant of sort C, a variable of sort C, and a new object constructor new $C()$ are terms of the sort C.*
- *If c is a term of sort C then a message of the form form $c.f(t_1, t_2, \ldots, t_n)$ is a term, where f is a method from Σ_C, and $t_1, t_2, \ldots, t_n$ are terms.*

– If c is a term of sort C, then an atom is of the form $c.p(t_1, t_2, \ldots, t_n)$, where p is a boolean method from Σ_C, and $t_1, t_2, \ldots, t_n$ are terms.

Note that since Σ_A necessarily contains A, the above definition includes terms of the form $a.f(a_1, a_2, \ldots, a_n)$ where a is a term of sort A, a_i is a term of sort C_i, where $C_i \in S_A$ and $f \in \Sigma_A$.

Definition 3 *(Σ sentences)*

– A Σ_A formula is obtained from Σ_A atoms according to the rules of a particular logical system.
– A Σ_A sentence is a closed formula, i.e., a formula with all variables quantified.

Note that the actual syntax of terms, atoms, formulae, and sentences depends upon a particular object-oriented language and the chosen logical system for expressing class constraints. The results of this paper are intended to be independent of both. This is why the definition of sentences is not more specific.

Definition 4 *(A class as a theory)*
A class as a theory $Th_A = (\Sigma_A, E_A)$ consists of a class signature Σ_A and a finite set E_A of Σ_A sentences.

The above definition 4 makes a class A a theory, denoted Th_A. A class A becomes a type, denoted M_A, by interpreting the method signatures from Σ_A as functions and by interpreting accordingly the sentences E_A in the chosen logical system. M_A is thus a model for Th_A if it satisfies all the sentences of Th_A. $\models$ denotes the satisfaction relation between models and sentences.

– If Σ is a signature, let $Sen(\Sigma)$ be the set of sentences over the signature Σ and $|\ Mod(\Sigma)\ |$ the set of all Σ models.
– A relation $\models_\Sigma\ \subseteq\ |\ Mod(\Sigma)\ | \times Sen(\Sigma)$ is called the satisfaction relation.
– If $Th_A = (\Sigma_A, E_A)$ is a class viewed as a theory and M_A is a Σ_A model, then M_A is a model for Th_A iff $M_A \models E_A$. Note that $E_A \subseteq Sen(\Sigma_A)$.

The above informal definitions are made precise in what follows. Specifically, models and satisfaction are discussed in detail in section 4.

3   Theory Morphisms

The notion of a theory morphism [19] plays a crucial role in this development. It specifies the semantic conditions for the inheritance of class signatures and of the associated class constraints. A theory morphism is, first of all, a morphism of method signatures.

Definition 5 *(Signature morphism)*
If A and B are classes, a morphism of method signatures consists of

- A function $\phi : S_A \to S_B$
- A function $\Sigma_A \to \Sigma_B$ (an extension of ϕ to method signatures), where
  $\phi(C\ m(C_1\ x_1,\ C_2\ x_2, \ldots,\ C_n\ x_n)) =$
  $\phi(C)\ m(\phi(C_1)\ \phi(x_1),\ \phi(C_2)\ \phi(x_2), \ldots,\ \phi(C_n)\ \phi(x_n))$

From now on we will just use ϕ for both functions that appear in the above definition. The above definition could be extended to allow for renaming of method signatures which we do not consider in this paper. Signature morphisms specify consistent functional transformations of method signatures. The semantic requirements for methods whose signatures are being transformed by signature morphisms are captured by a much more general notion of a morphism. Theory morphisms specify the conditions on the transformations of class sentences which guarantee the semantic compatibility of methods. The notion of a theory morphism comes from [19] and [18].

Let $closure(E)$ be defined as follows:
$P \in closure(E) \Leftrightarrow M \models P$, for all models M such that $M \models E$.

Then we have:

Definition 6 *(Theory morphism)*
  If $Th_A = (\Sigma_A, E_A)$ and $Th_B = (\Sigma_B, E_B)$ are classes as theories,
  $\phi : Th_A \to Th_B$ is a theory morphism iff

- *$\phi : \Sigma_A \to \Sigma_B$ is a signature morphism*
- *$e \in E_A \Rightarrow \phi(e) \in closure(E_B)$*

Note that ϕ maps sentences according to the rule $\phi(x_s) = x_{\phi(s)}$ where s is a sort and x_s is a variable of sort s. This means that a theory morphism does not necessarily guarantee type safety. Based on the definition of closure given above, an equivalent model-theoretic definition of a theory morphism is

Definition 7 *(Theory morphism)*
  If $Th_A = (\Sigma_A, E_A)$ and $Th_B = (\Sigma_B, E_B)$ are classes as theories,
  $\phi : Th_A \to Th_B$ is a theory morphism iff

- *$\phi : \Sigma_A \to \Sigma_B$ is a signature morphism*
- *For all Th_B models M_B (hence $M_B \models E_B$):*
  $M_B \models \phi(e)$ for each $e \in E_A$

The notion of a theory morphism plays such a critical role in the results of this paper because it specifies model-theoretic requirements for the inheritance of class sentences. $\phi(e)$ denotes the sentence e of Th_A inherited in Th_B. A model for a class B viewed as a theory is required to satisfy all the sentences of Th_B (i.e., $M_B \models E_B$), as well as all the sentences inherited from Th_A (i.e., $M_B \models \phi(E_A)$).

In addition, the importance of the notion of a theory morphism comes from its associated substitution (or abstraction) function $\phi^* : Mod(\Sigma_B) \to Mod(\Sigma_A)$ which maps objects of type B into objects of type A. The requirement for behavioral compatibility of objects of type B when substituted in place of objects of type A has the form $\phi^*(M_B) \models E_A$. This is fully elaborated in section 7.

4   Categories of Models

The results of this paper are on purpose independent of the choice of suitable models for object types. This is why the results of this paper are expected to be applicable to any well-defined notions of a model and a model morphism.

In general, a method m will be interpreted as a suitable function. The collection of all Th_A models will be denoted as Mod_A, and a particular Th_A model as M_A. If M_A and M'_A are models for a class A, then a morphism of models $M_A \to M'_A$ is required to map correctly the interpreted methods. In fact, the collection of models of a given type constitutes a category.

Definition 8 *(Σ models)*
A model for a class signature Σ_A consists of the following:

- *A collection of sets $\{M_s \mid s \in S_A\}$ where S_A is the set of sorts of A.*
- *For each method m in Σ_A with the signature $C\ m(C_1\ x_1, C_2\ x_2, \ldots, C_n\ x_n)$ a function $f_m : M_w \to M_C$ where $M_w = M_A \times M_{C_1} \times \ldots \times M_{C_n}$ with $w = AC_1 \ldots C_n$.*

A *category* [32] consists of a collection of *objects* together with their *morphisms*. Every object of a category is equipped with the *identity morphism*. When the codomain of one morphism is identical to the domain of another morphism, the two are composed in a new morphism. This *composition* is naturally *associative*.

Definition 9 *(Model morphisms)*
A morphism of Σ_A models $h : M_A \to M'_A$ is a family of functions $h_s : M_s \to M'_s$ for $s \in S_A$, where S_A is the set of sorts of Σ_A.

- *For each method m of a class signature Σ_A with signature $C\ m(C_1\ x_1, C_2\ x_2, \ldots, C_n\ x_n)$ and $a \in M_w$, $h_C(f_m(a)) = f'_m(h_w(a))$ holds, where h_w is a product of functions $h_A \times h_{C_1} \times \ldots \times h_{C_n}$ when $w = AC_1C_2 \ldots C_n$, as in the following diagram:*

$$
\begin{array}{ccc}
M_w & \xrightarrow{f_m} & M_C \\
h_w \downarrow & & \downarrow h_C \\
M'_w & \xrightarrow{f'_m} & M'_C
\end{array}
$$

Functors are *morphisms of categories* [32]. A *functor* $F : \mathbf{A} \to \mathbf{B}$ maps a morphism $f : A_1 \to A_2$, where A_1 and A_2 are objects of the category $\mathbf{A}$, to a morphism $F(f) : F(A_1) \to F(A_2)$ of the category $\mathbf{B}$. In addition, F preserves the identity morphism, and commutes with the composition of morphisms:

- $F(1_A) = 1_{F(A)}$ where 1 denotes the identity morphism.
- If $f : A_1 \to A_2$ and $g : A_2 \to A_3$ are morphisms of $\mathbf{A}$, then $F(gf) = F(g)F(f)$.

A Σ model M satisfies a Σ sentence $\forall X(e)$ if for any substitution of variables $\theta_s : X_s \to M_s$, $s \in S, S$ *sorts of* Σ, $e < \theta >$ evaluates to true. $eval(e < \theta >)$ stands for the results of evaluation of the expression e in which variables are substituted according to θ. The evaluation function $eval$ is based on a family of term evaluation functions $h_s : T_s^\Sigma \to M_s$, $s \in S$ where T_s^Σ denotes the set of Σ terms of the sort s defined inductively as follows:

Definition 10 *(Σ terms)*
 Given a class signature Σ_A with a set of sorts S_A, the set of Σ_A terms T_C^Σ of sort $C \in S_A$ is defined inductively as follows:

- $X_C \subseteq T_C^\Sigma$ *(X_C are variables of sort C)*
- *new* $C() \in T_C^\Sigma$
- *If $C\ m(C_1\ x_1, C_2\ x_2, \ldots, C_n\ x_n) \in \Sigma_{A_k}$, $a \in T_{A_k}^\Sigma$ ($A_k \in S_A$), $t_i \in T_{C_i}^\Sigma$, $C_i \in S_{A_k}$, $i = 1, \ldots, n$, then $a.m(t_1, t_2, \ldots, t_n) \in T_C^\Sigma$.*

Terms of the form $a.m(t_1, t_2, \ldots, t_n)$ will be called method terms.

Definition 11 *(Σ term evaluation)*
 Let Σ be a class signature with a set of sorts S and M a Σ model. The term evaluation function is a family of functions $h_s : T_s^\Sigma \to M_s$, $s \in S$ defined inductively as follows:
- $h_s(x_s) = \theta(x_s), x_s \in X_s$
- $h_s(new\ s()) = new\ s()$
- $h_s(a.m(t_1, t_2, \ldots, t_n)) = f_m(h_A(a), h_{C_1}(t_1), h_{C_2}(t_2), \ldots, h_{C_n}(t_n))$ *where $A \in S$ is the sort of the term a and $m \in \Sigma_A$.*

Σ sentences are constructed from Σ terms using the rules of a particular logic. The definition of the evaluation function for sentences depends upon the chosen logic. This is illustrated below for Horn clause logics:

Definition 12 *(Σ Horn clause evaluation)*
 Let Σ_A be a class signature with a set of sorts S_A and let h be the Σ_A term evaluation function defined according to 11.

- $eval(p < \theta >) = h_{boolean}(p)$ *where p is a boolean method term of a method in Σ_A.*
- $eval((p_1, p_2, \ldots, p_n) < \theta >) = true$ *iff $h_{boolean}(p_i) = true$ for p_i a Boolean method term ($i = 1, 2, \ldots, n$) of a method in Σ_{A_k} where $A_k \in S_A$.*
- $eval((p \leftarrow p_1, p_2, \ldots, p_n) < \theta >) = true$ *iff $eval((p_1, p_2, \ldots, p_n) < \theta >) = true$ implies $eval(p < \theta >) = true$.*

The above definition contains a subtlety: an atom in the head of a clause over a class signature Σ_A is necessarily a boolean method term of a method from Σ_A. The reason for this is that sentences of a class A should not specify the semantics of methods from other classes.

Definition 13 *(Satisfaction)*
 With the above definitions 10 and 11 we have:

– A Σ model M satisfies a Σ sentence $\forall X(e)$, iff $eval(e < \theta >) = true$ for any substitution of variables θ.
– The satisfaction relation is $(M, Sen(\Sigma)_M) \in \models_\Sigma$ where $Sen(\Sigma)_M \subseteq Sen(\Sigma)$ and $Sen(\Sigma)_M = \{\forall(e) \mid eval(e < \theta >= true)\}$ for any substitution of variables θ.

The above definitions are in fact based on the notion of the initial Σ model [20], but this point will not be elaborated in this paper.

5   Matching

Matching has been introduced as a more flexible typing discipline in comparison with subtyping ([13], [2]). It applies to type systems based on self types. When self typing is used, the inheritance and the subtyping orderings of classes do not coincide ([12], [16]). Identifying inheritance with subtyping when self typing is used leads to well-known problems [15] of the Eiffel type system ([33], [34]). Matching does not guarantee type safety of assignments with static type checking. But it has other important uses in parametric classes with bounded type constraints where subtyping does not necessarily apply.

Definition 14 *(Self-typed signatures)*

– A self-typed class signature $\Sigma_A^{thisType}$ is a class signature over the set of sorts $S_A \cup \{thisType\}$.
– An interpretation of a self-typed signature $\Sigma_A^{thisType}$ is a signature morphism $\phi : \Sigma_A^{thisType} \to \Sigma_A$ defined as $\phi(thisType) = A$ and $\phi(C) = C$ for $C \neq thisType$.

Definition 15 *(Matching)*
    Matching is a partial order $< \sharp$ of the set of sorts $S \cup \{thisType\}$ which extends to class signatures as follows:
    A class signature $\Sigma_B^{thisType}$ matches a class signature $\Sigma_A^{thisType}$, denoted $\Sigma_B^{thisType} < \sharp \Sigma_A^{thisType}$ iff the following is satisfied:

– Let $C_A\ m(C_{A1}\ x_1, C_{A2}\ x_2, ..., C_{An}\ x_n)$ be a signature of a method m in $\Sigma_A^{thisType}$.
– Then $\Sigma_B^{thisType}$ has a method m with the signature $C_B\ m(C_{B1}\ x_1, C_{B2}\ x_2, ..., C_{Bn}\ x_n)$ such that:
– $C_{Ai} < \sharp C_{Bi}$ $(i=1,2,...,n)$ (contravariance) and $C_B < \sharp C_A$ (covariance).

If the above conditions are satisfied, we say that a class B matches a class A.

Proposition 1 *Matching is not a morphism of method signatures.*

Proof 1 *The notion of a signature morphism $\Sigma_A^{thisType} \to \Sigma_B^{thisType}$ requires the existence of a function $S_A \cup \{thisType\} \to S_B \cup \{thisType\}$ for self-typed signatures. Likewise, if we consider interpreted self-typed signatures a function*

$S_A \to S_B$ is required. But matching guarantees only the existence of a relation in both cases.

In fact, if the underlying class is denoted both by *thisType* as well as explicitly by its name, the requirements for a signature morphism (and thus a theory morphism as well) will be violated. Indeed, consider the following classes:

class A {
  thisType $m(A\ a)$;
}

class B **extends** A {
  thisType $m(A\ a)$;
}

We have that B matches A. However, the mapping of the interpreted method signatures is such that $A \to A$ and $A \to B$. This follows from the fact that *thisType* denotes A in the class A and B in the class B. Hence $\Sigma_A \to \Sigma_B$ is not a signature morphism, and thus not a theory morphism either. This completes the proof.

Corollary 1 *Matching does not extend to a theory morphism.*

The above negative results are the consequence of the definition 5. Definition 5 is object-oriented, but it is still given in the spirit of the original definition ([19], [18]) targeted to many sorted algebras as models. Alternative object-oriented definitions of a theory morphism are possible that would lead to results that are different with respect to the results of this paper.

A restricted form of matching introduced in [8] requires that *thisType* is always used to denote the underlying type. Explicit usage of the name of the underlying type is not allowed. The reason for this is that using both *thisType* and the name of the underlying type leads to non-functional transformations of method signatures. In addition, this constrained matching [8] requires that the automatic change of the interpretation of *thisType* is the only change in the method signatures. All other types in the method signatures are required to remain the same. These restrictions are specified formally in the following definition.

Definition 16 *(Constrained self-typed signatures)*
A self-typed class signature $\Sigma_A^{thisType}$ is a constrained self-typed signature if it satisfies the following condition:

- If $C\ m(C_1\ x_1, C_2\ x_2, \ldots, C_n\ x_n)$ is a method in $\Sigma_A^{thisType}$ then $C_i \neq A$ and $C \neq A$.

Definition 17 *(Constrained matching)*
If $\Sigma_A^{thisType}$ and $\Sigma_A^{thisType}$ are constrained self-typed signatures we say that a class B is a constrained match for a class A, denoted $B <| A$, iff

- $\Sigma_A^{thisType} \subseteq \Sigma_B^{thisType}$ *(and thus $S_A \subseteq S_B$)*

Contrary to matching, the above restrictions in fact guarantee that constrained matching is a morphism of method signatures.

Proposition 2 *(Constrained matching)*
Constrained matching is a morphism of method signatures.

Proof 2 *If a class B is a constrained match for a class A we can construct a class signature morphism $\phi : \Sigma_A^{thisType} \to \Sigma_B^{thisType}$ as follows: For every class $C \in S_A \cup \{thisType\}$ we have:*

- *If $C \neq thisType$ then $\phi(C) = C$.*
- *If $C = thisType$ then $\phi(thisType) = thisType$.*

The above extends to $\phi : \Sigma_A^{thisType} \to \Sigma_B^{thisType}$ according to the definition 5. Likewise, for the interpreted signatures we also obtain a signature morphism $\phi : \Sigma_A \to \Sigma_B$ by setting $\phi(A) = B$ and $\phi(C) = C$ if $C \neq A$.

6   Behavioral Matching

In this section we extend the notion of a morphism of method signatures (as defined by constrained matching) with the semantic compatibility constraints. These constraints naturally apply to class sentences. The newly introduced behavioral compatibility notion is called behavioral matching.

Definition 18 *(Behavioral matching)*
If a class Th_B is a constrained match for a class Th_A such that

- $E_B = E_A < A/B > \sqcup E_B'$

where $\sqcup$ denotes disjoint union, then Th_B is a behavioral match for Th_A.

E_B' in the above definition are the sentences of Th_B which are not inherited from Th_A, i.e., these are the additional sentences introduced in Th_B.
An alternative and equivalent definition is:

Definition 19 *(Behavioral matching)*
A class Th_B is a behavioral match for a class Th_A iff

- *B is a constrained match for A*
- *$\phi : \Sigma_A \to \Sigma_B$ satisfies $\phi(E_A) \subseteq E_B$*

The above definition is in fact a particular case of a theory morphism, hence the following result:

Proposition 3 *(Behavioral matching and theory morphisms)*
If a class Th_B is a behavioral match for a class Th_A, then $\phi : \Sigma_A \to \Sigma_B$ is a theory morphism.

Proof 3 *If Th_B is a behavioral match for Th_A, then $\phi : \Sigma_A \to \Sigma_B$ is a signature morphism by the proposition 2. In addition, if $\phi(E_A) \subseteq E_B$, we necessarily have $\phi(E_A) \subseteq closure(E_B)$. This means that ϕ satisfies the definition 6 of a theory morphism.*

In this paper we do not consider the implications of parametric classes and their interfaces. However, we do provide an example of behavioral matching used to express the semantic compatibility with the bound type when bounded parametric classes are used.

Example 2 *(Behavioral matching)*
class *Comparable* {
   boolean lessEq(thisType x);
constraints:
   forAll thisType x,y,z require
   (x.lessEq(x)),
   (x.lessEq(z) $\leftarrow$ x.lessEq(y), y.lessEq(z))
}
   Note that the underlying type Comparable is never used explicitly. Rather, thisType is always used to denote the underlying class. The same discipline is used for the class Employee which is now a behavioral match for Comparable.

class *Employee* **extends** *Comparable* {
   int ssn();
   float salary();
   boolean equal(thisType x);
   boolean lessEq(thisType x);
constraints:
   forAll thisType x, y require
   (x.lessEq(y) $\leftarrow$ x.ssn() $\leq$ y.ssn())
}
   A parametric class OrderedSet given below follows the rules of behavioral matching for the type parameter constraint.

class *OrderedSet* $<T$ **extends** *Comparable* $>$ {
   boolean belongs(T a);
   int ordinal(T a);
   boolean insert(T a);
   boolean delete(T a);
constraints:
   forAll thisType this; T x,y require
   (this.belongs(x) $\leftarrow$ this.insert(x)),
   (this.ordinal(x) $\leq$ this.ordinal(y) $\leftarrow$ this.belongs(x), this.belongs(y), x.lessEq(y))
}

The following proposition is addressing the problem of verification of the condition for a theory morphism in such a way that the change of interpretation of *thisType* is properly taken into account.

Proposition 4 *(Interpreting thisType)*

- *Let Th_B be a behavioral match for Th_A and let $\phi : Th_A \to Th_B$ be the associated theory morphism.*
- *Let $\phi' : \Sigma_A \to \Sigma_B$ be a signature morphism induced by the substitution $A \to B$.*
- *Let $f : \Sigma_A^{thisType} \to \Sigma_A$ be a signature morphism induced by the substitution thisType $\to A$, and $g : \Sigma_B^{thisType} \to \Sigma_B$ a signature morphism induced by the substitution thisType $\to B$.*

All the arrows in the diagram below are in fact theory morphisms, and the diagram commutes.

$$
\begin{array}{ccc}
Th_A & \xrightarrow{\phi} & Th_B \\
f \downarrow & & g \downarrow \\
Th_A < thisType/A > & \xrightarrow{\phi'} & Th_B < thisType/B >
\end{array}
$$

Proof 4 *For all $C \in S_A$ we have $f(C) = C$ and $f(thisType) = A$. Likewise, for all $C \in S_B$ we have $g(C) = C$ and $g(thisType) = B$.*

For any sentence e in E_A, $f(e)$ is a sentence in $E_A < thisType/A >$. $f(e)$ is obtained from e by replacing every occurrence of thisType with A. This is why f is not only a signature morphism, but in fact a theory morphism $Th_A \to Th_A < thisType/A >$. The same applies to g.

Let us now define $\phi' : Th_A < thisType/A > \to Th_B < thisType/B >$ as follows:

- *for any $C \in S_A < thisType/A >$, such that $C \neq A$, $\phi'(C) = C$*
- *$\phi'(A) = B$.*

With these definitions, we actually have $\phi'(f(C)) = g(\phi(C))$ for any $C \in S_A$ including the case $C = thisType$.

We still need to show that ϕ' is a theory morphism, i.e., for any sentence $e' \in E_A < thisType/A > \phi'(e')$ is in $E_B < thisType/B >$. Note that $\phi'(e')$ is obtained by mapping a type C in e' to $\phi'(C)$ in accordance with the above definition of ϕ'.

Any sentence e' in $E_A < thisType/A >$ is actually $f(e)$, where e is in E_A, i.e., $e' = f(e)$. Thus $\phi'(e') = \phi'(f(e)) = g(\phi(e))$, using the property that $\phi'(f(C)) = g(\phi(C))$ for any class $C \in S_A$.

This shows that e' is mapped by ϕ' to $g(\phi(e))$. By the assumption of the proposition, $\phi(e)$ is in E_B, and by the definition of g, $g(\phi(e))$ is in $E_B < thisType/B >$. Hence $\phi'(e')$ belongs to $E_B < thisType/B >$. So $\phi' : Th_A < thisType/A > \to Th_B < thisType/B >$ is a theory morphism, and the diagram commutes.

7   Institutions

The results of this paper are intended to be independent of a particular logical system for expressing class constraints. The notion of an institution ([19], [18]) has been proposed to cover a variety of logical systems used for expressing the semantics of programming paradigms. The main requirement for a logical system to be an institution is the existence of the satisfaction relation between models and sentences that is consistent under change of notation. Throughout this paper the logic for expressing constraints will, as a rule, be an institution. The change of notation that is in the focus of our interest in this paper is caused by the rules that apply to method signatures in inheritance hierarchies when self typing is used.

The notion of an institution allows us to abstract over all applicable logical systems suitable for viewing classes as theories. Two functors play a crucial role in accomplishing this level of generality.

The first one is $Sen :$ **Sign** $\rightarrow$ **Set** where **Set** denotes the category of sets. If Σ is a class signature, then $Sen(\Sigma)$ is the set of all well-formed sentences (class constraints) over Σ. Many constraint languages, hence many Sen functors, are possible. Sen is determined by the choice of logic that specifies the syntax of sentences of the constraint language. This syntax is defined starting with the features of a class signature. The class signature determines the terms of the constraint language, and the logic determines the formulae based on those terms. This is why Sen maps a class signature into a set of sentences over that signature. Sen also maps a signature morphism to a function that transforms the sets of sentences.

The second functor is $Mod :$ **Sign** $\rightarrow$ **Cat**^{op}. For each class signature Σ, $Mod(\Sigma)$ is the category of Σ models, together with their morphisms. **Cat** denotes the category of categories. To me more precise about it, the term category of all small categories should be used [32] in order to avoid the well-know set-theoretic paradox. Objects of **Cat** are categories and arrows of **Cat** are functors. **Cat**^{op} differs from **Cat** only to the extent that the direction of its arrows is reversed. Unlike Sen, Mod is a contravariant functor. This reversal of the direction of arrows that happens going from class signatures to their models represents correctly the situation in the object-oriented model: object substitutability has the opposite direction with respect to class extensions via inheritance.

Definition 20 *(Institutions)*
An institution consists of

- *A category of signatures* **Sign**. *This category consists of objects representing class signatures together with their morphisms.*
- *A functor Sen :* **Sign** $\rightarrow$ **Set**. *If Σ is a signature, then $Sen(\Sigma)$ is a set of sentences over the signature Σ.*
- *A functor Mod :* **Sign** $\rightarrow$ **Cat**^{op}. *For each signature Σ, $Mod(\Sigma)$ is the category of Σ models, together with their morphisms.*
- *For each signature Σ a relation $\models_{\Sigma} \subseteq \mid Mod(\Sigma) \mid \times Sen(\Sigma)$ called the satisfaction relation. $\mid Mod(\Sigma) \mid$ denotes the set of objects of the category $Mod(\Sigma)$.*
- *For each signature morphism $\phi : \Sigma_A \rightarrow \Sigma_B$ the following* Satisfaction Condition *holds for each Σ_B model M_B and each sentence $e \in Sen(\Sigma_A)$:*

$$M_B \models_{\Sigma_B} Sen(\phi)(e) \quad \textit{iff} \quad Mod(\phi)(M_B) \models_{\Sigma_A} e.$$

A shorthand notation that we will use for $Mod(\phi)$ is ϕ^*. Note that this notation indicates that $Mod(\phi)$ is the model theoretic counterpart of the abstraction function used in the notion of behavioral subtyping [31]. An alternative notation for $Sen(\phi)(e)$ is just $\phi(e)$. $Mod(\Sigma_A)$ is abbreviated as Mod_A. An object of the category Mod_A is denoted as M_A.

The relationships in the above definition are represented by the following diagrams:

$$
\begin{array}{ccc}
\mathbf{Sign} & \xrightarrow{Sen} & \mathbf{Set} \\
= & & \models \\
\mathbf{Sign} & \xrightarrow{Mod} & \mathbf{Cat}^{op}
\end{array}
$$

$$
\begin{array}{ccc}
Mod(\Sigma_A) & \models_{\Sigma_A} & Sen(\Sigma_A) \\
Mod(\phi)\uparrow & & \downarrow Sen(\phi) \\
Mod(\Sigma_B) & \models_{\Sigma_B} & Sen(\Sigma_B)
\end{array}
$$

Note that the definition of the notion of an institution requires that signature morphisms are interpreted as functions. Indeed, the codomain of the functor *Sen* is the category of sets. Morphisms of the category of sets are functions.

A key observation of this paper is that in the object-oriented paradigm the *Satisfaction Condition* ties together the inheritance of class constraints and semantically correct object substitutability.

If A and B are classes viewed as theories and B is a subclass of A, then the left part of the *Satisfaction Condition*:

$M_B \models_{\Sigma_B} Sen(\phi)(e)$ or in the abbreviated notation

$M_B \models_{\Sigma_B} \phi(e)$ for $e \in E_A$

deals with the inheritance of the A-sentences in B. This condition states that a model for B satisfies the sentences inherited from A.

The right part of the *Satisfaction Condition* deals with semantic substitutability. It states that objects of type B when viewed as objects of type A satisfy the sentences of A:

$Mod(\phi)(M_B) \models_{\Sigma_A} e$, or in the abbreviated notation

$\phi^*(M_B) \models_{\Sigma_A} e$ for $e \in E_A$.

This means that substituting objects of type B where objects of type A are expected will cause no behavioral incompatibilities.

Proposition 5 *The formal system underlying matching is in general not an institution.*

Proof 5 *The proof follows immediately from the proposition 1 which establishes the fact that matching in general is not a morphism of method signatures.*

Definition 21 *(Preservation of semantics)*
Given classes $Th_A = (\Sigma_A, E_A)$ and $Th_B = (\Sigma_B, E_B)$, we say that the abstraction function $\phi^* : Mod_B \to Mod_A$ preserves semantics iff it is in fact a functor. This in particular means:

  - $\phi^*(M_B)$ is a (Σ_A, E_A) model, i.e., $\phi^*(M_B) \models E_A$
  - If $f : M'_B \to M''_B$ is a morphism of B models, then $\phi^*(f) : \phi^*(M'_B) \to \phi^*(M''_B)$ is a morphism of A models.

For transformations of method signatures that are in fact signature morphisms, the condition for the preservation of semantics coincides with the condition for a theory morphism. However, this holds only as long as the underlying logic for expressing constraints is an institution.

Theorem 1 *(Theory morphisms and institutions)*
    If $\phi : \Sigma_A \to \Sigma_B$ is a signature morphism, and the underlying logical system is an institution, then the abstraction function $\phi^* : Mod_B \to Mod_A$ preserves semantics iff ϕ is in fact a theory morphism: $(\Sigma_A, E_A) \to (\Sigma_B, E_B)$.

Proof 6 *Suppose that $\phi : (\Sigma_A, E_A) \to (\Sigma_B, E_B)$ is a theory morphism. For any (Σ_B, E_B) model M_B we have $M_B \models E_B \Rightarrow M_B \models \phi(e)$, for each sentence $e \in E_A$. Since ϕ is a signature morphism, the Satisfaction Condition holds. The Satisfaction Condition implies that ϕ^* is a functor, so that $M_B \models \phi(e) \Rightarrow \phi^*(M_B) \models e$, for all $e \in E_A$. This means that semantics is preserved.*
    Suppose now that the semantics is preserved, i.e., that we have a functor ϕ^* so that $\phi^*(M_B) \models e$ for all $e \in E_A$ and for any (Σ_B, E_B) model M_B. By the definition of an institution the Satisfaction Condition holds for any signature morphism ϕ. This implies $\phi^*(M_B) \models e \Rightarrow M_B \models \phi(e)$. This means that for any $e \in E_A$, $\phi(e) \in closure(E_B)$. This proves that ϕ is a theory morphism.

Definition 22 *(Behavioral compatibility for classes as theories)*
    A class B viewed as a theory is behaviorally compatible with a class A viewed as a theory iff there exists a theory morphism $\phi : Th_A \to Th_B$, and its associated functor $\phi^* : Mod_B \to Mod_A$.

Note that the existence of ϕ^* is guaranteed by the *Satisfaction Condition*.
    The above definition of behavioral compatibility for classes as theories is significantly different in comparison with the definition of behavioral subtyping [31]. It requires that the mapping of signatures is a theory morphism, and that the abstraction function is in fact a functor, i.e., a morphism of the categories of models. In addition, the above definition, since it applies to theories, is based on sentences rather than on assertions.

Corollary 2 *(Behavioral compatibility and preservation of semantics)*
    If a class B is behaviorally compatible with a class A according to the definition 22 then the abstraction function $\phi^* : Mod_B \to Mod_A$ preserves semantics.

Proof 7 *The proof is immediate from the definitions 21 and 22.*

The theorem that follows establishes that the logical system underlying behavioral matching is an institution. This result holds as long as the logic for expressing sentences (constraints) is itself an institution. Of course, this condition is satisfied by a variety of logics such as equational logic [20], Horn clause logic (with and without equality) ([21], [22], [23], [10], [11]), first-order predicate calculus, temporal logic in ([7], [6], [8]) and [9], the rewriting logic ([35], [36]), etc. However, this condition in these logics is in general guaranteed only under trivial changes of notation. It is a non-trivial problem to establish the *Satisfaction Condition* under no-trivial changes of notation. This is precisely what this paper does for the changes of method signatures in inheritance hierarchies when self typing is used.

Theorem 2 *(Behavioral matching is an institution)*

- *Let **Sign** be a category of interpreted self-typed class signatures (definition 14).*
- *Let Sen be a sentence functor where $Sen(\Sigma)$ is a set of sentences (definition 3) over an interpreted self-typed signature Σ.*
- *Let the functor Mod : **Sign** $\rightarrow$ **Cat**^{op} be defined in such a way that the category $Mod(\Sigma)$ is defined according to the definitions 8 and 9.*
- *The satisfaction relation is defined according to 13.*

The above formal system is an institution.

Proof 8 *In the proof of this theorem we concentrate on the most critical part: the proof that the SatisfactionCondition holds.*

Let M_B be a Th_B model. Then $M_B \models E_A < A/B >$. From this Th_B model we obtain a Th_A model by reinterpreting B as A in the signatures of the methods of Th_B that are in fact inherited from Th_A. These are methods with signatures $\sigma_{w,s}$ from Σ_B such that $\sigma_{w<B/A>,s<B/A>} \in \Sigma_A$. The resulting model is $\phi^*(M_B)$ and $\phi^*(M_B) \models E_A$. The same technique produces a morphism of Th_A models $\phi^*(f)$ from a morphism of Th_B models f. A morphism of Th_A models $\phi^*(f)$ is obtained from a morphism of Th_B models f by dropping the classes $S_B \setminus S_A$ from f and mapping B into A. This proves that ϕ^* is a functor, and so we have the following part of the Satisfaction Condition:

$$M_B \models E_A < A/B > \Rightarrow \phi^*(M_B) \models E_A$$

The other direction follows from the fact that starting with a Th_A model $\phi^*(M_B)$ we obtain a Th_B model M_B by reversing the above construction. Hence we have:

$$\phi^*(M_B) \models E_A \Rightarrow M_B \models E_A < A/B >.$$

Example 3 *(Satisfaction Condition)*

The classes Collection and Set are given in the example 1. Note that Set is a behavioral match for Collection.

A model for (Σ_{Set}, E_{Set}) is a model for $(\Sigma_{Collection}, E_{Collection})$. The additional structure which M_{Set} has with respect to $M_{Collection}$ consists of additional operators on sets, and the associated sentences, i.e., those that do not belong to $(\Sigma_{Collection}, E_{Collection})$. This means that M_{Set} satisfies all the sentences of $E_{Collection}$, as well as the additional sentences from E_{Set}.

$S_{Collection} = \{Object, Collection, boolean\}$

$S_{Set} = \{Object, Set, boolean\}$

The signature morphism ϕ is specified as follows:

$\phi(Object) = Object,$

$\phi(Collection) = Set,$

$\phi(boolean) = boolean.$

The mapping of sentences is defined as follows:

$\phi(e) = e < Collection/Set >$

The abstraction functor

$\phi^* : Mod_{Set} \to Mod_{Collection}$

is in fact the forgetful functor which forgets the additional methods and constraints that sets have in comparison with collections.

The Satisfaction Condition holds. In particular, it means:

$M_{Set} \models (\forall this : Set, \forall x : Object \; (this.copy().belongs(x) \leftarrow this.belongs(x)))$

iff

$\phi^*(M_{Set}) \models (\forall this : Collection, \forall x : Object$
$\quad (this.copy().belongs(x) \leftarrow this.belongs(x)))$

$M_{Set} \models (\forall this : Set, \forall x : Object \; (this.belongs(x) \leftarrow this.insert(x)))$ *iff*

$\phi^*(M_{Set}) \models (\forall this : Collection, \forall x : Object$
$\quad (this.belongs(x) \leftarrow this.insert(x)))$

The notion of behavioral matching has been introduced with the idea of the preservation of the model semantics in mind.

Corollary 3 *(Behavioral matching preserves semantics)*

If a class Th_B is a behavioral match for a class Th_A, then there exists a functor $\phi^* : Mod_B \to Mod_A$, i.e., the semantics is preserved.

Proof 9 *Proof of this proposition follows from the theorems 1 and 2, and the proposition 3.*

8   A Variety of Logics

The generality of the approach and the results from the previous section become particularly important when we consider more expressive logics in comparison with the simple Horn clause logic used in the illustrative examples so far. The institution-based approach does not depend upon a particular logic paradigm and more expressive logics allow specification of some true object-oriented features such as object-state changes. A suitable temporal logic may be used for that purpose as indicated in a number of our earlier results [8], [6], [9], [5]. All the results established in this paper still hold.

A simple temporal constraint language would contain two temporal operators. The operator *always* is denoted as $\square$. If c is a constraint, then $\square c$ is true iff c evaluates to true in the current and in all the future object states. The operator *next time* is denoted as $\bigcirc$. The constraint $\bigcirc c$ is true in the current state iff the constraint c is true in the next object state. The constraints may be expressed by temporal Horn clauses of the form:

$$\forall X(\Box(\bigcirc p \leftarrow p_1, p_2, \ldots, p_n))$$

where $p, p_1, p_2, \ldots, p_n$ are atoms, invocations of boolean methods.

This explains why a temporal logic is well-suited for the object-oriented paradigm: it allows constraints on sequences of object state. In particular, it allows constraints on two subsequent object states. These constraints would in particular correspond to the classical pre and post-conditions expressed as temporal sentences. Unlike the well-established notion of behavioral subtyping, this approach makes the view of classes as theories work. An illustrative example of behavioral matching of classes as temporal theories is given below:

Example 4 *(Classes as temporal theories)*
A class Bag given below is a behavioral match for the class Collection. The constraints are expressed in temporal Horn clause logic.

class *Collection* {
  boolean belongs(Object x, int N);
  boolean insert(Object x);
  boolean delete(Object x);
constraints
  forAll thisType this, Object X; int N require
  $\Box(\bigcirc$*this.belongs(X, N+1)* $\leftarrow$ *this.belongs(X, N), this.insert(X)),*
  $\Box(\bigcirc$*this.belongs(X, N)* $\leftarrow$ *this.belongs(X, N+1), this.delete(X))*
}

class *Bag* **extends** *Collection*
  thisType union(thisType B);
  thisType intersect(thisType B);
constraints
  forAll thisType this, B; Object X; int M,N require
  $\Box$*(this.union(B).belongs(X, M.max(N))* $\leftarrow$ *this.belongs(X, M), B.belongs(X,N)),*
  $\Box$*(this.intersect(B).belongs(X, M.min(N))* $\leftarrow$ *this.belongs(X, M), B.belongs(X, N))*
}

Consider now the definition of the sentence functor for this particular temporal logic.

Definition 23 *(Temporal Sen functor)*

- If Σ is a class signature with a set of sorts S, then
  $Sen(\Sigma) = \{\forall X(\Box(\bigcirc p \leftarrow p_1, p_2, \ldots, p_n))\}$
  where $p, p_1, p_2, \ldots, p_n$ are atoms, invocations of boolean methods from Σ.
- If $\phi : \Sigma_A \rightarrow \Sigma_B$ is a signature morphism, then
  $Sen(\phi) = \{\forall \phi(X)(\Box(\bigcirc \phi(p) \leftarrow \phi(p_1), \phi(p_2), \ldots, \phi(p_n)))\}$
  where $\phi(X) = \{X_{\phi(s)} \mid X_s \subseteq X, s \in S\}$.

Proposition 6 *(Temporal Sen functor)*
Sen as defined in 23 is a functor.

9   Multiple Inheritance

The result that behavioral matching is an institution has several implications. In this section we will consider particularly subtle problems of behavioral compatibility in multiple inheritance. The most complex case is the case of diamond inheritance where a class D extends classes B and C which in turn extend a common superclass A.

There are two behavioral compatibility issues here. The first is that an object of type D should be substitutable where either an object of type B is expected or an object of type C is expected with no behavioral incompatibilities. This is why a pair of theory morphisms ϕ_{CD} and ϕ_{BD} is required.

The second issue is that an object of type D viewed either as an object of type B or an object of type C should be substitutable where an object of type A is expected with no behavioral discrepancies between the two options. The condition that guarantees the above behavioral properties is specified as follows:

Proposition 7 *(Behavioral compatibility for multiple inheritance)*

If a class D extends classes B and C which extend a common superclass A, then the condition for behavioral compatibility is expressed by the following commutative diagram of theory morphisms:

1.

$$
\begin{array}{ccc}
Th_A & \xrightarrow{\phi_{AB}} & Th_B \\
\phi_{AC}\downarrow & & \phi_{BD}\downarrow \\
Th_C & \xrightarrow{\phi_{CD}} & Th_D
\end{array}
$$

2. *If the above condition is satisfied then an object of type D may be substituted in place of an object of type A either as an object of type B or an object of type C with no behavioral discrepancies.*

Proof 10 *The proof follows from the following diagram:*

$$
\begin{array}{ccc}
Mod(\Sigma_D) & \xrightarrow{Mod(\phi_{BD})} & Mod(\Sigma_B) \\
Mod(\phi_{CD})\downarrow & & Mod(\phi_{AB})\downarrow \\
Mod(\Sigma_C) & \xrightarrow{Mod(\phi_{AC})} & Mod(\Sigma_A)
\end{array}
$$

The above diagram commutes because the diagram (1) above commutes and Mod is a functor.

Let M_D be a Σ_D model such that $M_D \models e$ for all $e \in E_D$. We have to prove:

$Mod(\phi_{AB})Mod(\phi_{BD})(M_D) \models e$

$Mod(\phi_{AC})Mod(\phi_{CD})(M_D) \models e$

for all $e \in E_A$. Since Mod is a functor the above two conditions may be rewritten as:

$Mod(\phi_{AB}\phi_{BD})(M_D) \models e$

$Mod(\phi_{AC}\phi_{CD})(M_D) \models e$

By the **Satisfaction Condition** *this is equivalent to the following two conditions:*

$M_D \models Sen(\phi_{AB}\phi_{BD})(e)$
$M_D \models Sen(\phi_{AC}\phi_{CD})(e)$

But the above conditions hold because $\phi_{AB}\phi_{BD}$ and $\phi_{AC}\phi_{CD}$ are (composite) theory morphisms.

10   Conclusions and Related Work

The main contributions of this paper are:

- A model-theoretic notion of behavioral compatibility that applies to self typing, and the associated results.
- A view of classes as theories.
- Object-oriented view of the notion of an institution which makes the results applicable to a variety of logical systems for expressing class constraints.
- A view of the relationship between the inheritance of class constraints and behaviorally acceptable object substitutability based on the *Satisfaction Condition*, the key component of the notion of an institution.
- Proof that the *Satisfaction Condition* holds for classes viewed as self-typed theories which makes behavioral matching an institution.
- The implications of this result, in particular those that apply to behavioral compatibility for multiple inheritance and classes as temporal theories.

The notion of behavioral matching introduced in this paper overcomes the semantic limitations of type systems based on self typing. Matching guarantees only the existence of methods with suitable signatures. Even if a match does exist, complete behavioral incompatibility is still undetectable in a formal system based on matching.

Behavioral matching guarantees semantic compatibility. Furthermore, these constraints make this form of matching a theory morphism. A fundamental implication is that behavioral compatibility may then be expressed by the *Satisfaction Condition* of the object-oriented interpretation of the notion of an institution. This is, in fact, the main result of this paper. The *Satisfaction Condition*, a key component of the notion of an institution, is proved to tie together inheritance of class constraints and semantically (behaviorally) correct object substitutability.

This model theoretic view developed in the paper is significantly different from the well-known approach based on behavioral subtyping. Although the idea of classes as theories was hinted in [31], this view is only fully developed in this paper.

Exploring the notions of a theory morphism and an institution is a distinctive feature of this paper in comparison with other object-oriented papers on the related subjects. For example, in [1] the notion of a specification (which would correspond to a theory) and a sub-specification (which would correspond to a subtheory) are used, but not at all in the precise sense defined by the notion of a theory morphism. The underlying model theory is not algebraic either.

Even in more algebraic (in fact, coalgebraic) logic-based approaches such as [26], the notions of a class as a theory and a theory morphism are not used.

Recent coalgebraic results on behavioral subtyping [37] do not use explicitly these notions either. These results are much closer in the spirit to the results of this paper. However, the results reported in [37] are directed toward subtyping, and even more specifically to type systems in which signatures of the inherited methods remain the same (as in Java). The focus of this paper is on self typing. In addition, the institution based approach is necessarily more general than the coalgebraic approach. Relating inheritance of class sentences with behaviorally compatible substitution of objects is difficult to capture in other approaches. This is precisely what the *Satisfaction Condition* achieves.

Other related research results are typically tied to a particular logic and even to a particular language [17]. A distinctive feature of the institution-based approach is that the results do not depend upon a particular logic or a particular language.

A major advantage of the approach based on the notion of an institution is that this makes the results independent of the choice of a particular logic for expressing assertions. The results also apply to a variety of models. The generality of the results is particularly important because of a wide variety of logics that have been applied to the object-oriented paradigm ([17], [22], [10], [11], [35], [41], [27], [8], [6], [9], [5]). The same applies to a variety of logic based declarative, constraint and assertion languages.

Proving that the Satisfaction Condition holds is non-trivial for non-trivial changes of notation. In fact, proofs of the Satisfaction Condition are hard to find in the original papers on institutions such as ([19], [18], [25], [24]). In addition, the notion of an institution has not been applied to the object-oriented paradigm. This is precisely what this paper does. In addition, this paper proves under what conditions the Satisfaction Condition holds for the changes of notation caused by self typing in inheritance hierarchies.

An interesting question is whether the *Satisfaction Condition* holds for logics proposed for the object-oriented paradigm, such as dynamic logic ([40], [41]) or F-logic [27]. Indeed, to our knowledge, F-logic follows the subtyping discipline for the redefined method signatures which does not match the notion of a signature morphism.

It is hoped that this paper will lead to a variety of institution-based object-oriented research results. The main attraction of such a development would be that the results are independent of the choice of a particular logic paradigm, and the actual language specifics and peculiarities. Two such results are already available: [4] and [3].

The core of a model theory based on institutions for generic schema management is developed in [4]. This theory has two distinctive features: it applies to a variety of categories of schemas, and it applies to transformations of both the schema structure and its integrity constraints. The overall theory is based entirely on schema morphisms that carry both structural and semantic properties. Duality results that apply to the two levels (i.e., the schema and the data levels) are established. Implications of this theory are established that apply to integrity problems in schema integration.

The results reported in [3] are directed toward a general model theory based on institutions for typed database paradigms equipped with a constraint language. Prime examples of the targeted models are the object-oriented models as well as XML models like XML Schema. A major challenge in developing such a unified model theory is in the requirement that it must be able to handle major structural differences that exist between the targeted models as well as significant differences in the logic basis of their constraint languages. This model theory is based on structural transformations within a particular category of models or across different categories with a fundamental requirement that the associated integrity constraints are managed in such a way that database integrity is preserved.

References

1. Abadi, M., Leino, K.R.M.: A Logic of Object-Oriented Programs. Proceedings of TAPSOFT '97. *Lecture Notes in Computer Science 1214.* Springer (1997) 682-696.
2. Abadi, M., Cardelli, L.: On Subtyping and Matching. Proceedings of ECOOP '96. *Lecture Notes in Computer Science 1098.* Springer (1996) 145-167.
3. Alagić, S.: Institutions: Integrating Objects, XML and Databases. *Information and Software Technology* (2002) (to appear).
4. Alagić S., Bernstein, P.A.: A Model Theory for Generic Schema Management. Proceedings of DBPL '01 (Database Programming Languages), 107 - 118. *Lecture Notes in Computer Science* (2002) (to appear).
5. Alagić, S.: Semantics of Temporal Classes. *Information and Computation* **163** (2000) 60-102.
6. Alagić, S., Solorzano J., Gitchell, D.: Orthogonal to the Java Imperative. Proceedings of ECOOP '98. *Lecture Notes in Computer Science 1445.* Springer (1998) 212-233.
7. Alagić, S., Alagić, M.,: Order-Sorted Model Theory for Temporal Executable Specifications. *Theoretical Computer Science* **179** (1997) 273-299.
8. Alagić, S.: Constrained Matching is Type Safe. Proceedings of the Sixth Int. Workshop on Database Programming Languages. *Lecture Notes in Computer Science 1369.* Springer (1998) 78 - 96.
9. Alagić, S.: Temporal Object-Oriented Programming. *Object-Oriented Systems* **6** (1999) 1-42. *Computer Journal* **43** (2001) 492-493.
10. Alagić, S., Sunderraman, R., Bagai, R. Declarative Object-Oriented Programming: Inheritance, Subtyping and Prototyping. Proceedings of ECOOP '94. *Lecture Notes in Computer Science 821.* Springer (1994) 236-259.
11. Alagić S., Sunderraman, R.: Expressibility of Typed Logic Paradigms for Object-Oriented Databases. Proceedings of BNCOD-12. *Lecture Notes in Computer Science 826.* Springer (1994) 73-89.
12. Bruce, K.: Safe Type Checking in a Statically Typed Object-Oriented Programming Language. Proceedings of the Conference on Functional Programming. ACM Press (1993) 285-298.
13. Bruce, K., Schuett, A., van Gent, R.: PolyTOIL: a Type-Safe Polymorphic Object-Oriented Language. Proceedings of ECOOP '95. *Lecture Notes in Computer Science 952.* Springer (1995) 27-51.

14. Bruce, K., Petersen, L., Feich, A.: Subtyping is not a Good Match for Object-Oriented Programming. Proceedings of ECOOP '96. *Lecture Notes in Computer Science 1241*. Springer (1996) 104-127.

15. Cook, W. R.: A Proposal for Making Eiffel Type Safe. *The Computer Journal* **32** (1989) 305-311.

16. Cook, W. R., Hill, W. L., Canning, P.S.: Inheritance is not Subtyping. Proceedings of the Conference on Principles of Programming Languages. ACM Press (1990) 125-135.

17. Futatsugi, K. Goguen, J., Jouannaud, J., Meseguer, J.: Principles of OBJ2. In: Reid, B.K. (ed): Proceedings of POPL '85. ACM Press (1985) 52-66.

18. Goguen, J., Burstall, R.: Institutions: Abstract Model Theory for Specification and Programming. *Journal of the ACM* **39** (1992) 92-146.

19. Goguen, J.: Types as Theories. In: Reed, G.M., Roscoe A.W., Wachter R.F. (eds.): *Topology and Category Theory in Computer Science*. Clarendon Press (1991) 357-390.

20. Goguen, J., Meseguer, J.: Order-Sorted Algebra I: Equational Deduction for Multiple Inheritance, Overloading, Exceptions and Partial Operations. *Theoretical Computer Science* **105** (1992) 217-273.

21. Goguen, J., Meseguer, J.: EQLOG: Equality, Types, and Generic Modules for Logic Programming. In: Degroot, D., Lindstrom, G. (eds.): *Logic Programming: Functions, Relations and Equations*. Prentice Hall (1986) 295-363.

22. Goguen J., Meseguer, J.: Unifying Functional, Object-Oriented and Relational Programming with Logical Semantics. In: Shriver, B., Wegner, P. (eds.): *Research Directions in Object-Oriented Programming*. MIT Press (1987) 417- 477.

23. Goguen J., Meseguer, J.: Models and Equality for Logical Programming. In: Ehrig, H., Levi, G., Kowalski, R., Montanari, U. (eds.): Proceedings of TAPSOFT '87. *Lecture Notes in Computer Science 250*. Springer (1987) 1-22.

24. Goguen, J., Burstall, R.: A Study in the Foundations of Programming Methodology: Specifications, Institutions, Charters and Parchments. In: Pitt, D., Abramsky, S., Poigne, A., Rydehard, D. (eds.): Proceedings of the Conference on Category Theory and Computer Programming. *Lecture Notes in Computer Science 240*. Springer (1986) 313-333.

25. Goguen, J., Burstall, R.: Introducing Institutions. In: Clarke E., Kozen, D. (eds.): Proceedings of the Logics of Programming Workshop. *Lecture Notes in Computer Science 164*. Springer (1984) 221-256.

26. Jacobs, B. van den Berg, L., Husiman, M., van Berkum, M.: Reasoning About Java Classes. Proceedings of OOPSLA '98. ACM (1998) 329-340.

27. Kifer, M., Lausen, G., Wu, J.: Logical Foundation of Object-Oriented and Frame-Based Languages. *Journal of the ACM*, **42** (1993) 741-843.

28. Lamport, L.: Specifying Concurrent Program Modules. *ACM Transactions on Programming Languages and Systems* **5** (1983) 190-222.

29. Leavens, G.T., Weihl, W.E.: Reasoning About Object-Oriented Programs that Use Subtypes. Proceedings of OOPSLA/ECOOP '90. ACM (1990) 212-223.

30. Leavens, G.T.: Modular Specification and Verification of Object-Oriented Programs. *IEE Software* July (1991) 72-80.

31. Liskov B., Wing, J.M.: A Behavioral Notion of Subtyping. *ACM Transactions on Programming Languages and Systems* **16** (1994) 1811-1841.

32. Mac Lane, S.: *Categories for a Working Mathematician*. Springer (1998).

33. Meyer, B.: *Eiffel: The Language*. Prentice Hall (1992).

34. Meyer, B.: *Object-Oriented Software Construction*. Prentice Hall (1997).

35. Meseguer, J.: Solving the Inheritance Anomaly in Concurrent Object-Oriented Programming. Proceedings of ECOOP '93. *Lecture Notes in Computer Science 707.* Springer (1993) 220-246.
36. Meseguer J., Qian, X.: A logical Semantics for Object-Oriented Databases. Proceedings of ACM SIGMOD Conference. ACM Press (1993) 89-98.
37. Poll, E.: A Coalgebraic Semantics of Subtyping. *Electronic Notes in Theoretical Computer Science* (2000).
38. Ruby, C., Leavens, G.: Creating Correct Subclasses Without Seeing Superclass Code. Proceedings of OOPSLA 2000. ACM (2000) pp. 208 - 228.
39. Stata, R., Guttag, J.V.: Modular Reasoning in the Presence of Subclassing. Proceedings of OOPSLA '95. ACM (1995) 200-214.
40. Spruit, P., Wieringa, R., Meyer, J-J.: Dynamic Database Logic: the First-Order Case. In: *Modeling Database Dynamics, Fourth Int. Workshop on Foundations of Models and Languages for Data and Objects.* Workshops in Computing. Springer (1993) 103-120.
41. Wieringa, R., de Jonge W., Spruit, P.: Roles and Dynamic Subclasses: A Modal Logic Approach. Proceedings of ECOOP '94. *Lecture Notes in Computer Science 821.* Springer (1994) 33-59.

A Formal Framework
for Java Separate Compilation

Davide Ancona, Giovanni Lagorio, and Elena Zucca*

DISI – Università di Genova
Via Dodecaneso, 35, 16146 Genova, Italy
{davide,lagorio,zucca}@disi.unige.it

Abstract. We define a formal notion, called *compilation schema*, suitable for specifying different possibilities for performing the overall process of Java compilation, which includes typechecking of source fragments with generation of corresponding binary code, typechecking of binary fragments, extraction of type information from fragments and definition of dependencies among them. We consider three compilation schemata of interest for Java, that is, *minimal, SDK* and *safe*, which correspond to a minimal set of checks, the checks performed by the SDK implementation, and all the checks needed to prevent run-time linkage errors, respectively. In order to demonstrate our approach, we define a kernel model for Java separate compilation and execution, consisting in a small Java subset, and a simple corresponding binary language for which we provide an operational semantics including run-time verification. We define a safe compilation schema for this language and formally prove type safety.

1 Introduction

In modern programming languages, the notion of "program" as a whole has become more and more obsolete. Now, the process of developing software typically consists in writing separate pieces of code, which we will call *fragments*, following [8], each one implementing some basic functionality and relying on other functionalities provided by other fragments. The language should provide facilities which allow the development of fragments to be as much modular as possible. In particular, a highly desirable property is *separate compilation*, which means, in its strongest formulation, that a single source fragment f can be typechecked in isolation, generating a corresponding binary fragment, in a context where only type information is available on the fragments it depends on, say $f_1, \ldots, f_n$, but no code. This phase is called *intra-checking* in [8]. Then, an executable application can be constructed linking together a collection of binary fragments s.t., for each fragment f, all the fragments $f_1, \ldots, f_n$ it depends on are available

---

* Partially supported by DART – Dynamic Assembly, Reconfiguration and Type-checking, Murst NAPOLI - Network Aware Programming: Oggetti, Linguaggi, Implementazioni, and APPlied SEMantics - Esprit Working Group 26142.

B. Magnusson (Ed.): ECOOP 2002, LNCS 2374, pp. 609–635, 2002.

and satisfy the required type assumptions. This phase is called *inter-checking* in [8]. Inter-checking should guarantee that the resulting application does not raise linkage errors (for instance, a fragment needed during execution either does not exist or does not provide some expected functionality).

Though Java is a widely known paradigmatic example of language supporting separate compilation, it does not match the above schema in many respects.

1. A fragment f which depends on $f_1, \ldots, f_n$ can be typechecked in absence of their sources, but at least the corresponding binaries must be available, since in Java class files play the dual roles of interfaces and object files.
2. If (some of) $f_1, \ldots, f_n$ are only available in source form, then Java compilers enforce their typechecking, hence generation of the corresponding code[1], too.
3. Linking is *dynamic*, in the sense that starting an application corresponds to running just one fragment f and then, during the execution, other needed fragments are loaded and linked on demand.

The fact (3) that linking is dynamic has a very strong impact on changing the schema we outlined above based on two distinct phases of intra-checking (separate compilation) and inter-checking (linking).

First of all, run-time inter-checks become necessary in order to guarantee that execution does not crash. For instance, the Java Virtual Machine (JVM from now on) has a bytecode verifier which finds linkage errors and throws corresponding exceptions.

On the other hand, since run-time checks are performed, inter-checks at compile-time are in a sense redundant, since in any case the fact that the execution does not crash is guaranteed by the bytecode verifier. Nevertheless, Java compilers try to anticipate at compile-time the detection of some linkage errors, performing *some* (but not all) inter-checks at compile-time. In other words, the overall compilation process is not solely specified by the typechecking rules for the source code, but some additional aspects must be modeled in order to fully capture the behavior of a compiler.

For instance, if the fragment f to be typechecked depends on a source fragment f', Java compilers act like a typical static linker, by enforcing the typechecking of f' too, in order to ensure that, if f' either is missing or does not satisfy the type requirements of f, then the error is detected before execution.

However, Java compilers take this approach only partially, and do not perform *all* the checks which would be actually possible (for instance, no checks are performed if f' is in binary form). As a consequence, as well-known to experienced Java programmers, standard Java compilers, as SDK and Jikes, are *not type safe* in the sense that they can generate binary fragments whose execution throws linkage errors. This seems in contradiction with the fact that type safety results have been proved for the Java language [19,10,18]; the explanation is that these formal type systems, and the related type safety results, are only related to

---

[1] In this paper, we will always use the terminology *typechecking* a fragment meaning the process that in the case of a source fragment also includes generation of binary code.

the special case when a closed set of source fragments is typechecked, while (1) and (2) are not taken into account (apart from [12], see Section 5). Even worse, there is *no* specification of separate compilation in [14], hence the outcome of compilations may strongly depend on the particular compiler implementation. Moreover, as will be shown in detail in the following, rules adopted by existing compilers are quite complex and cannot be easily explained informally.

For all these reasons, we believe necessary the definition of a formal framework for Java separate compilation, providing a rigorous basis for:

- defining and investigating different possibilities for the overall compilation process (for instance: a minimal set of checks, the checks performed by standard Java compilers, as many checks as possible)
- proving desirable properties, like type safety, for a compilation process.

This is what we achieve in this paper, by modeling the overall compilation process via the formal notion of *compilation schema*. A compilation schema defines two different judgments, a *source type judgment* $\Gamma \vdash S \leadsto B$ and a *binary type judgment* $\Gamma \vdash B \diamond$ modeling typechecking, in a given type environment Γ, of source code S and binary code B, respectively; in the former case the corresponding binary code B is also generated. These two components model the part of Java compilation which corresponds to truly separate compilation in the sense of [8]. The fact (2) that in Java typechecking of a fragment may enforce typechecking of other fragments is modeled by another component of a compilation schema, that is, a *dependency function*. Finally, the fact (1) that in Java type information for a fragment cannot be provided separately from code is modeled by a *type extraction function* which extracts from a compilation environment *ce* (collection of source and binary fragments) a type environment Γ providing the type information needed for typechecking fragments in *ce*.

We consider three different compilation schemata for Java. The first, which we call *minimal*, corresponds to true separate typechecking, in the sense that no other fragment is typechecked when compilation is invoked on a fragment f. In this case, all inter-checks are left to the run-time verifier. However, note that some of the fragments f depends on *must* be available, since some of the type information needed for typechecking f has to be extracted from them (see Section 5 for some more comments).

The second compilation schema is that used by standard Java compilers (at least for what we have been able to understand by experiments, since no specification is available). In this case only some inter-checks are performed: invoking compilation on f enforces typechecking of other fragments, but not of all those which could be possibly loaded at run-time; moreover no checks are performed on binary fragments, that is, the type judgment $\Gamma \vdash B \diamond$ is always trivially valid. As a consequence, binaries obtained as result of the compilation are not guaranteed to safely link at run-time, as we will show by the examples in Section 2. Finally, we propose a compilation schema which is type safe, that is, guarantees safe linking at run-time. For this last schema we provide a full definition of the four components for a small Java subset and we prove type safety.

The paper is organized as follows. In Section 2 we illustrate by means of some examples the three different schemata. In Section 3 we introduce our framework, formally defining the notion of compilation schema and the related type safety property. In Section 4 we define, for a small subset of Java, a type safe compilation schema. Note that this implies that we not only define the syntax for the source level, but also for the binary level, for which we also provide, in order to express and prove type safety, a simple execution model, partly inspired by those defined in [11,9], but much simpler, since our aim here is not to provide a realistic model of Java dynamic loading and linking, but to focus on type safety. Hence a contribution of the paper is also to define a kernel calculus for the Java Virtual Machine, in the spirit of other calculi that have been defined for modeling in isolation relevant aspects of the Java language [15,3]. In Section 5 we discuss related work. Finally, Section 6 summarizes the contribution of this paper and outlines further work.

2   Some Motivating Examples

In this section we illustrate, by means of some examples, three different Java compilation schemata, called *minimal*, *SDK* and *safe*, respectively.

As already explained, the minimal compilation schema requires the minimal amount of checks over fragments: typechecking is performed only for those source fragments on which the compiler has been explicitly invoked and no checks (except those strictly necessary for compiling the sources) are performed on binary fragments. This schema fits well in open environments where source fragments to be compiled are expected to be later dynamically linked with fragments that are not available at compile-time. For instance, assume that the class C1 we want to compile depends on a class C2. Even in the case the source of C2 is available, it could be sensible avoiding typechecking of C2 if there is a high probability that it does not correspond to the actual code that will be linked with C1 at runtime.

The SDK schema simply corresponds to the SDK implementation of Java[2]. As already said, this schema falls in between the minimal and the safe schemata: it enforces more checks than the former but less than the latter. For instance, the compilation of a class C requires that all source fragments[3] directly used by C must be typechecked, while for all binary fragments[4] directly used by C, only their existence and format is checked (but no real typecheck is performed).

Finally, the safe schema can be sensibly applied when we expect that the fragments that will be linked at run-time are those available after the compilation; under this assumption, it makes sense to typecheck all fragments (either source or binary) used (either directly or indirectly) by a class C, in order to ensure that no execution of C will throw a linkage error (like, for instance, NoClassDefFoundError or NoSuchMethodError). To this aim, the compilation

---

[2] The examples in this paper are based on version 1.4 beta 2 of SDK.
[3] Whose corresponding binary fragment is either unavailable or older.
[4] Which either are more recent than the corresponding source fragment or do not have a corresponding source fragment.

schema must include all those checks on binary fragments that a safe linker would perform if Java classes were statically linked[5].

While all these three schemata share the same source type judgment and type extraction function (corresponding to the Java type system defined in [14] and formalized in, e.g., [10]), they remarkably differ in the other two components (that is, dependency function and binary type judgment) as described in the following examples.

Consider the following class declarations, that we assume each one contained in a single .java file:

```
class Main {
  static void main(String[] args){new Used().m();}
  void g (UsedAsType x) {}
}
class Used extends UsedParent {
  int m(){return new TransUsed().m();}
}
class UsedParent{
  int m(){return 1;}
}
class TransUsed {
  int m(){return 1;}
}
class UsedAsType { ... }
```

As already stated, the same type extraction function is shared by the three schemata. The definition is straightforward: the type environment is a mapping associating to each available class C the type information which can be extracted from its code, that is, a pair consisting of the direct superclass of C and the list of method signatures[6] directly declared in C, which we will call the *direct type* of C.

Assume now that we want to compile Main. In the minimal schema, our aim is just to perform the separate typechecking (intra-checking), hence we only need the type information necessary to typecheck the source code of Main. In particular, for each class used in Main, there are two possible situations: either the class is used only as a type, like in the method g, and in this case we only need the existence of the class in the type environment, or it is used as the receiver's type in a method call, like in new Used().m(). In this case we need to know which are *all* the method signatures of the class (either directly declared or inherited). This information, which we will call the *full type* of a class, can be safely constructed having all the direct types of the classes in its ancestor

---

[5] Of course, such checks are usually performed at run-time by the JVM.

[6] In these examples we will consider for simplicity only instance method declarations, as in the Java subset defined in Section 4; in full Java the direct type of a class would also include other declared members. We assume that the method main is just used for starting execution.

hierarchy and provided that this hierarchy is acyclic[7] (this will be formalized in Figure 5 later on). In summary, Main.java can be successfully typechecked, producing a corresponding Main.class, in the type environment Γ defined by

$\{$Main $\mapsto \langle$Object, void g(UsedAsType)$\rangle$, Used $\mapsto \langle$UsedParent, int m()$\rangle$,
UsedParent $\mapsto \langle$Object, int m()$\rangle$, UsedAsType $\mapsto \ldots\}$,

which can be extracted from a compilation environment ce_1 where only the source files Main.java, Used.java, UsedParent.java and UsedAsType.java are available. This is formalized by the validity of the judgment $\Gamma \vdash S \rightsquigarrow B$ that will be defined in Figure 3. Note that, since, as already said, in Java type information on fragments cannot be provided separately from their code, either the .java or .class files for Used, UsedParent and UsedAsType must be available, even though no typechecking is performed on their code (for UsedAsType not even the type information is used). In the minimal schema, indeed, the set of dependencies of Main.java is $\{$Main$\}$, reflecting the fact that we are only interested in typechecking Main.java.

In both the SDK and safe schema, the set of dependencies of Main in ce_1 includes also Used, UsedParent, UsedAsType and TransUsed. As a consequence, compilation of Main.java in ce_1 fails for both the SDK and safe schema.

Let us consider now two compilation environments able to discriminate between the SDK and the safe schemata. First consider ce_2 which contains the source files Main.java, Used.class, UsedParent.class, UsedAsType.class[8], and a changed version of TransUsed.java which does not satisfy intra-checks (for instance, the body of method m returns a boolean). The type environment extracted from ce_2 is still Γ. However, the set of dependencies of Main in ce_2 is $\{$Main, Used, UsedParent, UsedAsType, TransUsed$\}$ in the safe schema, while it is $\{$Main, Used, UsedParent, UsedAsType$\}$ in the SDK schema.

Hence, in SDK the source of class TransUsed is not typechecked; then, a new binary fragment Main.class is produced. However, in the new environment obtained by enriching ce_2 with the fragment Main.class, the execution of class Main throws the error NoClassDefFoundError (note that this error is raised instead of a type error since the class has not been compiled, hence there is no corresponding binary), whereas this error is detected at compile-time by the safe schema which performs the typechecking of the source code of TransUsed.

In this case the difference between the Java and the safe schema is given by the dependency function. However, even in the case dependencies are the same, the two schemata can still behave differently due to the fact that the safe schema also performs a significant binary typechecking (formalized by the validity of the judgment $\Gamma \vdash B \diamond$ that will be defined in Figure 6). For instance, invoking the compilation of both Main and TransUsed in the compilation environment ce_3 which contains Main.java, Used.class, UsedParent.class, UsedAsType.class and a changed version of TransUsed.java which does not satisfy type requirements in Used (for instance, declaring boolean m() {return

---

[7] However, in SDK 1.4 beta 2 the compiler loops if a used binary class has a cyclic inheritance hierarchy!

[8] Obtained, e.g., by compiling the whole program in the example.

`true;}`), in SDK no checks are performed on the the binary code of `Used`. Hence, again, in the binary environment obtained after the compilation, the execution of class `Main` throws the exception `NoSuchMethodError`, whereas this error is detected at compile-time by the safe schema.

3 Framework

We now formally define our framework for modeling the Java overall compilation process. Consistently with this aim, we will everywhere use a Java-related terminology. However, most of the notions presented here could be generalized to model the compilation process of other languages, as we will briefly discuss in Section 5.

Let us denote by $\mathbb{C}$ the set of fragment names, that is, in Java, class/interface names[9], ranged over by C, and by $\mathbb{S}$ and $\mathbb{B}$ the set of source and binary fragments, respectively. We assume that source fragments are `.java` files containing (for simplicity) exactly one class/interface declaration, and binary fragments are `.class` files.

A *compilation environment* ce is a pair[10]

$$\langle ce_b, ce_s \rangle \in CE = [\mathbb{C} \to_{fin} \mathbb{B}] \times [\mathbb{C} \to_{fin} \mathbb{S}]$$

s.t. $Def(ce_b) \cap Def(ce_s) = \emptyset$. We will call ce_b and ce_s a *binary* and a *source environment*, respectively. Note that the assumption $Def(ce_b) \cap Def(ce_s) = \emptyset$ means that, even in the case a class has both a binary and a source definition, the compiler considers only one of them, according to some rule.

The results of (successful) compilations are binary environments. Hence, we can model the compilation process by a (partial) function, called *compilation function*:

$$\mathcal{C} : CE \times \wp(\mathbb{C}) \to [\mathbb{C} \to_{fin} \mathbb{B}]$$

where $\mathcal{C}(\langle ce_b, ce_s \rangle, \mathtt{CS}) = ce'_b$ intuitively means that the compilation, invoked on fragments with names in $\mathtt{CS}$, in the compilation environment consisting of binary fragments ce_b and source fragments ce_s, generates binary fragments ce'_b.

We introduce now the formal notion of *compilation schema*, meant to express different Java compilation processes.

A compilation schema consists of the following four components.

- A *dependency function* $\mathcal{D}$ which gives, for any compilation environment ce and set of fragment names $\mathtt{CS}$, the set $\mathtt{CS}'$ of all the fragment names on which typechecking is enforced when the compilation is invoked on $\mathtt{CS}$.
- A *type extraction function* $\mathcal{T}$ which extracts from a compilation environment ce a *type environment* Γ providing the type information necessary to typecheck fragments in ce.

---

[9] We will consider only classes in the Java subset in Section 4.

[10] We denote by $[A \to_{fin} B]$ the set of *finite partial functions* from A into B, that is, functions f from A into B which are defined on a finite subset of A, denoted $Def(f)$.

616   Davide Ancona, Giovanni Lagorio, and Elena Zucca

- A *source type judgment* $\Gamma \vdash S \rightsquigarrow B$ expressing that in the type environment Γ the source fragment S is successfully typechecked generating the binary fragment B.
- A *binary type judgment* $\Gamma \vdash B \diamond$ expressing that in the type environment Γ the binary fragment B is successfully typechecked.

To compile a set of fragments CS in a compilation environment ce, first the needed type environment Γ is extracted applying $\mathcal{T}$ to ce. Then, all the fragments in the set CS_d computed from CS using $\mathcal{D}$ are typechecked generating corresponding binaries for those which were in source form. This can be formalized by the inference rule in Figure 1 which defines a compilation function $\mathcal{C}$ in terms of the four components of a compilation schema. The second side condition, $CS \subseteq Def(ce_s)$, states that a compilation can be only invoked on a set of existing sources.

$$\frac{\forall C \in CS_b\ \Gamma \vdash ce_b(C) \diamond \quad \forall C \in CS_s\ \Gamma \vdash ce_s(C) \rightsquigarrow B_C}{\mathcal{C}(\langle ce_b, ce_s \rangle, CS) = \{C \mapsto B_C \mid C \in CS_s\}}$$

$$\Gamma = \mathcal{T}(\langle ce_b, ce_s \rangle)$$
$$CS \subseteq Def(ce_s)$$
$$CS_d = \mathcal{D}(\langle ce_b, ce_s \rangle, CS)$$
$$CS_b = CS_d \cap Def(ce_b)$$
$$CS_s = CS_d \cap Def(ce_s)$$

Fig. 1. Definition of compilation function

Let us now apply the above definitions for specifying the three different compilation schemata informally introduced in Section 2.

The type extraction function is the same for the three schemata: the type environment extracted from a compilation environment $ce = \langle ce_b, ce_s \rangle$ is a finite partial function which associates to each $C \in Def(ce_b) \cup Def(ce_s)$ its *direct type*, that is, a pair consisting of the superclass of C and the list of the method signatures declared in C (see the formal definition in Figure 15 in the Appendix).

Again, the source type judgment is the same for the three schemata, and corresponds to the Java type system defined in [14] and formalized, e.g., in [10]. The formalization for the small Java subset for which we define a type safe compilation schema is given in Figure 3 in the Appendix.

On the contrary, the three schemata remarkably differ in the other two components.

For what concerns the dependency function, $\mathcal{D}(ce, \{C\})$ contains only C in the minimal schema; in the safe schema $\mathcal{D}(ce, \{C\})$ contains C and all the classes transitively used by C, regardless that C is in source or binary form (see the formal definition in Figure 14 later on). In the SDK schema the definition is much more involved. First of all, $\mathcal{D}(ce, \{C\})$ contains C and all the classes directly used by C. For each of these classes, say C', $\mathcal{D}(ce, \{C\})$ also (recursively) contains $\mathcal{D}(ce, \{C'\})$ if C' is in source form. If C' is in binary form, then the behavior is different depending whether C' is only used in C as "abstract" type (for instance, field type, parameter type, method return type) or information on the components provided by C is also needed (for instance, there is a method call with receiver's type C). In the former case $\mathcal{D}(ce, \{C\})$ contains only C', in the latter it contains C', all the ancestor classes of C' and (recursively) $\mathcal{D}(ce, \{C''\})$ for each ancestor C'' which is in source form.

This rule is quite complex, and has been extrapolated only by performing a number of compilation tests, since it is hard to deduce it from the compiler source and no other form of documentation seems to be available.

The binary type judgment also differs from schema to schema. In the minimal schema no typechecks are performed (that is, the judgment $\Gamma \vdash B \diamond$ trivially holds). In the safe schema the checks performed on a binary fragment are similar to those performed on a source fragment. A difference is, for instance, the way a method invocation is checked. In the source case the method must be found searching in all the ancestor classes, and overloading must be resolved, while in the binary case a method call is already annotated with the class where the method should be found together with its signature. The formalization for the small Java subset for which we define a type safe compilation schema is given in Figure 3 (last rule) and Figure 4 for the source case and in Figure 6 (last rule) for the binary case.

In the SDK schema no typechecks are performed on binary code. The only checks which are performed, together with the existence check on C', when type-checking a class C which uses C', are on the format of the binary (analogous to the fact that Java grammar is respected in the source case) and on the correspondence between the fragment name and the name of the class defined inside. In the formal model in Section 4 we assume for simplicity that fragments are well-formed in this sense.

We introduce now the formal property of type safety for separate compilation. We assume a judgment of the form $C \leadsto_{ce_b} V$ which is valid if and only if execution of class C in the binary environment ce_b terminates producing a value V which can be either a normal value or a linkage exception. Intuitively, this judgment corresponds to start the execution from class C in an environment ce_b corresponding to the set of all available binaries that can be dynamically linked during the execution.

The formal definition of this judgment for the small Java subset for which we define a type safe compilation schema is given in Figure 13. Let us denote with $ce_b[ce_b']$ the partial function f s.t. $Def(f) = Def(ce_b) \cup Def(ce_b')$ and for any $C \in Def(f)$ $f(C) = ce_b'(C)$ if $C \in Def(ce_b')$ and $f(C) = ce_b(C)$ otherwise.

Definition 1. *A compilation function $\mathcal{C}$ is type safe iff for any compilation environment $\langle ce_b, ce_s \rangle$ and set of class names CS, if $\mathcal{C}(CS, \langle ce_b, ce_s \rangle) = ce_b'$, then, for all class names $C \in Def(ce_b')$ and values V, if $C \leadsto_{ce_b[ce_b']} V$, then V is not a (linkage) exception.*

Note that type safety requires that execution does not throw linkage errors only when started from classes that are the product of the compilation. Indeed, an error raised by an execution started from a class C present in the original binary environment ce_b can be either an error which was already present, hence not due to the compilation, or an error due to the fact that some binary used by C has

$$
\begin{aligned}
\text{S} &::= \texttt{class C extends C}'\ \{\ \text{MDS}^s\ \}\ \texttt{main E}^s\\
\text{MDS}^s &::= \text{MD}_1^s \dots \text{MD}_n^s\\
\text{MD}^s &::= \text{MH}\ \{\ \texttt{return E}^s;\ \}\\
\text{MH} &::= \text{T}_0\ \texttt{m}(\text{T}_1\ \texttt{x}_1, \dots, \text{T}_n\ \texttt{x}_n)\\
\text{E}^s &::= \texttt{new C}\ |\ \texttt{x}\ |\ \texttt{N}\ |\\
&\qquad \text{E}_0^s.\texttt{m}(\text{E}_1^s, \dots, \text{E}_n^s)\\[4pt]
\text{T} &::= \texttt{C}\ |\ \texttt{int}\\[6pt]
\text{B} &::= \langle \texttt{C}, \texttt{C}', \text{MDS}^b, \text{E}^b \rangle\\
\text{MDS}^b &::= \text{MD}_1^b \dots \text{MD}_n^b\\
\text{MD}^b &::= \text{MH}\ \{\ \texttt{return E}^b;\ \}\\
V &::= \texttt{new C}\ |\ \texttt{N}\ |\ \varepsilon\\
\text{E}^b &::= V\ |\ \texttt{x}\ |\ \text{E}_0^b.\texttt{m} \prec \boxed{\texttt{C}}, \text{T}_1 \dots \text{T}_n, \text{T} \succ (\text{E}_1^b, \dots, \text{E}_n^b)\\
&\qquad \text{E}_0^b.\texttt{m} \prec \texttt{C}, \text{T}_1 \dots \text{T}_n, \text{T} \succ (\text{E}_1^b, \dots, \text{E}_n^b)\ |\ \texttt{new}\ \boxed{\texttt{C}}\\
\varepsilon &::= \textit{ClassNotFound}\ |\ \textit{ClassCircularityError}\ |\ \textit{VerifyError}\ |\ \textit{NoSuchMethod}\\[6pt]
\text{MS} &::= \text{T}\ \texttt{m}(\text{T}_1 \dots \text{T}_n)\\
\text{AMS} &::= \texttt{C}\ \text{MS}\\
\text{AMSS} &::= \text{AMS}_1 \dots \text{AMS}_n
\end{aligned}
$$

Fig. 2. Syntax and types

been modified. In this case we will say that the compilation function does not satisfy a different property, which we call *contextual binary compatibility* (see the Conclusion).

4   A Safe Compilation Schema for Java

The language we consider is reminiscent of Featherweight Java [15], in the sense that is a small functional subset of Java (see Figure 2); however, since here we are mainly interested in code generation and bytecode execution, we present a simple binary language as well, together with its reduction semantics. The dynamic semantics of our Java subset is indirectly defined by a compilation function mapping well-typed source fragments into well-typed binary fragments.

Metavariables $\texttt{C}$, $\texttt{m}$, $\texttt{x}$ and $\texttt{N}$ range over sets of class, method and parameter names, and integer literals, respectively.

A source fragment S is a class declaration consisting of the class name, the name of the superclass, a sequence of method declarations MDS^s, and an expression E^s playing the role of the (static) $\texttt{main}$ method, that for simplicity we assume present in all classes. A method declaration MD^s consists of a method header and a method body (an expression). A method header MH consists of a (return) type, a method name and a sequence of parameter types and names. There are four kinds of expression: instance creation, parameter name, integer literal and method invocation. A type is either a class name or $\texttt{int}$. We will use the abbreviation $\bar{\text{T}}$ for $\text{T}_1 \dots \text{T}_n$ in the following.

Our description of bytecode is rather abstract: we basically enrich the source language with two kinds of annotation. Each method invocation is annotated with a method descriptor, which is a triple describing the method which has been statically selected for the call: the first component corresponds to the static type of the receiver[11], the second to the type of the parameters and the third to the return type. Moreover, each class name mentioned either in class creation or as the first component of method descriptors in method call is (initially) boxed. The idea is that a reference to a class is "sealed" in a box until it has been verified (at runtime). Such a reference cannot be used until it has been unboxed.

A binary fragment B consists of the name of the class, the name of the superclass, a set of binary method declarations MDS^b and the binary expression corresponding to the method **main**. This expression is used as the starting point of the execution when the class is run. A binary method declaration MD^b is structurally equivalent to a source method declaration except that the body is a binary expression.

Binary expressions can be either *values*, or parameters, or (either boxed or unboxed) method calls, or a boxed creation expression. Values correspond to the normal forms of the reduction semantics of binary fragments (defined in Figure 13), and can be either unboxed creation expressions, or integer literals, or exceptions (in case of abnormal termination).

Note that exceptions and unboxed method invocation and creation are only needed for defining the rewriting rules for bytecode execution (see Figure 13), but they are not considered valid binary formats, even though for sake of simplicity we do not have introduced two separate syntactic categories corresponding to valid binary format and valid run-time expressions, respectively.

In the last part of Figure 2 we define *method signatures* and *annotated method signatures*, which are not part of the syntax but will be used in the type judgments. A method signature MS is a method header without the argument names; an annotated method signature AMS is a method signature prefixed by an annotation indicating the class which contains the method declaration.

We start now the formal definition of the four components of our safe compilation schema, which will be used (as shown in Figure 1 in Section 3 to define the corresponding compilation function.

The dependency function $\mathcal{D}$ is defined as follows:

$$\mathcal{D}(ce, \text{CS}) = \{\text{C}' \mid \exists \text{C} \in \text{CS} \ s.t. \ \text{C} \xrightarrow{*}_{ce} \text{C}'\}$$

where $\xrightarrow{*}_{ce}$ is the reflexive and transitive closure of the relation $\rightarrow_{ce}$ defined by $\text{C} \rightarrow_{ce} \text{C}'$ iff $\text{C}' \in \text{refClasses}(\text{C}, ce)$. This latter function, defined in Figure 14 in the Appendix, gives the set of all classes explicitly mentioned in the code of C.

A type environment Γ is a finite (partial) function from class names into *direct types* of classes, that is, pairs $\langle \text{C}', \text{MS}_1 \dots \text{MS}_n \rangle$ where C' is the (direct)

---

[11] This is a change introduced in SDK 1.4, since in the previous versions the first component of method descriptors corresponded to the class where the method was statically found.

$$\frac{\Gamma \vdash \mathtt{C} ::_\diamond \_ \quad \Gamma \vdash \mathtt{MDS}^s \rightsquigarrow \mathtt{MDS}^b \quad \Gamma; \emptyset \vdash \mathtt{E}^s : \_ \rightsquigarrow \mathtt{E}^b}{\Gamma \vdash \mathtt{class\ C\ extends\ C'\ \{\ MDS}^s\ \}\ \mathtt{main\ E}^s \rightsquigarrow \langle \mathtt{C}, \mathtt{C}', \mathtt{MDS}^b, \mathtt{E}^b \rangle}$$

$$\frac{\forall i \in 1..n \quad \Gamma \vdash \mathtt{MD}_i^s \rightsquigarrow \mathtt{MD}_i^b}{\Gamma \vdash \mathtt{MD}_1^s \ \ldots \ \mathtt{MD}_n^s \rightsquigarrow \mathtt{MD}_1^b \ldots \mathtt{MD}_n^b}$$

$$\frac{\begin{array}{c} \Gamma; \{\mathtt{x}_1 \mapsto \mathtt{T}_1, \ldots, \mathtt{x}_n \mapsto \mathtt{T}_n\} \vdash \mathtt{E}^s : \mathtt{T} \rightsquigarrow \mathtt{E}^b \\ \Gamma \vdash \mathtt{T} \leq \mathtt{T}_0 \end{array}}{\begin{array}{c} \Gamma \vdash \mathtt{T}_0\ \mathtt{m}(\mathtt{T}_1\ \mathtt{x}_1, \ldots, \mathtt{T}_n\ \mathtt{x}_n)\ \{\ \mathtt{return\ E}^s;\ \} \rightsquigarrow \\ \mathtt{T}_0\ \mathtt{m}(\mathtt{T}_1\ \mathtt{x}_1, \ldots, \mathtt{T}_n\ \mathtt{x}_n)\ \{\ \mathtt{return\ E}^b;\ \} \end{array}} \quad \forall i \in 1..n\ \mathtt{T}_i \in Def(\Gamma) \cup \{\mathtt{int}\}$$

$$\frac{}{\Gamma; \Pi \vdash \mathtt{new\ C} : \mathtt{C} \rightsquigarrow \mathtt{new}\ \boxed{\mathtt{C}}} \quad \mathtt{C} \in Def(\Gamma)$$

$$\frac{}{\Gamma; \Pi \vdash \mathtt{N} : \mathtt{int} \rightsquigarrow \mathtt{N}}$$

$$\frac{}{\Gamma; \Pi \vdash \mathtt{x} : \mathtt{T} \rightsquigarrow \mathtt{x}} \quad \Pi(\mathtt{x}) = \mathtt{T}$$

$$\frac{\begin{array}{c} \Gamma; \Pi \vdash \mathtt{E}_0^s : \mathtt{C} \rightsquigarrow \mathtt{E}_0^b \\ \forall i \in 1..n\ \Gamma; \Pi \vdash \mathtt{E}_i^s : \mathtt{T}_i \rightsquigarrow \mathtt{E}_i^b \end{array}}{\begin{array}{c} \Gamma; \Pi \vdash \mathtt{E}_0^s.m(\mathtt{E}_1^s, \ldots, \mathtt{E}_n^s) : \mathtt{T}' \rightsquigarrow \\ \mathtt{E}_0^b.m \prec \boxed{\mathtt{C}}, \bar{\mathtt{T}}', \mathtt{T}' \succ (\mathtt{E}_1^b, \ldots, \mathtt{E}_n^b) \end{array}} \quad \langle \bar{\mathtt{T}}', \mathtt{T}' \rangle = methRes(\Gamma, \mathtt{C}, m, \mathtt{T}_1 \ldots \mathtt{T}_n)$$

Fig. 3. Source type-judgment

superclass of C and $\mathtt{MS}_1 \ldots \mathtt{MS}_n$ is the list of the signatures of methods declared in C.

The type extraction function $\mathcal{T}$, defined in Figure 15 in the Appendix, simply throws away method bodies and parameter names, retaining type information from all classes in the compilation environment.

In Figure 3 are defined the rules for typechecking, in a given type environment, source fragments (with generation of the corresponding binary code).

The first rule defines the typechecking of a class declaration.

First, it is checked that C has a well-formed *full type* in Γ. The full type of a class is the list of all the annotated method signatures of the class, either directly declared or inherited, and it can be safely constructed if there are no cycles in the inheritance hierarchy of C and the Java rules on method overriding are respected. This is formalized by the judgment $\Gamma \vdash \mathtt{C} ::_\diamond \_$ defined in Figure 5.

Then, the method bodies and the main expression are checked and compiled.

The second rule defines the typechecking of a sequence of method declarations. Each method declaration is correct (third rule) if the type of the expression body is a subtype of the declared return type (premises) and all argument types exist in Γ (note that *no* check is performed on the fact that they have well-formed full types). The judgment $\Gamma \vdash \mathtt{T} \leq \mathtt{T}'$ is valid whenever T is a subtype of $\mathtt{T}'$ in the type environment Γ, and is defined in Figure 7.

$$methRes(\Gamma, \mathtt{C}, \mathtt{m}, \bar{\mathtt{T}}) = \begin{cases} <\bar{\mathtt{T}}', \mathtt{T}'> \text{ if } \Gamma \vdash \mathtt{C} :: \mathtt{AMSS} \land \\ \qquad mostSpec(\Gamma, appMeth(\Gamma, \mathtt{AMSS}, \mathtt{m}, \bar{\mathtt{T}})) = \mathtt{C}' \; \mathtt{T}' \; \mathtt{m}(\bar{\mathtt{T}}') \\ \bot \qquad \text{ otherwise} \end{cases}$$

$$appMeth(\Gamma, \Lambda, \mathtt{m}, \bar{\mathtt{T}}) = \Lambda$$
$$appMeth(\Gamma, \mathtt{C} \; \mathtt{T} \; \mathtt{m}'(\bar{\mathtt{T}}') \; \mathtt{AMSS}, \mathtt{m}, \bar{\mathtt{T}}) =$$
$$\begin{cases} \mathtt{C} \; \mathtt{T} \; \mathtt{m}'(\bar{\mathtt{T}}') \; appMeth(\Gamma, \mathtt{AMSS}, \mathtt{m}, \bar{\mathtt{T}}) \text{ if } \mathtt{m} = \mathtt{m}' \land \Gamma \vdash \bar{\mathtt{T}} \le \bar{\mathtt{T}}' \\ appMeth(\Gamma, \mathtt{AMSS}, \mathtt{m}, \bar{\mathtt{T}}) \qquad \text{ otherwise} \end{cases}$$

$$mostSpec(\Gamma, \Lambda) = \bot$$
$$mostSpec(\Gamma, \mathtt{C} \; \mathtt{T} \; \mathtt{m}(\bar{\mathtt{T}})) = \mathtt{C} \; \mathtt{T} \; \mathtt{m}(\bar{\mathtt{T}})$$
$$mostSpec(\Gamma, \mathtt{C} \; \mathtt{T} \; \mathtt{m}(\bar{\mathtt{T}}) \; \mathtt{AMSS}) = min(\Gamma, \mathtt{C} \; \mathtt{T} \; \mathtt{m}(\bar{\mathtt{T}}), mostSpec(\Gamma, \mathtt{AMSS})) \text{ with } \mathtt{AMSS} \ne \Lambda$$

$$min(\Gamma, \mathtt{C} \; \mathtt{T} \; \mathtt{m}(\bar{\mathtt{T}}), \mathtt{C}' \; \mathtt{T}' \; \mathtt{m}(\bar{\mathtt{T}}')) = \begin{cases} \mathtt{C} \; \mathtt{T} \; \mathtt{m}(\bar{\mathtt{T}}) \quad \text{ if } \Gamma \vdash \mathtt{C} \; \bar{\mathtt{T}} \le \mathtt{C}' \; \bar{\mathtt{T}}' \\ \mathtt{C}' \; \mathtt{T}' \; \mathtt{m}(\bar{\mathtt{T}}') \text{ if } \Gamma \vdash \mathtt{C}' \; \bar{\mathtt{T}}' \le \mathtt{C} \; \bar{\mathtt{T}} \\ \bot \qquad \qquad \text{ otherwise} \end{cases}$$

Fig. 4. Definition of *methRes*

Other rules define the typechecking of expressions, which also needs a local type environment Π which is a (partial) function from parameters into types.

An instance creation expression, new C, is well-typed, and has type C, in Γ and Π if C exists in Γ. An integer literal is trivially well-typed, and has type int, in every Γ and Π.

A parameter is well-typed in Γ and Π if it belongs to the domain of the local type environment, and it has the corresponding type.

A method call expression is typechecked in two steps: first, the receiver expression and all the argument expressions are typechecked finding their types $\mathtt{T}_i$ (and generating the corresponding binary expressions $\mathtt{E}_i^b$). Then, using this information, the most specific among the applicable methods is selected, as formally defined by the function *methRes*, defined in Figure 4, which returns a pair consisting of the type of parameters and returned value used to annotate the binary method call produced as the result of the compilation; the annotation is used at runtime by the JVM (see Figure 13). Recall that in SDK 1.4 the first component of the descriptor which annotates the method call is the static type of the receiver (C in the rule).

In Figure 5 we define the judgment $\Gamma \vdash \mathtt{C} :: \mathtt{AMSS}$, associating to a class its full type AMSS, and the judgment $\Gamma \vdash \mathtt{C} ::_\diamond \mathtt{AMSS}$, which is valid only if AMSS is well-formed.

As already said, the full type of a class consists of the sequence of the annotated signatures of the methods either directly declared in C or inherited.

A full class type AMSS is well-formed if it does not contain duplicate method signatures (predicate *noRep*) and if the Java rules on overriding are satisfied (predicate *okOverride*).

$$\Gamma \vdash \texttt{Object} :: \Lambda$$

$$\frac{\Gamma \vdash \texttt{C}' :: \text{AMSS}'}{\Gamma \vdash \texttt{C} :: \text{AMSS}' \ \texttt{C} \ \text{MS}_1 \ \dots \ \texttt{C} \ \text{MS}_n} \qquad \Gamma(\texttt{C}) = \langle \texttt{C}', \text{MS}_1 \dots \text{MS}_n \rangle$$

$$\frac{\Gamma \vdash \texttt{C} :: \text{AMSS}}{\Gamma \vdash \texttt{C} ::_\diamond \text{AMSS}} \qquad noRep(\text{AMSS}) \land okOverride(\text{AMSS})$$

$$noRep(\text{AMS}_1 \dots \text{AMS}_n) \iff \forall i, j \in 1..n \ \text{AMS}_i = \text{AMS}_j \implies i = j$$

$$okOverride(\text{AMSS}) \iff$$
$$\forall \text{AMS}, \text{AMS}' \in \text{AMSS} \ \text{AMS} = \texttt{C} \ \texttt{T} \ \texttt{m}(\bar{\texttt{T}}) \land \text{AMS}' = \texttt{C}' \ \texttt{T}' \ \texttt{m}(\bar{\texttt{T}}) \implies \texttt{T} = \texttt{T}'$$

Fig. 5. Full type of a class

$$\frac{\Gamma \vdash \texttt{C} ::_\diamond \_ \quad \Gamma \vdash \text{MDS}^b \diamond \quad \Gamma; \emptyset \vdash \texttt{E}^b : \_\diamond}{\Gamma \vdash \langle \texttt{C}, \texttt{C}', \text{MDS}^b, \texttt{E}^b \rangle \diamond}$$

$$\frac{\forall i \in 1..n \ \Gamma \vdash \text{MD}_i^b \diamond}{\Gamma \vdash \text{MD}_1^b \ \dots \ \text{MD}_n^b \diamond}$$

$$\frac{\Gamma; \{\texttt{x}_1 \mapsto \texttt{T}_1, \dots, \texttt{x}_n \mapsto \texttt{T}_n\} \vdash \texttt{E}^b : \texttt{T} \diamond \quad \Gamma \vdash \texttt{T} \leq \texttt{T}_0}{\Gamma \vdash \texttt{T}_0 \ \texttt{m}(\texttt{T}_1 \ \texttt{x}_1, \dots, \texttt{T}_n \ \texttt{x}_n) \ \{ \ \textbf{return} \ \texttt{E}^b; \ \} \diamond} \qquad \forall i \in 1..n \ \texttt{T}_i \in Def(\Gamma) \cup \{\textbf{int}\}$$

$$\frac{}{\Gamma; \Pi \vdash \textbf{new} \ \boxed{\texttt{C}} : \texttt{C} \diamond} \qquad \texttt{C} \in Def(\Gamma)$$

$$\frac{}{\Gamma; \Pi \vdash \texttt{N} : \textbf{int} \diamond}$$

$$\frac{}{\Gamma; \Pi \vdash \texttt{x} : \texttt{T} \diamond} \qquad \Pi(\texttt{x}) = \texttt{T}$$

$$\frac{\begin{array}{c} \Gamma; \Pi \vdash \texttt{E}_0^b : \texttt{C} \diamond \\ \forall i \in 1..n \ \Gamma; \Pi \vdash \texttt{E}_i^b : \texttt{T}_i \diamond \\ \forall i \in 1..n \ \Gamma \vdash \texttt{T}_i \leq \texttt{T}_i' \\ \Gamma \vdash \texttt{C} \triangleleft \texttt{C}' \ \texttt{T}' \ \texttt{m}(\texttt{T}_1' \dots \texttt{T}_n') \end{array}}{\Gamma; \Pi \vdash \texttt{E}_0^b.\texttt{m} \prec \boxed{\texttt{C}'}, \texttt{T}_1' \dots \texttt{T}_n', \texttt{T}' \succ (\texttt{E}_1^b, \dots, \texttt{E}_n^b) : \texttt{T}' \diamond}$$

Fig. 6. Binary type-judgment

In Figure 5 the notation AMS $\in$ AMSS is a shortcut for $\exists \text{AMSS}_0, \text{AMSS}_1 : \text{AMSS} = \text{AMSS}_0 \ \text{AMS} \ \text{AMSS}_1$.

Note that neither $\Gamma \vdash \texttt{C} :: \text{AMSS}$ nor $\Gamma \vdash \texttt{C} ::_\diamond \text{AMSS}$ can be deduced for C if it has a cyclic inheritance hierarchy in Γ.

Figure 6 shows the rules for typechecking binary fragments, which are analogous to those for source fragments shown in Figure 3, except for the last rule, concerning method calls.

$$\frac{}{\Gamma \vdash \texttt{int} \leq \texttt{int}}$$

$$\frac{}{\Gamma \vdash \texttt{C} \leq \texttt{C}} \quad \texttt{C} \in \mathit{Def}(\Gamma)$$

$$\frac{\Gamma \vdash \texttt{C}' :: \_}{\Gamma \vdash \texttt{C} \leq \texttt{C}'} \quad \Gamma(\texttt{C}) = \langle \texttt{C}', \_ \rangle$$

$$\frac{\Gamma \vdash \texttt{C} \leq \texttt{C}' \quad \Gamma \vdash \texttt{C}' \leq \texttt{C}''}{\Gamma \vdash \texttt{C} \leq \texttt{C}'}$$

$$\frac{\forall i \in 1..n \;\; \Gamma \vdash \texttt{T}_i \leq \texttt{T}'_i}{\Gamma \vdash \texttt{T}_1 \ldots \texttt{T}_n \leq \texttt{T}'_1 \ldots \texttt{T}'_n}$$

$$\frac{\Gamma \vdash \texttt{C} \leq \texttt{C}_k}{\Gamma \vdash \{\texttt{C}_1 \; \texttt{MS}_1, \ldots, \texttt{C}_n \; \texttt{MS}_n\} \lhd \texttt{C} \; \texttt{MS}} \quad k \in 1..n \wedge \texttt{MS} = \texttt{MS}_k$$

$$\frac{\Gamma \vdash \texttt{C} :: \texttt{AMSS} \quad \Gamma \vdash \texttt{AMSS} \lhd \texttt{AMS}}{\Gamma \vdash \texttt{C} \lhd \texttt{AMS}}$$

Fig. 7. Implementation and widening

Indeed, as already mentioned, in a binary method call the descriptor annotation indicates exactly which method to look for, and we only have to check that the types of the receiver expression and of the parameters are subtypes of those specified in the descriptor, and the class of the actual receiver C still implements such a method (premise $\Gamma \vdash \texttt{C} \lhd \texttt{C}' \; \texttt{T}' \; m(\texttt{T}'_1 \ldots \texttt{T}'_n)$, see Figure 7 above for the definition of this judgment); this informally means that class C must inherit method $\texttt{T}' \; m(\texttt{T}'_1 \ldots \texttt{T}'_n)$ from C' or any of C' superclasses (of course, if C' = C, then the method can also be defined in C itself). Note that this corresponds to the run-time check performed by the JVM when invoking methods, therefore requiring method $\texttt{T}' \; m(\texttt{T}'_1 \ldots \texttt{T}'_n)$ to be exactly defined in C' would be too strong. The judgment $\Gamma \vdash \texttt{int} \leq \texttt{int}$ is trivially valid in every Γ.

Every class C defined in Γ is a subtype of itself (second rule) and of its (direct) superclass (third rule). Note that every class in Γ is considered subclass of itself, even if its inheritance hierarchy is cyclical, because this does not lead to wrong type assumption. Vice versa, a class C is considered subclass of C' only if its inheritance relation is acyclic.

Subtyping relation is transitive, fourth rule. The fifth rule extends the subtype relation to tuples of types.

The judgment $\Gamma \vdash \{\texttt{C}_1 \; \texttt{MS}_1, \ldots, \texttt{C}_n \; \texttt{MS}_n\} \lhd \texttt{C} \; \texttt{MS}$ is valid whenever one of the annotated method signatures $\texttt{C}_i \; \texttt{MS}_i$ "implements" the annotated method signature C MS, that is, there is a method with the same signature in C or any of its superclasses. If a class has full type AMSS and the latter implements the method signature AMS', then the class is said to implement AMS'.

The last rule defines the judgment $\Gamma \vdash \texttt{C} \lhd \texttt{AMS}'$, that is valid whenever class C implements AMS'.

$$S_1 \cup^E S_2 =_{\mathrm{def}} \begin{cases} S_1 & \text{if } S_1 \in \varepsilon \\ S_2 & \text{if } S_2 \in \varepsilon, S_1 \notin \varepsilon \\ S_1 \cup S_2 & \text{otherwise} \end{cases}$$

$$b_1 \wedge^E b_2 =_{\mathrm{def}} \begin{cases} b_1 & \text{if } b_1 \in \varepsilon \\ b_2 & \text{if } b_2 \in \varepsilon, b_1 \notin \varepsilon \\ Ok & \text{otherwise} \end{cases}$$

Fig. 8. Exception-aware union and disjunction

We define now execution and verification of binary fragments. We anticipate some auxiliary definitions.

Figure 8 shows the definition of the two operations $\cup^E$ and $\wedge^E$, whose arguments are either set of class names or exceptions.

The former is just set union when both arguments are not exceptions, whereas it returns one of its arguments when it is an exception (giving priority to the left argument).

The latter is similar to a boolean conjunction; it returns Ok when both arguments are Ok and one of its argument when it is an exception (again, giving priority to the left argument).

$$MBody(ce_b, \mathtt{C}, \mathtt{m}, \mathtt{T}_1 \dots \mathtt{T}_n, \mathtt{T}) =$$
$$\begin{cases} NoSuchMethod & \text{if } \mathtt{C} = \mathtt{Object} \\ ClassNotFound & \text{if } \mathtt{C} \neq \mathtt{Object}, \mathtt{C} \notin Def(ce_b) \\ \langle \mathtt{E}^b, \mathtt{x}_1 \dots \mathtt{x}_n \rangle & \text{if } \mathtt{T}\ \mathtt{m}(\mathtt{T}_1\ \mathtt{x}_1, \dots, \mathtt{T}_n\ \mathtt{x}_n)\{\mathtt{E}^b\} \in code(ce_b(\mathtt{C})) \\ MBody(ce_b, superclass(ce_b(\mathtt{C})), \mathtt{m}, \mathtt{T}_1 \dots \mathtt{T}_n, \mathtt{T}) & \text{otherwise} \end{cases}$$

$$code(\langle \_, \_, \mathtt{MDS}^b, \_ \rangle) = \mathtt{MDS}^b$$

$$superclass(\langle \_, \mathtt{C}', \_, \_ \rangle) = \mathtt{C}'$$

Fig. 9. Definition of *MBody*

The function $MBody(ce_b, \mathtt{C}, \mathtt{m}, \mathtt{T}_1 \dots \mathtt{T}_n, \mathtt{T})$, defined in Figure 9, models method look-up at run-time; it searches in the binary environment ce_b for the body of a method named $\mathtt{m}$ whose argument types are $\mathtt{T}_1 \dots \mathtt{T}_n$ and return type is $\mathtt{T}$, starting from class $\mathtt{C}$. If such a method is not found in $\mathtt{C}$, then it is searched, recursively, in its superclass.

The result of *MBody* can be either the body of the method (if found) or an exception if it is not found. There are two kinds of error that can happen during the method look-up: if $\mathtt{C} = \mathtt{Object}$ then this means that the method cannot be found, so the exception *NoSuchMethod* is returned. Otherwise, if $\mathtt{C}$ cannot be found in the binary environment, then the exception *ClassNotFound* is returned.

In Figure 10 we introduce two kinds of contexts: expression contexts $[\cdot]^{Exp}$ and type contexts $[\cdot]^{Type}$. In rewrite semantics, given in Figure 13, the former

$$[\cdot]^{Exp} ::= [\cdot].m \prec \boxed{\mathtt{C}}, \mathtt{T}_1 \ldots \mathtt{T}_n, \mathtt{T} \succ (\mathtt{E}^b_1, \ldots, \mathtt{E}^b_n) \mid$$
$$\mathtt{new}\ \mathtt{C}.m \prec \boxed{\mathtt{C'}}, \mathtt{T}_1 \ldots \mathtt{T}_n, \mathtt{T} \succ (v_1, \ldots, v_{i-1}, [\cdot], \mathtt{E}^b_{i+1}, \ldots, \mathtt{E}^b_n)$$
$$[\cdot]^{Type} ::= \mathtt{new}\ \mathtt{C}.m \prec [\cdot], \mathtt{T}_1 \ldots \mathtt{T}_n, \mathtt{T} \succ (v_1, \ldots, v_n) \mid$$
$$\mathtt{new}\ [\cdot]$$

Fig. 10. Contexts

$$Weak\_subtype(\mathtt{T}, \mathtt{T'}, ce_b) = \begin{cases} Ok & \text{if } \mathtt{T} = \mathtt{T'} \\ \varepsilon & \text{if } \mathtt{T} \neq \mathtt{T'}, Supertypes(\mathtt{T}, ce_b) = \varepsilon \\ Ok & \text{if } \mathtt{T} \neq \mathtt{T'}, \mathtt{T'} \in Def(ce_b), \\ & \quad \mathtt{T'} \in Supertypes(\mathtt{T}, ce_b) \\ VerifyError & \text{if } \mathtt{T} \neq \mathtt{T'}, \mathtt{T'} \in Def(ce_b), \\ & \quad \mathtt{T'} \notin Supertypes(\mathtt{T}, ce_b) \\ ClassNotFound & \text{otherwise} \end{cases}$$

$Supertypes(\mathtt{T}, ce_b) = Supertypes_{aux}(\mathtt{T}, \emptyset, ce_b)$
$Supertypes_{aux}(\mathtt{T}, LC, ce_b) =$
$$\begin{cases} ClassCircularityError & \text{if } \mathtt{T} \in LC \\ ClassNotFound & \text{if } \mathtt{T} \notin Def(ce_b) \cup \{\mathtt{int}, \mathtt{Object}\} \\ \{\mathtt{Object}\} \cup LC & \text{if } \mathtt{T} = \mathtt{Object} \\ \{\mathtt{int}\} & \text{if } \mathtt{T} = \mathtt{int} \\ \{\mathtt{T}\} \cup^E Supertypes_{aux}(superclass(ce_b(\mathtt{T})), \{\mathtt{T}\} \cup LC, ce_b) & \text{if } \mathtt{T} \notin LC, \mathtt{T} \in Def(ce_b) \end{cases}$$

Fig. 11. *Weak_subtype* and *Supertypes* definitions

are used to propagate execution to sub-expressions and the latter to verify class references in order to unbox them (making it possible to "normal" execution to proceed). The function *Weak_subtype* is used, at verification time, to check whether a type is subtype of another; $Weak\_subtype(\mathtt{T}, \mathtt{T'}, ce_b)$, defined in Figure 11, returns Ok when the type $\mathtt{T}$ is a subtype of $\mathtt{T'}$ in the binary environment ce_b or an appropriate exception when it is not. The subtype is "weak" because of the special case $\mathtt{T} = \mathtt{T'}$: any type $\mathtt{T}$ is *always* considered subtype of itself; it does not even matter whether $\mathtt{T}$ exists or not in the binary environment ce_b. In all the other cases both $\mathtt{T}$ and $\mathtt{T'}$ must exist, otherwise an exception *ClassNotFound* is returned. When both exist in ce_b, the auxiliary function *Supertypes* is used to check the relationship between $\mathtt{T}$ and $\mathtt{T'}$; indeed, $\mathtt{T}$ is subtype of $\mathtt{T'}$ iff $\mathtt{T'}$ is a supertype of $\mathtt{T}$. The function $Supertypes(\mathtt{T}, ce_b)$ can either return the set of supertypes of $\mathtt{T}$ in ce_b, when they can be computed, or an exception in case of error. There are two possible error situations: when a class (directly or indirectly) extends itself and when a parent class is not found in ce_b; in these cases the exceptions *ClassCircularityError* and *ClassNotFound* are, respectively, returned. Figure 12 shows the verification judgments. The top-level judgment $\vdash_{ce_b} \mathtt{C} : Ok$ is valid whenever the class $\mathtt{C}$ can be verified in the binary environment cc_b, otherwise it is valid a judgment $\vdash_{ce_b} \mathtt{C} : \varepsilon$, where ε indicates the error occurred in the verification steps. Indeed, it can be proved that the verification process is deterministic and always terminates (either with Ok or with an exception).

$$\frac{\forall i \in 1..n \ \vdash_{ce_b} \text{MD}_i^b : b_i \quad \emptyset \vdash_{ce_b} \text{E}^b : \langle \_, b \rangle}{\vdash_{ce_b} \text{C} : noDup(\text{MD}^b{}_1 \ldots \text{MD}^b{}_n) \bigwedge_{i \in 1..n}^E b_i \wedge^E b} \qquad ce_b(\text{C}) = \langle \_, \_, \text{MD}^b{}_1 \ldots \text{MD}^b{}_n, \text{E}^b \rangle$$

$$\frac{}{\vdash_{ce_b} \text{C} : ClassNotFound} \qquad \text{C} \notin Def(ce_b)$$

$$\frac{\{x_1 \mapsto \text{T}_1, \ldots, x_n \mapsto \text{T}_n\} \vdash_{ce_b} \text{E}^b : \langle \text{T}, b \rangle}{\vdash_{ce_b} \text{T}_0 \ \text{m}(\text{T}_1 \ x_1, \ldots, \text{T}_n \ x_n) \ \{\text{return } \text{E}^b; \} : b \wedge^E Weak\_subtype(\text{T}, \text{T}_0, ce_b)}$$

$$\frac{\forall i \in 0..n \ \sigma \vdash_{ce_b} \text{E}_i^b : \langle \text{T}_i, b_i \rangle}{\sigma \vdash_{ce_b} \text{E}_0^b.\text{m} \prec \boxed{\text{T}_0'}, \bar{\text{T}}', \text{T} \succ (\text{E}^b{}_1, \ldots, \text{E}^b{}_n) : \langle \text{T}, \bigwedge_{i \in 0..n}^E s_i \rangle} \qquad \begin{array}{l} \bar{\text{T}}' = \text{T}'_1 \ldots \text{T}'_n \\ s_i = b_i \wedge^E \\ Weak\_subtype(\text{T}_i, \text{T}'_i, ce_b) \end{array}$$

$$\frac{}{\sigma \vdash_{ce_b} \text{E}_0^b.\text{m} \prec \boxed{\text{T}_0'}, \text{T}'_1 \ldots \text{T}'_n, \text{T} \succ (\text{E}^b{}_1, \ldots, \text{E}^b{}_k) : \langle \text{T}, VerifyError \rangle} \qquad k \neq n$$

$$\frac{}{\sigma \vdash_{ce_b} n : \langle \text{int}, Ok \rangle} \qquad n = 0, 1, -1, 2, -2, \ldots$$

$$\frac{}{\sigma \vdash_{ce_b} \text{new } \boxed{\text{C}} : \langle \text{C}, Ok \rangle}$$

$$\frac{}{\sigma \vdash_{ce_b} x : \langle \sigma(x), Ok \rangle} \qquad x \in Def(\sigma)$$

$$noDup(\text{MD}^b{}_1 \ldots \text{MD}^b{}_n) = \begin{cases} Ok & \text{if } \forall i, j \in 1..n \ methSig(\text{MD}_i^b) = methSig(\text{MD}_j^b) \implies i = j \\ VerifyError & \text{otherwise} \end{cases}$$

$$methSig(\text{T } \text{m}(\text{T}_1 \ x_1, \ldots, \text{T}_n \ x_n)\{\text{E}^b\}) = \text{T } \text{m}(\text{T}_1 \ldots \text{T}_n)$$

Fig. 12. Verification

Note the interesting relation between verification and typechecking of binaries as defined in Figure 6; the former corresponds to dynamic typechecking of binaries, whereas the latter to static typechecking, and, hence, is more conservative than the former. This relation is formalized by Theorem 4 below.

When a class exists in the current binary environment ce_b its verification consists of: checking that there are no different method declarations with the same signature in the code of the class (predicate $noDup$) and verifying that all method declarations ($\vdash_{ce_b} \text{MD}_i^b : b_i$) and the main expression ($\emptyset \vdash_{ce_b} \text{E}^b : \langle \_, b \rangle$) are Ok.

When a class does not exists in a binary environment ce_b its verification simply gives $ClassNotFound$ (second metarule).

The judgment $\sigma \vdash_{ce_b} \text{E}^b : \langle \text{T}, b \rangle$ is valid whenever the expression E^b in a binary context ce_b and local type environment σ has type T and the result of its verification is b. The value b can be either Ok, when the verification succeeds, or an exception, indicating the problem, when the verification fails. In this latter

$$\frac{\vdash_{ce_b} \texttt{C}: Ok \quad \texttt{E}^b \stackrel{*}{\leadsto}_{ce_b} V}{\texttt{C} \leadsto_{ce_b} V} \qquad ce_b(\texttt{C}) = \langle -, -, -, \texttt{E}^b \rangle$$

$$\frac{\vdash_{ce_b} \texttt{C}: \varepsilon}{\texttt{C} \leadsto_{ce_b} \varepsilon}$$

$$\frac{\vdash_{ce_b} \texttt{C}: \varepsilon}{[\boxed{\texttt{C}}]^{Type} \leadsto_{ce_b} \varepsilon}$$

$$\frac{\vdash_{ce_b} \texttt{C}: Ok}{[\boxed{\texttt{C}}]^{Type} \leadsto_{ce_b} [\texttt{C}]^{Type}}$$

$$\frac{\texttt{E}^b \leadsto_{ce_b} \texttt{E}^b_1}{[\texttt{E}^b]^{Exp} \leadsto_{ce_b} [\texttt{E}^b_1]^{Exp}} \qquad \texttt{E}^b_1 \neq \varepsilon$$

$$\frac{\texttt{E}^b \leadsto_{ce_b} \varepsilon}{[\texttt{E}^b]^{Exp} \leadsto_{ce_b} \varepsilon}$$

$$\frac{}{\texttt{new C}.m \prec \texttt{C}', \bar{\texttt{T}}, \texttt{T} \succ (v_1, \ldots, v_n) \leadsto_{ce_b} \varepsilon} \qquad \begin{array}{l} \bar{\texttt{T}} = \texttt{T}_1 \ldots \texttt{T}_n \\ MBody(ce_b, \texttt{C}', m, \bar{\texttt{T}}, \texttt{T}) = \varepsilon \end{array}$$

$$\frac{\texttt{E}^b[v_1/\texttt{x}_1, \ldots, v_n/\texttt{x}_n] \leadsto_{ce_b} \texttt{E}^b_1}{\texttt{new C}.m \prec \texttt{C}', \bar{\texttt{T}}, \texttt{T} \succ (v_1, \ldots, v_n) \leadsto_{ce_b} \texttt{E}^b_1} \qquad \begin{array}{l} \bar{\texttt{T}} = \texttt{T}_1 \ldots \texttt{T}_n \\ MBody(ce_b, \texttt{C}', m, \bar{\texttt{T}}, \texttt{T}) \neq \varepsilon \\ MBody(ce_b, \texttt{C}, m, \bar{\texttt{T}}, \texttt{T}) = \langle \texttt{E}^b, \texttt{x}_1 \ldots \texttt{x}_n \rangle \end{array}$$

Fig. 13. Rewriting

case the value of T is immaterial. A local type environment σ is a (partial) function from argument names to types.

The verification of a method declaration (third rule) succeeds when the verification of its body succeeds and the type of the body is a subtype of the declared return type.

The verification of a method invocation succeeds when the number of arguments coincides with the number of parameter types in the method descriptor, the verification of the receiver and of each argument type succeeds and the type of the receiver and of each argument is a (weak) subtype of the corresponding type contained in the method descriptor (fourth rule).

The fifth rule covers the case when the numbers of arguments differs (side condition $k \neq n$). Note that if a binary fragment is the result of the compilation of a source fragment, the number of arguments is indeed equal to the number of parameter types in the descriptor; such a mismatch may only be found in "malicious" binary fragments.

Figure 13 shows the rewriting rules for the program execution. The first two rules deal with the execution of the main method of a class C; the former covers the case when class C is verified, whereas the latter considers the case when C does not pass verification.

The third and fourth rules cover the loading/verification process. The former is used in case of error: the whole term is rewritten in the exception thrown by the verifier. The latter is used when the verification is carried out successfully; in this case the term is rewritten in itself except for the reference to the class C that is unboxed.

The third rule is just the standard closure.

The fourth rule propagates an exception rewriting an entire term containing an exception ε in the exception itself.

The fifth and the sixth rules deal with method invocation. When the method cannot be found starting the search from the class contained in the method descriptor the entire expression is rewritten in the exception; otherwise a second call to *MBody*, passing as starting class the dynamic type of the receiver, returns the method body and the name of the arguments. These information are used to expand the method call.

4.1   Main Results

We prove three main theorems claiming the safety of source and binary type-checking and of the safe compilation schema, respectively; the former two theorems are necessary for proving the latter.

Theorem 1 (Safe Source Typechecking). *For all type environments Γ, sources S and binaries B, if $\Gamma \vdash S \leadsto B$, then $\Gamma \vdash B \diamond$.*

Theorem 2 (Safe Binary Typechecking). *Let $\langle ce_b, ce_s \rangle$ and C be a compilation environment and a class name, respectively. For all values V, if*
$$\forall C' \in \mathcal{D}(\langle ce_b, ce_s \rangle, \{C\}) \quad \mathcal{T}(\langle ce_b, ce_s \rangle) \vdash ce_b(C') \diamond \text{ and } C \leadsto_{ce_b} V, \text{ then } V \text{ is not}$$
an exception.

We can state now the main property of the safe compilation schema: if a set of classes is successfully compiled w.r.t. the safe schema, then the execution of any binary produced by such compilation in the updated binary environment never throws a linkage exception.

Theorem 3 (Safety). *Let $\langle ce_b, ce_s \rangle$, CS and ce'_b be a compilation environment, a set of class names and a binary environment, respectively. For all class names $C \in Def(ce'_b)$ and values V, if $C(\langle ce_b, ce_s \rangle, CS) = ce'_b$ and $C \leadsto_{ce_b[ce'_b]} V$, then V is not an exception.*

4.2   Formal Proofs (Sketched)

Safe Source Typechecking: For reasons of space we omit the proof, which is by induction over the rules defining the source typechecking judgment $\Gamma \vdash S \leadsto B$. The proof uses a number of lemmas claiming the same property for all kinds of subcomponents of a source; the most interesting one concerns expressions.

Lemma 1. *For all type and variable environments Γ and Π, source and binary expressions E^s and E^b and types T, if $\Gamma; \Pi \vdash E^s : T \leadsto E^b$ then $\Gamma; \Pi \vdash E^b : T \diamond$.*

Safe Binary Typechecking: Safety of binary typechecking comes from the following two theorems, the former connecting static with dynamic binary typechecking (that is, the binary typechecking judgment $\Gamma \vdash B \diamond$ with the verification judgment $\vdash_{ce_b} C : b$), the latter expressing subject reduction for binary expressions. For reasons of space we omit the proofs of these two theorems; the former can be proved by induction over the rules for binary typechecking, while the latter can be proved by induction over the rewriting rules for binary expressions.

Theorem 4 (Binary Typechecking Implies Verification). *Let $\langle ce_b, ce_s \rangle$ and C be a compilation environment and a class name, respectively, s.t. the following condition holds: $\mathcal{D}(\langle ce_b, ce_s \rangle, \{C\}) \subseteq Def(ce_b)$. If $\mathcal{T}(\langle ce_b, ce_s \rangle) \vdash ce_b(C) \diamond$, then $\vdash_{ce_b} C : Ok$.*

Note that the converse implication does not hold, since typechecking at (dynamic) load time is more accurate than that at compile time. For instance, typechecking of a binary declaration of a class C requires the check of all classes explicitly mentioned in C, whereas the JVM only checks those classes that are actually needed by that particular execution.

Theorem 5 (Binary Subject Reduction). *Let $\langle ce_b, ce_s \rangle$ and E^b be a compilation environment and a binary expression, respectively. If $\mathcal{T}(\langle ce_b, ce_s \rangle); \emptyset \vdash E^b : T \diamond$ and $E^b \leadsto_{ce_b} E^{b'}$, then there exists a type T' s.t. $\mathcal{T}(\langle ce_b, ce_s \rangle); \emptyset \vdash E^{b'} : T' \diamond$ and $\mathcal{T}(\langle ce_b, ce_s \rangle) \vdash T' \leq T$.*

We are now able to prove safety of binary typechecking. Let us assume that $\forall C' \in \mathcal{D}(\langle ce_b, ce_s \rangle, \{C\})$ $\mathcal{T}(\langle ce_b, ce_s \rangle) \vdash ce_b(C') \diamond$ and $C \leadsto_{ce_b} V$. From the first assumption we easily deduce $\mathcal{D}(\langle ce_b, ce_s \rangle, \{C\}) \subseteq Def(ce_b)$ and $\mathcal{T}(\langle ce_b, ce_s \rangle) \vdash ce_b(C) \diamond$ (since, trivially, $C \in \mathcal{D}(\langle ce_b, ce_s \rangle, \{C\})$).

As a consequence, Theorem 4 can be applied, therefore $\vdash_{ce_b} C : Ok$ holds. This means that $C \leadsto_{ce_b} V$ has been deduced by instantiating the first (and not the second) meta-rule in Figure 13, so $E^b \overset{*}{\leadsto}_{ce_b} V$ must hold. Furthermore, the validity of $\mathcal{T}(\langle ce_b, ce_s \rangle) \vdash ce_b(C) \diamond$ implies the validity of $\mathcal{T}(\langle ce_b, ce_s \rangle); \emptyset \vdash E^b : T \diamond$, since there is only one meta-rule that can be instantiated in Figure 6. Therefore we can apply Theorem 5 and deduce the validity of $\mathcal{T}(\langle ce_b, ce_s \rangle); \emptyset \vdash V : T' \diamond$, with T' subtype of T. Since exceptions do not typecheck (see rules in Figure 6), we can conclude that V is not an exception.

Safety: To prove safety we need two lemmas claiming that both the dependency and type extraction functions are invariant w.r.t. source typechecking. These lemmas can be proved by induction over the definition of $\mathcal{D}$ and $\mathcal{T}$, respectively; for reasons of space we omit their proofs.

In what follows, let $ce_{s \setminus C}$ denotes the partial function obtained by restricting the definition domain of ce_s to the set $Def(ce_s) \setminus C$.

Lemma 2. *Let $\langle ce_b, ce_s \rangle$, C and B be a compilation environment, a class name, and a binary fragment, respectively. If $\mathcal{T}(\langle ce_b, ce_s \rangle) \vdash ce_b(C) \leadsto B$, then for all class name C' the following equality holds:*

$$\mathcal{D}(\langle ce_b, ce_s \rangle, \{C'\}) = \mathcal{D}(\langle ce_b[C \mapsto B], ce_{s \setminus C} \rangle, \{C'\}).$$

Lemma 3. *Let $\langle ce_b, ce_s \rangle$, C and B be a compilation environment, a class name, and a binary fragment, respectively. If $\mathcal{T}(\langle ce_b, ce_s \rangle) \vdash ce_b(C) \leadsto B$, then the following equality holds:*

$$\mathcal{T}(\langle ce_b, ce_s \rangle) = \mathcal{T}(\langle ce_b[C \mapsto B], ce_{s \backslash C} \rangle).$$

Now assume that $\mathcal{C}(\langle ce_b, ce_s \rangle, \mathsf{CS}) = ce_b'$. By virtue of the top-level rule in Figure 1, the following judgments are valid:

$$\forall \mathsf{C} \in \mathsf{CS}_b \; \Gamma \vdash ce_b(\mathsf{C}) \diamond$$
$$\forall \mathsf{C} \in \mathsf{CS}_s \; \Gamma \vdash ce_s(\mathsf{C}) \leadsto \mathsf{B}_\mathsf{C}$$

where $\mathsf{CS}_b = \mathsf{CS}_d \cap \mathit{Def}(ce_b)$, $\mathsf{CS}_s = \mathsf{CS}_d \cap \mathit{Def}(ce_s)$, $\mathsf{CS}_d = \mathcal{D}(\langle ce_b, ce_s \rangle, \mathsf{CS})$ and $\Gamma = \mathcal{T}(\langle ce_b, ce_s \rangle)$. Furthermore, $ce_b'(\mathsf{C}) = \{\mathsf{C} \mapsto \mathsf{B}_\mathsf{C} \mid \mathsf{C} \in \mathsf{CS}_s\}$.

By Theorem 1, $\Gamma \vdash ce_b'(\mathsf{C}) \diamond$ for all $\mathsf{C} \in \mathsf{CS}_s$, therefore we can easily deduce $\Gamma \vdash ce_b[ce_b'](\mathsf{C}) \diamond$ for all $\mathsf{C} \in \mathsf{CS}_d$.

Let us now prove the main theorem by assuming that C is a class name in CS_b (recall that $\mathit{Def}(ce_b') = \mathsf{CS}_b$) and that $\mathsf{C} \leadsto_{ce_b[ce_b']} V$ for a certain value V. By lemmas 2 and 3 and by induction on the cardinality of CS, $\mathcal{D}(\langle ce_b, ce_s \rangle, \{\mathsf{C}\}) = \mathcal{D}(\langle ce_b[ce_b'], ce_{s \backslash \mathsf{CS}} \rangle, \{\mathsf{C}\})$ and $\mathcal{T}(\langle ce_b, ce_s \rangle) = \mathcal{T}(\langle ce_b[ce_b'], ce_{s \backslash \mathsf{CS}} \rangle)$. Therefore we can apply Theorem 2 and conclude that V cannot be an exception.

5   Related Work

We already mentioned in the Introduction that the seminal paper on separate typecheck of fragments is [8]. There, the basic idea is to distinguish a phase of *intra-checking*, which models separate compilation, in which a single fragment is type-checked w.r.t. a typing environment (which expresses the interface of the fragment in terms of both imported and exported services), and a phase of *inter-checking* which models (static) linking, in which it is checked that all the fragments we want to link have been type-checked w.r.t. compatible type environments.

Formally[12], intra-checking is modeled by a judgment $\Gamma \vdash f : T$ (in [8] issues of code generation are avoided by always working at the source level, even when discussing linking), expressing that the fragment f has type T in the type environment Γ. Inter-checking takes place on *linksets* which are, roughly, collections of named fragment $x_i \mapsto \Gamma_i \vdash f_i : T_i^{i \in 1..n}$, and succeeds if and only if intra-checking succeeds (that is, each $\Gamma_i \vdash f_i : T_i$ holds) and, moreover, for each $j, k \in 1..n$, x_j has type T_j in Γ_k. This corresponds to require *exact* agreement among the actual interface of a fragment and that assumed in another: in realistic systems, this condition should be weakened, for instance requiring some subtyping relation (see below for the Java case).

As already discussed in the Introduction, Java has many features which make this view not immediately applicable: class files play the dual roles of interfaces

---

[12] We use slightly different notations from [8] in order to conform to those used in this paper.

(type environments) and object files; there is no separate linking phase, since linking takes place at run-time; compilers usually incorporate *some* inter-checks, but not enough to guarantee safe run-time linking.

In this paper, we present a framework which models separate compilation in the Java sense. Though a detailed formal comparison of our framework with that in [8] is matter of further work, we can list the main contact points and differences.

- The intra-checking phase is modeled in the same way, apart from the fact that here we are interested in distinguishing source and code fragments, hence in modeling code generation.
- Instead of starting from a fixed linkset, here we assume that the set of fragments to be linked is determined by the dependency function.
- Most importantly, instead of having that each fragment f_i is equipped with its own type environment Γ_i (expressing its interface), here we assume a *global* type environment. This reflects the fact that in Java there is no separate notion of interface[13] of a fragment (class C) describing both imported and exported services, but this interface must in some way be extracted from the code. Here, since our aim was to model separate compilation as it happens in Java rather than to compare with truly separate compilation in the sense of [8], we have taken the simpler approach to type-check all the fragments in the same type environment, which trivially consists in the compilation environment where we drop method bodies. Hence inter-checking is trivial. An approach more in the spirit of [8] consists in extracting the interface Γ_i for each class C_i containing the minimal assumptions needed for successfully typecheck C_i, and then to check that different interfaces are compatible. This approach poses non trivial problems both on how to perform the type extraction and how to define the "right" subtyping relation among interfaces. However, the investigation is very interesting because it could lead to innovative techniques for Java compilation supporting truly separate compilation and then the possibility of performing static checks on binaries. We refer to [6,2] for a more complete treatment in this direction.

Another important stream of research related to this paper is that devoted to the formal definition of Java (see [1] for a survey). As already mentioned, the type judgment which we consider at the source level is based (though much simpler, since we consider a small Java subset) on the many existing formal Java type systems, in particular those in [10]. For what concerns an integrated formal model covering all Java aspects, the most remarkable amount of work in this direction is that of Sophia Drossopoulou and her group. The already cited [10] provides a formal type system at the source level for a substantial subset Java[s] of Java and a translation of this language into a binary language Java[b], which is in turn a subset of a language Java[r] of run-time terms for which an operational semantics is given. This allows to prove type safety of the Java subset. In [13] the focus is on binary compatibility. In [9] a model is defined for dynamic loading and

---

[13] Not to be confused with a Java interface.

linking, distinguishing five components in a Java implementation: evaluation, resolution, loading, verification, and preparation, with their associated checks. These five together are proved to guarantee type soundness. This paper is the most important reference for the execution model of our small binary language; however, in our case the main aim is not to define a realistic model of the JVM, taking into account all features, but to show how absence of linkage errors can be guaranteed by a compilation schema, so we take a much more abstract view. Finally, [12] enhances the previous formal description of Java in [10], introducing, among other improvements, an account of separate compilation. Indeed, type information used in typechecking Java^s can also be extracted from the binary language Java^r, analogously to what we do in this paper by means of the $\mathcal{T}$ function. However, the judgment for typechecking source classes defined in [12] do not correspond to separate compilation as happens in our framework, simply because its validity requires the type environment extracted from the compilation environment to be well-formed.

Finally, several interesting papers can be found in literature on separate compilation for ML (see among many others [17,16,7]). All these papers clearly show that separate compilation in ML is not a simple issue, and for this reason, needs to be properly formalized. However, ML separate compilation is based on traditional static linking, therefore many problems arising in Java disappear in ML; for instance, the static type-checks proposed in [17] are sensible for a static linker, but cannot be performed at run-time by a virtual machine without seriously compromising efficiency. Furthermore, it seems that no unifying frameworks have been defined for investigating ML separate compilation, and in fact, this would be useful to compare all the technical results and to understand how they can contribute all together to the design of a better compiler/linker for ML. For instance, using the terminology used in our paper to model the overall compilation process, [17] is mainly concerned with the definition of the type extraction function, while [16] with the typechecking of sources and [7] with the definition of the dependency function.

6   Conclusion

We have introduced a formal framework modeling Java separate compilation. The overall compilation process is modeled by the formal notion of compilation schema, in which the aspects which concern truly separate typechecking of fragments (source type judgment and binary type judgment) are isolated from the definition of dependencies and extraction of the type information from the fragments. We have considered three compilation schemata of interest for Java, that is, minimal, SDK, and safe, correspondingly to perform, when a single fragment is typechecked, no typechecks on other fragments, only the typechecks performed by SDK, and enough typechecks in order to ensure absence of linkage errors at run-time.

In order to demonstrate our approach, we have defined a kernel model for Java separate compilation and execution, consisting in a small Java subset, and a simple corresponding binary language for which we provide an operational semantics including run-time verification. We have defined a safe compilation schema for this language and formally proved type safety.

In this paper we have focused on the safety property (a preliminary work pointing out that Java compilers are not safe in the context of separate compilation was [4]); however, there are other interesting properties of compilation schemata we want to investigate, like *monotonicity* and *contextual binary compatibility*. By monotonicity we mean the fact that, when a subset of the source fragments composing a program is changed, re-compiling only this set gives the same result as re-compiling the whole program (this property is mentioned as desirable in [8], and a preliminary formalization is given in [5]). By *contextual binary compatibility* we mean a property analogous to Java binary compatibility, but related to compilation: we say that a compilation schema respects contextual binary compatibility if all the binary fragments which could be safely linked before compilation still safely link after. Note that, even though a formal analysis of their relation is still matter of further work (see below), these three properties seem at a first sight to be independent.

The work presented in this paper is a first step, and many interesting research directions are open. On the more theoretical side, we plan to formally analyze the difference between separate compilation in the Java sense, modeled in this paper, and truly separate compilation in the sense of, e.g., [8] (see [6,2]). This should lead to the definition of a very abstract framework, like that in [8], but including dynamic linking and verification, in which we will express formal properties like type safety, monotonicity and contextual binary compatibility and analyze their relations. Furthermore, the interesting relation between verification and binary typechecking deserves further investigation in order to better understand the deep issue of binary compatibility.

On the side of application to Java, we plan to extend the safe type system defined here to more substantial Java subsets and to develop extended compilers which satisfy good properties like type safety.

Acknowledgment We are extremely grateful to Sophia Drossopoulou for her stimulating discussions and for her precious suggestions on preliminary drafts of this paper.

References

1. J. Alves-Foss, editor. *Formal Syntax and Semantics of Java*. Number 1523 in Lecture Notes in Computer Science. Springer, 1999.
2. D. Ancona and G. Lagorio. Supporting true separate compilation in Java: A modular approach. Technical report, Dipartimento di Informatica e Scienze dell'Informazione, Università di Genova, 2002. Submitted for publication.
3. D. Ancona, G. Lagorio, and E. Zucca. A core calculus for Java exceptions. In *ACM Symp. on Object-Oriented Programming: Systems, Languages and Applications 2001*. ACM Press, October 2001. SIGPLAN Notices.
4. D. Ancona, G. Lagorio, and E. Zucca. Java separate type checking is not safe. In *3th Intl. Workshop on Formal Techniques for Java Programs 2001*, June 2001.

5. D. Ancona, G. Lagorio, and E. Zucca. Separate compilation in Java: Avoiding ambiguity via monotonicity. Technical Report, DISI, July 2001.
6. D. Ancona, G. Lagorio, and E. Zucca. True separate compilation of Java classes. Technical report, Dipartimento di Informatica e Scienze dell'Informazione, Università di Genova, 2002. Submitted for publication.
7. M. Blume. Dependency analysis for standard ML. *ACM Transactions on Programming Languages and Systems*, 21(4):790–812, 1999.
8. L. Cardelli. Program fragments, linking, and modularization. In *ACM Symp. on Principles of Programming Languages 1997*, pages 266–277. ACM Press, 1997.
9. S. Drossopoulou. Towards an abstract model of Java dynamic linking and verification. In R. Harper, editor, *TIC'00 - Third Workshop on Types in Compilation (Selected Papers)*, volume 2071 of *Lecture Notes in Computer Science*, pages 53–84. Springer, 2001.
10. S. Drossopoulou and S. Eisenbach. Describing the semantics of Java and proving type soundness. In J. Alves-Foss, editor, *Formal Syntax and Semantics of Java*, number 1523 in Lecture Notes in Computer Science, pages 41–82. Springer, 1999.
11. S. Drossopoulou, S. Eisenbach, and D. Wragg. A fragment calculus - towards a model of separate compilation, linking and binary compatibility. In *Proc. 14th Ann. IEEE Symp. on Logic in Computer Science*, July 1999.
12. S. Drossopoulou, T. Valkevych, and S. Eisenbach. Java type soundness revisited. Technical report, Dept. of Computing - Imperial College of Science, Technology and Medicine, September 2000.
13. S. Drossopoulou, D. Wragg, and S. Eisenbach. What *is* Java Binary Compatibility? In *ACM Symp. on Object-Oriented Programming: Systems, Languages and Applications 1998*, volume 33(10) of *ACM SIGPLAN Notices*, pages 341–358, October 1998.
14. J. Gosling, B. Joy, G. Steele, and G. Bracha. *The Java™ Language Specification, Second Edition*. Addison-Wesley, 2000.
15. A. Igarashi, B. Pierce, and P. Wadler. Featherweight Java: A minimal core calculus for Java and GJ. In *ACM Symp. on Object-Oriented Programming: Systems, Languages and Applications 1999*, pages 132–146, November 1999.
16. X. Leroy. Manifest types, modules and separate compilation. In *ACM Symp. on Principles of Programming Languages 1994*, pages 109–122. ACM Press, 1994.
17. Z. Shao and A.W. Appel. Smartest recompilation. In *ACM Symp. on Principles of Programming Languages 1993*, pages 439–450. ACM Press, 1993.
18. D. Syme. Proving Java type sound. In Jim Alves-Foss, editor, *Formal Syntax and Semantics of Java*, number 1523 in Lecture Notes in Computer Science, pages 83–118. Springer, 1999.
19. D. von Oheimb and T. Nipkow. Machine-checking the Java specification: Proving type-safety. In Jim Alves-Foss, editor, *Formal Syntax and Semantics of Java*, number 1523 in Lecture Notes in Computer Science, pages 119–156. Springer, 1999.

A   Appendix

$$refClasses(\texttt{C}, \langle ce_b, ce_s \rangle) = \begin{cases} refClasses(ce_b(\texttt{C})) \text{ if } \texttt{C} \in Def(ce_b) \\ refClasses(ce_s(\texttt{C})) \text{ if } \texttt{C} \in Def(ce_s) \\ \emptyset \qquad\qquad\qquad\quad \text{otherwise} \end{cases}$$

$refClasses(\texttt{class C extends C' \{ MDS}^s \texttt{ \} main E}^s) =$
$\quad \{\texttt{C}, \texttt{C}'\} \cup refClasses(\texttt{MDS}^s) \cup refClasses(\texttt{E}^s)$

$refClasses(\texttt{MD}_1^s \ldots \texttt{MD}_n^s) = \bigcup_{i \in 1..n} refClasses(\texttt{MD}_i^s)$

$refClasses(\texttt{MH \{ return E}^s\texttt{; \}}) = refClasses(\texttt{MH}) \cup refClasses(\texttt{E}^s)$

$refClasses(\texttt{T}_0 \texttt{ m(T}_1 \texttt{ x}_1, \ldots, \texttt{T}_n \texttt{ x}_n)) = \{\texttt{T}_0, \ldots, \texttt{T}_n\}$

$refClasses(\texttt{new C}) = \{\texttt{C}\}$

$refClasses(\texttt{x}) = refClasses(\texttt{N}) = \emptyset$

$refClasses(\texttt{E}_0^s.\texttt{m(E}_1^s, \ldots, \texttt{E}_n^s)) = \bigcup_{i \in 0..n} refClasses(\texttt{E}_i^s)$

$refClasses(\langle \texttt{C}, \texttt{C}', \texttt{MDS}^b, \texttt{E}^b \rangle) = \{\texttt{C}, \texttt{C}'\} \cup refClasses(\texttt{MDS}^b) \cup refClasses(\texttt{E}^b)$

$refClasses(\texttt{MD}_1^b \ldots \texttt{MD}_n^b) = \bigcup_{i \in 1..n} refClasses(\texttt{MD}_i^b)$

$refClasses(\texttt{MH \{ return E}^b\texttt{; \}}) = refClasses(\texttt{MH}) \cup refClasses(\texttt{E}^b)$

$refClasses(\texttt{E}_0^b.\texttt{m} \prec \boxed{\texttt{C}}, \texttt{T}_1 \ldots \texttt{T}_n, \texttt{T}_0 \succ (\texttt{E}_1^b, \ldots, \texttt{E}_n^b))$
$\qquad\qquad = \{\texttt{C}\} \cup \bigcup_{i \in 0..n}(refClasses(\texttt{E}_i^b) \cup \{\texttt{T}_i\})$

$refClasses(\texttt{new } \boxed{\texttt{C}}) = \{\texttt{C}\}$

Fig. 14. Definition of the dependency function

$$\forall \texttt{C} \ \mathcal{T}(\langle ce_b, ce_s \rangle)(\texttt{C}) = \begin{cases} \langle \texttt{C}', \mathcal{T}(\texttt{MDS}^b) \rangle \text{ if } ce_b(\texttt{C}) = \langle \texttt{C}, \texttt{C}', \texttt{MDS}^b, \texttt{E}^b \rangle \\ \langle \texttt{C}', \mathcal{T}(\texttt{MDS}^s) \rangle \text{ if } ce_s(\texttt{C}) = \texttt{class C extends} \\ \qquad\qquad\qquad\qquad\qquad\quad \texttt{C' \{ MDS}^s \texttt{ \} main E}^s \\ \bot \qquad\qquad\qquad \text{otherwise} \end{cases}$$

$\mathcal{T}(\texttt{MD}_1^s \ldots \texttt{MD}_n^s) = \mathcal{T}(\texttt{MD}_1^s) \ldots \mathcal{T}(\texttt{MD}_n^s)$

$\mathcal{T}(\texttt{MD}_1^b \ldots \texttt{MD}_n^b) = \mathcal{T}(\texttt{MD}_1^b) \ldots \mathcal{T}(\texttt{MD}_n^b)$

$\mathcal{T}(\texttt{MH \{ return E}^s\texttt{; \}}) = \mathcal{T}(\texttt{MH})$

$\mathcal{T}(\texttt{MH \{ return E}^b\texttt{; \}}) = \mathcal{T}(\texttt{MH})$

$\mathcal{T}(\texttt{T}_0 \texttt{ m(T}_1 \texttt{ x}_1, \ldots, \texttt{T}_n \texttt{ x}_n)) = \texttt{T}_0 \texttt{ m(T}_1 \ldots \texttt{T}_n)$

Fig. 15. Definition of the type extraction function

Author Index

Lecture Notes in Computer Science

For information about Vols. 1–2275
please contact your bookseller or Springer-Verlag

Vol. 2312: T. Arts, M. Mohnen (Eds.), Implementation of Functional Languages. Proceedings, 2001. VII, 187 pages. 2002.

Vol. 2313: C.A. Coello Coello, A. de Albornoz, L.E. Sucar, O.Cairó Battistutti (Eds.), MICAI 2002: Advances in Artificial Intelligence. Proceedings, 2002. XIII, 548 pages. 2002. (Subseries LNAI).

Vol. 2314: S.-K. Chang, Z. Chen, S.-Y. Lee (Eds.), Recent Advances in Visual Information Systems. Proceedings, 2002. XI, 323 pages. 2002.

Vol. 2315: F. Arhab, C. Talcott (Eds.), Coordination Models and Languages. Proceedings, 2002. XI, 406 pages. 2002.

Vol. 2316: J. Domingo-Ferrer (Ed.), Inference Control in Statistical Databases. VIII, 231 pages. 2002.

Vol. 2317: M. Hegarty, B. Meyer, N. Hari Narayanan (Eds.), Diagrammatic Representation and Inference. Proceedings, 2002. XIV, 362 pages. 2002. (Subseries LNAI).

Vol. 2318: D. Bošnački, S. Leue (Eds.), Model Checking Software. Proceedings, 2002. X, 259 pages. 2002.

Vol. 2319: C. Gacek (Ed.), Software Reuse: Methods, Techniques, and Tools. Proceedings, 2002. XI, 353 pages. 2002.

Vol.2320: T. Sander (Ed.), Security and Privacy in Digital Rights Management. Proceedings, 2001. X, 245 pages. 2002.

Vol. 2322: V. Mařík, O. Štěpánková, H. Krautwurmová, M. Luck (Eds.), Multi-Agent Systems and Applications II. Proceedings, 2001. XII, 377 pages. 2002. (Subseries LNAI).

Vol. 2323: À. Frohner (Ed.), Object-Oriented Technology. Proceedings, 2001. IX, 225 pages. 2002.

Vol. 2324: T. Field, P.G. Harrison, J. Bradley, U. Harder (Eds.), Computer Performance Evaluation. Proceedings, 2002. XI, 349 pages. 2002.

Vol 2326: D. Grigoras, A. Nicolau, B. Toursel, B. Folliot (Eds.), Advanced Environments, Tools, and Applications for Cluster Computing. Proceedings, 2001. XIII, 321 pages. 2002.

Vol. 2327: H.P. Zima, K. Joe, M. Sato, Y. Seo, M. Shimasaki (Eds.), High Performance Computing. Proceedings, 2002. XV, 564 pages. 2002.

Vol. 2329: P.M.A. Sloot, C.J.K. Tan, J.J. Dongarra, A.G. Hoekstra (Eds.), Computational Science – ICCS 2002. Proceedings, Part I. XLI, 1095 pages. 2002.

Vol. 2330: P.M.A. Sloot, C.J.K. Tan, J.J. Dongarra, A.G. Hoekstra (Eds.), Computational Science – ICCS 2002. Proceedings, Part II. XLI, 1115 pages. 2002.

Vol. 2331: P.M.A. Sloot, C.J.K. Tan, J.J. Dongarra, A.G. Hoekstra (Eds.), Computational Science – ICCS 2002. Proceedings, Part III. XLI, 1227 pages. 2002.

Vol. 2332: L. Knudsen (Ed.), Advances in Cryptology – EUROCRYPT 2002. Proceedings, 2002. XII, 547 pages. 2002.

Vol. 2334: G. Carle, M. Zitterbart (Eds.), Protocols for High Speed Networks. Proceedings, 2002. X, 267 pages. 2002.

Vol. 2335: M. Butler, L. Petre, K. Sere (Eds.), Integrated Formal Methods. Proceedings, 2002. X, 401 pages. 2002.

Vol. 2336: M.-S. Chen, P.S. Yu, B. Liu (Eds.), Advances in Knowledge Discovery and Data Mining. Proceedings, 2002. XIII, 568 pages. 2002. (Subseries LNAI).

Vol. 2337: W.J. Cook, A.S. Schulz (Eds.), Integer Programming and Combinatorial Optimization. Proceedings, 2002. XI, 487 pages. 2002.

Vol. 2338: R. Cohen, B. Spencer (Eds.), Advances in Artificial Intelligence. Proceedings, 2002. X, 197 pages. 2002. (Subseries LNAI).

Vol. 2340: N. Jonoska, N.C. Seeman (Eds.), DNA Computing. Proceedings, 2001. XI, 392 pages. 2002.

Vol. 2342: I. Horrocks, J. Hendler (Eds.), The Semantic Web – ISCW 2002. Proceedings, 2002. XVI, 476 pages. 2002.

Vol. 2345: E. Gregori, M. Conti, A.T. Campbell, G. Omidyar, M. Zukerman (Eds.), NETWORKING 2002. Proceedings, 2002. XXVI, 1256 pages. 2002.

Vol. 2346: H. Unger, T., Böhme, A. Mikler (Eds.), Innovative Internet Computing Systems. Proceedings, 2002. VIII, 251 pages. 2002.

Vol. 2347: P. De Bra, P. Brusilovsky, R. Conejo (Eds.), Adaptive Hypermedia and Adaptive Web-Based Systems. Proceedings, 2002. XV, 615 pages. 2002.

Vol. 2348: A. Banks Pidduck, J. Mylopoulos, C.C. Woo, M. Tamer Ozsu (Eds.), Advanced Information Systems Engineering. Proceedings, 2002. XIV, 799 pages. 2002.

Vol. 2349: J. Kontio, R. Conradi (Eds.), Software Quality – ECSQ 2002. Proceedings, 2002. XIV, 363 pages. 2002.

Vol. 2350: A. Heyden, G. Sparr, M. Nielsen, P. Johansen (Eds.), Computer Vision – ECCV 2002. Proceedings, Part I. XXVIII, 817 pages. 2002.

Vol. 2351: A. Heyden, G. Sparr, M. Nielsen, P. Johansen (Eds.), Computer Vision – ECCV 2002. Proceedings, Part II. XXVIII, 903 pages. 2002.

Vol. 2352: A. Heyden, G. Sparr, M. Nielsen, P. Johansen (Eds.), Computer Vision – ECCV 2002. Proceedings, Part III. XXVIII, 919 pages. 2002.

Vol. 2353: A. Heyden, G. Sparr, M. Nielsen, P. Johansen (Eds.), Computer Vision – ECCV 2002. Proceedings, Part IV. XXVIII, 841 pages. 2002.

Vol. 2358: T. Hendtlass, M. Ali (Eds.), Developments in Applied Artificial Intelligence. Proceedings, 2002 XIII, 833 pages. 2002. (Subseries LNAI).

Vol. 2359: M. Tistarelli, J. Bigun, A.K. Jain (Eds.), Biometric Authentication. Proceedings, 2002. XII, 373 pages. 2002.

Vol. 2361: J. Blieberger, A. Strohmeier (Eds.), Reliable Software Technologies – Ada-Europe 2002. Proceedings, 2002 XIII, 367 pages. 2002.

Vol. 2363: S.A. Cerri, G. Gouardères, F. Paraguaçu (Eds.), Intelligent Tutoring Systems. Proceedings, 2002. XXVIII, 1016 pages. 2002.

Vol. 2367: J. Fagerholm, J. Haataja, J. Järvinen, M. Lyly. P. Råback, V. Savolainen (Eds.), Applied Parallel Computing. Proceedings, 2002. XIV, 612 pages. 2002.

Vol. 2374: B. Magnusson (Ed.), ECOOP 2002 – Object-Oriented Programming. XI, 637 pages. 2002.